OCÉANO

ATLÁNTICO

Estrecho de la Florida

LAS BAHAMAS

La Habana ⊛ • Matanzas

ar del Río •

Cienfuegos •   **CUBA**

Camagüey •

Guantánamo •

Santiago
de Cuba •

Canal de Yucatán

umel

Kingston
⊛

JAMAICA

**REPÚBLICA
DOMINICANA**

HAITÍ

Port-au-
Prince ⊛

Santo
Domingo •

*Islas
Vírgenes*

San
Juan
⊛

Mayagüez •

• Ponce

**PUERTO
RICO**

Antillas Menores

Antigua

Guadalupe

Dominica

Martinica
Santa Lucía

Barbados

San Vicente

Granada

**Trinidad y
Tobago**

Mar Caribe

ONDURAS

ucigalpa

NICARAGUA

ón

⊛ Managua

L. de Nicaragua

ntarenas

**COSTA
RICA** ⊛

San José •

PANAMÁ

*Canal de
Panamá*

• Colón

⊛ • Panamá

*Golfo
de
Panamá*

Curaçao

Aruba

Bonaire

*Isla
Margarita*

⊛
Caracas

Río Orinoco

VENEZUELA

GUYANA

Río Magdalena

COLOMBIA

⊛ Bogotá

B R A S I L

ECUADOR

PERÚ

¡Trato hecho!
Spanish for Real Life

THIRD EDITION

JOHN T. MCMINN
Austin Community College

NURIA ALONSO GARCÍA
Providence College

PEARSON

Prentice
Hall

Upper Saddle River, New Jersey 07458

Senior Acquisitions Editor: Bob Hemmer
Director of Editorial Development: Julia Caballero
Development Editor: Natalie Hansen, Seven Worldwide Publishing Solutions
Senior Director of Market Development: Kristine Suárez
Assistant Director of Production: Mary Rottino
Production Editor: Nancy Stevenson
Assistant Editor: Meriel Martínez Moctezuma
Media Editor: Samantha Alducin
Composition/Full-Service Project Management: Natalie Hansen, Sue Katkus, and Kathy Zander, Seven Worldwide Publishing Solutions

Prepress and Manufacturing Buyer: Brian Mackey
Prepress and Manufacturing Assistant Manager: Mary Ann Gloriande
Interior and Cover Design: Van Mua, Seven Worldwide Publishing Solutions
Director, Image Resource Center: Melinda Reo
Image Coordinator: Craig Jones
Interior Image Specialist: Beth Boyd Brenzel
Manager, Rights & Permissions IRC: Zina Arabia
Photo Research: Emily Tietz
Line Art Coordinator: Mirella Signoretto
Publisher: Phil Miller

Photo Credits appear on pp. 430–431, which constitutes a continuation of the copyright page.

This book was set in 10.5/12 Berkeley Book by Seven Worldwide Publishing Solutions, and was printed and bound by Courier Kendallville. The cover was printed by Coral Graphics.

 © 2006, 2000, 1996 by Pearson Education Upper Saddle River, New Jersey 07458

Printed in the United States of America
10 9 8 7 6 5 4 3 2 1

Student Text: ISBN 0-13-191408-1
Annotated Instructor's Edition: ISBN 0-13-191411-1
Student Text (Paperback): ISBN 0-13-193705-7

Prentice-Hall International (UK) Limited, London
Prentice-Hall of Australia Pty. Limited, Sydney
Prentice-Hall Canada Inc., Toronto
Prentice-Hall Hispanoamericana, S.A., Mexico
Prentice-Hall of India Private Limited, New Delhi
Prentice-Hall of Japan, Inc., Tokyo
Pearson Education Asia Pte. Ltd., Singapore
Editora Prentice-Hall do Brasil, Ltda., Rio de Janeiro

BRIEF CONTENTS

SCOPE AND SEQUENCE

¡Trato hecho! Spanish for Real Life, **Third Edition,** is an innovative beginning Spanish program completely driven by pedagogical priorities for students who want to put Spanish to immediate use in their community or place of work.

The main goals of **¡Trato hecho!** are to develop proficiency in and appreciation for the Spanish language, to foster students' understanding of Hispanic cultures and their growing importance in the world, and to provide contexts that emphasize the usefulness of Spanish in today's communities, particularly in North America.

Students today are aware of the important role Spanish plays and will continue to play in North America's economy and society. The global economy, with its ever-increasing opportunities in international business, has sparked a renewed interest in the study of languages. **¡Trato hecho!** responds to this surging interest by stressing the features of Spanish needed for everyday communication and applying these features immediately to realistic settings around the world.

The Modular Organization

At the heart of **¡Trato hecho!** is its flexible, modular organization. The main theme of each of the twelve chapters is divided into five interrelated **Temas,** each of which corresponds to a language function and comprises a two-page vocabulary module and a two-page grammar module.

MODULAR ORGANIZATION		
Chapter	Tema 1	Vocabulary Module
		Grammar Module
	Tema 1	Vocabulary Module
		Grammar Module
	Tema 3	Vocabulary Module
		Grammar Module
	Tema 4	Vocabulary Module
		Grammar Module
	Tema 5	Vocabulary Module
		Grammar Module

After the five **Temas,** an eight-page **¡Trato hecho!** cultural magazine, divided into four sections, heightens interest in learning Spanish through cultural readings, integrated video segments portraying the Hispanic community, and personalized writing activities that stress the value of Spanish and cultural understanding in daily life in North America, as well as when traveling around the world.

The modular organization of **¡Trato hecho!** was developed in response to the requests of busy students who need material organized into clear and functional step-by-step sections. Students who work full- or part-time in addition to attending college benefit from the compact modules because material is more manageable when learners can test their abilities and apply new material in one module before moving on to the next one. Students find smaller, clear-cut chunks of material better suited to their fragmented schedules. Instructors are drawn to the modular organization because each module contains presentational material and its related practice, which provides flexibility in planning and personalizing a course, and particularly in streamlining it to the needs of their students.

Development and Design

The development and design of *¡Trato hecho!* implement a process completely driven by pedagogical priorities. New material is presented through illustrations, photos, realia, and other graphics that are integrated with text so that each reinforces the other. Developing a language program with fully integrated text and graphics poses a serious challenge for authors and publishers. In the traditional textbook-writing process, an author usually completes a manuscript before designers, artists, and photo researchers create the design and format and add the visual support of illustrations and photographs. This process often results in photographs with limited functional or pedagogical value or in materials that are difficult (or impossible) to use.

To address this situation, the publishing team worked simultaneously on the writing and design of the program. We custom designed each two-page spread so that text and graphics not only fit in the space allocated for each module but also work together in a dynamic and pedagogically effective manner. The result is a new way of presenting Spanish that invigorates instructors and students and provides instant visual cues for learning and remembering material.

Chapter Organization

The material in the twelve chapters is organized into five interrelated, color-coded **Temas** that emphasize a particular communicative skill. Each color-coded topic contains one two-page vocabulary module and one two-page grammar module. This modular, color-coded format provides an extremely focused and flexible framework

CHAPTER ORGANIZATION	
Chapter opener with communicative objectives	
Tema 1	Vocabulary Module
	Grammar Module
Tema 2	Vocabulary Module
	Grammar Module
Tema 3	Vocabulary Module
	Grammar Module
Tema 4	Vocabulary Module
	Grammar Module
Tema 5	Vocabulary Module
	Grammar Module
Cultural Magazine: *¡Trato hecho!*	En Portada
	De puertas abiertas a la comunidad
	Escapadas
	En palabras de...
Vocabulary summary	

for presenting and learning new material within the limited blocks of time available to today's students and instructors. The end-of-chapter vocabulary list is broken into five color-coded sections corresponding to the five **Temas** so that students can acquire the material from the chapter one section at a time while associating it with the communicative function of each **Tema.**

Vocabulary Modules. *¡Trato hecho!* teaches useful vocabulary and expressions in contexts in which a broad range of students—traditional college-aged students, working people completing coursework at night, or retirees returning to school— might realistically find themselves or someone they know. The illustrations and photographs in the vocabulary module of each **Tema** make it possible to present new lexical structures entirely in Spanish while building a rich cultural framework. Presentation of new material is interwoven with contextualized and personalized activities that give students immediate practice. A limited number of new structures are previewed lexically in each vocabulary module, which lays the groundwork for their formal presentation in the grammar modules that follow. *¿Cómo se pronuncia?* sections are integrated as needed into presentations of new material at points where students are likely to have particular questions about pronunciation or spelling. For example, the difference between the use of **qu** and **cu** is introduced with the presentation of question words that illustrate the **qu/cu** alternation.

Grammar Modules. The grammar module of each **Tema** presents and practices a new structure that is useful for the communicative theme. Grammar explanations are very accessible and straightforward, with numerous charts and examples to facilitate study and review. In addition, self-check questions (*Para averiguar*) appear in the margins of the text to help students focus on essential points of each explanation and to enable them to verify that they have assimilated an explanation after they have read it.

We encourage students to look over these self-check questions before proceeding to the activities, which provide immediate, contextualized reinforcement of new structures.

All activities in both the vocabulary and grammar modules are designed to promote meaningful communication on topics about which students really have something to say. Students must understand what they are saying in order to answer correctly, and no activities allow students to manipulate grammatical forms without understanding what they are communicating. Activities are sequenced from simple recognition to more global activities that allow students to use new material in more creative ways.

Cultural Magazine. The eight-page cultural magazine called *¡Trato hecho!* expands on the theme of each chapter, guiding students to a better understanding of Hispanic cultures and their growing importance in our society, while also encouraging their dreams of visiting exciting places around the globe where students can use their Spanish and broaden their view of the world. Accompanying reading and writing strategies help students handle more challenging uses of Spanish. The cultural magazine uses dynamic art and graphics and a rich variety of charts, articles, authentic video segments, and other documents in a magazine-style presentation with the following sections:

- **En portada** (two pages). A cultural reading invites students to make cross-cultural comparisons related to the theme of the chapter. Reading strategies guide students through the text and help them approach the material in a more meaningful and effective way.
- **De puertas abiertas a la comunidad** (two pages). Authentic video segments feature Hispanics in the United States using Spanish in different sectors of the community and emphasize the growing value of being bilingual in our society.

- **Escapadas** (three pages). This visually appealing travelogue takes students on a virtual voyage to tourist sites from all over the Hispanic world with the hope that the beauty and cultural and historical interest of these places will encourage them to travel.

- **En palabras de…** (one page). Writing activities offer students opportunities to apply their steadily growing lexical and grammatical competence to situations that require practical and creative expression.

Vocabulary Summary. The last two-page module of each chapter presents a cumulative list of new, active vocabulary divided into color-coded sections that correspond to the **Temas** in which they appear. The color-coded format of the chapter vocabulary list makes it easy for students to study for quizzes and exams and for instructors to develop them.

Program Components

The essential goal of each component of **¡Trato hecho!** is simple: to make teaching and learning Spanish a meaningful, successful, and gratifying experience. Each component is carefully and logically woven into the program in order to provide students with a global understanding of the Spanish language and the Hispanic people.

Student Resources

¡Trato hecho! Third Edition, Student Text in Paperback   0-13-193705-7
A paperback version of the text is available. It weighs less and costs less but contains exactly the same materials as the hardcover version.

Student Activities Manual   0-13-191410-3
The organization of the **Student Activities Manual** (SAM) parallels that of the student text. There are activities corresponding to each **Tema** in the textbook; writing exercises and listening activities that recycle and reinforce vocabulary, grammar topics, cultural information, and communicative functions presented in the student text. A new *Diario* feature guides students in writing paragraphs on the topic of each **Tema,** which are later revised, combined, and refined in the final composition in the *¡Trato hecho!* section of the SAM. The *¡Trato hecho!* cultural magazine from the textbook has a corresponding section in the SAM, *En la red* Web activities that encourage students to investigate related topics and questions about Hispanic culture and Hispanics living in the United States on the Internet, and a guided composition in which students revise paragraphs written in the *Diario* sections of the **Temas** and combine them into a longer composition.

Answer Key to Accompany Student Activities Manual   0-13-191416-2
A separate, optional **Answer Key to Accompany Student Activities Manual** allows students to check their own work if the instructor wishes.

Audio CDs to Accompany Student Activities Manual   0-13-191414-6
CD recordings provide easy access to each listening comprehension activity in the Student Activities Manual.

Audio CD to Accompany Student Text   0-13-191423-5
CD recordings corresponding to each listening activity in the textbook as well as the dialogues and the vocabulary words allow students flexibility in practicing listening comprehension and pronunciation at home.

Student Video CD-ROM   0-13-191415-4
Filmed especially for **¡Trato hecho!,** the *De puertas abiertas a la comunidad* video features interviews with approximately 25 Spanish speakers from various

Spanish-speaking countries and from diverse backgrounds and professions on various issues and topics related to Spanish in the community. Students can listen firsthand to the personal and professional experiences of journalists, students, artists, and business owners among others living in New York City. Pre-, during-, and post-viewing activities are featured in the *¡Trato hecho!* section of each chapter. The video script is also available for self-checking of the activities or to facilitate comprehension of the video content.

Review Booklet   0-13-155502-2

Two review chapters available as a paper supplement or online can serve as an end-of-semester review before the final exam or may be used to reactivate previously learned material at the beginning of the next semester. The first review chapter combines vocabulary, structures, functions, and cultural information in applied settings to offer a systematic review of all material covered in the first half of the book. The second review chapter does the same for material from the last six chapters.

Situation Task Cards   0-13-189603-2

Task-based activities and situations promote meaningful interaction in the Spanish as a second language classroom.

Gramática viva: Interactive Student Grammar CD-ROM   0-13-111796-3

This interactive CD-ROM is designed for students to learn and practice grammar outside class, which helps prepare them for a highly interactive, communicative classroom experience. An instructional video on the CD-ROM delivers detailed grammar explanations and examples for 60 grammatical structures. The instruction is immediately followed by (1) oral drill practice with voice recording capability, which allows students to practice their pronunciation; (2) written activities with immediate feedback to practice the grammar forms in context; (3) an oral activity in which students develop and practice their oral skills; (4) a guided, open-ended writing activity to enable students to use the grammatical structures in increasingly more demanding contexts.

Instructor Resources

Annotated Instructor's Edition   0-13-191411-1

Numerous marginal annotations in the **Annotated Instructor's Edition** include warm-up and expansion activities as well as additional cultural information. Also included are an array of tips and ideas designed specifically for graduate teaching assistants or adjunct faculty who may have limited preparation time or who may be teaching Spanish for the first time in many years.

Instructor's Resource Manual   0-13-191421-9

In addition to sample syllabi and lesson plans, the scripts for the audio program and the video, and strategies for integrating multimedia into the course, the **Instructor's Resource Manual** (IRM) includes an array of extra in-class activities with many engaging, interactive, game-like activities that may be presented on transparencies. The IRM also includes the testing program, which uses a variety of techniques to evaluate students' skills in listening, speaking, reading, writing, and cultural awareness. The testing program consists of alternative tests for each chapter and final examinations for the end of each semester.

Audio CD to Accompany Testing Program   0-13-191409-X

This CD contains the audio that accompanies the listening comprehension section for each test.

VHS Video Cassette   0-13-191418-9
The *¡Trato hecho!* video features interviews with approximately 25 Spanish speakers from various Spanish-speaking countries and diverse backgrounds and professions on various issues and topics related to Spanish in the community. Students can listen firsthand to personal and professional experiences described by journalists, students, artists, and business-owners among others living in New York City. Pre-, during-, and post-viewing activities are featured in the *¡Trato hecho!* section of each chapter. The video on the VHS cassette is the same as the video on the Student Video CD-ROM.

Image Resource CD   0-13-191413-8
This CD-ROM contains the line drawings in the textbook. Instructors can use these images to create their own activities, tests, and transparencies.

Picture File   0-13-931313-3
This beautifully crafted photo file of 50 color photographs mounted on cardboard can be used to aid instructors to provide comprehensible input of vocabulary themes such as family life or to stimulate conversation when discussing topics such as jobs, sports, and travel.

Online Resources

Companion Website™

A Web site **www.prenhall.com/trato** has been specifically created to accompany *¡Trato hecho!* and contains a wealth of activities and cultural resources. Students can practice and review their vocabulary and grammar through self-test exercises, the results of which they can communicate to their instructor via e-mail. Students may also do guided research on topics related to the chapter themes, answering brief essay questions, which give them further writing practice. The complete audio program, games, and interactive flashcards are included to enhance self-study. Finally, video-based listening comprehension activities extend the student's interaction with the culturally rich *De puertas abiertas a la comunidad* video.

 **OneKey**

This resource features everything your students need for out-of-class work, conveniently organized to match your syllabus. **OneKey** includes the online **Student Activities Manual** with integrated audio linked to an automated gradebook, in addition to video and Web resources. Your students will save money too!

ACKNOWLEDGMENTS

We would like to thank everyone who has helped us turn our years of teaching experience into ¡*Trato hecho!*

First we would like to express our appreciation to our students and colleagues, who are always an inspiration. Special thanks go to Maisa Taha for her work on the testing program. We are also indebted to the many members of the teaching community who reviewed manuscript and whose comments and suggestions helped us shape, reshape, and fine-tune every chapter. Their many eyes helped us to see more clearly. We gratefully acknowledge and thank:

Catherine L. Angell, Austin Community College
Enrica J. Ardemagni, Indiana University-Purdue University Indianapolis
M. Ellen Blossman, Armstrong Atlantic State University
Darren Broome, Gordon College
Elaine Marie Coney, Southwest Mississippi Community College
Jane Marcus-Delgado, College of Staten Island, City University of New York
Kim A. Eherenman, University of San Diego
Laurie Huffman, Los Medanos College
Teresa Dee Kennedy, Lenoir Community College
Lynne Flora Margolies, Manchester College
Vija G. Mendelson, University of Massachusetts–Amherst
Krystyna P. Musik, University of Delaware
Francisco R. Pérez, Midlands Technical College
Richard Seybolt, University of Minnesota–Duluth
Jorge W. Suazo, Georgia Southern University
Germán Torres, Georgia State University
Joanna Vargas, Columbia College
Francisco Vivar, University of Memphis
Richard F. Williams, Benedict College
Janice Wright, College of Charleston

As always, it has been a pleasure to work with our friends from Prentice Hall: Publisher, Phil Miller; Senior Acquisitions Editor, Bob Hemmer; Director of Development, Julia Caballero; Production Editor, Nancy Stevenson; Assistant Director of Production, Mary Rottino; Supplements Editor, Meriel Martínez Moctezuma; Media Editor, Samantha Alducin; Media Production Manager, Roberto Fernández; Sponsoring Editor for Spanish, María F. García; and Senior Director of Market Development, Kristine Suárez. Their support and dedication allowed us to create the book we had always envisioned.

Words cannot express our thanks to Natalie Hansen and her production staff at Seven Worldwide. Her extraordinary skill and talent guided the development and production of ¡*Trato hecho!* with tireless dedication and admirable professionalism. We also gratefully recognize the contributions of Kathy Zander, Cathy Townsend, Sue Katkus, Sue McKinnon, Van Mua, and Barb Knospe at Seven Worldwide. We are equally happy to acknowledge the assistance of Seven Worldwide partners: our native readers, proofreaders, and our wonderful copy editor.

Last, but not least, we extend a big hug to our friends and family for their support throughout it all, especially Daniel, Joel, Aram, and our dear friends and colleagues of the Providence College and Austin Community College communities.

¡Trato hecho!

1

¡A conocernos!

In this chapter you will learn to...

- introduce yourself and get to know others
- introduce and describe acquaintances
- describe the university
- count and exchange phone numbers
- talk about your classes
- describe your schedule
- better understand Hispanics in the United States

You will use...

- formal **usted** and familiar **tú** to say *you*
- the verb **ser** and adjectives
- the articles **el, la, los, las**
- numbers 1–100
- **me, te, le gusta** and **mi(s), tu(s), su(s)**
- days of the week and expressions for telling time

VOCABULARIO
¿Cómo te llamas? ¿Cómo estás?

Suggestions. A. Tell students that in this course they will learn the vocabulary and grammar that is most useful to carry on everyday conversations. To illustrate, have students brainstorm in pairs to think of the first ten questions in English they would probably ask a student they had just met. (*What is your name? Where are you from?*, etc.) Point out that most of these questions will be learned in the next few weeks. To create a friendly, interactive atmosphere in the class, have students use the questions to interview and present their partner to the class in English. Keep a list of the questions, and tell students that you will check midsemester to see how many they can ask in Spanish.
B. Write useful expressions on the board for meeting and greeting people. Have students go through a greeting line. Students stand in two lines facing one another. They shake hands, greet each other, ask names, and ask how the other is doing. When they have met the person facing them, they greet the next person in the line facing them. At the end of the line they shift to the other side, until they have gone in a full circle and met everyone. (Students shifting sides at the ends of lines have to wait out one turn.) Afterward, present the question *¿Quién es?* and ask students names of classmates. If they don't recall, let them ask again.

Use these expressions to introduce yourself to a classmate or to other people with whom you have an informal relationship.

— **Buenos días. Soy** Antonio.
  ¿Y tú? ¿Cómo te llamas?
— **Hola.** Me llamo David.
— **Mucho gusto,** David.
— **Igualmente. ¿De dónde eres,** Antonio?
— Soy **de aquí.** ¿Y tú?
— Soy de Miami.

Use the following expressions to ask how a classmate is doing.

— **Buenas tardes. ¿Cómo estás?**
— **Estoy…**

bien   **regular**   **mal**

You use a different verb form and a different word for *you* when talking to someone to whom you want to show respect, such as a professor or an adult you do not know well.

— **Buenas noches.** Soy Carlos González. ¿Y usted? ¿Cómo se llama?
— Me llamo María Delgado.
— Mucho gusto.
— Igualmente. ¿Cómo está usted?
— Estoy **muy** bien, gracias. ¿Y usted?
— Muy bien. ¿De dónde es usted, señor González?
— Soy de México. ¿Y usted, señora Delgado?
— Soy de Puerto Rico.

¡Ojo!

Use **señora** to address married women and **señorita** for unmarried women. There is no equivalent for *Ms.* in Spanish.

Buenos días. *Good morning.* **soy** *I am* **¿Y tú?** *And you?* **¿Cómo te llamas?** *What's your name?* **Hola.** *Hi.* **Mucho gusto.** *Pleased to meet you.* **Igualmente.** *Likewise.* **¿De dónde eres?** *Where are you from?* **de** *from* **aquí** *here* **Buenas tardes.** *Good afternoon.* **¿Cómo estás?** *How are you?* **estoy** *I am* **bien** *well* **Buenas noches.** *Good evening.* **muy** *very*

Here is how you can ask people to spell their name.

¿Cómo se escribe González? ¿Se escribe **con** acento **o sin** acento? Se escribe…

a	a	**k**	ka	**s**	ese
b	be (grande)	**l**	ele	**t**	te
c	ce	**m**	eme	**u**	u
d	de	**n**	ene	**v**	uve, ve (chica), ve
e	e	**ñ**	eñe		(corta)
f	efe	**o**	o	**w**	uve doble, doble
g	ge	**p**	pe		ve, doble u
h	hache	**q**	cu	**x**	equis
i	i	**r**	ere	**y**	i griega
j	jota	**rr**	erre	**z**	zeta

1-1 Respuestas. Which responses from the box are logical?

> Me llamo Anita López.   Soy de aquí.   Igualmente.   Mucho gusto.
> Buenos días.   Soy Daniel Reyna.   Buenas tardes.   Estoy muy bien, gracias.
> Estoy regular.   Se escribe con **z**.   Hola.

1. ¡Hola!
2. ¿Cómo te llamas?
3. ¿Cómo se llama usted?
4. ¿De dónde eres?
5. Soy Carlos González.
6. ¿González se escribe con z o s?
7. Mucho gusto.
8. ¿Cómo estás?
9. ¿Cómo está usted?
10. Buenas tardes.

1-2 ¿Cómo se escribe? Spell your favorite people and things in Spanish. Your classmates will try to name them.

1. su restaurante favorito
2. su actor favorito
3. su actriz favorita
4. su auto favorito

P **Conversaciones.** Role-play the following conversation with a classmate, changing the words in italics so that it describes you.

— *Buenos días.*
— Hola. ¿Cómo te llamas?
— Me llamo *Isabel Ramos.* ¿Y tú?
— Soy *Juan Mosquera.*
— ¿Cómo se escribe *Mosquera?*
— Se escribe *M-O-S-Q-U-E-R-A.* ¿De dónde eres, *Isabel?*
— Soy de *Denver.* ¿Y tú, *Juan?*
— Soy de *aquí.*

Suggestions. A. Point out that *ch* and *ll* used to be considered separate letters and that some dictionaries will have them alphabetized as such. **B.** Spell cognates aloud and have students write them down and give the English equivalent. **C.** Write the names of the following Hispanic countries on the board in a random order. Spell the names of their capitals and have students write them down and name the country. 1. Nicaragua (Managua) 2. España (Madrid) 3. Colombia (Bogotá) 4. México (Ciudad de México) 5. Honduras (Tegucigalpa) 6. Guatemala (Guatemala) 7. Perú (Lima) 8. Paraguay (Asunción) 9. Argentina (Buenos Aires) 10. Ecuador (Quito) 11. Uruguay (Montevideo) 12. Chile (Santiago) **D.** Ask oral questions such as the following about words on the preceding page or students' names. *¿Cómo se escribe **llamo,** con **ll** o con **y**? ¿Cómo se escribe **días,** con acento o sin acento? ¿Cómo se escribe **aquí,** con acento o sin acento?*

Follow-up for 1-2. *¿Cómo se escribe?* Continue the activity by having students spell their name, hometown, favorite singer, and street name.

Suggestion. When working in pairs, randomly group students by counting off half of the class. Then count off the other half, starting again at *uno.* The two students who get the same number are partners.

AUDIO ¡A escuchar!

Listen to another conversation in which two students meet. What are their names and where are they from?

Note. An icon with the letter **P** appearing next to an activity means that it is recommended for students to do the activity in pairs.

---

cómo *how*   **se escribe…** *(it) is written…*   **con** *with*   **o** *or*   **sin** *without*

Para averiguar

There are **Para averiguar** self-check questions with each grammar explanation. After reading the explanation, you should be able to answer these questions.

1. What does **tú** mean? What does **usted** mean? With whom do you use each one?
2. Do you usually use subject pronouns like **yo** (*I*) and **tú** (*you*) in Spanish?
3. What are the two ways of saying *I am, you are* (*familiar*), and *you are* (*formal*)? When do you use **soy** to say *I am*? When do you use **estoy**?

Note. *Ser* and *estar* are explained in more detail in *Capítulo 2*.

Suggestion. Read these statements aloud and have students write *yo* if a student is talking about himself/herself, *tú* if talking to another student, and *usted* if addressing a professor. 1. Me llamo María. 2. Soy de España. 3. ¿Cómo te llamas? 4. ¿De dónde eres? 5. ¿Es usted de México? 6. ¿Cómo se llama usted? 7. ¿Eres de aquí? 8. ¿Cómo está usted? 9. Estoy muy bien hoy. 10. ¿Estás bien?

GRAMÁTICA
Los tratamientos: ¿*tú* o *usted*?

There are two ways to say *you* in Spanish. Use the familiar form **tú** when talking to a friend, a classmate, a family member, or a child. Use the formal form **usted** to address an adult you do not know or someone to whom you wish to show respect. **Usted** is often abbreviated **Ud.** Verb forms are different for each of the subject pronouns.

YO (*I*)	TÚ (*YOU*, FAMILIAR)	USTED (*YOU*, FORMAL)
(Yo) me llamo…	¿Cómo te llamas (tú)?	¿Cómo se llama (Ud.)?
(Yo) soy…	(Tú) eres…	(Ud.) es…
(Yo) estoy…	(Tú) estás…	(Ud.) está…

In Spanish the words **yo** (*I*) and **tú** (*you*, familiar) are normally omitted because the verb ending indicates who the subject is. The pronoun **usted** (*you*, formal) is used more often than **yo** and **tú**. Both **soy** and **yo soy** are translated as *I am*. The word **yo** is included only when you want to put emphasis on the word *I*. As you can see, you should not expect to be able to translate word for word from English to Spanish. The lack of one-to-one correspondence can also be seen in the expressions used to give names.

SPANISH	LITERAL TRANSLATION	ENGLISH EQUIVALENT
(Yo) me llamo…	*(I) myself call…*	*My name is…*

There are also two ways to say *to be* in Spanish, **ser** and **estar**. Use the forms of **ser** (**soy, eres,** and **es**) to say *I am, you are* (familiar), and *you are* (formal) when saying who someone is or where one is from originally. Use the forms of **estar** (**estoy, estás,** and **está**) when saying how one is feeling or doing or where one is at a given moment.

Soy María Delgado.	***I am*** *María Delgado.*
Soy de México.	***I am*** *from Mexico.*
Estoy muy bien hoy.	***I am*** *very well today.*

1-3 **¿Tú o usted?** In which situation would you more likely use the following phrases, **A** or **B**?

1. ¿Cómo te llamas?
2. ¿Cómo se llama usted?
3. ¿Cómo está usted?
4. ¿Cómo estás?
5. Me llamo Pablo Zamora, ¿y usted?
6. Me llamo Alicia, ¿y tú?
7. ¿De dónde es usted?
8. ¿Eres de México?
9. ¿De dónde eres?
10. ¿Es usted de Miami?

A

B

1-4 ¿Cómo se llama usted? / ¿Cómo te llamas? How would you ask these people their name?

> **Modelo**   an elderly neighbor
> **¿Cómo se llama usted?**

1. a professor
2. a classmate
3. your classmate's little brother
4. a salesclerk
5. your roommate's grandmother
6. your roommate's girlfriend/boyfriend
7. your father's boss
8. your mother's secretary

1-5 ¿Cómo estás? ¿De dónde eres? How would you ask the people in the preceding activity how they are and where they are from?

> **Modelo**   an elderly neighbor
> **¿Cómo está usted? ¿De dónde es usted?**

P 1-6 ¿Cómo estás? With a partner, prepare brief exchanges where these people greet each other and ask how they are doing. Do they use **¿Cómo estás?** or **¿Cómo está usted?**

> **Modelo**   — Buenas tardes. ¿Cómo está usted?
> — Estoy muy bien, gracias. ¿Y usted?
> — Estoy bien, gracias.

P 1-7 ¿Y tú? Get acquainted with a classmate, using the following conversation as a model. Change the formal **usted** forms to familiar **tú** forms and make it true for you.

— Buenas tardes. Soy Ximena Duarte. ¿Y usted? ¿Cómo se llama?
— Me llamo Enrique Contreras.
— Mucho gusto, señor Contreras.
— Igualmente. ¿Cómo está usted?
— Estoy muy bien. ¿Y usted?
— Bien, gracias. ¿De dónde es usted, señora Duarte?
— Soy de Miami. ¿Y usted, señor Contreras?
— Soy de aquí.

Follow-up for 1-3. *¿Tú o usted?* With partners, have students imagine what the people in the photos are saying. They should prepare two conversations to present to the class.

Suggestions. A. Write names of celebrities on pieces of paper. Try to think of people who have had good or bad things happen to them lately. Randomly distribute the slips of paper and pick pairs of students to introduce themselves as the celebrities whose names they received. They should shake hands, greet each other, ask each other's name, and how each other is doing. **B.** Have students open their books to the maps of the Spanish-speaking world inside the front cover. Read the following sentences and have students say what city these people would say they are from if they are from their nation's capital. 1. Soy de Venezuela. (Soy de Caracas.) 2. Soy de Nicaragua. (Soy de Managua.) 3. Soy de Cuba. (Soy de La Habana.) 4. Soy de la República Dominicana. (Soy de Santo Domingo.) 5. Soy de Costa Rica. (Soy de San José.) 6. Soy de Honduras. (Soy de Tegucigalpa.) 7. Soy de Chile. (Soy de Santiago.) 8. Soy de Bolivia. (Soy de Sucre. o Soy de La Paz.) 9. Soy de Uruguay. (Soy de Montevideo.) 10. Soy de Paraguay. (Soy de Asunción.) 11. Soy de Ecuador. (Soy de Quito.) **C.** In random order, write the names of the following Hispanic celebrities (or others) on the board. Read the statements and have students say who you are. 1. Soy de la República Dominicana. Ahora estoy en Chicago. (Sammy Sosa) 2. Soy actriz. Soy de México. Ahora estoy en California. (Salma Hayek) 3. Soy de Nueva York. Mi familia es de Puerto Rico. (Jennifer López) 4. Soy de Madrid, España. (Enrique Iglesias) 5. Soy de San Francisco, California. Mi familia es de Perú. (Benjamin Bratt) 6. Soy de Colombia. (Shakira) 7. Soy de Nueva York. Mi familia es de Ecuador. (Christina Aguilera) 8. Soy de San Juan, Puerto Rico. (Ricky Martin)

Note. An icon with the letter **P** appearing next to an activity means that it is recommended for students to do the activity in pairs.

VOCABULARIO

Quiero presentarte a... / Quiero presentarle a...

mis hermanas (No tengo ningún hermano.)

mi madre

mis padres

mi padre

mi compañera de clase

mi profesora

mi compañero de clase

mi mejor amigo   mi mejor amiga   mi novia   mi novio

¡Ojo!

You will be able to understand a lot of Spanish that you read because many words, like the adjectives presented here, look like English words and have the same meaning. Such words are called cognates. Many nouns and adjectives have different forms to describe males or females. Where two endings are given, use the **-o** to describe males and the **-a** for females.

¿Cómo eres?
Yo soy **muy** extrovertido/a.
Yo soy **menos** intelectual **que** él/ella.
Yo soy serio/a y él/ella **también.**

¿Cómo es tu mejor amigo/a?
Él/Ella es **un poco** tímido/a.
Él/Ella es **más** inteligente **que** yo.
Él/Ella es **tan** serio/a **como** yo.

atlético/a	egoísta	emocional
cómico/a	optimista	intelectual
romántico/a	pesimista	liberal
organizado/a	ambicioso/a	inteligente
extrovertido/a	religioso/a	paciente
tímido/a	serio/a	responsable
impulsivo/a	rebelde	interesante

Quiero presentarte a… (familiar)/**Quiero presentarle a…** (formal) *I want you to meet…*   **No tengo ningún hermano. (No tengo ninguna hermana.)** *I have no brother. (I have no sister.)*   **mi mejor amigo/a** *my best friend*   **muy** *very*   **él** *he*   **ella** *she*   **un poco** *a little*   **menos… que** *less… than*   **más… que** *more… than*   **también** *too, also*   **tan… como** *as… as*

¿Cómo se pronuncia? Las vocales *a, e, i, o, u*

There are five basic vowels in Spanish: **a, e, i, o, u.** Whereas the tongue and lips move as you pronounce vowels in English, you must hold your tongue and lips firmly in the same position when pronouncing vowels in Spanish. This gives vowels in Spanish a purer and often shorter, clipped sound. When pronouncing **o** and **u,** round your lips in a puckered position. Spread the corners of your lips to pronounce **e** and **i.**

a: aquí, mal, madre, atlética, amiga, Panamá
e: me, te, se, rebelde, eres, Venezuela
i: mi, tímido, inteligente, Chile
o: novio, honesto, organizado, Colombia, optimista
u: tú, usted, impulsivo, Uruguay

1-8 ¿Cómo es usted? Pick three adjectives that describe you from the list on the preceding page. Then pick one that does not. If you are female, replace the **-o** ending with **-a.**

> Modelo   **Soy extrovertido/a, liberal y rebelde. No soy atlético/a.**

Now describe a friend or a family member.

> Modelo   **Mi madre es religiosa, responsable y seria. No es paciente.**

1-9 Personalidades. Complete the following sentences with adjectives, comparing you and your best friend.

Yo soy más _____ que mi mejor amigo/a.
Yo soy menos _____ que mi mejor amigo/a.
Yo soy tan _____ como mi mejor amigo/a.

G   **Conversaciones.** In groups of three, read aloud the following conversation in which a student introduces his wife to a friend. Then redo it, introducing two classmates.

E1:   Hola, Juan. Quiero presentarte a mi **esposa,** Anita.
E2:   Mucho gusto, Anita. Soy Juan. ¿Cómo estás?
E3:   Bien, gracias. ¿Y tú, Juan?
E2:   Bien, gracias. ¿Eres de aquí, Anita?
E3:   Soy de Puerto Rico. ¿Y tú, Juan? ¿De dónde eres?
E2:   Soy de Arizona.
E1:   Bien, Juan, **hasta mañana.** Tengo clase **ahora.**
E2:   Sí, **hasta luego.**
E3:   **Adiós.**

Suggestion for *¿Cómo se pronuncia?*
Have students pronounce the words *eight* and *think* very slowly, feeling that the tongue rises as the vowels are pronounced in English. Compare those vowels to the pure [e] and [i] sounds of Spanish. Then have students pronounce *spoke* and *clue* very slowly. Point out that the lips become more rounded during the pronunciation of [o] and [u] in English, whereas the lips must be rounded from the start in Spanish. Have students practice pronouncing the vowels with the list of cognates on the preceding page.

Follow-ups for 1-9. *Personalidades.*
A. Give students the following adjectives and have them compare themselves to their best friend. *Modelo:* paciente > *Yo soy más paciente que mi mejor amigo/a./Yo soy menos paciente que mi mejor amigo/a./Yo soy tan paciente como mi mejor amigo/a.*
1. atlético/a 2. ambicioso/a 3. tímido/a 4. optimista 5. serio/a 6. cómico/a 7. organizado/a 8. liberal
B. Read sentences such as the following ones about celebrities and have students repeat them if they agree or change them to express their opinion. 1. Jay Leno es más cómico que David Letterman. 2. Brad Pitt es menos romántico que Harrison Ford. 3. Madonna es menos rebelde que Britney Spears. 4. Dan Rather es tan inteligente como Peter Jennings. 5. Katie Couric es más intelectual que Oprah Winfrey.

AUDIO ¡A escuchar!

Listen to another conversation in which a student introduces two acquaintances. Who are they, what are their names, and where are they from?

Note. An icon with the letter **G** means that it is recommended to do the activity in groups.

---

esposo/a *husband/wife, spouse* **Hasta mañana.** *See you tomorrow.* **ahora** *now* **Hasta luego.** *See you later.*
Adiós. *Good-bye.*

Para averiguar

1. What are three uses of the verb **ser** (to be)?
2. What are the forms of **ser** that go with each subject pronoun?
3. When do you use the **-as** ending instead of **-os** in **nosotros, vosotros,** or **ellos**? What form of these pronouns is used for mixed groups?
4. Where is **vosotros** used? What is used in American Spanish?
5. Which adjectives have distinct masculine and feminine forms? Which do not? How do you make adjectives plural?

¡Ojo!

The **usted, él,** and **ella** forms of verbs are always the same, as are the **ustedes, ellos,** and **ellas** forms. You often need to use these pronouns to clarify who the subject is. If **usted se llama** means *your name is,* what would **él se llama** and **ella se llama** mean?

Suggestions. A. Ask students to give the pronoun they would use instead of the following names: *María, Juan, María y Anita, Juan y Carlos, Juan y María, Juan y yo, tú y yo, María y tú, María y yo.* **B.** Reusing the subjects in section *A,* have students give the corresponding form of *ser* for each one.

GRAMÁTICA

La identidad y las descripciones: *ser* y los adjetivos

Use the following forms of the verb **ser** (*to be*) to identify people, to say where they are from, or to describe what they are like.

SER (*TO BE*)					
yo	**soy**	*I am*	nosotros/as	**somos**	*we are*
tú	**eres**	*you are (familiar)*	vosotros/as	**sois**	*you are (plural)*
usted	**es**	*you are (formal)*	ustedes	**son**	*you are (plural)*
él	**es**	*he is*	ellos	**son**	*they are*
ella	**es**	*she is*	ellas	**son**	*they are*

With names of people or things as the subject of a sentence, use the **él/ella** form of the verb if it is singular and **ellos/ellas** if it is plural. Use the **nosotros/as** form when including yourself in a group. Place **no** before verbs to negate them.

Carlos **es** mi mejor amigo.   *Carlos is my best friend.*
Mis amigos **son** un poco rebeldes.   *My friends are a little rebellious.*
Mis amigos y yo **no somos** atléticos.   *My friends and I are not athletic.*

Subject pronouns are generally not used, unless they are needed for clarity or to emphasize who you are talking about.

Somos amigos. *We are friends.*   ¿Eres de aquí? *Are you from here?*

The feminine pronouns **nosotras, vosotras,** and **ellas** are used for all-female groups. For groups containing males, use **nosotros, vosotros,** and **ellos**. In Spain, **vosotros/as** is used as the plural of familiar **tú** to talk to a group of friends or classmates, and **ustedes** is the plural of formal **usted. Vosotros/as** is not used in American Spanish. **Ustedes** is used to say *you* (plural) to all groups, formal or familiar, and is often abbreviated **Uds.**

Use adjectives with the verb **ser** to describe people. Adjectives have different forms, depending on whether they describe males or females, and whether the noun is singular or plural. Generally adjectives ending with **-o** in the masculine form end with **-a** in the feminine. Adjectives ending with other letters or **-ista** have just one form for both masculine and feminine.

	MASCULINE	FEMININE	MASCULINE	FEMININE
SINGULAR	tímid**o**	tímid**a**	inteligent**e**	inteligent**e**
PLURAL	tímid**os**	tímid**as**	inteligent**es**	inteligent**es**

Mi novio es **inteligente** y **romántico** pero (*but*) es **egoísta** también.
Mi novia es **inteligente** y **romántica** pero es **egoísta** también.

Make adjectives and nouns plural by adding **-s** if they end with a vowel and **-es** if they end with a consonant. Use the masculine plural form of adjectives to describe a group with both males and females.

Juan es **intelectual** y **serio.**   >   Juan y María son **intelectuales** y **serios.**

1-10 **¿Cierto o falso?** Complete the following sentences with the correct form of **ser.** Then say whether each one is true (**cierto**) or false (**falso**) for you.

> **Modelo**   Mi padre ____es____ liberal.
> **Cierto. Mi padre es liberal.**
> **Falso. Mi padre no es liberal. / Falso. No tengo padre.**

1. Yo _____ tímido/a.

2. Mis amigos y yo _____ un poco rebeldes.

3. Mis profesores _____ intelectuales.

4. Mi hermano _____ muy egoísta.

5. Mi mejor amigo/a _____ de México.

6. Mis padres _____ de California.

7. Mi madre _____ un poco tímida.

8. Mis compañeros de clase y yo _____ muy inteligentes.

℗ 1-11 **Descripciones.** A friend is telling you who these people are and describing them. Work with a partner to prepare descriptions.

> **Modelo**   **Juan es mi compañero de clase. No es muy organizado.**

1-12 **Comparaciones.** You are talking to your best friend. Write sentences comparing your friends and family members. Use an item from each column and change the adjectives to the appropriate forms. You may also insert other adjectives of your choice.

> **Modelo**   **Tú y yo somos más rebeldes que mi hermana.**

		egoísta		
Yo...		emocional		yo
Tú...	soy	paciente		tú
Mi padre...	eres	organizado	que	mi padre
Mi madre...	es	romántico	como	mi madre
Mi hermano/a...	somos	rebelde	que	mi hermano/a
Tú y yo...	son	atlético		tú y yo
Mis padres...		serio		mis padres
Mis profesores...		intelectual		mis profesores

Suggestion for 1-10. *¿Cierto o falso?* Point out in *7* that *un poco* does not agree for feminine because it is not an adjective.

Suggestions. **A.** Have students change the verb and adjective to the plural form in the following sentences. *Modelo: Soy liberal. > Somos liberales.* 1. Soy serio. 2. Eres egoísta. 3. Ud. es pesimista. 4. Él es rebelde. 5. Ella es religiosa. 6. No soy atlético. 7. No eres serio. 8. Él no es romántico. **B.** Have students change the following sentences from plural to singular. 1. Somos rebeldes. 2. Ellos son impulsivos. 3. Ellas son inteligentes. 4. Somos intelectuales. 5. Ellos son optimistas. 6. Somos tímidas. **C.** Contradict what I say. *Modelo: Ella es tímida. > No, ella no es tímida. Ella es extrovertida.* 1. Ellos son pesimistas. 2. Él es serio. 3. Somos optimistas. 4. Ella es muy cómica. 5. Ellos son extrovertidos. **D.** Tell students that a friend is talking about his parents. Have them write the following columns on a sheet of paper: *mi padre, mi madre, mis padres, ???.* Students write the number of each sentence they hear in the column of the person it describes. If they cannot tell, they write it under ???. 1. Es muy serio. 2. Es cómico. 3. Son intelectuales. 4. Es muy inteligente. 5. Es muy optimista. 6. Es religioso. 7. Es muy organizada. 8. Son ambiciosos. 9. No es paciente. 10. Es atlética. **E.** Have students compare themselves now to when they were 15 years old. Give them the word *antes* = before. *Modelo: responsable > Soy más responsable ahora que antes./Soy menos responsable ahora que antes./Soy tan responsable ahora como antes. (paciente, atlético/a, optimista, intelectual, egoísta, ambicioso/a, organizado/a, emocional, rebelde, serio/a)*

VOCABULARIO

¿Cómo es la universidad? ¿Qué clases tienes?

TEMA 3

Suggestions. A. Make statements such as the following about your university and have students say whether they are *cierto* or *falso*. 1. La universidad es pequeña. 2. La universidad es vieja. 3. Los edificios son nuevos. 4. Los edificios son feos. 5. La biblioteca es grande. 6. La biblioteca es buena. 7. Los estudiantes son viejos. 8. La cafetería es buena. 9. El laboratorio de lenguas es moderno. 10. El gimnasio es grande. 11. Las residencias son nuevas. 12. El gimnasio es más grande que el laboratorio de lenguas. 13. La biblioteca es más moderna que el laboratorio de lenguas. 14. Los profesores son más trabajadores que los estudiantes. 15. Los estudiantes son más intelectuales que los profesores. **B.** Have students say whether these adjectives describe their best friend *(viejo/a > No, mi mejor amigo/a no es viejo/a.)*: *viejo/a, grande, pequeño/a, feo/a, antipático/a, simpático/a, aburrido/a, interesante, perezoso/a, trabajador/a, bueno/a, malo/a.* Repeat with celebrities such as Cameron Diaz, David Letterman, Barbara Walters, Tom Cruise, or Arnold Schwarzenegger.

¿Cómo es la universidad? ¿Cómo es la cafetería? ¿el laboratorio de **lenguas**? ¿el gimnasio?

Los edificios son...

nuevos y modernos

viejos

La biblioteca es...

grande

pequeña

Los residencias son...

bonitas

feas

Los profesores son...

simpáticos e interesantes

antipáticos y aburridos

¡Ojo!

Use **y** to say *and*, except when the next word begins with **i** or **hi.** In that case use **e** instead.

¿Como es la universidad? *What is the university like?* **lenguas** *languages* **simpático/a** *nice* **e = y** *(and)* **antipático/a** *unpleasant*

Las clases son…

fáciles   **difíciles**

Los estudiantes son…

buenos y trabajadores   **malos y perezosos**

¿**Qué** clases **tienes** este semestre?
Tengo…

ciencias: biología, **química,** física
humanidades: literatura, filosofía
lenguas: inglés, español, francés
ciencias sociales: historia, ciencias políticas, (p)sicología
bellas artes: arte, música
administración de empresas: economía, **contabilidad**
cursos técnicos: matemáticas, **informática**

1-13   En la universidad perfecta. Complete the sentences to describe the ideal university.

1. La biblioteca es… (grande, pequeña)
2. La biblioteca es… (moderna, vieja)
3. Las clases son… (aburridas, interesantes)
4. Los profesores son… (buenos, malos)
5. Los profesores son… (simpáticos, antipáticos)
6. Los estudiantes son… (perezosos, trabajadores)
7. Los edificios son… (nuevos, viejos)
8. Los edificios son… (bonitos, feos)

1-14   Las clases. Replace the words in italics so that the following sentences describe you. If a sentence is already true for you, read it as it is.

1. Este semestre (trimestre) tengo *matemáticas, historia y español.*
2. Mi clase favorita es la clase de *historia.*
3. Mi clase de *matemáticas* es *más* difícil *que* mi clase de *español.*
4. La clase de *historia* es muy interesante.
5. Mi profesor/a de *español* es *simpático/a.*
6. Los estudiantes de la clase de *matemáticas* son *simpáticos.*

P **Conversaciones.** Read the following conversation in which two students talk about their classes. Then redo it with a partner, making it true for you. After you have finished, change roles and do it again.

— ¿Qué clases tienes este semestre (trimestre)?
— Tengo matemáticas, historia, física y español.
— ¿Son interesantes?
— Mis clases de física e historia son interesantes, **pero** mi clase de matemáticas no es muy interesante y es muy grande. La clase de español es mi favorita. Es muy importante y **útil** y la clase es **divertida.**

Suggestions. A. Point out that the *p* in *(p)sicología* is dropped in many regions. **B.** Ask students in what course they would study the following people: *Pablo Picasso y Frida Kahlo (arte), Cervantes (literatura, español), Jean-Paul Sartre (literatura, francés, filosofía), Bill Gates (informática, administración de empresas), Hernán Cortés y Alvar Núñez Cabeza de Vaca (historia), Plácido Domingo y José Carreras (música), Isaac Newton (física), Aristóteles y Sócrates (filosofía), Charles Darwin (biología).* **C.** Have students give the logical answer. 1. Tengo A en mi clase de biología. ¿Es fácil o difícil? 2. Tengo F en mi clase de física. ¿Es fácil o difícil? 3. Mi profesora de literatura es organizada e interesante. ¿Es buena o mala? 4. En mi clase de inglés, los estudiantes son perezosos. ¿Son buenos o malos? 5. La biblioteca es nueva. ¿Es moderna o vieja? 6. La biblioteca es grande y moderna. ¿Es buena o mala? 7. Mi mejor amigo es muy cómico. ¿Es divertido o aburrido? 8. Mi hermano es muy serio y ambicioso. ¿Es trabajador o perezoso? 9. La clase de español es mi mejor clase. ¿Es interesante o aburrida? 10. Mi clase de historia es aburrida. ¿Es buena o mala? 11. Mi profesor de economía es egoísta y no es paciente. ¿Es simpático o antipático? 12. En mi clase de economía, los estudiantes son muy inteligentes. ¿Son buenos o malos?

AUDIO ¡A escuchar!

Listen to another conversation in which one student asks another about her classes this semester. What is she taking and how is each class? Which is her favorite?

---

bueno/a *good*   **trabajador/a** *hardworking*   **malo/a** *bad*   **perezoso/a** *lazy*   **qué** *what*   **tienes** *(do) you have*
tengo *I have*   **química** *chemistry*   **administración de empresas** *business (administration)*   **contabilidad**
accounting   **informática** *computer science*   **pero** *but*   **útil** *useful*   **divertido/a** *fun*

GRAMÁTICA

Hablar de personas y cosas específicas: el artículo definido

Para averiguar

1. For nouns that do not refer to humans or animals, can you tell their gender from what they mean?
2. What endings generally indicate that a noun is masculine? feminine? Are the following cognates masculine or feminine: **familia, actividad, vídeo, definición, televisión, discurso**?
3. What are the four forms of the word for *the* in Spanish? When do you use each?
4. What is a case where the definite article is used in Spanish, but not in English?
5. Which nouns and adjectives generally have different forms for masculine and feminine? Which do not? What are three exceptions?

All nouns in Spanish have gender, even nouns referring to things. This means that they are classified as masculine or feminine. Nouns naming humans or animals are generally masculine or feminine according to their sex, but you cannot guess the gender of nouns naming things from their meaning. For example, the word for *dress* (**vestido**) is masculine.

There are four ways to say *the* (the definite article) in Spanish. The form you use depends on whether a noun is masculine or feminine and singular or plural.

THE DEFINITE ARTICLE		
	MASCULINE	**FEMININE**
SINGULAR	**el** edificio	**la** residencia
PLURAL	**los** edificios	**las** residencias

The definite article is not only used to translate the word *the*, it is also used when making a generalized description of a category of people or things. In such cases, there is no article in English. Adjectives describing things must agree for gender and plurality, just like those describing people.

Los cursos técnicos son difíciles.	*Technical courses are difficult.*
Los amigos son importantes.	*Friends are important.*

Generally, nouns ending with **-o** or **-l** are masculine and those ending with **-a**, **-dad**, **-tad**, **-sión**, or **-ción** are feminine. There are exceptions, such as **el día** (*the day*). The gender of nouns ending with other vowels or consonants is usually not predictable, so you should learn them with the article to help you remember whether they are masculine or feminine. Can you fill in the blanks with **el** or **la**?

_la_ economía	_la_ contabilidad	_la_ administración
_el_ español	_el_ curso	_la_ historia

Like adjectives, most nouns referring to people or animals have distinct forms for masculine or feminine if they end with **-o/-a.** Otherwise, they have the same form for both males and females.

el novio/la novia   el amigo/la amiga   but: el estudiante/la estudiante

Exceptions: Adjectives and nouns ending with **-ista** have **-a** in the masculine form (**el economista/la economista**). Adjectives and nouns ending with **-or** (**el profesor/la profesora, trabajador/trabajadora**) and nationalities (**español/española, francés/francesa**) have feminine forms with **-a.**

1-15   Mi universidad. Complete the following statements with the correct form of the definite article and say whether each statement is true (**cierto**) or false (**falso**) for your university. Correct the false statements. To say there is not something at your university use **No hay...**

> **Modelo**   _____ residencias son modernas.
> **Cierto. Las residencias son modernas. / Falso. Las residencias son viejas. / Falso. No hay residencias.**

1. _____ universidad es grande.
2. _____ edificios son nuevos.
3. _____ clase de español es fácil.
4. _____ estudiantes son trabajadores.
5. _____ biblioteca es nueva y moderna.
6. _____ laboratorio de lenguas es viejo.

1-16 Los cursos. Give your opinions of the following things as in the model.

> **Modelo**   biología / español (fácil)
> **La biología es más fácil que el español. /**
> **La biología es menos fácil que el español. /**
> **La biología es tan fácil como el español.**

1. lenguas / cursos técnicos (interesantes)
2. química / contabilidad (aburrida)
3. español / inglés (difícil)
4. ciencias / lenguas (útiles)
5. administración de empresas / música (divertida)
6. francés / español (útil)
7. clases / amigos (importantes)
8. estudiantes / profesores (trabajadores)

G 1-17 Dos universidades. In groups, write sentences comparing these two universities. Which group can make the most complete comparisons?

> **Modelo**   **Los edificios son modernos en la universidad A pero son viejos en la universidad B.**

La universidad A

La universidad B

VOCABULARIO

TEMA ④ ¿Te gustan las clases? ¿Cuántos estudiantes hay?

Suggestions for presenting and practicing numbers. A. Model pronunciation by saying pairs of numbers and having students repeat the one that is larger. **B.** Have students write 5 numbers between 1 and 30 on a sheet of paper. Randomly call out numbers, and the first student to have all five numbers called out wins. Play again, having students write five multiples of 5 between 1 and 100. **C.** Have students secretly write a number between 1 and 100 on a sheet of paper. As other students guess the number, the student who wrote it answers *más* or *menos* to indicate whether the number is greater or smaller. Students continue taking turns guessing until they narrow it down to the correct number. **D.** Say numbers and have students give the number that is greater by 10. **E.** Give math problems with two possible answers and have students repeat the answer that is correct. 7 + 8 = 14/15 (*¿Siete más ocho son catorce o quince?*) **F.** Send groups of students to the board. Give math problems aloud and have students write them and give the answer. Students at their desks should do the same problems on paper.

¿**Te gusta** la universidad? Hay…

mucha tarea

muchos exámenes

muchas actividades sociales

¡Ojo!

The single word **hay** is used to translate *there is, there are, is there,* and *are there.*

When followed directly by a noun, **uno** changes to **un** for masculine and to **una** for feminine: **un profesor, una profesora.**

— ¿Qué clase te gusta más?
— Me gusta más la clase de historia.
— ¿**Por qué** te gusta?
— Me gusta **porque** es interesante y no hay muchos estudiantes como en las **otras** clases.
— ¿Cuántos estudiantes hay?
— Hay…

0 cero	14 catorce	28 veintiocho
1 uno	15 quince	29 veintinueve
2 dos	16 dieciséis	30 treinta
3 tres	17 diecisiete	31 treinta y uno
4 cuatro	18 dieciocho	32 treinta y dos…
5 cinco	19 diecinueve	
6 seis	20 veinte	40 cuarenta
7 siete	21 veintiuno	50 cincuenta
8 ocho	22 veintidós	60 sesenta
9 nueve	23 veintitrés	70 setenta
10 diez	24 veinticuatro	80 ochenta
11 once	25 veinticinco	90 noventa
12 doce	26 veintiséis	100 cien
13 trece	27 veintisiete	

---

te gusta(n) *do you like* **por qué** *why* **porque** *because* **otro/a** *other*

1-18 En la clase de geografía. Guess which population in millions (**millones**) goes with each of these Hispanic countries. Your instructor will answer **más** (*more*) or **menos** (*less*) until you give the correct answer.

4, 6, 7, 11, 13, 16, 24, 28, 38, 40, 41, un poco más de 100

1. México	**5.** Argentina	**9.** Colombia
2. España	**6.** Venezuela	**10.** Honduras
3. Perú	**7.** Costa Rica	**11.** Chile
4. Guatemala	**8.** Cuba	**12.** El Salvador

1-19 En la clase de matemáticas. Complete the following math problems.

> **Modelo** 10 + 12 =
> **Diez más doce son veintidós.**

1. 8 + 7 =	**5.** 15 + 12 =	**9.** 61 + 15 =
2. 6 + 10 =	**6.** 34 + 22 =	**10.** 84 + 15 =
3. 4 + 14 =	**7.** 49 + 13 =	**11.** 91 + 7 =
4. 13 + 11 =	**8.** 58 + 24 =	**12.** 63 + 47 =

(P) 1-20 ¿Cuántos hay? Ask a classmate these questions.

1. ¿Cuántas clases tienes este semestre? ¿Tienes mucha tarea?
2. ¿Cuántos estudiantes hay en tus clases? ¿Hay más estudiantes en la clase de español o en las otras clases?
3. ¿Cuántos exámenes hay este semestre/trimestre en tus clases?
4. ¿Cuántas clases de español hay en la universidad?

1-21 ¿Cuál es tu número de teléfono? Read the following phone numbers aloud. After you have finished, ask three classmates their phone numbers.

> **Modelo** 223-7607 (**dos, veintitrés, setenta y seis, cero, siete**)

1. 907-1531	**4.** 305-6484	**7.** 257-1707
2. 759-4152	**5.** 414-9099	**8.** 654-1511
3. 878-9505	**6.** 302-1213	**9.** 512-6743

(P) Conversaciones. Read the following conversation in which two students talk about their favorite classes. Then redo it with a partner, making it true for you. After you have finished, change roles and do it again.

— ¿Qué clase te gusta más este semestre (trimestre)?
— Me gusta mucho la clase de historia. Es un poco difícil pero es interesante.
— ¿Hay muchos estudiantes?
— Hay **unos** cincuenta.
— **¿Quieres estudiar conmigo para** el examen?
— **¡Claro!** No me gusta estudiar **solo en casa.** ¿Cuál es tu número de teléfono?
— Es 645-5108 (seis, cuarenta y cinco, cincuenta y uno, cero, ocho).

Answers for 1-18. *En la clase de geografía.* (Populations are rounded to the nearest million.) 1. México: un poco más de 100 2. España: *40* 3. Perú: *28* 4. Guatemala: *13* 5. Argentina: *38* 6. Venezuela: *24* 7. Costa Rica: *4* 8. Cuba: *11* 9. Colombia: *41* 10. Honduras: *7* 11. Chile: *16* 12. El Salvador: *6*

Follow-up for 1-18. *En la clase de geografía.* Have students guess the following statistics about the population of the United States, answering *más* or *menos* until they narrow them down to the correct answer. 1. the number of Hispanics in millions (*39*) 2. the number of Spanish speakers in millions (*28*) (Point out that of the many Spanish-speaking nations, only Mexico, Colombia, Spain, and Argentina have more Spanish speakers than the U.S.) 3. the percentage of U.S. Hispanics that are of Mexican origin (*66*) 4. the percentage that are of Puerto Rican origin (*9*) 5. the percentage that are of Cuban origin (*4*)

AUDIO ¡A escuchar!

Listen to another conversation in which two students talk about their classes and make plans to study together. What are their favorite classes and what are they like? What are the two students' telephone numbers?

---

unos *some*   **¿Quieres…?** *Do you want…?*   **estudiar** *to study*   **conmigo** *with me*   **para** *for*   **¡Claro!** *Sure!*
solo/a *alone*   **en casa** *at home*

GRAMÁTICA

Expresar preferencias y posesión: *me, te, le gusta y mi(s), tu(s), su(s)*

Use the expression **me gusta** to say what you like. Literally **me gusta** means that something *is pleasing to me*. Notice that the subject of the sentence is generally placed after the verb and **me** is placed before it.

Me gusta mi clase de español.
My Spanish class pleases me. = *I like my Spanish class.*

Add **-n** to **gusta** if what you like is plural. Use **gusta** without **-n** if what you like is singular or before a verb. Place **no** before **me** to negate **me gusta.**

Me gust**an** mis clases de historia y español, pero **no** me gust**a** mi clase de inglés.
I like my history and Spanish classes, but I don't like my English class.

When used without a following noun or verb, **me gusta** means *I like it* and **me gustan** means *I like them.*

Me gusta la universidad. **Me gusta** mucho.   *I like the university.* **I like it** *a lot.*

Use **te gusta(n)** to say *you like* to a friend or a classmate, and **le gusta(n)** for *you like* (formal), *he likes,* or *she likes.*

¿Te gusta estudiar?	¿Le gusta estudiar?
Do you (familiar) *like to study?*	*Do you* (formal) *like to study? /*
	Does he like to study? /
	Does she like to study?

Use the definite article (**el, la, los, las**) with the noun naming what you like, where there is no article in English.

Me gusta **la** literatura.	No me gustan **los** exámenes.
I like literature.	*I don't like exams.*

You can replace the definite article with a possessive adjective like **mi(s)** (*my*), **tu(s)** (*your:* familiar), and **su(s)** (*your:* formal, *his, her*) before nouns to indicate to whom something belongs. Add an **-s** to them before plural nouns. Note that **su(s),** like **le gusta(n),** can have three meanings.

Me gusta **mi** clase.	*I like **my** class.*
¿Te gusta **tu** clase?	*Do you like **your** class?* (familiar)
	⎧ *Do you like **your** class?* (formal)
¿Le gusta **su** clase?	⎨ *Does he like **his** class?*
	⎩ *Does she like **her** class?*

1-22 ¿Qué le gusta? Which ending goes with each sentence?

1. Mi mejor amiga es extrovertida. Le gusta…   d   **a.** las comedias.
2. Mi mejor amigo es muy atlético. Le gustan… b   **b.** el tenis y el fútbol.
3. Mi hermana es muy intelectual. Le gustan… f   **c.** estar solo.
4. Mi madre es muy cómica. Le gustan… a   **d.** estar con sus amigos.
5. Mi padre es muy tímido. Le gusta… c   **e.** estar con su novia.
6. Mi hermano es muy romántico. Le gusta… e   **f.** la literatura y la filosofía.

1-23 ¿Qué te gusta estudiar? Ask whether a classmate likes to study these subjects. Your partner will answer and explain why.

Modelo	E1	**¿Te gusta estudiar economía?**
	E2	**No, no me gusta estudiar economía porque es difícil.**

1.

2.

3.

4.

5.

6.

7.

8.

Suggestions. A. Oral questions. *¿Qué le gusta más a usted? ¿Estudiar matemáticas o estudiar biología? ¿Estudiar música o estudiar filosofía? ¿Estudiar español o estudiar contabilidad? ¿Estudiar en casa o estudiar en la biblioteca? ¿Estudiar solo/a o estudiar con dos o tres amigos?* **B.** ¿Es lógico? 1. Me gusta mi clase de matemáticas. La profesora no es muy organizada. 2. Mis compañeros de clase son muy simpáticos. Me gusta estudiar con ellos. 3. Me gustan mis clases este semestre. Mis profesores son muy interesantes. 4. Me gusta estudiar solo/a. Soy muy tímido/a. 5. No me gusta estudiar ciencias. La clase de química es mi favorita. 6. Me gusta estudiar con mi hermano. Es muy inteligente. 7. Mi mejor amigo no es muy intelectual. No le gusta estudiar. 8. Mi mejor amigo/a es muy simpático/a. No me gusta estar con él/ella.

Now describe your partner to the class as in the model.

Modelo	**A Cristina no le gusta la economía porque es difícil. Le gusta el arte porque…**

1-24 Entrevista. Ask a partner the following questions. Be prepared to tell the class about your partner, using **su(s)** or **le gusta(n).**

1. ¿Cómo son tus clases? ¿Qué clases te gustan? ¿Qué clases no te gustan?
2. ¿Cómo son tus profesores? ¿estrictos? ¿simpáticos? ¿interesantes?
3. ¿Te gustan más las clases con muchos estudiantes o con pocos estudiantes? ¿Te gusta hablar (*to talk*) mucho en clase?
4. ¿Te gusta más estudiar solo/a o con tus amigos? ¿Dónde te gusta estudiar? ¿en casa? ¿en la biblioteca? ¿en un café?

VOCABULARIO

TEMA ⑤

¿Qué hora es? ¿Cuándo son tus clases?

¡Ojo!

Use **es la una** to say *it is one o'clock*, but **son las** to say *it is* with the other hours. Use **a la una** to say *at one o'clock* and **a las** to say *at* with other hours.

Suggestions for presenting telling time. A. Create clocks using paper plates. Present telling time using one of the clocks. Then call out times and have students show the time on their clocks. **B.** Give two times and have students repeat the one that is later. 1. Es la una./Son las dos. 2. Son las once./Son las nueve. 3. Son las ocho y diez./Son las ocho y cuarto. 4. Es la una y media./Es la una y cuarto. 5. Son las siete menos diez./Son las siete menos cinco. 6. Son las tres y cuarto./Son las tres menos cuarto. 7. Son las nueve de la mañana./Son las nueve de la noche. **C.** Give the following times and have students say what time it really is if your watch is thirty minutes behind. *Modelo: Son las dos y diez. > Son las tres menos veinte.* 1. Es la una y media. 2. Son las dos y cuarto. 3. Son las tres menos diez. 4. Son las diez y diez. 5. Son las cuatro y cuarto. 6. Son las seis y veinte. 7. Son las siete menos cinco. 8. Son las ocho. 9. Es la una menos veinte. 10. Son las diez y veintiocho.

¿Qué hora es?

Son las ocho.

Son las nueve y diez.

Son las diez y cuarto.

Son las once y veinte.

Es la una.

Es la una y media.

Son las dos menos veinte.

Son las cinco menos cuarto.

¿Te gusta tu **horario**? ¿Qué días son tus clases? ¿A qué hora son?

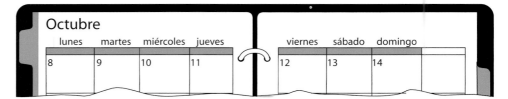

Octubre							
lunes	martes	miércoles	jueves		viernes	sábado	domingo
8	9	10	11		12	13	14

¿Dónde estás generalmente los lunes a las nueve **de la mañana**? ¿a la una **de la tarde**? ¿a las diez **de la noche**? ¿en casa? ¿en clase? ¿en la biblioteca? ¿con tus amigos? **¿en el trabajo?**

¿Cómo se pronuncia? El acento tónico y los acentos gráficos

If words ending with a vowel or the consonants **s** or **n** are not stressed on the *next-to-last* syllable, there is a written accent mark on the vowel of the syllable that is stressed.

(no accent): do-**min**-go, **lu**-nes, se-**ma**-na, im-pul-**si**-vo, **gus**-tan
(written accent): **sá**-ba-do, **miér**-co-les, ma-te-**má**-ti-cas, in-**glés**

If words ending with consonants other than **s** or **n** are not stressed on the *last* syllable, there is a written accent mark on the vowel of the syllable that is stressed.

(no accent): us-**ted**, pro-fe-**sor**, li-be-**ral**, es-tu-**diar**
(written accent): di-**fí**-cil, **fá**-cil, Gon-**zá**-lez, **Pé**-rez

---

horario *schedule* **de la mañana** *in the morning* **de la tarde** *in the afternoon* **de la noche** *at night* **en el trabajo** *at work*

When the letter **i** is adjacent to another vowel, it normally has a -y- sound and combines with the other vowel to form one syllable: **bien, historia, novio.** If **i** is next to another vowel, but remains a separate syllable with the -i- sound, it has a written accent mark: **día, biología.**

1-25 **¿Dónde está?** Read each sentence aloud and use **estoy** to say where you generally are at the indicated times: **¿en casa? ¿en clase? ¿en la universidad pero no en clase? ¿en la biblioteca? ¿con sus amigos? ¿con su familia? ¿en el trabajo?**

> Modelo   Los sábados a las 10:30 de la noche...
> **Los sábados a las diez y media de la noche, generalmente estoy con mis amigos.**

1. Los lunes a las 9:00 de la mañana…
2. Los martes a la 1:15 de la tarde…
3. Los miércoles a las 6:30 de la mañana…
4. Los jueves a las 11:30 de la noche…
5. Los viernes a las 5:45 de la tarde…
6. Los sábados a las 10:30 de la noche…
7. Los domingos a las 3:20 de la tarde…

1-26 **Mis clases.** Change the words in italics in the following sentences so that they describe you. If they are already true for you, read them as they are.

1. Mi clase de español es los *lunes y miércoles.*
2. Mi clase de español es a *las diez y cuarto de la mañana.*
3. Tengo *una clase* los martes y jueves.
4. No tengo clases los *viernes, sábados y domingos.*
5. Me gustan más las clases a *las nueve o diez de la mañana.*
6. No me gustan las clases a *las cuatro de la tarde.*

P   **Conversaciones.** Read the following conversation in which two students talk about their schedule. Then redo it with a partner, making it true for you. After you have finished, change roles and do it again.

— ¿Qué días son tus clases?
— Mis clases de literatura, historia y biología son los lunes, miércoles y viernes y mi clase de ciencias políticas es los martes y jueves.
— ¿A qué hora son tus clases?
— Los martes y jueves, mi clase de ciencias políticas es a las nueve. Los lunes, miércoles y viernes estoy en clase **todo el día de** diez **a** tres.
— ¿Qué días **trabajas**?
— **Esta semana trabajo** cuatro **horas** el lunes, miércoles y viernes y todo el día el sábado. Normalmente trabajo los domingos también, pero **este fin de semana** no trabajo el domingo.

Suggestion. Write these cognates on the board without the accents, showing syllabification. Have the class underline the syllables that would be stressed without an accent mark. Then read the words aloud and have students indicate whether they need a written accent because another syllable is stressed. 1. au-to-má-ti-co 2. a-gre-si-vo 3. co-lor 4. Ca-na-dá 5. Mé-xi-co 6. fre-cuen-te 7. au-to-mó-vil 8. am-bi-ción 9. su-per-mer-ca-do 10. co-mu-ni-dad 11. fan-tás-ti-co 12. dó-lar

---

AUDIO ¡A escuchar!

Listen to another conversation in which one student asks another about her schedule this semester. What classes does she have, what days, and at what times? When does she work?

---

todo el día *all day*   **de… a…** *from… to…*   **trabajas** *(do) you work*   **esta semana** *this week*   **trabajo** *I work*
horas *hours*   **este fin de semana** *this weekend*

GRAMÁTICA
La hora y los días de la semana

Para averiguar

1. When do you use **es** instead of **son** to say what time it is?
2. When would you say **son las dos**? **a las dos**?
3. When do you say **de la mañana** for *in the morning*? When do you say **por la mañana**?
4. When do you use **el** with a day of the week? When do you use **los**?

¡Ojo!

Some speakers will say **¿Qué hora son?** instead of **¿Qué hora es?** and **en la mañana/tarde/noche** for **por la mañana/tarde/noche.**

Use **¿Qué hora es?** to ask *What time is it (now)?* Say **Es la una** for *It's one o'clock,* **Es mediodía** for *It's noon,* and **Es medianoche** for *It's midnight.* With all other hours, use **Son las…**

— ¿Qué hora es?   — Es la una y cuarto. (1:15)
     — Son las tres menos diez. (2:50)
     — Son las ocho y media. (8:30)

To ask *at what time* something will take place, use **¿A qué hora…?** To answer, use **a la una, a mediodía, a medianoche,** or **a las…** with other hours.

— **¿A** qué hora es tu clase de historia?   — Es **a** las diez.

You may use the following expressions to distinguish times in the morning, afternoon, or evening.

de la mañana	A las ocho de la mañana.	*At eight in the morning.*
de la tarde	A la una de la tarde.	*At one in the afternoon.*
de la noche	A las once de la noche.	*At eleven in the evening.*

If you are not giving a specific hour, use **por la mañana, por la tarde,** and **por la noche** to say *in the morning, in the afternoon,* and *in the evening/at night.* Notice that **mañana** can mean both *morning* and *tomorrow.* Context will clarify the meaning.

Specific hour:	Trabajo a las ocho y media **de la mañana.**
	*I work at eight thirty **in the morning.***
No hour given:	Trabajo **por la mañana.**
	*I work **in the morning.***

Use the following expressions to ask and tell what day it is. Days of the week are not capitalized in Spanish.

— ¿Qué día es hoy?
— Hoy es lunes (martes, miércoles, jueves, viernes, sábado, domingo).

Use **el** to say that something will occur *on* a particular day.

Esta semana, no tengo clase **el** miércoles.   *This week, I don't have class **on** Wednesday.*

To say that something normally happens every week *on* a day, use **los.** Add **-s** to **sábado** and **domingo** to make them plural, but not to days that already end with **-s.**

Trabajo **los** viernes, sábados y domingos.   *I work **on** Fridays, Saturdays, and Sundays.*

1-27 **¿Qué hora es?** Say what time it is.

Modelo   **Son las once y media de la mañana.**

1.

2.

3.

4.

5.

6.

7.

8.

Suggestions. A. Distribute photocopies of daily planners for a week. Working in pairs, have students take turns describing their class and work schedules. Their partner fills in their schedule. Afterward, the other student checks that it is correct. **B.** Oral questions: *¿Qué día es hoy? ¿Qué día es mañana? ¿Qué día de la semana le gusta más? ¿Qué días trabaja usted? ¿Qué días está usted en casa todo el día? ¿Dónde está usted generalmente los lunes por la mañana? ¿por la tarde? ¿por la noche? ¿Dónde está usted generalmente los sábados por la mañana? ¿Le gusta más estudiar por la mañana, por la tarde o por la noche? ¿Qué hora es ahora? ¿Está usted en clase todo el día hoy? ¿De qué hora a qué hora está usted en clase hoy? ¿y mañana? ¿Tiene usted más clases por la mañana, por la tarde o por la noche?*

Follow-up for 1-28. *¿Qué palabra?* Have students adapt the conversation with a partner to talk about their schedules and make plans to study together.

P **1-28** **¿Qué palabra?** Complete the following conversation by choosing the correct words in parentheses.

— ¿Tienes más clases (*de, por*) la mañana o (*de, por*) la tarde este semestre/trimestre?

— Tengo química (*el, los*) martes y jueves (*son, a*) las diez de la mañana. (*Mi, Mis*) clases de matemáticas (*y, e*) inglés son (*de, por*) la tarde (*el, los*) lunes, miércoles (*y, e*) viernes.

— ¿Quieres estudiar química conmigo en la biblioteca este fin de semana?

— ¡Claro! ¿(*El, Los*) sábado o (*el, los*) domingo?

— ¿(*El, Los*) domingo (*a, son*) las tres (*de, por*) la tarde está bien?

— Me gusta más estudiar (*son, a*) las siete (*el, los*) domingos.

— Está bien (*son, a*) las siete. ¿Qué hora es ahora?

— (*Son, A*) las dos y veinte.

— Tengo clase (*son, a*) las dos y media. Hasta el domingo.

— Hasta luego.

P **1-29** **Entrevista.** Ask another student the following questions. Afterward, be prepared to tell the class about your partner. You will need these verb forms to talk about him or her to the class: **le gusta(n), él/ella está, él/ella tiene, él/ella trabaja.**

1. ¿Te gusta tu horario este semestre? ¿Qué días estás en clase? ¿Qué días no tienes clase?

2. ¿Tienes más clases por la mañana, por la tarde o por la noche? ¿A qué hora te gustan más las clases? ¿A qué hora son tus clases este semestre?

3. ¿De qué hora a qué hora estás en la universidad todos los días (*every day*)? ¿Qué días no estás en la universidad?

4. ¿Qué días trabajas? ¿a qué hora?

En portada

REVISTA CULTURAL

The **¡Trato hecho!** section always opens with the **En portada** reading. The accompanying activities follow on the right page. Be sure to complete the **Antes de leer** activities (on the right page) before proceeding with the reading.

¡CELEBREMOS LA HERENCIA HISPANA!

Durante el **Mes Nacional de la Herencia Hispana** (15 de septiembre–15 de octubre) Estados Unidos celebra la cultura hispánica y la contribución de la comunidad hispana a las artes, la economía, la educación y la política de la nación.

Desfile anual del Día de Puerto Rico, Nueva York

La comunidad hispana en Estados Unidos. Con treinta y nueve millones de personas, la comunidad hispana representa el 13 **por ciento** de la población total de Estados Unidos.

La comunidad hispana es especialmente visible en los estados de California, Texas, Nueva York, Florida, Illinois, Arizona y Nueva Jersey. La mayor parte de la población hispana es **de ascendencia mexicana,** puertorriqueña y cubana.

Carnaval en la Calle Ocho, Miami, Florida

¡Celebremos la herencia hispana!
Es esencial respetar y apreciar la diversidad sociocultural única de la nación norteamericana. Hablar inglés y español favorece la comunicación con el 50% de la población **del mundo.** Durante el Mes Nacional de la Herencia Hispana, celebramos la importancia de la herencia indígena, africana y española de los hispanoamericanos y **descubrimos la riqueza** de otras culturas y **el valor de** las diferencias.

Celebración del Cinco de Mayo, Austin, Texas

Note: The vocabulary in the *Revista cultural* sections is not included in the end-of-chapter vocabulary list and is presented for recognition only. Let students know if you expect them to learn it as active vocabulary.

la herencia *heritage*   **por ciento** *percent*   **de ascendencia mexicana** *of Mexican ancestry*   **del mundo** *of the world*
descubrimos la riqueza *we discover the richness*   **el valor de** *the value of*

Antes de leer

Take a look at the official poster for the Hispanic Heritage Festival 2003. What are the main elements that make up the poster? What do you think they represent? Can you identify the flags of the different Spanish-speaking countries?

Reading strategies: Recognizing cognates. Cognates often make the reading process in a foreign language easier. There are numerous words in English that have been adopted from the Spanish language or that are similar to Spanish words. By recognizing cognates in a text, we take advantage of the linguistic ground shared by both languages, and we expand our lexical competence in the foreign language.

1-30 Ahora Ud. Glance at the reading and identify as many cognates as possible. Classify them in three categories: Verbos, Sustantivos (*Nouns*), and Adjetivos.

Después de leer

P 1-31 Aires de fiesta. Look at the pictures that accompany the *¡Celebremos la herencia hispana!* article and describe the people, the atmosphere, and the celebrations using the verb **ser** that you learned in this chapter.

1. ¿Dónde son las celebraciones?
2. ¿De dónde son las personas en las fotos?
3. ¿Qué similitudes observa entre las distintas fotos?

P 1-32 La población hispana por estados (*states*). Take a look at the map of the United States below and indicate if the following statements are true (**cierto**) or false (**falso**). Correct the false statements.

	Cierto	Falso
1. Nueva Jersey es el estado con más población hispana.	☐	☐
2. El número de hispanos en Florida y Nueva York es similar.	☐	☐
3. Illinois es el estado con el porcentaje más pequeño de hispanos.	☐	☐
4. El estado de Arizona aparece con el segundo porcentaje más alto (*high*) de hispanos.	☐	☐
5. La población hispana está concentrada en el suroeste (*southwest*) de Estados Unidos.	☐	☐
6. El número de hispanos en Colorado es más pequeño que en Illinois.	☐	☐

G 1-33 Artistas. In groups, develop a poster for the Hispanic Heritage Festival next year using drawings, photos, text… and your imagination. Try to communicate what's in your poster to your classmates using as much Spanish as you can. A jury formed by selected members of your class will evaluate and rate the poster, and select the most original. Be creative!

Verbos	Sustantivos
celebra	la cultura
_____	_____
_____	_____
_____	_____
_____	_____

Adjetivos

hispánica
_____
_____
_____
_____
_____
_____

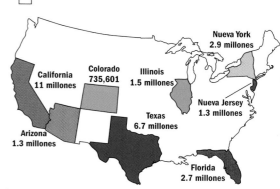

Nueva York
2.9 millones

California
11 millones

Colorado
735,601

Illinois
1.5 millones

Nueva Jersey
1.3 millones

Texas
6.7 millones

Arizona
1.3 millones

Florida
2.7 millones

Suggestion for 1-32. Encourage students to find some interesting facts about Hispanics in the United States in magazines, newspapers, or on the Web, and bring the information to the next class session.

De puertas abiertas a la comunidad

📹 SEÑAS DE IDENTIDAD

1-34 Entrando en materia. What are some indicators of the Hispanic presence in today's American society? Besides Hispanics, what other cultures are represented in the United States? What percentage of the American population does the Hispanic community represent?

Go to the Web and research the number of Hispanics in the United States in relation with other ethnic groups, and prepare a chart with percentages regarding ethnic distribution for the next class.

Hoy en día no es necesario viajar muy lejos para encontrarnos con personas de origen hispano. Viven en nuestras comunidades, están en nuestros lugares de trabajo, **sentimos** su presencia y la influencia de su cultura en **nuestro vivir diario.**

Y es que los hispanos forman una parte integral de la sociedad norteamericana.

Escuchen sus **voces,** sus experiencias, sus **sueños. Déjense cautivar por sus pensamientos,** por sus sentimientos, por su **orgullo** latino.

Estados Unidos es **el hogar** de muchos inmigrantes de origen hispano y de muchos hispanos nativos del **suroeste** del actual Estados Unidos. Los hispanoamericanos preservan sus tradiciones y su lengua, y la herencia hispana está integrada **ya** en la sociedad norteamericana, donde **convive** con otras culturas.

Les presentamos a varios latinos de orígenes diferentes. Escuchen sus testimonios y sus señas de identidad.

Answers for 1-35. ¿De Dónde son?
es, El Paso; son, la Ciudad de México; es, Paraguay; es, Nicaragua; es, Costa Rica

1-35 ¿Dé dónde son? Complete the following sentences indicating the origin of the Hispanics from the video. Use the appropriate form of **ser** and the place of origin or residence.

Analissa Martinez _____ de _____ , Texas.

Michelle y Alejandro _____ de _____ .

Edgar Alcaraz _____ de _____ .

Gloria Celaya _____ de _____ y su esposo Héctor _____ de _____ .

---

señas *signs* **sentimos** *we feel* **nuestro vivir diario** *our daily living* **escuchen** *listen to* **voces** *voices* **sueños** *dreams* **Déjense cautivar por sus pensamientos** *Let yourself be captivated by their thoughts* **orgullo** *pride* **el hogar** *home* **suroeste** *southwest* **ya** *already* **convive** *coexists*

1-36 Cualidades esenciales. Choose one person's occupation from the video and list all the adjectives describing traits needed to work in this profession. Search for new words in the dictionary and start a *vocabulary journal* in Spanish. This will be the first entry: **los adjetivos de personalidad.**

Vocabulary learning strategies: Creating a vocabulary journal. Using the dictionary will help you to familiarize yourself with new words in Spanish. By creating a vocabulary journal you will group new words under lexical categories for easy remembering and reference. You should review your vocabulary journal periodically and add new words to the existing categories of words.

1-37 Comparaciones. Select two people from the video and write sentences comparing them. Use the structures for comparing and the adjectives that you learned in the chapter.

Modelo   **Jorge es más extrovertido que Héctor.**

1-38 ¿Qué dicen? Read the following statements from the video segment and match each one to the correct picture.

1. "Soy periodista (*journalist*), vivo en Nueva York, soy mitad colombiano, mitad argentino, escribo para revistas como *Urban Latino* magazine."
2. "Como músico, me encanta estar con mi chelo, primeramente, tocar mi instrumento."
3. "¡Hola! Mi nombre es Jorge Merced. Soy puertorriqueño. Vivo aquí en el Bronx, en Nueva York."
4. "Soy pintor y [...] estamos aquí en Queens, Nueva York, y estamos muy contentos de estar aquí."

_____3_____   _____1_____   _____4_____   _____2_____

1-39 Quiero presentarte a... Select a person from the video and introduce him/her to the class using what you learned in the chapter. Show the class the video image of the person who you are introducing.

Escapadas

CIUDADES CON HERENCIA HISPANA

San Antonio: vestigios misioneros San Antonio, Texas, preserva como vestigios de la colonización española **varias** misiones de gran interés histórico.

El Álamo es una de **las** misiones **más antiguas** de Estados Unidos, establecida en 1718. En 1836 El Álamo **fue** durante trece días el escenario de la revolución texana contra **el ejército** mexicano. El Álamo es un símbolo de **la lucha** por la libertad y la identidad de Texas.

Otras misiones de gran interés son la Misión San José, San Juan, Concepción y Espada, fundadas originalmente en **el este** de Texas y establecidas más tarde en San Antonio.

El Álamo, San Antonio, Texas

Misión San José, San Antonio, Texas

Ybor City: un legado multicultural Es una ciudad con un pasado fascinante. Marcada por la influencia de las culturas cubana, española, italiana y **alemana,** Ybor City es hoy el distrito histórico de Tampa. Ybor City es especialmente famosa por la **industria tabacalera** y es **conocida como** "la capital **mundial** del cigarro". Entre 1881 y 1895, el revolucionario José Martí visita Ybor City con frecuencia y proclama con fervor la independencia de Cuba de España **entre los trabajadores** cubanos. El *Ybor City Museum State Park* ofrece exhibiciones sobre el pasado fascinante de esta ciudad.

Real Fábrica de Tabacos Partagás, Ybor City, Tampa, Florida

La atmósfera festiva de Ybor City es **otro** de sus atractivos. Son famosos los festivales del *Día de Fiesta* en febrero y el de *Guavaween* en octubre. El *Día de Fiesta* es una celebración de la cultura y las tradiciones cubanas y el *Guavaween* es la celebración de Halloween al estilo hispánico con **un desfile** extravagante por **las calles** de la ciudad.

Mural urbano, Los Ángeles, California

Los Ángeles: un arte urbano Los Ángeles es conocida como "la capital mundial de los murales". En Los Ángeles hay aproximadamente 2.500 murales de artistas hispanos inspirados en los muralistas mexicanos Rivera, Orozco y Siqueiros.

Mural "La Ofrenda", por Yreina Cervantez, Los Ángeles, California

---

varias *several* **las más antiguas** *the oldest* **fue** *was* **el ejército** *the army* **la lucha** *the struggle* **el este** *the east* **alemana** *German* **industria tabacalera** *tobacco industry* **conocida coma** *known as* **mundial** *world (wide)* **entre los trabajadores** *among the workers* **otro** *another* **un desfile** *a parade* **las calles** *the streets*

Los murales son un arte urbano accesible al público general y están en edificios públicos, parques, **autopistas** y residencias privadas. Los murales presentan escenas de la historia y la cultura mexicana, chicana y estadounidense, e inspiran a la comunidad latina a **enorgullecerse** de su pasado y de su futuro.

Albuquerque: foco cultural hispánico Albuquerque, Nuevo México, es hoy un activo centro para la cultura hispánica. El Centro Nacional de Cultura Hispana de Nuevo México en Albuquerque organiza eventos sociales y culturales para preservar la herencia hispana en Nuevo México y **difundir** la cultura y el arte latinos.

La institución ofrece un centro de artes visuales con fotografías y **pinturas,** esculturas de artistas latinos, y un centro de artes escénicas con **representaciones** de danza, música y teatro hispánicos tradicionales y contemporáneos.

Old Town Plaza, Albuquerque, Nuevo México

1-40 Trivia. Test yourself with the following trivia questions about *Ciudades con herencia hispana.*

Follow-up for 1-40. Ask the students to create new endings for the trivia sentences: *Ybor City es...; Los murales son...; En Albuquerque está...; El Álamo es...; El Día de Fiesta...; Los muralistas hispanos...*

1. Ybor City es…
  a. una ciudad con influencia francesa.
  b. el área metropolitana con más cubanos de Florida.
  c. el distrito histórico de Tampa, Florida.

2. Los murales son…
  a. una manifestación de arte urbano.
  b. inusuales en las calles de Los Ángeles.
  c. inaccesibles al público general.

3. En Albuquerque está…
  a. la misión más antigua de América del Norte.
  b. la tumba de José Martí.
  c. el Centro Nacional de Cultura Hispana de Nuevo México.

4. El Álamo es hoy…
  a. un centro de artes escénicas.
  b. un símbolo de la lucha por la libertad de Texas.
  c. un museo de murales mexicanos.

5. El Día de Fiesta conmemora…
  a. la herencia cubana de Ybor City.
  b. la independencia de Cuba.
  c. el heroísmo de José Martí.

6. Los muralistas hispanos…
  a. no se inspiran en los artistas mexicanos Rivera, Orozco y Siqueiros.
  b. representan en sus murales escenas de la historia y la cultura mexicanas, chicanas y estadounidenses.
  c. no usan edificios públicos para presentar sus murales al público.

autopistas *highways*   **enorgullecerse de** *to be proud of*   **difundir** *to spread*   **pinturas** *paintings*
representaciones *performances*

1-41 Vacaciones para todos los gustos. Your friends have different preferences for their traveling destinations. Read the following descriptions and choose the place from the *Escapadas* section that best fits each personality.

1. A Elena le gusta el arte mexicano.
2. Óscar está interesado en la historia de los misioneros españoles.
3. A Miriam le gustan las representaciones de teatro y danza hispánicos.
4. Ernesto es muy divertido y le gustan las fiestas latinas.
5. A Lidia le gusta estudiar las tradiciones cubanas.

(P) **1-42 Compañeros de viaje.** Imagine that you are traveling to one of the destinations described in the *Escapadas* reading and you want to start a conversation with the people sitting next to you: an elderly lady and a college student. Write two separate conversations greeting the other person, introducing yourself, and talking a little bit about your travel destination.

(G) **1-43 Horarios de visita.** When you travel it is essential to know the visiting hours of the monuments and sites that you would like to tour. Make up visiting schedules with days and times for the different sites mentioned in the *Escapadas* section. Make sure that you write out the times.

El Álamo

Horario de visita

_____
_____
_____
_____

El Parque Estetal del Museo de Ybor city

Horario de visita

_____
_____
_____
_____

Centro Nacional de Cultura Hispana de Nuevo México

Horario de visita

_____
_____
_____
_____

www **1-44 El arte urbano.** Mural painting is one of the most important forms of artistic, political, and social expression. You read about the muralist movement in Los Angeles and its mission to reach the general public. Search the Web for a photograph of a mural painting, and prepare a description of it answering the following questions:

1. ¿Qué hay en el mural?
2. ¿Cuántas personas hay en el mural?
3. ¿Cómo son las personas del mural?
4. ¿Qué representa el mural?

En palabras de...

MI AUTOBIOGRAFÍA

You are going to write a brief autobiography focusing on yourself and the people in your life. When you write your autobiography, reflect about who you are, where you are in life, and be yourself.

Writing strategies: Writing an autobiography. When you prepare to write an autobiography, you should think about yourself as the main character in a play. There is certain information that is essential in an autobiography, such as your name and origins, your personality, your education, and something about your family and friends. By setting up a list of topics to address, you will ensure a complete and organized autobiography.

Antes de escribir

P Think about possible questions in Spanish that you would ask a new roommate and write them down. Review your questions and make sure that you ask for personal information: name, origin, preferences, personality, family, and classes at school (type of classes, class schedule, etc.). Once you feel the list is complete, answer the questions as if your roommate had asked them and write the first draft of your autobiography.

Después de escribir

After you finish answering the questions, review your first draft using the checklist below.

> ✅ **Lista de control:**
>
> ___ Did you use the verb **ser** to say who you are, where you are from, and to describe what you are like?
> ___ Did you make the adjectives agree with the nouns in your descriptions?
> ___ Did you use the appropriate forms when comparing yourself and your family members?
> ___ Did you use the verb **gustar** to talk about your preferences?
> ___ Did you make **gustar** agree with the subject placed after it?

Before you hand in your autobiography, read it over, check for any misspelled words, and be sure that you have made all the necessary changes.

En la red

Go to the Web and select the biography of a Hispanic personality in the United States. Break the biography into short sections related to personal information: name, origin, preferences, personality, family information, and information about his/her career. In the next session introduce the person to your classmates.

All the sources consulted for the readings are cited on the *¡Trato hecho!* Web site at **www.prenhall.com/trato**

VOCABULARIO

T E M A ❶

Saludos
Buenos días. *Good morning.*
Buenas tardes. *Good afternoon.*
Buenas noches. *Good evening.*
   Good night.
Hola. *Hi.*
¿Cómo estás? *How are you?*
   (familiar)
¿Cómo está usted? *How are you?*
   (formal)
estoy *I am, I'm (doing)*
(muy) bien *(very) well*
regular *as usual*
mal *badly*
gracias *thank you*

Para el alfabeto, vea la página 5.

Presentaciones
¿Cómo te llamas? *What is your*
   name? (familiar)
¿Cómo se llama usted? *What is*
   your name? (formal)
Me llamo... *My name is...*
Soy... *I am, I'm...*
Mucho gusto. *Pleased to meet you.*
Igualmente. *Likewise.*
¿De dónde eres? *Where are you*
   from? (familiar)
¿De dónde es usted? *Where are*
   you from? (formal)
de *from*
aquí *here*

¿Y tú/usted? *And you?*
   (familiar/formal)
señor *Mr., sir*
señora *Mrs., Mme.*
señorita *Miss*

Otras expresiones
¿Cómo se escribe...? *How is…*
   written?
Se escribe... *It's written...*
con o sin acento *with or without*
   an accent

T E M A ❷

Presentaciones
Quiero presentarte a…/Quiero
   presentarle a… *I want you to*
   meet… (familiar/formal)
mi compañero/a de clase *my*
   classmate
mi familia *my family*
mi esposo/a *my husband/wife,*
   spouse
mi hermano/a *my brother/sister*
mi mejor amigo/a *my best friend*
mi novio/a *my boyfriend/girlfriend*
mi padre/madre *my father/mother*

Para los adjetivos, vea la página 8.

mi profesor/a *my professor*
(No) tengo *I (don't) have*

Descripciones y comparaciones
¿Cómo es...? *What's... like?*
ser *to be*
yo soy *I am*
tú eres *you are (familiar)*
usted es *you are (formal)*
él es *he is*
ella es *she is*
nosotros/as somos *we are*
vosotros/as sois *you are (familiar*
   plural in Spain)

ustedes son *you are (plural)*
ellos/as son *they are*
más... que *more... than*
menos... que *less... than*
muy *very*
también *too, also*
tan... como *as... as*
un poco *a little*

Despedidas
Adiós. *Good-bye.*
Hasta luego. *See you later.*
Hasta mañana. *See you tomorrow.*

T E M A ❸

La universidad
la biblioteca *the library*
la cafetería *the cafeteria*
la clase *the class*
el edificio *the building*
el/la estudiante *the student*
el gimnasio *the gymnasium*
el laboratorio de lenguas *the*
   language lab

el/la profesor/a *the professor*
la residencia *the residence hall,*
   dormitory
la universidad *the university*

Adjetivos
aburrido/a *boring*
antipático/a *unpleasant*
bonito/a *pretty*

bueno/a *good*
divertido/a *fun*
fácil *easy*
feo/a *ugly*
difícil *difficult*
grande *big*
interesante *interesting*
malo/a *bad*
moderno/a *modern*

nuevo/a *new*
pequeño/a *little, small*
perezoso/a *lazy*
simpático/a *nice*
trabajador/a *hardworking*
útil *useful*
viejo/a *old*

Para las clases, vea la página 13.

Los gustos
me gusta(n) *I like*
te gusta(n) *you like (familiar)*
le gusta(n) *you like (formal), he likes, she likes*

¿Cuántos?
¿cuántos/as? *how many*
hay *there is, there are, is there, are there*
mucho/a *much, a lot (of)*
muchos/as *many, a lot (of)*

Para los números de 0 a 100, vea la página 16.

La hora
¿Qué hora es? *What time is it?*
ahora *now*
Es la una. *It's one o'clock.*
Es mediodía. *It's noon.*
Es medianoche. *It's midnight.*
Son las dos (tres…) *It's two (three…) o'clock.*
Es la/Son las… y cuarto. *It's a quarter past…*
Es la/Son las… y media. *It's half past…*
¿A qué hora? *At what time?*
a la una *at one o'clock*
a las dos (tres…) *at two (three…) o'clock*
de/por la mañana *in the morning*

Las clases
¿Qué clases tienes este semestre/trimestre? *What classes do you have this semester/trimester?*
Tengo… *I have...*

T E M A ④

Sustantivos
la tarea *the homework*
el examen *the exam*
las actividades sociales *the social activities*
el número de teléfono *the telephone number*

Posesión
mi(s) *my*
tu(s) *your (familiar)*
su(s) *your (formal), his, her*

T E M A ⑤

de/por la tarde *in the afternoon*
de/por la noche *in the evening, at night*
de… a… *from... to...*
el horario *the schedule*
una hora *one hour*

El día
¿Qué día es hoy? *What day is today?*
lunes *Monday*
martes *Tuesday*
miércoles *Wednesday*
jueves *Thursday*
viernes *Friday*
sábado *Saturday*
domingo *Sunday*

Otras palabras
y (e) *and (The alternative* **e** *is used before the letters* **i** *and* **hi**).
pero *but*

Otras palabras y expresiones
¡Claro! *Sure!*
conmigo *with me*
en *in, at*
en casa *at home*
estudiar *to study*
otro/a *other, another*
para *for*
¿por qué? *why?*
porque *because*
¿Quieres…? *Do you want...?*
solo/a *alone*

¿Qué días trabajas? *What days do you work?*
Trabajo el (lunes…) *I work on (Monday...) (a particular week)*
Trabajo los (lunes…) *I work on (Mondays...) (every week)*
todo el día *all day*

Otras palabras y expresiones
con *with*
¿dónde? *where?*
generalmente *generally*
en clase *in class*
en el trabajo *at work*
esta semana *this week*
este fin de semana *this weekend*

2

En la universidad

In this chapter you will learn to...

- follow classroom instructions
- say what's near the university
- describe yourself and classmates
- say what you like to do after class
- ask classmates about how they spend the day
- discuss education among Hispanics

You will use...

- **hay** with the indefinite article
- the verb **estar** with prepositions of location
- the verbs **ser** and **estar**
- **-ar** verbs and adverbs indicating how often
- question words

VOCABULARIO

¿Qué hay?

TEMA 1

Suggestions. A. Give students the question and response *¿Qué es esto? Es un/a...* With books closed, present objects in the classroom, saying what they are. Follow up by asking *either/or* questions such as *¿Qué es esto? ¿Es un lápiz o un bolígrafo? ¿Es una silla o una mesa?* Students repeat the correct answer. Afterwards, go back around the room asking students to name objects from memory. **B.** Ask students if there are certain objects in the classroom, on your desk, in their backpacks, or in their room at home. If so, ask how many. **C.** Give students pairs of objects such as the following and have them repeat the one that is generally more expensive, larger, or smaller: *un lápiz/un libro, un cuaderno/un libro de español, una mochila/un bolígrafo, una computadora/una calculadora, una silla/un escritorio.* **D.** Collect classroom objects such as pens, notebooks, pencils, and textbooks from students when they are not looking. Select a student to pick one of the items and to ask a classmate if it is his/hers. If it does not belong to the student asked, that student must ask another student if it is his/hers until the owner is found. **E.** Have students say whether the following items are possibly found in a backpack. (*un libro, una silla, un cuaderno, lápices, una calculadora, una mesa, un escritorio, papel, un profesor, un estante, una pizarra, un bolígrafo, la tarea, un salón de clase, una computadora*) Have students go back and respond *sí* or *no* whether each of the preceding items is sold at the university bookstore.

En el salón de clase, hay…

En mi cuarto, en el escritorio tengo…

¡Ojo!

In Mexico, people say **una pluma** instead of **un bolígrafo**. In Spain, one hears **un ordenador** instead of **una computadora**.

Instrucciones en clase:

¡Abran el libro en la página 37!	*Open the book to page 37!*
¡Saquen papel y un bolígrafo!	*Take out paper and a pen!*
¡Lean cada oración!	*Read each sentence!*
¡Repitan las siguientes palabras, por favor!	*Repeat the following words, please!*
¡Hagan el ejercicio A en parejas!	*Do exercise A in pairs!*
¡Contesten las mismas preguntas!	*Answer the same questions!*
¡Vayan a la pizarra!	*Go to the board!*
¡Escriban las respuestas de la tarea!	*Write the answers from the homework!*

2-1 ¿Dónde están? Which item is logically in or on the other? Use **está** (*is*) after a singular noun and **están** (*are*) after a plural noun. **En** can mean both *in* and *on*.

> **Modelo**   mesa / mochila   →   **La mochila está en la mesa.**
>   libros / estante   →   **Los libros están en el estante.**

1. lápices / mesa
2. tarea / pizarra
3. cuaderno / papel
4. sillas / estudiantes
5. libro / preguntas

6. libros / mochila
7. página 41 / ejercicio
8. respuestas / pizarra
9. profesor / salón de clase

Suggestion for 2-1. *¿Dónde están?* Point out that it is not necessarily the first item that is on or in the other.

2-2 ¿Qué necesitamos hacer? Complete the following commands with only the logical nouns listed in parentheses.

> **Modelo**   Escriban (las respuestas, las oraciones, las ventanas).
>   **Escriban las respuestas. Escriban las oraciones.**

1. Abran (el libro, la puerta, la palabra, las ventanas, el cuaderno).
2. Escuchen (la mochila, las preguntas, la oración, la silla, las respuestas).
3. Escriban (las respuestas, la calculadora, el ejercicio, las preguntas).
4. Lean (el libro, la computadora, la pizarra, la mochila, las preguntas).
5. Hagan (el escritorio, el ejercicio, la tarea, el lápiz).
6. Repitan (la calculadora, las palabras, las preguntas, las respuestas).
7. Saquen (la pizarra, la tarea, el libro, un lápiz, un bolígrafo).

P 2-3 Instrucciones. Working with a partner, how many logical commands can you form using words from each column? Include the article **el, la, los,** or **las** before each noun.

> **Modelo**   **Hagan los ejercicios en el cuaderno.**

Abran	oraciones		página 54.
Hagan	respuestas		pizarra.
Escriban	tarea		cuaderno.
Repitan	libro	en	escritorio.
Lean	ejercicios		libro.
Contesten	palabras		computadora.
	preguntas		

Suggestion for 2-3. *Instrucciones.* Have students do this activity in pairs with a time limit to see which group can compose the most logical commands.

Follow-ups for 2-3. *Instrucciones.*
A. Review numbers by telling students to open their books to different pages from 1 to 100 and read something from that page. (*Abran el libro en la página 39. Lean el modelo del ejercicio 2-5.*) B. Give commands such as the following and have students repeat the one that would be done first. 1. Lean las palabras en la página 38. / Abran el libro en la página 38. 2. Escuchen las preguntas. / Escriban las respuestas en la pizarra. 3. Repitan cada palabra. / Escuchen las palabras. 4. Saquen papel y un bolígrafo. / Escriban las respuestas en el papel. 5. Hagan el ejercicio A en parejas. / Abran el libro en la página 72. 6. Hagan el ejercicio A en parejas. / Escriban las respuestas en la pizarra.

P Conversaciones. Read the following conversation in pairs. Then prepare a similar conversation explaining the homework for your own class.

— Profesor, ¿cuál es la tarea para la **próxima** clase?
— Bueno, **primero,** lean de la página 25 a la página 29 del libro y **aprendan** el vocabulario en la página 25 para **una pruebita.**
— ¿**Necesitamos hacer algo** en el **cuaderno de ejercicios**?
— Sí, hagan los ejercicios en las páginas 20 y 21 y contesten **todas** las preguntas con oraciones completas.

AUDIO ¡A escuchar!

Now listen to ten sentences in which an instructor is giving students instructions. Indicate whether she probably wants them to do each task at home or in class by writing **en casa** or **en clase** on a sheet of paper.

Suggestion for *Conversaciones.* Write the homework assignment for the next class on the board and have students change the conversation accordingly. Have students also pretend that it is the previous class and talk about the assignment for today.

---

próximo/a *next*   **primero** *first*   **¡Aprendan…!** *Learn…!*   **una pruebita** *a quiz*   **¿Necesitamos hacer algo?** *Do we need to do something?*   **cuaderno de ejercicios** *workbook*   **todo/a/os/as** *all*

1. What are the two forms of the word for *a* in Spanish? When do you use each one?
2. How do you say *some, many, few,* and *several*?
3. What happens to a final **-z** when you add the plural ending **-es**?
4. What single word can translate *there is, there are, is there,* and *are there*?
5. Is there any difference in how you say *other* and *another* in Spanish?

Supplemental activity. Have students say whether there are items such as the following in your class, using *un, una, unos, unas, mucho/a/os/as, poco/a/os/as,* or *varios/as* to say how much/many of each there is/are *(estudiantes, hombres, mujeres, profesores/as, tarea, puertas, ventanas, sillas, mesas, escritorios, estantes, libros, pizarras, computadoras, mochilas, cuadernos de ejercicios, ejercicios en parejas, exámenes, preguntas difíciles, palabras nuevas, pruebitas).* Repeat the activity describing your university with the following nouns *(clases de español, clases de francés, profesores de español, estudiantes de México, edificios nuevos, edificios viejos, bibliotecas, libros en español en la biblioteca, computadoras en la biblioteca, gimnasios, cafeterías).*

GRAMÁTICA
Hablar de personas y cosas no específicas: los indefinidos

The words for *a* and *some* have different forms, depending on whether the following noun is masculine or feminine.

	MASCULINE		FEMININE	
SINGULAR	un libro	*a book*	una mesa	*a table*
PLURAL	unos libros	*some books*	unas mesas	*some tables*

The word for *one* is the same as the word for *a*. When counting, use **uno** to say *one*, but before a noun, use **un** or **una.**

uno, dos, tres, cuatro…	*one, two, three, four…*
un libro	*a book, one book*
una mesa	*a table, one table*

Remember to pluralize adjectives and nouns by adding **-s** if they end with a vowel and **-es** if they end with a consonant. A final **-z** changes to **-c-** before the **-es** plural ending.

una mesa	→	unas mesas
un profesor	→	unos profesores
un lápiz	→	unos lápices

Hay is used with both singular and plural nouns and can have four different translations: *there is, there are, is there, are there.*

Hay un diccionario en mi mochila.	**There is** a dictionary in my backpack.
¿**Hay** muchos estudiantes en tu clase?	**Are there** a lot of students in your class?

The following words are also used to say *how much / many* or *what else there is / there are.* They agree with the noun for gender and number.

mucho/a/os/as	*much, many, a lot of*
poco/a/os/as	*little, few*
varios/as	*several*
otro/a/os/as	*other, another*

Hay muchas ventanas.	*There are a lot of windows.*
Hay poca tarea.	*There is little homework.*
Hay varios libros en español.	*There are several books in Spanish.*
Hay otro examen mañana.	*There is another exam tomorrow.*

Do not use **un** or **una** before **otro/a** to say *another*.

Tengo otra pregunta.	*I have another question.*

2-4 ¿Qué cosas? Complete las oraciones con la forma singular o plural de todas las palabras apropiadas. Use **un, una, unos** o **unas.**

Modelo   En mi mochila, tengo (libro, lápiz, calculadora, bolígrafo).
En mi mochila, tengo unos libros y un bolígrafo.

1. En la clase de español, hay (profesor, profesora, estudiante, libro, cuaderno de ejercicios).
2. En el salón de clase, hay (pizarra, silla, estante, reloj, ventana, puerta).
3. En la pizarra, hay (pregunta, oración, ejercicio, respuesta, palabra).
4. En mi cuarto, tengo (estante, silla, mesa, escritorio, libro, computadora).
5. En la universidad, hay (biblioteca, gimnasio, residencia, edificio nuevo, edificio viejo, cafetería).

2-5 ¿Qué hay? ¿Qué hay en esta biblioteca? Use las palabras **un/a, unos/as, muchos/as** o **varios/as.**

Modelo   **En la biblioteca, hay muchos libros.**

P 2-6 Preguntas. Complete las siguientes preguntas con el artículo **el, la, los, las** o el indefinido **un, una, unos, unas.** Luego (*then*), use las preguntas para entrevistar (*to interview*) a otro/a estudiante.

1. ¿Te gusta _____ universidad?
2. ¿Te gusta más _____ clase de español o te gusta más otra clase?
3. ¿Te gusta más estudiar con _____ compañero de clase o solo/a?
4. ¿Hay _____ biblioteca grande o pequeña en _____ universidad?
5. ¿Te gusta más estudiar en _____ biblioteca o en tu cuarto?
6. ¿Tienes _____ cuarto grande o pequeño? ¿Está en _____ residencia de _____ universidad?
7. ¿Dónde está _____ oficina (*office,* f.) del (de la) profesor/a? ¿Está en _____ mismo edificio que _____ salón de clase o está en otro edificio?
8. ¿Tienes _____ clases aburridas este semestre? ¿Cuáles (*Which ones*)? ¿Te gustan más _____ ciencias o _____ lenguas? ¿Cuál es _____ clase más difícil para ti (*you*) este semestre?

Note. From this point on, directions to activities will generally be in Spanish. It is important to check that students understand what they are to do. Depending on the needs of your students, you may also give students the directions in English, or you may ask a student to translate them.

Suggestions for 2-5. *¿Qué hay?*
A. Make this a chain activity in which students list all of the items named before and add a new noun until all items are listed. **B.** Do other chain activities where students complete the following statements. 1. En el salón de clase, hay... 2. En la universidad, hay... 3. En la mochila de un estudiante típico, hay...

Follow-up for 2-6. *Preguntas*. Remind students that *otro/a* means *another* as well as *other* and not to use *un/a* with it. Then ask the following questions. 1. ¿Hay clases de otras lenguas en la universidad? ¿Cuáles? 2. ¿Hay otras clases de Español I este semestre? ¿Cuántas? ¿muchas? ¿pocas? ¿varias? 3. ¿Hay más clases de español o de otra lengua? 4. ¿Quiere Ud. estudiar otra lengua? ¿Cuál? 5. ¿Cuántas clases más tiene Ud. este semestre? 6. ¿Tiene más clases en este mismo edificio o en otro edificio? 7. ¿Tiene otras clases con estudiantes de la clase de español? 8. ¿Tiene otra clase hoy? 9. ¿Tiene más clases hoy u otro día? 10. ¿Tiene más tarea para la clase de español o para otra clase? 11. ¿Tiene exámenes en otras clases esta semana? 12. ¿Tiene más exámenes en la clase de español o en otra clase este semestre?

VOCABULARIO

TEMA ❷

¿Qué hay cerca de la universidad?

una librería

un cine con películas extranjeras
(de aventuras, de terror)

un club nocturno con música latina (música popular, música rock, música country, jazz)

un parque

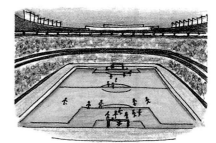

un estadio (un partido de fútbol / de fútbol americano)

una tienda de ropa

una escuela (primaria, secundaria)

un restaurante (de comida mexicana, de comida italiana)

un supermercado

Supplemental activities. A. Create several statements such as the following and have students give classmates' names. *¿Quién está delante de Daniel? ¿Quién está detrás de él? ¿Quién está a su derecha? ¿Quién está a su izquierda? ¿Quién está entre Daniel y Cristina? ¿Quién está enfrente de mí? ¿Quién está detrás de él/ella? ¿Qué hay detrás de mí? ¿Quién está más lejos de la puerta? ¿Quién está al lado de la ventana?* **B.** Present *cerca de* from the title of this *Tema* and ask questions such as the following about the university area. 1. ¿Hay muchos restaurantes cerca de la universidad? 2. ¿Hay más restaurantes de comida mexicana o de comida italiana cerca de aquí? 3. ¿Le gusta más la comida mexicana o la comida italiana? 4. ¿Hay cafetería en la universidad? 5. ¿Le gusta la comida de la cafetería? 6. ¿Cuál es su restaurante favorito cerca de la universidad? 7. ¿Cuál es su tienda de ropa favorita? 8. ¿Hay una librería o hay varias librerías en la universidad o cerca de la universidad? 9. ¿Hay muchos clubes nocturnos cerca de aquí? 10. ¿Cuál es el club más popular? 11. ¿Hay un parque cerca de la universidad? 12. ¿Le gusta estudiar en el parque? 13. ¿Le gusta la universidad más que la escuela secundaria? 14. ¿Las clases son más difíciles o menos difíciles en la universidad que en la escuela secundaria? 15. ¿Hay estadio en la universidad? 16. ¿Hay estadio en las escuelas primarias? 17. ¿Hay gimnasio en las escuelas primarias? ¿Hay cafetería? 18. ¿Hay cafetería en todas las residencias de la universidad? 19. ¿Le gustan las películas extranjeras? 20. ¿Hay muchas películas extranjeras en los cines cerca de aquí? 21. ¿Le gustan las películas románticas? 22. ¿Cuál es su película favorita? 23. ¿Le gusta más la música rock o el jazz? ¿la música latina o la música country?

¿Dónde está?

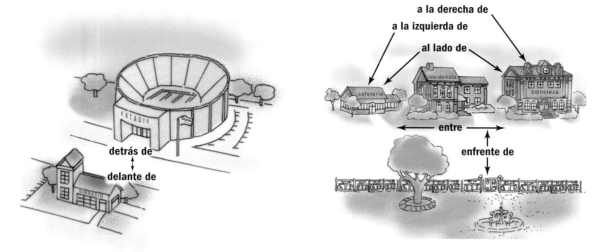

2-7 Lugares. ¿Qué está localizado en estos lugares en las ilustraciones anteriores?

> **Modelo**   Está detrás del gimnasio.
> **El estadio está detrás del gimnasio.**

1. Está delante del estadio.
2. Están al lado de la residencia.
3. Está enfrente de la residencia.
4. Está a la izquierda de la residencia.
5. Está entre la cafetería y la biblioteca.
6. Está a la derecha de la residencia.

2-8 Mis lugares favoritos. Nombre sus lugares favoritos y diga en qué calle (*street*) están.

> **Modelo**   un club nocturno
> **Mi club nocturno favorito es *La Bamba*. Está en la calle Seis. /**
> **No me gustan los clubes nocturnos.**

1. un supermercado
2. un cine
3. una tienda de ropa
4. una librería
5. un parque
6. un restaurante

Ⓟ   **Conversaciones.** En parejas, lean la siguiente conversación en la cual (*in which*) dos estudiantes hacen planes para estudiar juntos. Luego (*Then*), haga planes para estudiar con su compañero/a.

— ¿Quieres estudiar **juntos** en mi apartamento **antes de**l examen?
— ¿Tu apartamento está **cerca de** aquí?
— Está un poco **lejos de** la universidad. Está en la calle Buena Vista.
— Prefiero estudiar en el café Java. Está **abierto** las 24 horas del día.
— ¿Dónde está?
— Está al lado de un edificio de **oficinas** en la calle Río Grande.
— Está bien. ¿A qué hora?
— Me gusta estudiar **después de la cena**. ¿Está bien a las ocho?
— Perfecto.

---

juntos/as *together* **antes de** *before* **cerca de** *near* **lejos de** *far from* **abierto/a** *open* **una oficina** *an office*
después de *after* **la cena** *dinner*

Follow-ups for *Conversaciones*.
A. Practice *antes de* and *después de* with the following questions. 1. ¿Está Ud. en otra clase antes de la clase de español? ¿en la biblioteca? ¿en casa? ¿en el trabajo? 2. ¿Está en otra clase después de la clase de español? ¿en la biblioteca? ¿en casa? ¿en el trabajo? 3. ¿Le gusta hacer la tarea para la clase de español antes o después de clase? 4. ¿Está muy nervioso/a antes de los exámenes? 5. ¿Está en la universidad antes de las ocho de la mañana? ¿después de las diez de la noche? 6. ¿Después de qué hora está en casa los lunes? ¿los martes? **B.** Have students say where they usually are at each time. *Estoy... en casa, en otra clase, en la biblioteca, en un café, en el trabajo, en mi coche, con mis amigos...* 1. antes de la clase de español 2. después de la clase de

🔊 ¡A escuchar!

Ahora escuchen otra conversación en la cual dos estudiantes hacen planes para estudiar juntos. ¿Dónde y cuándo deciden estudiar?

español 3. los lunes, antes de las seis de la mañana 4. los lunes, después de las once de la noche 5. los sábados por la tarde 6. los sábados por la noche 7. los viernes por la noche **C.** Ask *either/or* questions about where well-known stores, restaurants, parks, clubs, cafés, cinemas, or bookstores are located in your city: *¿Dónde está el supermercado Whole Foods? ¿En la calle Ocho o en la calle Guadalupe?*

GRAMÁTICA

Situar en el espacio: *estar*, las contracciones con *de*, los pronombres preposicionales

Para averiguar

1. What are two uses of the verb **estar**?
2. What happens to the word **de** when it is followed by **el** (*the*)? Does **de** contract with **la, los,** or **las**?
3. Which two pronouns used after prepositions are not the same as the subject pronouns?
4. How do you say *with me* and *with you* (to a friend)?

Use **estar** (*to be*) to say where someone or something is located or with adjectives to describe physical or mental states or conditions.

ESTAR (*TO BE*)					
yo	**estoy**	*I am*	nosotros/as	**estamos**	*we are*
tú	**estás**	*you are (familiar)*	vosotros/as	**estáis**	*you are (plural)*
usted	**está**	*you are (formal)*	ustedes	**están**	*you are (plural)*
él	**está**	*he is*	ellos	**están**	*they are*
ella	**está**	*she is*	ellas	**están**	*they are*

Use **estar** with these prepositions to say where something is.

cerca de	*near*	**lejos de**	*far from*
encima de	*on top of*	**debajo de**	*below, under*
delante de	*ahead of, in front of*	**detrás de**	*behind*
al lado de	*next to*	**enfrente de**	*across from, facing*
a la derecha de	*to the right of*	**a la izquierda de**	*to the left of*
en	*at, in, on*	**entre**	*between*
con	*with*	**sin**	*without*

De contracts with the singular article **el** (*the*) to form **del**. **De** does not contract with **la, los,** or **las**.

Tu lápiz está debajo **del** libro.
Your pencil is under the book.

Mi mochila está encima **de la** mesa.
My backpack is on top of the table.

The pronouns used after prepositions are the same as the subject pronouns, except for **mí** and **ti,** which are used instead of **yo** and **tú**. There is a written accent on **mí** to distinguish it from the possessive adjective **mi** (*my*). Unlike with **el** (*the*), there is no contraction of **de** with **él** (*him*).

sin **mí (ti, usted, él, ella, nosotros/as, vosotros/as, ustedes, ellos, ellas)**
without **me** *(you, you, him, her, us, you, you, them, them)*

Use the irregular forms **conmigo** and **contigo** to say *with me* and *with you* (singular, familiar). Otherwise, use the regular prepositional pronouns after **con**.

¿Quieres estudiar **conmigo** o **con ellos**?
Do you want to study **with me** *or* **with them**?

¿Cómo se pronuncia? La consonante *d*

When **d** is the first sound in a phrase, or after the letters **n** or **l** in Spanish, it is pronounced much as in English, but with the tongue closer to the upper teeth. In all other positions, it is pronounced similarly to the *th* sound of the English word *they*.

— ¿**D**ón**d**e está tu resi**d**encia?
— Está **d**etrás **d**e la biblioteca y al la**d**o **d**e la cafetería.

Suggestions. A. Have students refer to the drawing of the classroom on p. 36 and read the following *true/false* statements. 1. El estante está delante de una ventana. 2. La profesora está delante de la pizarra. 3. Hay un papel encima del escritorio de la profesora. 4. Hay cuatro libros encima de la mesa. 5. Hay unos lápices encima de la mesa. 6. Hay una mochila debajo de la silla de una estudiante. 7. La puerta está al lado de la pizarra. Continue by asking the following *either/or* questions. 1. ¿La pizarra está enfrente de los estudiantes o a su derecha? 2. ¿Las ventanas están a la derecha del estante o a la izquierda del estante? 3. ¿Las ventanas están a la derecha del reloj o a la izquierda del reloj? 4. ¿La pizarra está enfrente de la profesora o detrás de ella? 5. ¿Hay unos libros o una computadora encima del estante? 6. En la mesa, ¿el papel está entre los libros y los lápices o está debajo de ellos? 7. ¿La profesora está enfrente de un estudiante o una estudiante? 8. ¿La mesa está entre los estudiantes o enfrente de ellos? **B.** Tell students that *pongan* is the command *put*. Then give them commands such as the following: *Pongan su bolígrafo encima de (a la derecha de, a la izquierda de, debajo de, detrás de) su libro. Pongan su libro debajo de (a la derecha de, a la izquierda de, encima de) su pupitre.* **C.** Give students pairs of objects / people such as the following and have them say where they are in relation to each other. *Modelo:* su mochila / su silla → *Mi mochila está debajo de (al lado de) mi silla.* 1. su libro / su cuaderno 2. su bolígrafo (su lápiz) / su libro 3. la puerta / la pizarra 4. Ud. / la puerta 5. Ud. / la(s) ventana(s) 6. yo (el profesor / la profesora) / mi escritorio 7. yo (el profesor / la profesora) / la pizarra 8. yo (el profesor / la profesora) / ustedes

2-9 **¿Sí o no?** Use el verbo **estar** para decir si las siguientes personas están en cada lugar.

Modelo   nosotros (en clase los domingos)
No, no estamos en clase los domingos.

1. yo (en clase de lunes a viernes, en otra clase antes de la clase de español, en la biblioteca por la tarde, en casa todo el día los domingos)
2. el profesor/la profesora (en clase ahora, en su oficina antes de la clase de español, en su oficina después de clase, delante de la pizarra ahora)
3. mis padres (en el trabajo los lunes, en casa ahora, cerca de aquí)
4. mi mejor amigo/a y yo (juntos todos los días, en todas las mismas clases)

Ⓟ **2-10** **En la calle Molino.** Sketch the following street twice on a sheet of paper. On the first sketch, write the names of the following places in Spanish on the different buildings in random order. Then, working in pairs, ask your partner questions as in the model about what is in each place on his/her paper. Write in the names on your empty sketch of **la calle Molino** until you have completed it. When you have finished, compare papers.

> un restaurante   un cine   un café   un gimnasio   un supermercado
> una librería   un club nocturno   una tienda de ropa   una biblioteca

Modelo   E1: **¿Qué está enfrente de la escuela?**
E2: **El restaurante está enfrente de la escuela.**

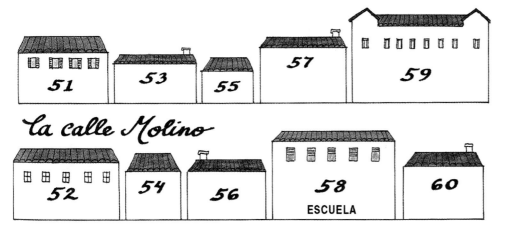

Ⓟ **2-11** **Entrevista.** Complete cada pregunta con la forma indicada del verbo **estar** para entrevistar a otro/a estudiante.

1. ¿Dónde _____ (tú) generalmente antes y después de la clase de español? ¿Dónde _____ tus padres generalmente a la hora de la clase de español? ¿en casa? ¿en el trabajo? ¿en un café o un restaurante?
2. ¿En qué calle _____ tu casa/apartamento/residencia? ¿_____ cerca o lejos de aquí?
3. ¿Te gusta más _____ con tus amigos, con tu familia o solo/a los fines de semana? ¿Cuándo (*When*) _____ (tú) con tus amigos generalmente? ¿Dónde _____ ustedes generalmente cuando _____ juntos?

Suggestion for 2-9. ¿Sí o no? If students answer *no*, ask them to say what is true. *Modelo: — No, no estamos en clase los domingos. — ¿Qué días estamos en clase? — Estamos en clase los lunes, miércoles y viernes.*

Follow-ups for 2-10. *En la calle Molino.* A. Have students sketch *la calle Molino* with five boxes on each side of the street. Read the following sentences and have students fill in the name of each place. 1. Enfrente de la escuela, hay una biblioteca. 2. A la derecha de la biblioteca, hay un supermercado. 3. Al otro lado de la biblioteca, hay un café. 4. A la izquierda del café, hay un restaurante. 5. El restaurante está entre el café y un club nocturno. 6. Enfrente del club nocturno, hay un cine. 7. Al lado del cine, hay una tienda de ropa. 8. Entre la tienda de ropa y la escuela, hay una librería. 9. A la derecha de la escuela hay un gimnasio. (**Quick reference answers:** 51–club nocturno, 52–cine, 53–restaurante, 54–tienda de ropa, 55–café, 56–librería, 57–biblioteca, 58–escuela, 59–supermercado, 60–gimnasio.) **B.** Have students write the name of a classmate on a sheet of paper. The other students ask questions such as the following until they guess who it is: *¿Está detrás de ti? ¿Está a la derecha de Raquel? ¿Está cerca de la puerta?...* **C.** Have students write three sentences describing the location of their favorite restaurant and read them aloud. Classmates guess the name of the restaurant. *Modelo: Está en la calle Riverside cerca de la calle Comal. Está al lado de un edificio grande. Está enfrente de otro restaurante.*

VOCABULARIO

TEMA 3

¿Están listos o necesitan más tiempo?

¿Cómo estás hoy?

¿Cansado/a?

¿Enfermo/a?   ¿Ocupado/a?

¿Estupendo/a?

¿Cómo estás en clase generalmente?

¿Contento/a,   triste   o enojado/a?

¿Aburrido/a o interesado/a?

¿Nervioso/a o bien?

¿Confundido/a o seguro/a
de la respuesta?

Expresiones útiles si algo no está claro en clase.

No sé.	*I don't know.*
No comprendo.	*I don't understand.*
Tengo una pregunta.	*I have a question.*
¿Cómo se dice… en español?	*How do you say… in Spanish?*
¿Cómo se escribe?	*How is it written?*
¿Qué significa… en inglés?	*What does… mean in English?*
No estoy listo/a. Necesito más tiempo.	*I'm not ready. I need more time.*
¿Cuál es la tarea para la próxima clase?	*What is the homework for the next class?*

2-12 ¿Cómo son? ¿Cómo están? Describa a estas personas con el verbo **estar** y un adjetivo de la caja según (*according to*) sus características.

> ocupado/a   enojado/a   cansado/a   contento/a   triste   confundido/a   listo/a

Modelo   Mi padre es muy trabajador.
Siempre (*Always*) **está ocupado.**

1. Mi hermano es antipático.
2. Mi madre es muy optimista.
3. Mi novio no es muy inteligente.
4. Mi mejor amiga es perezosa.
5. Mi hermano es pesimista.
6. Yo soy organizado/a.

2-13 ¿Cómo estás? Complete cada oración con la forma correcta del adjetivo lógico de la lista: **aburrido, ocupado, confundido, listo, contento, seguro, enfermo.**

1. No comprendo. Estoy _____.
2. Mi clase de contabilidad no es muy interesante. A veces los estudiantes están _____.
3. Tengo mucha tarea hoy. Estoy muy _____.
4. No sé. No estoy _____ de la respuesta.
5. ¿Necesitan ustedes más tiempo para este ejercicio o están _____?
6. Hoy estamos estupendos. Estamos _____ porque es viernes y no hay mucha tarea este fin de semana.
7. Muchos estudiantes no están en clase hoy porque están _____.

2-14 ¿Es cierto? ¿Son ciertas o falsas las siguientes oraciones? Cambie (*Change*) las palabras indicadas de las oraciones falsas para describir su propia (*own*) situación.

1. Generalmente, estoy cansado/a *los lunes por la mañana.*
2. Generalmente, estoy *estupendo/a los sábados por la noche.*
3. Estoy más ocupado/a *los lunes, miércoles y viernes.*
4. A veces, estoy aburrido/a cuando *estoy con mis padres.*
5. Muchos de mis amigos están interesados en *el fútbol americano.*
6. Estoy muy contento/a cuando *no tengo mucha tarea.*
7. Me gusta estar solo/a cuando estoy *enojado/a.*
8. Estoy nervioso/a cuando *no estoy seguro/a de una respuesta en clase.*

(P)

Conversaciones. Dos estudiantes hablan de sus clases. En parejas, lean su conversación, luego preparen dos conversaciones sobre sus propias clases.

— En tus clases, ¿te gusta estar cerca del profesor o **al fondo,** lejos del profesor?
— Eso depende de la clase. En la clase de español me gusta estar cerca de la profesora, pero en la clase de química, no me gusta **hablar** y prefiero estar lejos del profesor.
— ¿Por qué no te gusta hablar en la clase de química?
— No sé. **Siempre** estoy confundido. **Nunca** sé las respuestas.

---

al fondo *at the back*   **hablar** *to talk, to speak*   **siempre** *always*   **nunca** *never*

AUDIO ¡A escuchar!

Ahora, escuchen otra conversación en la cual (*in which*) una estudiante habla de sus clases con un amigo. ¿Cómo está ahora? ¿Cómo está con frecuencia en sus clases? ¿Por qué?

GRAMÁTICA
Más descripciones: ¿*ser* o *estar*?

Para averiguar

1. What are two uses of **estar**?
2. What are four uses of **ser**?
3. What does **¿Cómo están tus padres?** mean? What does **¿Cómo son tus padres?** mean?

Suggestions. A. Tell students to remember the uses of *estar*, and by process of elimination use *ser* elsewhere. **B.** You may wish to explain to students that *estar* is derived from the Latin verb *stare*, from which the English words *status* and *state* are derived. The verb *ser* is derived from the Latin verb *esse*, from which the English word *essence* is derived. Thus, you use *estar* with adjectives describing physical and mental states or the status of something. You use *ser* with adjectives describing its essence. **C.** Tell students that you generally use *estar* with adjectives describing conditions that are expected to change from time to time. **D.** Point out to students that *ser* is always used with nouns when saying who someone is or what something is, even if talking about something that is likely to change. (*Soy estudiante. Son novios...*)

Although **ser** and **estar** both mean *to be*, the two verbs are not interchangeable. Here is a summary of the main uses of each.

Use **estar**:

1) to describe mental and physical states or conditions with adjectives.	— ¿Estás listo para el examen? — No, y estoy muy nervioso.
2) to say where or with whom someone or something is.	— ¿Dónde está la profesora? — Está en su oficina. Está con otro estudiante.

Use **ser**:

1) to say what someone or something is like with adjectives describing general characteristics.	— ¿Tus profesores son buenos? — Sí, son muy inteligentes y simpáticos.
2) to say where someone is from.	— ¿De dónde eres? — Soy de Estados Unidos.
3) to say who someone is or what something is with a noun.	— ¿Quiénes son ellos? — Son mis compañeros de clase.
4) to talk about time.	— ¿A qué hora son tus clases? — Son a las diez y a la una.

Some adjectives can be used with either **ser** or **estar,** but have different meanings with each one.

estar aburrido/a *to be bored*	ser aburrido/a *to be boring*
estar listo/a *to be ready*	ser listo/a *to be smart, clever*
estar seguro/a *to be sure*	ser seguro/a *to be safe*

Compare these sentences.

¿Cómo está tu padre? *How is your father doing?*	¿Cómo es tu padre? *What is your father like?*
Tu novia está bonita. *Your girlfriend looks pretty.* (*She's pretty on a specific occasion.*)	Tu novia es bonita. *Your girlfriend is pretty.* (*She's a pretty woman in general.*)

Suggestion for 2-15. ¿*Ser o estar*? A. Have students explain why they use *ser* or *estar* in each case. **B.** Have students write a similar paragraph about themselves.

2-15 ¿Ser o estar? ¿Se usa **ser** o **estar** en las siguientes oraciones?

[1](Soy / Estoy) Joel Martínez y mi familia [2](es / está) de Guatemala. Ahora [3](somos / estamos) en Texas porque mi padre [4](es / está) profesor de español en una universidad aquí. Él [5](es / está) muy ocupado y siempre [6](es / está) en clase o en su oficina. Yo [7](soy / estoy) estudiante en la misma universidad. [8](Soy / Estoy) un poco nervioso hoy porque el primer examen de mi clase de física [9](es / está) esta tarde y no [10](soy / estoy) listo. La física [11](es / está) muy difícil para mí y a veces [12](soy / estoy) confundido en clase. Mis padres [13](son / están) muy estrictos y no [14](son / están) contentos si saco malas notas (*if I get bad grades*) en mis clases.

2-16 Descripciones. Use el verbo **ser** o **estar** para describir a estas personas con las palabras indicadas.

Modelo	mi hermana, sola, con su novio, en un club, tímida

Es mi hermana. No está sola. Está con su novio. Está en un club. No es tímida.

1. mi hermano, trabajador, perezoso, en casa, ocupado, aburrido

2. mi otro hermano, en el gimnasio, con sus amigos, solo, atlético

3. mis padres, viejos, juntos, en un restaurante, simpáticos

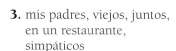 **2-17 Entrevista.** Complete las siguientes preguntas con la forma correcta del verbo **ser** o **estar.** Luego entreviste a un/a compañero/a de clase.

1. ¿_____ (tú) muy cansado/a los fines de semana? ¿Dónde _____ (tú) generalmente los sábados por la noche? ¿en casa? ¿con los amigos?

2. ¿Quién _____ tu mejor amigo/a? ¿De dónde _____ (él/ella)? ¿_____ estudiante? ¿Dónde _____ su casa/apartamento? ¿_____ (tú) con él/ella con frecuencia? ¿_____ ustedes muy similares?

3. ¿Cuál _____ tu restaurante favorito? ¿_____ cerca de aquí? ¿En qué calle _____? ¿_____ un restaurante de comida mexicana? ¿_____ abierto las veinticuatro horas del día?

Supplemental activities. A. Ask students how they would translate the verb *to be* in the following sentences. 1. Today is Wednesday. 2. I'm very busy on Wednesdays. 3. I'm at the university in the morning. 4. My last class is at eleven o'clock. 5. I'm at work in the afternoon. 6. The office where I work is next to the university. 7. My work is very difficult. 8. Sometimes I'm bored at work. 9. I'm not home until late. 10. I'm very tired after work. 11. It's ten o'clock when I arrive at my apartment. 12. My apartment is very far from my work. 13. It's a beautiful apartment. 14. It's not very big. 15. I'm almost never at home. B. Have students choose between (*no*) *soy* and (*no*) *estoy* to say whether these adjectives describe them: *cansado/a, trabajador/a, triste, emocional, tímido/a, intelectual, confundido/a, enojado/a, responsable, atlético/a, ocupado/a, enfermo/a, liberal, enojado/a, impulsivo/a.* Continue with the following nouns or phrases: *estudiante, en clase ahora, en clase todos los días, de California, padre/madre, mexicano/a, el/la novio/a de otro/a estudiante de la clase, al fondo del salón de clase, cerca de la pizarra.*

VOCABULARIO

TEMA **4**   **¿Qué te gusta hacer después de clase?**

Hoy después de clase, quiero…

estudiar

tomar algo con mis amigos

hablar por teléfono

comprar ropa

Hoy después de clase, necesito…

trabajar

limpiar la casa

preparar la cena

regresar a casa en autobús / en mi coche

Los fines de semana, prefiero…

escuchar música y bailar

tocar la guitarra y cantar

pasar mucho tiempo en casa y descansar

mirar partidos de básquetbol en la televisión

Supplemental activities. A. ¿Deseo o necesidad? Generalmente, ¿quiere o necesita hacer las siguientes cosas? *Modelo:* mirar la televisión > *Generalmente, quiero mirar la televisión. (descansar después de clase, estudiar, limpiar la casa, trabajar, pasar mucho tiempo con los amigos, pasar mucho tiempo en la biblioteca, escuchar música, tomar algo con los amigos)* **B.** Have students complete the following sentences logically. 1. Quiero ir a un club nocturno. Quiero… 2. Quiero ir a un café con mis amigos. Quiero… 3. Me gusta ir a las tiendas de ropa. Me gusta… 4. Quiero ir al estadio. Quiero… 5. Estoy muy cansado/a. Necesito… 6. Necesito ir al supermercado. Esta noche, quiero… 7. Hay un examen mañana. Necesito… 8. Necesito ir a la oficina. Necesito…

el tiempo *time*   **descansar** *to rest*

¿Cómo se pronuncia? *r* y *rr*

In Spanish, a single **r** between vowels is pronounced by tapping the tip of the tongue just behind the upper teeth. This is similar to the tapping sound of *dd* when you pronounce the English word *ladder* quickly.

quiero   quieres   eres   pero   prefiero   prefieres

The double **rr** is pronounced by tapping the tip of the tongue behind the upper teeth in a series of rapid vibrations. When a single **r** appears at the beginning of a word or after **l, n,** or **s,** it is pronounced like **rr.**

aburrido   pizarra   repitan   residencia   regresar   Enrique

When **r** appears at the end of a syllable, the tendency is to pronounce it as a single **r,** but for emphasis, it can be pronounced as **rr.**

hablar   descansar   mirar   tarde   miércoles   viernes

2-18   ¿Qué hace usted? Diga si las siguientes oraciones son ciertas (*true*) o falsas. Cambie (*Change*) las palabras indicadas de las oraciones falsas para describir su propia situación.

1. Hoy, después de clase, necesito *trabajar.*
2. Generalmente, después de clase, me gusta *descansar.*
3. No me gusta *bailar* con mis amigos.
4. Los fines de semana, me gusta *mirar la televisión.*
5. Tengo mucho tiempo para descansar *los jueves.*
6. Generalmente, necesito estudiar mucho *los lunes, miércoles y sábados.*
7. Me gusta pasar mucho tiempo con mis amigos *los viernes por la noche.*

(P) 2-19   Entrevista. Entreviste a otro/a estudiante con estas preguntas.

1. ¿En qué tienda te gusta comprar ropa? ¿En qué librería te gusta comprar libros? ¿Dónde te gusta pasar tiempo con tus amigos?
2. ¿Te gusta más los partidos de fútbol americano o de básquetbol? ¿Te gustan más mirar un partido de fútbol americano en un estadio o en la televisión?
3. ¿Te gusta escuchar música clásica? ¿jazz? ¿rock? ¿música popular? ¿Te gusta más escuchar música en la radio o en un concierto?

(P)   Conversaciones. En parejas, lean la siguiente conversación en la cual dos amigos hablan de los fines de semana. Luego, preparen dos conversaciones sobre los fines de semana de ustedes.

— ¿Qué te gusta hacer los fines de semana?
— Los viernes **casi siempre** estoy cansado. Trabajo **hasta** las siete y después del trabajo, prefiero pasar la noche en casa.
— ¿No trabajas los sábados **ni** los domingos?
— No, los sábados me gusta **salir.** Me gusta **ir al cine** o a un café con mis amigos. A veces me gusta **comer** en un restaurante.
— ¿Te gusta descansar los domingos?
— Sí, me gusta mirar **los deportes** en la televisión, pero casi siempre necesito hacer mucha tarea.

---

casi *almost* **siempre** *always* **hasta** *until* **ni** *nor* **salir** *to go out* **ir al cine** *to go to the movies* **comer** *to eat*
los deportes *sports*

Suggestion for ¿Cómo se pronuncia? Give students the following *trabalenguas* along with the translations. First have students decide whether each single *r* is pronounced like *rr*. Then have students practice saying each tongue twister. 1. 'Erre' con 'erre' cigarro, 'erre' con 'erre' barril. Rápido corren los carros, cargados de azúcar del ferrocarril. (*'R' with 'r' cigar, 'r' with 'r' barrel. Rapidly run the railroad cars loaded with sugar.*) 2. ¿Cuánta madera roería un roedor si los roedores royeran madera? (*How much wood would a rodent gnaw, if rodents could gnaw wood?*) 3. El perro de Rosa no tiene rabo porque Ramón Ramírez se lo ha cortado. (*Rosa's dog has no tail because Ramón Ramírez has cut it off.*) 4. Rosa Rizo reza ruso, ruso reza Rosa Rizo. (*Rosa Rizo prays in Russian, in Russian prays Rosa Rizo.*)

Suggestions for 2-19. Entrevista. A. Remind students that *le gusta(n)* is used to say both *he likes* and *she likes* and ask them about their partners' answers. **B.** Continue with these questions. *¿Con quién le gusta tomar algo en un café? ¿Con quién le gusta hablar por teléfono? ¿Le gusta hablar por teléfono en su coche? ¿Dónde prefiere trabajar, en una tienda de ropa o en un supermercado? ¿en un restaurante o en una tienda de ropa? ¿en una librería o en un restaurante? ¿Cuándo prefiere trabajar, por la mañana, por la tarde o por la noche? ¿Qué día de la semana le gusta limpiar la casa? ¿Le gusta más limpiar la casa o preparar la comida? ¿Le gusta bailar? ¿En qué club le gusta bailar? ¿Le gusta más bailar o cantar? ¿Le gusta más regresar a casa en autobús, en su coche o con un amigo? ¿Le gusta pasar mucho tiempo en*

AUDIO **¡A escuchar!**

Ahora, escuchen otra conversación en la cual dos estudiantes hablan de sus actividades después de clase. ¿Qué le gusta hacer a cada uno y cuándo trabajan?

casa los fines de semana? Los sábados por la noche, ¿le gusta más pasar tiempo con su familia o con sus amigos? ¿Qué días le gusta descansar? Para descansar, ¿le gusta más escuchar música o mirar la televisión? ¿Le gusta más mirar el fútbol americano o una película romántica? ¿Le gustan más las películas de aventuras o las películas de terror?

GRAMÁTICA
Las acciones: los verbos en *-ar* y la frecuencia

Para averiguar

1. What is an infinitive?
2. What are the three infinitive endings in Spanish?
3. What are the endings of regular **-ar** verbs that go with each of the subject pronouns? How do you determine the stem to which you attach these endings?
4. What adverbs can you use to say how often something occurs? Where do you place them in a sentence?

¡Ojo!

You will learn later how to conjugate non **-ar** verbs like **ir** (*to go*), **comer** (*to eat*), and **hacer** (*to do, to make*). Until then, just use them in the infinitive to say what you need, want, or like to do. (**Necesito comer. Quiero ir a la cafetería. Me gusta hacer mi tarea en un café.**)

Infinitives. The form of the verb that you find in dictionaries or vocabulary lists is called the infinitive. Some examples of infinitives in English are *to work*, *to do*, and *to write*. Spanish infinitives consist of single words that end in **-ar**, **-er**, or **-ir**: trabaj**ar**, hac**er**, escrib**ir**. The part of the verb that carries the meaning is called the *stem*. The *ending* is the part that indicates who the subject is. For example, in **trabajo** and **trabajas**, the stem is **trabaj-** and the endings are **-o** (for *I*) and **-as** (for *you*).

-ar verbs. To indicate the subject of **-ar** verbs you must conjugate them by dropping the **-ar** ending of the infinitive and adding the endings below. As with all verbs, the subject pronouns are not used, unless they are needed for clarity or emphasis.

TRABAJAR (*TO WORK*)					
yo	trabaj**o**	*I work*	nosotros/as	trabaj**amos**	*we work*
tú	trabaj**as**	*you work*	vosotros/as	trabaj**áis**	*you work*
usted	trabaj**a**	*you work*	ustedes	trabaj**an**	*you work*
él	trabaj**a**	*he works*	ellos	trabaj**an**	*they work*
ella	trabaj**a**	*she works*	ellas	trabaj**an**	*they work*

These **-ar** verbs follow the same pattern as **trabajar.**

bailar	*to dance*	**limpiar**	*to clean*
cantar	*to sing*	**llegar**	*to arrive*
comprar	*to buy*	**mirar**	*to watch, to look at*
contestar	*to answer*	**necesitar**	*to need*
descansar	*to rest*	**pasar**	*to pass, to spend* (time)
enseñar	*to teach*	**preparar**	*to prepare*
escuchar	*to listen (to)*	**regresar**	*to return*
estudiar	*to study*	**tocar**	*to play* (el piano, la guitarra)
hablar	*to speak*	**tomar**	*to drink, to take*

— ¿A qué hora **regresan** ustedes a casa?   — *At what time do you return home?*
— **Regresamos** a las seis.   — *We return at six.*

Use the following adverbs to say how often one does something. Place **siempre** and **nunca** just before the verb. The other adverbs may go at the beginning or end of phrases.

(casi) siempre	*(almost) always*
(casi) nunca	*(almost) never*
todos los días	*every day*
con frecuencia	*frequently*
a veces	*sometimes, at times*
una vez a la semana	*once per week*
dos veces al mes / al año	*twice per month / per year*

— ¿**Siempre** trabajas por la tarde?
— Trabajo de la una a las seis **todos los días. Nunca** trabajo por la mañana.

Supplemental activities. A. ¿Cuál es lógico? 1. ¿Mi hermano pasa mucho tiempo solo porque es tímido o extrovertido? 2. ¿Los estudiantes no escuchan en clase porque están interesados o aburridos? 3. Estoy muy cansado/a. ¿Necesito trabajar o descansar? 4. ¿Siempre estoy listo/a para mis clases porque estudio mucho o poco? 5. ¿Mi hermano nunca está confundido en sus clases porque estudia mucho o poco? 6. Mi hermano toma clases de biología, química y física. ¿Le gustan las ciencias o las humanidades? 7. Mi hermana habla mucho en sus clases. ¿Es muy tímida o extrovertida? 8. ¿Ella contesta todas las preguntas porque está confundida o está segura de las respuestas? B. Write activities with -ar verbs such as the following on slips of paper. Have students draw a slip of paper and mime the verb. (cantar, tocar el piano, tocar la guitarra, bailar, hablar por teléfono, comprar un libro, contestar una pregunta, contestar el teléfono, escuchar música, preparar la comida, limpiar la casa, tomar un café, mirar la televisión)

2-20 **¿Qué hacen?** ¿Con qué frecuencia hacen estas personas las cosas indicadas entre paréntesis?

> **Modelo**   Yo… (estudiar en la biblioteca)
> **Estudio en la biblioteca (casi) todos los días. / Estudio en la biblioteca con frecuencia. / Estudio en la biblioteca a veces. / (Casi) Nunca estudio en la biblioteca.**

1. Yo… (llegar tarde [*late*] a la universidad, regresar a casa después de la clase de español, descansar los sábados por la noche, limpiar la casa)

2. Mi mejor amigo/a… (estudiar conmigo, hablar conmigo por teléfono, trabajar los fines de semana, tocar la guitarra, escuchar música clásica)

3. Mis amigos y yo… (bailar juntos, tomar algo en un café, estudiar en un café, cantar en un karaoke, regresar a casa muy tarde los sábados)

P **2-21** **¿Quién?** Pregúntele a un/a compañero/a de clase quién de su familia hace las siguientes cosas con más frecuencia.

> **Modelo**   E1: **¿Quién de tu familia compra la comida con más frecuencia?**
> E2: **Mi padre compra la comida con más frecuencia. /**
> **Yo compro la comida con más frecuencia. /**
> **Todos compramos la comida a veces. /**
> **Nadie** (*Nobody*) **compra la comida.**

1.

2.

3.

4.

5.

6.

7.

P **2-22** **Entrevista.** Use estas preguntas para entrevistar a otro/a estudiante.

1. ¿Qué días trabajas, por lo general? ¿Qué días descansas? ¿Pasas mucho tiempo en casa? ¿Cuándo limpias la casa? ¿Necesitas limpiar la casa ahora?

2. ¿Miras mucho la televisión? ¿Qué programas miras con frecuencia? ¿Miras la tele mientras (*while*) estudias?

3. ¿Escuchas música mientras estudias? ¿Qué música escuchas más? ¿Tocas la guitarra o el piano? ¿Cantas bien? ¿Compras muchos discos compactos? ¿Quién canta bien? ¿Quién canta mal?

Supplemental activity. Using the verbs from the list on the preceding page, have students make a list of things they do in the following places. Encourage them to list several activities for each place if possible. (en un café, en un club, en una tienda de ropa, en un supermercado, en una biblioteca, en una oficina, en un concierto, en casa) Afterward, ask questions such as the following for each place. ¿Estudia Ud. en un café a veces? ¿En qué café pasa mucho tiempo? ¿Baila mucho? ¿En qué club tocan buena música? ¿En qué tiendas compra Ud. mucha ropa? ¿En qué supermercado compra comida generalmente? ¿Pasa Ud. mucho tiempo en la biblioteca? ¿Estudia más en casa o en la biblioteca? ¿Trabaja Ud. en una oficina? ¿A qué hora regresa del trabajo? ¿de la universidad? ¿Trabajan sus padres en una oficina? ¿Escucha Ud. mucha música? ¿Le gusta más escuchar música rock o jazz? ¿Prepara Ud. la comida en casa todos los días o le gusta comer en un restaurante a veces? ¿Prepara Ud. comida mexicana a veces? ¿comida italiana?

TEMA 5

VOCABULARIO
¿Cómo pasas el día?

Supplemental activities. A. Point out that **tarde** can mean both *late* and *afternoon.* **B.** Have students ask one another the questions on this page. Remind them that *su(s)* means *his* and *her* and have them report back to the class about what they find out. **C.** Oral questions. Ask students the following questions about your class. Tell them that they may need to refer to their syllabus for some answers. 1. ¿Quién es? (*Point at a student.*) 2. ¿Dónde está? (*Name a student.*) 3. ¿Cuántos estudiantes hay en clase hoy? 4. ¿Qué día es hoy? 5. ¿Qué hora es ahora? 6. ¿Dónde está mi oficina? 7. ¿Cuál es mi número de teléfono? 8. ¿Cuándo estoy en mi oficina? 9. ¿Cuántos exámenes hay este semestre? 10. ¿Cuántas semanas de clase hay? 11. ¿Cuándo estudia Ud. más, por la mañana, por la tarde o por la noche? 12. ¿De qué hora a qué hora está en la universidad hoy? 13. ¿Cuántas clases tiene hoy? 14. ¿Cuál es su día favorito? ¿Por qué es su favorito?

Suggestion for ¿Cómo se pronuncia? Give students the following *trabalenguas:* Cuando cuentas cuentos nunca cuentas cuántos cuentos cuentas porque cuando cuentas cuentos nunca cuentas cuántos cuentos cuentas. (*When you tell tales you never tell how many tales you tell, because when you tell tales you never count how many tales you tell.*)

¿Cómo pasas el día generalmente?	Estoy en clase y **luego** trabajo.
¿Cuándo estás en clase, por la mañana o por la tarde?	Estoy en clase por la mañana y trabajo por la tarde.
¿A qué hora llegas a la universidad?	Llego a la universidad a las nueve de la mañana. Nunca llego **tarde.**
¿Qué estudias?	Estudio química, historia y español.
¿Cuál es tu clase favorita?	La clase de español es mi favorita.
¿Por qué es tu favorita?	Porque el profesor (la profesora) es muy bueno/a y la clase es **divertida.**
¿Quién es tu profesor/a?	Es el profesor (la profesora) Gómez.
¿Dónde trabajas?	Trabajo **en** un hospital, **para** un doctor.
¿Cuántas horas trabajas a la semana?	Trabajo veinte horas a la semana.
¿Qué te gusta hacer después del trabajo?	Si no tengo tarea, me gusta escuchar música.

¿Cómo se pronuncia? Más sobre los acentos gráficos, *cu* y *qu*

Written accents are used to indicate which syllable is stressed (see pages 20–21). They are also used to distinguish in writing a few sets of words that otherwise are spelled alike. *All* question words have written accent marks for this reason, as well as the following words.

sí	*yes*	si	*if*
él	*he*	el	*the*
tú	*you*	tu	*your*
mí	*me*	mi	*my*
sólo	*only*	solo/a	*alone*
cómo	*how*	como	*like, as*
por qué	*why*	porque	*because*
qué	*what*	que	*that, than*

Most question words begin with **cu** and **qu.** Words spelled with **cu** have a [w] sound when they are pronounced.

cuál	cuándo	cuántos	cuatro	frecuente	escuela

There is no [w] sound with **qu.** The **u** of **qu** is silent.

quién	qué	quince	quiero	aquí	química

---

luego *then, next* **tarde** *late* **divertido/a** *fun* **en** *at* **para** *for*

2-23   ¿Cuál es la pregunta? ¿Qué palabra interrogativa se usa para obtener la información indicada?

> **Modelo**   Trabajo *en un restaurante.*   →   **¿dónde?**

1. Mis clases son *difíciles.*
2. Me gusta estudiar *biología.*
3. Me gusta *porque es interesante.*
4. Hay *treinta* estudiantes.

5. Trabajo *mucho.*
6. Trabajo *todos los días.*
7. Mi mejor amiga es *Ana.*
8. Ana es muy *simpática.*

P **2-24   La tarde de Ramón.** Complete cada pregunta con la palabra interrogativa lógica. Luego, hágale las preguntas a otro/a estudiante.

1. ¿A _____ hora regresa Ramón del trabajo?

2. ¿_____ regresa? ¿en su coche o en el autobús?

3. ¿_____ compra antes de regresar a su casa? ¿ropa, un libro o comida?

4. ¿_____ compra eso? ¿en una tienda de ropa, en una librería o en un supermercado?

5. ¿_____ paga (*pay*)? ¿más de veinticinco dólares o menos?

6. ¿_____ prepara la comida, Ramón o su esposa?

7. ¿_____ prepara la comida? ¿en la casa o en el patio?

P   **Conversaciones.** En parejas, lean la siguiente conversación entre dos estudiantes. Luego, cambien la conversación para describir uno de sus días de clase.

— ¿Hasta qué hora estás en casa los lunes por la mañana?
— Estoy en casa hasta las siete y media.
— ¿A qué hora llegas a la universidad?
— No llego hasta las nueve menos cuarto porque mi casa está muy lejos de la universidad. Llego quince minutos antes de mi **primera** clase.
— ¿Cuánto tiempo estás en clase los lunes?
— Cinco horas. Estoy en clase todo el día.
— ¿Regresas a tu casa después de tu **última** clase?
— No, regreso después de las diez de la noche.
— ¿Por qué regresas **tan** tarde?
— Porque trabajo cinco horas.

AUDIO ¡A escuchar!

Ahora, escuchen otra conversación en la cual una estudiante habla de cuándo trabaja. ¿Qué días trabaja y de qué hora a qué hora?

---
primero/a *first* **último/a** *last* **tan** *so*

GRAMÁTICA
Formar preguntas: la formación de preguntas

Para averiguar

1. Where do you generally place the subject in a question?
2. How do you translate tag questions such as *isn't he?*, *can't she?*, and *don't they?*
3. Which question words have written accents? Which ones have plural forms?
4. What does **qué** mean? What does **cuál(es)** mean? When do you use **cuál(es)** instead of **qué** to say *what*?

Supplemental activity. Have students see how many logical questions they can think of for another student with the following verbs in a set time: *estudiar, trabajar, hablar por teléfono, bailar, comprar mucha ropa, descansar, tocar.* (*Modelo:* preparar la comida: *¿Quién prepara la comida? ¿Con quién preparas la comida? ¿Cuándo preparas la comida? ¿Dónde preparas la comida? ¿Qué comida preparas? ¿Cuánta comida preparas? ¿Por qué preparas la comida? ¿Cómo preparas la comida?*)

To ask a question that may be answered *yes* or *no*, use rising intonation. The word *do*, used to ask questions in English, is not translated in Spanish. Questions are preceded by an inverted question mark (¿).

¿Trabajas todos los días?   *Do you work every day?*

When the subject of a verb is stated, it is generally placed after the verb in a question. It may be placed at the end of very short questions.

Statements	**Questions**
Daniel estudia más que tú.	¿Estudia Daniel más que tú?
Daniel estudia mucho.	¿Estudia mucho Daniel?

If you think you already know the answer to a question and you are just asking to be sure, attach **¿verdad?** or **¿no?** to the end of a statement.

Daniel es tu novio, **¿verdad?**   *Daniel is your boyfriend, **isn't he**?*
Es de Guatemala, **¿no?**   *He's from Guatemala, **right**?*

Use the following interrogative words to ask questions that will be answered with new information, such as *where*, *when*, or *with whom*. Unlike *yes/no* questions, information questions have falling intonation. **Cuál(es)** and **quién(es)** have plural forms and **cuánto/a** and **cuántos/as** agree for plurality and gender. All question words have written accents.

¿cuál(es)?	*which?, what?*
¿cuándo?	*when?*
¿cuánto/a?	*how much?*
¿cuántos/as?	*how many?*
¿cómo?	*how?*
¿dónde?	*where?*
¿de dónde?	*from where?*
¿por qué?	*why?*
¿quién(es)?	*who?*
¿con quién(es)?	*with whom?*
¿qué?	*what?*

Generally **qué** translates the English word *what*; however, **cuál(es)** translates *what* when it is followed by the verb *to be* (**ser**) and one is making a selection from a group. Use **qué** to say *what* with other verbs and with **ser** when asking for a definition.

Selection: ¿Cuál es tu clase favorita?   *What is your favorite class?*
Definition: ¿Qué es un infinitivo?   *What is an infinitive?*

Use **qué** rather than **cuál(es)** directly before a noun.

¿Qué días trabajas?   *What/Which days do you work?*

2-25 **¿Qué? o ¿Cuál(es)?** Complete las siguientes preguntas para el/la profesor/a con **qué** o **cuál(es).**

1. ¿_____ es la tarea para la próxima clase?
2. ¿_____ necesitamos estudiar para mañana?
3. ¿_____ es un infinitivo?
4. ¿_____ es el infinitivo del verbo **miran**?
5. ¿_____ son los verbos que necesitamos estudiar para el próximo examen?
6. ¿_____ significa el verbo **llegar**?
7. ¿_____ son sus horas de oficina?
8. ¿_____ le gusta hacer después del trabajo?

(P) 2-26 **El día de Carlos.** Escriba cinco preguntas para un/a compañero/a de clase sobre esta descripción del día de Carlos. Luego, hágale las preguntas.

> Hoy es jueves. Tengo muchas clases hoy. Mi clase de matemáticas es a las 9:00 de la mañana. Es una clase muy difícil. Me gusta mucho la clase de literatura hispanoamericana. Es interesante y la profesora es muy buena. Antes de mi clase de literatura, estudio una hora en la biblioteca con mi amigo Alejandro, y después, estoy en la cafetería hasta las 2:00. Me gusta comer en mi casa porque la comida de la cafetería es muy mala, pero sólo tengo treinta minutos para comer antes de ir a otra clase. Es una clase de historia y el profesor es viejo y aburrido. Trabajo después de la clase de historia y regreso a mi casa a las nueve de la noche.

2-27 **¿Y tú?** ¿Qué se pregunta para obtener las siguientes respuestas? Primero, escriba las preguntas, y luego, use las preguntas para entrevistar a otro/a estudiante.

Modelo   Soy de *Baltimore.*
                    E1: **¿De dónde eres?**
                    E2: **Soy de Boston.**

1. Soy *tímido/a, paciente y optimista.*
2. Este semestre, tomo *tres* clases.
3. Tengo clases de *francés, matemáticas e historia.*
4. Estoy en clase *todo el día los lunes, miércoles y viernes.*
5. Llego a la universidad *a las ocho y media.*
6. Mi clase favorita es *la clase de matemáticas.*
7. Me gusta más *porque es divertida y el profesor es interesante.*
8. Hay *veinticinco* estudiantes en mi clase favorita.
9. Trabajo *en una tienda.*
10. Estudio con *mi mejor amigo.*
11. Necesito estudiar más para mis clases *de matemáticas y francés.*
12. Hoy, regreso a casa *después de clase.*

Supplemental activities. A. Give students the following questions in English and have them say whether they would use *qué* or *cuál(es)* to translate the word *what.* 1. What is your telephone number? 2. What are you studying this semester? 3. What is your favorite class? 4. What do you like to study? 5. What is your address? 6. What is a past participle? 7. What is the past participle in this sentence? 8. What is the date today? 9. What do you need? 10. What is the answer? **B.** Have students make three statements of what they know about you or their classmates and check that they are right using *¿verdad?* or *¿no?.*

Follow-up for 2-26. *El día de Carlos.* Have students reread the paragraph in activity *2-15. ¿Ser o estar?* on p. 46 and write questions about Joel Martínez.

Suggestions for 2-27. A. *¿Y tú?* Have students report back what they find out about their partners. Remind them that **su(s)** is used to say both *his* and *her.* **B.** Have students ask one another about their partners: *¿De dónde es Verónica?* **C.** Using the sentences as a guide, have students write a description of themselves on a sheet of paper with their name at the top. Collect the papers and read them aloud. Students say who they think it is, using a question with *¿verdad?* or *¿no? (Es Patricia, ¿verdad?).*

REVISTA CULTURAL

Note: Have students complete the *Antes de leer, Reading strategies,* and *Ahora Ud.* activities before reading this article.

¿EDUCACIÓN BILINGÜE EN LAS ESCUELAS?

Escuela elemental, Santa Ana, California.

En los años 90 llegan más inmigrantes a Estados Unidos que en otras décadas y hay muchos niños que necesitan instrucción lingüística adicional en las escuelas públicas.

Hablar inglés es para muchos inmigrantes un **desafío** grande. En los datos de la Agenda Pública 2003, un 63% de los inmigrantes opina que las escuelas públicas de Estados Unidos **deben** enseñar todas las clases en inglés y un 32% opina que deben enseñar **algunas** clases en la lengua nativa de los estudiantes extranjeros.

Aprender en colaboración.

Algunas escuelas usan la lengua nativa para enseñar en los **niveles** elementales, y en los niveles superiores incorporan el inglés en las clases. Cada estado y cada distrito formulan **las reglas sobre** la lengua de instrucción en las clases. Nuevo México es un ejemplo de multilingüismo y multiculturalismo. Es el único estado que **apoya** la educación bilingüe en su constitución. En otros estados como Georgia, Maryland, Missouri, Carolina del Sur y Virginia enseñan las clases **sólo** en inglés. El debate sobre la educación bilingüe es complejo y no hay **aún** soluciones definitivas.

En una clase de *Educación para la salud.*

---

desafío *challenge*   **deben** *should, ought to*   **algunas** *some*   **niveles** *levels*   **las reglas sobre** *the rules on*   **apoya** *supports*   **sólo** *only*   **aún** *yet*

Antes de leer

Take a look at the photos that accompany the article. What kind of information do they provide about the reading? Describe the people that appear in the photos. In what kind of setting are they presented?

Reading strategies: Inferring from the title. The title of an article can be a clear indicator of the content of the reading, and it can often help you anticipate the main themes of the text. Before starting a reading in Spanish, consider for a few minutes the title and its possible implications in the text that you are about to read. By using this technique, you will develop clues about the topic that will lead you more easily through the reading process.

2-28 Ahora Ud. Look at the title of the reading and think about the possible topics that are going to be mentioned in the reading and the issues that are going to be raised. Why do you think that the title appears as a question?

Después de leer

2-29 ¿Cierto o falso? ¿Son ciertas o falsas las siguientes oraciones? Corrija las oraciones falsas.

1. En las escuelas de Estados Unidos no hay niños de diferentes nacionalidades.
2. Aprender una nueva lengua es un desafío grande para el inmigrante.
3. La mayoría (*majority*) de los estudiantes extranjeros no necesita instrucción adicional en su lengua nativa.
4. Muchos inmigrantes opinan que es mejor enseñar a los niños sólo en inglés.
5. Algunas escuelas usan la lengua nativa del estudiante en los grados elementales y el inglés en los grados superiores.
6. El estado de Virginia es un ejemplo de bilingüismo en las escuelas.

Answers for 2-29. *¿Cierto o falso?*
1. falso: Las escuelas públicas de Estados Unidos son multiculturales. 2. cierto. 3. falso: La mayoría de los estudiantes extranjeros necesita instrucción lingüística adicional. 4. cierto. 5. cierto. 6. falso: Nuevo México es un ejemplo de bilingüismo en las escuelas.

2-30 ¿Cómo están? Complete las oraciones con el verbo **estar** y un adjetivo lógico.

Answers for 2-30. *¿Cómo están?*
1. están confundidos/aburridos 2. está ocupado 3. está seguro 4. están confundidos/aburridos 5. está contento

> aburrido   ocupado   confundido   contento   seguro

1. Los estudiantes extranjeros no comprenden las explicaciones del profesor.

   Los estudiantes _____ _____.

2. El profesor trabaja mucho en las escuelas públicas con programas bilingües.

   El profesor _____ _____.

3. Nuevo México es un ejemplo de multiculturalismo y multilingüismo.

   El gobierno (*government*) _____ _____ del éxito (*success*) de la educación bilingüe.

4. Las clases en inglés son difíciles para los estudiantes extranjeros.

   A veces los estudiantes _____ _____.

5. Los profesores en los programas bilingües trabajan con los niños en dos lenguas y los progresos académicos son buenos.

   El estudiante _____ _____ con su progreso académico.

G 2-31 Español para la educación. In groups, try to think of possible situations in which you might need Spanish in an educational setting. Summarize your discussion and present it to the class.

La educación bilingüe por estados. Ask students to go to the Web and find out the position of the different states on bilingual education. Have them prepare a brief report and bring it to the next class.

De puertas abiertas a la comunidad

VIDEO ¡YO SÍ PUEDO!

2-32 Entrando en materia. Do you think that minorities are well represented in American colleges and universities? How many students of Hispanic heritage attend your school? Go to the Web and do some research about the number of Hispanics in universities, community colleges, and technical schools. What other information can you find related to Hispanics in higher education?

> La educación es una parte esencial del **desarrollo** del individuo. Los **maestros** dedican sus **vidas** a trabajar con los estudiantes, **ayudándolos** a formar su **propia** identidad y a **pensar por sí mismos.** En el vídeo les presentamos a Pietro González y Bárbara Bonilla, dos maestros hispanos de español en escuelas de Estados Unidos. Escuchen sus testimonios sobre su experiencia en la clase y los **desafíos** que **enfrentan** como educadores hoy.

2-33 La educación. Listen carefully to the entire segment of the video where Pietro and Bárbara talk about their experience as teachers, and note all the vocabulary that you understand related to education. This will be the second entry for your vocabulary journal: **la educación.**

2-34 ¿Quién es quién? Link the following information to the teacher that it describes. Write the letters of the statements that correspond to each person next to the appropriate photo.

_b, d, f, g_   _a, c, e, h_

    a. Es de origen chileno.
    b. Es de origen cubano.
    c. Enseña en una escuela pública bilingüe para niños hispanos.
    d. Enseña todos los niveles de español, de Español 1 a Español 5.
    e. Sus estudiantes hablan poco inglés.

---

desarrollo *development*   **maestros** *teachers*   **vidas** *lives*   **ayudándolos** *by helping them*   **propia** *own*   **pensar por sí mismos** *to think for themselves*   **desafíos** *challenges*   **enfrentan** *face*

f. Sus estudiantes estudian español.
g. Quiere enseñar a sus estudiantes que hay diferentes latinos.
h. Le gusta enseñar porque hace algo importante por los jóvenes (*young people*).

2-35 Desafíos. What are some of the challenges that Pietro and Bárbara have to face as educators? Think about other challenges that teachers have to face in today's society.

2-36 Falta de motivación. Look at the following scene and describe the characters in the picture by answering the following questions in Spanish:

1. ¿Cuántas personas hay en la ilustración?
2. ¿Dónde están?
3. ¿Cómo son las personas en la ilustración?
4. ¿De qué hablan?
5. ¿Tienen la misma opinión?

Answers for 2-35. *Desafíos.* la disciplina, la falta de motivación, la fundación de la familia

2-37 Un buen maestro. What are the characteristics that Bárbara thinks that a good teacher should possess? What is your idea of a good teacher? List six adjectives that, in your opinion, describe a good teacher.

(G) 2-38 El futuro del español. What does Pietro think about the future of the Spanish language in the United States? In groups, discuss the impact of the Spanish language in our society today.

Answers for 2-37. *Un buen maestro.* cariño hacia los muchachos, paciencia, saber cómo enseñar, y un buen sentido del humor

Answers for 2-38. *El futuro del español.* Pietro opina que el español tiene un gran futuro acá en Estados Unidos, debido principalmente a la cantidad de gente que ha venido de países donde se habla el idioma. Los padres se preocupan de que los hijos mantengan sus raíces y el idioma español.

Escapadas

UNIVERSIDADES CON HISTORIA

La Universidad de Salamanca. La Universidad de Salamanca, fundada en 1218 por el rey Alfonso IX de León, es la universidad **más antigua** de España. La universidad es famosa por su dedicación a la enseñanza del español como lengua extranjera. En Salamanca estudian anualmente aproximadamente 40.000 estudiantes de diferentes nacionalidades.

Salamanca es un importante centro cultural y la atmósfera universitaria está en todos **los rincones.** Estudiar en Salamanca es **descubrir** un pasado **rico** en arte y en tradiciones.

Universidad de Salamanca. Plaza Anaya.

Interior de la Universidad de Salamanca.

---

más antigua *oldest*   **los rincones** *corners*   **descubrir** *to discover*   **rico** *rich*

La Real Pontificia Universidad de Santo Tomás de Aquino. La Real Pontificia Universidad de Santo Tomás de Aquino es la *"Primada de América"* fundada por una orden de dominicos en el año 1538 en Santo Domingo. La República Dominicana es la primera colonia europea en América y allí se establece la primera universidad y la primera catedral, la Catedral Metropolitana Santa María de la Encarnación. La Universidad Autónoma de Santo Domingo, **como se**

Catedral de Santo Domingo.

conoce hoy en día, no es **ya** una institución religiosa, **sino** un centro **laico,** público y democrático.

La Universidad Mayor de San Marcos. La Universidad Mayor de San Marcos en Lima, Perú, **fue** fundada en 1551 y es la universidad más antigua de Sudamérica. La actividad académica y cultural de la Universidad Mayor de San Marcos es extensa y **además de las licenciaturas** tradicionales en ciencias sociales, **derecho,** economía, educación, humanidades, matemáticas, medicina y psicología, tiene un instituto de medicina tropical especializado en **investigaciones** innovadoras.

Claustro de la Universidad de San Marcos, Lima.

como se conoce hoy *as it is known today*   **ya** *now*   **sino** *rather*   **laico** *secular*   **fue** *was*   **adémas de** *besides*
las licenciaturas *degrees*   **derecho** *law*   **investigaciones** *research*

2-39 Test de universidades. Conteste las siguientes preguntas con información del artículo *Universidades con historia.*

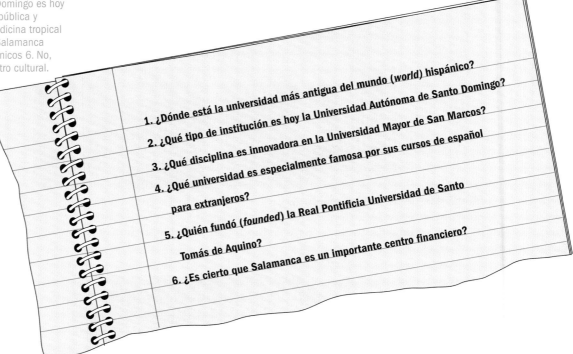

1. ¿Dónde está la universidad más antigua del mundo (*world*) hispánico?

2. ¿Qué tipo de institución es hoy la Universidad Autónoma de Santo Domingo?

3. ¿Qué disciplina es innovadora en la Universidad Mayor de San Marcos?

4. ¿Qué universidad es especialmente famosa por sus cursos de español para extranjeros?

5. ¿Quién fundó (*founded*) la Real Pontificia Universidad de Santo Tomás de Aquino?

6. ¿Es cierto que Salamanca es un importante centro financiero?

2-40 Preguntas. You are thinking about the possibility of studying abroad in a Spanish-speaking country. Prepare a list of five questions in Spanish that you would like to ask the study abroad counselor regarding the university program. Use the question words that you learned in this chapter.

2-41 Otras opciones. Language immersion programs are ideal for developing foreign language skills, but there are also very interesting options for studying Spanish during the summer in the United States, without going abroad. Go to the Web and select a program that seems exciting to you and prepare a brief description of it in Spanish for the next class.

Estudiar con amigos.

En palabras de...

SU UNIVERSIDAD

Your school is developing a new website, and students are invited to post their comments about the university for prospective students to read.

Writing strategy: Brainstorming. Brainstorming is a freely thinking exercise that will help you activate existing knowledge in your own mind. The purpose of brainstorming is to generate a profusion of ideas connected to a topic in order to better organize the writing activity. By brainstorming you will be better orientated to the topic that you are going to write about and aware of the gaps that you have to fill.

Mural de David Alfaro Siqueiros, *El pueblo a la universidad y la universidad al pueblo*, Universidad Nacional Autónoma de México.

Antes de escribir

When you think about the university and aspects of university life, what words and ideas come to your mind? Write down these words and ideas as they occur to you. When you finish, evaluate the list that you generated and select those items that are relevant for writing a paragraph in Spanish about you and your school describing the campus and its location, the courses offered, your daily schedule, the extracurricular activities, and what you like to do.

Ⓟ Después de escribir

Working with a partner, edit each other's compositions and discuss possible errors or areas that are unclear. Use the checklist below:

> ### ☑️ Lista de control:
> ___ Did you use **ser** to describe the campus and **estar** with prepositions to tell its location?
> ___ Did you use **hay** to talk about the classes offered?
> ___ Did you use **-ar** verbs to describe your daily activities and how often you perform them?

After you have finished the review, tell about your partner's schedule and activities, using the information you read in the composition.

 En la red

Compare the actual website from your school to some websites from universities in Spain and Latin America. Do they have a comparable organization? What are some of the similarities? How are they different?

All the sources consulted for the readings are cited on the *¡Trato hecho!* Web site at **www.prenhall.com/trato**

VOCABULARIO

TEMA 1

Sustantivos
un bolígrafo *a pen*
una calculadora *a calculator*
una computadora *a computer*
un cuaderno *a notebook*
un cuaderno de ejercicios *a workbook*
un cuarto *a room*
un ejercicio *an exercise*
un escritorio *a desk*
un estante *a shelf*
un lápiz *a pencil*
un libro *a book*
una mesa *a table*
una mochila *a bookbag, a backpack*
una oración (completa) *a (complete) sentence*

una página *a page*
una palabra *a word*
un papel *a piece of paper*
una pizarra *a blackboard*
una pregunta *a question*
una pruebita *a quiz*
una puerta *a door*
un reloj *a clock, a watch*
una respuesta *an answer*
un salón de clase *a classroom*
una silla *a chair*
una ventana *a window*
el vocabulario *the vocabulary*

Otras palabras y expresiones
algo *something*
¡Aprendan...! *Learn...!*

cada *each*
de *of, from*
en parejas *in pairs*
hacer *to do*
mismo/a *same*
mucho/a/os/as *much, many, a lot of*
¿Necesitamos...? *Do we need...?*
otro/a *other, another*
poco/a/os/as *little, few*
por favor *please*
primero *first*
próximo/a *next*
siguiente *following*
todo/a/os/as *all, every*
un/a/os/as *a, an, some*
varios/as *several*

Para las instrucciones en clase, vea la página 36.

TEMA 2

Sustantivos
un apartamento *an apartment*
un café *a café*
una calle *a street*
la cena *the dinner*
un cine *a movie theater, a cinema*
un club nocturno *a night club*
una escuela (primaria, secundaria) *a (primary, secondary) school*
un estadio *a stadium*
una librería *a bookstore*
una oficina *an office*

un parque *a park*
un partido de fútbol (fútbol americano, básquetbol) *a soccer (football, basketball) game*
una película (extranjera, de aventuras, de terror) *a (foreign, adventure, horror) movie*
un restaurante (de comida mexicana/italiana) *a (Mexican/Italian food) restaurant*
un supermercado *a supermarket*
una tienda (de ropa) *a (clothing) store*

Otras palabras y expresiones
abierto/a *open*
antes de *before*
conmigo *with me*
contigo *with you*
después de *after*
¿Está bien? *Okay?*
estar *to be*
juntos/as *together*
(cerca de) mí *(near) me*
perfecto/a *perfect*
(detrás de) ti *(behind) you*

Para las preposiciones, vea la página 42.

Adjetivos

aburrido/a *bored, boring*
cansado/a *tired*
confundido/a *confused*
contento/a *happy*
enfermo/a *sick, ill*
enojado/a *angry, mad*
estupendo/a *great*
interesado/a *interested*
listo/a *ready, smart*
nervioso/a *nervous*
ocupado/a *busy*

Sustantivos

un deporte *a sport*
la guitarra *the guitar*
la televisión, la tele *the television, the TV*
el tiempo *the time*

Verbos

bailar *to dance*
cantar *to sing*
comer *to eat*
comprar *to buy*
contestar *to answer*
descansar *to rest*
enseñar *to teach*
escuchar *to listen (to)*
estudiar *to study*

Palabras interrogativas

¿cómo? *how?*
¿con quién(es)? *with whom?*
¿cuál(es)? *which?, what?*
¿cuándo? *when?*
¿cuánto/a? *how much?*
¿cuántos/as? *how many?*
¿de dónde? *from where?*

TEMA 3

seguro/a *sure, safe*
triste *sad*

Otras palabras y expresiones

al fondo (de) *at the back (of)*
¿Cómo se dice... en español? *How do you say... in Spanish?*
¿Cómo se escribe? *How is it written?*
¿Cuál es la tarea para la próxima clase? *What is the homework for the next class?*

TEMA 4

hablar (por teléfono) *to speak, to talk (on the phone)*
ir (al cine) *to go (to the movies)*
limpiar *to clean*
llegar *to arrive*
mirar *to look at, to watch*
necesitar *to need*
pasar *to pass, to spend (time)*
preparar *to prepare*
regresar *to return*
salir *to go out*
tocar *to play (an instrument)*
tomar *to drink, to take*
trabajar *to work*

La frecuencia

a veces *sometimes, at times*

TEMA 5

¿dónde? *where?*
¿por qué? *why?*
¿qué? *what?*
¿quién(es)? *who?*

Otras palabras y expresiones

divertido/a *fun*
en *at, in, on*

(TEMA 3 continued)

Eso depende de... *That depends on...*
hablar *to speak, to talk*
Necesito más tiempo. *I need more time.*
No comprendo. *I don't understand.*
No sé. *I don't know.*
nunca *never*
¿Qué significa... en inglés? *What does... mean in English?*
siempre *always*
Tengo una pregunta. *I have a question.*

(TEMA 4 continued)

(casi) nunca *(almost) never*
(casi) siempre *(almost) always*
con frecuencia *frequently*
los fines de semana *weekends*
todos los días *every day*
una vez (dos veces) a la semana / al mes / al año *once (twice) per week / per month / per year*

Otras palabras y expresiones

en autobús *by bus*
en mi coche *in my car*
hasta *until*
ni *nor*
Quiero... *I want...*
Prefiero... *I prefer...*

(TEMA 5 continued)

favorito/a *favorite*
luego *then, next*
para *for*
primero/a *first*
tan *so*
tarde *late*
último/a *last*

3

En casa

● **In this chapter you will learn to...**

- give information about where you live
- describe your belongings
- talk about your family
- say what you do on school days
- say what you do on the weekend
- better understand Hispanic families

● **You will use...**

- numbers above 100
- the verb **tener** and possessive adjectives
- adjectives and comparatives
- **-er** and **-ir** verbs
- verbs with irregular **yo** forms and the personal **a**

VOCABULARIO

TEMA 1

¿Dónde vives? ¿Cuál es tu dirección?

— ¿Dónde prefieres **vivir**?
— Prefiero vivir en el centro de **una ciudad** grande (en **las afueras** de una ciudad, en **el campo**).
— ¿En qué calle vives?
— Vivo en la calle Comal.
— ¿Cuánto pagas de **alquiler**? ¿Es **caro**?
— **Pago** $650 (seiscientos cincuenta) al mes.
  (No pago nada. Vivo con mis padres.)
— ¿Cómo es tu casa?
— Hay una sala grande, una cocina, un comedor y tres dormitorios con **armarios** grandes. También hay un jardín con muchos árboles.

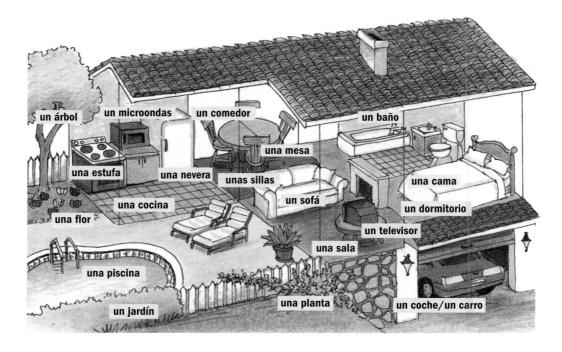

3-1 ¿Qué es? ¿Qué hay en estos lugares (*places*) en la ilustración de la casa?

Modelo   Está entre la cocina y el baño.
El comedor está entre la cocina y el baño.

1. Está detrás del dormitorio y al lado del comedor.
2. Está al lado de la cocina, en el jardín.
3. Están debajo del árbol.
4. Está en la cocina entre la estufa y la nevera.
5. Está a la izquierda del microondas.
6. Está a la derecha del microondas.
7. Está en el garaje debajo del dormitorio.
8. Está enfrente del televisor, en la sala.

---

vivir *to live*   **una ciudad** *a city*   **las afueras** *the outskirts*   **el campo** *the country*   **el alquiler** *the rent*   **caro/a** *expensive*   **pagar** *to pay*   **un armario** *a closet, a wardrobe*

3-2 Una casa nueva. Describa esta casa completando las oraciones con las palabras correctas.

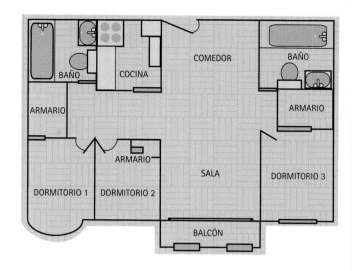

1. Hay *dos / tres / cuatro* dormitorios.
2. El armario es grande en *todos los / dos / un* dormitorio(s).
3. Hay *un / dos / tres* baño(s).
4. Los baños son *más grandes que / menos* grandes *que / casi tan* grandes *como* la cocina.
5. No hay pared (*wall*) entre el comedor y *la cocina / la sala*.
6. El comedor es *más grande que / menos* grande *que / casi tan* grande *como* la sala.

Ahora cambie las oraciones anteriores para describir su propio/a apartamento/casa.

P 3-3 Entrevista. Entreviste a otro/a estudiante con estas preguntas.

1. ¿Prefieres vivir en un apartamento, una casa o un cuarto en una residencia? ¿Tienes apartamento, casa o cuarto en una residencia? ¿Está cerca de aquí? ¿En qué calle está?
2. ¿Cómo es tu casa (apartamento, residencia)? ¿nuevo/a o viejo/a? ¿bonito/a o feo/a? ¿caro/a? ¿Cuántos dormitorios hay? ¿Cuántos baños? ¿Hay piscina? ¿Qué te gusta de tu casa (apartamento, residencia)? ¿Qué no te gusta?
3. ¿Vives con tu familia, con un compañero o una compañera de cuarto o de casa o vives solo/a?
4. ¿Prefieres vivir en el centro de una ciudad grande, en las afueras o en el campo?

P Conversaciones. Dos futuros compañeros de casa hablan. En parejas, lean la conversación. Luego, cambien la conversación para hablar de ustedes.

— ¿Dónde vives ahora?
— Ahora vivo en una casa pequeña en las afueras. **Me gustaría** vivir en un apartamento más cerca del centro porque no me gusta trabajar en el jardín y quiero estar más cerca de la universidad y más cerca de las tiendas y los restaurantes. Y tú, ¿dónde vives?
— **Alquilo** un apartamento no muy lejos de aquí. Me gusta **el barrio.** Es muy **agradable** y tengo **vecinos** simpáticos, pero me gustaría tener un apartamento un poco más grande.
— ¿Tienes **un perro** o **un gato**?
— No, no tengo animales. ¿y tú?
— Tengo un perro, pero nunca está en la casa. Siempre está **afuera.**
— **¿Fumas?**
— No, ¿y tú?
— Yo **tampoco.**

Follow-ups for *Conversaciones.*
A. Point out the difference between *me gusta* and *me gustaría.* Have students say whether they would like to have the following. *¿Le gustaría tener una casa o un apartamento más grande (más cerca/lejos del centro/de la universidad)? ¿Le gustaría tener un jardín muy grande con muchos árboles (con muchas flores)? ¿Le gustaría tener otro/a compañero/a de cuarto/casa (otros vecinos, un perro, un gato)? ¿Le gustaría más vivir solo/a y pagar más*

AUDIO ¡A escuchar!

Ahora, escuchen otra conversación en la cual un hombre llama por el anuncio (*ad*) de alquiler de un apartamento. ¿Dónde está el apartamento? ¿Cómo es? ¿Quiere ver (*Does he want to see*) el apartamento? ¿Por qué (no)?

o tener un/a compañero/a de casa y pagar menos? ¿Le gustaría más vivir en Nueva York o California (en México o en Canadá)? ¿Le gustaría más vivir en un apartamento en un edificio grande del centro o en una casa pequeña lejos de todo? **B.** Ask the following questions. *¿Cómo es el/la compañero/a de cuarto ideal para Ud.? ¿Fuma o no fuma? ¿Le gustan los animales o no le gustan? ¿Es liberal o no es liberal? ¿Es más intelectual o más atlético/a? ¿Insiste en tener la casa limpia o no insiste en tener la casa limpia? ¿Le gustan las fiestas y estudia poco o no le gustan las fiestas y estudia mucho? ¿Pasa mucho tiempo con Ud. en casa o no pasa mucho tiempo con Ud. en casa?*

me gustaría(n) *I would like* **alquilar** *to rent* **el barrio** *the neighborhood* **agradable** *pleasant, nice* **un/a vecino/a** *a neighbor* **un perro** *a dog* **un gato** *a cat* **afuera** *outside* **fumar** *to smoke* **tampoco** *neither*

GRAMÁTICA
Los números 100 y más

Para averiguar

1. In which of the following numbers do you translate the word *one: one hundred, one thousand, one million*?
2. Which of these numbers has no plural form: **cien/ciento, mil, un millón**? Which has feminine plural forms?
3. When do you use a period with numbers in Spanish? a comma?
4. How do you express years in Spanish?
5. When do you use **de** after **millón/millones**?

Here are the numbers from 100 to 999.

100 cien	500 quinientos/as
101 ciento uno (un/una)	600 seiscientos/as
102 ciento dos…	700 setecientos/as
200 doscientos/as	800 ochocientos/as
300 trescientos/as	900 novecientos/as
400 cuatrocientos/as	999 novecientos/as noventa y nueve

Use **cien** to say *one hundred* exactly, but use **ciento** in 101 to 199. Do not use the word **un** before **cien** or **ciento**. Although **cien** and **ciento** do not change forms before feminine nouns, multiples of 100 (200, 300…) have a form with **-a/-as** before feminine nouns.

	WITH MASCULINE NOUNS	WITH FEMININE NOUNS
100:	cien libros	cien páginas
101:	ciento un libros	ciento un**a** páginas
200:	doscientos libros	doscient**as** páginas
720:	setecientos veinte libros	setecient**as** veinte páginas

As opposed to English, in Spanish one uses a period (.) to designate numbers in the thousands, and a comma (,) for decimal points.

Spanish 1.543 (English 1,543)	mil quinientos cuarenta y tres
Spanish 3,25 (English 3.25)	tres con veinticinco

The word for *thousand* is **mil. Mil** is not pluralized, nor is **un** used before it. Do not use the word **y** immediately after the words **mil** or **cien/ciento,** nor their multiples.

1.000	mil
1.914	mil novecientos catorce
2.007	dos mil siete

Years are expressed using **mil,** not hundreds.

1492	mil cuatrocientos noventa y dos
1989	mil novecientos ochenta y nueve
2001	dos mil uno

When counting in the millions, say **un millón, dos millones, tres millones….** Use **de** before nouns that directly follow the word **millón/millones.** If another number is between the word **millón/millones** and the noun, **de** is not needed.

un millón de dólares	un millón doscientos mil dólares
dos millones de euros	dos millones novecientos euros

3-4 El alquiler. ¿Cuánto paga de alquiler al mes?

Modelo $1.100 **Pago mil cien dólares al mes.**

1. $150	**3.** $275	**5.** $515	**7.** $750	**9.** $1.000	**11.** $1.545
2. $199	**4.** $440	**6.** $685	**8.** $995	**10.** $1.250	**12.** $2.100

Supplemental activity. Have a trivia contest with students working in teams. Within a time limit, each team writes out the numbers on a sheet of paper, spelling out the numbers. They all show their papers at the same time after each question. All teams with correct numbers get a point. 1. ¿Cuántas horas hay en una semana? (168) 2. ¿Cuántos segundos hay en una hora? (3.600) 3. ¿Cuántos segundos hay en un día? (86.400) 4. ¿Cuántos días hay en un año bisiesto (*leap year*)? (366) 5. ¿Cuántos senadores hay en el Senado de Estados Unidos? (100) 6. ¿Cuántos representantes hay en la Cámara de Representantes de Estados Unidos? (435) 7. ¿Cuál es la dirección de la Casa Blanca donde vive el presidente en Washington? (1.600 Pennsylvania Avenue) 8. ¿Cuántos metros hay en un kilómetro? (1.000) 9. ¿Cuántos centímetros hay en un kilómetro? (100.000) 10. ¿Cuántas yardas hay en una milla? (1760) 11. ¿Cuántos pies (*feet*) hay en una milla? (5.280) 12. ¿Cuál es el código postal de la universidad? (*Check for your university.*) 13. ¿Cuál es el año de fundación de nuestra universidad? (*Check for your university.*) 14. ¿Cuál es el año del asesinato de John Kennedy? (1963) 15.-17. ¿Cuál es el año de la elección de Jimmy Carter? (1976) ¿de Harry Truman? (1948) ¿de Herbert Hoover? (1928)

Suggestion. Explain to students how to convert currencies. Give them the current exchange rates for various Hispanic countries and have them convert numbers such as $10; $100; $1,000; $500; $5,000; $1,000,000.

3-5 Un poco de historia. ¿En qué año ocurren estos eventos históricos?

1492   1519   1821   1836   1846   1898   1917   1959

1. México declara su independencia de España.
2. El presidente cubano Fulgencio Batista es derrocado (*toppled*) por Fidel Castro.
3. Los puertorriqueños obtienen la nacionalidad estadounidense.
4. Cristóbal Colón llega a América por primera vez.
5. El emperador azteca, Moctezuma, se somete al conquistador español Hernán Cortés.
6. Texas se independiza de México.
7. Estados Unidos declara la guerra (*war*) contra España.
8. Estados Unidos declara la guerra contra México.

3-6 ¿Y Ud.? Cambie las siguientes oraciones para describir su situación o sus preferencias.

1. Soy de *San Antonio*. La población es de más o menos *1.150.000* habitantes.
2. Prefiero vivir en una ciudad *pequeña*, de *no más de 25.000* habitantes.
3. Mi dirección es *calle Mérida*, número *1257*.
4. Pago *$750* de alquiler al mes.
5. Para estudiar en la universidad pago más o menos *$3.500* cada semestre.
6. Hay más de *15.000* estudiantes en esta universidad.
7. Generalmente, pago *entre $350 y $450* por mis libros cada semestre.
8. Hay muchos estudiantes en mi clase de historia. Hay unos *150*.

3-7 Anuncios clasificados. Conteste las siguientes preguntas sobre estos apartamentos que se alquilan en Puerto Rico.

¿Cuántos dormitorios hay?   ¿Cuál es el teléfono?
¿Cuántos baños hay?   ¿Cuánto es el alquiler al mes?

1. Bonito apartamento en el segundo piso. Tres dormitorios, dos baños en excelentes condiciones. El complejo tiene piscina y cancha de tenis. $900 al mes. Teléfono: (787) 640-5823

2. Apartamento agradable y muy céntrico. 1 dormitorio/1 baño. A 5 minutos del centro. $575 al mes. Incluye agua y luz. Teléfono: (939) 644-3499

3. Precioso apartamento, 3 cuartos, 1 baño, cocina, sala, comedor, balcón. Situado en Carolina, cerca de Plaza Carolina. Acceso controlado. Precio mensual: $650. Para más información: (787) 531-7004

4. Apartamento amueblado, 2 dormitorios, 2 baños, terraza. Cerca de la piscina, cancha de tenis y playa. En excelentes condiciones. $1.200 al mes. Teléfono: (787) 864-7667

VOCABULARIO
TEMA ② ¿Cómo es tu cuarto?

¿Qué **muebles** hay en tu cuarto? ¿Está **limpio** o **sucio**? ¿**ordenado** o **desordenado**?

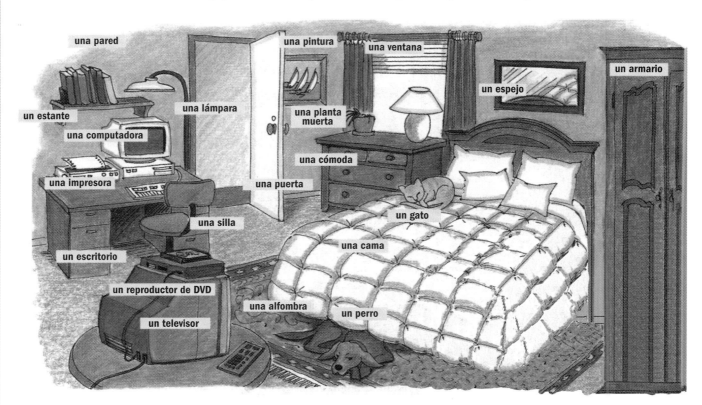

¿De qué color es tu cuarto/tu sala?

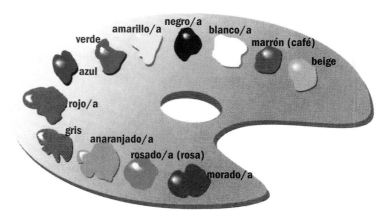

los muebles *furniture* **limpio/a** *clean* **sucio/a** *dirty* **ordenado/a** *neat, straightened up* **desordenado/a** *messy*
muerto/a *dead*

3-8 ¿Dónde están? ¿Dónde están estas cosas la una en relación a la otra en el cuarto de la página anterior?

> **Modelo**   la planta muerta / la ventana
> **La planta muerta está delante de la ventana.**

1. la computadora / la impresora
2. el televisor / la cama
3. el gato / la cama
4. la pintura / la puerta

5. el televisor / el reproductor de DVD
6. la cómoda / la cama
7. el armario / la cama
8. la ventana / la cómoda

3-9 Los colores. ¿De qué color(es) son las siguientes cosas?

> **Modelo**   la casa del presidente de Estados Unidos
> **Es blanca.**

1. las paredes del salón de clase
2. las sillas del salón de clase
3. la puerta del salón de clase
4. el escritorio del/de la profesor/a
5. las plantas

6. las plantas muertas
7. las flores
8. una piscina
9. el coche de usted
10. la ropa de usted

Continuation for 3-9. *Los colores.* el libro de español, el cuaderno de ejercicios, el papel, el bolígrafo del/de la profesor/a, un día bonito, un día feo, la noche, un árbol, un pingüino, una jirafa, un tigre, un elefante, un gorila

P 3-10   Entrevista. Entreviste a otro/a estudiante con las siguientes preguntas.

1. ¿De qué color son las paredes de tu cuarto? ¿De qué color es la alfombra? ¿De qué color son las paredes de tu sala? ¿De qué color es el sofá?
2. ¿Pasas más tiempo en tu cuarto o en la sala? ¿Qué muebles tienes en tu cuarto? Generalmente, ¿está ordenado o desordenado tu cuarto? ¿Limpias la casa todos los días?
3. ¿Tienes un perro o un gato? ¿Te gustan los animales?

Follow-up for *Conversaciones.* Read the following pairs of sentences and have students repeat the sentence from each pair that is true for them. 1. Vivo con alguien. / Vivo solo/a. 2. Comparto un baño con alguien. /

P Conversaciones. Dos amigos hablan del compañero de casa de uno de ellos. Primero lean la conversación en parejas. Luego cambien la conversación para describir su propia situación.

— ¿Vives con **alguien** o vives solo?
— Vivo con un compañero de casa.
— ¿Te gusta vivir con él?
— Sí y no. Es simpático, pero a veces no tiene **dinero** para pagar el alquiler y es una persona un poco desordenada. Su cuarto siempre está sucio. **Deja** su ropa en **el suelo** y hay papeles y libros **por todos lados.**
— ¿Limpias la casa más que él?
— Sí, mi cuarto siempre está limpio y ordenado.
— ¿**Comparten** ustedes baño o tienes tu **propio** baño?
— Sí, **desafortunadamente, tenemos que usar** el mismo baño.

AUDIO ¡A escuchar!

Ahora, escuchen otra conversación en la cual una estudiante habla de su casa y de sus compañeras de casa. ¿Cuánto paga al mes y cómo son sus compañeras de casa? ¿Hay problemas con ellas?

Tengo mi propio baño. 3. Comparto un cuarto con alguien. / Tengo mi propio cuarto. 4. Generalmente, mi cuarto está desordenado. / Generalmente, mi cuarto está ordenado. 5. Dejo mi ropa en el suelo a veces. / Nunca dejo mi ropa en el suelo. 6. Mi baño está limpio ahora. / Mi baño no está limpio. 7. Mi cocina está limpia ahora. / Mi cocina no está limpia. 8. Dejo platos (*dishes*) sucios en la cocina por un día a veces. / Nunca dejo platos sucios en la cocina. 9. Limpio la casa con frecuencia. / No limpio la casa con frecuencia. 10. En mi cuarto hay libros por todos lados. / No hay muchos libros en mi cuarto.

---

alguien *someone, anyone* **el dinero** *money* **dejar** *to leave* **el suelo** *the ground, the floor* **por todos lados** *everywhere* **compartir** *to share* **propio/a** *own* **desafortunadamente** *unfortunately* **tener que usar** *to have to use*

GRAMÁTICA
Más sobre la posesión: el verbo *tener* y los adjetivos posesivos

Para averiguar

1. How do you say *to have* in Spanish? What are its forms?
2. How do you say *my, your, his, her, its, our,* and *their* in Spanish?
3. What do you use in Spanish instead of 's to show possession?
4. What can **su(s)** mean? How can you clarify its meaning?

The verb **tener** (*to have*) is useful when describing family or possessions. You have already seen the forms **tengo** (*I have*) and **tienes** (*you have*).

TENER (*TO HAVE*)			
yo	tengo	nosotros/as	tenemos
tú	tienes	vosodd/as	tenéis
usted, él, ella	tiene	ustedes, ellos, ellas	tienen

Tengo dos hermanas y un hermano.   *I have two sisters and one brother.*

Use **tener que** followed by an infinitive to say that someone has to do something.

Tenemos que limpiar la casa.   *We have to clean the house.*

Possessive adjectives are also useful when talking about family and belongings. You have already seen **mi(s)**, **tu(s)**, and **su(s)**.

SUBJECT	POSSESSIVE ADJECTIVE		SUBJECT	POSSESSIVE ADJECTIVE	
yo	**mi(s)**	*my*	nosotros/as	**nuestro/a(s)**	*our*
tú	**tu(s)**	*your*	vosotros/as	**vuestro/a(s)**	*your*
usted	**su(s)**	*your*	ustedes	**su(s)**	*your*
él	**su(s)**	*his/its*	ellos	**su(s)**	*their*
ella	**su(s)**	*her/its*	ellas	**su(s)**	*their*

Possessive adjectives end with **-s** before plural nouns. Only **nuestro/a** and **vuestro/a** have different forms for masculine and feminine nouns.

Mis padres tienen cinco gatos.   *My parents have five cats.*
Nuestra casa no está lejos de aquí.   *Our house isn't far from here.*

Use **el/la/los/las** + *noun* + **de** instead of 's to show possession in Spanish. Remember that **de** contracts with **el** (*the*) to form **del**.

Es **la casa de** Ramón.   *It's Ramón's house.*
Son **los perros del** vecino.   *They are the neighbor's dogs.*

Since **su(s)** can mean *your, his, her, its,* or *their;* it is often rephrased as shown below. **De** contracts with **el** (*the*) but not with **él** (*he, him*).

sus cosas {
las cosas de usted(es)   *your things*
las cosas de él   *his things*
las cosas de ella   *her things*
las cosas de ellos/ellas   *their things*

¿Es **la casa de él** o es **la casa de ella**?   *Is it **his house** or **her house**?*

3-11 **¿Qué tienen?** ¿Tienen estas personas las cosas indicadas?

Modelo   mis padres (una casa grande, animales)
Mis padres no tienen una casa grande. Tienen dos perros.

1. mis padres (tres dormitorios, muchas plantas, más de un televisor)
2. yo (un gato, un coche nuevo, una cocina grande, muchas ventanas)
3. en esta clase, nosotros (mesas grandes, sillas azules, un televisor, un reproductor de DVD, una pizarra verde)
4. el/la profesor/a (un escritorio grande, una silla nueva, muchas preguntas)
5. [a otro estudiante] ¿…(tú)? (una casa o un apartamento, animales, un buen estéreo, una buena computadora, un buen diccionario de español)

3-12 **¿De quién?** ¿Son las pertenencias (*belongings*) de Juan, de Mario o de los dos?

Modelo   Su alfombra es azul.
La alfombra de Juan es azul.

el cuarto de Juan   **el cuarto de Mario**

1. Su cuarto está ordenado.
2. Sus paredes son blancas.
3. Su escritorio está desordenado.
4. Su ropa está en el suelo.
5. Sus gatos están en su cuarto.
6. No hay pinturas en sus paredes.
7. Todos sus libros están en el estante.
8. Hay una lámpara al lado de su cama.
9. No hay nada encima de su cama.
10. La puerta de su armario está abierta.

3-13 **Posesiones.** Complete las siguientes oraciones con el verbo **tener** en el primer espacio en blanco y el adjetivo posesivo correspondiente en el segundo.

Modelo   Mi compañera de casa y yo **tenemos** una casa en las afueras. Hay tres dormitorios en **nuestra** casa.

1. (Yo) _____ una casa cerca de aquí. _____ casa está en la calle Comal.
2. Mis padres _____ muebles nuevos en la sala. _____ sofá es verde.
3. Mi mejor amigo _____ un coche nuevo. _____ coche es rojo.
4. Mi compañero de cuarto y yo _____ vecinos simpáticos. _____ vecinos pasan mucho tiempo con nosotros.
5. Mis vecinos _____ un perro grande. _____ perro siempre está afuera.
6. Nosotros _____ muchos árboles y flores en _____ jardín.
7. (Yo) _____ una computadora nueva. _____ computadora está en la sala.

Ahora cambie las oraciones anteriores para describir su propia situación.

Modelo   **Vivo solo/a y tengo un apartamento cerca de la universidad. Sólo hay un dormitorio en mi apartamento.**

Follow-up for 3-11. *¿Qué tienen?* Remind students of the words *nadie* and *todos* and the form of the verb used with each. Then have them say who has the following things in your class. *Modelo:* ropa azul > *Todos tenemos ropa azul. David y yo tenemos ropa azul. David y Verónica tienen ropa azul. Nadie tiene ropa azul.* (ropa roja/morada/negra/verde/amarilla; una mochila azul/roja/morada/negra/verde/amarilla; flores en su ropa; un cuaderno azul/rojo/morado/negro/verde/amarillo; un cuaderno abierto; un libro abierto; algo en el suelo al lado/debajo de su silla.

Follow-ups for 3-12. *¿De quién?* **A.** Have students say whether each statement from the reading is true about their room at this moment. *Modelo: Sí, mi alfombra es azul. / No, mi alfombra es verde. / No tengo alfombra.* **B.** Have students, working in pairs, pretend that they are Juan and write sentences with *tener* comparing what he has with what Mario has. *Modelo: Yo no tengo muchos libros en mi cuarto, pero Mario tiene libros por todos lados en su cuarto. Nosotros dos tenemos una ventana en nuestro cuarto.* **C.** Have students name people the following sentences describe. *Modelo:* Me gusta su música. > *Me gusta la música de Sting. / No me gusta su música.* > *No me gusta la música de Jennifer López. (No) Me gusta(n) su música (sus conciertos, sus películas, su programa de televisión, sus libros).*

VOCABULARIO
¿Cómo es tu familia?

TEMA ❸

¡Ojo!

Use the expression **tener... años** (*to have... years*), rather than *to be*, to express age in Spanish.

Supplemental activities. **A.** Ask students the following questions about Alicia in the family tree. 1. ¿Quiénes son los abuelos de Alicia? 2. ¿Manuel y Rosa son los padres de su padre o de su madre? 3. ¿Cómo se llama el tío de Alicia? 4. ¿Su tío es el esposo de quién? 5. ¿Su tía Carmen es la hermana de la madre o del padre de Alicia? 6. ¿Cuántos hijos tienen los tíos de Alicia? 7. ¿Cómo se llama su primo? 8. ¿Cómo se llama su prima? 9. ¿Cuántos hermanos tiene Alicia? 10. ¿Cuántos hijos tienen los padres de Alicia? 11. ¿Cuántos nietos tienen sus padres? 12. ¿Quién es mayor, el hermano o la hermana de Alicia? 13. ¿Quién tiene hijos, el hermano o la hermana de Alicia? 14. ¿Quién es Lorena? **B.** Review the adjectives describing personalities from *Capítulo 1* and have students complete the following sentences with antonyms. *Modelo: Mi mejor amigo no es alto, es bajo.* 1. No es feo... 2. No es joven ni de mediana edad... 3. No es menor que yo... 4. No es optimista... 5. No es desordenado... 6. No es delgado... 7. No es rubio ni pelirrojo... 8. No es impaciente... 9. No es serio... 10. No es tímido... 11. No es perezoso... 12. No es aburrido... 13. No es pequeño... 14. No es reservado... 15. No es malo... **C.** Go back and ask students which antonym from each sentence in section *B* describes their best friend. *Modelo: ¿Su mejor amigo/a es alto/a o bajo/a?*

LOS ABUELOS
mi abuelo Manuel   mi abuela Rosa

LOS PADRES
mi madre Isabel   mi padre Eduardo   mi tía Carmen   mi tío Alfredo

LOS HIJOS
mi hermano mayor Felipe   yo (Alicia)   mi hermana menor Delia   mi primo Javier   mi prima Raquel

LOS NIETOS
mi sobrino Ángel   mi sobrina Lorena

¿Eres más **como** tu padre o como tu madre? ¿Cómo es él/ella?

pelirrojo/a   moreno/a   rubio/a
gordo/a   delgado/a
de estatura mediana   bajo/a   alto/a

de mediana edad (Tiene 44 años.)
viejo/a (Tiene 86 años.)
guapo/a   feo/a   joven (Tiene 4 años.)   casado/a   soltero/a   divorciado/a

mayor *older*   **menor** *younger*   **como** *like*

¿Tiene el pelo corto o largo? ¿Tiene los ojos marrones (color café), verdes o azules? ¿Tiene el pelo negro, **castaño,** rubio, rojo o **canoso**? ¿Usa gafas?

3-14 Parentescos. Hay muchas palabras para hablar de los parientes (*relatives*). ¿Qué significan las palabras en letra cursiva (*italics*) de estas oraciones?

1. Mi *cuñado* es el hermano de mi esposo y mi *cuñada* es su hermana.
2. Mi *suegra* es la madre de mi esposo y mi *suegro* es su padre.
3. Mi *yerno* es el esposo de mi hija y mi *nuera* es la esposa de mi hijo.
4. Mis padres están divorciados. El nuevo esposo de mi madre es mi *padrastro*. La nueva esposa de mi padre es mi *madrastra*.
5. El hijo de mi padre y mi madrastra es mi *medio hermano* y su hija es mi *media hermana*.
6. Los hijos de mi madrastra y su primer esposo son mis *hermanastros*, mi *hermanastro* y mi *hermanastra*.

el pelo
las gafas
los ojos
el bigote
la barba

3-15 Descripciones. Diga si estas oraciones son ciertas o falsas para usted. Corrija (*Correct*) las oraciones falsas, cambiando las palabras en letra cursiva.

1. Soy *alto/a*.
2. Tengo los ojos *azules y uso gafas*.
3. Tengo el pelo *corto y rojo*.
4. Tengo *22 años*.
5. Estoy *casado*.
6. Tengo *dos hijos*.

Ahora cambie las oraciones anteriores para describir a un familiar (*family member*).

Modelo **Mi padre es alto. Tiene los ojos marrones y no usa gafas...**

3-16 ¿Y tú? Entreviste a otro/a estudiante con estas preguntas.

1. ¿Tienes una familia grande o una familia pequeña? ¿Cuántos hermanos tienes? ¿Cuántos son mayores que tú? ¿Cuántos son menores? ¿Cuántos años tienen? ¿Viven con tus padres? ¿Con qué miembro de tu familia pasas más tiempo?
2. En tu familia, ¿qué color de ojos es más común? ¿Qué color de pelo es más común? ¿Tienen tus abuelos el pelo canoso?
3. ¿Tienes muchos tíos? ¿Quién tiene más hermanos, tu madre o tu padre? ¿Cuántos primos tienes? ¿Pasas mucho tiempo con ellos?

Conversaciones. Dos amigos hablan de sus familias. Primero, lean su conversación en parejas. Luego, cambien la conversación para describir a las familias de ustedes.

— ¿Cuántos son ustedes en la familia?
— Somos cinco, mis padres, mi hermana mayor, mi hermano menor y yo.
— ¿Cómo se llaman tus hermanos?
— Mi hermana mayor se llama Anita y mi hermano menor se llama Joel.
— ¿Cuántos años tienen?
— Anita tiene veintiún años y Joel catorce.
— ¿Qué miembro de tu familia **se parece más a ti**?
— En el aspecto físico, soy más como mi padre. Es alto, tiene el pelo castaño y los ojos verdes como yo. En el carácter, soy más como mi hermano. Es cómico, extrovertido e impulsivo.

---

castaño *brown* **canoso** *gray, white (hair)* **se parece más a ti** *looks more like you*

Note for 3-14. *Parentescos.* The italicized names of family members are not considered active vocabulary and do not appear in the end-of-chapter vocabulary list. Tell students if you expect them to learn these words.

Continuation for 3-14. *Parentescos.* 1. Mi *hijastro* es el hijo de mi esposo/a y su primer/a esposo/a. ¿Qué significa *hijastro*? 2. Mis *bisabuelos* son los abuelos de mis padres. ¿Cómo se dice *bisabuelos* en inglés? 3. Mis *tatarabuelos* son los abuelos de mis abuelos. ¿Qué significa *tatarabuelos*? 4. Mi *sobrina nieta* es la hija de mi sobrina. ¿Cómo se dice *sobrina nieta* en inglés?

Supplemental activities. A. Have students guess who is older from each pair/group of the following celebrities and then guess their age. Their date of birth is given in parentheses. Also have students describe what they look like. 1. Jennifer López (7-24-70) / Salma

AUDIO ¡A escuchar!

Ahora, escuchen otra conversación en la cual dos amigos hablan de sus familias. ¿Cómo es la familia de él? ¿y la de ella? ¿Cuál de los dos quiere tener más hijos?

Hayek (9-2-68) 2. Antonio Banderas (8-10-60) / Brad Pitt (12-18-63) 3. Dan Rather (10-31-31) / Tom Brokaw (2-6-40) / Peter Jennings (7-29-38) 4. Jay Leno (4-28-50) / David Letterman (4-12-47) 5. Barbra Streisand (4-24-42) / Dolly Parton (5-17-44) 6. Steve Martin (8-14-45) / Arnold Schwarzenegger (7-30-45) 7. Cameron Díaz (8-30-72) / Halle Berry (8-14-68) 8. Oprah Winfrey (1-29-54) / Katie Couric (1-7-57) 9. Christina Aguilera (12-18-80) / Britney Spears (12-2-81)

GRAMÁTICA

Más descripciones: la posición del adjetivo y los comparativos

When describing people or things in Spanish, most adjectives are placed after the noun they describe.

Tengo **una familia grande.** Mis padres tienen **una casa muy bonita.**

The adjectives **bueno, malo, mejor,** and **peor** (*worse*) can be placed before nouns. Like the number **uno, bueno** and **malo** drop the **-o** when followed by a masculine noun, but they end with **-a** before feminine nouns. The adjective **grande** changes meaning, depending on whether it is placed before or after nouns. Before both masculine and feminine singular nouns, it shortens to **gran** and it means *great*. After nouns, **grande** means *big*.

Tengo un **buen** padre. No es un hombre **grande** pero es una **gran** persona.
I have a good father. He isn't a big man but he is a great person.

Use the following expressions to compare people or things.

más... que	*more... than, -er... than*
menos... que	*less... than, fewer... than*
tan... como	*as... as*
tanto/a/os/as... como	*as much... as, as many... as*

Soy **más estudioso que** mi hermano.	*I am more studious than my brother.*
¿Es **más alto que** tú?	*Is he taller than you?*
Yo tengo **menos paciencia que** tú.	*I have less patience than you.*
Mi madre es **tan alta como** mi padre.	*My mother is as tall as my father.*
Limpio **tanto como** tú.	*I clean as much as you.*

The following adjectives (adverbs) have irregular comparatives, instead of using **más... que.**

bueno/a (bien)	*good (well)*	mejor	*better*
malo/a (mal)	*bad (badly)*	peor	*worse*
joven	*young*	menor	*younger*
viejo/a	*old*	mayor	*older*

Mi hermano **mayor** canta **mejor** que yo.   *My **older** brother sings **better** than I do.*

Tanto (*As much, as many*) can be an adjective or an adverb. As an adjective, it must agree with a following noun for gender and number. As an adverb, it always ends with **-o.**

(adjective)	Tengo **tantas tías** como tíos.
(adverb)	Hablo **tanto** con mis tías como con mis primas.

3-17 Descripciones. ¿Cuál de los adjetivos describe sus cosas?

> Modelo   un cuarto (ordenado, desordenado)
> **Tengo un cuarto desordenado.**

1. un cuarto (grande, pequeño)
2. muebles (nuevos, viejos)
3. un sofá (bonito, feo)
4. un barrio (agradable, desagradable)
5. el pelo (corto, largo)
6. un coche (grande, pequeño)
7. un coche (bueno, malo)
8. una cocina (limpia, sucia)

3-18 Comparaciones. Exprese su opinión como en el modelo.

> Modelo   los coches rojos / los coches azules (bonitos)
> **Los coches rojos son más (menos) bonitos que los coches azules. /
> Los coches rojos son tan bonitos como los coches azules.**

1. los coches japoneses / los coches norteamericanos (buenos)
2. un sofá / un coche (caro)
3. los sofás negros / los sofás blancos (elegantes)
4. las paredes amarillas / las paredes moradas (feas)
5. los perros / los gatos (inteligentes)
6. las casas / los apartamentos (caras)
7. un televisor / una computadora (útil)
8. el precio (*price*) de una casa nueva / el barrio (importante)
9. las ciudades grandes / el campo (interesantes)
10. el centro de la ciudad / las afueras (tranquilo)

P 3-19 Una casa nueva. Ud. habla con un agente inmobilario (*real estate agent*) de su casa ideal. Conteste sus preguntas haciendo comparaciones con el lugar donde vive ahora. Use **más, menos, tan** o **tanto/a/os/as.**

> Modelo   E1: ¿Quiere tener Ud. un jardín grande?
> E2: **Quiero tener un jardín más (menos) grande que ahora. /
> Quiero tener un jardín tan grande como ahora.**

1. ¿Quiere tener Ud. una cocina grande?
2. ¿Quiere tener Ud. muchos árboles?
3. ¿Cuántos baños necesita Ud.?
4. ¿Cuánto le gustaría pagar al mes?
5. ¿Cuántos dormitorios quiere Ud.?
6. ¿Cuántas ventanas quiere en la sala?
7. ¿Quiere vivir en una ciudad grande?
8. ¿Le gustaría estar cerca del centro?

G 3-20 Juan y Mario. En grupos, escriban oraciones comparando a Juan y Mario. ¿Cuántas oraciones pueden escribir?

> Modelo   **Juan es más serio que Mario.**

Juan, 22 años   **Mario, 21 años**

Follow-up for 3-17. *Descripciones.* Have students use the same cues to compare their best friend's things to their own. *Modelo: Generalmente, mi mejor amigo tiene un cuarto más (menos) desordenado que mi cuarto. / Generalmente, mi mejor amigo tiene un cuarto tan desordenado como mi cuarto.*

Continuation for 3-18. *Comparaciones.* Have students say whether the following statements are true about their home. 1. Mi cuarto es tan grande como la sala. 2. Paso tanto tiempo en la sala como en mi cuarto. 3. Paso tanto tiempo en casa los lunes como los domingos. 4. Vivo tan cerca de la universidad como mi mejor amigo. 5. Estudio tanto en la biblioteca como en mi casa. 6. Miro la televisión tanto en mi cuarto como en la sala. 7. Hay tantos muebles en mi cuarto como en la sala. 8. Por lo general, mi cuarto está tan ordenado como la sala.

Follow-ups for 3-20. *Juan y Mario.* **A.** Have students refer to the illustrations of Juan's and Mario's rooms on p. 75 and say whether the following sentences are true or false. Then change the ones that are false. 1. El cuarto de Juan está tan desordenado como el cuarto de Mario. 2. Juan tiene tantas ventanas en su cuarto como Mario. 3. Juan tiene tantos libros como Mario. 4. Juan tiene tantas pinturas en las paredes como Mario. 5. Juan tiene tantos gatos en su cuarto como Mario. 6. La cama de Juan es tan grande como la cama de Mario. 7. El cuarto de Juan es tan grande como el cuarto de Mario. 8. Juan tiene tanta ropa en el suelo como Mario. 9. Juan tiene tantos muebles en su cuarto como Mario. 10. El escritorio de Juan está tan ordenado como el escritorio de Mario. 11. Juan tiene tantas cosas en su escritorio como Mario. **B.** Have students write sentences with *más... que, menos... que, tan... como,* and *tanto/a/os/as... como* comparing themselves to their best friend or to someone else.

VOCABULARIO
¿Qué haces los días de clase?

TEMA 4

Por la mañana…

Como solo/a generalmente.   **Leo el periódico y bebo café.**   **Corro por el parque.**

Por la tarde…

Asisto a mis clases.   **Aprendo vocabulario para mi clase de español.**   **Leo mis libros de texto y revistas. Escribo ensayos y cartas.**

Por la noche…

Como con mis amigos.   **Escribo y leo mis correos electrónicos. Recibo muchos correos electrónicos.**

Veo una película o un vídeo.

---

asistir a *to attend*   **una revista** *a magazine*   **un ensayo** *an essay, a paper*   **una carta** *a letter*

¿Cómo se pronuncia? *b y v*

In Spanish, the letters **b** and **v** are pronounced the same. When they are the first sound after a pause, or after an **m** or an **n,** they are pronounced similarly to an English **b,** with the upper lip, not the teeth, pressed against the lower lip.

ver	vídeo	ventana	viernes
baño	bueno	bien	también

In any other position, **b** and **v** are still pronounced with both lips, but they are not pressed as tightly together.

Mi no**v**ia **B**eti **viv**e con su **b**uena amiga **V**erónica.
Mis a**b**uelos **b**e**b**en **v**ino a **v**eces para cele**b**rar.
Veo un ár**b**ol muy **b**onito por la **v**entana a**b**ierta.

3-21 ¿Con qué frecuencia? ¿Con qué frecuencia hace usted las siguientes cosas?

> (casi) siempre   todos los días   con frecuencia   a veces   (casi) nunca

Modelo   Como mucho por la mañana.
   Nunca como mucho por la mañana.

1. Como cereales por la mañana.
2. Bebo café por la mañana.
3. Asisto a mi clase de español.
4. Corro por el parque o la calle.
5. Aprendo mucho en mis clases.
6. Escribo ensayos para mis clases.
7. Como pizza.
8. Recibo correos electrónicos.
9. Leo novelas románticas.
10. Escribo poemas.
11. Veo vídeos en mis clases.
12. Leo el periódico.

P

Conversaciones. Dos estudiantes hablan de sus clases. En parejas, lean la conversación. Luego, cambien la conversación para hablar de las clases de ustedes.

— ¿Siempre asistes a todas tus clases?
— A veces no asisto a mi clase de contabilidad. Es a las siete y media de la mañana.
— ¿Para qué clases tienes que leer mucho?
— Leo mucho para mis clases de inglés y ciencias políticas. No tengo que leer mucho para las otras clases.
— ¿Escribes muchos ensayos?
— Sí, tengo que escribir tres para mi clase de inglés, uno para mi clase de historia y otro para mi clase de ciencias políticas.
— ¿Comprendes mucho cuando el profesor **sólo** habla español en esta clase?
— Sí, por lo general comprendo muy bien porque siempre aprendo todo el vocabulario.

---

sólo *only*

Suggestions. A. Point out that *vino* can mean both *wine* and *came* and give students the tongue twister: *El vino vino, pero el vino no vino vino. El vino vino vinagre.* **B.** Have students practice pronouncing the letters *b* and *v* in the following sentences. Afterward, have them say whether each sentence is true. 1. Vivo en un barrio bonito con nuevos vecinos jóvenes y divertidos. 2. Trabajo en la biblioteca los viernes y sábados a veces. 3. Hay una pruebita sobre las nuevas palabras de vocabulario el jueves.

Follow-up for *Conversaciones.* ¿Es lógico? 1. Leo muchos libros para mi clase de literatura. 2. Corro a mi próxima clase porque hay dos horas entre las clases. 3. A veces no asisto a mis clases si estoy enfermo/a. 4. Escribo muchos poemas sentimentales para mi clase de contabilidad. 5. Escribo un ensayo sobre el socialismo para mi clase de ciencias políticas. 6. Comprendo bien en mi clase de sociología porque es fácil. 7. Aprendo mucho en mi clase de historia porque el profesor no es muy bueno. 8. Veo muchos vídeos en mi clase de historia. El profesor no habla mucho.

AUDIO ¡A escuchar!

Ahora, escuchen otra conversación en la cual alguien habla de sus actividades los lunes después de las clases. ¿Dónde corre? ¿Con quién come a veces? ¿Qué lee? ¿Qué escribe? ¿Cuándo ve la tele?

Para averiguar

1. How do **-er** verb endings differ from those for **-ar** verbs?
2. Verbs ending with **-ir** are conjugated like **-er** verbs except in two forms. Which ones?
3. What is the irregular **yo** form for **ver**?

Supplemental activities. A. Point out that *deber* is often followed by an infinitive. 1. ¿Debo o no debo hacer las siguientes cosas si quiero bajar de peso (*lose weight*)? (*comer menos, comer mucha comida mexicana, beber muchos refrescos, correr todos los días, ver la tele todo el día, pasar más tiempo en el gimnasio*) 2. ¿Deben o no deben hacer los estudiantes las siguientes cosas si quieren sacar buenas notas (*get good grades*) en la clase de español? (*asistir a sus clases, leer el libro, leer el periódico durante la clase, hablar sólo inglés en clase, abrir el libro durante los exámenes, abrir el libro entre los exámenes, aprender todo el vocabulario*) **B.** ¿Le gustaría hacer las siguientes cosas en sus clases? (*aprender mucho, aprender más vocabulario en la clase de español, aprender más sobre la historia de México, escribir más ensayos en la clase de inglés, escribir más en la pizarra, comer en clase, beber café en clase, leer libros más interesantes, leer revistas en clase, comprender mejor, asistir a clase los sábados, recibir las preguntas de los exámenes antes de los exámenes para estudiar, ver vídeos todos los días*)

GRAMÁTICA
Más acciones: los verbos en -er/-ir

The endings for regular **-er** verbs are similar to those for **-ar** verbs. Just replace the letter **a** in the **-ar** verb endings with an **e**. Regular **-ir** verbs are conjugated like **-er** verbs, except in the **nosotros/as** and **vosotros/as** forms.

COMER (*TO EAT*)		VIVIR (*TO LIVE*)	
yo	com**o**	yo	viv**o**
tú	com**es**	tú	viv**es**
usted, él, ella	com**e**	usted, él, ella	viv**e**
nosotros/as	com**emos**	nosotros/as	viv**imos**
vosotros/as	com**éis**	vosotros/as	viv**ís**
ustedes, ellos, ellas	com**en**	ustedes, ellos, ellas	viv**en**

The following **-er** and **-ir** verbs are conjugated like **comer** and **vivir.**

aprender (a…)	to learn (to…)	**abrir**	to open
beber	to drink	**asistir (a)**	to attend
comprender	to understand	**compartir**	to share
correr	to run	**escribir**	to write
creer	to believe	**recibir**	to receive
deber	should, ought to, to owe		
leer	to read		
vender	to sell		

Use the preposition **a** before infinitives following **aprender** and before nouns after **asistir.**

Aprendemos a hablar español.	*We're learning to speak Spanish.*
Asisto a clase todos los días.	*I attend class every day.*

The verb **ver** (*to see*) has an irregular form for **yo.**

veo, ves, ve, vemos, veis, ven

3-22 **¿Sí o no?** Diga si estas personas de la clase de español hacen las cosas indicadas entre paréntesis.

1. Yo… (comprender todas las preguntas en clase, deber estudiar mucho, vender mis libros al final del semestre, leer todas las explicaciones del libro, aprender el vocabulario fácilmente)
2. Nosotros… (aprender francés, leer muchos libros, comer en clase, asistir a clase todos los días, abrir los libros durante los exámenes, escribir muchos ensayos)
3. El profesor… (escribir mucho en la pizarra, beber café en clase, deber hablar más inglés en clase, recibir a muchos estudiantes en su oficina)

3-23 Una familia de diplomáticos. Diga que usted y su familia reciben correos electrónicos de los familiares (*family members*) que viven en estas capitales.

> **Modelo** Asunción, Paraguay
> **Recibimos muchos correos electrónicos de nuestros primos que viven en Asunción, Paraguay.**

1. Caracas, Venezuela
2. La Paz, Bolivia
3. Buenos Aires, Argentina
4. Lima, Perú
5. Quito, Ecuador
6. Bogotá, Colombia
7. Santiago, Chile
8. Montevideo, Uruguay

3-24 ¿Quién? ¿Qué miembro(s) de su familia hace(n) las siguientes cosas?

> **Modelo** leer mucho
> **Mi hermano lee mucho. / Yo leo mucho. / Todos leemos mucho. / Nadie lee mucho.**

1. comer mucha pizza
2. correr con frecuencia
3. asistir a muchos conciertos
4. creer en Santa Claus
5. escribir muchas cartas
6. deber trabajar menos
7. leer el periódico todos los días
8. recibir muchos correos electrónicos
9. beber mucho café
10. comer mucha comida mexicana
11. aprender español
12. vivir solo/a
13. comprender otra lengua
14. ver muchas películas

P 3-25 Entrevista. Entreviste a otro/a estudiante con estas preguntas.

1. ¿Vives con tus padres? ¿Comen ustedes juntos con frecuencia? ¿Beben tus padres mucho café? ¿Quién de tu familia comprende mejor tus problemas? ¿Recibes muchos regalos (*gifts*) de tu familia?
2. ¿Para qué clase lees más? ¿Para qué clase escribes más? ¿Para qué clase(s) debes estudiar más? ¿Siempre asistes a todas tus clases? ¿En qué clases comprendes bien? ¿En qué clases no comprendes a veces? ¿En qué clases aprendes mucho? ¿En qué clases no aprendes mucho?
3. ¿Lees mucho? ¿Lees un libro ahora? ¿Cómo se llama? ¿Quién escribe libros interesantes? ¿Lees muchos libros de ciencia ficción?
4. ¿Crees en los extraterrestres? ¿en los fantasmas (*ghosts*)? ¿en la reencarnación?

Follow-up for 3-23. *Una familia de diplomáticos.* ¿En qué país (*country*) viven sus amigos si viven en estas capitales? *Modelo:* Mis amigos viven en Madrid. > *Viven en España.* Mis amigos viven en (Managua, Guatemala, San Salvador, San José, La Habana, Santo Domingo, Tegucigalpa, Panamá)

Supplemental questions. ¿Lee Ud. más el periódico o las revistas? ¿Qué revistas lee Ud. con frecuencia? ¿Lee Ud. más libros o ve Ud. más la tele? ¿Qué programas de televisión ve Ud. con frecuencia? ¿Escribe Ud. más correos electrónicos o más cartas? ¿Escribe Ud. más correos electrónicos o recibe Ud. más correos electrónicos? ¿Escribe o recibe Ud. correos electrónicos en español a veces? ¿Ve Ud. películas o la televisión en español a veces? ¿Ve Ud. más películas de acción o más comedias? ¿Ve Ud. muchas películas extranjeras? ¿Comprende Ud. otras lenguas? ¿Aprende Ud. otra lengua? ¿Qué desea aprender a hacer? ¿tocar un instrumento musical? ¿bailar? ¿cocinar? ¿En qué restaurante come Ud. con frecuencia? ¿Come Ud. más comida mexicana o más comida italiana? ¿Come Ud. antes o después de clase? ¿Come Ud. mucho por la mañana? ¿Necesita beber café por la mañana? ¿Bebe Ud. mucho café? ¿Debe beber menos café? ¿Bebe Ud. café cuando estudia? ¿Aprende Ud. mejor si bebe café? Generalmente, ¿aprende Ud. mejor si estudia por la mañana, por la tarde o por la noche?

VOCABULARIO
TEMA 5
¿Qué haces los sábados?

A veces, traigo mucho trabajo a casa los fines de semana.

Hago ejercicio.

Asisto a un concierto o un partido de fútbol.

Pongo un CD o la radio y oigo música.

Salgo con mis amigos a un restaurante (al cine, a un bar, a bailar).

A veces, hago un viaje a la montaña o a la playa.

Si estoy cansado/a no hago nada en especial. Paso mucho tiempo en casa.

¿Cómo se pronuncia? La letra *g*

Before **e** or **i**, the letter **g** is pronounced like the Spanish letter **j**. This is similar to a harsh English *h* sound pronounced with the tongue arched high in the back of the mouth.

general   biolo**g**ía   **G**eraldo

When **g** is the first sound of a phrase or after **n**, and is before **a, o,** or **u**, it is pronounced similarly to an English *g* before **a, o,** or **u.**

pon**g**o   **g**ato   **g**usto   un **g**araje

When **g** is not the first sound of a phrase or after **n,** place the tongue in the same position before **a, o,** or **u**, but do not press it tightly against the roof of your mouth as in English.

ha**g**o   oi**g**o   trai**g**o   sal**g**o   ami**g**a   del**g**ado   bi**g**ote

---

traigo *I bring*   **la playa** *the beach*

3-26 ¿Dónde? ¿En qué parte de la casa hace usted las siguientes cosas?

| Modelo | Hago ejercicio. |

Hago ejercicio en la sala. / Nunca hago ejercicio en casa.

1. Como.
2. Bebo café.
3. Oigo música.
4. Hago mi tarea.
5. Leo el periódico.
6. Veo la televisión.
7. Leo mis libros de texto.
8. Escribo correos electrónicos.
9. Pongo música para bailar.
10. Pongo la mesa.

Ahora diga si usted hace estas cosas más por la mañana, por la tarde o por la noche.

| Modelo | **Hago más ejercicio por la mañana. / Nunca hago ejercicio.** |

3-27 ¿Y usted? Seleccione o cambie las palabras en letra cursiva para describir sus pasatiempos.

1. Oigo más _música clásica / jazz / rock / música popular / rap / ???._
2. Cuando oigo música en el coche, generalmente pongo _la radio / un CD / un casete._
3. Cuando oigo la radio, generalmente pongo la emisora (_station_) _90.5 (noventa punto cinco) FM._
4. Veo más _películas de terror / dramas / comedias / películas de aventuras / películas de acción._
5. Veo más partidos de _fútbol americano / fútbol / básquetbol / béisbol / tenis_ en la televisión.
6. Hago más viajes _a la playa / a la montaña / a Nueva York / ???._
7. Generalmente los fines de semana, no hago nada en especial _los sábados por la noche / los domingos por la tarde / ???._
8. Salgo más con mis amigos _los sábados por la noche / los domingos por la tarde / ???._
9. Salgo más con mis amigos _al cine / a bailar / a un café / a un restaurante / ???._

P **Conversaciones.** Dos estudiantes hablan de los fines de semana. En parejas, lean la conversación. Luego, cambien la conversación para hablar de sus propios fines de semana.

— ¿Qué haces generalmente los fines de semana?
— **Pues,** con frecuencia los sábados y a veces los viernes por la noche salgo con mis amigos a comer o a bailar. Si estoy cansado, a veces no hago nada en especial los viernes. Veo la tele o un vídeo en casa.
— ¿Regresas muy tarde a casa a veces?
— Sí, a veces regreso a las dos o las tres de la mañana.
— ¿Qué haces los domingos por la tarde?
— Los domingos hago mi tarea y leo mucho para mis clases. Si no tengo mucha tarea, a veces veo un partido de fútbol americano en la tele.

Supplemental activities. A. Repita las siguientes oraciones si son ciertas para usted o cambie las oraciones falsas para decir la verdad. 1. Oigo el estéreo tanto como veo la televisión. 2. Oigo música clásica (música popular, música country) tanto como oigo jazz (rap, música latina). 3. Veo la televisión tanto por la mañana como por la noche. 4. Veo tantas películas en español como en inglés. 5. Hago tantas fiestas en mi casa como mi mejor amigo/a. 6. Salgo a bailar tanto como salgo a un restaurante. 7. Salgo a comer tanto con mis padres como con mis amigos. 8. Salgo con mis amigos tanto los lunes como los sábados. 9. Hago tanta tarea los sábados como los lunes. 10. Hago tanta tarea para mis otras clases como para la clase de español. 11. Traigo tantos libros a mis otras clases como a la clase de español.

Follow-up for _Conversaciones._ ¿Es lógico? 1. No hago nada en especial ahora. Estoy muy ocupado/a. 2. No salgo mucho con mis amigos los fines de semana. Me gusta descansar. 3. Si estoy muy cansado/a los sábados, salgo con mis amigos y regreso muy tarde. 4. No salgo mucho al cine. Veo más vídeos en casa. 5. Nunca salgo a los clubes nocturnos porque no me gusta bailar. 6. Casi siempre salgo a un restaurante a comer porque no me gusta cocinar.

AUDIO ¡A escuchar!

Ahora, escuchen otra conversación en la cual dos amigos hablan de este fin de semana. ¿Qué deciden hacer? ¿Cuándo?

7. No hago nada interesante. Estoy aburrido/a. 8. Pongo un CD de Mozart porque no me gusta la música clásica. 9. Nunca pongo la televisión los fines de semana porque veo mi programa favorito los sábados.

_____

Pues,... _Well,..._

GRAMÁTICA

Las acciones: los verbos con primera persona irregular; la *a* personal

Para averiguar

1. What is irregular about the verbs **hacer, poner, traer,** and **salir** in the present tense?
2. What are the forms of the verb **oír**? What does **oír** mean?
3. What are three idiomatic expressions with **hacer**?
4. What word precedes direct objects referring to people? What happens to **a** when it is followed by **el** (*the*)?

Supplemental activities. A. (You may wish to have students open their books to the maps inside the front and back covers.) ¿A qué país (*country*) hacen estas personas un viaje si visitan estas capitales? *Modelo:* Nosotros visitamos Asunción. > *Hacemos un viaje a Paraguay.* 1. Mi hermano visita San José. 2. Mis amigos visitan Managua. 3. Yo visito La Paz también. 4. Mis padres visitan Montevideo. 5. Mi prima visita Quito. 6. Todos visitamos Buenos Aires. 7. Nadie visita Bogotá. 8. Mis amigos visitan Caracas. **B.** Practice *personal a* with the following questions. *Modelo:* ¿Ve Ud. a alguien todos los días? > *Veo a mi amigo Eric todos los días. / No veo a nadie todos los días.* 1. ¿Visita Ud. a su mejor amigo/a con frecuencia? 2. ¿Trae Ud. a alguien a la universidad en su coche? 3. ¿Ve Ud. más a sus padres o a su mejor amigo/a los fines de semana? 4. ¿Ve Ud. a sus vecinos con frecuencia? 5. ¿Oye Ud. a sus vecinos a veces cuando escuchan música o hablan muy fuerte (*loud*)? 6. ¿Invita Ud. a los vecinos a comer a veces? 7. ¿Siempre comprende a su mejor amigo/a? 8. ¿Cuándo no quiere ver Ud. a nadie?

The following verbs are conjugated like regular **-er** and **-ir** verbs in the present indicative, except for the **yo** form.

	HACER (*TO DO/MAKE*)	PONER (*TO PUT/SET*)	TRAER (*TO BRING*)	SALIR (*TO GO OUT/LEAVE*)
yo	**hago**	**pongo**	**traigo**	**salgo**
tú	haces	pones	traes	sales
usted, él, ella	hace	pone	trae	sale
nosotros/as	hacemos	ponemos	traemos	salimos
vosotros/as	hacéis	ponéis	traéis	salís
ustedes, ellos, ellas	hacen	ponen	traen	salen

— ¿Qué **haces** los fines de semana?   — *What do you do on the weekend?*
— No **hago** nada en especial. ¿Y tú?   — *I don't do anything special. And you?*
— Casi siempre **salgo** con mis amigos los sábados.   — *I almost always go out with my friends on Saturdays.*

The verb **oír** (*to hear*) has a slightly different pattern. It can also be used instead of **escuchar** to talk about listening to music.

oigo, o**y**es, o**y**e, o**í**mos, o**í**s, o**y**en

Oigo a los vecinos a veces.
I hear the neighbors sometimes.

¿Oyes música mientras estudias?
Do you listen to music while you study?

Hacer is also used in the following idiomatic expressions:

hacer una pregunta	*to ask a question*
hacer un viaje	*to take a trip*
hacer una fiesta	*to have a party*

The preposition **a** precedes direct objects referring to people, but not things. In this context, it is called the *personal* **a**. Direct objects are people or objects to which something is being done. When **a** is followed by **el** (*the*), the two words contract to form **al.** In the following sentences, **el profesor** and **mis hijos** are direct objects because they are being heard or brought.

¿Oyen ustedes bien **al profesor**?
Can you hear the professor well?

Siempre traigo **a mis hijos.**
I always bring my children.

3-28 ¿Con qué frecuencia? ¿Con qué frecuencia hace usted estas cosas en la clase de español?

> Modelo
>
> salir de clase temprano (*early*)
> **Nunca salgo de clase temprano. / Salgo de clase temprano a veces. / Salgo de clase temprano con frecuencia.**

1. traer su libro a clase
2. poner algo debajo de su silla
3. hacer preguntas
4. traer un diccionario a clase
5. oír bien al profesor (a la profesora)
6. salir de clase durante los exámenes
7. oír música
8. hacer la tarea durante la clase

3-29 ¿Y tú? Pregúntele a otro/a estudiante si las siguientes personas hacen las cosas indicadas.

> Modelo
>
> tú (hacer la comida en casa)
> E1: **¿Haces la comida en casa?**
> E2: **A veces yo hago la comida y a veces mi esposo hace la comida. / No, no hago la comida en casa generalmente. Casi siempre como en un restaurante.**

1. tú (hacer la cama todos los días)
2. tus amigos y tú (oír más música rock o más música latina)
3. tú (oír música en español a veces)
4. tú (poner más un CD o la radio)
5. tus amigos (traer discos compactos para oír en tu casa a veces)
6. tú (salir más con los amigos los viernes o los sábados)
7. tus amigos y tú (salir a bailar con frecuencia)
8. tus padres (salir mucho a comer)
9. tus amigos (hacer algo en especial para tu cumpleaños [*birthday*])

3-30 Una fiesta. En grupos, preparen descripciones de lo que hacen en esta fiesta. Usen los verbos **hacer, poner, traer, salir** y **oír.**

> Palabras útiles: un regalo (*a present*), un/a invitado/a (*a guest*), un pastel (*a cake*), una chaqueta (*a jacket*)

Supplemental activities. A. 1. ¿Trae Ud. las siguientes cosas en su mochila a la clase de español? (el cuaderno de ejercicios, el libro de español, un libro de matemáticas (biología...), un bolígrafo rojo (azul, negro), un cuaderno verde (amarillo...), un lápiz, mucho dinero, comida, una calculadora, una computadora, un teléfono celular) 2. ¿Oye Ud. estas cosas en la clase de español a veces? (teléfonos celulares, música, muchas preguntas en español, mucho inglés, un CD, el/la profesor/a del salón de clase de al lado, los coches de afuera) 3. ¿Hacemos nosotros las siguientes cosas en esta clase? (muchos ejercicios en grupos, más ejercicios en grupos o más con toda la clase, muchos ejercicios en la pizarra, mucha tarea, tanta tarea como en las otras clases de usted, muchos exámenes, muchas preguntas, muchas fiestas) **B.** Preguntas. 1. ¿Qué hace Ud. después de las clases generalmente? ¿Hace Ud. ejercicio a veces? ¿Hace Ud. más ejercicio en un gimnasio o corre Ud. más? ¿A qué hora sale Ud. de su última clase hoy? ¿A qué hora sale Ud. de la casa para su primera clase los lunes (los martes)? 2. ¿Aprende Ud. español porque le gusta hacer viajes? ¿Hace usted muchos viajes? ¿Hace Ud. más viajes a la playa, a la montaña o a otra ciudad? ¿Le gustaría más hacer un viaje a México o a España? ¿a Puerto Rico o a Bolivia? ¿Hay más playas (montañas altas) en Puerto Rico o en Bolivia? 3. ¿Hace Ud. muchas fiestas en su casa? ¿Qué hacen sus amigos y Ud. en las fiestas generalmente? ¿Traen sus amigos algo a las fiestas? ¿Qué música oye Ud. más en las fiestas?

Suggestion for 3-30. *Una fiesta.* Remind students to use words like *alguien, nadie, un hombre,* and *una mujer.*

¡Trato hecho!

En portada

REVISTA CULTURAL

Note. Have students complete the *Antes de leer, Reading strategies,* and *Ahora Ud.* activities before reading the *En familia* article.

Tres generaciones.

Ventura, California.

EN FAMILIA

La identidad familiar. Una parte importante de la identidad latina es la familia: vivir en familia **crecer** en familia, y **morir** en familia. Los latinos **sienten** la responsabilidad de mantener sus **raíces** y sus tradiciones **dentro de** la familia.

El núcleo familiar en la cultura hispana es muy **fuerte.** Generalmente, la familia es una comunidad extendida de **parientes** (padres, hijos, abuelos, **padrinos,** primos, tíos, sobrinos, nietos) que tienen relaciones muy **cercanas.** Por lo general, la familia latina **valora** la unidad y el respeto entre sus miembros.

Desafíos familiares. Las familias de inmigrantes hispanos en Estados Unidos viven entre dos culturas. No es siempre fácil para el inmigrante hispano preservar sus tradiciones familiares, **aunque** muchas veces **aprovechan** lo mejor de las dos culturas para la educación de sus hijos.

Estructuras familiares. En los **hogares** hispanos de Estados Unidos, la estructura familiar es variada. Muchas veces la madre **lleva**

Compañía Telefónica Iberoamericana

En las largas distancias, te acercamos a los tuyos.

- Servicio de llamadas al extranjero.
- Tarjetas telefónicas prepagadas.
- Mensajería y correo electrónico.

sola las responsabilidades familiares, pero **la pareja casada** es todavía el núcleo familiar más común entre los hispanos.

El español en casa. En muchos hogares hispanos de Estados Unidos, el español es la lengua de comunicación familiar porque los padres comprenden que preservar el español es preservar sus raíces. Santa Ana, California, El Paso, Texas, y Miami, Florida, son las tres ciudades donde el español se habla con más frecuencia en las casas hispanas.

LANTANA
Viajar es compartir

Mobifam
Muévete en familia

GASNAT
llega a todos los hogares

Vive cada instante al calor de la familia

Consume gas natural, bueno para ti, bueno para el medioambiente

---

crecer *to grow up*   **morir** *to die*   **sienten** *feel*   **raíces** *roots*   **dentro de** *within*   **fuerte** *strong*   **parientes** *relatives*   **padrinos** *godparents*   **cercanas** *close*
valora *values*   **desafíos** *challenges*   **aunque** *although*   **aprovechan** *they make the most of*   **hogares** *homes*   **lleva** *carries*   **la pareja casada** *the married couple*

Antes de leer

Think about times when your family gathers together. Are the gatherings similar to those shown in the photos on these two pages? How are they different? Mention other activities that families share when they get together.

Reading strategies: Anticipating content in a reading.   One approach to reading in a foreign language is to predict upcoming information. Predicting involves using knowledge one already has about a topic to anticipate the content of the succeeding portions of the text, and calls for the reader to think ahead. Readers can use this knowledge to trigger personal associations, which can help them anticipate the likely information discussed in the passage.

G **3-31** **Ahora Ud.** *En familia.* Examinen en grupos las diferentes secciones del artículo y piensen en las posibles ideas que se van a mencionar (*think about the possible ideas that are going to be mentioned*).

Después de leer

3-32 **Finales con sentido.** Complete las oraciones con los finales apropiados según la lectura (*according to the reading*).

1. Preservar las raíces y las tradiciones… b
2. La familia hispana valora… e
3. Las familias de inmigrantes hispanos en Estados Unidos… c
4. El núcleo familiar hispano está formado… a
5. El español es… d

a. generalmente por la pareja casada.
b. es esencial en la cultura hispana.
c. observan los contrastes entre su cultura y la cultura norteamericana.
d. una parte muy importante de la identidad latina.
e. la unión de sus miembros.

P **3-33** **Anuncios en español.** Observen con atención los anuncios (*ads*) que acompañan la lectura. ¿Qué servicios/productos ofrecen? ¿Cómo reflejan la identidad latina?

3-34 **Parentescos.** Defina en español las siguientes palabras relacionadas con la familia según las relaciones entre los miembros.

Modelo   sobrino
Es el hijo de mi hermano o de mi hermana.

1. abuela   2. tío   3. prima   4. hermano   5. nietos

En familia.

De puertas abiertas a la comunidad

 CRECER EN UNA FAMILIA HISPANA

3-35 Entrando en materia. Cuando piensa en una familia hispana, ¿cómo la imagina? ¿Qué actividades cree que hacen en su tiempo libre (*free*)? ¿Qué valores (*values*) cree que son importantes en general para la familia hispana?

> La familia tiene una importancia enorme para los hispanos. Las familias hispanas son generalmente numerosas y las reuniones familiares son un gran evento, una ocasión para compartir. En este segmento de vídeo les presentamos a varias personas de origen hispano que nos hablan de sus familias, de sus relaciones familiares y de lo importante que es tener siempre **el apoyo** de **los seres queridos**.

3-36 ¿Cierto o falso? Indique cuáles de las siguientes afirmaciones son ciertas y cuáles son falsas según (*according to*) el vídeo. Corrija las falsas con la información correcta.

	Cierto	Falso
1. Rafael está divorciado y tiene un hijo de veintiún años de una relación previa.	X	☐
2. Rosal es puertorriqueña y sus padres trabajan en el teatro.	X	☐
3. Alejandro tiene familia en Argentina, Paraguay y Brasil.	X	☐
4. Jorge tiene familia en Puerto Rico y pasa siempre las Navidades allá.	X	☐
5. La esposa de Rafael es brasileña, hija de emigrantes.	X	☐

Answers for 3-37. *Bueno, mi familia...* **Rafael:** uruguayo; cinco, su esposa y sus tres hijos, Bianca, Claudia y Rafael; tiene una familia muy bonita; **Itandehui:** de padre mexicano y de madre norteamericana; son cuatro hermanos; tiene una familia muy interesante; **Analissa:** mexicanoamericana; son seis, cinco mujeres y un hombre, y muchos primos, once sobrinos, dos sobrinas, muchos tíos y tías; tiene una familia muy cariñosa, que apoya mucho; **Edgar:** paraguayo; son cuatro hermanos y cuatro hermanas, más sus padres; son una familia muy numerosa, como es muy típico en Latinoamérica.

3-37 Bueno, mi familia... Escuche con atención a las siguientes personas hablando de su familia y escriba la información adecuada en cada caso.

Rafael   Itandehui   Analissa   Edgar

¿Cuál es su origen?
¿Cuántos son en la familia?
¿Cómo describe a su familia?

---

el apoyo *the support*   **los seres queridos** *loved ones*

3-38 En familia. Observe la foto de familia de los Escansini y describa a la familia de Rafael utilizando el vocabulario nuevo del capítulo.

(G) 3-39 En sus ratos libres. Imaginen lo que hacen las siguientes personas del vídeo en sus ratos libres (*free time*).

1. Itandehui es estudiante de literatura y medios de comunicación. En sus ratos libres…

_____
_____
_____

2. Rosal va a comenzar sus estudios en la universidad y quiere ser actriz. En sus ratos libres…

_____
_____
_____

3. Rafael es bombero (*fireman*). En sus ratos libres…

_____
_____
_____

4. Alejandro trabaja en una bodega (*grocery store*). En sus ratos libres…

_____
_____
_____

3-40 En el plano personal. Seleccione a una de las personas del vídeo y compare su familia con la familia de usted utilizando la gramática y el vocabulario del capítulo. Presente después su comparación al resto de la clase.

Escapadas

CANCÚN PARA TODAS LAS EDADES

Cancún, en el estado de Quintana Roo, México, es un paraíso que forma parte del Caribe mexicano. Cancún es un destino ideal para las familias. El turismo en Cancún combina las actividades de aventura con la exploración del arte y la cultura mayas. Aquí les presentamos algunos sitios de interés de la región.

Cancún, México.

Figura precolombina en la playa de Chac Mool, Cancún.

El Parque Natural de Xcaret.   Xcaret es un parque natural con ecosistemas extraordinarios: el Acuario de Arrecife de Coral, con especies de plantas y animales únicos; **el mariposario** más grande del mundo con mariposas **volando libremente** y una **laguna** natural con **peces** tropicales, lugar **sagrado** de los mayas. Xcaret tiene también sitios arqueológicos, donde el visitante aprende sobre la historia viviente del **pueblo** maya.

Pareja de mariposas.

Cobá.   Cobá es un destino muy interesante y misterioso, pero no muy turístico. Allí está una de las pirámides más altas y **más antiguas** de la península de Yucatán: Nohoch Mul, **de** 136 **pies de altura.**

Ruinas del Rey, Península de Yucatán.

Tulum.   Tulum es el sitio arqueológico prehispánico más visitado de la península de Yucatán. Las ruinas mayas de Tulum están situadas en un **acantilado** sobre el Caribe y las **vistas** son impresionantes. Las construcciones más importantes son El Castillo, **la torre** que domina el sitio, y el Templo de los Frescos, que contiene **pinturas** sagradas.

---

el mariposario *the butterfly pavilion*   **volando libremente** *flying freely*   **laguna** *lagoon*   **peces** *fish*
sagrado *sacred*   **pueblo** *people*   **más antiguas** *oldest*   **de...pies de altura** *...feet high*   **acantilado** *cliff*
vistas *views*   **la torre** *the tower*   **pinturas** *paintings*

Ruinas mayas de Tulum con vistas de la playa de Quintana Roo.

3-41　Un Cancún muy familiar. Responda a las siguientes preguntas con la información que aparece en la lectura *Cancún para todas las edades.*

1. ¿Por qué es Cancún un destino ideal para los viajes en familia?
2. ¿Cuál es una cultura prehispánica de México en la Península de Yucatán?
3. ¿Qué actividades ofrece el Parque Natural de Xcaret?
4. ¿Qué es el Nohoch Mul?
5. ¿Dónde hay más turistas, en Cobá o en Tulum?
6. ¿Qué tienen de especial las ruinas de Tulum?

P **3-42　Viajes en familia.** Entreviste a otro/a estudiante con estas preguntas.

1. ¿Prefieres hacer un viaje con tu familia o con amigos? ¿Por qué?
2. ¿Cuáles son algunos de los destinos familiares preferidos (*some of the preferred family vacation destinations*) en Estados Unidos?
3. ¿Adónde viajas con frecuencia con tu familia?
4. Generalmente, ¿cómo son tus vacaciones en familia?

www **3-43　Más opciones.** En grupos, busquen en la red otras opciones de viajes familiares en los distintos países hispánicos y preparen una descripción con fotos de los lugares (*places*) para presentar en la próxima sesión de clase.

En palabras de...

MIS COSTUMBRES

Un estudiante hispano va a (*is going to*) vivir con su familia el próximo verano (*next summer*) y desea obtener información sobre los miembros de su familia, su casa, sus costumbres familiares y su rutina del verano. Escriba una carta al estudiante con información personal y de su familia.

Writing strategies: Composing an informal letter. When writing an informal letter in Spanish, one usually includes personal information, delivered in a casual style and with a cordial tone. There are certain conventional greetings and farewells that are commonly used. You can use the expressions listed below to open and close your letter.

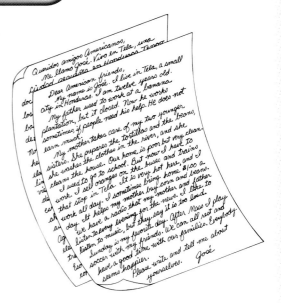

For opening your letter:
hola
querido/a... (*dear*)

For closing your letter:
adiós
hasta pronto (*see you soon*)
un saludo (*greetings*)
un abrazo (*a hug*)
besos (*kisses*)

Antes de escribir

En preparación a su carta, anote ideas relacionadas con las cuatro categorías siguientes:

- los miembros de su familia
- las características de su casa
- sus costumbres familiares
- su rutina en el verano

Escriba ahora su carta distribuida en cuatro párrafos correspondientes a las categorías mencionadas.

Después de escribir

Ahora examine su carta otra vez y compruebe (*make sure*) que contiene los siguientes puntos:

- ✓ el vocabulario apropiado para hablar de los miembros de la familia
- ✓ las palabras para describir las diferentes partes de una casa
- ✓ las estructuras que expresan posesión
- ✓ las expresiones para hablar de un día típico de su fin de semana

En la red

Busque ejemplos de cartas de familias anfitrionas (*host families*) a estudiantes extranjeros. ¿Son similares a su carta? ¿Contienen información adicional y útil para incorporar a su carta?

All the sources consulted for the readings are cited on the *¡Trato hecho!* Web site at **www.prenhall.com/trato**

VOCABULARIO

TEMA 1

En casa
las afueras *the outskirts*
el alquiler *the rent*
un animal *an animal*
un árbol *a tree*
un armario *a closet, a wardrobe*
un baño *a bathroom*
un barrio *a neighborhood*
una cama *a bed*
el campo *the country*
una casa *a house*
el centro *the center, downtown*
una ciudad *a city*
un coche (un carro) *a car*
una cocina *a kitchen*
un comedor *a dining room*
una dirección *an address*

Para los números, vea la página 70.

un dormitorio *a bedroom*
una estufa *a stove*
una flor *a flower*
un garaje *a garage*
un gato *a cat*
un jardín *a garden, a yard*
un microondas *a microwave oven*
una nevera *a refrigerator*
un perro *a dog*
una piscina *a swimming pool*
una planta *a plant*
un restaurante *a restaurant*
una sala *a living room*
un sofá *a sofa*
un televisor *a television set*
un/a vecino/a *a neighbor*

Verbos
alquilar *to rent*
fumar *to smoke*
pagar *to pay*
vivir *to live*
Me/Te/Le gustaría(n)... *I/You (familiar)/He, She, You (formal) would like...*

Otras palabras y expresiones
afuera *outside*
agradable *pleasant, nice*
caro/a *expensive*
no... nada *not... anything*
tampoco *neither, not either*

TEMA 2

Sustantivos
una alfombra *a rug*
una cómoda *a chest (of drawers)*
un/a compañero/a de casa *a housemate*
el dinero *money*
un espejo *a mirror*
una impresora *a printer*
una lámpara *a lamp*
los muebles *furniture*
una pared *a wall*
una persona *a person*

una pintura *a painting*
un reproductor de DVD *a DVD player*
el suelo *the ground, the floor*

Adjetivos
desordenado/a *messy*
limpio/a *clean*
muerto/a *dead*
ordenado/a *neat, straightened up*
propio/a *own*
sucio/a *dirty*

Verbos
compartir *to share*
dejar *to leave (something somewhere)*
tener *to have*
tener que + infinitive *to have to + verb*
usar *to use*

Otras palabras y expresiones
alguien *someone, somebody*
desafortunadamente *unfortunately*
por todos lados *everywhere*

Para los colores, vea la página 72.
Para los adjetivos posesivos, vea la página 74.

T E M A 3

La familia

¿Cuántos son en...? *How many are there in...?*

el/la abuelo/a (los abuelos) *the grandfather/grandmother (grandparents)*

el/la hermano/a (los hermanos) *the brother/sister (brothers and sisters)*

el/la hijo/a (los hijos) *the son/ daughter (children)*

el/la nieto/a (los nietos) *the grandson/granddaughter (grandchildren)*

el padre/la madre (los padres) *the father/mother (parents)*

el/la primo/a (los primos) *the cousin (cousins)*

el/la sobrino/a (los sobrinos) *the nephew/niece (nephews and nieces)*

el/la tío/a (los tíos) *the uncle/aunt (aunts and uncles)*

Descripciones

alto/a *tall*

bajo/a *short (in height)*

casado/a *married*

como *like*

corto/a *short (in length)*

de estatura mediana *of medium height*

delgado/a *thin*

de mediana edad *middle-aged*

divorciado/a *divorced*

en el aspecto físico *in appearance*

en el carácter *as for personality*

gordo/a *fat*

guapo/a *handsome/beautiful*

joven *young*

largo/a *long*

mayor *older, oldest*

mejor *better, best*

menor *younger, youngest*

moreno/a *dark-haired, dark-skinned*

pelirrojo/a *redheaded*

peor *worse, worst*

rubio/a *blond/e*

Se llama (Se llaman)... *His/Her name is (Their names are)...*

Se parece a... *He/She looks like...*

soltero/a *single*

tener... años *to be... years old*

tener bigote/barba *to have a mustache/beard*

tener el pelo negro/castaño/ rubio/rojo/canoso *to have black/ brown/blond/red/gray (white) hair*

tener los ojos marrones (color café)/verdes/azules *to have brown/green/blue eyes*

usar gafas *to use/wear glasses*

Comparaciones

más... que *more... than, -er... than*

menos... que *less... than, fewer... than*

tan... como *as... as*

tanto/a/os/as... como *as much... as, as many... as*

T E M A 4

Sustantivos

el café *coffee*

una carta *a letter*

el correo electrónico *e-mail, the e-mail message*

un ensayo *an essay, a paper*

un libro de texto *a textbook*

un periódico *a newspaper*

una revista *a magazine*

un vídeo *a video*

Verbos

abrir *to open*

aprender (a...) *to learn (to...)*

asistir (a) *to attend*

beber *to drink*

compartir *to share*

comprender *to understand*

correr *to run*

creer *to believe*

deber *should, ought to, to owe*

escribir *to write*

leer *to read*

recibir *to receive*

vender *to sell*

ver *to see*

Adverbio

sólo *only*

T E M A 5

Sustantivos

un bar *a bar*

un CD *a CD*

un concierto *a concert*

una montaña *a mountain*

una playa *a beach*

la radio *the radio*

Expresiones verbales

hacer *to do, to make*

hacer ejercicio *to exercise*

hacer una fiesta *to have a party*

hacer una pregunta *to ask a question*

hacer un viaje *to take a trip*

oír *to hear; to listen to*

poner *to put, to place, to set, to turn on*

salir *to leave, to go out*

traer *to bring*

Otra expresión

nada en especial *nothing in particular*

4

En los ratos libres

VOCABULARIO

¿Adónde vas en tus ratos libres?

Voy…

a la playa (al lago, a la piscina) para nadar, hacer esquí acuático y tomar el sol

a la montaña para esquiar

al teatro para ver una obra de teatro

al museo para ver una exposición

al parque para pasear, correr y jugar al tenis (fútbol, fútbol americano, baloncesto, voléibol)

a un club o a un bar para tomar una copa y bailar

a la iglesia (a la sinagoga, a la mezquita, al templo) para cantar y rezar

a un café para tomar un café y hablar con los amigos

al gimnasio para levantar pesas, hacer ejercicio aeróbico y hacer yoga

¡Ojo!

La palabra **fútbol** significa *soccer* y se usa **fútbol americano** para hablar de *football*. También se dice **básquetbol** y **vólibol** en vez de **baloncesto** y **voléibol**.

---

voy *I go*   **para** *(in order) to*   **tomar el sol** *to sunbathe*   **al** (= a + el) *to the*   **pasear** *to walk, to go for a walk*
baloncesto = básquetbol   **tomar una copa** *to have a drink*   **rezar** *to pray*

4-1 **¿Dónde?** ¿Dónde prefiere usted hacer estas cosas?

Modelo   levantar pesas (en casa, en el gimnasio)
Generalmente, prefiero levantar pesas en el gimnasio.
No me gusta levantar pesas.

1. nadar (en la piscina, en el lago, en la playa)
2. hacer ejercicio (en casa, en el gimnasio)
3. correr (en el parque, en el estadio, en la calle)
4. tomar una copa con los amigos (en casa, en un club, en un café)
5. tomar el sol (en la piscina, en el lago, en la playa, en el patio)

4-2 **¿Y tú?** Invite a otro/a estudiante a hacer estas cosas.

Modelo   **¿Quieres ir al gimnasio conmigo para hacer ejercicio?**

1.

2.

3.

4.

5.

4-3 **Entrevista.** Entreviste a otro/a estudiante con estas preguntas.

1. ¿Eres atlético/a? ¿Te gusta jugar al tenis? ¿al vóleibol? ¿al baloncesto?
2. ¿Haces ejercicio con frecuencia? ¿Prefieres levantar pesas o hacer ejercicio aeróbico? ¿Prefieres correr o nadar?
3. ¿Prefieres ir a la playa o a la montaña? ¿Te gusta tomar el sol? ¿Te gusta nadar? ¿Te gusta jugar al vóleibol en la playa? ¿Te gusta esquiar?

Conversaciones. Dos amigos hablan de sus planes para esta noche. Lean la conversación en parejas. Luego, cambien la conversación, haciendo planes para salir con su compañero/a.

— ¿Qué quieres hacer esta noche?
— No sé. ¿Por qué no **vamos** al centro comercial?
— No, no **tengo ganas de ir de compras.** ¡Vamos al cine! Quiero ver la nueva película de Antonio Banderas.
— Está bien. ¿Quieres ir a comer algo antes?
— ¡Buena idea! ¿A qué restaurante quieres ir?
— Vamos a *Tien Hong.* Tengo ganas de comer comida china.
— Sí, me gusta mucho **ese** restaurante. ¿A qué hora paso por tu casa?
— ¿A las seis y media?
— Muy bien. **Entonces,** hasta las seis y media.
— Sí. Hasta luego.

----

vamos *we go*   **tener ganas de** *to feel like*   **ir de compras** *to go shopping*   **ese/a** *that*   **entonces** *so, then*

Continuation for 4-1. *¿Dónde?*
¿Dónde prefiere usted...? 1. jugar al vóleibol (en la playa, en el gimnasio, en el parque) 2. ver una obra de teatro (en el teatro, en la televisión) 3. ver un partido de fútbol americano (en la televisión, en el estadio) 4. jugar al baloncesto (en el parque, en el gimnasio) 5. pasear (en el parque, en la calle) 6. cantar (en el baño, en la iglesia, en un bar) 7. ver una exposición (en un museo de arte, en un museo de historia) 8. hablar con los amigos (en casa, en un café, en un club nocturno, por teléfono)

Supplemental activities. A. Have students rank the following activities in order of interest (10 for the most interesting and 1 for the least), collect the papers, and tally the numbers for each activity. The next day have the class guess each activity's overall ranking. *(nadar, tomar el sol, ver una exposición de arte, ver una obra de teatro,*

AUDIO **¡A escuchar!**

Ahora, escuchen otra conversación en la cual dos amigos hacen planes para este fin de semana. ¿Qué deciden hacer, con quiénes y cuándo?

ver una película, jugar al vóleibol, jugar al baloncesto, tomar una copa con los amigos, bailar, ir a la iglesia)
B. (Supplemental questions.) ¿Cuál es un estado de Estados Unidos con muchas playas? ¿con muchas montañas? ¿Cuál es una ciudad con muchos teatros? ¿Ve usted muchas obras de teatro? ¿En qué ciudad hay muchos museos? ¿Ve Ud. muchas exposiciones? ¿Dónde está el museo Smithsonian? En el Smithsonian, ¿tienen más exposiciones de arte o de historia? ¿Hay un teatro (una piscina, un museo) en la universidad? ¿Dónde le gusta pasar su tiempo libre? ¿Qué le gusta hacer?

GRAMÁTICA

Hablar de destinos y hacer planes: *ir*, las contracciones con *a*

Para averiguar

1. You use **dónde** to ask where something is located. What question word do you use to ask where someone is going?
2. What happens to the preposition **a** when it is followed by the article **el**?
3. When do you use **para** before an infinitive?

Use the verb **ir** to say where people go.

IR (*TO GO*)			
yo	**voy**	nosotros/as	**vamos**
tú	**vas**	vosotros/as	**vais**
usted, él, ella	**va**	ustedes, ellos, ellas	**van**

Voy a la universidad los lunes, miércoles y viernes.
Mis amigos y yo casi nunca **vamos** al cine.

Use **adónde** with verbs such as **ir** or **salir** to ask *where* someone goes. To answer, use the preposition **a** (*to*), which contracts with the article **el** to form **al.** It does not contract with **la, los,** or **las.**

— ¿**Adónde van** Uds.?   — *Where are you going?*
— **Vamos al** parque.   — *We're going to the park.*

Use **para** (*for, in order to*) with an infinitive to explain for what purpose you are doing something.

— Voy a Los Ángeles el sábado.   — *I'm going to Los Angeles on Saturday.*
— ¿Sí? ¿Para qué?   — *Really? What for?*
— **Para asistir** a un concierto.   — *To attend a concert.*

¡Ojo!

Use the preposition **a** to say that someone is going *to* a place, but use the preposition **en** to say what someone does or what happens *at* a place.

Voy **a** una tienda.
*I'm going **to** a store.*

Trabajo **en** una tienda.
*I work **at** a store.*

P **4-4** ¿**Qué?** ¿Para qué van estas personas a los lugares indicados?

> levantar pesas   jugar al tenis   ver un partido de fútbol americano
> estudiar   bailar   nadar y hacer esquí acuático   comprar unas cosas
> asistir a una conferencia   trabajar

Modelo después de clase, mis amigos y yo / la biblioteca
Después de clase, mis amigos y yo vamos a la biblioteca para estudiar.

1. esta tarde, mi padre / la oficina
2. mi mejor amigo y yo / el gimnasio
3. mañana, (yo) / la universidad
4. mis amigos / el parque
5. este sábado por la tarde, (yo) / el estadio
6. este sábado por la noche, mis amigos y yo / un club
7. el domingo, mis hermanos / el lago
8. esta mañana, mi mamá / el centro comercial

Supplemental activity. Have students complete the following statements about themselves, then ask a classmate the same things, using *dónde* or *adónde. Modelo: Me gusta comer en el restaurante* [name a nearby restaurant]. *Monica, ¿dónde te gusta comer?* 1. Después de clase voy a... 2. Esta noche quiero ir a... 3. Esta noche quiero comer en... 4. Con frecuencia salgo con mis amigos a... 5. Generalmente, los sábados a las diez de la noche estoy en... 6. Compro mucha ropa en la tienda... 7. Para comprar comida, voy a... 8. Me gusta pasar mucho tiempo en... 9. Para pasar una tarde tranquila, generalmente, voy a... 10. Me gusta tomar una copa con los amigos en...

4-5　¿Con qué frecuencia? ¿Con qué frecuencia van estas personas a cada lugar: **(casi) todos los días, con frecuencia, a veces, (casi) nunca**?

Modelo　mi madre
Mi madre va al parque a veces para pasear al perro. / Mi madre casi nunca va al parque.

Supplemental activity. Refer students to the map of South America on p. 83. Tell students that after a family reunion, a family is returning home. Students say to what capital city each one is going. *Modelo: Los abuelos van a Caracas, Venezuela.*

1. yo

2. mi padre

3. mi mejor amigo/a

4. mis amigos y yo

5. mis amigos y yo

6. mi familia

4-6　¿Adónde vas? Complete las siguientes oraciones con el verbo **ir** y el nombre de un lugar específico.

Modelo　Para bailar, muchos estudiantes…
Para bailar, muchos estudiantes **van al club Carnaval.**
Para comer comida italiana, yo…
Para comer comida italiana, yo **voy al restaurante Casa Toscana.**

1. Para ver una película, mis amigos y yo…
2. Para nadar, yo…
3. Para hacer ejercicio, mi mejor amigo/a…
4. Para comprar ropa, mi madre…
5. Para tomar algo, mis amigos y yo…
6. Para comprar libros, muchos estudiantes…
7. Para comer comida mexicana, yo…

Continuation for 4-6. *¿Adónde vas?*
1. Para comprar comida, mis padres...
2. Para comer comida china, yo...
3. Para descansar, yo... 4. Para tomar un café, muchos estudiantes... 5. Para oír música, muchos estudiantes...
6. Para comprar los CDs, yo... 7. Para practicar español, mis compañeros de clase y yo... 8. Para pasear, yo...
9. Para jugar al fútbol, muchas personas... 10. Para esquiar, muchas personas... 11. Para alquilar vídeos, yo... 12. Para correr, muchas personas... 13. Para estudiar juntos, mis amigos y yo...

ⓟ 4-7　Entrevista. Complete las siguientes preguntas con la forma correcta del verbo **ir** y luego entreviste a otro/a estudiante.

1. ¿Adónde _____ (tú) generalmente después de la clase de español? ¿a casa? ¿a otra clase? ¿al trabajo? ¿a la biblioteca?
2. ¿_____ (tú) a nadar con frecuencia? ¿Prefieres _____ a la playa, al lago o a una piscina? ¿Quién _____ contigo generalmente?
3. Cuando sales con tus amigos los fines de semana, ¿adónde _____ ustedes generalmente? ¿_____ (tú) allí con tus amigos todos los fines de semana? ¿_____ (ustedes) en tu coche, en el coche de un amigo o en el autobús?

VOCABULARIO
¿Qué tiempo hace? ¿Qué vas a hacer?

TEMA **2**

¡Ojo!

In Spanish-speaking countries outside the United States, temperatures are given in centigrade, rather than Fahrenheit. To convert from Fahrenheit to centigrade, subtract 32 and multiply by ⅝. To convert from centigrade to Fahrenheit, multiply by ⅝ and add 32.

¿Qué tiempo hace?

En (el) verano (junio, julio, agosto)…

El verano en una playa de Puerto Rico.

…hace sol.
…el cielo está despejado.

…hace (mucho) calor.

En (el) otoño (septiembre, octubre, noviembre)…

El otoño en el Parque del Retiro de Madrid, España.

…hace (mucho) viento.

…hace fresco

En (el) invierno (diciembre, enero, febrero)…

Cuando es invierno en Bariloche, Argentina, es verano aquí.

…nieva.

…hace (mucho) frío.

En (la) primavera (marzo, abril, mayo)…

En Taxco, México, cada día es como un día de primavera.

…llueve.

…el cielo está nublado.

…hace buen tiempo.

¿Qué tiempo hace? *What's the weather like?*

4-8 ¿Es lógico? Complete cada oración con la terminación lógica.

Modelo   Hace frío y… (hace calor, nieva).
          Hace frío y **nieva.**

1. El cielo está nublado y… (llueve, hace sol).
2. El cielo está despejado y… (llueve, hace sol).
3. Hace sol y… (hace buen tiempo, nieva).
4. Hace calor y… (hace fresco, hace sol).
5. Hace fresco y… (hace viento, hace calor).
6. Llueve y… (hace mal tiempo, hace sol).

4-9 ¿Cuándo? ¿En qué mes (*month*) hace el tiempo indicado en su región?

Modelo   Hace más frío en…
          Hace más frío en **enero. / Nunca hace frío aquí.**

1. Llueve más en…   **5.** Nieva más en…
2. Llueve menos en…   **6.** Hace mejor tiempo en…
3. Hace más frío en…   **7.** Hace muy mal tiempo en…
4. Hace más calor en…   **8.** Hace mucho sol en…

4-10 ¿Qué tiempo hace? Describa el tiempo
ilustrado.

Modelo   **El cielo está nublado.**

1.

2.

3.

4.

5.

6.

P 4-11 Entrevista. Entreviste a otro/a estudiante con estas preguntas.

1. ¿Qué tiempo hace hoy? ¿Te gusta más el frío o el calor? ¿Prefieres los días nublados o despejados? ¿Qué te gusta hacer cuando hace mal tiempo? ¿Qué te gusta hacer cuando hace buen tiempo?
2. ¿Prefieres el verano, el otoño, el invierno o la primavera? ¿Por qué? ¿Qué estación (*season*) te gusta menos? ¿Por qué?

P Conversaciones. Dos amigos hablan de sus planes para mañana. Lean la conversación en parejas. Luego, hablen de sus propios planes para mañana.

— ¿Qué **vas a hacer** mañana?
— Tengo que trabajar por la mañana. Por la tarde, quiero ir al parque si hace buen tiempo. Si llueve, voy a estudiar. ¿Y tú? ¿Qué vas a hacer?
— Nada en especial. Si hace mal tiempo, voy a pasar el día en casa. Quiero **dormir** hasta tarde. Si hace buen tiempo, tengo ganas de ir de compras.

vas a + infinitive *are you going to* + verb   **dormir** *to sleep*

Supplemental activities. A. Have students complete the following sentence with logical activities for different weather conditions. *Cuando hace sol (nieva, hace frío, hace buen tiempo, hace mucho calor, llueve) me gusta…* B. Ask questions about the photos on the previous page. 1. En la foto del verano, ¿hace buen tiempo o hace mal tiempo? ¿Hace mucho calor? ¿Hace viento? ¿Dónde están? ¿Hacen esquí acuático? ¿Nadan? ¿Toman el sol? 2. En la foto del otoño, ¿hace frío, hace fresco o hace calor? ¿Hace viento? ¿Llueve? ¿Es una ciudad grande o el campo? ¿La señora pasea o hace un picnic? ¿Dónde está? 3. En la foto del invierno, ¿dónde está esa persona? ¿Qué hace? ¿El cielo está nublado o despejado? ¿Hace mucho viento? ¿Nieva mucho en esa región? 4. En la foto de la primavera, ¿qué tiempo hace? ¿Llueve? ¿Está nublado?

Follow-up for *Conversaciones.* Generalmente, ¿son éstas cosas que los estudiantes tienen ganas de hacer o que tienen que hacer? *Modelo:* estudiar > *Tienen que estudiar.* 1. ir al café 2. hacer la tarea 3. ir a la playa 4. ir a clase 5. jugar al tenis 6. hacer ejercicio 7. trabajar 8. ir de compras 9. ir a la biblioteca 10. limpiar la casa 11. ver un vídeo 12. asistir a un concierto 13. hacer exámenes 14. tomar una copa con los amigos

AUDIO ¡A escuchar!

Ahora, escuchen otra conversación en la cual una mujer va a visitar a una amiga que vive muy lejos. ¿Cuándo llega? ¿Qué tiempo hace? ¿Qué van a hacer si hace mal tiempo?

GRAMÁTICA
Hacer planes: *ir a* con los infinitivos, la fecha

To say what someone is going to do, conjugate **ir** followed by the preposition **a** and an infinitive.

— ¿**Vas a comer** en casa?　　　　— *Are you going to eat at home?*
— No, **voy a comer** con mi novia.　— *No, I'm going to eat with my girlfriend.*
— ¿Qué **van a hacer** después?　　— *What are you going to do afterwards?*
— **Vamos a ir** a bailar.　　　　　— *We're going to go dancing.*

Use these infinitives to say how the weather is going to be.

Va a hacer sol (viento, calor, frío, fresco).　*It's going to be sunny (windy, hot, cold, cool).*
Va a llover (nevar).　*It's going to rain (snow).*

The following adverbs express when something is going to happen.

esta mañana / tarde	*this morning / afternoon*
esta noche	*tonight*
mañana (por la mañana, por la tarde, por la noche)	*tomorrow (morning, afternoon, night)*
la semana (el mes, el año) que viene	*next week (month, year)*
en enero (febrero, marzo, abril, mayo, junio, julio, agosto, septiembre, octubre, noviembre, diciembre)	*in January (February, March, April, May, June, July, August, September, October, November, December)*

To give the date, use the ordinal number **primero** for the first of a month, but use the cardinal numbers (**dos, tres, cuatro...**) for the other days. The names of months are not capitalized in Spanish.

— ¿Cuál es la fecha hoy?　　　　　— *What's the date today?*
— Es **el veinte de diciembre.**　　— *It's December twentieth.*
— ¿Qué vas a hacer para la Navidad?　— *What are you going to do for Christmas?*
— Voy a estar en México hasta 　　— *I'm going to be in Mexico*
　el primero de enero.　　　　　*until January first.*

4-12　Predicciones. ¿Van a hacer estas personas las cosas indicadas mañana?

> **Modelo**　Yo… (salir temprano de casa, ir al trabajo)
> **Voy a salir temprano de casa. No voy a ir al trabajo.**

1. Yo… (estar ocupado/a, ir al parque, correr, hacer ejercicio, esquiar)
2. Mi mejor amigo/a… (trabajar, ir a la universidad, pasar el día conmigo, comer conmigo, salir a bailar, levantar pesas, estudiar mucho)
3. Mi mejor amigo/a y yo… (hablar por teléfono, tomar una copa, ver una exposición en un museo, ir a la playa, jugar al tenis, ir de compras)
4. Mis padres… (trabajar, estar en casa por la mañana, comer conmigo, descansar, ir a la casa de mis abuelos)

4-13 Pronóstico del tiempo. ¿Qué tiempo va a hacer cada día en Santiago, Chile?

Modelo **El lunes, dos de agosto el cielo va a estar nublado y va a hacer fresco.**

Santiago, Chile	jueves	viernes	sábado	domingo	lunes	martes	miércoles
	29 de julio	30 de julio	31 de julio	1º de agosto	2 de agosto	3 de agosto	4 de agosto
Mínima	-6°C	-4°C	2°C	6°C	5°C	4°C	3°C
Máxima	0°C	3°C	12°C	13°C	12°C	11°C	9°C

4-14 Un calendario. ¿Qué planes tiene esta persona para este mes?

Modelo **Va a visitar a su abuelita el primero de mayo.**

Mayo

lunes	martes	miércoles	jueves	viernes	sábado	domingo
				1 visitar a abuelita	2	3 fiesta en San Antonio
4	5	6	7	8 ESTUDIAR	9	10
11 exámenes	12	13	14	15 playa	16	17 viaje a México
18	19	20	21	22 regresar de México	23 trabajo	24
25 trabajo	26	27	28	29 exposición de arte	30	31

P 4-15 ¿Qué vas a hacer? Pregúntele a otro/a estudiante qué va a hacer en los momentos indicados.

Modelo esta noche
> **E1: ¿Qué vas a hacer esta noche?**
> **E2: Voy a pasar esta noche en casa. No voy a hacer nada en especial.**

1. esta tarde
2. mañana por la tarde
3. mañana por la noche
4. este fin de semana
5. el verano que viene
6. el 25 de diciembre
7. el 31 de diciembre
8. el 1º de enero
9. el 14 de febrero

P 4-16 Entrevista. Entreviste a un/a compañero/a de clase.

1. ¿Cuál es la fecha de este sábado? ¿Qué tiempo va a hacer este fin de semana? ¿Qué vas a hacer si hace buen tiempo? ¿si hace mal tiempo?
2. ¿Cuál es la fecha de tu cumpleaños (*birthday*)? ¿Qué tiempo hace generalmente ese día? ¿Vas a hacer algo en especial este año para tu cumpleaños?
3. ¿Cuál es la fecha del último (*last*) día de clase este semestre? ¿Vas a estudiar aquí el año que viene? ¿Vas a estudiar español? ¿Cuántos semestres/trimestres de español vas a tomar? ¿Vas a aprender otras lenguas? ¿Cuáles?

Suggestion for 4-13. *Pronóstico del tiempo.* Have students predict whether the weather tomorrow is going to be as in each picture where you live.

Supplemental activities. A. Have students refer to their syllabus and answer questions such as the following. 1. ¿En qué fecha vamos a hacer el examen sobre este capítulo? 2. ¿Cuántos exámenes vamos a tener este semestre? 3. ¿Cuándo vamos a hacer el examen final? 4. ¿Va a estudiar Ud. mucho para el examen final? 5. ¿Vamos a hacer un examen oral este mes? 6. ¿Cuántos capítulos del libro vamos a estudiar este semestre? 7. ¿Quiénes van a estudiar español el semestre que viene? 8. ¿Cuántos semestres vamos a usar este libro? **B.** Haga las siguientes preguntas. *¿Cuándo va a hacer Ud. las siguientes cosas la próxima vez o en el futuro? (comer en un restaurante, ver a sus padres, trabajar, pasar el día en casa, ir al supermercado, hacer ejercicio, ir a la playa, ir al centro comercial, terminar sus estudios, tener un hijo, comprar un coche, comprar una casa, hablar español con fluidez [fluently]).* **C.** Put students in groups of 3-5 and have them work together to make predictions about the future for someone from each of the other groups. **D.** *Horóscopos.* Write the Spanish names of zodiac signs on the board. Read each sign's dates in random order and have students say what sign it is: Acuario (20 de enero – 19 de febrero), Piscis (20 de febrero – 20 de marzo), Aries (21 de marzo – 19 de abril), Tauro (20 de abril – 20 de mayo), Géminis (21 de mayo – 21 de junio), Cáncer (22 de junio – 22 de julio), Leo (23 de julio – 22 de agosto), Virgo (23 de agosto – 21 de septiembre), Libra (22 de septiembre – 22 de octubre), Escorpión (23 de octubre – 21 de noviembre), Sagitario (22 de noviembre – 21 de diciembre), Capricornio (22 de diciembre – 19 de enero). Print out current horoscopes from the Internet by searching *horóscopos* and have students summarize theirs using the immediate future.

VOCABULARIO
TEMA ❸
¿Qué quieres hacer? ¿Puedes...?

¿Qué quieres hacer mañana por la mañana?

dormir hasta tarde

empezar el día temprano con ejercicio

desayunar en casa

¿Qué prefieres hacer por la tarde?

almorzar en el parque

jugar al ajedrez (a las cartas, a los videojuegos)

¿Por la noche vas a…?

cenar con unos amigos

volver a casa después de cenar

volver a salir con otros amigos

---

empezar *to begin, to start*   **temprano** *early*   **desayunar** *to eat breakfast*   **almorzar** *to eat lunch*
cenar *to eat dinner*   **volver** *to return*   **volver a hacer algo** *to do something again*

4-17 ¿Y Ud.? Complete cada oración con la terminación lógica. Luego diga si la oración es cierta o falsa para usted.

Modelo   Esta noche voy a comer en casa. Voy a **cenar con mis padres.**
          Falso. Voy a cenar en casa, pero voy a cenar solo/a.

1. Para no estar cansado/a por la mañana, necesito...
2. Nunca quiero comer por la mañana. No tengo ganas de...
3. Me gusta comer entre las once y las once y media. Prefiero...
4. No tengo coche. Tengo que...
5. Prefiero descansar un poco después de las clases. Me gusta...
6. No me gusta dejar las cosas para más tarde. Prefiero...
7. A veces no comprendo los ejercicios del cuaderno. Tengo que...
8. No me gustan los deportes. Prefiero...

a. desayunar
b. almorzar temprano
c. cenar con mis padres
d. dormir nueve o diez horas
e. dormir la siesta
f. jugar a los videojuegos
g. volver a casa hoy en autobús
h. volver a leer las preguntas dos o tres veces
i. empezar mi tarea temprano

4-18 Mañana. Cambie las palabras en letra cursiva para describir sus planes para mañana.

1. Mañana, voy a dormir hasta *las nueve.*
2. Voy a dormir *seis o siete* horas.
3. Voy a desayunar *en The Golden Omelet.*
4. Voy a almorzar *con mi novio.*
5. Por la tarde, voy a ir *al parque* y voy a *jugar al tenis.*
6. Voy a volver a casa *a las cinco y media.*
7. Voy a cenar *en casa a las siete y media.*
8. Después de cenar, voy a *jugar a los videojuegos.*

Ⓟ   **Conversaciones.** En parejas, lean la siguiente invitación. Luego, invite a su pareja a hacer algo con usted.

— ¿Quieres estudiar conmigo después de clase?
— **No puedo** hoy después de clase. Tengo que trabajar.
— ¿Quieres estudiar conmigo después del trabajo?
— Sí, ¿a qué hora?
— ¿A qué hora vuelves del trabajo?
— A las seis.
— Entonces, a las siete o las siete y media en la biblioteca.
— Está bien a las siete.

Follow-ups for *Conversaciones*. A. Point out the verb form *(no) puedo* from the conversation and have students say whether they can do the following things tomorrow. Remind students how to use *tengo que* and have them give a reason why if they cannot do something. *Modelo: dormir hasta tarde > Sí, puedo dormir hasta tarde. / No, no puedo dormir hasta tarde porque tengo que ir a una clase a las ocho. (dormir hasta las diez, empezar el día a las once de la mañana, desayunar con su mejor amigo/a, almorzar en su restaurante favorito, jugar a los videojuegos todo el día, dormir una siesta por la tarde, cenar con sus padres, cenar en su restaurante favorito, volver a casa antes de las tres de la tarde, salir con sus amigos por la noche, volver a casa muy tarde)* **B.** Ask students which days they can do the things listed in section **A**. **C.** Practice turning down invitations by having students complete sentences such as the following. 1. No puedo salir esta noche. Hay un examen mañana en mi clase de física y tengo que... 2. No puedo ir al cine hoy porque mis padres vienen a mi casa esta noche y está muy sucia. Tengo que... 3. No puedo ir de compras este sábado. Voy a estar en la oficina. Tengo que... 4. No puedo ir a tomar una copa ahora. Voy al gimnasio. Tengo que... 5. No puedo ir al parque ahora. Estoy muy cansado/a. Tengo que...

AUDIO ¡A escuchar!

Ahora, escuchen otra conversación en la cual dos esposos van a cenar. ¿Con quiénes van a comer, cuándo y dónde?

_____
no puedo *I can't*

GRAMÁTICA
Las acciones: los verbos con alteraciones vocálicas

Some verbs have vowel changes in the stem when they are conjugated in the present tense. The last **e** of the stem becomes **ie** or **i**, and the last **o** of the stem becomes **ue** in all of the forms except **nosotros** and **vosotros**.

	EMPEZAR (*TO BEGIN*)	PODER (*TO BE ABLE, CAN, MAY*)	PEDIR (*TO ASK FOR, TO ORDER*)
yo	emp**ie**zo	p**ue**do	p**i**do
tú	emp**ie**zas	p**ue**des	p**i**des
usted, él, ella	emp**ie**za	p**ue**de	p**i**de
nosotros/as	empezamos	podemos	pedimos
vosotros/as	empezáis	podéis	pedís
ustedes, ellos, ellas	emp**ie**zan	p**ue**den	p**i**den

Other verbs that follow this pattern are:

e → ie
cerrar *to close*
entender *to understand*
pensar *to think, to intend*
perder *to lose, to miss*
preferir *to prefer*
querer *to want*
venir* *to come*

o (u) → ue
almorzar *to eat lunch*
contar *to count, to tell*
dormir *to sleep*
encontrar *to find*
jugar* *to play*
volver *to return*

e → i
decir* *to say, to tell*
repetir *to repeat*
servir *to serve*

***Jugar** is the only verb where **u** becomes **ue. Decir** and **venir** have irregular forms for **yo** (**yo digo** *I say,* **yo vengo** *I come*). Use **decir** to say *to tell* when telling a piece of information, but **contar** when telling or recounting a story.

Use **pensar** followed by an infinitive to say what you *intend* or *plan* to do. Use the preposition **a** after **empezar** and **volver** before infinitives. **Volver** is used with infinitives to say one *re*does something or does something *again.*

Pienso estudiar francés también.	*I intend to study French too.*
Empiezo **a** entender.	*I'm beginning to understand.*
Vuelvo **a** leer todo dos o tres veces.	*I reread everything two or three times.*

4-19 **¿Sí o no?** ¿Hacen ustedes estas cosas en la clase de español?

1. Yo… (dormir, entender bien, decir muchas cosas en español, empezar a entender más español, almorzar antes de clase, querer mucha tarea, venir a cada clase, perder la paciencia, encontrar el español difícil, pensar en español a veces, poder hacer preguntas)
2. El/La profesor/a… (decir muchas cosas en español, preferir hablar español, repetir mucho, contar muchos chistes (*jokes*) en clase, querer buenos estudiantes)
3. Nosotros… (poder comer, venir a clase los sábados, volver a clase mañana, encontrar los exámenes difíciles, querer exámenes más difíciles, repetir muchas palabras, cerrar los libros durante los exámenes)

4-20 **¿Y Ud.?** Dos amigos describen su rutina diaria (*daily*). ¿Hace usted lo mismo?

Modelo   Dormimos hasta las nueve todos los días.
Yo duermo hasta las seis y media o las siete.

1. Almorzamos en McDonalds por lo general.
2. Jugamos al tenis todos los días.
3. Volvemos a casa a las tres de la tarde.
4. Empezamos nuestra tarea a las cuatro y media de la tarde.
5. Preferimos cenar a las ocho o las nueve.
6. Pedimos una pizza dos o tres veces a la semana.
7. Dormimos nueve horas todas las noches.
8. Repetimos las mismas actividades de lunes a viernes pero podemos hacer otras cosas los fines de semana.

4-21 **En mi familia.** ¿Qué miembros de su familia hacen estas cosas? Use uno de los verbos de la página anterior.

Modelo   muy tarde / primero / antes de las tres
Mi padre y yo volvemos muy tarde a casa a veces.
Mi hermano vuelve primero a casa.
Nadie (*Nobody*) **de mi familia vuelve antes de las tres.**

1. bien / todos los días / a veces   **2.** hasta tarde / mucho / poco   **3.** vino (*wine*) para tomar / cola / café

4. en el trabajo / en la universidad o en la escuela / solo(a)   **5.** con los amigos / solo(a) a veces

P **4-22** **Entrevista.** Entreviste a un/a compañero/a de clase con estas preguntas.

1. ¿Prefieres nadar en una piscina o en un lago? ¿Hay piscina donde vives? ¿A qué hora cierran la piscina? ¿Duermes al lado de la piscina a veces?
2. ¿A qué deportes juegas a veces? ¿Con quién juegas? ¿Quién pierde generalmente? ¿Pierdes la paciencia a veces cuando juegas?
3. ¿A qué hora vuelves a casa hoy? ¿Dónde piensas cenar esta noche? ¿Qué quieres hacer después de la cena? ¿Vienes a la universidad mañana?

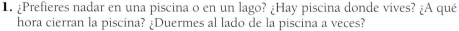

Supplemental questions. ¿Duerme usted mejor cuando hace frío o cuando hace calor? ¿Duerme Ud. bien cuando llueve? ¿Hasta qué hora le gusta dormir? ¿Qué días puede dormir hasta tarde? ¿Vuelve a dormir una siesta por la tarde? ¿Qué días no puede dormir mucho? ¿Por qué? ¿A qué hora empieza su primera clase todos los días? ¿Prefiere Ud. tener clases por la mañana, por la tarde o por la noche? ¿Viene Ud. a la universidad todos los días? ¿Viene Ud. en el autobús? ¿Pierde el autobús a veces? ¿Cómo encuentra Ud. sus clases este semestre? ¿Dicen sus profesores cosas que Ud. no entiende a veces? ¿Hace Ud. preguntas si no entiende algo? ¿En qué clases prefiere hablar mucho? ¿En qué clases prefiere no hablar? ¿Son pacientes sus profesores o pierden la paciencia a veces? ¿Pierde Ud. la paciencia con otros estudiantes a veces? ¿Duermen los estudiantes a veces en sus clases? ¿Almuerza Ud. en la universidad? ¿A qué hora

prefiere almorzar? ¿Dónde sirven la mejor comida cerca de la universidad? ¿Sirven pizza? ¿A qué hora empiezan a servir el almuerzo? ¿Empieza Ud. su tarea antes o después de cenar? ¿Vuelve Ud. a la universidad por la noche para estudiar en la biblioteca? ¿A qué hora cierran la biblioteca? ¿Piensa Ud. estudiar mucho esta noche o puede descansar? ¿Piensa Ud. volver a estudiar aquí el semestre que viene? ¿Cuándo empieza el semestre que viene? ¿Piensa Ud. tomar otra clase de español? ¿Qué otras clases piensa tomar? ¿Quiere estudiar otra lengua?

Suggestion. Have students prepare a conversation in pairs in which one talks about plans for this weekend and invites the other to do something. The person invited cannot go at the suggested time, so they discuss and decide on an alternate time.

VOCABULARIO

TEMA ④ ¿Qué están haciendo ahora?

¿Qué están haciendo en la fiesta?

Está tocando la guitarra y cantando.

Está sacando una foto.

Están oyendo música y bailando.

Están viendo un vídeo.

Están jugando a los videojuegos.

Están tomando y comiendo./ Están hablando y contando chistes.

Están sirviendo la comida (papitas fritas, pizza, galletas, pastel y helado.)

Está durmiendo.

¡Ojo!

In this **Tema,** you will learn a new verb form ending with **-ando** or **-iendo.** Note how it is used here to say what someone *is doing*.

papitas fritas *potato chips* **galletas** *cookies* **pastel** *cake* **helado** *ice cream* **un chiste** *a joke*

4-23 ¿Qué tal la fiesta? ¿Es una fiesta divertida o aburrida si los invitados están haciendo estas cosas? ¿Qué opina usted?

Modelo Todos están hablando.
Es una fiesta divertida.

1. Nadie está hablando.
2. Están jugando a la charada.
3. Están oyendo música y todos están bailando.
4. Están escuchando una ópera.
5. Todos están jugando a los videojuegos.
6. Están viendo vídeos y todos están durmiendo.
7. Todos están contando chistes.
8. Están cantando karaoke.

4-24 ¿Dónde están? ¿Dónde está su amigo si está haciendo estas cosas?

Modelo Está comprando un libro.
Está en la librería.

Hay muchas exposiciones en el Museo del Prado de Madrid.

1. Está levantando pesas.
2. Está nadando.
3. Está durmiendo.
4. Está asistiendo a una clase.
5. Está tomando el sol.
6. Está visitando una exposición de arte.
7. Está esquiando.
8. Está tomando una copa con los amigos.
9. Está viendo una obra de teatro.
10. Está viendo una película.

P **4-25 Entrevista.** Entreviste a un/a compañero/a de clase con estas preguntas.

1. ¿Vas a muchas fiestas? ¿Haces muchas fiestas en tu casa o apartamento? ¿Eres tímido/a en grupos grandes? ¿Qué te gusta hacer en las fiestas? ¿Qué no te gusta hacer? ¿Cuentas muchos chistes? ¿Sacas muchas fotos?
2. ¿Comes mucha pizza? ¿Cuál es la mejor pizzería cerca de aquí? ¿Cuántas veces al mes comes pizza? ¿Almuerzas o cenas con más frecuencia en una pizzería?
3. ¿Tocas la guitarra o el piano? ¿Te gusta la música salsa?

P **Conversaciones.** Dos amigos hablan por teléfono. En parejas, lean su conversación. Luego, cambien la conversación para invitar a su pareja a hacer algo.

— ¿Aló?
— ¿Puedo hablar con María, por favor?
— Soy yo. ¿Eres tú, Carlos?
— Hola María, ¿cómo estás?
— Bien, Carlos. ¿Y tú?
— Bien. ¿Estás ocupada? ¿Qué estás haciendo?
— Nada en especial. ¿Por qué?
— Mis amigos y yo estamos en el café El Rincón y después vamos a una fiesta a la casa de mi primo. ¿Quieres ir con nosotros?
— Sí, cómo no. Llego en veinte minutos.
— Está bien. Hasta luego.
— Chau.

Continuation for 4-23. *¿Qué tal la fiesta?*
1. Están hablando de política. 2. Están jugando al vóleibol. 3. Están jugando al Scrabble. 4. Están viendo el Superbowl en la tele. 5. Todos están haciendo yoga. 6. Están tocando música clásica. 7. Están jugando a las cartas. 8. Están leyendo poemas.

Follow-up for 4-24. *¿Dónde están?*
¿Qué hora es si está haciendo estas cosas los días de clase? *Modelo:* Está desayunando. > *Son entre las siete y media y las ocho de la mañana. / Nunca desayuno los días de clase.* 1. Está asistiendo a su primera clase. 2. Está almorzando. 3. Está haciendo su tarea. 4. Está trabajando. 5. Está durmiendo una siesta. 6. Está haciendo ejercicio. 7. Está viendo la televisión. 8. Está cenando.

AUDIO ¡A escuchar!

Ahora, escuchen otra conversación telefónica entre dos amigos. ¿Dónde están? ¿Qué están haciendo?

Supplemental activity. En las fiestas, ¿con qué frecuencia hace Ud. estas cosas: (casi) siempre, a veces o (casi) nunca? *(bailar toda la noche, cantar, tocar la guitarra, tomar una copa, comer pizza, comer mucho pastel, galletas o helado, comer mucho, tomar mucho, jugar a los videojuegos, jugar a las cartas, contar chistes, escuchar chistes, sacar fotos, dormir, oír música clásica, ver vídeos, volver tarde de la fiesta a casa, estar enfermo/a al día siguiente)*

GRAMÁTICA

Expresar acciones en curso: el presente progresivo

Para averiguar

1. What is the ending of the present participle of **-ar** verbs in Spanish? of **-er** and **-ir** verbs? These endings correspond to what verb ending in English?
2. Which verb meaning *to be* do you use with present participles to say what is happening?
3. Are there stem changes in present participles of **-ar, -er,** or **-ir** verbs? What do **o** and **e** become?
4. When does the **i** of the **-iendo** ending change to **y**?
5. What are two cases where the present progressive is used in English, but not in Spanish?

Suggestion. You may wish to point out to students that present participles cannot be used as nouns in Spanish, and that you use infinitives instead: *Ver es creer.* (Seeing is believing.)

Supplemental activity. Write verbs such as those that follow on slips of paper. A student draws one and mimes the verb. The rest of the class says what he/she is doing using the present progressive. *(jugar al tenis, jugar al baloncesto, jugar al ajedrez, hacer ejercicio, levantar pesas, dormir, servir comida, comer, beber, escuchar música, escribir, leer, nadar, cantar, esquiar, correr, bailar, abrir la puerta, cerrar la puerta, ver la televisión, hablar por teléfono, fumar, comprar algo, tocar la guitarra, tocar el piano, limpiar la casa)*

Use the present progressive to say what someone is in the process of doing at a particular moment. The present progressive is composed of a conjugated form of **estar** followed by the present participle, which is the equivalent of the *-ing* form of the verb in English. The present participle is formed by replacing the **-ar** ending of infinitives with **-ando,** and **-er** or **-ir** with **-iendo.**

hablar → **hablando**	¿Quién está hablando?	*Who is talking?*
comer → **comiendo**	Estamos comiendo.	*We're eating.*
escribir → **escribiendo**	¿Qué estás escribiendo?	*What are you writing?*

There is no stem change in the present participle of **-ar** and **-er** stem-changing verbs.

almorzar → **almorzando**	¿Estás almorzando?	*Are you having lunch?*
nevar → **nevando**	Está nevando.	*It's snowing.*
perder → **perdiendo**	Estamos perdiendo.	*We're losing.*
llover → **lloviendo**	Está lloviendo.	*It's raining.*

Stem-changing **-ir** verbs have the following changes in the present participle.

o → u: dormir → **durmiendo**	Todos están durmiendo.	*Everyone is sleeping.*
e → i: servir → **sirviendo**	Están sirviendo la comida.	*They're serving the food.*

Other stem-changing **-ir** verbs you have seen include: **decir (diciendo), pedir (pidendo), preferir (prefiriendo), repetir (repitiendo),** and **venir (viniendo).**

The initial **i** of the **-iendo** ending changes to **y** when it falls between two vowels.

leer → **leyendo**	¿Qué estás leyendo?	*What are you reading?*

This also occurs with **oir (oyendo)** and **creer (creyendo).**

In Spanish, the present progressive is rarely used with verbs that indicate *coming* and *going*. The simple present tense is used instead.

Vamos con ustedes.	*We're going with you.*
Vienen ahora.	*They're coming now.*

Do not use the present progressive to express future actions as you do in English. Use the immediate future (**ir a** + infinitive) instead.

Voy a trabajar este fin de semana.	*I'm working this weekend.*

4-26 **En el centro estudiantil.** ¿Está haciendo alguien las siguientes cosas?

> Modelo   leer el periódico
> **Sí, alguien** (*someone*) **está leyendo el periódico.**
> leer un libro de texto
> **No, nadie** (*nobody*) **está leyendo un libro de texto.**

1. comer
2. dormir
3. hablar por teléfono
4. jugar al ajedrez
5. escuchar música

6. ver la televisión
7. abrir la ventana
8. escribir algo
9. usar una computadora

P **4-27** **Una fiesta.** Un amigo da una fiesta. ¿Qué están haciendo todos? Complete las oraciones con un verbo lógico como en el modelo.

> Modelo   Mi amigo **está sirviendo** la comida.

1. Unos amigos y yo… un vídeo.
2. Yo… una cola.
3. Dos novios… un tango.
4. Nadie… por teléfono.
5. Alguien… el piano y… canciones.
6. El gato… la comida de un invitado.
7. Unos invitados… a los videojuegos.

4-28 **¿Dónde estás?** Usted está en los siguientes lugares y alguien lo/la llama (*calls you*) a su celular. En parejas, hagan conversaciones como en el modelo.

> Modelo   en un club nocturno
> E1: **¿Dónde estás?**
> E2: **Estoy en un club nocturno.**
> E1: **¿Qué estás haciendo?**
> E2: **Estoy bailando con mis amigos.**

1. en un café
2. en la playa
3. en la biblioteca
4. en el parque
5. en una fiesta
6. en el centro comercial

7. en el teatro
8. en el gimnasio
9. en una librería
10. en un restaurante
11. en el estadio
12. en el museo

Follow-up for 4-26. *En el centro estudiantil.* ¿Quién está haciendo estas cosas ahora en nuestra clase? *Modelo:* comiendo > *Todos estamos comiendo. Mónica y Lisa están comiendo. Nadie está comiendo.* (hablando, durmiendo, escuchando las preguntas, escuchando las respuestas, haciendo las preguntas, escribiendo, comiendo, tomando café, buscando algo, abriendo su libro, leyendo, fumando, mirando al (a la) profesor(a), haciendo este ejercicio, diciendo algo)

Suggestion. Explain to students how present participles can be used without *estar* and ask the following questions. 1. ¿Aprende Ud. mejor haciendo su tarea solo/a o con otros estudiantes (escuchando en clase o leyendo las explicaciones del libro, trabajando en parejas o trabajando con toda la clase, haciendo tarea en casa o practicando en clase, hablando inglés a veces en clase o hablando español todo el tiempo)? 2. ¿Pasa Ud. más tiempo oyendo música o viendo la televisión (hablando por teléfono o escribiendo correos electrónicos, leyendo libros o practicando deportes, leyendo revistas o leyendo libros de texto, durmiendo o estudiando, trabajando o estudiando, limpiando la casa o trabajando en el jardín, desayunando o cenando)? 3. En las fiestas, ¿pasa Ud. más tiempo... (bailando o comiendo, contando chistes o hablando de política, cantando o escuchando música, jugando a las cartas o tocando música)? 4. En la playa, ¿pasa Ud. más tiempo... (tomando el sol o nadando, jugando o durmiendo, nadando o hablando con los amigos, haciendo esquí acuático o tomando el sol)?

TEMA ⑤

VOCABULARIO
¿Quieres ir al café?

¡Ojo!

Use the masculine articles **el** and **un** with feminine nouns beginning with a stressed **a**, as with **un agua**. Adjectives modifying such nouns will be in the feminine form.

El agua está frí**a**.

Note. More foods and beverages are taught in *Capítulo 8*.

Supplemental activities. A. ¿Prefiere Ud. estas bebidas con hielo, del tiempo (*at room temperature*) o calientes? *(el té, el café, el vino tinto, los refrescos, el agua, el jugo de naranja, la cerveza, el chocolate, la limonada)* **B.** ¿Tengo hambre o tengo sed si digo las siguientes cosas?
1. Quiero agua mineral, por favor.
2. Un bocadillo de jamón, por favor.
3. Para mí, una cerveza bien fría, por favor. 4. Prefiero un té con mucho hielo. 5. Quiero una ensalada, por favor. 6. Una cola, por favor. 7. Quiero un flan, por favor. 8. Tengo ganas de comer helado de vainilla. 9. Una limonada con mucho hielo, por favor. 10. ¿Tienen pastel de queso?
C. ¿Cuál es mejor para la salud (*health*)? ¿el jugo de naranja o el café? ¿el vino o el agua mineral? ¿el jugo de naranja o los refrescos? ¿la cerveza o la limonada? ¿la ensalada o la pizza? ¿el helado o los bocadillos? **D.** Give students the words *cafeína* and *alcohol* and ask: ¿*Tiene cafeína, alcohol o azúcar?* (*el té, la cerveza, el jugo de naranja, la limonada, el café, la cola, el chocolate, el vino tinto, el agua mineral, el vino blanco*) **E.** Quiero beber algo frío. ¿Pido una cerveza o un vino tinto (un café o un refresco, un vino tinto o un vino blanco, un té con hielo o sin hielo, un agua mineral o un café)? **F.** Have students complete the following statements with a drink name. 1. En el desayuno, me gusta tomar... 2. En una fiesta, generalmente, tomo... 3. Después de hacer ejercicio, me gusta tomar... 4. Con los amigos en un café, prefiero... 5. Casi nunca tomo... 6. Mi bebida favorita es...

¿Tienes sed? ¿Quieres tomar algo?

un refresco

una limonada con hielo

un café con leche (crema, azúcar)

un té o un chocolate caliente

una cerveza

un jugo de naranja

un vino (tinto/blanco)

un agua mineral

¿Tienes hambre? ¿Quieres comer algo?

un trozo de pizza

un bocadillo (de queso, de jamón)

un trozo de pastel

una ensalada

un flan

un helado de chocolate/vainilla

---

tener sed *to be thirsty* **la leche** *milk* **el azúcar** *sugar* **tener hambre** *to be hungry*

4-29 **¿Tienes hambre o sed?** Pregúntele a otro/a estudiante si tiene hambre o sed. Luego pregúntele cuál de las comidas o bebidas prefiere.

> Modelo   E1: **¿Tienes sed? ¿Quieres una limonada o un café?**
> E2: — **Prefiero un café. / No quiero nada de beber, gracias.**

1.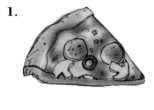

2.

3.

4.

5.

6.

Suggestion for 4-30. ¿Y Ud.? Give students the noun *la cena* and have them change the sentences to describe their favorite restaurant for dinner.

4-30 **¿Y Ud.?** Lea cada oración y conteste **cierto** o **falso.** Cambie las palabras en letra cursiva de las oraciones falsas para describir el restaurante donde prefiere almorzar.

1. Almuerzo con frecuencia en el restaurante *Golden Steak House* porque *está cerca de mi trabajo.*
2. Almuerzo allí *cinco o seis veces al mes.*
3. Sirven *de todo: comida norteamericana, mexicana, italiana, china, ensaladas, bocadillos y hamburguesas.*
4. Empiezan a servir el almuerzo a *las once de la mañana.*
5. Cierran a *las diez de la noche.*
6. Almuerzo *con mi mejor amiga* en ese restaurante con frecuencia.
7. Prefiero almorzar a *las once de la mañana.*
8. Para beber, pido *agua* generalmente. Nunca pido *un refresco.*
9. Como ensalada *a veces.*
10. Generalmente, después de almorzar, quiero *dormir una siesta.*

Supplemental questions. 1. En la cafetería universitaria, ¿sirven café (cerveza, jugo de naranja, vino)? 2. ¿De qué hora a qué hora sirven el desayuno (el almuerzo, la cena)? 3. ¿Necesita Ud. tomar café por la mañana? ¿Puede dormir después de tomar café? ¿Prefiere Ud. el café con leche, con crema, con azúcar o sin nada? 4. ¿Cuál es su refresco favorito? ¿Prefiere Ud. los refrescos con azúcar o los dietéticos? 5. ¿Prefiere Ud. el té con hielo o caliente? ¿con azúcar o sin azúcar? ¿Toma Ud. más té o más café? 6. ¿Bebe Ud. vino? ¿Prefiere el vino blanco o el vino tinto? 7. ¿Tiene Ud. hambre o sed ahora? ¿Qué tiene ganas de comer (beber)? ¿Almuerza (Desayuna, Cena) Ud. antes de clase? 8. ¿En qué clases tiene Ud. hambre o sed a veces? ¿A qué hora son?

Conversaciones. En grupos de tres, lean la siguiente conversación en un café entre un **mesero** y dos amigos. Luego, cambien la conversación, pidiendo sus bebidas favoritas.

MESERO:	Buenas noches. ¿Qué desean tomar?
JUAN:	Una limonada para mí, por favor.
MARCO:	Yo quiero un capuchino, por favor.
MESERO:	Una limonada y un capuchino. **¿Algo más?**
JUAN:	Nada para mí, gracias.
MARCO:	Nada para mí **tampoco.**
MESERO:	Vuelvo en un momento con sus bebidas.

AUDIO **¡A escuchar!**

Ahora, escuchen otra conversación en una fiesta. ¿Qué hay de beber y comer? ¿Qué desea la invitada?

9. ¿Come Ud. más pizza o más ensalada? ¿más pastel o más helado? ¿Prefiere Ud. el helado de chocolate o de vainilla?

---

un/a mesero/a server, waiter   **¿Algo más?** Anything else?   **tampoco** neither

GRAMÁTICA

Expresar negación: *algo/nada, alguien/nadie, también/tampoco, alguno/ninguno*

Unlike English, Spanish has double negatives. When the negative expressions below follow the verb, **no** must be placed before the verb. **No** is not required when negative expressions precede the verb.

AFIRMATIVO		NEGATIVO	
algo	*something*	**nada**	*nothing, (not) anything*
alguien, todos	*someone, everyone*	**nadie**	*nobody, (not) anyone*
alguno/a(s)	*some, any*	**ninguno/a**	*none, not any*
también	*also, too*	**tampoco**	*neither*
y, o	*and, or*	**ni... ni...**	*neither... nor...*
siempre, a veces	*always, sometimes*	**nunca**	*never*

— ¿Con quién hablas?
— **No** hablo con **nadie.**
— Entonces, ¿quién está hablando?
— **Nadie** habla. Es la televisión.

— *With whom are you speaking?*
— *I'm not talking with anyone.*
— *Then who's talking?*
— *Nobody's talking. It's the TV.*

— ¿Tienes **algo** para el cumpleaños de tu novia?
— No, **no** tengo **nada.**

— *Do you have something for your girlfriend's birthday?*
— *No, I don't have anything.*

Alguno and **ninguno** must agree in number and gender with nouns they describe. They become **algún** and **ningún** before masculine singular nouns. **Ninguno/a** is usually used in the singular, even as response to the plural forms **algunos/as.**

— ¿Tienes **algunos** amigos aquí?
— No, no tengo **ningún** amigo aquí.

— *Do you have some friends here?*
— *No, I don't have any friends here.*

4-31 En una fiesta. Usted está en una fiesta y alguien le hace las siguientes preguntas. Complete las preguntas con una palabra lógica de la lista.

> algunos   alguien   o   algo   y   siempre   también

1. ¿Estás solo/a o estás con _____?
2. ¿Tienes _____ amigos en la fiesta?
3. ¿Tienes hambre? ¿Quieres comer _____? ¿Tienes sed _____?
4. ¿Te gusta el vino blanco _____ el vino tinto?
5. ¿_____ vas a muchas fiestas?
6. ¿Te gusta tocar la guitarra _____ cantar?

Ahora conteste cada pregunta con el antónimo negativo de las palabras de la lista.

4-32 **¿Cierto o falso?** ¿Qué pasa hoy en el parque? Lea cada oración y conteste **cierto** o **falso.** Corrija las oraciones falsas.

1. Nadie está corriendo.
2. Hay algunos hombres jugando al ajedrez.
3. Hay algunas personas tomando el sol.
4. Nadie está durmiendo.
5. No hay ni perros ni gatos en el parque.
6. Alguien está jugando al baloncesto y al fútbol también.
7. Algunas personas están almorzando.
8. No hay ningún árbol en el parque.

4-33 **¡Al contrario!** Un esposo se queja de las fiestas de su cuñada (*sister-in-law*) y su esposa dice lo contrario. ¿Qué dice la esposa? Use el antónimo de las palabras en letra cursiva.

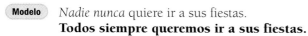 *Nadie nunca* quiere ir a sus fiestas.
Todos siempre queremos ir a sus fiestas.

1. *Nunca* hay *nadie* interesante en las fiestas.
2. *Alguien siempre* cuenta historias aburridas.
3. *Nunca* hay *nada* bueno de comer *tampoco.*
4. *Nunca* hay *ni* comida buena *ni* música interesante.
5. *Todos siempre* estamos aburridos.
6. *Nadie* habla *ni* baila *tampoco.*
7. *Siempre* hay *algunos* problemas.
8. *Todos siempre* salen temprano de las fiestas.

℗ **4-34** **Entrevista.** Entreviste a un/a compañero/a de clase.

1. ¿Tienes algunos planes para este fin de semana? ¿Tienes alguna idea de qué tiempo va a hacer este fin de semana? ¿Va a nevar o va a llover? ¿Qué piensas hacer? ¿Vas a salir con alguien el viernes? ¿el sábado?
2. ¿Quieres ir al cine este fin de semana? ¿Tienes ganas de ver alguna película en especial? ¿Vas a comer en un restaurante? ¿Quieres comer en algún restaurante en especial? ¿Quieres ir de compras? ¿Necesitas comprar algo en particular? ¿Quieres ir a alguna tienda en especial?
3. ¿Tienes algo que hacer el domingo o no tienes que hacer nada en especial? ¿Trabajas el domingo por la mañana o por la tarde? ¿Viene alguien a tu casa el domingo? ¿Vas a preparar algo especial de comer?

Ⓖ **4-35** **Hoy en clase.** En grupos, usen todas las expresiones afirmativas y negativas de la página anterior para escribir oraciones describiendo su clase en este momento.

Modelo **Algunos estudiantes no están en clase hoy.**
Ningún estudiante está durmiendo.
Todos estamos trabajando en grupos. Alguien está…

Supplemental activities. A. Have students briefly look around the room. Then have them close their eyes and ask them questions such as the following: *¿Hay algunos papeles (libros, cuadernos, lápices) en mi escritorio / en la mesa de (name a student)? ¿Hay algunas palabras (preguntas) en la pizarra? ¿Hay algunos estudiantes detrás (delante) de usted? ¿Hay algunos estudiantes ausentes (absent) hoy? ¿Hay algunos estudiantes con el libro cerrado? ¿sin libro?* **B.** Name a street with some businesses or public places on it near your campus and give true / false statements such the following. *Hay algunos restaurantes en la calle Buena Vista. > Cierto. Hay algunos restaurantes. / Falso, no hay ningún restaurante en la calle Buena Vista.* **C.** 1. *¿Vive Ud. con alguien o no vive con nadie?* 2. *¿Viene Ud. a la universidad con alguien o no viene con nadie?* 3. *¿Come Ud. algo antes de salir para la universidad o no come nada?* 4. *¿Trae Ud. algo de comer a la universidad o no trae nada?* 5. *¿Prefiere Ud. almorzar en algún restaurante en particular o no tiene ningún restaurante favorito para almorzar?* 6. *¿Almuerza (Cena) Ud. con alguien hoy o no almuerza (cena) con nadie?* 7. *¿Viene alguien a su casa esta noche o no viene nadie?* 8. *¿Va a salir Ud. con alguien este fin de semana o no va a salir con nadie?* 9. *¿Hace Ud. algo en especial este fin de semana o no hace nada en especial?* 10. *¿Va Ud. a alguna fiesta este fin de semana o no va a ninguna fiesta?* 11. *¿Quiere ir a alguna exposición este fin de semana o no hay ninguna exposición interesante?*

En portada

REVISTA CULTURAL

Note: Have students complete the *Antes de leer,* *Reading strategies,* and *Ahora Ud.* activities before reading this article.

LOS HISPANOS DE ESTADOS UNIDOS EN SUS RATOS LIBRES

VIVE.com

Mi correo
Mis fotos
Mi música
Buscador

Música   Cine y Televisión   Gente   Lo último   De viajes   Deportes

Música
Apoteosis hace su aparición en la escena musical con su nuevo álbum Radical. Apoteosis presentará su nuevo trabajo de rock de la frontera en una gira de conciertos por el sur de Estados Unidos. Visita su página web www.apoteosis.com para conocer más de su música y para comprar boletos para los conciertos.

Cine y Televisión
Panavisión presenta su nueva serie Entre amigas, que cuenta las historias de un grupo de jóvenes profesionales mejicanas, Guadalupe, Verónica y Catalina, que empiezan su vida como mujeres independientes en Los Angeles. Dificultades en el trabajo, líos amorosos, diferencias culturales, son algunos de los ingredientes que aseguran el éxito de esta nueva serie que se emitirá los jueves a las 8.00 de la noche.

Lo último en moda
Rosas, violetas, berenjena, son los tonos que marcan la nueva temporada. Los grandes modistos presentan su colección otoño-invierno en la Pasarela Cervantes, donde se reúnen expertos en moda de todo el mundo. No te pierdas las mejores fotos del evento.

De viajes
No dejes escapar las ofertas que Viajes de primera te ofrece este otoño. Playas, turismo de aventura, viajes culturales, escapadas románticas.... Todo lo que quieras al alcance de tu bolsillo. Boletos de avión, tren y autobús. ¡Ofertas especiales para estudiantes! Visita la página web de esta nueva agencia de viajes en línea y haz la reserva para tus próximas vacaciones. Precios especiales para grupos. ¡Viaja de primera!

La popularización de Internet **influye** ciertamente en los hábitos de **ocio** de la población hispana de Estados Unidos. Un estudio reciente indica que 14 millones de latinos de Estados Unidos están conectados a **la red,** número mayor al de los usuarios de Internet de México, España, Argentina, Francia y Colombia, y es similar a los de **Alemania.**

La comunicación familiar es un aspecto muy importante de la cultura hispana. En la sociedad tecnológica de hoy, los hispanos usan Internet para comunicarse con su familia por correo electrónico y por **mensajería instantánea.**

En Internet jóvenes y adultos latinos se informan de las **noticias** nacionales e internacionales, **hacen compras en línea,** escuchan música, **descargan archivos** MP3 y buscan vídeo clips de las nuevas películas o de las nuevas **canciones de moda.**

Internet en casa.

Toda la música en la red.

En línea.

---

influye *influences*   **ocio** *free time*   **la red** *Internet*   **Alemania** *Germany*   **mensajería instantánea** *instant messaging*   **noticias** *news*   **hacen compras en línea** *shop on line*   **descargan archivos** *download files*   **canciones de moda** *popular songs*

Tarde de novela.

Ir al cine y ver la televisión son otros pasatiempos de los hispanos de Estados Unidos. Los programas de televisión preferidos por **la audiencia familiar** y adolescente son **las novelas,** un género típicamente hispano que presenta dramas de intriga, **traición** y romance.

Los deportes son una actividad de tiempo libre muy común entre los hispanos. Como resultado del contacto con la cultura norteamericana, el béisbol es hoy el deporte más popular entre los hispanos de Estados Unidos, **seguido por** el *soccer*, y el fútbol americano. ESPN es el primer canal estadounidense con información deportiva en español dirigida al público hispano.

¡A salvo!

Antes de leer

Piensen en cómo la tecnología influye nuestra sociedad actual y nuestros hábitos de ocio (*free time*). ¿Qué pasatiempos nuevos tienen los jóvenes y los adultos derivados del uso de las tecnologías?

Reading strategies: Using visual aids. Pictures, graphics, drawings, and other visual materials play a vital role in the active learning of a foreign language. Visual aids facilitate the overall understanding of a text by providing clues about the main topics and situations presented in the piece. When reading in a foreign language, take into account the non-textual information accompanying the passage and allow yourself to gather information from the visuals.

P **4-36 Ahora Ud.** Miren las fotos que acompañan al artículo y expliquen qué actividades están haciendo las personas que aparecen en ellas.

P **4-37 Una página web.** Examinen con atención la página web que aparece con el artículo e indiquen las secciones que se mencionan. ¿Les gusta el diseño de la página? ¿Qué les gusta y qué no les gusta?

Después de leer

4-38 En sus ratos libres… Indique las actividades que hacen los hispanos en sus ratos libres según la información presentada en el artículo.

> Modelo   **En sus ratos libres muchos hispanos hablan con su familia por correo electrónico.**

P **4-39 ¿Y Uds.?** Entreviste a su compañero/a sobre las actividades que él/ella hace con sus familiares o con sus amigos en su tiempo libre. Puede usar estas preguntas y otras de su creación. Después, presente a la clase un informe con los datos (*information*) de su compañero/a.

¿Practicas algún deporte? ¿Qué deporte practicas?

¿Usas mucho Internet? ¿Qué te gusta hacer en Internet?

¿Haces viajes con tu familia y/o con tus amigos? ¿Con qué frecuencia?

la audiencia familiar *family audiences*   **las novelas** *soap operas*   **traición** *betrayal*   **seguido por** *followed by*

De puertas abiertas a la comunidad

VIDEO CENTROS SOCIALES COMUNITARIOS

4-40 Entrando en materia. ¿Cuál cree que es la labor de un centro comunitario? ¿Qué actividades cree que organiza? ¿Hay algún centro comunitario en su área?

El sentimiento de comunidad es muy **fuerte** entre los hispanos y hay muchas personas dedicadas a servir a esta comunidad **a través de** las artes y otras actividades sociales y educativas. En este segmento van a conocer a Jorge Merced, director del Teatro Pregones, **comprometido** a llevar piezas teatrales en español a la audiencia hispana.

　　También van a escuchar a Jane Delgado, subdirectora del centro comunitario Abrons Art Center, parte del Henry Street Settlement en la ciudad de Nueva York, que ofrece programas educativos a miembros de **todas las edades.** Jane **siente** una gran pasión por las artes y está muy dedicada a las labores que el centro realiza para la comunidad. La comunidad hispana puede encontrar en estos centros **un espacio de encuentro** y **apoyo.**

4-41 ¿Qué están haciendo? Observe las imágenes que abren el segmento de vídeo y describa el ambiente y las personas que aparecen en estas imágenes.

4-42 El Abrons Art Center. Escuche con atención la información que Jane Delgado ofrece sobre el Abrons Art Center y complete las siguientes afirmaciones con la opción adecuada en cada caso.

1. El Abrons Art Center está situado en...
  a. Manhattan.
  b. el Harlem.
  c. Queens.
  d. Lower East Side.

2. La misión del centro es...
  a. política.
  b. educativa.
  c. comercial.
  d. artística.

3. El centro promueve...
  a. la enseñanza del baile, la música, el teatro y las artes plásticas.
  b. el desarrollo de las ciencias.
  c. el desarrollo de la creatividad de los jóvenes.
  d. la enseñanza de la tecnología.

---

fuerte *strong*　**a través de** *through the use of*　**comprometido** *committed*　**todas las edades** *all ages*
siente *feels*　**un espacio de encuentro** *a meeting place*　**apoyo** *support*

4. Las personas que van al centro son...
- **a.** sólo mujeres.
- **b.** sólo hombres.
- **c.** adolescentes.
- (**d.**) desde niños hasta ancianos.

5. El centro recibe...
- **a.** sólo a estudiantes del vecindario (*neighborhood*).
- **b.** sólo a estudiantes hispanos.
- (**c.**) a estudiantes de todos los condados (*counties*) de Nueva York.
- **d.** sólo a estudiantes afroamericanos.

4-43 Este año... ¿Por qué es importante este año para el Abrons Art Center? ¿Qué va a celebrar? ¿Cómo lo van a celebrar?

Answers for 4-43. *Este año...* Este año el Abrons Art Center va a celebrar 30 años. Van a tener un proyecto titulado ¿*Qué es la casa?*, también una feria artesanal, con varios artesanos compartiendo su arte y su cultura.

4-44 En los ratos libres. ¿Qué opina del trabajo realizado en los centros sociales? Mencione los programas de educación y ocio (*leisure*) que ofrecen los distintos centros comunitarios. ¿Son similares en los distintos centros? ¿Participa usted o conoce (*do you know*) a alguien involucrado (*involved*) en algún centro comunitario? Describa esa participación.

4-45 El Teatro Pregones. Escuche las palabras de Jorge Merced, director del Teatro Pregones, y determine si las siguientes afirmaciones son ciertas o falsas. Corrija las que sean falsas.

Answers for 4-45. *El Teatro Pregones.* 1. el Teatro Pregones está celebrando 25 años de labor 3. la misión del Teatro Pregones es presentar teatro contemporáneo de raíz puertorriqueña y latina

	Cierto	Falso
1. El Teatro Pregones va a celebrar diez años de trabajo continuado en Estados Unidos.	☐	☒
2. El Teatro Pregones es fundado en 1979 como una compañía itinerante.	☒	☐
3. La misión del Teatro Pregones es crear y presentar teatro clásico en español.	☐	☒
4. Muchas de las piezas que representa el Teatro Pregones son puertorriqueñas.	☒	☐
5. El Teatro Pregones viaja a pueblos y universidades, llevando el teatro a lugares donde no siempre llega.	☒	☐

G **4-46 ¡A escena!** Observen con atención la fotografía de una de las representaciones (*performances*) del Teatro Pregones y Jorge Merced. Describan lo que ven, lo que están haciendo las personas, la atmósfera de la función.

Escapadas

PANAMÁ, ZONA FRANCA

La República de Panamá, en Centroamérica, es **país** vecino de Colombia, al este, y Costa Rica, al oeste. Panamá, colonia española hasta 1821, se independiza de Colombia en 1903, año en el que Panamá y Estados Unidos firman un acuerdo para la construcción del Canal de Panamá.

Vista aérea del Canal de Panamá.

El Canal de Panamá es una parte esencial en la economía del país y del comercio **mundial.**
Panamá es hoy la segunda zona franca más grande del mundo. El turista encuentra allí innumerables tiendas libres de impuestos. La magnitud del canal puede admirarse desde **las esclusas** de Miraflores, al noreste de la ciudad de Panamá, **desde** donde se observan **los barcos** pasar por el canal.

Las esclusas de Miraflores en el Canal de Panamá.

El tráfico internacional de **pasajeros** y **mercancías** hace de los panameños gente muy cosmopolita, con un pasado muy rico, **mezcla** de tradiciones españolas, africanas y también orientales y europeas **traídas** por los trabajadores del canal.

Panamá posee, además de una moderna infraestructura, **una** gran **belleza** natural. La biodiversidad del país es uno de los atractivos principales para **los amantes** del ecoturismo, con más de 5 millones de acres de **selvas tropicales** y parques naturales y 944 especies de **aves.**

Selva de Los Quetzales, Guadalupe, Panamá.

Las islas de Panamá son especialmente **bellas.** El Archipiélago de San Blas, a veinte minutos en avión de la ciudad de Panamá, es **la tierra** de los indios cunas, que aún hoy preservan sus tradiciones **milenarias.**

Madre cuna y su hija cosiendo una mola, Archipiélago de San Blas, Panamá.

Isla Taboga, o Isla de las Flores, a una hora en barco de la ciudad de Panamá, con su **hermosa** y serena playa y **su bosque de lluvia alberga** una de las colonias de pelícanos marrones más grandes de Latinoamérica. Allí llega Pizarro desde Perú en 1524.

Las Islas de Bocas del Toro son un archipiélago tropical descubierto por Colón en 1502, con hermosas playas y **arrecifes de coral,** fascinantes para **los aficionados al buceo** y al esnórquel.

---

zona franca *free trade zone*   **país** *country*   **mundial** *world(wide)*   **las esclusas** *the locks*   **desde** *from*
los barcos *ships*   **pasajeros** *passengers*   **mercancías** *merchandise*   **mezcla** *a mixture*   **traídas** *brought*
una belleza *a beauty*   **los amantes** *lovers*   **selvas tropicales** *tropical forests*   **aves** *birds*   **bellas** *beautiful*
la tierra *land*   **milenarias** *a thousand years old*   **hermosa** *beautiful*   **su bosque de lluvia** *its rainforest*
alberga *is home to*   **arrecifes de coral** *coral reefs*   **los aficionados al buceo** *diving fans*

4-47 ¿Qué sabes de Panamá? Seleccione la respuesta o respuestas correctas de las opciones presentadas.

1. Panamá es hoy…
   a. una colonia norteamericana.
   b. un territorio colombiano.
   c. parte del estado español.
   d. un país independiente.

2. Panamá es famoso por…
   a. sus actividades comerciales.
   b. sus museos de arte moderno.
   c. sus montañas.
   d. su biodiversidad natural.

3. El Canal de Panamá…
   a. es una parte esencial en la economía del país y del comercio mundial.
   b. no tiene mucha actividad comercial.
   c. es un parque natural.
   d. es administrado y mantenido por la República de Panamá.

4. En Panamá el turista puede…
   a. practicar el buceo y el esnórquel en las aguas del Mar Caribe.
   b. esquiar en las montañas.
   c. observar las distintas especies de aves.
   d. pasear por hermosas playas.

Isla de Nia Tupu, Archipiélago de San Blas, Panamá.

4-48 Negativas. Complete la siguiente conversación entre dos amigas utilizando las estructuras para expresar negación presentadas en el capítulo.

> nadie   ni... ni...   ningún   nada   nunca

En un cibercafé….

— Hola, Graciela, qué sorpresa. ¿Quieres tomar algo?

— No, gracias, no quiero tomar (1) ___nada___. Voy a usar el Internet. Estoy preparando un viaje a la ciudad de Panamá en febrero.

—¿En serio? ¡Qué bien! ¿Tienes algunos amigos en Panamá?

— No, no tengo (2) ___ningún___ amigo allí.

— Entonces, ¿con quién vas?

— No voy con (3) ___nadie___. Voy sola. Y tú, ¿siempre haces viajes con otras personas?

— Sí, la verdad es que (4) ___nunca___ hago viajes sola. ¿Y vas a tener un guía (*guide*) para visitar la ciudad?

— No, (5) ___ni___ voy a tener guía, (6) ___ni___ voy a hacer excursiones de grupo. Quiero descubrir la ciudad con mis propios (*own*) ojos.

4-49 Un viaje a Panamá… Busque más información cultural sobre Panamá y su gente en Internet y prepare un plan de viaje para una semana en el país con varios amigos. Utilice las estructuras para hacer planes y expresar preferencias de este capítulo.

Octubre

1	Lunes	Vamos a llegar al aeropuerto internacional de Tocumén.
2	Martes	
3	Miércoles	
4	Jueves	
5	Viernes	
6	Sábado	
7	Domingo	

Avenida Balboa. Ciudad de Panamá.

En palabras de...

ENCUESTA DE VIAJES Y VACACIONES

¿Qué prefieren hacer los estudiantes en sus períodos de vacaciones? Prepare una encuesta (*survey*) para obtener información sobre las preferencias de sus compañeros en sus períodos de descanso (*breaks*) de las clases.

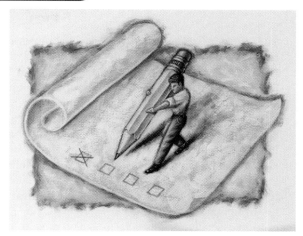

Writing strategies: Developing a questionnaire. When developing a questionnaire, it is important to use clear language and to avoid ambiguous questions. Make sure that the questions are directly related to the targeted topic and that the answers include all possibilities of response.

Antes de escribir

Piense en posibles puntos relacionados con los viajes y las vacaciones sobre los que quiere obtener información en la encuesta. Éstos son algunos aspectos importantes para el cuestionario.

- Frecuencia de los viajes
- Vacaciones/Fechas preferidas para el viaje
- Actividades preferidas para el viaje
- Rutina durante las vacaciones (actividades por la mañana, por la tarde, por la noche)

Después prepare seis preguntas de elección múltiple (*multiple choice*) con la información que desea obtener sobre los hábitos de viajes y vacaciones. Pase la encuesta a cinco compañeros y escriba una conclusión con los resultados obtenidos para presentar en su próxima sesión de clase.

Después de escribir

Revise sus conclusiones asegurándose que contienen los siguientes puntos.

 Lista de control:

___ Las estructuras para expresar la frecuencia con la que se realiza una acción.
___ Las estructuras para expresar preferencias.
___ El vocabulario relacionado con las estaciones del año y las fechas.
___ Las expresiones verbales para hablar de actividades diarias.

 En la red

Busque información en la red relacionada con los hábitos de viaje de los estudiantes universitarios y compárelos con los obtenidos en su encuesta. ¿Hay puntos en común? ¿Hay diferencias? Puede usar en sus comparaciones las estructuras para expresar afirmación y negación de este capítulo.

All the sources consulted for the readings are cited on the *¡Trato hecho!* Web site at **www.prenhall.com/trato**

VOCABULARIO

TEMA 1

Sustantivos
el centro comercial *the mall, the shopping center*
la comida china Chinese *food*
la exposición *the exhibition*
la iglesia *the church*
el lago *the lake*
la mezquita *the mosque*
el museo *the museum*
la obra de teatro *the play*
los ratos libres *free time*
la sinagoga *the synagogue*
el teatro *the theater* (for live performances)
el templo *the temple*

Expresiones verbales
correr *to run*
esquiar *to ski*
hacer ejercicio aeróbico / yoga *to do aerobics / yoga*
hacer esquí acuático *to waterski*
ir de compras *to go shopping*
jugar al tenis / al baloncesto / al vóleibol *to play tennis / basketball / volleyball*
levantar pesas *to lift weights*
nadar *to swim*
pasear *to walk, to go for a walk*
rezar *to pray*

tener ganas de + infinitive *to feel like …ing*
tomar el sol *to sunbathe*
tomar una copa *to have a drink*

Otras expresiones
a *to*
adónde *(to) where*
entonces *so, then*
ese/a *that*
esta noche *tonight*
para + infinitive *(in order) to + verb*

TEMA 2

El tiempo
¿Qué tiempo hace? *What's the weather like?*
El cielo está despejado / nublado. *The sky's clear / cloudy.*
Hace buen / mal tiempo. *The weather's good / bad.*
Hace (mucho) calor. *It's (very) hot.*
Hace fresco. *It's cool.*
Hace (mucho) frío. *It's (very) cold.*
Hace sol. *It's sunny.*
Hace viento. *It's windy.*
Llueve. *It rains., It's raining.*
Nieva. *It snows., It's snowing.*
Va a llover / nevar. *It's going to rain / to snow.*

La fecha
¿Cuál es la fecha (de…)? *What is the date (of…)?*

Es el primero (dos, tres…) de… *It's the first (second, third…) of…*
enero *January*
febrero *February*
marzo *March*
abril *April*
mayo *May*
junio *June*
julio *July*
agosto *August*
septiembre *September*
octubre *October*
noviembre *November*
diciembre *December*

Las estaciones del año
la primavera *the spring*
el verano *the summer*
el otoño *the autumn, the fall*
el invierno *the winter*

Expresiones verbales
dormir hasta tarde *to sleep late*
ir a + infinitive *to be going to + verb*

¿Cuándo?
esta mañana *this morning*
esta noche *tonight, this evening*
esta tarde *this afternoon*
mañana (por la mañana, por la tarde, por la noche) *tomorrow (morning, afternoon, night)*
la semana (el mes, el año) que viene *next week (month, year)*

Verbos

almorzar (o > ue) *to eat lunch, to have lunch*
cenar *to eat dinner, to have dinner*
cerrar (e > ie) *to close*
contar (o > ue) *to count, to tell*
decir (e > i, yo digo) *to say, to tell*
desayunar *to eat breakfast, to have breakfast*
dormir (o > ue) *to sleep*
dormir (o > ue) una siesta *to take a nap*

T E M A 3

empezar (e > ie) *to begin*
encontrar (o > ue) *to find*
entender (e > ie) *to understand*
jugar (u > ue) (al ajedrez, a las cartas, a los videojuegos) *to play (chess, cards, video games)*
pedir (e > i) *to ask for, to order*
pensar (e > ie) *to think*
pensar (e > ie) *+ infinitive to intend to + verb*
perder (e > ie) *to lose, to miss*
poder (o > ue) *to be able, can*

preferir (e > ie) *to prefer*
querer (e > ie) *to want*
repetir (e > i) *to repeat*
servir (e > i) *to serve*
venir (e > ie, yo vengo) *to come*
volver (o > ue) *to return*
volver (o > ue) a + infinitive *to + verb again*

Otra palabra
temprano *early*

T E M A 4

La comida
las galletas *cookies*
el helado *ice cream*
las papitas fritas *potato chips*
el pastel *cake*
la pizza *pizza*

Expresiones verbales
contar chistes *to tell jokes*
sacar una foto *to take a picture*
tocar la guitarra *to play the guitar*

Otras palabras
aló *hello (on the phone)*
Chau. *Ciao., Bye.*

T E M A 5

Las bebidas
tener sed *to be thirsty*
el agua (*f*) **mineral** *mineral water*
el azúcar *sugar*
el café *coffee*
el capuchino *cappuccino*
la cerveza *beer*
el chocolate caliente *hot chocolate*
la crema *cream*
la leche *milk*
la limonada con hielo *lemonade with ice*
los refrescos *soft drinks*
el té *tea*
el vino (tinto/blanco) *(red/white) wine*

La comida
tener hambre *to be hungry*
un bocadillo (de queso / de jamón) *a (cheese/ham) sandwich*
la ensalada *salad*
el flan *flan*
el helado (de vainilla / de chocolate) *(chocolate / vanilla) ice cream*
un trozo *a slice*

Expresiones afirmativas y negativas
algo *something*
alguien *someone*
alguno/a(s) (algún) *some, any*
a veces *sometimes*

nada *nothing, (not) anything*
nadie *nobody, (not) anyone*
ni… ni… *neither… nor*
ninguno/a (ningún) *none, not any*
nunca *never*
siempre *always*
también *also, too*
tampoco *neither*
todos *everyone*

Otras expresiones
¿Algo más? *Anything else?*
desear *to wish, to desire*
un/a mesero/a *a server*
un momento *a moment*
para mí *for me*

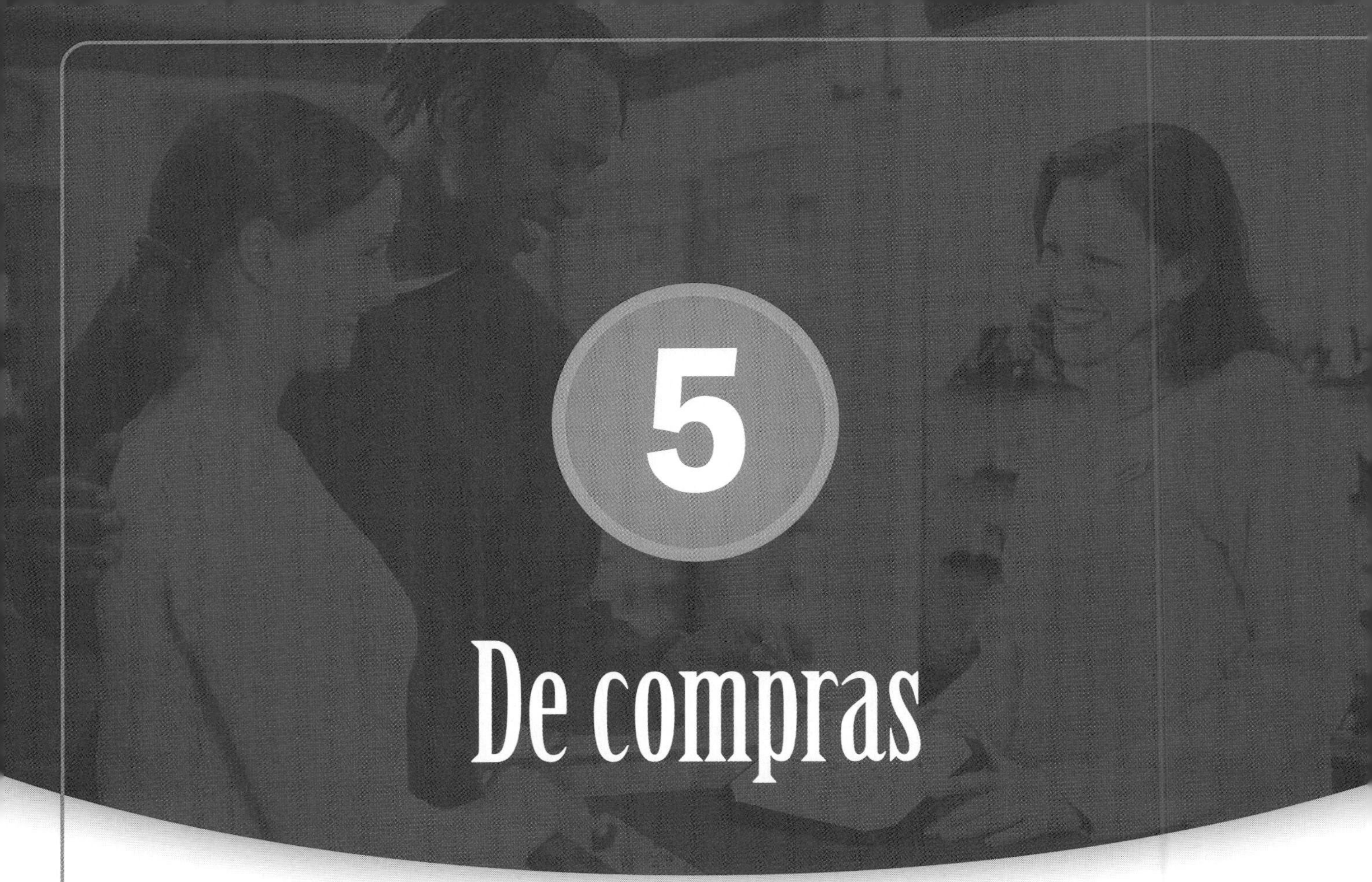

5

De compras

In this chapter you will learn to...

- talk about your daily routine
- describe your daily interactions with others
- say what you wear
- go shopping for clothes
- talk about stores
- understand more about the daily life of young Hispanics

You will use...

- reflexive verbs
- reciprocal verbs
- demonstrative adjectives
- direct object pronouns
- the prepositions **por** and **para**

TEMA ❶

Vocabulario
¿Qué haces los sábados?

Gramática
Las acciones reflexivas y recíprocas:
  los verbos reflexivos y recíprocos

TEMA ❷

Vocabulario
¿Qué haces con los amigos y los
  seres queridos?

Gramática
Más acciones reflexivas y recíprocas:
  el uso del infinitivo y del gerundio
  de los verbos reflexivos y
  recíprocos

TEMA ❸

Vocabulario
¿Qué te vas a poner?

Gramática
La selección: los demostrativos

TEMA ❹

Vocabulario
¿Cuánto cuesta?

Gramática
Evitar la redundancia: los
  pronombres de complemento
  directo

TEMA ❺

Vocabulario
¿Para quién es?

Gramática
Dar explicaciones: ¿**por** o **para**?

¡TRATO HECHO!

Revista cultural
En portada: ¿Cuándo se marchan
  de casa?
**De puertas abiertas a la
  comunidad:** Bocados de realidad
Escapadas: Toledo: La ciudad de las
  tres culturas
En palabras de…: Diseñadores de
  moda

VOCABULARIO
¿Qué haces los sábados?

TEMA **1**

¡Ojo!

The verbs presented on this page have reflexive pronouns (**me, te, se...**) before them. In the following grammar explanation you will learn when to include such pronouns. In this vocabulary presentation use them where they appear and focus on the meaning of the verbs.

Supplemental activities. **A.** ¿Hace Ud. las siguientes cosas los sábados o los lunes? Complete las oraciones. *Modelo:* Me despierto más temprano *los lunes. (Me despierto a la misma hora los dos días.)* 1. Me levanto más temprano... 2. Me quedo en la cama hasta más tarde... 3. Me quedo más en casa... 4. Me siento más cansado/a... 5. Me relajo más... 6. Me divierto más... 7. Mis amigos y yo nos encontramos más... 8. Me acuesto más temprano... **B.** ¿Hace Ud. estas cosas más por la mañana, por la tarde o por la noche? Complete las oraciones. *Modelo:* Me baño... > *Me baño más por la mañana. / Me baño tanto por la mañana como por la noche.* 1. Me baño más... 2. Me lavo los dientes... 3. Me quedo en casa más... 4. Me relajo más... 5. Mis amigos y yo nos encontramos más... 6. Me divierto más... 7. Me siento más cansado/a... 8. Me siento más aburrido/a... **C.** ¿Cuáles de los verbos de esta página asocia Ud. con estas palabras? *Modelo:* agua > *Me baño con agua. Me lavo el pelo con agua.* 1. ropa 2. la cama 3. el baño 4. el pelo 5. los dientes 6. los amigos 7. una fiesta 8. el sofá

Duermo hasta tarde.
Me despierto a las diez.

Me quedo un poco en la cama
y me levanto a las diez y media.

Me baño o me ducho por
la mañana. Me lavo el pelo.

Me lavo los dientes.

Me relajo en casa
por la tarde.

Me maquillo y me
visto para salir.

Mis amigos y yo nos
encontramos en el centro.
Me divierto mucho.

Cuando me siento cansada,
me voy a la casa y me acuesto.

5-1 ¿Qué se hace primero? Una estudiante habla de su rutina diaria. ¿En qué orden dice que hace las siguientes cosas?

Modelo   Me levanto. / Me despierto. / Desayuno.
Me despierto, me levanto y luego desayuno.

1. Me visto. / Me maquillo. / Me lavo la cara (*face*).
2. Me levanto. / Me voy a la universidad. / Me visto.
3. Ceno. / Vuelvo a la casa. / Me acuesto después de estudiar.
4. Me levanto después de quince minutos. / Me despierto. / Me quedo un poco en la cama.
5. Me lavo los dientes. / Desayuno. / Me despierto.
6. Nos relajamos un poco después de comer. / Mis amigos y yo nos encontramos en la cafetería. / Almorzamos.

5-2 Mi rutina. Cambie las palabras en letra cursiva para describir su rutina los sábados.

1. Me despierto a *las ocho / las nueve / las diez / ???* y me levanto *inmediatamente / después de quince minutos / ???*
2. Me despierto *fácilmente / con dificultad.*
3. Me baño *por la mañana / por la tarde / por la noche.*
4. Me visto en *mi cuarto / el baño.*
5. Para relajarme, me gusta *escuchar música / leer una revista / ???*
6. Generalmente, me quedo en casa *los sábados por la noche / los domingos por la tarde / todo el fin de semana / ???*
7. Me divierto mucho cuando mis amigos y yo *vamos a bailar / vamos al café / jugamos al vóleibol / ???*
8. No me divierto mucho cuando mis amigos y yo *vamos al centro comercial / hablamos de política / ???*
9. Los sábados me acuesto a *las diez / las once / ???*

P

Conversaciones. En parejas, lean la siguiente conversación en la cual dos amigos hablan de su rutina de los sábados. Luego, cambien la conversación para hablar de su rutina los sábados.

— ¿Te despiertas tarde los sábados?
— No, me levanto a las seis y media. Trabajo a las ocho los sábados y me ducho antes de salir.
— ¿Trabajas todo el día?
— No, vuelvo a casa a las dos.
— ¿Qué haces por la tarde?
— Generalmente, me quedo en casa y me relajo. A veces duermo una siesta.
— ¿Te quedas en casa por la noche también?
— Los sábados por la noche, prefiero salir con mis amigos a cenar o a bailar.
— ¿Te acuestas tarde?
— Sí, casi siempre me acuesto tarde los sábados porque puedo dormir hasta tarde los domingos.

Supplemental activity. ¿Quién habla, el señor Elegante o el señor Sucio? *Modelo:* Me lavo el pelo dos o tres veces al año. > *El señor Sucio.* 1. Me lavo el pelo todos los días. 2. Me baño una vez por la mañana y otra vez por la noche. 3. Me baño una vez los sábados y otra vez los jueves. 4. Me lavo los dientes sólo si voy a ver al dentista. 5. Me lavo los dientes después de cada comida. 6. Uso la misma ropa todos los días por una semana. 7. Me visto con ropa nueva todos los días. 8. Me acuesto en la misma cama con mis cinco perros.

Suggestion for *Conversaciones.* Have students change the conversation another time, talking about a typical Monday.

AUDIO ¡A escuchar!

Escuchen otra conversación en la cual dos amigos hablan de su rutina de los lunes. ¿Quién se levanta más temprano, él o ella? ¿Quién vuelve a casa primero? ¿A qué hora se acuesta cada uno?

GRAMÁTICA
Las acciones reflexivas y recíprocas: los verbos reflexivos y recíprocos

Para averiguar

1. What is a reflexive verb?
2. Which reflexive pronoun is used with each subject?
3. Where do you place reflexive pronouns with verbs conjugated in the present tense? with an infinitive?
4. What are two types of verbs that are often reflexive in Spanish, but not in English?
5. What are reciprocal verbs? Do the pronouns used with these verbs differ from reflexive pronouns?

Note. More reciprocal verbs are presented in the next *Tema*, where reflexive/reciprocal verbs used in the infinitive after conjugated verbs are introduced.

Suggestion. Use the illustrations of Adela to explain the difference between reflexive and non-reflexive use of verbs. Then give students the following sentences, asking if the verb would be reflexive or not. 1. I wake up at 6:00 in the morning. 2. I wake my children up at 6:45. 3. I bathe every morning. 4. I have to bathe my youngest son too. 5. I wash clothes three times a week. 6. I wash my hair every day. 7. My children get dressed before breakfast. 8. I get dressed after breakfast. 9. I always sit down with my children to eat breakfast. 10. I always seat my youngest son to my right. 11. My oldest son amuses everyone with his jokes. 12. I always amuse myself with my children. 13. I put my children to bed at 8:30. 14. I go to bed at 10:30. (After having students decide whether the verbs are reflexive, you may wish to remind them of the use of personal **a** and have them translate the preceding sentences.)

Reflexive verbs describe actions that people do to or for themselves.

REFLEXIVE

Adela se baña.
Adela is bathing (herself).

NON-REFLEXIVE

Adela baña al perro.
Adela is bathing the dog.

Reflexive pronouns are attached to the end of infinitives. When conjugating reflexive verbs, remove the reflexive pronoun from the infinitive and place the reflexive pronoun corresponding to the subject before the verb: **me** (*myself*), **te** (*yourself*), **nos** (*ourselves*), **os** (*yourselves*), **se** (*himself, herself, oneself, yourself, yourselves, themselves*).

LAVARSE (*TO WASH ONESELF*)					
yo	**me**	lavo	nosotros/as	**nos**	lavamos
tú	**te**	lavas	vosotros/as	**os**	laváis
usted, él, ella	**se**	lava	ustedes, ellos, ellas	**se**	lavan

Verbs that are reflexive in English will generally be reflexive in Spanish. In addition, verbs are generally reflexive in Spanish when describing a change in mental or physical state or people doing something to their own body, including changing its position. Some common reflexive verbs include:

acostarse	*to lie down, to go to bed*	**levantarse**	*to get up*
bañarse	*to bathe*	**maquillarse**	*to put on make-up*
despertarse (ie)	*to wake up*	**quedarse**	*to stay*
divertirse (ie)	*to have fun, to amuse oneself*	**relajarse**	*to relax*
irse (para)	*to go away, to leave (for)*	**sentarse (ie)**	*to sit down*
lavarse (el pelo)	*to wash (one's hair)*	**sentirse (ie)**	*to feel*
llamarse	*to be called / named*	**vestirse (i)**	*to get dressed*

Reciprocal verbs look like reflexive verbs and have the same pronouns (**nos, os, se**). Whereas reflexive verbs indicate that someone is doing something to or for oneself, reciprocal verbs indicate that two or more people are doing something to or for one another. Many verbs can be made reciprocal by adding the reflexive/reciprocal pronouns.

Mis padres nunca **se** hablan.	*My parents never talk **to each other.***
Nos vemos con frecuencia.	*We see **one another** frequently.*
Mi novia y yo **nos** queremos.	*My girlfriend and I love **each other.***

5-3   El extraterrestre. Un extraterrestre llega a su casa y no entiende cómo se hacen las cosas en la Tierra (*Earth*). Explíquele qué hacen los seres humanos normalmente.

> Modelo   ¿Me acuesto en la mesa?
> **Nosotros nos acostamos en la cama.**

1. ¿Me levanto durante la noche?   **4.** ¿Me baño en la cocina?
2. ¿Me acuesto durante el día?   **5.** ¿Me lavo el pelo en la piscina?
3. ¿Me visto y después me baño?   **6.** ¿Me visto en el patio?

5-4   El día de Alejandro. Describa la rutina diaria de Alejandro.

> Modelo   a las 6:00
> **Alejandro se despierta a las seis.**

1. inmediatamente

2. por la mañana

3. en quince minutos

4. temprano por la mañana

5-5   ¿Y tú? Pregúntele a un/a compañero/a de clase si hace las mismas cosas que Alejandro del ejercicio anterior los días que ustedes van a la clase de español.

> Modelo   E1: **¿Te despiertas a las seis?**
> E2: **No, me despierto a las ocho.**
> E1: **¿Te levantas inmediatamente?…**

5-6   En clase. ¿Quiénes de su clase hacen las siguientes cosas?

> Modelo   sentarse cerca del profesor / de la profesora
> **Dominique y Jeff se sientan cerca de la profesora.**
> ayudarse con el español
> **Todos nos ayudamos con el español.**

1. sentarse cerca de la puerta   **5.** quedarse enfrente de la clase
2. divertirse en clase   **6.** ayudarse durante los exámenes
3. verse los días de clase   **7.** sentirse nervioso/a(s) durante los exámenes
4. sentirse bien hoy   **8.** irse después de clase

Supplemental activities. A. Distribute slips of paper with the following verbs on them. Students mime the action, and the class guesses what they are doing. *(lavarse el pelo, lavarse los dientes, maquillarse, vestirse, despertarse, acostarse, divertirse, sentarse, levantarse, bañarse)* **B.** ¿Cuál es el antónimo de acostarse (estar aburrido, irse, sentarse, dormir hasta tarde, sentirse mal)? **C.** Make statements such as the following about yourself, then have students change them so that they are true for themselves. 1. Me visto antes de desayunar. 2. Me visto en menos de quince minutos por la mañana. 3. Me baño en diez minutos. 4. Me relajo escuchando música clásica. 5. Me siento aburrido/a viendo la televisión. 6. Me divierto bailando con mis amigos. **D.** Have students complete the following sentences. 1. Me divierto mucho cuando... 2. No me divierto mucho cuando... 3. Me siento nervioso/a cuando... 4. Me relajo cuando... 5. No me siento bien cuando... **E.** Additional oral questions. 1. ¿Cuántas horas duerme Ud. generalmente? ¿A qué hora se acuesta y a qué hora se levanta generalmente? 2. ¿Se siente Ud. cansado/a por la mañana? ¿Necesita tomar café para despertarse? 3. ¿Qué hace Ud. si se queda en casa por la mañana? ¿Qué días se queda en casa? 4. ¿Tiene Ud. compañero/a de cuarto o de casa? ¿Cómo se llama? ¿Se queda más en su cuarto o pasa mucho tiempo en la sala? ¿Se ven Uds. todos los días? ¿Quién se despierta más temprano generalmente, su compañero/a de cuarto/casa o Ud.? ¿Quién se acuesta más tarde? ¿Quién se va de la casa más temprano por la mañana? ¿Quién vuelve primero?

VOCABULARIO
TEMA ❷ ¿Qué haces con los amigos y los seres queridos?

¡Ojo!

En la cultura hispánica, los amigos casi siempre se dan un beso o se dan la mano cuando se ven. ¿Qué hace usted cuando ve a sus amigos?

Supplemental activities. **A.** ¿Se llevan bien o se llevan mal dos esposos si hacen las siguientes cosas? 1. Se pelean todos los días. 2. Se abrazan todo el tiempo. 3. Nunca se hablan. 4. Se quieren mucho. 5. Se encuentran todos los días para almorzar. 6. Nunca se besan. 7. Se compran muchos regalos. 8. Se dicen cosas feas. 9. Se escriben poemas. 10. Se sienten muy tristes cuando se despiden por la mañana. 11. Se hablan por teléfono o se comunican por Internet cinco o seis veces mientras están en el trabajo. 12. Nunca se miran a los ojos. 13. Siempre se ayudan en casa. 14. Quieren casarse con otras personas. 15. Se hablan de todo. **B.** ¿Describen estas oraciones una relación ideal con su compañero/a de cuarto? Conteste: *Está bien. / No me gusta. / No me importa.* (*It doesn't matter to me.*) 1. Uds. se ven poco. 2. Su compañero/a de cuarto siempre se acuesta en el sofá de la sala. 3. Se llevan bien. 4. Comparten un cuarto. 5. Él/Ella se enoja con Ud. todo el tiempo. 6. Uds. nunca se pelean. 7. Siempre se divierten juntos. 8. Su compañero/a de cuarto y la/el novia/o de él/ella se abrazan y se besan todo el tiempo enfrente de Ud.. 9. Él/Ella se lava los dientes en la cocina. 10. Él/Ella se queda en casa todo el tiempo. 11. Él/Ella nunca se viste cuando pasa el día en casa. 12. Él/Ella se sienta en el piso de la sala para hacer su tarea. **C.** Have students say whom these sentences might describe. *Modelo:* Nos hablamos mucho por teléfono. > *Mi madre y yo nos hablamos mucho por teléfono. / No hablo mucho por teléfono con nadie.* 1. Nos comunicamos con frecuencia por Internet. 2. Nos vemos todos los días. 3. Nos abrazamos con frecuencia. 4. Nos llevamos bien. 5. Nos peleamos con frecuencia. 6. Nos ayudamos con el español.

Mi novio/a y yo nos hablamos por teléfono o nos comunicamos por correo electrónico varias veces al día.

Nos vemos casi todos los días. Nos encontramos en un café después del trabajo.

Nos abrazamos y nos besamos.

Generalmente nos llevamos bien, pero a veces nos enojamos y nos peleamos.

Siempre nos reconciliamos antes de despedirnos.

Nos queremos mucho y nos vamos a casar algún día.

5-7 Mi mejor amigo y yo. ¿Describen las siguientes oraciones su relación con su mejor amigo/a? Conteste **cierto** o **falso** y corrija las oraciones falsas.

1. Nos hablamos por teléfono todos los días.
2. Nos comunicamos más por correo electrónico que por teléfono.
3. Nos vemos en la universidad.
4. Nos vemos todos los días.
5. Nos encontramos a veces en un café.

6. Nos encontramos todos los días después de esta clase.
7. Nos abrazamos cuando nos vemos.
8. Siempre nos llevamos bien y casi nunca nos peleamos.
9. Cuando nos peleamos, siempre nos reconciliamos inmediatamente.
10. Nos abrazamos a veces cuando nos despedimos.

G **5-8 Una pareja feliz.** Usando los verbos de la lista, cuente una historia de amor entre Pablo y Felicia. Trabajen en grupos e incluyan muchos detalles.

Modelo **Pablo y Felicia se ven por primera vez en un café. Él mira a Felicia y se sienta en la mesa de al lado...**

verse por primera vez	no separarse hasta tarde	nunca pelearse
mirarse a los ojos	pedirse los números de teléfono	abrazarse
levantarse	despedirse con un beso (*a kiss*)	quererse
presentarse	empezar a llamarse	casarse
hablarse por horas	encontrarse todos los días	

Follow-up questions for
Conversaciones. 1. Cuando Ud. sale con los amigos los fines de semana, ¿dónde se encuentran Uds.? ¿Se dan un abrazo o un beso cuando se ven? ¿Se dan la mano? ¿Se abrazan o se dan la mano cuando se despiden? ¿A veces se van algunos de sus amigos sin despedirse? 2. ¿Se pelean a veces algunos de sus amigos? ¿Se reconcilian rápidamente? ¿Se abrazan después de reconciliarse? 3. ¿Con quién se enoja Ud. a veces? ¿Por qué? ¿Se

P **Conversaciones.** En parejas, lean la siguiente conversación en la cual un estudiante habla de su círculo de amigos. Luego, cambien la conversación dos veces para hablar de sus amigos y de los de su pareja.

— Cuando sales con tus amigos, ¿dónde se encuentran ustedes **por lo general**?
— Generalmente, nos encontramos en un café.
— ¿Siempre **se dan un abrazo** o **un beso** cuando se ven?
— Sí, o **nos damos la mano.**
— ¿Todos tus amigos se llevan bien?
— A veces mis amigas Alicia y Érica se pelean, pero siempre se reconcilian.

AUDIO ¡A escuchar!

Escuchen otra conversación en la cual una estudiante habla de su compañera de cuarto. ¿Se llevan bien? ¿Por qué sí o por qué no? ¿Se ven con frecuencia?

llevan Uds. bien generalmente? 4. ¿Se siente Ud. cómodo/a (*comfortable*) cuando dos personas se besan enfrente de todos? ¿Se siente Ud. cómodo/a cuando dos personas se pelean enfrente de todos? Para Ud., ¿es romántico o es tonto si dos novios se miran románticamente a los ojos por mucho tiempo sin hablar? 5. ¿Es importante casarse? ¿Es importante quedarse con la misma persona por toda la vida (*life*)?

---

por lo general *in general* **darse un abrazo/un beso** *to give each other a hug/a kiss* **darse la mano** *to shake hands*

GRAMÁTICA

Más acciones reflexivas y recíprocas: el uso del infinitivo y del gerundio de los verbos reflexivos y recíprocos

Para averiguar

1. When you use a reflexive verb in the infinitive following a conjugated verb, where are the two possible placements of the reflexive pronoun? Does the pronoun change to correspond to the subject?
2. What does **acabar de** + *infinitive* mean?
3. In the present progressive, what are the two possible placements of the reflexive pronoun? When the pronoun is attached to the end of the present participle, what do you write on the stressed syllable of the verb?

Supplemental activities. A. Write the following sentences on the board or on a transparency and have students complete them in a logical way. Tell students that they may also use non-reflexive verbs. *Modelo:* No tenemos sed. Acabamos de *tomar algo.* 1. No tengo hambre. Acabo de... 2. No tenemos sueño. Acabamos de... 3. ¿Estás listo para el examen? ¿Acabas de...? 4. Voy a lavarme los dientes. Acabo de... 5. ¿Estás cansado/a? ¿Acabas de...? 6. Nadie está en casa. Todos acaban de... 7. Nadie duerme. Todos acabamos de... 8. Estoy contento/a. Acabo de... **B.** Generalmente, ¿a qué hora acaba de hacer Ud. las siguientes cosas los días que va a la clase de español? Complete las oraciones con una hora. *Modelo:* Acabo de despertarme a... *Acabo de despertarme a las siete de la mañana. (Me acabo de despertar a las siete de la mañana.)* 1. Me acabo de levantar a... 2. Acabo de bañarme a... 3. Acabo de irme para la universidad a... 4. Acabo de almorzar a... 5. Acabo de salir de mi primera clase a... 6. Acabo de acostarme a...

When a conjugated verb is followed by a reflexive/reciprocal verb in the infinitive, the reflexive/reciprocal pronoun may be placed either before the conjugated verb or attached to the end of the infinitive without changing the meaning of the sentence. The pronoun must correspond to the subject of the conjugated verb.

Me voy a levantar temprano. = Voy a levantar**me** temprano.
I'm going to get up early.

To say what someone just did, use **acabar de** followed by an infinitive. **Acabar** is conjugated like a regular **-ar** verb.

Acabamos de comer.   Acabo de levantar**me**. / **Me** acabo de levantar.
We just ate.   *I just got up.*

In the present progressive, there are two possible placements of reflexive/reciprocal pronouns. They may be placed either before the conjugated form of **estar** or attached to the end of the present participle. When they are attached to the present participle, there is an accent on the stressed vowel of the verb.

Los niños **se** están bañando. = Los niños están bañ**á**ndo**se**.
The children are bathing.

5-9 ¿Qué acaban de hacer? ¿Alejandro y su esposa Petra acaban de hacer o están haciendo las cosas indicadas?

Modelo **A.** lavarse el pelo
**Petra está lavándose el pelo. /
Petra se está lavando el pelo.**

Modelo **B.** lavarse el pelo
**Petra acaba de lavarse el pelo. /
Petra se acaba de lavar el pelo.**

1. despertarse

2. bañarse

3. bañarse

4. lavarse los dientes

5. maquillarse   **6.** vestirse   **7.** acostarse

Supplemental activities. **A.** ¿Va a hacer Ud. las siguientes cosas mañana? *Modelo:* levantarse temprano > *Sí, voy a levantarme temprano mañana. (Sí, me voy a levantar temprano mañana.)* (despertarse antes de las seis, quedarse en la casa, irse temprano de la casa, lavarse el pelo antes de salir, maquillarse por la mañana, relajarse por la tarde, divertirse por la noche, acostarse temprano)
B. ¿Cuántas veces van a hacer Ud. y su mejor amigo/a las siguientes cosas esta semana? *Modelo:* verse > *Nos vamos a ver tres o cuatro veces. / No vamos a vernos esta semana.* (encontrarse después de clase, encontrarse en un café, hablarse por teléfono, abrazarse, darse un beso, pelearse, comunicarse por Internet, verse en la universidad) **C.** Una mujer habla con su esposo. Complete las siguientes oraciones de manera lógica con un verbo reflexivo. *Modelo:* No puedes pasar toda la mañana en la cama. Necesitas *levantarte*. 1. Los niños duermen mucho. Necesitan... 2. No quiero estar aburrida esta noche. Quiero... 3. Tengo el pelo muy sucio. Quiero... 4. Los niños no pueden salir a jugar sin ropa. Tienen que... 5. Los niños siempre se llevan muy mal. Necesitan... 6. Los niños no pueden pelearse toda la tarde. Necesitan... 7. ¿Vamos a salir esta noche o vamos a...? 8. Ya es muy tarde y todos estamos cansados. Necesitamos... 9. Estoy muy sucia. Antes de acostarme necesito...

5-10 **¿En qué orden?** Un padre habla de lo que (*what*) acaban de hacer y lo que están haciendo ahora en su familia. ¿Cuál es el orden lógico?

> **Modelo**   yo (vestirse / bañarse)
> **Acabo de bañarme. Ahora estoy vistiéndome.**
> **(Me acabo de bañar. Ahora me estoy vistiendo.)**

1. yo (despertarse / preparar el desayuno)
2. mi esposa (bañarse / levantarse)
3. mis hijos (pelearse / reconciliarse)
4. nosotros (almorzar / sentarse a comer)
5. mi esposa y yo (lavar los platos / comer)
6. mi esposa (sentarse en el sofá / dormir una siesta)
7. mi hija mayor (salir para una fiesta / divertirse con los amigos)
8. mis hijos menores (acostarse / dormir)

P **5-11** **Mis amigos y yo.** Forme preguntas para otro/a estudiante describiendo a las personas indicadas.

> **Modelo**   (tú) / poder / levantarse tarde / todos los días
> E1: **¿Puedes levantarte tarde todos los días? (¿Te puedes levantar tarde todos los días?)**
> E2: **Puedo levantarme tarde sólo los sábados. (Me puedo levantar tarde sólo los sábados.)**

1. (tú) / preferir / bañarse / por la mañana o por la noche
2. (tú) / tener que / levantarse temprano / los sábados
3. tus padres / preferir / quedarse en casa / los fines de semana
4. tus amigos y tú / preferir / encontrarse / en un café o en un club nocturno
5. tus amigos y tú / querer / divertirse esta noche
6. tu mejor amigo/a y tú / ir a / verse / mañana
7. (tú) / poder / relajarse / hoy después de clase
8. (tú) / necesitar / acostarse / más temprano todos los días

P **5-12** **Entrevista.** Entreviste a otro/a estudiante con estas preguntas.

1. ¿A qué hora te vas a acostar esta noche? ¿Tienes que levantarte temprano mañana? ¿Vas a quedarte en casa mañana por la mañana? ¿A qué hora te vas a ir de la casa mañana?
2. ¿Vas a relajarte esta noche o tienes que estudiar o trabajar? ¿Qué haces para relajarte? ¿Escuchas música? ¿Lees un libro? ¿Ves la televisión?
3. ¿Qué haces para divertirte con los amigos? ¿Dónde prefieren encontrarse tus amigos y tú generalmente cuando salen? ¿Con qué frecuencia se ven tu mejor amigo/a y tú? ¿Se van a ver este fin de semana? ¿Siempre se dan un abrazo cuando se ven?

VOCABULARIO
¿Qué te vas a poner?

¡Ojo!

También se dice **los zapatos de tenis** o **las zapatillas de tenis** en vez de **los tenis.**

No compro mucha ropa cara. Prefiero comprar ropa **barata.**

En la playa **llevo traje de baño** y sandalias.

Para hacer ejercicio, uso tenis, **camiseta** y pantalones cortos.

Cuando salgo con mis amigos, **me pongo…**

Supplemental activities. **A.** Name pieces of clothing and have students say whether they are *para hombre, para mujer,* or *para los dos.* **B.** Review names of colors and ask students the color of classmates' clothes. **C.** ¿Cuál se pone uno primero? *Modelo:* ¿la camisa o la corbata? > *Se pone uno la camisa primero y luego la corbata.* 1. ¿los calcetines o los zapatos? 2. ¿el cinturón o los pantalones? 3. ¿la camisa o la chaqueta? 4. ¿la camisa o el traje? 5. ¿los zapatos o los pantalones? 6. ¿la camiseta o el sombrero? 7. ¿el suéter o la camisa? 8. ¿el suéter o el abrigo? **D.** ¿Cuál no se usa con los otros? (*The answers are italicized for quick reference.*) 1. una falda, una blusa, *un traje de baño* 2. *botas,* una camiseta, pantalones cortos 3. un traje de baño, *un abrigo,* sandalias 4. *un traje de baño,* un abrigo, botas 5. *un vestido,* una camisa, pantalones 6. calcetines, zapatos, *sandalias* 7. una blusa, *un vestido,* una falda 8. un cinturón, zapatos, *un traje de baño* 9. *un vestido,* tenis, una camiseta 10. un suéter, una chaqueta, *pantalones cortos* **E.** ¿Cuál de estas cosas es de cuero? *(los calcetines o los zapatos, un cinturón o una corbata, las botas o un suéter, una camisa o una chaqueta, una blusa o una bolsa)* ¿Cuál es de seda? *(un traje de baño o una corbata, una blusa o una camiseta)* ¿Cuál es de lana? *(una blusa o un suéter, un traje o un cinturón, los zapatos o los calcetines)* ¿Cuál es de mezclilla? *(los pantalones o los calcetines, las sandalias o una chaqueta)* ¿Cuál es de algodón? *(una camisa o una bolsa, las botas o una falda, las sandalias o una camiseta)*

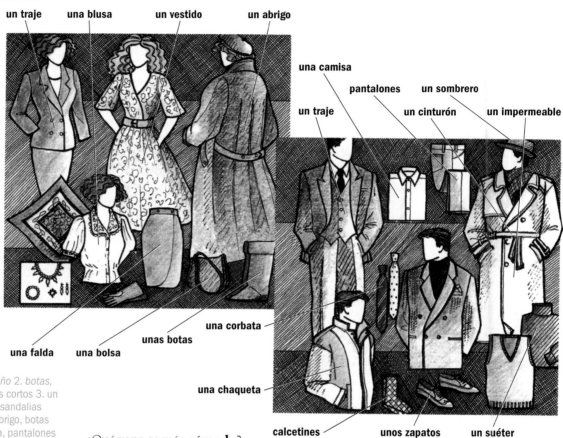

un traje · una blusa · un vestido · un abrigo

una camisa · pantalones · un sombrero · un traje · un cinturón · un impermeable

una corbata · unas botas · una falda · una bolsa · una chaqueta · calcetines · unos zapatos · un suéter

¿Qué ropa es más **cómoda**?

¿Prefieres las blusas de **algodón** o de **seda**?

¿Prefieres las chaquetas de **cuero,** de **lana** o de **mezclilla**?

¿Está de moda la ropa… ?

de un solo color

de rayas

de cuadros

---

barato/a *cheap*   **llevar** *to wear, to carry, to take*   **un traje de baño** *a swimsuit*   **una camiseta** *a T-shirt*
ponerse *to put on*   **cómodo/a** *comfortable*   **el algodón** *cotton*   **la seda** *silk*   **el cuero** *leather*   **la lana** *wool*
la mezclilla *denim*   **estar de moda** *to be in fashion*

5-13 ¿Qué se pone usted? ¿Qué ropa se pone usted en estas situaciones?

Modelo Hace sol y usted va a la playa.
Me pongo un traje de baño.

1. Hace mucho frío y usted sale de la casa.
2. Usted se queda en casa todo el día y quiere relajarse.
3. Está nevando y usted va a esquiar.
4. Hace calor y usted va al parque para correr.
5. Usted va a una entrevista (*interview*) importante.
6. Usted sale a bailar con unos amigos.
7. Usted va a la clase de español.

5-14 De compras. Usted está de compras con una amiga. Contéstele que la ropa que usted está mirando es lo opuesto (*the opposite*) de lo que cree.

Modelo ¿Ese (*That*) vestido es demasiado (*too*) largo?
No, es demasiado corto.

1. ¿Esos (*Those*) zapatos son demasiado grandes?
2. ¿Esa camisa es muy barata?
3. ¿Esa falda es demasiado larga?
4. ¿Ese traje es muy feo?
5. ¿Ese cinturón es demasiado corto?
6. ¿Esos suéteres son muy caros?
7. ¿Esas botas son de buena calidad (*quality*)?

5-15 ¿Quién es? Describa la ropa de alguien de su clase, y sus compañeros de clase adivinarán (*will guess*) quién es.

Modelo E1: **Hoy lleva pantalones negros, camisa amarilla y botas.**
E2: **Es Cristina, ¿verdad?**
E1: **Sí, es ella.**

(P)

Conversaciones. En parejas, lean la siguiente conversación. Luego, cambien la conversación para hablar de algo que ustedes quieren comprar.

— Necesito ir al centro comercial. Quiero comprar un vestido para llevar a **la boda** de mi prima.
— Yo también necesito ir de compras. Quiero comprar **vaqueros** nuevos y **una sudadera.** No puedo usar **la que** tengo. Está **rota.**
— ¿A qué tienda quieres ir?
— Me gusta ir al **almacén** Martínez. Tienen ropa de buena calidad a **precios razonables.** ¿Adónde quieres ir para comprar el vestido?
— Hay una boutique que se llama La Onda que me gusta mucho. Es un poco cara, pero siempre tienen **cosas** bonitas.

---

la boda *the wedding* **los vaqueros** *jeans* **una sudadera** *a sweatshirt* **el/la (los/las) que** *the one (ones) that*
roto/a *torn* **el almacén** *the department store* **el precio** *the price* **razonable** *reasonable* **cosas** *things*

Supplemental activity. Preguntas. ¿Prefiere Ud. las camisas de algodón o las camisas de seda? ¿las chaquetas de mezclilla o las chaquetas de cuero? ¿los trajes de seda o los trajes de lana? ¿los calcetines de algodón o los calcetines de lana? ¿los tenis o los zapatos de cuero? ¿los tenis blancos o negros? ¿las faldas de cuero o las faldas de algodón? ¿las camisas de un solo color o las camisas de rayas? ¿las camisas blancas o las camisas azules? ¿las camisas de rayas o de cuadros? ¿las corbatas de un solo color o las corbatas de rayas?

Follow-up for *Conversaciones*. Point out the new vocabulary presented in the conversation, then ask questions such as the following. 1. ¿Qué almacén de aquí tiene ropa cara / barata / de buena calidad / de mala calidad? Para Ud., ¿cuál es más importante, el precio o la calidad? ¿Cuál es su almacén favorito? ¿Cuál es su boutique favorita? ¿Compra Ud. más ropa en almacenes grandes o en boutiques pequeñas? 2. ¿Lleva alguien de la clase una sudadera hoy? ¿Cuándo se pone Ud. una sudadera? ¿para hacer ejercicio? ¿para dormir? 3. ¿Usa Ud. ropa rota a veces? ¿Está de moda usar pantalones rotos? ¿Qué ropa está de moda ahora? ¿Qué está de moda siempre para los estudiantes?

AUDIO ¡A escuchar!

Escuchen otra conversación en la cual dos amigas hablan de la ropa que se van a poner. ¿Adónde van? ¿Qué ropa van a llevar?

GRAMÁTICA
La selección: los demostrativos

Use demonstrative adjectives to say *this/these* or *that/those*. There are two ways to say *that/those* in Spanish: **ese/esa/esos/esas** and **aquel/aquella/aquellos/aquellas**. **Aquel** is generally used to describe something at a greater distance than **ese**.

ESTE (*THIS/THESE*)		ESE (*THAT/THOSE*)		AQUEL (*THAT/THOSE*)	
este sombrero	*this hat*	ese sombrero	*that hat*	aquel sombrero	*that hat*
esta falda	*this skirt*	esa falda	*that skirt*	aquella falda	*that skirt*
estos zapatos	*these shoes*	esos zapatos	*those shoes*	aquellos zapatos	*those shoes*
estas botas	*these boots*	esas botas	*those boots*	aquellas botas	*those boots*

¿Te gustan **estos** zapatos?	*Do you like **these** shoes?*
Me gusta **esa** blusa con **esa** falda.	*I like **that** blouse with **that** skirt.*
¿Puedo probarme **aquel** traje?	*May I try on **that** suit (**over there**)?*

The demonstrative pronouns look just like the demonstrative adjectives, except that they have a written accent on the stressed **e**, and the noun is omitted.

¿Te gustan estos zapatos?	*Do you like these shoes?*
No, prefiero **éstos**.	*No, I prefer **these**.*
Este reloj es más barato que **ése**.	*This watch is cheaper than **that one**.*

To say *this* or *that* referring to a general idea or a situation rather than to a specific noun, or when referring to a noun that has not yet been identified, use the neuter form of the demonstratives: **esto, eso,** or **aquello**.

Eso es imposible.	**That** *is impossible.*
Esto es muy importante.	**This** *is very important.*
¿Qué es **aquello**?	*What is **that** (**over there**)?*

5-16 Preferencias. Imagine que Ud. está de compras con un/a amigo/a. Usando la forma correcta de los adjetivos demostrativos, pregúntele a un/a compañero/a de clase cuál de los artículos de ropa prefiere. Su compañero/a debe contestar según sus gustos (*according to his/her tastes*).

Modelo

este/a/os/as	ese/a/os/as	aquel/aquella/os/as
pantalones negros	vaqueros	pantalones blancos

E1: **¿Prefieres estos pantalones negros, esos vaqueros o aquellos pantalones blancos?**
E2: **Prefiero los vaqueros.**

ESTE/A/OS/AS	ESE/A/OS/AS	AQUEL/AQUELLA/OS/AS
1. corbata roja	corbata azul	corbata verde
2. camisa de rayas	camisa de cuadros	camisa blanca
3. sandalias	tenis	botas
4. falda corta	falda larga	vestido
5. traje gris	traje negro	traje blanco
6. corbata amarilla	corbata rosada	corbata roja
7. camisa de mezclilla	blusa de algodón	blusa de seda
8. chaqueta de cuero	chaqueta de algodón	chaqueta de mezclilla

5-17   Mi ropa y mis cosas. Use **este, esta, estos** o **estas** y describa tres artículos de ropa o cosas que usted tiene.

> **Modelo**   **Esta camisa es nueva.**
> **Estos zapatos son mis favoritos.**
> **Este bolígrafo no escribe bien.**

Follow-up for 5-17. *Mi ropa y mis cosas.* Have students give classmates three compliments about their clothes. *Modelo: Me gustan esas botas. Ese suéter es bonito. El color de esa camisa es muy bonito.*

5-18   Mis favoritos. Pregúntele a un/a compañero/a de clase sobre sus cosas y personas favoritas. Luego reaccione a su respuesta como en el modelo.

> **Modelo**   su tienda favorita
> E1: **¿Cuál es tu tienda favorita?**
> E2: **Mi tienda favorita es Macy's.**
> E1: **Esa tienda me gusta también. Tiene ropa bonita. /**
> **Esa tienda no me gusta. Tiene precios altos. /**
> **No conozco** (*I'm not familiar with*) **esa tienda.**

1. su restaurante favorito
2. su película favorita
3. su color favorito
4. su actor favorito
5. su actriz favorita
6. su ciudad favorita
7. su programa de televisión favorito
8. su canción (*song*) favorita

5-19   ¿Cuál prefieres? En parejas, imaginen la conversación entre estas personas.

> **Modelo**   E1: **¿Me debo comprar este vestido?**
> E2: **Ese vestido no me gusta mucho. Prefiero esta falda y cuesta menos. ¿Te gusta esta falda de cuadros?…**

VOCABULARIO
¿Cuánto cuesta?

En la tienda

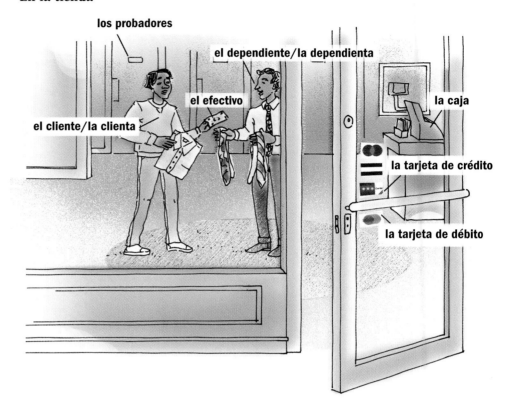

los probadores

el dependiente/la dependienta

el efectivo

la caja

el cliente/la clienta

la tarjeta de crédito

la tarjeta de débito

EL DEPENDIENTE (LA DEPENDIENTA) DICE:	EL CLIENTE (LA CLIENTA) DICE:
¿En qué puedo servirle?	**Busco…**
¿Cuánto desea **gastar**?	¿Tiene usted algo menos caro / más barato / **de oferta**?
¿Cómo desea pagar?	¿Cuánto cuesta(n)?
¿Qué color prefiere usted?	**¿Me** puedo **probar** este/a/os/as…?
¿Qué **talla** lleva usted?	**Me** voy a **llevar** este/a/os/as…
	¿Acepta usted tarjetas de crédito?

Las tallas en Estados Unidos no corresponden a las tallas en los países hispanos.

ROPA DE MUJER		ROPA DE HOMBRE		CAMISA DE HOMBRE	
PAÍSES HISPANOS	EEUU	PAÍSES HISPANOS	EEUU	PAÍSES HISPANOS	EEUU
38	8	40	30	36	14
40	10	42	32	38	15
42	12	44	34	41	16
44	14	46	36	43	17
46	16	48	38	46	18
48	18	50	40		

¿En qué puedo servirle? *How may I help you?* **buscar** *to look for* **gastar** *to spend* **de oferta** *on sale* **probarse (ue)** *to try on* **la talla** *the size* **llevar(se)** *to take, to carry, to wear*

5-20 Respuestas lógicas. ¿Cuál es la respuesta lógica del cliente a cada pregunta del dependiente?

EL DEPENDIENTE:
1. ¿En qué puedo servirle?
2. ¿Cuánto desea gastar?
3. ¿Qué talla lleva Ud.?
4. ¿Qué color prefiere usted?
5. ¿Le gustan las rayas o los cuadros?
6. ¿Le gusta ésta?
7. ¿Necesita algo más?
8. ¿Cómo desea pagar?

EL CLIENTE:
a. Necesito la talla 43.
b. No gracias. Eso es todo.
c. Busco una camisa.
d. ¿Tiene algo de rayas?
e. No quiero nada muy caro.
f. Quiero algo en azul o blanco.
g. Voy a pagar con tarjeta de crédito.
h. Sí, es muy bonita.

P **5-21 Entrevista.** Entreviste a otro/a estudiante con estas preguntas.

1. ¿Te gusta llevar ropa elegante o informal cuando sales con los amigos los sábados? ¿En qué ocasiones te pones un traje (un vestido)?
2. ¿En qué tienda compras mucha ropa? ¿En qué tienda venden ropa barata de buena calidad? ¿Compras ropa usada a veces?
3. ¿Usas camisetas de talla grande, mediana o pequeña? ¿De qué color es tu camiseta favorita? Cuando te pones una camiseta, ¿usas tenis, sandalias o zapatos de cuero generalmente? ¿Prefieres usar vaqueros o pantalones cortos si no hace frío?
4. ¿Prefieres camisas de algodón o de seda? ¿chaquetas de cuero o de mezclilla? ¿calcetines de algodón o de lana?

P **Conversaciones.** En parejas, lean la siguiente conversación en la cual una mujer compra un vestido. Luego, cambien la conversación para comprar un traje o un abrigo.

— ¿En qué puedo servirle?
— Busco un vestido.
— ¿Qué color prefiere usted?
— Algo en amarillo o rosado si tiene.
— ¿Qué talla lleva usted?
— Llevo la talla 42.
— ¿Le gusta éste? Cuesta 415 pesos.
— Sí, ¿me **lo** puedo probar?
— Sí, **cómo no.** Los probadores están **por acá.**

Después de probarse el vestido

— Me gusta mucho. Me lo voy a llevar.
— ¿Cómo desea pagar?
— Con mi tarjeta de crédito. **Aquí la tiene.**

AUDIO ¡A escuchar!

Escuchen otra conversación en la cual un hombre compra ropa. ¿Qué busca? ¿De qué color es lo que compra? ¿Cuánto cuesta?

Suggestion for *Conversaciones*.
Remind students that *llevar* can mean *to wear, to take,* or *to carry,* and point out that it is used reflexively when saying someone is taking something away, as when buying things. Also explain to students that both *aquí* and *acá* mean *here,* and that *aquí* indicates a more precise location, whereas *acá* indicates a general area. You may wish to also give them *allá* and contrast it with *allí.*

---

lo *it* **cómo no** *of course* **por acá** *over/through here* **Aquí la tiene.** *Here it is.*

GRAMÁTICA
Evitar la redundancia: los pronombres de complemento directo

Para averiguar

1. What is a direct object? What are the direct object pronouns in Spanish?
2. Where do you place direct object pronouns with a conjugated verb in the present tense? What are the two possible placements when there is an infinitive following a conjugated verb or in the present progressive? Do these placement rules differ from those of reflexive/reciprocal pronouns?
3. Do you place direct object pronouns before or after reflexive/reciprocal pronouns?

Suggestion. Point out that the direct object pronouns look like reflexive pronouns, except for **se**. Give examples such as the following to illustrate the different uses: *Mi amigo **se** despierta. [My friend wakes **himself** up .]*, *Mi amigo **lo** despierta. [My friend wakes **him** (= someone else) up]*. Also point out the different verb endings in **Me** despierto. [I wake myself up.] and **Me** despierta. [He wakes **me** up.]

Supplemental activities. A. ¿Trae Ud. las siguientes cosas a clase generalmente? Conteste con un pronombre de complemento directo. *Modelo: su mochila > Sí, la traigo. / No, no la traigo. (su libro de español, el cuaderno de ejercicios, su diccionario, el periódico, su celular, su computadora, su reloj, sus tarjetas de crédito, comida, café)* **B.** Ud. se muda (*are moving*) a otro/a apartamento/casa. ¿Dónde pone Ud. las siguientes cosas? *Modelo: el televisor > Lo pongo en la sala. (la mesa, la cama, el sofá, su ropa, el microondas, la comida, las plantas, sus zapatos, la computadora, el escritorio, sus libros)*

Direct objects refer to people, places, or things that are acted on by the subject of a sentence or a question. The words in bold type below are direct objects. Remember that human direct objects are preceded by the personal **a.**

Siempre compramos **nuestra ropa** en esa tienda.
¿Tienes **mis tarjetas de crédito**?
Necesito **a Juan y María.**
¿Buscan **al dependiente**?

Use the following direct object pronouns to replace direct objects.

LOS PRONOMBRES DE COMPLEMENTO DIRECTO			
me	*me*	nos	*us*
te	*you* (familiar, singular)	os	*you* (familiar, plural)
lo	*you* (formal, singular), *him, it*	los	*you* (plural), *them*
la	*you* (formal, singular), *her, it*	las	*you* (plural), *them*

Use **lo** to say *it* for masculine nouns and **la** for feminine nouns. Use **las** to say *them* when replacing all feminine nouns. Use **los** to say *them* for masculine nouns or a mixed group of masculine and feminine nouns.

The placement rules for direct object pronouns are the same as those for the reflexive/reciprocal pronouns. They go immediately before the conjugated verb.

— ¿Tienes mi tarjeta de crédito?
— Sí, **la** tengo. / No, no **la** tengo.

They may also be placed on the end of infinitives or present participles. There is a written accent mark on present participles with pronouns attached to them.

— ¿Vas a comprar **esos zapatos**?
— Sí, **los** voy a comprar. / Sí, voy a comprar**los.**

— ¿Dónde está **mi ropa**?
— **La** estoy lavando. / Estoy lavándo**la.**

When used with reflexive/reciprocal verbs, direct object pronouns are placed after the reflexive/reciprocal pronoun. There is a written accent mark on infinitives with two pronouns attached to them.

— ¿Te vas a llevar **esta camisa**?
— Sí, **me la** voy a llevar. / Sí, voy a llevár**mela.**

5-22 **¿Qué es?** ¿A qué ropa de la lista se refieren los pronombres indicados?

> una chaqueta   tenis   botas   un impermeable   una corbata
> un traje de baño   pantalones cortos   una camiseta

Modelo   Me *las* pongo para caminar en la nieve.
         Me pongo botas para caminar en la nieve.

1. *Lo* necesito si va a llover.   **4.** Me *los* pongo para jugar al tenis.
2. Me *la* pongo con mi traje.   **5.** Me *la* pongo porque hace fresco.
3. *Los* llevo cuando hace calor.   **6.** *Lo* llevo a la playa o a la piscina.

5-23 **Un crucero.** ¿Va a llevar Ud. estas cosas para un crucero (*cruise*) a Puerto Rico?

Modelo   ropa formal
         Sí, voy a llevarla. (Sí, la voy a llevar.)

1. su traje de baño   **6.** unas camisetas
2. su abrigo   **7.** sandalias
3. mucho dinero   **8.** botas
4. muchos suéteres   **9.** un DVD de *Titanic*
5. su cámara   **10.** su libro de español

Ⓟ 5-24 **¿Quién?** Pregúntele a otro/a estudiante quién hace estas acciones, usando el pronombre **te** como en el modelo.

Modelo   llamar por teléfono con frecuencia
         E1: **¿Quién te llama por teléfono con frecuencia?**
         E2: **Mi hermana me llama dos o tres veces a la semana. / Nadie me**
             llama.

1. ayudar con el español   **4.** comprender bien
2. ver todos los días   **5.** invitar a salir
3. visitar a veces en casa   **6.** poner nervioso/a

Ahora diga si su profesor/a hace estas cosas con relación a usted y sus compañeros de clase.

Modelo   llamar por teléfono con frecuencia
         No, nunca nos llama por teléfono. / Nos llama a veces.

Ⓟ 5-25 **Entrevista.** Entreviste a un/a compañero/a de clase. Conteste las preguntas usando pronombres para sustituir las palabras en letra cursiva.

1. ¿En qué tiendas prefieres comprar *zapatos*? ¿Siempre te pruebas *los zapatos* antes de comprarlas? ¿y *los calcetines*? ¿y *las camisas*?
2. ¿Necesitas lavar *la ropa* esta noche? ¿Con qué frecuencia lavas *la ropa*? ¿Te pones *los vaqueros* más de una vez sin lavarlos? ¿y *las camisetas*?
3. ¿Siempre llevas *zapatos* en casa? ¿Llevan muchos estudiantes *sandalias* a clase? ¿Te pones *zapatos* sin calcetines a veces? ¿Te pones *calcetines* con las sandalias? ¿Llevas *botas* a veces?

Supplemental activities. A. Remind students that direct object pronouns are placed after the reflexive pronouns and have them answer the following questions using direct object pronouns. *Ud. va a comprar las siguientes cosas. ¿Se las prueba primero? (una camisa, calcetines, zapatos, una corbata, un vestido, una camiseta, un traje, un cinturón, un reloj)* **B.** ¿Se pone Ud. estas cosas cuando hace frío o cuando hace calor? Conteste usando pronombres de complemento directo. *Modelo: las sandalias > Me las pongo cuando hace calor. (el traje de baño, el abrigo, un suéter, una camiseta, calcetines de lana, pantalones cortos, botas, una chaqueta de cuero)* **C.** ¿Quién hace las siguientes cosas en una tienda, el cliente o el dependiente? Conteste con pronombres de complemento directo. *Modelo: ¿Quién se prueba la ropa? > El cliente se la prueba.* 1. ¿Quién vende la ropa? 2. ¿Quién compra la ropa? 3. ¿Quién busca los probadores? 4. ¿Quién limpia los probadores? 5. ¿Quién necesita dinero para pagar? 6. ¿Quién abre la caja? 7. ¿Quién cierra la tienda? 8. ¿Quién se lleva la ropa a la casa? 9. ¿Quién gasta dinero?

VOCABULARIO

TEMA ⑤

¿Para quién es?

Tengo que pasar por esta calle para **hacer unos mandados.**
¿Qué venden en estas tiendas? ¿Dónde puedo **cortarme el pelo**?

Necesito pasar por **la joyería.** Necesito comprar **un regalo** para mi novia.

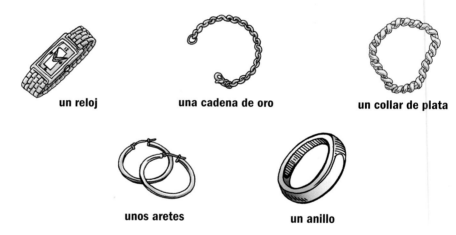

un reloj   **una cadena de oro**   **un collar de plata**

unos aretes   **un anillo**

También necesito comprar regalos para mi familia.

un paraguas   **una gorra**   **una cartera**   **unos juguetes**

---

hacer mandados *to run errands*   **cortarse el pelo** *to cut one's hair, to get one's hair cut*   **la joyería** *the jewelry store*   **un regalo** *a gift, a present*

5-26 ¿Por qué tienda? ¿Por qué tienda necesita pasar si quiere comprar estas cosas?

Modelo	zapatos

Necesito pasar por la zapatería.

1. un pastel
2. un collar
3. un libro

4. una falda
5. jamón
6. un anillo

7. sandalias
8. un diccionario
9. unos aretes

5-27 ¿Qué venden? Adivine (*Guess*) qué venden en estas tiendas.

Modelo	una mueblería

Venden muebles en una mueblería.

1. una relojería
2. una juguetería

3. una perfumería
4. una pizzería

5. una papelería
6. una heladería

Ⓟ **5-28** Pregúntele a otro/a estudiante si le gustan más estas cosas aquí o las cosas de la página anterior. ¿En qué son distintas?

Modelo	E1: **¿Te gusta más este reloj de plata aquí o aquel reloj de oro de la otra página?** E2: **Me gusta más este reloj de plata.**

1.

2.

3.

4.

Ⓟ **Conversaciones.** En parejas, lean la siguiente conversación en la cual una mujer compra un regalo para un amigo en una joyería. Luego, cambien la conversación para comprar algo para su mejor amigo/a o un familiar.

— Buenas tardes, señorita. ¿En qué puedo servirle?
— Deseo comprar un regalo para un amigo, **tal vez** un reloj.
— ¿Le gustan estos relojes? Tienen un descuento del 25 por ciento.
— **Me parecen** un poco grandes para mi amigo. ¿Qué precio tienen esos relojes que están al lado de los que están de oferta?
— Cuestan cincuenta dólares.
— Me voy a llevar el de plata.
— ¿Desea pagar en efectivo, con cheque o con tarjeta de crédito?
— Con mi tarjeta de crédito.
— ¿Puede **firmar** aquí? Gracias. Aquí tiene su **recibo.**
— Gracias, hasta luego.
— Adiós, señorita.

---

tal vez *maybe* **Me parece(n)…** *It seems (they seem)… to me* **firmar** *to sign* **un recibo** *a receipt*

Follow-up for 5-27. *¿Qué venden?* Conteste las preguntas con un pronombre de complemento directo. 1. ¿Venden las siguientes cosas en una mueblería? *Modelo:* camisas > *No, no las venden en una mueblería.* (*camas, sillas, faldas, libros, mesas, lámparas, perfume*) 2. ¿Venden estas cosas en una zapatería? (*botas, camisas, zapatos, sandalias, helado, calcetines, relojes*) 3. ¿Venden estas cosas en una joyería? (*cadenas de oro, aretes, relojes, trajes de baño, anillos, collares, café*) 4. ¿Venden estas cosas en un almacén? (*trajes, coches, abrigos, zapatos, pizza, muebles, casas*)

Follow-up for *Conversaciones.* Put these phrases on the board and have students use them to react to the following situations. *Eso me parece (caro, barato, normal, ridículo, muy bien).* 1. Una camiseta cuesta cincuenta dólares. 2. Ud. encuentra una cadena de oro por cinco dólares. 3. Toda la ropa que Ud. quiere comprar está de oferta con un descuento del cincuenta por ciento. 4. Un par de vaqueros cuesta treinta dólares. 5. Ud. quiere comprar una camisa, pero sólo tienen camisas de rayas rosadas y moradas. 6. Ud.

AUDIO ¡A escuchar!

Escuchen otra conversación en la cual una mujer está de compras. ¿Está en una joyería, una zapatería o una librería? ¿Qué compra? ¿Para quién es? ¿Cuánto paga y cómo?

quiere comprar un traje, y la tienda tiene más de cincuenta trajes de su talla de oferta. 7. No aceptan su tarjeta de crédito sin identificación. 8. Ud. quiere probarse algo en una tienda de ropa, pero no hay probadores en la tienda. 9. El dependiente siempre entra al probador con los clientes. 10. Los clientes no pueden probarse los zapatos sin calcetines. 11. Los clientes no pueden probarse la ropa sin bañarse primero en el baño de la tienda.

GRAMÁTICA
Dar explicaciones: ¿*por* o *para*?

Para averiguar

1. Do you use **por** or **para** to say something is true throughout an area of space or a period of time? Which do you use to talk about a destination point or a point in time?
2. Do you use **por** or **para** to express cause? to express purpose? What does **para** mean when it is followed by an infinitive?
3. Do you use **por** or **para** to express means? an exchange? a recipient?
4. Do you use **por** or **para** to say *for* what type of person or thing something is true? when clarifying whose point of view you are describing?

¡Ojo!

Remember that the pronouns used after prepositions look like the subject pronouns, except you use **mí** and **ti** instead of **yo** and **tú: por/para mí (ti, usted, él, ella, nosotros/as, vosotros/as, ustedes, ellos/as).**

— Voy a traer el regalo para **él.**
¿Paso por **ti** a las siete para ir a la fiesta?
— Es un poco temprano para **mí.**

The prepositions **por** and **para** can both mean *for* in English.

Use **por** to express:

1. during what period of time or for how long (*during, for*)	Voy de compras **por la tarde.** Vamos a estar en el centro comercial **por tres horas.**
2. through where one passes or the general area (*through, along, by, around*)	Vamos **por esta calle** y pasamos **por esta tienda.** Hay muchas tiendas **por acá.**
3. a cause (*on account of, because of, for*)	Esa tienda es famosa **por su ropa.** Estoy muy sorprendido **por los precios.**
4. an exchange (*for*)	No pago mucho **por mi ropa.** Gracias **por el regalo.**
5. means (*by, by way of, via*)	Hago muchas compras **por Internet.**
6. who or what is being picked up (*for*)	Vamos a la tienda **por las cosas** que necesitamos. Paso **por ti** a las ocho.

Use **para** to express:

1. a point in time, an occasion, or a deadline (*for, by*)	Necesito un traje nuevo **para el sábado.** Tenemos la reserva **para las seis.**
2. a destination (*for*)	Me voy **para el centro comercial.** ¿Cuál es el autobús **para el centro**?
3. a recipient or for whom or what something is intended (*for*)	Este regalo es **para ti.** Necesito una bolsa **para estas cosas.**
4. for what category of person or thing (*for*)	Este traje es muy elegante **para un niño de seis años.** Es muy barato **para un vestido de seda.**
5. from whose point of view (*for*)	**Para papá** es muy aburrido ir de compras. Es un poco caro **para mí.**
6. a purpose, goal, or intent (*to, in order to*)	Busco los probadores **para probarme** este traje. ¿Adónde vamos **para pagar**?

5-29 **¿Cierto o falso?** Lea las siguientes oraciones y decida por qué se usa **por** o **para.** ¿Es el uso 1, 2, 3, 4, 5 o 6 de la página anterior? Luego, diga si la oración es cierta o falsa para usted. Cambie las oraciones falsas para describir su propia (*own*) situación.

> Modelo
> Nunca pago más de cincuenta dólares *por* un par de zapatos.
> **Es el uso 4 de *por*. Para mí la oración es falsa. A veces, pago más de cincuenta dólares por un par de zapatos.**

1. A veces compro ropa *para* mi mejor amigo/a. 3
2. Hay muchas tiendas de ropa *por* acá. 2
3. Voy a estar en la universidad *por* tres horas hoy. 1
4. Voy a pasar *por* el centro comercial antes de regresar a casa hoy. 2
5. Compro muchas cosas *por* Internet. 5
6. *Para* mí, las camisas de seda son más cómodas que las de algodón. 5
7. *Para* salir a bailar, prefiero ponerme una falda corta. 6
8. Necesito comprar un traje de baño *para* mis próximas vacaciones. 1
9. Casi siempre salgo *para* la playa *por* unos días en el verano. 2, 1

5-30 **¿Para quién es?** Diga cuánto quieren por los siguientes artículos de ropa, si cada artículo es para hombre o para mujer y si es para el verano o el invierno.

> Modelo
> **Quieren noventa dólares por estas botas. Son para mujer y para el invierno.**

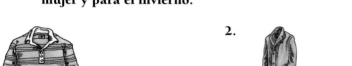

1.

2.

3.

4.

5.

6.

Supplemental activities. A. Have students say whether you use *por* or *para* to translate the following sentences. 1. Is the party for your wife? 2. It's for her birthday. 3. We are inviting several friends (in order) to celebrate. 4. I'm leaving for the bakery for the cake. 5. You need to pass by the ice cream shop (*heladería*) for ice cream for the cake. 6. I need the cake for tomorrow for a party. 7. I'm going to buy a gold chain for her birthday. 8. It's on sale for 70 dollars. 9. It's a cheap price for a chain of that quality. 10. It's a good gift for her. **B.** Completen las siguientes oraciones de manera lógica. 1. Hoy estoy en clase por... 2. Después de las clases, salgo de la universidad para... 3. Para regresar a casa, paso por... 4. No tengo planes para... 5. Necesito más tiempo para... 6. Necesito ir a la tienda por... 7. Pago mucho dinero por... 8. Me pongo ropa formal a veces para...

P **5-31** **¿Por o para?** En parejas, completen las siguientes preguntas con **por** o **para.** Luego, usen las preguntas para entrevistarse.

1. ¿Qué tienda prefieres _____ comprar ropa? ¿Prefieres esa tienda _____ sus bajos precios o _____ su buena selección? ¿Necesitas pasar _____ la tienda hoy? ¿_____ qué?

2. ¿Compras ropa _____ Internet a veces? ¿Usas tarjeta de crédito _____ pagar? ¿Estás preocupado/a _____ la seguridad (*security*)?

3. ¿Tienes más ropa _____ el verano o _____ el invierno? ¿Qué ropa te pones _____ ir a clase cuando hace calor? ¿Cuándo hace frío? ¿Qué ropa usas _____ varios días sin lavarla?

4. ¿Qué te pones generalmente _____ ocasiones formales? ¿Es muy importante _____ ti llevar ropa que está de moda?

¡Trato hecho!

En portada

Note: Have students complete the *Antes de leer, Reading strategies,* and *Ahora Ud.* activities before reading this article.

REVISTA CULTURAL

¿CUÁNDO SE MARCHAN DE CASA?

Una situación **bastante** habitual en España y en muchos **países** de Latinoamérica es **la permanencia** de los hijos solteros en la casa de sus padres. Prolongan los estudios, **tardan en** encontrar trabajo, en casarse, y viven más tiempo en casa de sus padres. En España, un 60% de los jóvenes entre 25 y 30 años que trabaja vive **todavía** en casa de los padres. ¿Cómo explicar esta tendencia?

La inestabilidad del mercado de trabajo y el alto precio de **la vivienda** son algunas de las razones que explican esta situación. **La juventud** hoy confronta un grave problema de **desempleo** y encuentra en su familia un gran **apoyo** económico y emocional. Los jóvenes se quedan en la casa de sus padres sin presión, hasta encontrar un buen trabajo.

También el cambio en la dinámica familiar puede explicar la **tardía** emancipación de los hijos. Las familias antes **eran** más tradicionales. Ahora padres e hijos hispánicos se entienden mejor en casa, se respetan más, no hay **barreras generacionales** tan grandes. Los horarios son flexibles y los jóvenes tienen su espacio personal y mucha libertad.

No existe entre los hijos hispanos ese **deseo** de independencia como ocurre en Estados Unidos, donde los hijos se marchan de casa cuando terminan la escuela secundaria, generalmente a la universidad o a vivir con compañeros de trabajo o con la pareja. Independizarse es la tendencia más común entre los jóvenes estadounidenses, muy diferente al estilo de vida de los jóvenes hispánicos.

---

se marchan *leave*   **bastante** *quite*   **países** *countries*   **la permanencia** *staying*   **tardan en** *take a long time to*   **todavía** *still*   **la vivienda** *housing*   **la juventud** *youth*   **desempleo** *unemployment*   **apoyo** *support*   **tardía** *late*   **eran** *were*   **barreras generacionales** *generation gaps*   **deseo** *desire*

Antes de leer

¿Vive usted en casa? ¿Vive con otros estudiantes de la universidad? ¿Cómo es la relación con su familia/sus compañeros de apartamento? ¿Qué hace con ellos?

Reading strategies: Skimming. Skimming allows for a rapid reading of a text to get the "gist" of its content. Glance over the title and first sentence of each paragraph to get an overview of the reading. What is the central theme, and what issues are being discussed in the text?

Después de leer

5-32 Ahora Ud. Lea la lectura e indique si las siguientes afirmaciones son ciertas o falsas.

Suggestion for 5-32. *Ahora Ud.* Have students do a first reading of the text without stopping before doing activities *5-32* and *5-33*. Then have them do a second reading of the text for greater comprehension of details before doing *5-34*.

	Cierto	Falso
1. El texto habla de las relaciones entre padres e hijos en los países hispánicos.	X	
2. Los hijos españoles no están contentos viviendo con sus padres.		X
3. Muchos hijos españoles no se marchan de casa de sus padres porque no tienen trabajo.	X	
4. Las familias españolas son ahora más liberales en las relaciones entre padres e hijos.	X	
5. El estilo de vida (*lifestyle*) de los jóvenes hispanos es diferente al estilo de vida de los jóvenes norteamericanos.	X	

5-33 ¿Se entienden? Complete las siguientes oraciones con el verbo reflexivo/recíproco apropiado al contexto.

> respetarse   casarse   marcharse   sentirse   entenderse

1. Los hijos hispanos no __se marchan__ de casa tan pronto como los hijos norteamericanos.

2. Los jóvenes españoles __se sienten__ cómodos viviendo en el hogar (*home*) familiar.

3. Padres e hijos en las familias hispanas __se entienden__ ahora mejor que en el pasado (*the past*).

4. Padres e hijos en las familias hispanas __se respetan__ en sus horarios y su espacio personal.

5. Los hijos españoles encuentran un trabajo más tarde y __se casan__ más tarde; por eso están más tiempo viviendo con sus padres.

5-34 En detalle. Conteste las siguientes preguntas de acuerdo con la lectura y su perspectiva personal.

1. ¿Cuál es la situación familiar habitual de los hijos solteros españoles de entre 25 y 30 años?

2. ¿Cuál es uno de los graves problemas que confrontan los jóvenes hispanos?

3. ¿Por qué es difícil para los jóvenes hispanos obtener su propia vivienda?

4. ¿Por qué se sienten tan cómodos los hijos españoles adultos quedándose en casa de sus padres?

5. ¿Cómo es la situación de los jóvenes norteamericanos? ¿Qué opina usted de estas diferencias?

P 5-35 Las diferentes rutinas. Compare las diferentes rutinas de los estudiantes que viven en casa de sus padres, los estudiantes que viven en una residencia universitaria en el campus y los estudiantes que viven en su propio apartamento.

Follow-up for 5-35. *Las diferentes rutinas.* Have students list the pros and cons of living with one's parents as a university student.

De puertas abiertas a la comunidad

VIDEO BOCADOS DE REALIDAD

G **5-36** **Entrando en materia.** Piensen en los distintos grupos étnicos que viven en Estados Unidos. ¿Cómo creen que viven su herencia (*heritage*) en su rutina diaria (*daily*)? Y ustedes ¿cómo viven su herencia familiar?

> Vivimos en **un mundo con fronteras cada vez más estrechas,** donde las tradiciones y las culturas se encuentran y donde la identidad de los pueblos **se hace** cada vez más global. Pero todavía las personas se sienten **orgullosas** de su origen y de sus **raíces** y viven su herencia de una manera peculiar.
> Escuchen **los bocados de realidad** recogidos en el vídeo y vean cómo viven su herencia, cómo piensan y sienten estas personas del mundo hispánico.

5-37 **Herencia hispana.** ¿Cuál es la herencia cultural de las personas que aparecen en el vídeo? Complete las siguientes oraciones con el adjetivo de nacionalidad apropiado en cada caso. Preste (*Pay*) atención al género del adjetivo.

> mexicano   costarricense   puertorriqueño   paraguayo

1. Analissa Martínez es _____ mexicana _____.

2. Jorge Merced es _____ puertorriqueño _____.

3. Itandehui Chávez es _____ mexicana _____.

4. Edgar Alcáraz es _____ paraguayo _____.

5. Rosal Colón es _____ puertorriqueña _____.

6. Héctor Marín es _____ costarricense _____.

5-38 **¿Se sienten orgullosos?** Escuche con atención las palabras de las personas en el vídeo que hablan sobre su herencia y sus raíces y responda de manera general a las siguientes preguntas con la información que nos ofrecen.

1. ¿Se sienten orgullosos de su herencia?

_____

2. ¿Se encuentran con gente de su mismo origen en la ciudad donde viven?

_____

3. ¿Se divierten viviendo su herencia en su vida diaria (*daily life*)? ¿Cómo se divierten?

_____

4. ¿Cómo se sienten viviendo en Nueva York?

_____

---

un mundo con fronteras cada vez más estrechas *a world with ever closer borders*   **se hace** *becomes*
orgullosas *proud*   **raíces** *roots*   **los bocados de realidad** *reality bites*

5-39 Descripciones. Describa a las personas que aparecen en las fotos e imagine qué hacen cuando están con sus seres queridos y cuando tienen tiempo libre.

Analissa Martínez, músico.

Edgar Alcáraz, estudiante de administración de empresas.

Héctor Marín, pintor.

5-40 Bocados de realidad. Escuche de nuevo el vídeo fijándose (*focusing*) en los detalles de los testimonios de estas personas y complete las siguientes reflexiones con las palabras que aparecen en la caja.

> comunidad mexicana   extraño   las artes   busco
> la cultura   satisfacción   puertorriqueño   me relaciono

Jorge Merced, actor.

"Mi herencia puertorriqueña aquí en Estados Unidos es una que se nutre diariamente de la labor que llevo a cabo a través de (*I carry out through*) _____ y _____. A través de la manera en que _____, pues, con mi familia también acá, porque tengo familia en Nueva York, también, donde pues continuamente nos nutrimos unos a los otros (*we inspire one another*) de lo que significa ser _____ viviendo en esta gran urbe de Nueva York."

Itandehui Chávez, estudiante de literatura y medios de comunicación.

"Bueno, tengo la fortuna de vivir en Nueva York, donde hay muchos mexicanos, este, entonces, pues siempre que _____ y _____ la cultura, es muy accesible en esta ciudad.[...] Pero en particular, ahorita lo que me da más _____ y más acceso a la _____ es mi trabajo con la Academia de Mariachi, que es una organización sin fines de lucro (*non-profit*), que empezamos (*we began*) hace un par de años y bueno, yo soy la coordinadora de ese proyecto."

Escapadas

TOLEDO: LA CIUDAD DE LAS TRES CULTURAS

Toledo, ciudad de las tres culturas.

España es un país interesante por **la mezcla** de tradiciones y **creencias** que allí **conviven** durante **siglos.** Toledo es un **bello** ejemplo de tolerancia de las tres religiones predominantes de occidente: el cristianismo, el judaísmo y el islamismo.

Toledo, situada en la actual región de Castilla La Mancha, a pocos kilómetros de Madrid, es una ciudad con un pasado fascinante. Toledo es **conquistada** por los romanos en el año 192 a.C. y después pasa a ser territorio **visigodo** en el año 411, hasta **la llegada** de los musulmanes en el año 711. El Islam domina Toledo hasta **la reconquista cristiana** con Alfonso VI en el año 1085.

Durante siglos Toledo acepta con tolerancia las costumbres y las religiones de sus habitantes —cristianos, judíos y musulmanes— que **crean** una gran **riqueza** cultural y económica.

Molinos de viento junto al Castillo de San Juan de los Caballeros, Toledo.

Cerámicas toledanas.

---

la mezcla *the mixture*   **creencias** *beliefs*   **conviven** *live together*   **siglos** *centuries*   **bello/a** *beautiful* **conquistada** *conquered*   **visigodo** *Visigothic*   **la llegada** *the arrival*   **la reconquista cristiana** *the Christian Reconquest*   **crean** *create*   **riqueza** *richness*

Ejemplos de la presencia del Islam son **el diseño** de la ciudad y edificios como la Mezquita del Cristo de la Luz, donde se celebra la primera **misa** cristiana después de la reconquista de la ciudad.

Los judíos, que viven en Toledo desde la época visigoda, dejan **muestras** de su cultura y de su religión en edificios como la Sinagoga del Tránsito, donde está hoy el Museo Sefardí, que ofrece una visión del pueblo judío y su relación con España.

La Catedral **se empieza a construir** en el siglo XII y no se completa hasta el siglo XV. Es de estilo gótico y refleja **el renacimiento** de la religión cristiana con Alfonso VI.

La Sinagoga del Tránsito, Toledo.

A partir del siglo XIV, el ambiente de tolerancia empieza a cambiar, y la llegada de los Reyes Católicos inicia un período de persecución religiosa que termina con la expulsión de los judíos y los musulmanes de España en el siglo XV.

La Catedral, Toledo.

Altar mayor de la Catedral de Toledo.

---

el diseño *the design* **misa** *mass* **muestras** *samples* **se empieza a construir** *starts to be built*
el renacimiento *the Renaissance* **A partir del siglo XIV, el ambiente** *Starting in the 14th century, the atmosphere*

5-41 **¿Por o para?** Complete las siguientes oraciones relacionadas con el texto sobre Toledo con la preposición **por** o **para** de acuerdo con el contexto. Después explique en cada caso el uso de la preposición. Indique después si las afirmaciones son ciertas o falsas, y corrija las falsas.

1. La ciudad de Toledo es interesante ____por____ su pasado fascinante. cierto
2. Toledo es conquistada ____por____ los visigodos en el año 711. falso
3. Musulmanes, budistas y cristianos viven juntos en Toledo ____por____ muchos siglos. falso
4. ____Para____ Alfonso VI no es importante reconquistar la ciudad de Toledo. falso
5. En una excursión ____por____ Toledo se observa la riqueza arquitectónica de las tres culturas. cierto
6. Durante el período de los Reyes Católicos se inicia una persecución religiosa ____para____ expulsar a los judíos y a los musulmanes de España. cierto

P **5-42** **Asociaciones.** ¿Con cuál de las tres culturas predominantes del Toledo de la época asocia las siguientes ideas? Puede asociar una idea con más de una cultura.

la riqueza cultural y económica

Alfonso VI

la Sinagoga del Tránsito

la persecución religiosa

la Reconquista

la Mezquita del Cristo de la Luz

la tolerancia religiosa

el Museo Sefardí

el diseño de la ciudad

los Reyes Católicos

la catedral

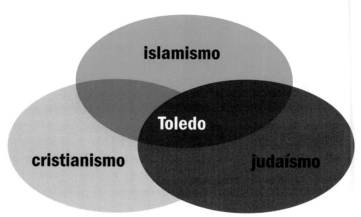

5-43 **Riqueza cultural.** Muchas ciudades de Estados Unidos se caracterizan por una gran mezcla cultural y religiosa. Busque información en la red sobre una ciudad que sea un ejemplo de esta mezcla y tolerancia cultural y prepare un breve informe (*a brief report*) para presentarlo a la clase.

En palabras de...

DISEÑADORES DE MODA

Imagine que trabaja para una compañía de diseño de ropa y tiene que preparar un informe (*report*) de la nueva línea para hombre y mujer de la próxima temporada (*season*). Describa las tendencias en colores, prendas y complementos (*garments and accessories*). Puede incluir fotos documentando su informe.

Writing strategies: Preparing a report. When writing a report about a topic, some basic steps should be followed. First, define the purpose of your report and make it clear and meaningful to the reader. Second, decide on the main ideas to include in your report. Third, decide on the logical order for your ideas. Fourth, create a content-oriented and informative title. Fifth, edit and proofread the report.

Antes de escribir

Imagine la nueva línea de ropa y complementos de la temporada. Piense en el vocabulario relacionado con la ropa para las distintas ocasiones: para las fiestas, para ir a trabajar, para ir a la universidad, para hacer deporte.

Luego, piense en el vocabulario relacionado con los colores, los tejidos (*fabrics*), la temporada del año —primavera, verano, otoño, invierno. Después prepare su informe siguiendo los pasos (*steps*) 1-4 sugeridos con anterioridad en la estrategia de escritura y utilizando estructuras para hablar del vestir (*wardrobe*) como: **está de moda, no está de moda, esta temporada...**

Después de escribir

Revise y edite su informe, asegurándose que contiene los siguientes puntos.

 Lista de control:

___ El vocabulario relacionado con la ropa, los colores, los tejidos.
___ Las estructuras para expresar selección: los demostrativos.
___ Las preposiciones *por* y *para* en sus distintos usos.

 **En la red**

G ¿Qué está de moda en el mundo hispánico? Visite las páginas de moda de algunos diseñadores hispanos y describa las tendencias femeninas y masculinas de esta temporada. ¿Qué diseñador/a le gusta más? ¿Por qué?

All the sources consulted for the readings are cited on the *¡Trato hecho!* Web site at **www.prenhall.com/trato**

VOCABULARIO

TEMA ❶

Expresiones verbales

acostarse (ue) *to lie down, to go to bed*

bañarse *to bathe, to take a bath*

despertarse (ie) *to wake up*

divertirse (ie) *to have fun, to amuse oneself*

ducharse *to shower, to take a shower*

encontrarse (ue) *to get together, to meet one another*

irse *to leave, to go away*

lavarse el pelo *to wash your hair*

lavarse los dientes *to brush your teeth*

levantarse *to get up*

llamarse *to be called/named*

maquillarse *to put on make-up*

quedarse *to stay*

relajarse *to relax*

sentarse (ie) *to sit down*

sentirse (ie) *to feel*

vestirse (i) *to get dressed*

Pronombres reflexivos y recíprocos

me *myself*

te *yourself*

se *himself, herself, yourself, yourselves, themselves, each other, one another*

nos *ourselves, each other, one another*

os *yourselves, each other, one another*

TEMA ❷

Expresiones verbales

abrazarse *to hug each other*

acabar de + infinitive *to have just* + past participle

besarse *to kiss each other*

casarse (con) *to get married (to)*

comunicarse *to get in touch with each other, to contact each other*

darse la mano *to shake hands*

darse un abrazo/un beso *to give each other a hug/a kiss*

despedirse (i) *to say good-bye*

enojarse *to get angry*

hablarse *to talk to each other*

llevarse bien/mal *to get along well/badly*

pelearse *to fight*

quererse (ie) *to love each other*

reconciliarse *to make up*

verse *to see one another*

Otra expresión

por lo general *in general*

TEMA ❸

De compras

un abrigo *an overcoat*

un almacén *a department store*

una blusa *a blouse*

una boda *a wedding*

una bolsa *a purse*

(unas) botas *(some) boots*

una boutique *a boutique*

(unos) calcetines *(some) socks*

una camisa *a shirt*

una camiseta *a T-shirt*

una chaqueta *a jacket*

un cinturón *a belt*

una corbata *a necktie*

una cosa *a thing*

una falda *a skirt*

un impermeable *a raincoat*

(unos) pantalones *(some) pants*

(unos) pantalones cortos *(some) shorts*

un precio *a price*

(unas) sandalias *(some) sandals*

un sombrero *a hat*

una sudadera *a sweatshirt*

un suéter *a sweater*

(unos) tenis *(some) tennis shoes*

un traje *a suit*

un traje de baño *a swimsuit*

(unos) vaqueros *(some) jeans*

un vestido *a dress*

(unos) zapatos *(some) shoes*

Adjetivos

aquel/aquella (aquellos/as) *that (those) (over there)*

barato/a *cheap*

cómodo/a *comfortable*

ese/esa (esos/as) *that (those)*

este/esta (estos/as) *this (these)*

razonable *reasonable*

roto/a *torn*

Otras palabras y expresiones

una camisa de cuadros (de rayas, de un solo color) *a checkered / plaid (striped, solid-colored) shirt*

el/la (los/las) que *the one (ones) that*

estar de moda *to be in fashion*

la ropa de algodón (de cuero, de lana, de mezclilla, de seda) *cotton (leather, wool, denim, silk) clothes*

llevar *to take, to carry, to wear*

ponerse (la ropa) *to put on (clothes)*

TEMA 4

En la tienda
la caja *the cash register*
el cliente/la clienta *the customer*
el dependiente/la dependienta
  the salesclerk
el efectivo *cash*
los probadores *the fitting rooms*
la talla *the size*
una tarjeta de crédito *a credit card*
una tarjeta de débito *a debit card*

Verbos
aceptar *to accept*

buscar *to look for*
gastar *to spend*
llevarse algo *to take something*
probarse (ue) *to try on*

Pronombres de complemento directo
me *me*
te *you (familiar, singular)*
lo *you (formal, singular), him, it*
la *you (formal, singular), her, it*
nos *us*
os *you (familiar, plural)*

los *you (plural), them*
las *you (plural), them*

Otras palabras y expresiones
Aquí lo/la tiene. *Here it is.*
¿Cuánto cuesta(n)? *How much does it (do they) cost?*
de oferta *on sale*
¿En qué puedo servirle? *How may I help you?*
por acá *over here, through here*
Sí, cómo no. *Yes, of course.*

TEMA 5

De compras
un anillo *a ring*
(unos) aretes *(some) earrings*
una cadena de oro *a golden chain*
una carnicería *a butcher's shop*
una cartera *a wallet, a billfold*
un collar de plata *a silver necklace*
un descuento del... por ciento
  a... percent discount
una gorra *a cap*
una joyería *a jewelry store*

un juguete *a toy*
un paraguas *an umbrella*
una pastelería *a pastry shop, a bakery*
una peluquería *a hair salon*
una pescadería *a seafood shop*
un recibo *a receipt*
un regalo *a gift, a present*
una zapatería *a shoe store*

Expresiones verbales
cortarse el pelo *to cut one's hair, to get one's hair cut*
firmar *to sign*
hacer mandados *to run errands*

Otras expresiones
Me parece(n)... *It seems (They seem)... to me*
tal vez *maybe, perhaps*

6

De viaje

TEMA 1

VOCABULARIO
¿Adónde fuiste de vacaciones?

¿Adónde fuiste de vacaciones? ¿Con quién **viajaste**? ¿Cuánto gastaste?

Plaza de Mayo, Buenos Aires, Argentina.

Fui a una ciudad grande.
Me alojé en un hotel grande.
Fui a un parque de atracciones.
Visité los museos.
Vi una obra de teatro.

Bosque nuboso de Monteverde, Costa Rica.

Fui al campo / a la montaña.
Acampé con mis amigos.
Descendí por el río en canoa.
Fui de excursión por **el bosque**.

Chichén Itzá, México.

Fui a un país extranjero.
Fui al mercado y compré **recuerdos**.
Visité los sitios históricos y las ruinas
   y **saqué** muchas fotos.
Aprendí mucho sobre la historia.
Comí en muchos restaurantes y probé
   los platos regionales.

Costa del Sol, España.

Fui a la playa.
Hice un crucero.
Tomé el sol y nadé.
Salí en **velero**.
Pesqué en **el mar**.

¿Qué hiciste antes de salir?

Consulté las guías turísticas y preparé un itinerario.

Compré los pasajes (los boletos, los billetes) de avión y reservé la habitación de hotel con unas semanas de antelación en una agencia de viajes.

¿Adónde fuiste? *Where did you go?*   **viajar** *to travel*   **alojarse en** *to stay at (on a trip)*   **Fui** *I went*   **ir de excursión** *to go on a hike / an outing*   **el bosque** *the forest, the woods*   **un recuerdo** *a souvenir*   **sacar** *to take, to take out, to get*   **un plato** *a dish, a plate*   **hacer un crucero** *to go on a cruise*   **un velero** *a sailboat*   **pescar** *to fish*   **el mar** *the sea*   **¿Qué hiciste?** *What did you do?*   **los pasajes, los boletos, los billetes** *the tickets*

Cambié dinero y compré cheques de viaje.   **Saqué un pasaporte y una visa.**

Compré una maleta, un saco de dormir, rollos de película,   **Hice la maleta.**
una cámara, gafas de sol, crema protectora solar.

¡Ojo!

En España se dice **un billete** en vez de **un pasaje** o **un boleto** (*a ticket*). En algunas regiones se dice **los lentes de sol** o **los anteojos de sol** en vez de **las gafas de sol** (*sunglasses*), **con anticipación** en vez de **con antelación** (*in advance*) y **un visado** en vez de **una visa** (*a visa*).

6-1   De vacaciones. Si un amigo dice que hizo (*he did*) estas cosas de vacaciones, ¿fue (*did he go*) a una ciudad grande, al campo, a un país extranjero o a la playa?

> Modelo   Visité las ruinas incas de Machu Picchu.
> **Fue a un país extranjero.**

1. Fui a ver tres obras de teatro.
2. Acampé en el bosque.
3. Saqué muchas fotos de las pirámides y otros sitios históricos.
4. Nadé y salí en velero.
5. Me divertí mucho en los parques de atracciones.
6. Pesqué y descendí por el río en canoa.

6-2   ¿Y usted? Cambie las oraciones para describir sus últimas vacaciones.

1. Fui *a Nueva York*.
2. Viajé *con mi novio*.
3. Pasé mucho tiempo *en los museos*.
4. Vi *muchas obras de teatro*.
5. Compré *muchos recuerdos y dos camisetas*.
6. Me divertí mucho *comiendo en los restaurantes*.

Supplemental activities.
A. Preguntas. 1. Generalmente, ¿cómo compra Ud. los pasajes de avión, por Internet, por teléfono o en una agencia de viajes? 2. ¿Reserva la habitación de hotel con mucho tiempo de antelación o busca un hotel después de llegar? ¿La reserva por Internet, por teléfono o en una agencia de viajes? ¿Cómo paga, con tarjeta de crédito, con dinero en efectivo o con cheque de viaje? 3. ¿Consulta una guía turística antes de salir? ¿Hace un itinerario antes de salir o día a día durante el viaje? 4. ¿Hace la maleta la noche antes de salir o el día del viaje? ¿Lleva muchas maletas? 5. ¿Llega Ud. al aeropuerto en el último momento? 6. ¿Desayuna en el hotel o en un restaurante? **B.** 1. ¿Cuál es un buen lugar para acampar (pescar) cerca de aquí? ¿Le gusta acampar o prefiere alojarse en un hotel, donde puede dormir en una cama y bañarse? 2. ¿En qué ciudad hay muchos parques de atracciones? ¿Cuál es su parque de atracciones preferido? 3. ¿Qué país extranjero desea visitar? ¿Por qué?

Ⓟ   **Conversaciones.** En parejas, lean la siguiente conversación en la cual dos amigos hablan de sus últimas vacaciones. Luego, cambien la conversación para hablar de sus vacaciones más interesantes.

— ¿Qué tal tus vacaciones?
— Muy bien. Fui a México.
— ¿Qué hiciste en México?
— Pasé cuatro días en Cancún donde fui a la playa todos los días. Luego, fui a Mérida por tres días. Me gustó mucho. Visité las ruinas mayas de Chichén Itzá. Y tú, ¿qué hiciste de vacaciones?
— No hice nada en especial. Me quedé aquí y descansé.

Chichén Itzá, México.

AUDIO ¡A escuchar!

Escuchen otra conversación en la cual una pareja habla de sus preparativos para las vacaciones. ¿Adónde van? ¿Qué van a hacer? ¿Qué preparativos están listos? ¿Qué necesitan hacer todavía (*still*)?

---

hacer la maleta *to pack one's suitcase*

GRAMÁTICA

Hablar de acontecimientos pasados: el pretérito de los verbos regulares y los verbos *ir* y *ser*

To say what someone did or what happened at some point in the past, use the preterite. Here are the preterite forms of regular **-ar, -er,** and **-ir** verbs. Note that the **nosotros** form of **-ar** and **-ir** verbs looks the same as the present tense. Context will clarify the meaning. The **nosotros** form of **-er** verbs has **i** instead of **e** in the ending of the preterite.

	HABLAR	COMER	ESCRIBIR
yo	habl**é**	com**í**	escrib**í**
tú	habl**aste**	com**iste**	escrib**iste**
usted, él, ella	habl**ó**	com**ió**	escrib**ió**
nosotros/as	habl**amos**	com**imos**	escrib**imos**
vosotros/as	habl**asteis**	com**isteis**	escrib**isteis**
ustedes, ellos/as	habl**aron**	com**ieron**	escrib**ieron**

— ¿**Compraste** los boletos?
— Sí, los **compré** ayer.

— *Did you buy the tickets?*
— *Yes, I bought them yesterday.*

— ¿Ya **comieron** ustedes?
— Sí, **comimos** en el avión.

— *Did you already eat?*
— *Yes, we ate on the plane.*

— ¿Quién **abrió** mi maleta?
— Yo la **abrí**.

— *Who opened my suitcase?*
— *I opened it.*

Ver and **salir** have regular **-er/-ir** preterite forms, except there is no accent on the **yo** form of **ver** (**yo vi**), because it is only one syllable.

The verbs **ir** and **ser** are irregular and look the same in the preterite.

	IR / SER		
yo	**fui**	nosotros/as	**fuimos**
tú	**fuiste**	vosotros/as	**fuisteis**
usted, él, ella	**fue**	ustedes, ellos/as	**fueron**

— ¿Adónde **fuiste** de vacaciones?
— **Fui** a Costa Rica.
— Anita **fue** contigo, ¿verdad?
— No, no **fue** Anita, **fue** Mari.

— *Where did you go on vacation?*
— *I went to Costa Rica.*
— *Anita went with you, right?*
— *No, it wasn't Anita, it was Mari.*

Here are some useful words to say when something happened.

ayer (por la mañana, por la tarde)	*yesterday (morning, afternoon)*
anoche	*last night*
la semana pasada	*last week*
el mes (el año, el sábado...) pasado	*last month (year, Saturday...)*
hace tres días (dos meses, mucho tiempo...)	*three days (two months, a long time...) ago*
por última vez	*the last time*

6-3 ¿Cuándo? Diga cuándo estas personas hicieron las cosas indicadas por última vez.

> **Modelo**   Yo… (salir con unos amigos)
> **Salí con unos amigos anoche (el fin de semana pasado…).**

1. Yo… (comer pizza, comprar algo, visitar otra ciudad, ir a un café, levantarme tarde, quedarme en casa todo el día, escribir un correo electrónico, viajar en autobús)
2. Mi mejor amigo/a… conmigo… (pasar todo el día, salir a bailar, cenar, desayunar, estudiar, ir a una fiesta, ver una película, pelearse)
3. Mis padres… (ir de vacaciones, comprar un coche nuevo, visitar a los abuelos, salir al cine, enojarse conmigo)
4. Mi madre y yo… juntos/as… (pasar las vacaciones, comer, ir a la playa, ver la televisión, ver una obra de teatro, ir de compras)

6-4 Un viaje. Dos personas fueron de vacaciones. ¿Hicieron estas cosas antes de salir o durante (*during*) el viaje?

> **Modelo**   comprar los boletos
> **Compraron los boletos antes de salir.**

1. comprar los cheques de viaje
2. cambiar los cheques de viaje
3. decidir adónde ir de vacaciones
4. reservar el hotel
5. comer en muchos restaurantes
6. ver muchos monumentos
7. ir a la agencia de viajes
8. preparar un itinerario

6-5 ¿Adónde fueron? Una joven dice adónde fueron los miembros de su familia el fin de semana pasado y cuáles de las siguientes cosas hicieron. ¿Qué dice?

> comprar ropa   salir en velero y pescar   escuchar música clásica
> correr   ver un partido de fútbol   comer y hablar con sus amigos

> **Modelo**   Mis padres…
> **Mis padres fueron al lago. Salieron en velero y pescaron.**

1. Mi hermana…

2. Mi abuela…

3. Mi abuelo y mi hermano…

4. Yo…

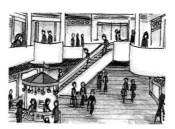

5. Mi novio y yo…

Supplemental activities.
A. Complete las siguientes oraciones, diciendo cuántas veces Ud. hizo estas cosas la semana pasada. *Modelo: Hablé con mis padres… > Hablé con mis padres una vez (dos veces, muchas veces) la semana pasada. / No hablé con mis padres la semana pasada.* 1. Lavé la ropa… 2. Trabajé… 3. Desayuné en un restaurante… 4. Cené en un restaurante… 5. Visité a mi mejor amigo/a… 6. Comí con mis padres… 7. Vi una película… 8. Fui a un concierto… 9. Leí el periódico… 10. Escribí un correo electrónico… 11. Salí a bailar… 12. Fui a la universidad… 13. Fui de compras… 14. Fui a la biblioteca…
B. En la última clase de español, ¿quiénes hicieron las siguientes cosas? *Modelo: comer en clase > Sara y Roberto comieron en clase. / Casi todos comimos en clase. / Nadie comió en clase.* (asistir a la clase de español, escribir en la pizarra, hablar mucho español, aprender algo nuevo, beber algo en clase, salir temprano de clase, ver un vídeo en clase, escuchar con atención, pelearse, comprenderlo todo)

Follow-up for 6-5. ¿*Adónde fueron?*
Diga cuándo Ud. fue a los siguientes lugares por última vez y qué hizo. *Modelo: al parque > Fui al parque hace dos semanas y corrí por treinta minutos. / No recuerdo (I don't recall) cuándo fui al parque por última vez. / Nunca fui al parque.* (al cine, al teatro, al centro comercial, a la biblioteca, al aeropuerto, al lago, a la playa, a la casa de su mejor amigo/a, a la casa de sus padres, a una fiesta, a otra ciudad grande, a un país extranjero, a otro estado, al gimnasio, al estadio).

VOCABULARIO

TEMA ❷ ¿Qué tal el vuelo?

¿Qué hiciste la última vez que viajaste en avión? ¿Cuánto tiempo **duró** el vuelo?

Llegué al aeropuerto dos horas antes del vuelo.

Facturé mi equipaje.

Fui a la sala de espera donde esperé un poco más de una hora.

Subí al avión y busqué mi asiento.

Durante el vuelo…

Me abroché el cinturón de seguridad para despegar.

Leí una guía turística.

Los asistentes de vuelo sirvieron la comida y almorcé.

Hablé con otros pasajeros y dormí un poco.

Después de **aterrizar**…

Bajé del avión.

Recogí mi equipaje.

Pasé por la aduana.

Busqué un taxi.

Supplemental activity. Write these nouns on the board and have students complete the following statements with one of them: *la sala de espera, la hora de llegada, la hora de salida, la entrada, la salida, pasajeros, viajes, servicio, un asiento, duración, la pista de aterrizaje* (the runway), *los despegues.* Point out that the verb/adjective and noun are from the same word family. 1. Muchos... pasan por el aeropuerto todos los días. 2. Los pasajeros entran al aeropuerto por... 3. Esperan el avión en... 4. En el avión, se sientan en... 5. El avión sale a... 6. El avión llega a... 7. El avión aterriza en... 8. Los pasajeros salen del aeropuerto por... 9. Me gusta viajar. Hago muchos... 10. Siempre tengo miedo cuando el avión va a despegar. No me gustan... 11. Generalmente, traigo una novela si el vuelo dura mucho tiempo pero leo una revista en el avión durante los vuelos de corta... 12. Generalmente, los asistentes de vuelo que sirven las bebidas y la comida son buenos pero a veces no hay buen...

durar *to last* **la sala de espera** *the waiting room* **un asiento** *a seat* **despegar** *to take off* **aterrizar** *to land*

6-6 **¿Qué tal el vuelo?** Un pasajero habla de su último viaje. ¿En qué orden dice que ocurrieron estas cosas?

> **Modelo** Hice mi maleta. / Salí para el aeropuerto. / Me levanté temprano.
> **Me levanté temprano, hice mi maleta y salí para el aeropuerto.**

1. Tomé un taxi al aeropuerto. / Llegué una hora antes del vuelo. / Salí temprano de casa.
2. Fui a la sala de espera. / Facturé mi equipaje. / Esperé el vuelo.
3. Subí al avión. / Anunciaron mi vuelo. / Busqué mi asiento.
4. Me senté. / El avión despegó. / Me abroché el cinturón de seguridad.
5. Sirvieron el almuerzo. / Almorcé. / Los asistentes de vuelo recogieron los platos y la basura (trash).
6. Recogí mi equipaje. / Bajé del avión. / Aterrizamos.
7. Fui a mi hotel. / Busqué un taxi. / Subí al taxi.

ⓟ 6-7 **Entrevista.** Entreviste a otro/a estudiante con las siguientes preguntas.

¿Cuándo viajaste en avión por última vez? ¿Adónde fuiste? ¿Llevaste mucho equipaje? ¿Quién viajó contigo? ¿Cuánto costó el boleto? ¿Lo compraste por Internet, por teléfono, en una agencia de viajes o en el aeropuerto? ¿Desayunaste, almorzaste o cenaste en el avión? ¿Llegaste a tiempo o con retraso (late)? ¿Adónde fuiste después de llegar? ¿Alguien te recogió en el aeropuerto o tomaste un taxi?

ⓟ **Conversaciones.** En parejas, lean la siguiente conversación en la cual un pasajero habla con una encargada de una aerolínea. Luego, imaginen que uno de ustedes hace un viaje entre dos países en América del Sur. Cambien la conversación para decir qué ciudad va a visitar y dónde prefiere sentarse.

> — Buenos días y **bienvenido** a Aerolíneas Encanto. Su pasaje y su pasaporte, por favor. ¿Adónde va usted esta mañana?
> — Voy a Lima en el vuelo 534. Aquí tiene mi pasaje y mi pasaporte. **Hacemos escala** en Quito, ¿verdad?
> — Sí, es correcto, hay escala en Quito. Veo que usted pidió un asiento **junto a la ventanilla,** ¿verdad?
> — Sí, pero decidí que prefiero estar junto **al pasillo** si hay algo **disponible.**
> — **Lo siento,** pero no tengo nada disponible junto al pasillo.
> — En ese caso me quedo con el asiento junto a la ventanilla.
> — ¿Cuántas maletas va a facturar?
> — Tengo estas dos.
> — Aquí tiene **el comprobante** de sus maletas y su **tarjeta de embarque.** La salida del vuelo 534 es por **la puerta** 18 y empiezan a abordar a las diez de la mañana.

---

bienvenido/a *welcome*   hacer escala *to make a stopover*   junto a *next to*   la ventanilla *the window (of a plane)*
el pasillo *the aisle*   disponible *available*   Lo siento *I'm sorry*   el comprobante *the receipt*   la tarjeta de
embarque *the boarding pass*   la puerta *the gate*

Supplemental activity. ¿Quiénes hacen estas cosas durante un vuelo, los asistentes de vuelo o los pasajeros? 1. Suben primero al avión. 2. Bajan primero del avión. 3. Necesitan un pasaje para subir al avión. 4. Sirven comida y bebidas. 5. Esperan el vuelo en la sala de espera. 6. Preparan el avión antes del vuelo. 7. Sólo se sientan para despegar y aterrizar. 8. Pueden dormir durante el vuelo. 9. Hablan con todos los pasajeros. 10. Toman el avión casi todos los días.

Follow-up for 6-6. *¿Qué tal el vuelo?* ¿Hizo un turista las siguientes cosas en la agencia de viajes o en el aeropuerto? 1. Compró su pasaje de avión con cuatro semanas de antelación. 2. Facturó su equipaje. 3. Consultó varias guías turísticas para hacer un itinerario para el viaje. 4. Reservó la habitación de hotel. 5. Esperó el avión en la sala de espera. 6. Subió al avión. 7. Comparó los vuelos y los precios. 8. Recogió su equipaje después de bajar del avión.

AUDIO ¡A escuchar!

Escuchen otra conversación en la cual una pareja habla de un viaje que van a hacer. ¿Adónde van y por qué? ¿Cuándo salen y cuándo vuelven? ¿Cuánto cuestan los boletos?

Follow-up for *Conversaciones.* Preguntas. 1. ¿Tiene miedo de viajar en avión? ¿Está más nervioso/a mientras el avión despega o mientras aterriza? 2. ¿Viaja por avión con frecuencia? ¿Cuántas veces viajó por avión el año pasado? 3. ¿Qué hace en el aeropuerto si tiene que esperar el avión por mucho tiempo? ¿Duerme? ¿Lee un libro? ¿Habla con otros pasajeros? ¿Toma una copa? ¿Visita las boutiques del aeropuerto? Generalmente, ¿salen los vuelos a tiempo aquí? 4. ¿Prefiere tomar un vuelo con escalas y pagar menos o tomar un vuelo sin escalas y pagar más? 5. ¿Prefiere sentarse en el fondo del avión, en el centro o en el frente? ¿Prefiere un asiento junto a la ventanilla, en el centro o junto al pasillo? 6. Si va a hacer escala y tiene que cambiar de avión, ¿prefiere facturar todo su equipaje o prefiere llevar una maleta pequeña con Ud.?

GRAMÁTICA

Más acciones pasadas: el pretérito de los verbos en -car, -gar, -zar y los verbos como *leer*

Verbs ending with **-car**, **-gar**, and **-zar** have the following spelling changes in the **yo** form of the preterite: **c → qu**, **g → gu**, and **z → c**. There is also a spelling change with **-er** and **-ir** verbs when the stem ends with a vowel, as in **leer: le-**. The **i** of the **-ió** and **-ieron** endings becomes **y** when it falls between vowels, and the **i** of all the other endings has a written accent mark.

	BUSCAR	PAGAR	EMPEZAR	LEER
yo	bus**qué**	pa**gué**	empe**cé**	le**í**
tú	buscaste	pagaste	empezaste	le**í**ste
usted, él, ella	buscó	pagó	empezó	le**y**ó
nosotros/as	buscamos	pagamos	empezamos	le**í**mos
vosotros/as	buscasteis	pagasteis	empezasteis	le**í**steis
ustedes, ellos/as	buscaron	pagaron	empezaron	le**y**eron

Here are the other verbs you have seen that follow these patterns:

Like **buscar: pescar, sacar, tocar.**
Like **pagar: despegar, jugar, llegar.**
Like **empezar: abrazar, almorzar, aterrizar, rezar.**
Like **leer: creer, oír.**

Almorcé con mi esposa en un restaurante que nos gustó mucho. Mi esposa lo encontró en una guía que **leyó.**

I had lunch with my wife in a restaurant that we really liked. My wife found it in a guidebook that she read.

¿Cómo se pronuncia? Las letras *c* y *g*

The pronunciation of **c** and **g** depends on the vowel that follows each letter.

Before **a, o,** or **u** } **c** is pronounced like a **k: buscar, campo, con**
g is pronounced as in **pagar, llego, gusta**

Before **e** or **i** } **c** is pronounced like **s** in Latin America and like the English *th* of *think* in Spain: **cerca, ciento, doce**
g is pronounced like a Spanish **j: general, biología**

Spelling changes occur in the preterite **yo** form of **-car** and **-gar** verbs due to the pronunciation of the **c** and **g** of the stem before the **-é** ending.

Bus**qu**é en todas las tiendas.
No pa**gu**é mucho.

For a similar reason **g** becomes **j** in the present tense **yo** form of verbs ending in **-ger**. Such verbs maintain the **g** in all forms of the preterite.

Present of **recoger:** reco**j**o, recoges, recoge, recogemos, recogéis, recogen
Preterite of **recoger:** recogí, recogiste, recogió, recogimos, recogisteis, recogieron

6-8 Mi último vuelo. Cambie las palabras en letra cursiva para describir un viaje que usted hizo en avión.

Fui a *Boston*.

Llegué al aeropuerto *una hora antes del vuelo*.

Facturé *dos maletas*.

Abordé el avión *en Denver e hice una escala en Chicago*.

Despegué en *Denver por la mañana* y aterricé en *Boston cinco horas más tarde*.

Almorcé en el avión.

Durante el vuelo, *hablé con otros pasajeros, dormí y leí*.

Llegué a Boston *por la tarde*.

Suggestion for 6-8. *Mi último vuelo.* Give students time to prepare their answers, then ask a few students to read the description of their flight. Students who cannot remember their last flight should make up a logical flight to a place they would like to have visited.

6-9 ¿En qué orden? Primero, ponga las oraciones en el orden lógico para describir un viaje. Luego, cambie los verbos al pretérito para contar lo que pasó.

Suggestion for 6-9. *¿En qué orden?* Give students time to prepare. Have them guess the meaning of *aterrizaje* from the verb *aterrizar*.

a. Después de sentarme, *me abrocho* el cinturón de seguridad y el avión *despega* unos minutos más tarde. 4
b. *Salgo* de la casa muy tarde y *llego* al aeropuerto treinta minutos antes de mi vuelo. 1
c. El avión *aterriza* con mucha turbulencia y la pasajera a mi lado *reza* durante todo el aterrizaje. 6
d. *Recojo* mi maleta y *salgo* del aeropuerto. 8
e. *Busco* un taxi y *voy* a mi hotel. 9
f. *Facturo* rápidamente mi equipaje y *voy* a la puerta de salida. 2
g. Todos *bajamos* del avión y *vamos* a recoger nuestro equipaje. 7
h. *Subo* al avión y *busco* mi asiento. 3
i. Después de despegar, los otros pasajeros y yo *hablamos* un poco. Luego, la pasajera a mi derecha *lee* un libro y el pasajero a mi izquierda *escucha* música. Yo *saco* mi computadora y *trabajo*. 5

6-10 Entrevista. Entreviste a otro/a estudiante sobre el día de ayer con estas preguntas.

1. ¿A qué hora te levantaste ayer? ¿Te quedaste en casa por la mañana o saliste? ¿Leíste el periódico por la mañana? ¿Dónde desayunaste? ¿Bebiste café?
2. ¿Trabajaste ayer? ¿Asististe a alguna clase? ¿Fuiste a la biblioteca? ¿Jugaste a algún deporte ayer? ¿a cuál?
3. ¿Dónde cenaste ayer? ¿Con quién comiste? ¿Qué bebiste? ¿Te gustó la comida?
4. ¿Qué hiciste anoche después de cenar? ¿Viste la televisión? ¿Estudiaste mucho? ¿Hablaste por teléfono? ¿Te bañaste anoche antes de acostarte?

VOCABULARIO

¿Te gustó el hotel?

¿Reservaste una habitación de hotel antes de salir o encontraste un hotel después de llegar?

¿Cuánto pagaste por noche?

- la escalera
- el ascensor
- la recepción
- el/la recepcionista
- el pasillo
- el botones
- un mensaje
- el/la huésped
- la llave

- con vistas al mar
- con balcón
- con cama matrimonial
- con ducha
- con baño
- una habitación sencilla/doble

¡Ojo!

En los países hispanos *the first floor/ground floor* es **la planta baja. El primer piso** es *the second floor* en Estados Unidos.

En algunas regiones también se dice **el elevador** (*the elevator*).

Suggestion. Explain the different masculine forms of *primer(o)* and *tercer(o)*.

la planta baja, el primer piso, el segundo piso, el tercer piso, el cuarto piso, el quinto piso el sexto piso, el séptimo piso el octavo piso, el noveno piso, el décimo piso

Supplemental activities. A. ¿Cómo se llaman las personas que se alojan en un hotel? ¿Cómo se llama la persona que ayuda a los huéspedes del hotel con su equipaje? ¿Cómo se llama la persona que trabaja en la recepción? Generalmente, ¿la recepción está en qué piso? Si no quiere subir la escalera, ¿qué puede usar para ir a los pisos más altos? ¿Qué se usa para abrir la puerta de su habitación? ¿Qué se usa para ducharse? **B.** Go over the *¡Ojo!* note with students, then ask: *¿Cuál es el piso más alto, el tercer piso o el quinto (el noveno o el sexto, el cuarto o el décimo, el octavo o el noveno...)?* En un hotel, si las habitaciones 100-199 están en el primer piso y las habitaciones 200-299 están en el segundo, etc., ¿en qué piso está la habitación 312 (928, 689, 299, 765, 1000, 845, 409, 564)?

¿Cómo pasaste el primer día de las vacaciones? ¿el segundo? ¿el tercero?

Me desperté temprano. Llamé al servicio de habitaciones y pedí algo de comer. Me sirvieron el desayuno en mi habitación pero preferí almorzar y cenar en un restaurante.

Me vestí y salí. Almorcé en un restaurante con mi amiga y probé un plato típico de la región. Vimos una obra de teatro por la tarde y me divertí mucho.

Volví al hotel después de cenar. Me acosté y dormí hasta tarde el día siguiente.

6-11 ¿En qué hotel? ¿Describen estas oraciones el hotel **A** o el hotel **B**?

1. Tiene varios pisos.
2. No hay ascensor.
3. No hay balcón en las habitaciones.
4. Muchas habitaciones tienen vistas al mar.
5. Muchas personas trabajan en la recepción.
6. Hay más de trescientos huéspedes en el hotel.
7. El botones ayuda a los huéspedes con su equipaje.
8. No hay restaurante en el hotel.

A

B

P **Conversaciones.** En parejas, lean la siguiente conversación en la cual un turista habla con el recepcionista de un hotel. Luego, recuerde su última habitación de hotel y prepare una conversación con un/a recepcionista (su pareja) en la cual pide una habitación similar.

— Buenas tardes. Necesitamos una habitación doble para esta noche y mañana.
— ¿Para cuántas personas?
— Dos.
— ¿Prefiere una habitación de fumadores o no fumadores?
— De no fumadores si hay.
— Tengo una habitación en el segundo piso a 750 pesos la noche con el desayuno incluido.
— Está bien.
— **Me permite** su identificación, por favor.
— Claro. Aquí tiene mi pasaporte y mi tarjeta de crédito también.
— Bueno, aquí tienen la llave para la habitación 214. Pueden tomar el ascensor o subir por la escalera. Están al fondo de este pasillo.
— Gracias.

_____
Me permite… *May I see…*

Supplemental activities. Point out that Monday is the first day on calendars in Hispanic countries and ask: *¿Cuál es el quinto (sexto, segundo, primer, tercer, séptimo, cuarto) día de la semana? ¿Cuál es el décimo (segundo, octavo, séptimo, tercer, cuarto, noveno, primer, quinto, sexto) mes del año?* (Remind students that ordinal numbers are not used with dates, except for the first of the month.)

Follow-up for 6-11. *¿En qué hotel?* Dos turistas se alojaron en los hoteles *A* y *B* de la actividad 6-11 *¿En qué hotel?* ¿Quién hizo las siguientes cosas, el huésped del hotel *A* o el huésped del hotel *B*? *Modelo:* salir al balcón para ver el mar > *El huésped del hotel B salió al balcón para ver el mar.* 1. salir de su cuarto para ver las flores 2. leer el periódico en el balcón 3. ir a la playa 4. bajar a la planta baja para desayunar 5. tomar café en el patio cerca de su habitación 6. oír a mucha gente en el pasillo por la noche 7. oír a dos gatos peleando cerca de su ventana por la noche 8. subir la escalera al cuarto piso para ir a su habitación 9. pasar la tarde en el bosque 10. nadar en el mar 11. tomar el sol toda la tarde 12. pescar en el mar 13. pescar en el río 14. pagar mucho por su habitación

AUDIO ¡A escuchar!

Escuchen otra conversación en la cual dos turistas buscan un hotel por Internet. ¿Adónde van? ¿Cómo son los dos hoteles que consideran? ¿En cuál de los dos deciden reservar una habitación?

Follow-up for *Conversaciones.*
¿Prefiere Ud. una habitación…?
1. de fumadores o de no fumadores
2. en la planta baja, el primer piso o el décimo piso 3. con balcón por $200 o sin balcón por $150
4. cerca del ascensor o lejos del ascensor 5. con vistas al mar o con vistas a las montañas 6. con vistas a la calle o con vistas a la piscina
7. con el desayuno incluido por $105 o sin desayuno por $100
8. en un hotel con piscina por $125 o sin piscina por $115

GRAMÁTICA

Más acciones pasadas: el pretérito de los verbos con irregularidades en la raíz

Para averiguar

1. Are there stem changes in the preterite with -ar, -er, or -ir verbs?
2. In which two forms of the preterite are there stem changes? What does o become in those forms? What does e become?
3. What are seven other verbs conjugated like pedir?

In the preterite, there are stem changes only in the **usted, él, ella** and **ustedes, ellos, ellas** forms of **-ir** verbs, where **e** becomes **i** and **o** becomes **u**. There are no stem changes in the other forms of **-ir** verbs or in any form of **-ar** and **-er** verbs.

	NO STEM CHANGE FOR -AR AND -ER VERBS.		STEM CHANGES ONLY IN TWO FORMS OF -IR VERBS.	
	ENCONTRAR	VOLVER	PEDIR	DORMIR
yo	encontré	volví	pedí	dormí
tú	encontraste	volviste	pediste	dormiste
usted, él, ella	encontró	volvió	**pidió**	**durmió**
nosotros/as	encontramos	volvimos	pedimos	dormimos
vosotros/as	encontrasteis	volvisteis	pedisteis	dormisteis
ustedes, ellos/as	encontraron	volvieron	**pidieron**	**durmieron**

These verbs follow the same pattern as **pedir: despedirse** (to say good-bye), **divertirse** (to have fun), **preferir** (to prefer), **repetir** (to repeat), **sentirse** (to feel), **servir** (to serve), **vestirse** (to get dressed).

— ¿Por qué **durmieron** ustedes en la estación del tren?

— No **encontramos** ningún hotel con habitaciones disponibles, entonces **volvimos** a la estación.

— Why did you sleep in the train station?

— We didn't find any hotel with available rooms, so we returned to the station.

6-12 Dos turistas. Una pareja pasó las vacaciones en un país extranjero. La esposa es una persona muy aburrida y no hizo nada interesante durante el viaje. El esposo, al contrario, es muy aventurero y siempre quiere probar cosas nuevas. ¿Quién hizo las siguientes cosas, el esposo o la esposa?

Modelo dormir mucho
La esposa durmió mucho.

1. despertarse temprano todos los días para salir
2. probar muchos platos nuevos
3. almorzar todos los días en McDonalds
4. pasar mucho tiempo viendo la tele en el hotel
5. preferir hacer algo diferente todos los días
6. sentirse aburrido/a durante todo el viaje
7. divertirse mucho

Ahora diga si usted hizo estas cosas la última vez que pasó las vacaciones en un hotel.

Modelo dormir mucho
Sí, dormí mucho. /
No, no dormí mucho.

Supplemental activity. ¿Cuál de las siguientes cosas hizo primero un turista? *Modelo:* Fue a un país extranjero./ Sacó un pasaporte. > *Primero sacó un pasaporte y luego fue a un país extranjero.* 1. Encontró un buen hotel. / Reservó una habitación. 2. Pidió unos días de vacaciones. / Salió de viaje. 3. Se vistió. / Bajó al restaurante del hotel para desayunar. 4. Se divirtió con los amigos. / Fue a una fiesta. 5. Volvió a su habitación. / Se despidió de los otros turistas de su grupo. 6. Se acostó. / Volvió a su habitación. 7. Se despertó a las siete de la mañana. / Durmió ocho horas. 8. Pidió su comida. / Se sentó en un restaurante. 9. Comió muchos jalapeños. / Se sintió enfermo. 10. Pidió instrucciones en la recepción del hotel para ir al museo. / Repitió las instrucciones para recordarlas. 11. Encontró sus cheques de viaje. / Perdió sus cheques de viaje. 12. Se divirtió durante las vacaciones. / Volvió al trabajo.

Follow-up for 6-12. *Dos turistas.* Una pareja pasó las mejores vacaciones de su vida (*life*) sin problema. ¿Hicieron o no las siguientes cosas? *Modelo:* llegar tarde para su vuelo > *No, no llegaron tarde para su vuelo.* (*encontrar boletos muy baratos, perder su equipaje, encontrar un buen hotel, dormir muy bien en el hotel, ver muchas cosas aburridas, ir a muchos sitios turísticos interesantes, aprender muchas cosas interesantes, perder todo su dinero, comer en muchos buenos restaurantes, sentirse mal por unos días después de comer en un restaurante, sentirse muy bien durante todas las vacaciones, divertirse, preferir volver temprano de las vacaciones, pedir un reembolso (refund) de su agencia de viajes, volver contentos de las vacaciones*)

P 6-13 ¿Qué hicieron? Hágale las siguientes preguntas a otro/a estudiante, completándolas con la forma correcta de los verbos entre paréntesis.

René

Modelo
E1: ¿Dónde **almorzó** (almorzar) René?
E2: **René almorzó en su oficina.**
E1: ¿ **Comió** (comer) con alguien?
E2: **No, no comió con nadie.**
E1: ¿A qué hora **empezó** (empezar) a comer?
E2: **Empezó a comer a las doce y media.**

1. ¿_____ (empezar) a trabajar Carlos a las nueve?
2. ¿_____ (despertarse) fácilmente?
3. ¿A qué hora _____ (levantarse)?
4. ¿_____ (dormir) en el sofá?

Carlos

Ramiro

5. ¿_____ (divertirse) Ramiro con los amigos hoy?
6. ¿_____ (quedarse) en casa o _____ (salir)?
7. ¿_____ (ver) la televisión?
8. ¿Con quién _____ (jugar) a las cartas?

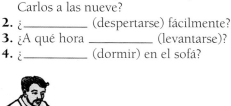

9. ¿_____ (almorzar) Juan y Ana en casa?
10. ¿_____ (vestirse) con ropa formal o informal?
11. ¿Qué _____ (pedir) de beber?
12. ¿_____ (empezar) a comer antes de pedir vino?

Juan y Ana

G 6-14 Comparaciones. En grupos de tres o cuatro, pregúnteles a los otros estudiantes de su grupo si hicieron estas cosas. Luego, prepare un informe para la clase comparando lo que hicieron.

Modelo
dormir mucho ayer
E1: **David, ¿dormiste mucho ayer?**
E2: **Sí, dormí mucho ayer. / No, no dormí mucho ayer.**
E3: **¿Y tú, Erica? ¿Dormiste mucho ayer?…**

Después, a la clase: **Juan y yo dormimos mucho ayer pero Erica no durmió mucho. / Juan y Erica durmieron mucho ayer pero yo no dormí mucho. / Todos dormimos mucho ayer. / Nadie durmió mucho ayer.**

1. dormir hasta tarde esta mañana
2. acostarse antes de las diez ayer
3. vestirse antes de desayunar hoy
4. almorzar en un restaurante ayer
5. jugar al tenis la semana pasada
6. divertirse el sábado pasado
7. volver tarde a casa el sábado
8. preferir quedarse en casa el sábado
9. despertarse temprano el domingo
10. sentirse mal el domingo

Supplemental activities. A. Put the following phrases on the board or a transparency and have students write a love story between two vacationers by putting the verbs in the preterite: *verse por primera vez en la playa durante las vacaciones, mirarse a los ojos, levantarse, presentarse, empezar a hablar, hablarse por horas, no separarse hasta tarde, pedirse los números de teléfono, llamarse al día siguiente, encontrarse en un restaurante, abrazarse por primera vez, pasar todas las vacaciones juntos, volver a casa, despedirse con un beso, empezar a escribirse correos electrónicos, casarse un año más tarde.* **B.** ¿Cuándo tomó el avión (fue a un parque de atracciones, fue a la playa, se alojó en un hotel) por última vez? ¿Fue la primera (segunda, tercera...) vez que tomó el avión (fue a un parque de atracciones, fue a la playa, se alojó en un hotel) este año? ¿Cuándo cenó en un restaurante (fue al cine, volvió a casa muy tarde, salió a bailar...) por última vez? ¿Fue la primera (segunda, tercera...) vez que cenó en un restaurante (fue al cine, volvió a casa muy tarde, salió a bailar...) este mes?

VOCABULARIO

TEMA **4**

¿Qué tal la habitación?

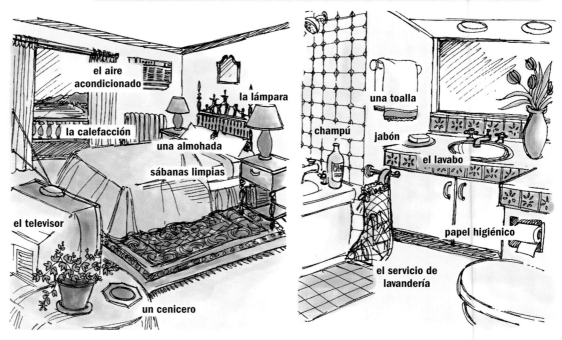

el aire acondicionado

la calefacción

el televisor

una almohada

sábanas limpias

la lámpara

un cenicero

una toalla

champú

jabón

el lavabo

papel higiénico

el servicio de lavandería

Supplemental activities. A. ¿Dónde están estas cosas en su casa? *(el lavabo, el televisor, las almohadas, las sábanas, el papel higiénico, el jabón, los ceniceros, las toallas, el champú)* **B.** ¿Los huéspedes de un hotel llaman a la recepción porque necesitan estas cosas o porque no funcionan? *(la calefacción, jabón, el televisor, el despertador, papel higiénico, toallas limpias, el aire acondicionado, champú, la lámpara, un cenicero, la ducha)* **C.** Ud. va a acampar este fin de semana. ¿Necesita las siguientes cosas? *(jabón, un televisor, un saco de dormir, sábanas, papel higiénico, el libro de español, crema protectora solar, vídeos)* **D.** ¿Qué se usa para hacer la cama? *(para lavarse el pelo, para fumar en la habitación, para leer por la noche, para dormir, para despertarse por la mañana, para ducharse, para comunicarse con la recepción, si hace calor, si hace frío, si su ropa está sucia)*

Suggestions. A. Have students search for web pages for hotels in Spanish and print out the most interesting one they find. Collect them and make copies to use as readings or for students to role play scenes where tourists are reserving a room and asking about the hotel. **B.** Have students work in groups to plan an imaginary trip to a Hispanic country, researching airfares and schedules, hotels, and tourist attractions on the web. Afterward, have them present their itinerary to the class.

Para comunicarse con la recepción

Necesitamos más toallas (jabón, papel higiénico…) en la habitación 512.

El aire acondicionado (el televisor, **el despertador,** la calefacción) de la habitación 512 no **funciona. ¿Podría mandar** a alguien para **arreglar**lo/la?

¿Podría llamarme a las seis para despertarme, por favor?

¿Podría comunicarme con la habitación…?

¿Hay algún mensaje para mí?

6-15 **En el hotel.** ¿Qué dice un/a huésped de un hotel? Complete las oraciones con una palabra lógica.

1. Hace mucho frío en la habitación. La _____ no funciona.
2. Mi ropa está sucia. ¿Tiene el hotel _____?
3. Quiero bañarme pero no hay ni _____ ni _____.
4. También quiero lavarme el pelo. ¿Hay _____?
5. Pedí una habitación de no fumadores. No comprendo por qué hay _____ en mi habitación.
6. Necesitan hacer la cama. Necesitamos _____ limpias.
7. Raramente hace calor aquí. Por eso, el hotel no tiene _____.

_____

el despertador *the alarm clock* **funcionar** *to work, to function* **¿Podría…?** *Could you…?* **mandar** *to send* **arreglar** *to fix* **¿Podría comunicarme con…?** *Could you connect me with…?*

6-16 ¿Quién habla? ¿Quién dice las siguientes cosas, el huésped de un hotel o el recepcionista?

1. ¿En qué le puedo servir?
2. Necesito una habitación para esta noche.
3. Prefiero una habitación de no fumadores.
4. El precio de la habitación más barata es de 125 euros la noche con el desayuno incluido.
5. Voy a tomar la habitación con vistas al mar.
6. ¿Cómo desea pagar?
7. Aquí tiene mi tarjeta de crédito.
8. ¿Me permite su pasaporte, por favor?
9. Tiene la habitación número 547. Está en el quinto piso, a la derecha al salir del ascensor.
10. ¿Dónde está el ascensor?
11. La calefacción de nuestra habitación no funciona.
12. ¿Necesitan algo más?

6-17 Con el recepcionista. ¿Qué le puede decir al recepcionista de un hotel en estas situaciones?

> Modelo   Hay algún problema con el aire acondicionado.
> **El aire acondicionado no funciona. ¿Podría mandar a alguien para arreglarlo?**

1. Hace mucho frío en la habitación y usted no entiende por qué.
2. Usted quiere llamar a otro huésped del hotel llamado Daniel Reyna, pero no sabe el número de su habitación.
3. Su oficina va a llamar hoy con información importante y usted vuelve a su habitación después de comer.
4. Usted necesita despertarse a las cinco y media de la mañana para ir al aeropuerto y no hay despertador en la habitación.

Ⓟ **Conversaciones.** En parejas, lean la siguiente conversación en la cual dos turistas vuelven a su habitación de hotel. Luego, imaginen la siguiente situación y preparen una conversación. Usted llega a su habitación y ve que nada está bien. No hay toallas ni jabón, el televisor y la calefacción no funcionan y hay/un cenicero en la habitación pero usted pidió una habitación en un piso de no fumadores. Usted llama al/a la recepcionista para resolver el problema.

— **Ya vino la camarera** a limpiar la habitación e hizo las camas.
— ¿Puso sábanas limpias?
— Sí, y trajo toallas limpias y jabón.
— Sí, pero sólo dejó dos toallas. Vamos a necesitar más.
— Tuve que pedir más toallas ayer también. Voy a llamar a la recepción.

Por teléfono…

— Sí, señora. ¿En qué puedo servirle?
— Señor, por favor, necesitamos más toallas para la habitación 214.
— **Con mucho gusto.** ¿Necesitan algo más?
— No, gracias.

Ya vino la camarera The maid already came   **Con mucho gusto.** *It would be a pleasure.*

AUDIO **¡A escuchar!**

Escuchen otra conversación en la cual dos amigos hablan de sus vacaciones. ¿Dónde se van a alojar? ¿Cuándo fue la última vez que pasaron la noche allí? ¿Qué necesitan llevar?

Para averiguar

1. What are the preterite stems for **tener, estar, poner, venir, querer, poder,** and **hacer**? In which form does the **c** in the preterite stem of **hacer** change to **z**?
2. What are the endings that go with all the verbs in the preceding question? Are there written accents on any of the endings, as with regular verbs?
3. What are the preterite stems for **decir** and **traer**? In which form does their ending differ from the other irregular verbs?

Supplemental activities. A. Have students repeat the sentence that is true about them the last day you had class. 1. Vine a clase. / No vine a clase. 2. Hice muchas preguntas. / No hice muchas preguntas. 3. Dije algo en inglés. / No dije nada en inglés. 4. Pude contestar todas las preguntas. / No pude contestar algunas preguntas. 5. Estuve nervioso(a). / No estuve nervioso(a). 6. Hice mucha tarea. / No hice mucha tarea. 7. Traje mi libro a clase. / No traje mi libro a clase. 8. Traje mi mochila a clase. / No traje mi mochila a clase. 9. Puse mi mochila en el piso. / Puse mi mochila en una silla. 10. Estuve enfermo(a). / No estuve enfermo(a). **B.** ¿Quién de la clase hizo las siguientes cosas hoy? 1. ¿Quién trajo una mochila verde (negra, azul)? 2. ¿Quién no vino a clase hoy? 3. ¿Quién vino tarde? 4. ¿Quién dijo algo que Ud. no entendió? 5. ¿Quién tuvo que repetir algo? 6. ¿Quién hizo muchas preguntas? 7. ¿Quién puso su libro en su mesa? 8. ¿Quién puso algo debajo de su asiento?

GRAMÁTICA
Más acciones pasadas: el pretérito de los verbos irregulares

You have already seen some of the forms of **hacer** in the preterite. Here is the full conjugation.

HACER			
yo	**hice**	nosotros/as	**hicimos**
tú	**hiciste**	vosotros/as	**hicisteis**
usted, él, ella	**hizo**	ustedes, ellos/as	**hicieron**

The following verbs have irregular stems in the preterite, but all take the same endings as in the preceding conjugation of **hacer** and the conjugation of **tener** that follows. Note that there are no accents on these irregular endings.

IRREGULAR PRETERITE STEMS		TENER	
tener:	tuv-	yo	tuv**e**
estar:	estuv-	tú	tuv**iste**
poner:	pus-	usted, él, ella	tuv**o**
venir:	vin-	nosotros/as	tuv**imos**
querer:	quis-	vosotros/as	tuv**isteis**
poder:	pud-	ustedes, ellos/as	tuv**ieron**

The irregular verbs **decir** and **traer** also have the same endings as the preceding verbs, except the ending for **ustedes, ellos,** and **ellas** is **-eron,** instead of **-ieron.**

decir: dij- dije, dijiste, dijo, dijimos, dijisteis, dij**eron**
traer: traj- traje, trajiste, trajo, trajimos, trajisteis, traj**eron**

— ¿Dónde **pusiste** nuestra cámara? — *Where did you put our camera?*
— No la **traje.** — *I didn't bring it.*
— ¿**Dijiste** que no la **trajiste**? — *Did you say you didn't bring it?*
  ¿Cómo sacaste estas fotos? *How did you take these photos?*
— **Tuve** que comprar una cámara desechable. — *I had to buy a disposable camera.*

6-18 ¿Cuándo? Diga cuándo estas personas hicieron las cosas indicadas por última vez antes de hoy: **ayer, hace tres días, el sábado pasado…**

1. (Yo)… (tener que trabajar, hacer una fiesta en mi casa, venir a la universidad, estar enfermo/a, poder descansar todo el día, ponerse el traje de baño, decir algo en la clase de español)
2. Mi mejor amigo/a… (venir a visitarme, traer un vídeo/DVD a mi casa, estar enojado/a conmigo, hacer un viaje conmigo, no querer salir conmigo)
3. En la clase de español, (nosotros)… (tener mucha tarea, venir a clase, estar muy ocupados, hacer muchos ejercicios en parejas, poder salir temprano de clase)
4. Mis padres (tener una semana de vacaciones, hacer un viaje en avión, hacer algo conmigo, estar en mi casa)

6-19 El día de René. Decida cuál de las descripciones corresponde a cada ilustración y ponga los verbos en el pretérito para hablar sobre el día de René.

1.

2.

3.

4.

5.

6.

Follow-up for 6-19. *El día de René.* Preguntas sobre las ilustraciones. 1. ¿Durmió René hasta tarde o se despertó temprano? ¿Se puso René corbata para ir al trabajo? ¿Trajo trabajo a la casa la noche anterior o dejó su maletín (*briefcase*) en la oficina? 2. ¿Tomó el autobús 25? ¿A qué hora subió al autobús? ¿Estuvo en el autobús más de treinta minutos o menos? 3. ¿A qué hora llegó a la oficina? ¿Subió a su oficina en el ascensor o subió por la escalera? ¿Salió alguien del ascensor con René? ¿Cómo salió René del ascensor, corriendo o caminando tranquilamente? 4. ¿Qué hizo René a las doce y media? ¿Comió un sándwich o una ensalada? ¿Trabajó durante el almuerzo? ¿Trabajó con la computadora o leyó algo? 5. ¿Vinieron cuatro clientes a la presentación de René? ¿René hizo la presentación usando una computadora? ¿Durmió uno de los clientes durante la presentación o todos escucharon con atención? ¿Cuántos clientes bebieron café? ¿Bebió René café también o no bebió nada? 6. ¿Cuánto tiempo estuvieron los clientes en la oficina de René? ¿Se despidieron en la oficina de René o en el pasillo, cerca del ascensor? ¿Se sintió René bien o mal después de la presentación?

a. Después del almuerzo, unos clientes *vienen* a la oficina y René *hace* una presentación que *dura* dos horas.

b. René *se levanta* tarde, *se pone* el traje y *sale* de la casa sin desayunar. No *tiene* tiempo para comer.

c. No *puede* salir a almorzar a un restaurante. *Pide* una ensalada por teléfono y *come* en la oficina.

d. René *va* al trabajo en autobús, pero *pierde* el primer autobús y *tiene* que esperar otro. El siguiente autobús *viene* después de quince minutos.

e. Los clientes *están* en la oficina hasta las cuatro, cuando *se despiden* y *se van*. Antes de irse, dos clientes le *dicen* a René que les *gustan* mucho sus ideas.

⑥ 6-20 El fin de semana pasado. Entreviste a varios compañeros de clase hasta que encuentre a dos que hicieron estas cosas el fin de semana pasado. Luego, informe a la clase de quiénes las hicieron.

> **Modelo**   estar muy ocupado/a
> E1: **Ivonne, ¿estuviste muy ocupada el fin de semana pasado?**
> E2: **Sí, estuve muy ocupada.**
> E1: **Roberto, ¿estuviste muy ocupado?**
> E3: **No, no estuve muy ocupado…**

Después, a la clase: **Ivonne y Sara estuvieron muy ocupadas. (Nadie de la clase estuvo muy ocupado.)**

1. tener que trabajar
2. ponerse ropa elegante para salir
3. estar con su mejor amigo/a
4. poder descansar el domingo
5. venir a la universidad
6. hacer un viaje
7. ir al cine
8. hacer algo con sus padres

Supplemental activity. Give students the following sentences and have them fill in the blanks. 1. La semana pasada quise _____ pero no pude hacerlo porque tuve que _____. 2. Recientemente alguien me invitó a _____ pero no quise hacerlo. 3. Estuve muy nervioso/a cuando tuve que _____. 4. Estuve aburrido/a cuando fui a _____. 5. El otro día debí _____ pero no quise hacerlo.

VOCABULARIO
¿Conoce usted bien la ciudad?

TEMA **5**

¡Ojo!

También se dice **timbres postales** o **estampillas** en vez de **sellos** (*stamps*).

¡Disculpe, señor / señora / señorita!

¿Hay un banco por aquí?

Hay un banco a dos **cuadras** de aquí. Si usted **sigue recto,** está en **la esquina** de la calle Granada con la calle Valencia.

Suggestion. Have students search the web for *currency exchange calculators* or *currency exchange convertors* to find names and exchange rates of currencies from Hispanic countries. Review numbers by having students calculate how much of each currency they will get for $10, $100, and $1000.

un hospital

una farmacia

una peluquería

una agencia de viajes

un quiosco de periódicos

una oficina de correos

un teléfono público

una estación de servicio/una gasolinera

Supplemental activities. A. ¿Dónde se puede comprar medicamentos (*crema protectora solar, revistas, champú, pasajes de avión, sellos, periódicos, tarjetas telefónicas, gasolina, guías turísticas*)? **B.** ¿Dónde hizo un turista las siguientes cosas? (*hacer una llamada internacional, hacer planes para un viaje, echar unas cartas al correo, cambiar cheques de viaje, cortarse el pelo, encontrar revistas de países extranjeros, comprar gasolina, estar muy enfermo por dos días, comprar medicamentos, mandar unos recuerdos a su casa, sacar dinero con su tarjeta de débito, comprar crema protectora solar para ir a la playa, buscar información sobre los vuelos*)

¿Dónde **se puede(n)...**?

● **cambiar** dinero
● comprar medicamentos (gasolina, periódicos internacionales, **un plano de la ciudad, sellos,** tarjetas telefónicas)
● hacer una llamada de larga distancia
● **echar** algo **al correo**

¡Disculpe! *Excuse me!* **una cuadra** *a (city) block* **seguir (i, i) recto** *to continue straight (ahead)* **la esquina** *the corner* **se puede** *can one* **cambiar** *to change, to exchange* **un plano de la ciudad** *a city map* **un sello** *a stamp* **echar al correo** *to mail*

P **6-21** **¡Disculpe!** Unos turistas buscan lugares cerca de la universidad. Complete las siguientes oraciones con el nombre de un lugar lógico. Luego, hágale la pregunta a otro estudiante.

¡Disculpe, señor / señora / señorita!…

Modelo   E1: Necesito sacar dinero con mi tarjeta de débito. ¿Hay __un banco__ cerca de aquí?
          E2: **Sí, hay un banco en la esquina de la calle Metric con la calle Parmer.**

1. Quiero comprar unos periódicos en español. ¿Hay _____ por aquí?
2. Necesito comprar unos medicamentos. ¿Me puede decir dónde hay _____?
3. Necesito gasolina. Busco _____.
4. Necesito comprar sellos y quiero echar algo al correo. ¿Dónde hay _____?
5. Tenemos hambre. ¿Nos puede recomendar _____?
6. Necesitamos un lugar para pasar la noche. Buscamos _____.
7. Quiero cortarme el pelo. ¿Hay _____ cerca de aquí?

6-22 **¿Por qué fue allí?** Diga cuándo usted fue a los siguientes lugares por última vez y qué hizo en cada lugar.

Modelo   el banco
          Fui al banco hace tres días. Saqué dinero con mi tarjeta de débito.

1. la oficina de correos
2. la gasolinera
3. la librería
4. el aeropuerto
5. la farmacia
6. la peluquería
7. el café
8. el parque

P **Conversaciones.** En parejas, lean la siguiente conversación en la cual una turista habla con un recepcionista de un hotel sobre los restaurantes del vecindario. Luego, preparen una conversación en la cual un/a turista busca un restaurante cerca de su universidad.

— ¡Disculpe, señor! ¿Puede recomendarme un buen restaurante cerca de aquí?
— *El Papagayo* es muy popular.
— Ya comí en ese restaurante ayer. Es un poco caro. **¿Conoce** usted algún restaurante un poco menos caro?
— *La Olla de Oro* tiene buena comida a buen precio.
— ¿Dónde está *la Olla de Oro*?
— En la calle Seis. Si va a la derecha **al salir** del hotel, está a tres cuadras, en la esquina de la calle Seis con la calle Guadalupe.

---

conocer *to know*   **al salir** *as you leave, upon leaving*

Suggestion for 6-21. *¡Disculpe!* Give students time to prepare the questions together. Remind them to talk about places near your university or in your city.

Follow-ups for *Conversaciones*.
A. Have students refer to the illustration on the preceding page to answer these questions. *Imagine que está en la agencia de viajes.* 1. Al salir de la agencia de viajes, ¿qué hay a su derecha? 2. Si va a la derecha y pasa por la peluquería, ¿qué hay en la siguiente esquina? 3. Al salir de la agencia de viajes, ¿dónde hay un quiosco de periódicos? ¿Dónde hay un café? 4. Al salir de la agencia de viajes, ¿dónde hay una gasolinera? 5. ¿La oficina de correos está a cuántas cuadras del hospital? 6. ¿Dónde hay teléfonos públicos? **B.** ¿En qué lugar de la ilustración de la página anterior dice alguien las siguientes cosas? *Modelo:* Si mando esta carta a Estados Unidos, ¿va a llegar en cuántos días? > la oficina de correos 1. ¿Vende Ud. revistas en inglés? 2. ¿Puede recomendarme algo para las alergias? Me siento muy mal. 3. Necesito un vuelo a Buenos Aires para el tres de enero. 4. Necesito cambiar $300 dólares por pesos. 5. Me puede cortar el pelo un poco más por los lados. 6. ¿Cuántos sellos necesito para esta carta? 7. ¿Cuánto cuesta un litro de gasolina? 8. Aquí tiene el itinerario para el viaje, y recuerde que necesita llevar su pasaporte.

AUDIO ¡A escuchar!

Escuchen otra conversación en la cual un huésped de un hotel habla con la recepcionista. ¿Qué lugares busca el turista? ¿Por qué? ¿Cómo se llega a cada lugar desde el hotel?

Supplemental activities. Review ordinal numbers by asking for directions with questions such as the following, inserting names of places in your area. 1. Si alguien está en la esquina de la calle... con la calle... y sube la calle..., ¿cuál es la primera (segunda, tercera...) calle que se encuentra después de la calle...? 2. En la carreterra (*highway*)..., ¿cuál es la primera (segunda, tercera...) salida después de la calle...? 3. Si alguien va de nuestra ciudad a [*a city to which students often drive*], ¿cuál es la primera (segunda, tercera...) ciudad que se encuentra en la carretera...?

GRAMÁTICA

Hablar de conocimientos: ¿*saber* o *conocer*?

Both **saber** and **conocer** mean *to know*. In the present tense they are irregular in the **yo** form, but have regular **-er** verb endings for the other forms.

SABER			CONOCER	
yo	**sé**		yo	**conozco**
tú	sabes		tú	conoces
usted, él, ella	sabe		usted, él, ella	conoce
nosotros/as	sabemos		nosotros/as	conocemos
vosotros/as	sabéis		vosotros/as	conocéis
ustedes, ellos/as	saben		ustedes, ellos/as	conocen

Use **saber** to say…

- you know facts or information. It is often followed by a question word such as **dónde, cuándo, quién…;** or it can be followed by **que** (*that*) or **si** (*if*).

  — ¿**Sabe** Ud. dónde se pueden cambiar unos cheques de viaje?
  — Sí, pero no **sé** la dirección.

  — *Do you know where one can change some traveler's checks?*
  — *Yes, but I don't know the address.*

- you know how to do something. It is followed by an infinitive.

  ¿**Sabes usar** el metro?

  Do you know how to use the subway?

Use **conocer** to say…

- you know a person, place, or thing. It may also be used to say *to be acquainted / familiar with* or *to meet* someone for the first time. Remember to use the personal **a** after **conocer** before nouns referring to specific people.

  No **conozco** bien la ciudad.
  ¿**Conoces** a mi agente de viajes?
  Quiero **conocer** a tu agente de viajes.

  I don't know the city well.
  Do you know my travel agent?
  I want to meet your travel agent.

In the preterite, **saber** usually means that you *found out* something and **conocer** means you *met* or *became acquainted* with someone or something. They are used in another past tense studied in the next chapter to say what or who you *knew* in the past. **Conocer** is conjugated as a regular **-er** verb in the preterite, but **saber** is irregular and has the same endings as **hacer.**

saber: **supe, supiste, supo, supimos, supisteis, supieron**
conocer: conoc**í**, conoc**iste**, conoc**ió**, conoc**imos**, conoc**isteis**, conoc**ieron**

¿Cómo **supiste** que salgo con el hombre que **conocí** durante las vacaciones?

*How **did you find out** that I'm going out with the man **I met** on vacation?*

6-23 ¿Lo saben? ¿Saben estas personas las cosas indicadas?

1. nosotros / el teléfono del profesor (de la profesora)
2. el profesor (la profesora) / mi nombre (*my name*)
3. yo / el cumpleaños del profesor (de la profesora)
4. nosotros / la fecha del examen final
5. mis padres / hablar español
6. yo / todo el vocabulario
7. el profesor (la profesora) / otras lenguas
8. yo / tocar el piano

6-24 ¿Los conocen? Diga si estas personas conocen bien a las personas o los lugares indicados entre paréntesis. Use la **a** personal si es necesario.

> **Modelo**   mis padres (mi mejor amigo/a)
> **No, mis padres no conocen bien a mi mejor amigo/a.**

1. yo (todos los estudiantes de la clase de español)
2. mi profesor/a de español (mis padres)
3. mi mejor amigo/a y yo (nuestra ciudad)
4. yo (la Ciudad de México)
5. mis padres (esta universidad)
6. mi mejor amigo/a (mi madre)
7. yo (los padres de mi mejor amigo/a)

Suggestion for 6-24. *¿Los conocen?*
Have students repeat the answer using direct object pronouns. *Modelo: No, mis padres no lo/la conocen bien.*

6-25 Un viaje a México. Usted va a visitar la Ciudad de México. ¿Sabe Ud. o conoce Ud. las siguientes cosas?

1. ¿Algún hotel en la ciudad?
2. ¿Usar el metro (*subway*) de la ciudad?
3. ¿Reservar una habitación de hotel en español?
4. ¿Cuánto cuesta un vuelo a la Ciudad de México?
5. ¿Si se necesita un pasaporte para ir a México?
6. ¿El número de su pasaporte?
7. ¿El centro de la Ciudad de México?
8. ¿Dónde está la catedral?
9. ¿Algunos sitios turísticos de la región?
10. ¿Regatear (*To haggle*) en el mercado?
11. ¿Las pirámides que están cerca de la Ciudad de México?
12. ¿Cómo se llaman esas pirámides?

La Catedral de la Ciudad de México.

ⓟ 6-26 Entrevista. Complete las siguientes preguntas con **sabes** o **conoces**. Luego, use las preguntas para entrevistar a un/a compañero/a de clase.

1. ¿_____ cuándo vas a tomar tus próximas vacaciones? ¿_____ adónde quieres ir? ¿Ya _____ ese lugar? ¿Qué sitios turísticos _____ en España? ¿_____ si los norteamericanos necesitan un pasaporte para visitar España?
2. ¿_____ una buena agencia de viajes cerca de aquí? ¿_____ cuántas horas dura un vuelo a Cancún? ¿_____ cuánto cuesta un vuelo a Cancún?
3. ¿Qué otras lenguas _____ hablar? ¿_____ en qué países de Sudamérica no se habla español? ¿_____ a alguien de Sudamérica?

Follow-ups for 6-25. *Un viaje a México.* **A.** ¿Un buen guía turístico *sabe* o *conoce* las siguientes cosas? 1. hablar varias lenguas 2. las calles de la ciudad 3. los mejores hoteles 4. cuánto cuestan los hoteles 5. los lugares más interesantes 6. mucho de la historia de la región 7. muchos restaurantes buenos 8. cuándo están abiertos los museos **B.** Have students work in pairs to think of four or five things/people that the following people know: *un buen agente de viajes, un buen profesor de español, un buen estudiante.*

¡Trato hecho!

En portada

Note: Have students complete the *Antes de leer, Reading strategies,* and *Ahora Ud.* activities before reading this article.

REVISTA CULTURAL

OPERACIÓN SALIDA

Operación salida.

Con la llegada del verano se inicia la operación salida de vacaciones. **Las carreteras,** los aeropuertos y las estaciones de trenes son escenario de esa **fiebre viajera** que siente el turista. El viajero español gasta una media de 489,4 euros en reservas de billetes de avión y una media de 1.478,7 euros en paquetes vacacionales.

Las agencias de viajes ofrecen una gran variedad de ofertas para satisfacer los gustos de todos los públicos. A la hora de planear sus vacaciones el viajero español usa en su mayoría los servicios de las agencias de viajes, donde los paquetes vacacionales son el producto más vendido. La reserva y compra directa de billetes de tren o de avión es el uso más extendido que el viajero individual hace de Internet.

Los destinos turísticos preferidos por el viajero español son, en el territorio nacional, las Islas Canarias y la Islas Baleares, zonas de playa por excelencia. En Europa, las ciudades más visitadas por el turista español son Amsterdam, Estambul, Londres, París, Praga y Roma, por su **riqueza** histórica y cultural. En **el ámbito** internacional, los destinos preferidos son Egipto y el Caribe, y en el continente americano, Nueva York, Buenos Aires y Caracas.

Cuando viajan, los españoles prefieren alojarse en hoteles; el alojamiento en apartamentos, campings y casas rurales es menos popular. Los paquetes vacacionales incluyen generalmente alojamiento en hotel y transporte en avión o autobús; por esta razón el turista generalmente decide quedarse en un hotel y **disfrutar de** sus comodidades.

Puerto de la Cruz, Tenerife. Islas Canarias, España.

Keizersgracht, Ámsterdam, Holanda.

Planes de viaje.

Estatua de la Libertad, Liberty Island, Nueva York.

---

las carreteras *roads* **fiebre viajera** *traveling frenzy* **riqueza** *richness* **el ámbito** *the area* **disfrutar de** *to enjoy*

Antes de leer

¿Cuáles son los hábitos de viaje del turista americano? ¿Cuál es el período principal de vacaciones? ¿Cuáles son sus destinos favoritos? ¿Qué medio de transporte prefiere para viajar? ¿Qué tipo de alojamiento prefiere?

Reading strategies: Recognizing words from the same family. As you develop your lexical proficiency in a foreign language, previously learned vocabulary can help you recognize words from the same family. You can often guess the meaning of new words you encounter in readings by using related words you have already learned with the same root.

6-27 Ahora Ud. Usando las palabras en cursiva que ya conoce, ¿puede inferir el significado de las palabras en negrita que aparecen en las siguientes oraciones?

1. *un plan / viajar:* A la hora de **planificar** sus vacaciones, **el viajero** español usa en su mayoría los servicios de las agencias de viajes.
2. *las vacaciones / vender:* **Los paquetes vacacionales** son el producto más **vendido** en las agencias de viajes.
3. *alojarse / estar cómodo/a:* Los paquetes incluyen generalmente **alojamiento** en hotel y transporte por avión o autobús; por esta razón el turista generalmente decide quedarse en un hotel y disfrutar de (*enjoy*) sus **comodidades.**
4. *último(a) / el estrés:* **Ultimar** todos los detalles de un viaje puede resultarnos **estresante.**
5. *entrar / visitar:* En ocasiones los viajes al extranjero requieren del turista documentación especial de **entrada** al país: visas de **visitante,** que pueden obtenerse en la embajada (*embassy*).
6. *funcionar:* En el vídeo **un funcionario** del consulado de Venezuela nos ofrece información específica sobre los documentos requeridos para viajar a ese país.

Después de leer

6-28 Diferencias y similitudes. Conteste las preguntas de acuerdo con la lectura y compare sus últimas vacaciones con lo que hacen los españoles.

1. ¿En qué estación del año prefieren ir de vacaciones los españoles? ¿En qué estación tomó usted sus últimas vacaciones?
2. ¿Cuánto gasta el español típico en billetes de avión y paquetes vacacionales cada año? ¿Cuánto gastó usted el año pasado?
3. ¿Usan muchos españoles las agencias de viajes para planificar las vacaciones? ¿Planificó usted sus últimas vacaciones en una agencia de viajes?
4. ¿Qué hacen muchos viajeros españoles por Internet? ¿Usó usted Internet para planificar sus últimas vacaciones? ¿Qué hizo por Internet?
5. ¿Dónde prefieren pasar las vacaciones los españoles? ¿Dónde pasó usted sus últimas vacaciones?
6. ¿Por qué prefieren los españoles alojarse en hoteles durante las vacaciones? ¿Dónde prefirió usted alojarse durante sus últimas vacaciones?

6-29 El peor viaje de mi vida. Describa el peor viaje que realizó. ¿Adónde fue? ¿Qué hizo o no hizo allí? ¿Viajó en avión, en tren, en carro, en autobús? ¿Qué tal el viaje? ¿Le gustó el hotel? ¿Conoció bien la ciudad? ¿Qué pasó?

Suggestion for *Antes de leer.* Point out to students that the -*ado/a* and -*ido/a* endings are often the same as -*ed* or irregular past participles in English and have them guess the meaning of the following past participles that appear in the readings here: *vendido/a, visitado/a, preferido/a, guiado/a, requerido/a, extendido/a.*

De puertas abiertas a la comunidad

VIDEO **DIME A DÓNDE VIAJAS Y...**

6-30 Entrando en materia. ¿Cuáles son las épocas en las que más viajan los estudiantes en su universidad? ¿Cuáles son los destinos más populares? ¿Por qué cree que son populares esos lugares? ¿Cuál fue el último viaje que realizó usted? ¿Qué actividades hizo durante el viaje? ¿Le gustó el hotel?

Planear unas vacaciones puede ser una actividad **emocionante,** pero al mismo tiempo finalizar todos los detalles del viaje puede resultarnos estresante. Las agencias de viajes **adquieren el compromiso** de encontrar las mejores ofertas de viaje, adecuadas a los intereses del viajero, y ayudar a planear sus vacaciones. En ocasiones los viajes al extranjero requieren del turista documentación especial de entrada al país: una visa de turismo que puede obtenerse en la embajada.

En el vídeo, van a escuchar los testimonios de Luis Barbieri, empleado en el departamento de visas del Consulado de Venezuela en Nueva York, y Fernando Carbone, dueño de Carbone Travel, quien nos habla de los hábitos del viajero hispano que vive en Estados Unidos.

Answers for 6-31. ¿Cierto o falso?
1. es un inmigrante argentino dueño de una agencia de viajes 3. trabajó en turismo en Argentina y también en Estados Unidos 4. en la oficina son siete en total

6-31 ¿Cierto o falso?. Escuche con atención la información personal y profesional que Fernando Carbone nos da e indique si las siguientes afirmaciones son ciertas o falsas. Corrija la información falsa.

	Cierto	Falso
1. Fernando Carbone es un inmigrante argentino, dueño de una compañía de taxis.	☐	☒
2. Fernando vino a Estados Unidos hace quince años.	☒	☐
3. Fernando Carbone nunca trabajó en turismo antes de tener la agencia Carbone Travel.	☐	☒
4. En la agencia de Fernando son nueve trabajadores en total.	☐	☒
5. La clientela de la agencia Carbone Travel puede recibir servicios en inglés o en español.	☒	☐

---

emocionante *exciting* **adquieren el compromiso** *make a commitment*

6-32   La biografía de Carbone. Complete la siguiente biografía de Fernando Carbone con las formas adecuadas del pretérito.

¡Hola! Mi nombre es Fernando Carbone. _____Nací_____ (1. Nacer) en Argentina, y _____vine_____ (2. venir) a Estados Unidos en 1989. Al llegar a Estados Unidos, _____decidí_____ (3. decidir) trabajar en agencias de viajes y _____empecé_____ (4. empezar) con la agencia Carbone Travel hace doce años. Mis empleados aquí en la agencia _____siguieron_____ (5. seguir) mis pasos en el negocio y ahora somos siete en total.

En Argentina también _____trabajé_____ (6. trabajar) en turismo, donde _____fui_____ (7. ser) empleado de Aerolíneas Argentinas. Mi interés _____estuvo_____ (8. estar) siempre en el negocio de los viajes y aquí en Nueva York me va bien.

Ⓖ 6-33   La clientela es lo primero. Contesten en grupos las siguientes preguntas relacionadas con el tipo de clientes que va a la agencia Carbone Travel.

1. ¿Qué tipo de clientela recibe Fernando en su agencia?
2. ¿Cuál es el propósito (*purpose*) principal de los viajes del hispano que vive en Estados Unidos?
3. ¿Por qué es atractiva Latinoamérica para el turista norteamericano?
4. ¿Conocen ustedes algún país de Latinoamérica? ¿Qué sitios les atraen (*attract*) más de Latinoamérica y por qué?

6-34   ¿Necesito una visa? Compruebe (*Check*) ahora la información que aprendió después de escuchar a nuestro operario de inmigración Luis Barbieri.

1. ¿Qué países no requieren una visa de turista para entrar en Venezuela?
2. ¿Qué documentos se necesitan para solicitar (*apply for*) una visa de turismo?
3. ¿Cuál es el precio de tramitación (*processing*) de la visa de turismo?
4. ¿Cuál es el objetivo de los viajes de negocios temporales (*temporary*)?
5. ¿Qué documento necesita una persona en viaje de negocios a Venezuela?

Ⓖ 6-35   ¡Cuánto papeleo! Usted y varios amigos van a viajar a Costa Rica y necesitan completar la siguiente solicitud de visa de visitante con sus datos personales. Visiten también la página web de la embajada de Costa Rica en Estados Unidos y averigüen el tiempo máximo de estancia (*stay*) en el país, y otros documentos de viaje que necesitan presentar.

Answers for 6-33. *La clientela es lo primero.* 1. En cuanto a la clientela, un 60% es de latinoamericanos viviendo en Estados Unidos y el resto es gente mayormente americana de Estados Unidos. 2. Ver a su familia de vacaciones. 3. Latinoamérica comparada con Estados Unidos es otra forma de hacer las cosas, la lengua es un atractivo muy grande, pero se encuentran con una forma totalmente nueva de vida, que mucha gente cuando va de vacaciones es lo que quiere. 4. *Answers will vary.*

Answers for 6-34. *Necesito una visa.* 1. Los países que no requieren de visa para entrar a Venezuela como turista son una lista grande, entre ellos, Argentina, Chile, Paraguay, Alemania, Gran Bretaña, Japón y muchos otros. 2. una carta del trabajo, una carta del banco, un *money order* por treinta dólares o un cheque certificado, copia o original de la tarjeta de residencia, más dos fotografías tamaño pasaporte de frente a color con fondo blanco. 3. treinta dólares 4. Ver qué posibilidades de negocios puede haber en Venezuela, o tener reuniones con empresas que ya están pautadas. 5. Una carta de la empresa que lo esté enviando a Venezuela.

Escapadas

EL CAMINO DE SANTIAGO

Garganta del Cares, Picos de Europa, Cantabria, España.

El Camino de Santiago es **una ruta** de gran belleza natural en el norte de España, que durante **la Edad Media, peregrinos** de toda Europa **recorrieron** para **redimir sus penas** y rezar al Apóstol Santiago. El itinerario tradicional de la ruta, conocido como *camino francés*, **une** Roncesvalles, en los Pirineos navarros, con Santiago de Compostela, Galicia.

La Catedral de Santiago de Compostela, La Coruña, España.

Los peregrinos de distintos lugares de Europa y de Oriente caminaban por las vías romanas que unían los distintos puntos del continente. Pero con el tiempo **se desarrolló** una infraestructura de **hospederías,** hospitales e iglesias, así como **pueblos en torno** a la ruta.

En la actualidad, el interés del camino no es sólo religioso, **sino** también cultural y gastronómico, y turistas de todas las nacionalidades se unen para recorrer este camino de 850 kilómetros **a pie,** en bicicleta, **a caballo** o en automóvil.

Puente Romano de Cangas de Onís, Asturias, España.

---

una ruta *a route* **la Edad Media** *the Middle Ages* **peregrinos** *pilgrims* **recorrieron** *traveled across* **redimir sus penas** *to redeem their sins* **une** *joins* **se desarrolló** *there developed* **hospederías** *lodges* **pueblos** *towns* **en torno** *around* **sino** *but, rather* **a pie** *walking* **a caballo** *riding horseback*

El visitante puede admirar los verdes **paisajes** montañosos del norte de España, muestras del arte prerrománico a su paso por Asturias y del arte románico en la arquitectura y pinturas de la Catedral de Santiago de Compostela. La gastronomía vasca y gallega es también otro actractivo de esta ruta.

Julio, agosto y septiembre —los meses de menos lluvia en el norte de España— son los mejores para **realizar** el camino, pero durante julio y agosto las avalanchas de turistas son impresionantes. **Los amantes** de la aventura que hacen el camino a pie o en bicicleta pueden alojarse **gratuitamente** en **los albergues** que hay por el camino, donde **se crea** una camaradería entre aquellos que comparten esta experiencia.

Un alto en el Camino. Callados y conchas de peregrinos en ruta a Santiago de Compostela.

6-36　¿Entendió Ud.?　Complete las siguientes afirmaciones con la opción u opciones correctas.

1. El Camino de Santiago es...
   a. una ruta natural en el norte de España.
   b. la carretera entre Madrid y Santiago de Compostela.
   c. una vía de peregrinaciones durante la Edad Media.
   d. una red de trenes española.
2. Los peregrinos desde (*since*) la Edad Media van a Santiago de Compostela para...
   a. visitar los museos de arte moderno.
   b. redimir sus penas.
   c. ir de pesca.
   d. rezar.
3. Hoy los turistas visitan Santiago de Compostela por...
   a. su riqueza histórica y cultural.
   b. las playas.
   c. los deportes de aventura.
   d. los paisajes verdes y la gastronomía.
4. Los turistas que hacen el Camino a pie o en bicicleta...
   a. son amantes de la naturaleza (*nature*).
   b. tienen el alojamiento gratis (*free*) en los albergues.
   c. no quieren volar (*to fly*).
   d. no saben conducir (*to drive*).
5. A lo largo del Camino, el turista puede admirar...
   a. manifestaciones del arte prerrománico asturiano.
   b. paisajes desérticos.
   c. grandes ciudades con arquitectura contemporánea.
   d. pueblos de atmósfera tradicional.

---

paisajes *landscapes*　**realizar** *to do, to carry out*　**los amantes** *lovers*　**gratuitamente** *for free*
los albergues *the hostals*　**se crea** *there is created*

6-37 ¿Saber o conocer? Complete las siguientes preguntas utilizando **saber** o **conocer** según convenga al contexto.

1. — Alberto, ¿___conoces___ el norte de España?
   — Sí, visité el País Vasco con mi familia hace unos años, pero no ___conozco___ la ciudad de Santiago.
2. — Sonia y Eduardo, ¿___saben___ que voy a hacer el Camino de Santiago en bicicleta?
   — ¡Impresionante! Vas a tener una experiencia maravillosa. ¿___Conoces___ a otras personas que vayan (*might be going*) contigo?
3. — Jorge, ¿___sabes___ ya la fecha de tu viaje?
   — Sí, ___supe___ que las mejores fechas para hacer el Camino eran (*were*) julio y agosto, así que voy a ir en julio.
4. — Jorge, ¿___sabes___ dónde vas a alojarte?
   — Todavía no, pero ___sé___ que hay albergues gratuitos para los viajeros que hacen el Camino en bicicleta.
5. — Sonia, ¿___conoces___ a Luis Ortiz? Él hizo el Camino de Santiago a caballo.
   — Sí, lo ___conozco___. Es el agente de viajes de la agencia Horizontes, ¿verdad?

6-38 Un viaje en bicicleta. ¿Hizo alguna vez un viaje en bicicleta? Prepare un breve diario, contando las experiencias que vivió y la gente y los lugares que conoció. Si nunca hizo un viaje en bicicleta, piense en una ruta turística que la gente puede realizar en bicicleta, e imagine que hizo usted esa ruta.

6-39 ¿Qué hacer? En grupos, imaginen que pasaron las vacaciones juntos en estos destinos. Mencionen son dos o tres cosas que hicieron en cada lugar:

1. En la ciudad de Barcelona.

Catedral de la Sagrada Familia, Barcelona, España.

2. En Jaca, los Pirineos.

Jaca, Pirineo Aragonés, España.

3. En la República Dominicana.

Cayo Levantado, la República Dominicana.

4. En Argentina.

Cataratas de Iguazú, Frontera de Argentina y Brasil.

Casa Rosada, Plaza de Mayo, Buenos Aires, Argentina.

Barrio de San Telmo, Buenos Aires, Argentina.

En palabras de...

UN FOLLETO TURÍSTICO

Imagine que está trabajando en una agencia de viajes y tiene que preparar un folleto (*brochure*) para un paquete vacacional. Piense en varios lugares turísticos y haga una lista de los puntos de interés de cada uno. Después elija (*select*) uno de esos lugares y prepare un folleto informativo para el viajero.

Writing strategies: Preparing a travel brochure. The purpose of a travel brochure is to attract potential travelers to a specific destination. When preparing a travel brochure, it is essential to identify the audience, the type of tourist that you want to attract, and to determine how to reach them. A successful brochure opens with a visual image of the destination that is being advertised, the name of the travel agency, and the services offered. The body of the brochure consists of three or four paragraphs about the site, including history, tourist attractions, shopping, weather, currency, and the itinerary with basic descriptions of each day's event. The last paragraph should provide information about the total cost of the package and departure dates and times. References to the website of the travel agency might be included as well.

Antes de escribir

Para la preparación de su folleto piense en los siguientes aspectos:

- A qué tipo de viajero va dirigido: a familias, a estudiantes, a recién casados (*newlyweds*), a personas mayores.
- Características del paquete vacacional: hotel + avión, apartamento + avión, hotel + autobús...
- Ubicación (*Location*) del destino turístico.
- Información de interés histórico, geográfico y cultural del destino.
- Las actividades culturales y/o deportivas que incluye el paquete: itinerario de viaje.
- Las razones por las cuales es un destino ideal.
- El precio total del paquete.

Después, prepare un folleto atractivo incluyendo las distintas secciones mencionadas arriba y fotos ilustrativas de la belleza (*beauty*) del lugar.

Después de escribir

Revise y edite su folleto prestando (*paying*) especial atención a su organización y a las estructuras de vocabulario relacionadas con los viajes y las vacaciones. Compruebe (*Check*) también que es atractivo y adecuado al tipo de viajero seleccionado.

En la red

Haga una búsqueda (*search*) de **agencias de viajes** o **paquetes de vacaciones** en Internet para ver ejemplos de folletos turísticos en español y compare su folleto con los de otras agencias. ¿Contienen información similar? ¿Tienen una organización parecida (*that's alike*)? ¿Qué tiene de especial su folleto en comparación con los de Internet?

All the sources consulted for the readings are cited on the *¡Trato hecho!* Web site at **www.prenhall.com/trato**

VOCABULARIO

TEMA 1

De vacaciones
una agencia de viajes *a travel agency*
el bosque *the woods, the forest*
una cámara *a camera*
una canoa *a canoe*
los cheques de viaje *the traveler's checks*
la crema protectora solar *sunscreen*
unas gafas de sol *sunglasses*
una guía turística *a tourist guide*
una habitación *a room*
un hotel *a hotel*
un itinerario *an itinerary*
una maleta *a suitcase*
el mar *the sea*
un mercado *a market (place)*
un país extranjero *a foreign country*
un parque de atracciones *an amusement park*
un pasaje (un boleto, un billete) de avión *a plane ticket*
un pasaporte *a passport*

un plato *a dish, a plate*
un recuerdo *a souvenir*
un río *a river*
un rollo de película *a roll of film*
las ruinas *the ruins*
un saco de dormir *a sleeping bag*
un sitio histórico *a historic site*
un velero *a sailboat*
una visa *a visa*

Expresiones verbales
acampar *to camp*
alojarse en *to stay at*
cambiar dinero *to change / exchange money*
consultar *to consult*
descender *to go down, to descend*
hacer la maleta *to pack your suitcase*
hacer un crucero *to take a cruise*
ir de excursión *to go on an outing, to go on a hike*
ir de vacaciones *to go on vacation*
pescar *to fish*
probar (ue) *to try*

reservar *to reserve*
sacar *to take, to take out, to get*
viajar *to travel*
visitar *to visit*

¿Cuándo?
anoche *last night*
ayer (por la mañana, por la tarde) *yesterday (morning, afternoon)*
hace (tres días, dos meses, mucho tiempo…) *(three days, two months, a long time…) ago*
(el mes, el año, el sábado, la semana…) pasado/a *last (month, year, Saturday, week…)*
por última vez *the last time*

Otras palabras y expresiones
con… de antelación *…in advance*
maya *Mayan*
¿Qué tal…? *How was/were…?*
regional *regional*

TEMA 2

Los vuelos
la aduana *customs*
una aerolínea *an airline*
un aeropuerto *an airport*
un asiento *a seat*
un/a asistente de vuelo *a flight attendant*
un avión *an airplane*
un comprobante *a receipt, proof*
una entrada *an entrance*
una llegada *a arrival*
un/a pasajero/a *a passenger*
un pasillo *an aisle, a hall*
una puerta *a gate*
una sala de espera *a waiting room*
una salida *a departure*
una tarjeta de embarque *a boarding pass*

un taxi *a taxi*
una ventanilla *a window (of a vehicle or a box office)*
un vuelo *a flight*

Expresiones verbales
abordar *to board*
abrocharse el cinturón de seguridad *to buckle your seatbelt*
aterrizar *to land*
bajar de *to get off / out of, to go down*
despegar *to take off*
durar *to last*
esperar *to wait (for)*
facturar el equipaje *to check your luggage*
hacer escala *to make a stopover*

recoger *to pick up, to gather*
subir a *to get on / in, to go up*

Otras palabras y expresiones
bienvenido/a *welcome*
correcto/a *right, correct*
disponible *available*
durante *during*
en ese caso *in that case*
junto a *next to*
Lo siento. *I'm sorry.*
más de + *number* *more than* + *number*
¿verdad? *right?*

TEMA 3

En el hotel
un ascensor *an elevator*
un balcón *a balcony*
un botones *a bellhop*
una cama matrimonial *a double bed*
el desayuno *breakfast*
una ducha *a shower*
la escalera *the stairs*
una habitación sencilla/doble *a single/double room*
un/a huésped *a guest*
la identificación *identification*
una llave *a key*

un mensaje *a message*
la planta baja *the ground floor*
la recepción *the front desk*
un/a recepcionista *a receptionist*
el servicio de habitaciones *room service*
una vista (a) *a view (of)*

Los números ordinales
primer(o)/a *first*
segundo/a *second*
tercer(o)/a *third*
cuarto/a *fourth*
quinto/a *fifth*

sexto/a *sixth*
séptimo/a *seventh*
octavo/a *eighth*
noveno/a *ninth*
décimo/a *tenth*

Otras palabras y expresiones
al día siguiente *on the next day*
de (no) fumadores *(non-)smoking*
decidir *to decide*
incluido/a *included*
llamar (a) *to call*
Me permite... *May I see...*
típico/a *typical*

TEMA 4

En el hotel
el aire acondicionado *the air conditioning*
la almohada *the pillow*
la calefacción *the heating*
la camarera *the maid*
el cenicero *the ashtray*
el champú *the shampoo*
el despertador *the alarm clock*
el jabón *the soap*
el lavabo *the sink*

el papel higiénico *the toilet paper*
las sábanas *the (bed)sheets*
el servicio de lavandería *the laundry service*
la toalla *the towel*

Verbos
arreglar *to fix, to repair*
funcionar *to work, to function*
mandar *to send*

Otras palabras y expresiones
Con mucho gusto. *Gladly., I'd be happy to.*
¿Podría comunicarme con...? *Could you connect me with...?*

TEMA 5

Los lugares
un banco *a bank*
una cuadra *a (city) block*
una esquina *a corner*
una estación de servicio (una gasolinera) *a service station, a gas station*
una farmacia *a pharmacy*
una oficina de correos *a post office*
un quiosco de periódicos *a newsstand*
un teléfono público *a public telephone*

Otros sustantivos
la gasolina *gasoline*
una llamada (de larga distancia) *a (long distance) call*
los medicamentos *medicine*
un periódico internacional *an international newspaper*
un plano de la ciudad *a city map*
un sello *a stamp*
una tarjeta telefónica *a phone card*

Expresiones verbales
cambiar *to change, to exchange*

conocer *to know, to be familiar with, to be acquainted with, to meet*
echar algo al correo *to mail something*
recomendar (ie) *to recommend*
saber *to know, to find out*
seguir (i, i) recto *to continue straight (ahead)*

Otras palabras y expresiones
al + infinitive *as soon as you + verb, upon ...ing*
¡Disculpe! *Excuse me!, Pardon me!*
popular *popular*
se puede... *one can...*

7

En la ciudad

CIRCUITO INTERIOR ↑
← CHAPULTEPEC

In this chapter you will learn to...

- talk about your childhood
- describe important events in your life
- tell stories
- describe the neighborhood where you grew up
- report what happened
- discuss features of Hispanic neighborhoods

You will use...

- the imperfect to say how things used to be
- the imperfect to say what was in progress
- the preterite with the imperfect to narrate
- the impersonal **se**

VOCABULARIO
¿Cómo eras de niño/a?

¡Ojo!

In this chapter you will learn a new past tense, the imperfect, which is used to talk about how things used to be. Here you see the endings for **yo** (-ar > aba, -er/-ir > ía).

Supplemental activities. A. ¿Hablo de mi vida de ahora o de niño/a? (Give statements such as the following, changing the boldfaced words so that they describe you.) *Modelos:* Me gustaba **mucho** la escuela. > *de niño* / Me gustan **mis clases**. > *ahora* 1. Vivo en **Boston**. 2. Vivía en **Santa Fe**. 3. Vivía **en una casa en el campo**. 4. Vivo en **un apartamento en una ciudad grande**. 5. Pasaba mucho tiempo **leyendo**. 6. Paso mucho tiempo **en el gimnasio**. 7. Paso mucho tiempo con **mi esposo/a**. 8. Pasaba mucho tiempo **con mis primos**. 9. Quería ser **cantante**. 10. Quiero ser **profesor/a de español**. 11. Soy **un poco tímido/a**. 12. Era **buen/a estudiante. B.** Reread the statements in the imperfect from the preceding activity and have students give the same information about themselves when they were young. *Modelo:* Me gustaba mucho la escuela de niño/a. Y a Ud., ¿le gustaba? **C.** ¿Quién gana más dinero generalmente? ¿un médico o un enfermero? ¿un jugador de fútbol americano o un agricultor? ¿un maestro de escuela primaria o un profesor universitario? ¿un cantante famoso o un programador de computadoras? ¿un obrero de la construcción o un abogado? ¿un hombre de negocios o un secretario? ¿un contador o un pintor?
D. ¿Quiénes trabajan en estos lugares? *Modelo:* en un teatro > *los actores (en el campo, en un estadio, en una universidad, en una escuela, en una fábrica, en una oficina)*

Ahora…
Vivo cerca de la universidad con un amigo.
Me gusta dormir hasta tarde.
Paso mucho tiempo estudiando en la biblioteca.
Estudio mucho.
Soy muy serio/a y trabajador/a.
Quiero ser…

De niño/a…
Vivía en Baltimore con mis padres.
Me gustaba levantarme temprano.
Pasaba mucho tiempo jugando en el parque.
Casi nunca estudiaba.
Era **travieso/a**. No **me portaba** bien.
Soñaba con ser…

médico/a, enfermero/a

artista: cantante, músico, actor (actriz), pintor/a

bombero/a, policía (mujer policía)

maestro/a de escuela primaria, profesor/a universitario/a

programador/a, diseñador/a de software

abogado/a, **hombre (mujer) de negocios,** contador/a, secretario/a

deportista: jugador/a de baloncesto/fútbol americano

agricultor/a

obrero/a de fábrica, obrero/a de la construcción

de niño/a *as a child*   **travieso/a** *mischievous*   **portarse** *to behave*   **soñar con** *to dream of/about*   **hombre/mujer de negocios** *businessman/woman*   **contador/a** *accountant*

7-1 ¿Ahora o de niño/a? ¿Cuál de las oraciones lo/la describe mejor a usted?

Modelo   Paso más tiempo con mis padres ahora. /
Pasaba más tiempo con mis padres de niño/a. /
Pasaba más tiempo con mis padres de niño/a. /
Paso tanto tiempo con mis padres ahora como de niño/a.

1. Paso más tiempo solo/a ahora. / Pasaba más tiempo solo/a de niño/a.
2. Me gusta más la universidad ahora. / Me gustaba más la escuela de niño/a.
3. Leo más ahora. / Leía más de niño/a.
4. Veo más la televisión ahora. / Veía más la televisión de niño/a.
5. Estoy más ocupado/a ahora. / Estaba más ocupado/a de niño/a.
6. Soy más tímido/a ahora. / Era más tímido/a de niño/a.
7. Me porto mejor ahora. / Me portaba mejor de niño/a.
8. Hablo más español ahora. / Hablaba más español de niño/a.

7-2 Profesiones. Un amigo habla de su familia cuando era (*he was*) pequeño.
Complete las oraciones con el nombre de una profesión.

Modelo   Me gustaba jugar al béisbol. Quería ser **jugador de béisbol.**

1. Mi padre trabajaba con los médicos en un hospital. Era…
2. Mi abuelo tenía un tractor y cultivaba tomates, maíz y algodón. Era…
3. Mi madre trabajaba con las computadoras. Era…
4. Mi abuela enseñaba en una escuela primaria. Era…
5. A mi hermana le gustaba cantar y quería ser famosa. Soñaba con ser…
6. Mi tío trabajaba en la construcción de edificios grandes. Era…
7. Mi hermano quería tener un negocio propio. Quería ser…

P   **Conversaciones.** En parejas, lean la siguiente conversación en la cual dos
amigos hablan de su **niñez.** Luego, cambien la conversación para hablar de su
propia niñez.

— ¿Te portabas bien cuando eras pequeña?
— De niña yo era un poco traviesa. ¿Y tú? ¿Cómo eras?
— Era muy tímido. No tenía muchos amigos y pasaba mucho tiempo en mi
   cuarto. Me gustaba leer y jugar con los videojuegos.
— Yo prefería jugar afuera. Era muy deportista y jugaba al béisbol con mis
   hermanos. En el verano pasaba todo el tiempo en la piscina.
— ¿Dónde vivía tu familia?
— Aquí. ¿Y tu familia?
— Mi familia vivía en San Diego.
— **¿A qué se dedicaban** tus padres?
— Los dos trabajaban en **un colegio.** ¿Y tus padres?
— Mi padre era asistente social y mi madre trabajaba en un hospital.

Supplemental activity. ¿Quién tiene
el trabajo más peligroso (*dangerous*)?
¿un policía o un contador? ¿un
obrero de la construcción o un
agricultor? ¿un profesor universitario o
un bombero? ¿un jugador de béisbol
o un jugador de fútbol americano?
¿un maestro de escuela primaria o de
escuela secundaria?

Follow-up for 7-1. *¿Ahora o de
niño/a?* Have students prepare four
other statements comparing
themselves now to ten years ago.
*Modelos: Ahora casi siempre salgo
con los amigos los sábados. Hace
diez años nunca salía los sábados.
Ahora soy más alto/a. Hace diez años
era bajo/a.*

Suggestion for 7-2. *Profesiones.* In
the *modelo,* point out the absence of
the indefinite article when naming a
person's profession.

Suggestion for *Conversaciones.* You
may wish to have students change the
conversation to describe themselves
after doing the grammar section that
follows.

AUDIO ¡A escuchar!

Escuchen otra conversación en la
cual alguien habla de su mejor
amigo cuando era niño. ¿Quién
era? ¿Cómo era? ¿Qué hacía
con su mejor amigo?

¡Ojo!

También se usa **el instituto** o **la
preparatoria** para decir *high
school.*

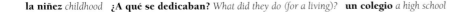

la niñez *childhood*   **¿A qué se dedicaban?** *What did they do (for a living)?*   **un colegio** *a high school*

GRAMÁTICA
Describir en el pasado: el imperfecto

To describe how things used to be, use the imperfect. Unlike the preterite, which focuses on the completion of an event, the imperfect describes the habitual or ongoing nature of past actions.

Preterite: **Visité** a mis abuelos la semana pasada.   *I visited my grandparents last week.*

(The activity was not ongoing, and it is clear when it was completed.)

Imperfect: **Visitaba** a mis abuelos cada verano cuando era pequeño.   *I visited my grandparents every summer when I was little.*

(The activity was ongoing, with no indication of when it was completed.)

All verbs are conjugated regularly with the following **-ar** or **-er/-ir** endings, except **ir, ser,** and **ver.** The ending for **yo** is the same as the **usted, él, ella** ending. Include the subject pronouns of these forms if it is not clear from the context who the subject is. The imperfect of **hay** is **había.**

	HABLAR	COMER	VIVIR
yo	habl**aba**	com**ía**	viv**ía**
tú	habl**abas**	com**ías**	viv**ías**
usted, él, ella	habl**aba**	com**ía**	viv**ía**
nosotros/as	habl**ábamos**	com**íamos**	viv**íamos**
vosotros/as	habl**abais**	com**íais**	viv**íais**
ustedes, ellos, ellas	habl**aban**	com**ían**	viv**ían**

There are only three irregular verbs in the imperfect.

	SER	IR	VER
yo	**era**	**iba**	**veía**
tú	**eras**	**ibas**	**veías**
usted, él, ella	**era**	**iba**	**veía**
nosotros/as	**éramos**	**íbamos**	**veíamos**
vosotros/as	**erais**	**ibais**	**veíais**
ustedes, ellos, ellas	**eran**	**iban**	**veían**

The imperfect may be expressed in a variety of ways in English.

Siempre **comíamos** temprano.

*We always **ate** early.*
*We always **used to eat** early.*
*We would always **eat** early.*

7-3 En el colegio y ayer. Diga si usted hacía las siguientes cosas cuando estaba en el colegio. Luego, diga si las hizo ayer.

Modelo
estar en clase todo el día
Sí, en el colegio estaba en clase todo el día.
No, ayer no estuve en clase todo el día.

1. levantarse temprano
2. salir de la casa antes de las ocho
3. hablar mucho en clase
4. hacer muchas preguntas en clase
5. comer en la cafetería
6. ir a la biblioteca por la tarde
7. regresar a casa antes de las cuatro
8. salir por la noche
9. acostarse después de las once
10. dormir mucho

7-4 ¿Y en tu familia? Pregúntele a otro/a estudiante quién hacía estas actividades con más frecuencia en su familia cuando era pequeño/a.

Modelo
E1: ¿Quién preparaba más la comida en tu familia cuando eras pequeño/a?
E2: **Mi padre preparaba más la comida. / Mi madre y yo preparábamos la comida. / Nadie preparaba la comida. Siempre comíamos en restaurantes.**

1.

2.

3.

4.

5.

6.

7.

7-5 ¿Cómo eran? Prepare tres preguntas para otro/a estudiante sobre cada una de las siguientes cosas o personas de su niñez. Luego, use las preguntas para entrevistar a un/a compañero/a de clase.

Modelo
su cuarto
E1: **¿Tenías tu propio cuarto o compartías un cuarto?**
E2: **Tenía mi propio cuarto.**
E1: **¿De qué color eran las paredes?**
E2: **Eran azules.**
E1: **¿Había un televisor en tu cuarto?**
E2: **No, no había ningún televisor.**

1. su barrio
2. sus vecinos de al lado
3. su escuela primaria
4. su mejor amigo/a de la escuela primaria
5. su clase preferida del colegio
6. su maestro/a preferido/a

VOCABULARIO

TEMA ❷ Los grandes acontecimientos de la vida

Mi hermano mayor tenía diez años cuando **nací**.

un nacimiento

la piñata / una fiesta de cumpleaños

Todos mis amigos vinieron a mi fiesta de cumpleaños cuando **cumplí** cinco años.

un concurso o un campeonato

Gané mi primer concurso de **patinaje** (arte, **belleza** ...) a **la edad** de diez años.

una quinceañera

Toda la familia vino a mi quinceañera.

una graduación

Me gradué de la escuela secundaria a la edad de dieciocho años.

la novia / el novio / una boda

Mi hermano mayor se casó cuando yo tenía quince años.

un funeral / una muerte

Mi abuelo **murió** cuando yo tenía dieciséis años.

una licencia de manejar

Saqué mi licencia de **manejar** a la edad de dieciocho años y tuve mi primer accidente poco después.

una jubilación

Mi padre **se jubiló** a la edad de sesenta y cinco años.

---

un acontecimiento *an event* **nacer** *to be born* **cumplir** *to turn (an age), to carry out* **ganar** *to win* **el patinaje** *skating* **la belleza** *beauty* **la edad** *the age* **morir (ue, u)** *to die* **manejar** *to drive* **jubilarse** *to retire*

℗ 7-6 Una boda terrible. Una amiga cuenta que su boda fue un desastre. En parejas, cambien su descripción para describir una boda perfecta. Use el mismo tiempo verbal (el pretérito o el imperfecto) que en la pregunta.

1. El día de mi boda *llovía y hacía muy mal tiempo.*
2. *Casi nadie fue* a mi boda.
3. Mi novio *llegó tarde a la iglesia.*
4. Al comienzo de la boda mi mamá *estaba triste e histérica.*
5. La comida de la recepción *estaba fría.*
6. Mi novio *perdió los pasajes de avión para la luna de miel (honeymoon) y llegamos tarde al aeropuerto.*
7. Mi esposo y yo *tuvimos que pasar la luna de miel en nuestro apartamento.*

℗ 7-7 Entrevista. Entreviste a un/a compañero/a de clase con las siguientes preguntas. Para contestar, use el mismo tiempo verbal (el pretérito o el imperfecto) que en la pregunta.

1. ¿Cómo celebrabas los cumpleaños cuando eras pequeño/a? ¿Hacían tus padres una fiesta? ¿Había una piñata a veces?
2. ¿En qué año te graduaste de la escuela secundaria? ¿Fue tu familia a la graduación? ¿Qué hiciste después de la ceremonia?
3. La última vez que fuiste a una boda, ¿quién se casó?
4. ¿Ya se jubilaron tus padres? ¿y tus abuelos? ¿Cuántos años tenían cuando se jubilaron?
5. ¿Ganaste alguna vez un concurso o campeonato? ¿Cuántos años tenías? ¿Hiciste algo para celebrarlo después?
6. ¿Qué otros acontecimientos importantes recuerdas de tu niñez? ¿Cuántos años tenías?

℗ Conversaciones. En parejas, lean la siguiente conversación en la cual dos amigos hablan de sus mejores recuerdos. Luego, cambien la conversación para hablar de un día importante de la vida de usted.

— ¿Cuáles son los mejores **recuerdos** de tu niñez?
— Tengo muchos buenos recuerdos pero sobre todo **recuerdo** el día en que mi **equipo** ganó el campeonato de fútbol.
— ¿Cuántos años tenías?
— Tenía nueve años.
— ¿Qué pasó ese día?
— Recuerdo que ese día llovía cuando me desperté e íbamos a jugar a las dos de la tarde. Estaba un poco **preocupado,** pero un poco antes del partido salió el sol y hacía buen tiempo cuando empezamos a jugar.
— ¿Cómo te sentías?
— **Al comienzo** estaba un poco nervioso pero muy **emocionado.** Cuando **marqué** el gol con que ganamos el partido me sentí muy **orgulloso.**

Supplemental activities. A. Give students the following verbs and phrases and have them say whether they did them with their best friend as children: *pasar mucho tiempo juntos/as, verse todos los días, abrazarse con frecuencia, pelearse, hablar mucho por teléfono, jugar juntos/as afuera, comprarse regalos, ir a la misma escuela, ir juntos/as al cine con frecuencia, divertirse juntos/as, enojarse a veces, decirse cosas feas a veces.* Have students prepare five sentences comparing themselves to their best friend as a child. *Modelos: Yo era más grande que él. Él tenía más hermanos que yo...* **B.** Preguntas auditivas. (Tell students to answer each question using the same tense as the verb in the question. You may wish to write each verb on the board and have students say which tense it is.) 1. ¿Tiene Ud. hermanos menores? ¿Cuántos años tenía cuando nacieron? ¿Jugaba Ud. más con sus hermanos, con otros niños del barrio, con sus primos o solo/a? 2. ¿Tiene Ud. hermanos mayores? ¿Ya se casaron? ¿Ya se graduaron de la universidad? ¿Tienen hijos? ¿Cuántos años tenía Ud. cuando sus sobrinos nacieron? 3. ¿Tiene abuelos? ¿Ya se jubilaron o todavía

AUDIO ¡A escuchar!

Escuchen otra conversación en la cual una joven habla de un recuerdo de su niñez. ¿Qué pasó ese día? ¿Cuántos años tenía? ¿Quiénes estaban con ella ese día?

trabajan? ¿Pasaba Ud. mucho tiempo con ellos de niño/a? ¿Iban Uds. más a la casa de sus abuelos o venían sus abuelos más a la casa de Uds.? ¿Venían ellos a sus fiestas de cumpleaños? 4. ¿Tiene licencia de manejar? ¿Cuántos años tenía cuando la sacó? ¿Cómo aprendió a manejar?

---

un recuerdo *a memory* **recordar (ue)** *to remember* **equipo** *team* **preocupado/a** *worried*
al comienzo *at the beginning* **emocionado/a** *excited* **marcar** *to score* **orgulloso/a** *proud*

GRAMÁTICA

Expresar sucesos instantáneos en el pasado: ¿el pretérito o el imperfecto?

Para averiguar

1. Do you use the imperfect or the preterite to describe something in progress in the past?
2. Which tense do you use for something that occurred, interrupting something in progress?

Supplemental activities. **A.** Refer students to *Activity 4-26 En el centro estudiantil*, p. 115, or make a transparency of it. Tell them that this was the scene when they walked into the student lounge, and using the cues listed in the activity have them say what was or was not happening. **B.** Ask questions such as the following about when students left home today. *Cuando Ud. salió de la casa hoy... ¿llovía o hacía sol? ¿hacía frío o hacía calor? ¿llevaba Ud. chaqueta o no llevaba chaqueta? ¿estaba solo/a o estaba con alguien? ¿era antes de las ocho o después de las ocho? ¿no tenía sueño o quería dormir más? ¿iba a la universidad o iba a otro lugar? ¿tenía mucho tiempo o iba a llegar tarde? ¿había muchos carros en las calles o no había muchos carros? ¿traía su mochila o no la traía? ¿tenía hambre o no tenía hambre? ¿estaba listo/a para la clase de español o necesitaba estudiar más? ¿tenía ganas de quedarse en casa o quería salir?* **C.** *¿Dónde estaba Ud. y qué hacía ayer a estas horas: a las seis / ocho / diez de la mañana, a las dos / cuatro / seis de la tarde, a las nueve / once de la noche?*

When describing an activity that was in progress when something else happened interrupting it, use the imperfect for the activity in progress and the preterite to say what occurred, interrupting it. In this context, the imperfect is often, but not always, translated as *was/were …ing* in English.

Íbamos a la tienda cuando **vimos** el accidente.

*We **were going** to the store when we **saw** the accident.*

____*We were going…* (imperfect: what was in progress)

we saw
(preterite: what occurred)

Conocí a mi novio mientras **esperaba** el autobús.

*I **met** my boyfriend while I **was waiting** for the bus.*

____*I was waiting…* (imperfect: what was in progress)

I met
(preterite: what occurred)

Mis padres **vivían** en San Antonio cuando yo **nací.**

*My parents **lived** in San Antonio when I **was born.***

____*My parents lived in…* (imperfect: what was in progress)

I was born
(preterite: what occurred)

Use two verbs in the imperfect to say that two activities were in progress at the same time. These two activities are often connected by **mientras** (*while*).

Yo **estudiaba** mientras mis amigos **jugaban.**

*I **was studying** while my friends **were playing.***

____*I was studying* (imperfect: what was in progress)

My friends were playing (imperfect: what was in progress)

To say what was going to happen in the past, use the imperfect of **ir** followed by **a** + *infinitive*.

Iba a levantarme temprano, pero no oí el despertador.

*I **was going to get up** early, but I didn't hear the alarm clock.*

7-8 En el pasado. Complete las siguientes oraciones usando el imperfecto para describir la acción en progreso, y el pretérito para hablar de la acción completada. Luego, cambie la oración para describir su propio pasado.

> **Modelo** Cuando ___**nací**___ (nacer: yo), mis padres ya ___**tenían**___ (tener) dos hijos.
> **Cuando nací, mis padres no tenían otros hijos.**

1. Mi familia _____ (estar) en Santa Fe cuando _____ (nacer: yo).
2. _____ (vivir: nosotros) en San Diego cuando _____ (empezar: yo) la escuela primaria.
3. _____ (conocer: yo) a mi mejor amigo mientras _____ (estar: yo) en la escuela secundaria.
4. _____ (tener: yo) dieciséis años cuando _____ (aprender: yo) a manejar.
5. Cuando _____ (graduarse: yo) de la escuela secundaria _____ (querer: yo) trabajar en un hospital.
6. _____ (tomar: yo) la clase de español porque _____ (necesitar: yo) una lengua extranjera para mi carrera (*degree*).

(P) 7-9 Las circunstancias. Hágale estas preguntas a otro/a estudiante sobre las circunstancias en las que realizó las siguientes actividades.

> | | |
> |---|---|
> | ¿Qué hora era? | ¿Cómo te sentías? |
> | ¿Quiénes estaban allí y qué hacían? | ¿Qué querías hacer después? |

> **Modelo** levantarse esta mañana
> E1: **¿Qué hora era cuando te levantaste esta mañana?**
> E2: **Eran las seis y media.**
> E1: **¿Quiénes estaban en tu casa?**
> E2: **Mi madre y mi hermano.**
> E1: **¿Qué hacían?**
> E2: **Mi madre se vestía y mi hermano dormía.**
> E1: **¿Cómo te sentías?**
> E2: **Tenía sueño.**
> E1: **¿Qué querías hacer después?**
> E2: **Quería dormir más.**

1. salir de la casa hoy
2. llegar a la clase de español hoy
3. volver a casa ayer
4. cenar anoche

(G) 7-10 Unas fotos. Imagine que Ud. acaba de vivir con una familia en México por un año y les muestra (*are showing*) estas dos fotos de la familia a unos/as amigos/as. Ellos le hacen preguntas acerca de lo que pasaba cuando sacó cada foto. Con dos compañeros de clase, preparen conversaciones imaginarias para cada foto, haciendo varias preguntas.

VOCABULARIO

TEMA 3

Mis cuentos preferidos

¿Le gustaba leer cuando era pequeño/a? ¿Le gustaban más los cuentos de terror? ¿de aventuras? ¿de amor? ¿Cuál era su cuento preferido? ¿Leyó **alguna vez** el cuento puertorriqueño de *La Guanina*?

Érase una vez una **hermosa** india que se llamaba Guanina. Guanina era la hermana de Guaybana, **un cacique**, y estaba **enamorada** de un soldado español que se llamaba don Cristóbal de Sotomayor. **El amor** entre Guanina y don Cristóbal era secreto porque el matrimonio entre los indios y los europeos no se aceptaba **en aquella época.**

Un día Guanina fue corriendo a la casa de don Cristóbal para decirle que los indios iban a atacar a los españoles. Don Cristóbal creía que Guanina estaba exagerando. Él dijo que los indios eran **felices** y que querían vivir en **paz**, pero ella contestó que no eran felices. Los españoles hacían trabajar mucho a los indios y eran crueles. Los indios no querían **someterse** más a los deseos de los españoles. Guanina le dijo a don Cristóbal que tenía que **huir.** Don Cristóbal se enojó y replicó que los hombres de la familia Sotomayor nunca huían. Guanina **se echó a llorar** y don Cristóbal la abrazó y la besó con **cariño.**

Al día siguiente, don Cristóbal llamó a Guaybana. Le dijo que iba a hacer un viaje a la Villa de Caparra y que necesitaba un grupo de indios para llevar su equipaje. Guaybana no estaba contento pero **obedeció** con cortesía. **Pronto** un grupo de indios llegó para llevar el equipaje de don Cristóbal.

En ruta a la Villa de Caparra, Guaybana y sus hombres esperaban a don Cristóbal y sus amigos y los atacaron. Don Cristóbal **luchó** con valor pero murió con todos sus hombres.

Guaybana les dijo a algunos hombres que quería **enterrar** a don Cristóbal con honor porque era **un guerrero** valiente. Cuando esos hombres volvieron al sitio de combate, encontraron a Guanina abrazando y besando **el cuerpo** de don Cristóbal. Los hombres regresaron para informar a Guaybana, y él les dijo que tenían que **matar** y enterrar a Guanina con su **amante,** don Cristóbal.

Pero no fue necesario matar a Guanina. Cuando volvieron al sitio de combate, Guanina ya estaba muerta. Los indios enterraron a Guanina junto a don Cristóbal. Y hasta nuestros días, cuando **los campesinos** de aquel **lugar** oyen la brisa por la noche, dicen que es el canto de amor de don Cristóbal y Guanina, que salen de la tumba para besarse **bajo el claro de luna.**

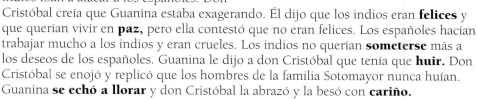

alguna vez *ever* **Érase una vez** *Once upon a time* **hermoso/a** *beautiful* **un cacique** *a chief* **enamorado/a** *in love* **el amor** *love* **en aquella época** *at that time* **feliz** *happy* **la paz** *peace* **someterse** *to submit* **huir** *to flee* **echarse a** *to start* **llorar** *to cry* **el cariño** *affection* **obedecer** *to obey* **Pronto** *soon* **luchar** *to fight, to struggle* **enterrar (ie)** *to bury* **un/a guerrero/a** *a warrior* **el cuerpo** *the body* **matar** *to kill* **un/a amante** *lover* **un/a campesino/a** *a country person, a peasant* **un lugar** *a place* **bajo** *under* **el claro de luna** *the moonlight*

7-11 Comprensión. Conteste las siguientes preguntas sobre *La Guanina*.

1. ¿Quiénes estaban enamorados? ¿Por qué era un amor secreto?
2. ¿Por qué no eran felices los indios?
3. ¿Cómo murió don Cristóbal?
4. ¿Por qué dijo Guaybana que quería enterrar a don Cristóbal?
5. ¿Quién estaba con don Cristóbal cuando fueron a enterrarlo? ¿Cómo reaccionó Guaybana cuando lo supo?
6. ¿Por qué no fue necesario matar a Guanina?

7-12 La Cenicienta. Cuente la historia de la Cenicienta usando el imperfecto para describir las situaciones en progreso y el pretérito para narrar lo que ocurrió.

1. Cuando su padre _____ (morir), Cenicienta _____ (quedarse) con su madrastra mala y dos hermanastras tontas y feas y _____ (tener) que hacer todo el trabajo.
2. Un día un mensajero _____ (venir) a la casa donde _____ (vivir) Cenicienta y _____ (anunciar) que el príncipe _____ (ir) a hacer una fiesta en el palacio.
3. La noche de la fiesta Cenicienta _____ (quedarse) en casa porque no _____ (poder) ir y _____ (llorar) cuando su hada madrina (*fairy godmother*) _____ (llegar) para ayudarla.
4. Cuando Cenicienta _____ (entrar) al palacio, el príncipe la _____ (mirar) con curiosidad porque no la _____ (conocer) y _____ (ser) la mujer más encantadora de todas.
5. El príncipe _____ (abrazar) a Cenicienta cuando _____ (empezar) a sonar las campanas (*bells*) de la medianoche. Cenicienta _____ (echar) a correr fuera del palacio y _____ (perder) uno de sus zapatos de cristal mientras _____ (salir).
6. El príncipe y sus hombres _____ (ir) de casa en casa buscando a la muchacha de la fiesta cuando _____ (llegar) a la casa de Cenicienta.
7. Cuando Cenicienta _____ (ponerse) el zapato de cristal, todos _____ (saber) que _____ (ser) la muchacha de la fiesta.

ⓟ Conversaciones. En parejas, lean la siguiente conversación en la cual una estudiante habla de sus cuentos preferidos de niña. Luego, cambien la conversación para hablar de un cuento o una película que le gustaba a Ud.

— ¿Te gustaba leer cuando eras pequeña?
— Sí, **me encantaba.** Leía mucho. También me gustaba escuchar los cuentos de mi abuela.
— ¿Todavía los recuerdas?
— Sí, cómo no. Mi preferido era **la historia** de *la Llorona*. ¿La conoces?
— No. ¿**De** qué **se trata**?
— Es **la leyenda** mexicana de una mujer que **ahogó** a sus hijos. Luego, **se arrepintió** y después de su muerte, su **fantasma** volvió y pasaba por las calles llorando y buscando a sus hijos. Si me portaba mal, mi abuelita me decía que la Llorona iba a venir por mí.

me encantaba *I loved it* **la historia** *the story* **tratarse de** *to be about, to deal with* **la leyenda** *the legend* **ahogar** *to drown* **arrepentirse (ie, i)** *to be sorry, to regret* **un fantasma** *a ghost*

AUDIO ¡A escuchar!

Escuchen otra conversación en la cual dos personas hablan de los programas de televisión que más les gustaban cuando eran pequeños. ¿Cómo se llamaban los programas y por qué les gustaban?

Suggestion. Have students first read *La Guanina* silently or as homework. Then put the following three headings on the board: *1. setting the scene / background information 2. what was in progress when something else happened 3. what happened next in the sequence of events.* Then have students find the verbs and write them under the corresponding heading. Afterwards, point out that the first two groups are in the imperfect, but the last is in the preterite.

GRAMÁTICA

Narrar en el pasado: ¿el pretérito o el imperfecto?

Para averiguar

1. Do you use the preterite or the imperfect to describe situations that continued in the past? Which tense do you use to say what happened and was finished?
2. What are four uses of the imperfect? What is a contrasting use of the preterite for each one?

Supplemental activities. **A.** Tell students that using the wrong tense can completely change the meaning of a sentence. Have them translate the following sentences into English to illustrate this point: 1. Cuando vi a mi novia nos besamos. / Cuando vi a mi novia nos besábamos. 2. Cuando mis amigos se casaron, tuvieron un bebé. / Cuando mis amigos se casaron, tenían un bebé. **B.** Put the names of the following tales for children on the board or a transparency and have them guess what they are in English: *La Bella y la Bestia, Caperucita Roja, El flautista de Hamelín, Ricitos de Oro y los tres osos, Los tres cerditos, El gato con botas, El patito feo, Blancanieves y los siete enanitos, La Bella Durmiente, Juanito y la planta de frijoles, La Sirenita*. Read the following summaries and have students identify the story from the preceding list of titles. (You may also give students the passages with verbs in the infinitive form for them to decide whether to use the preterite or imperfect.) 1. Es la historia de una muchacha que vivía con su madre en el bosque. Su abuela vivía en el otro lado del bosque. Siempre llevaba una caperuza roja. Un día le llevaba algo de comer a su abuelita enferma cuando encontró a un lobo en el bosque. 2. Tres osos vivían en un bosque en una casa pequeña. Un día la mamá preparó una sopa para almorzar pero estaba muy caliente y no podían comerla. Entonces los tres osos decidieron dar un paseo por el bosque. Mientras estaban en el bosque, una muchacha con el pelo largo y rubio llegó a la casa de ellos. Probó la sopa y se durmió. 3. Una mujer pobre vivía con su hijo de doce años. Sólo tenían una vaca vieja. Un día no había nada de comer en la casa y tenían hambre y por eso la mamá mandó a su hijo al mercado a vender la vaca para comprar comida. Pero en vez de comprar comida, el niño compró tres frijoles mágicos.

While the preterite and imperfect are both used to talk about the past, they are not interchangeable. Each gives a different message about time frames.

Contrast the following uses of each tense.

Note. This grammar module is four pages long.

Use the…

imperfect: for something that continued or was repeated for an unspecified duration.

preterite: for something that happened for a specified duration or for a specific number of times, or was completed at a precise moment.

En el año 2000, yo vivía en Florida y estudiaba en la universidad.
In the year 2000, I was living in Florida and I was studying at the university.

Me gradué de la universidad en el año 2003.
I graduated from the university in the year 2003.

imperfect: for continuing conditions, such as when describing mental or physical states.

preterite: for changes in conditions and states or reactions.

Era el día de mi boda y me sentía muy nervioso.
It was the day of my wedding and I was feeling very nervous.

Después de la boda, me sentí muy feliz.
After the wedding, I felt very happy.

imperfect: for something in progress that was interrupted.

preterite: for what happened, interrupting an action in progress.

Tenía 30 años cuando me casé.
I was thirty when I got married.

imperfect: in narration, to set the scene and describe things that continued to be true.

preterite: in narration, to state the sequence of events that advance the story line.

Era una noche de invierno y hacía mucho frío. Había mucha nieve en las calles, estaba solo en el carro y tenía mucha hambre. Vi un restaurante y decidí ir a comer algo…

It was a winter night and it was very cold. There was a lot of snow on the streets, I was alone in the car, and I was hungry. I saw a restaurant and I decided to go eat something…

When telling a story in the past, ask yourself: *Is it background information that continued to be true though a sequence of events* (imperfect), *or is it the next thing that happened in the sequence of events* (preterite)?

7-13 Un examen. Una estudiante habla de su último examen en una clase. Ponga los verbos en la forma de **yo** del imperfecto para describir un estado mental o físico prolongado y en el pretérito para describir una reacción momentánea.

> Modelo   Cuando me levanté el día del examen **me sentía** (sentirse) un poco enferma.

1. Cuando llegué a la clase, _____ (estar) un poco nerviosa y no _____ (querer) tomar el examen.

2. Justo antes de empezar el examen _____ (creer) que _____ (estar) lista.

3. Cuando vi las preguntas del examen, _____ (tener) un ataque de pánico, pero después _____ (calmarse).

4. _____ (saber) casi todas las respuestas.

5. Después de terminar el examen _____ (sentirse) aliviada (*relieved*).

6. Cuando recibí mi nota (*grade*) del examen _____ (querer) gritar de alegría (*to shout for joy*).

Ahora escriba un párrafo describiendo la última vez que Ud. tomó un examen en una de sus clases.

> Modelo   **Estudié hasta muy tarde la noche anterior y cuando me levanté el día del examen tenía mucho sueño…**

7-14 Pocahontas. Hay muchas leyendas en América parecidas a la de la Guanina de la página 204. Complete el cuento de Pocahontas, escogiendo (*choosing*) la forma correcta de cada verbo (imperfecto = una acción en progreso o las circunstancias, pretérito = lo que ocurrió después).

Érase una vez una princesa que (1. se llamaba, se llamó) Pocahontas. (2. Era, Fue) una muchacha muy inteligente y curiosa. Un día los guerreros de su padre (3. regresaban, regresaron) del bosque con un prisionero extranjero. Cuando (4. llegaban, llegaron) al pueblo, Pocahontas (5. veía, vio) por primera vez a un hombre blanco. (6. Tenía, Tuvo) los ojos azules y el pelo rubio y (7. se llamaba, se llamó) John Smith.

Después de hablar un poco, el padre de Pocahontas (8. decía, dijo) que John Smith (9. tenía, tuvo) que morir. Pocahontas (10. intercedía, intercedió) y le (11. salvaba, salvó) la vida a John Smith. John Smith se quedó con la tribu unos días y habló mucho de su país. Pocahontas se enamoró de él pero pronto John Smith (12. volvía, volvió) con los ingleses.

Los ingleses no (13. sabían, supieron) cultivar la tierra (*earth*) como los indios y (14. pasaban, pasaron) hambre (*were going hungry*). Pocahontas (15. empezaba, empezó) a llevarles comida a John Smith y a sus hombres en Jamestown. Pero al padre de Pocahontas no le (16. gustaba, gustó) la amistad entre Pocahontas y los ingleses, y cuando John Smith (17. volvía, volvió) a Inglaterra, Pocahontas (18. dejaba, dejó) de ir (*stopped going*) a Jamestown.

En la primavera, más hombres (19. llegaban, llegaron) de Inglaterra. Uno de ellos (20. era, fue) el Capitán Samuel Argall. Un día (21. encontraba, encontró) a Pocahontas y la (22. invitaba, invitó) a vivir en Jamestown. Allí (23. conocía, conoció) a John Rolfe, con quien (24. se casaba, se casó). Tres años después de casarse, Pocahontas (25. iba, fue) a Inglaterra con Rolfe, y allí (26. veía, vio) a John Smith otra vez.

Supplemental activities. A. Have students work in groups to complete one of the stories begun on the preceding page or have them tell one of the other stories listed in that section. **B.** Using the sentences from activity *7-12 La Cenicienta* on page 205 as a guide, have students complete the story by filling in the missing details.

Note for 7-14. *Pocahontas.* This activity and others for this section continue on the next page.

A Pocahontas le (27. gustó, gustaba) mucho Inglaterra, pero (28. quería, quiso) volver a América. En 1617, su esposo y ella (29. salían, salieron) para Jamestown, pero (30. tenían, tuvieron) que abandonar el viaje porque Pocahontas (31. se enfermaba, se enfermó). Ella nunca (32. volvía, volvió) a ver su país y (33. moría, murió) a la edad de veintidós años.

7-15 ¿Qué hizo? Las siguientes oraciones describen el día de una joven. Ponga los verbos de la columna izquierda en el pretérito para explicar lo que hizo y en qué orden. Ponga los verbos de la columna derecha en el imperfecto para describir las circunstancias. Luego, usando palabras como **y, pero, luego, como** (*since*), **por eso** (*therefore, that's why*) o **porque,** combine las oraciones de manera lógica para contar su día de ayer.

> **Modelo** **Ayer por la mañana, se levantó a las siete y media. Tenía sueño y quería dormir un poco más…**

PRETERITE (SEQUENCE OF EVENTS)	IMPERFECT (BACKGROUND, CIRCUMSTANCES, SITUATION)
POR LA MAÑANA	**POR LA MAÑANA**
Se levanta a las siete y media.	Tiene mucho sueño y quiere dormir un poco más.
Prepara el desayuno.	Su madre duerme todavía.
Come cereales con fruta y toma café.	No tiene tiempo para comer mucho.
Sale de la casa para el trabajo.	Hace sol pero hace un poco de frío.
Pierde el autobús y tiene que esperar al siguiente.	En el autobús hay mucha gente y no puede sentarse.
Llega tarde a la oficina a las nueve y cuarto.	Casi todos los pasajeros leen el periódico o duermen.
Trabaja desde las nueve y veinte hasta las doce y media.	Su jefe (*boss*) está esperándola.
POR LA TARDE	**POR LA TARDE**
A la hora del almuerzo va a una agencia de viajes.	La agencia no está lejos.
Compra un boleto para Buenos Aires.	La agente es muy simpática.
Regresa al trabajo a la una y media.	El boleto más barato cuesta $500.
Trabaja sólo hasta las cuatro.	No hay mucho que hacer en la oficina.
Después de trabajar, corre una hora por el parque.	Como hace buen tiempo, tiene mucha energía.
Regresa a casa a las seis.	
POR LA NOCHE	**POR LA NOCHE**
Cena pizza.	No tiene ganas de cocinar.
Después de cenar, descansa y ve la televisión.	Su madre no quiere comer.
Se acuesta temprano.	No hay nada interesante en la tele.
	Está aburrida y tiene mucho sueño.

Suggestion for 7-15. ¿Qué hizo? Point out to students that they do not always take one sentence from the left column followed by the sentence next to it in the right column. Remind them to think about what they are saying and combine the sentences in the most logical order.

Follow up for 7-15. ¿Qué hizo? Have students use this activity as a model to write a composition about their day yesterday. First, have them write a list of the sequence of events as in the left column. Then, have them write descriptions of the circumstances as in the right column. Finally, have them combine them into a composition.

7-16 La Llorona. Complete el cuento de la leyenda de la Llorona, cambiando los verbos a la forma apropiada del pretérito o del imperfecto.

Hay (1) una hermosa muchacha que *vive* (2) en un pueblo pobre. Dicen que *es* (3) la muchacha más hermosa de todo el mundo pero también dicen que *es* (4) muy orgullosa y que *se cree* (5) mejor que todos los demás (*everybody else*). Todos los muchachos del pueblo *quieren* (6) ser su novio pero ella siempre *dice* (7) que *son* (8) muy pobres y feos y que *va* (9) a casarse con el hombre más rico y guapo del mundo. Un día *llega* (10) al pueblo el hijo de un ranchero rico. *Es* (11) guapo y encantador y la muchacha *decide* (12) que *va* (13) a casarse con él.

Encantado por la belleza de la muchacha, el ranchero *viene* (14) cada noche y *toca* (15) la guitarra y *canta* (16) cerca de la ventana de ella. Al principio, la muchacha *finge* (*pretends*) (17) no estar interesada y nunca *mira* (18) al joven ranchero. El ranchero *decide* (19) que *va* (20) a ganarse el corazón (*heart*) de esa muchacha y finalmente los dos *se enamoran* (21).

Después de un corto noviazgo, la muchacha y el ranchero *se casan* (22). Al principio, los recién casados (*newlyweds*) *parecen* (23) felices. *Nacen* (24) dos hijos y *tienen* (25) una casa bonita. Pero al pasar unos años todo *cambia* (26), y el ranchero *empieza* (27) a pasar mucho tiempo fuera de casa. *Hay* (28) rumores de que *está* (29) con otras mujeres y sólo *vuelve* (30) a casa para ver a sus hijos.

Cada vez que la joven esposa *ve* (31) a su esposo *se enoja* (32) y los dos *pelean* (33). Un día, la esposa *sale* (34) con los hijos a pasear cerca del río y *ve* (35) a su esposo con una dama elegante. Él *viene* (36) a darles un abrazo a sus hijos, pero no le *dice* (37) nada a su esposa antes de irse con la otra mujer. Cuando *ve* (38) que su esposo *quiere* (39) a sus hijos pero a ella no, la esposa *siente* (40) una rabia celosa (*jealous rage*). *Lleva* (41) a sus hijos y los *tira* (*throws*) (42) al río.

Al verlos arrastrados por la corriente (*swept away by the current*), *se arrepiente* (43) y *echa* (44) a correr por la orilla (*edge*) del río tratando de salvarlos, pero ya *es* (45) demasiado tarde y los niños *mueren* (46).

Al día siguiente, unos niños del pueblo *encuentran* (47) a la joven esposa muerta en la orilla (*bank*) del río. Los muchachos pobres del pueblo *vienen* (48) y la *entierran* (49) allí donde *está* (50). Después de ese día, cada noche todos *oyen* (51) un llanto (*crying*) triste que *viene* (52) desde el río y que *dice* (53) — *Aaaah… mis hijos, dónde están mis hijos. Aaah… mis hijos…*— y algunos *ven* (54) el reflejo de una mujer vestida de blanco en el agua del río. Le *ponen* (55) el nombre (*give her the name*) de La Llorona porque *llora* (56) tanto. Hasta hoy día dicen que el fantasma de La Llorona sale en las noches oscuras buscando a sus niños.

Suggestion for 7-16. *La Llorona.* First, have students read through the story in the present tense for comprehension before putting the verbs in the preterite or imperfect. Remind students to use the imperfect to set the scene and for actions that were in progress, and the preterite for the sequence of events that took place, changes in mental states, or reactions.

Follow-up for 7-16. *La Llorona.* Conteste las siguientes preguntas sobre *La Llorona.* 1. ¿Dónde vivía la muchacha de este cuento? 2. ¿Cómo era la muchacha? 3. ¿Con quién quería casarse? 4. ¿De quién se enamoró? 5. ¿Qué hacía el ranchero cada noche para ganarse el corazón de la muchacha? 6. ¿Cuántos hijos tuvieron el ranchero y la muchacha? 7. ¿Por qué empezaron a pelearse después de unos años? 8. ¿Por qué mató la Llorona a sus hijos? 9. ¿Dónde se murieron los hijos? 10. ¿Dónde se murió la madre? 11. ¿Por qué le pusieron el nombre de la Llorona después de su muerte?

VOCABULARIO
¿Cómo era el vecindario?

Supplemental activities.
A. ¿Qué se necesita en el campus o cerca del campus? ¿más estacionamientos? ¿más semáforos? ¿dónde? ¿límites de velocidad más altos / bajos? ¿en qué calle? ¿más aceras para los peatones? ¿dónde? ¿más paradas de autobús? ¿Dónde se necesita una parada de autobús? ¿Se encuentra una parada de autobús cerca de este edificio? ¿Hay muchos espacios verdes en o cerca de la universidad? ¿Se ven animales a veces en el campus? ¿Vienen muchos estudiantes a la universidad a pie? ¿Traen muchos su carro? En la cafetería, ¿sirven más comida fresca o productos procesados? **B.** ¿Qué palabra corresponde a las siguientes definiciones? 1. el lugar donde se espera el autobús 2. una persona que anda a pie 3. una persona que maneja un coche o un autobús 4. una señal con una luz roja, una luz amarilla y una luz verde 5. la parte de la calle donde caminan los peatones 6. un vehículo que transporta los autos después de un choque 7. un lugar donde se pueden dejar los autos 8. una calle donde se puede manejar a grandes velocidades **C.** ¿Cierto o falso? Hace cincuenta años... 1. Se veían más espacios verdes que ahora. 2. Se jugaba más afuera. 3. Se veía más la televisión. 4. Se comían menos productos procesados. 5. Se comía más en restaurantes. 6. Había menos tráfico. 7. Se divertía uno más. 8. Se trabajaba más. 9. Todo costaba más.

¡Ojo!

El verbo **andar** (*to go, to walk*) es irregular en el pretérito: **anduve, anduviste, anduvo, anduvimos, anduvisteis, anduvieron.** También se dice **la banqueta** en vez de **la acera.**

¿Cómo era la ciudad dónde **creciste**? ¿Qué había en **el vecindario/el barrio**?

¿Cómo era **la vida** cuando tus padres eran niños?

Se veían más espacios verdes y más animales y se jugaba más afuera.

Se comía más en casa y menos en restaurantes. Se comía más comida fresca y había menos productos procesados.

Había menos tráfico. Se manejaba menos y se **andaba** más **a pie.**

---

crecer *to grow (up)*   **el vecindario** *the neighborhood*   **el barrio** *the neighborhood*   **la vida** *life*   **Se veía(n)...** *One saw...*   **Se comía(n)...** *One ate...*   **andar a pie** *to go on foot, to walk*

7-17 **Entrevista.** Complete las siguientes preguntas con la forma del pretérito o del imperfecto de cada verbo. Luego, use las preguntas para entrevistar a un/a compañero/a de clase.

1. ¿_____ (tomar: tú) el autobús escolar para ir a la escuela cuando _____ (ser: tú) pequeño/a? ¿Dónde _____ (estar) la parada de autobús?
2. ¿Dónde _____ (vivir: tú) cuando _____ (aprender: tú) a manejar? ¿_____ (haber) mucho tráfico? ¿Te _____ (gustar) manejar? ¿Cuántos años _____ (tener: tú) cuando _____ (sacar: tú) la licencia de manejar?
3. ¿Cuántos años _____ (tener: tú) cuando _____ (tener: tú) tu primer accidente automovilístico? ¿_____ (estar: tú) en la autopista cuando lo _____ (tener: tú)?
4. ¿Cuándo _____ (recibir: tú) tu última multa (*ticket*)? ¿Por qué?

7-18 **Un día de mala suerte.** En grupos, describan lo que pasó el día de esta boda usando uno de los verbos indicados en el pretérito y el otro en el imperfecto.

Modelo   salir, haber
Cuando el novio salió para la iglesia había mucho tráfico.

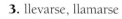

1. ir, tener   **2.** estar, llegar

3. llevarse, llamarse   **4.** llegar, esperar   **5.** manejar, ver

Conversaciones. En parejas, lean la siguiente conversación en la cual dos vecinos hablan de los cambios en su vecindario. Luego, cambien la conversación para hablar de los cambios en su ciudad.

— El vecindario era muy diferente hace diez años.
— Sí, antes había muchos espacios verdes y ahora sólo hay edificios altos y **carreteras.** Recuerdo que se veían muchos animales en el parque pero ahora casi no se ve ninguno.
— Y ahora hay **demasiado** tráfico. Recuerdo que antes se podía llegar al centro en veinte minutos. Ahora se necesita casi una hora.
— A veces hay tanta **contaminación** en el aire que no se puede **respirar.**

AUDIO ¡A escuchar!

Escuchen otra conversación en la cual una persona compara el lugar donde creció con el lugar donde vive ahora. ¿Dónde creció? ¿Dónde vive ahora? ¿Cuáles son las diferencias?

una carretera *a road*   **demasiado/a** *too much*   **la contaminación** *pollution*   **respirar** *to breathe*

GRAMÁTICA
Las normas y las acciones pasivas: *se impersonal*

Para averiguar

1. What are three ways you might express **Eso no se dice** in English?
2. Which two verb forms are used with the impersonal **se**? Which one is used when followed by verbs in the infinitive? when followed by the personal **a** before a group of people?
3. How do you form a phrase with the impersonal **se** when using reflexive verbs?

Supplemental activities. A. Un extraterrestre llega a su casa. Explíquele qué se hace con las siguientes cosas. *Modelos: el café > El café se toma. / los libros > Los libros se leen. (la pizza, el periódico, el vino, la música, los instrumentos musicales, las revistas)* Explíquele al extraterrestre qué se hace en estos lugares. *(en la biblioteca, en la librería, en el supermercado, en la piscina, en el parque, en la playa, en una fiesta, en una escuela, en un museo, en un aeropuerto, en una agencia de viajes, en una farmacia, en un restaurante, en un estadio, en una oficina de correos)* Explíquele al extraterrestre para qué se usan los siguientes productos. *Modelo: Dawn > Se lavan los platos con Dawn. (Windex, Dove, Crest, Tide)* **B.** ¿A qué edad se hacen estas cosas generalmente? *Modelo: celebrar la quinceañera > Se celebra la quinceañera a la edad de quince años. (sacar la licencia de manejar, graduarse de la escuela secundaria, jubilarse, poder comprar bebidas alcohólicas, poder casarse sin el permiso de los padres, votar por primera vez, aprender a hablar, aprender a caminar, aprender a leer)*

Use the impersonal **se** to state what people do or used to do as a general rule. Phrases with **se** may be expressed in a variety of ways in English.

Se habla español allí.
> *People speak Spanish there.*
> *They speak Spanish there.*
> *Spanish is spoken there.*

Eso no **se hacía**.
> *People didn't do that.*
> *One didn't do that.*
> *That wasn't done.*

No **se usaban** las computadoras.
> *People didn't use computers.*
> *One didn't use computers.*
> *Computers weren't used.*

With **se**, use the third-person form (**él, ella, ellos, ellas**) of the verb. It may be singular or plural, depending on the subject, which most commonly follows the verb.

Se come paella en España.   *Paella is eaten in Spain.*
Se comen tacos en México.   *Tacos are eaten in Mexico.*
Se necesita uno más.   *One more is needed.*
Se necesitan dos más.   *Two more are needed.*

A verb with the impersonal **se** is in the singular form when it is followed by infinitives or with a group of people introduced by the personal **a**, even though you are referring to more than one action or person.

Se puede oír música y **bailar** allí.   *You can hear music and dance there.*
Se ve a muchas personas en el parque   *One sees many people in the park on*
   los sábados.   *Saturdays.*

When using a verb that is normally reflexive in an impersonal **se** construction, the word **uno** is added as the subject.

Uno se divertía mucho.   *One used to have a good time.*

7-19 ¿Dónde? Nombre un lugar donde se hacen estas cosas en su ciudad.

> **Modelo**   Se come bien.
>   **Se come bien en el restaurante El Patio. / Se come bien en la casa de mi abuela.**

1. Se aprende mucho.
2. Se puede nadar.
3. Se prohíbe fumar.
4. Se habla mucho español.
5. Uno se divierte mucho.
6. Se conoce a muchachos y muchachas interesantes.
7. Se toma mucha cerveza.

7-20   **¿Y en el colegio?** Ahora diga si cada cosa de *7-19 ¿Dónde?* se hacía en su colegio.

Modelo   **No se comía bien en la cafetería.**

Ⓖ **7-21**   **De vacaciones.** En grupos, imaginen que usted y sus compañeros de clase viajaron a Oaxaca o a uno de los lugares presentados en las secciones de *Escapadas*. Escriban oraciones con **se** impersonal explicando lo que se hacía en ese lugar.

Se veía(n)…	Se podía(n)…	Se comía(n)…	…
Se hablaba(n)…	No se permitía(n)…	Se prohibía(n)…	…
Se necesitaba(n)…	Se oía(n)…	Se vendía(n)…	

Oaxaca, México.

Ⓟ **7-22**   **Entrevista.** Complete las siguientes preguntas con la forma correcta del verbo entre paréntesis y entreviste a un/a compañero/a de clase.

1. ¿(Se habla / Se hablan) mucho español en tu vecindario? ¿(Se encuentra / Se encuentran) muchos restaurantes de comida mexicana en el vecindario? ¿(Se vende / Se venden) revistas en español en los supermercados? ¿(Se oye / Se oyen) a mucha gente (*people*) hablando español en los supermercados?
2. ¿(Se usa / Se usan) mucho el transporte público en tu vecindario? ¿(Se encuentra / Se encuentran) una parada de autobús cerca de tu casa? ¿(Se ve / Se ven) muchos accidentes en las calles?

Ahora vuelva a hacer las mismas preguntas en el imperfecto, hablando del vecindario de su compañero/a cuando él/ella era pequeño/a.

Ⓖ **7-23**   **Cambios.** En grupos de tres, hagan listas de los siguientes cambios. Escriban oraciones con **se** impersonal. ¿Qué grupo puede hacer las listas más largas?

1. ¿Qué se hace en la universidad que no se hacía en el colegio y viceversa?
2. ¿Qué se hace ahora que no se hacía cuando sus padres tenían su edad?
3. ¿Qué se encuentra / se ve en su ciudad que no se encontraba / se veía hace veinte años?

VOCABULARIO

TEMA 5

¿Vio usted lo que pasó?

7-24 Definiciones. ¿Qué palabra corresponde a las siguientes definiciones?

1. una persona que sufre un accidente o un crimen
2. una persona que comete un crimen
3. los gases grises y negros que salen de un incendio
4. una persona que maneja una ambulancia
5. un caso urgente
6. una persona que vio un accidente o un crimen
7. un informe policial sobre un crimen
8. la detención de un criminal

7-25 **Un informe.** Complete los espacios en blanco con las palabras lógicas de la lista y seleccione la forma correcta de los verbos entre paréntesis.

> heridos   víctimas   humo   bombero   escalera   incendio

REPORTERO: Buenas noches, estoy aquí en la calle 24. Detrás de mí hay un edificio destruido por un _____. Estoy con Salvador Zavala, _____ de la ciudad de Los Ángeles. Señor Zavala, cuando Uds. (*llegaron, llegaban*), (*hubo, había*) una familia atrapada en el tercer piso, ¿verdad?

BOMBERO: Sí, cuando (*llegamos, llegábamos*), (*salió, salía*) mucho _____ negro de la planta baja y nadie podía entrar ni salir. (*Pudimos, Podíamos*) rescatar a la familia a través de una ventana con una _____ .

REPORTERO: ¿Hubo _____?

BOMBERO: No, gracias a Dios, todos (*salieron, salían*) sanos y salvos, pero esta familia lo (*perdió, perdía*) todo.

REPORTERO: Como (*oyeron, oían*), no les queda nada a las _____ de este incendio. Si alguien quisiera ayudarles, puede llamar al 929-4085. Martín López informando desde la calle 24.

P **7-26** **Entrevista.** Entreviste a otro/a estudiante con estas preguntas.

1. ¿Tienes detectores de humo en tu casa/apartamento? ¿Hay detectores de humo en todos los edificios de la universidad? ¿Sabes por dónde debemos salir de este edificio en caso de incendio? ¿Se debe usar el ascensor o la escalera?
2. ¿Sabes cómo administrar los primeros auxilios? ¿Te gustaría trabajar como paramédico/a? ¿enfermero/a? ¿médico/a? ¿Cómo reaccionas cuando ves una ambulancia? ¿Siempre la dejas (*let*) pasar? ¿Cuál es el hospital con sala de emergencia más cercano?
3. ¿Se ve a la policía con frecuencia en el barrio universitario? ¿Se oyen más las sirenas de las ambulancias, de los bomberos o de la policía?

P **Conversaciones.** En parejas, lean la siguiente conversación en la cual un policía habla con un conductor que acaba de **chocar** con otro carro. Luego, cambien la conversación para hablar de un accidente automovilístico que usted vio.

— ¿Necesito llamar una ambulancia o todos están bien?
— No, nadie de nuestro carro **resultó herido.**
— ¿Me puede contar cómo ocurrió el accidente?
— El semáforo estaba en rojo y esperaba en este **carril** porque iba a seguir recto. Ese señor venía en la dirección opuesta. El semáforo cambió a verde y empecé a **cruzar** la calle. Él no me vio y **giró** a la izquierda y chocó conmigo.

---

chocar *to have a wreck, to crash*   **resultar herido/a** *to get injured* (**resultar** *to turn out*)   **un carril** *a lane*
cruzar *to cross*   **girar** *to turn*

Follow-up for 7-25. *Un informe.* Have students work in pairs to prepare an interview about a real news/sports event that recently took place in your city. One student plays the reporter and the other a witness.

Supplemental activity. Tell students that they have been hired as a courtroom interpreter and they have to ask the following questions in Spanish. 1. *Were you driving the night of the accident?* 2. *Did you go to a bar that night?* 3. *How much did you drink?* 4. *How did you feel when you left the bar?* 5. *How many people were with you in the car?* 6. *Did you know the victims of the accident?* 7. *Did you meet them that night?* 8. *Do you remember what happened when you hit the other car?* 9. *At what speed were you driving when you had the accident?* 10. *What did you remember when you woke up in the hospital?* (You may wish to share with your students that court interpreting for Spanish is a fast-growing profession. From July 1, 2002 to June 31, 2003, of the 71,370 events requiring interpreters in New Jersey superior courts, 61,980 were for Spanish. Pay for staff interpreters varies across the country from $30,000 to $80,000 per year, depending on where you work. Most interpreters are freelancers. Hardworking freelancers can make over $100,000 per year. Federal courts pay interpreters $305 per day. Qualifications for interpreters vary greatly and depend on the state where one lives. Not only does court interpreting require fluency in two

AUDIO **¡A escuchar!**

Escuchen otra conversación en la cual un policía habla con la víctima de un crimen. ¿Qué pasó? ¿En qué circunstancias ocurrió el suceso (*incident*)?

languages, it also requires familiarity with legal terms and the legal system. Certification to interpret in federal courts is determined by an exam. Students can learn more by researching the *Federal Court Interpreter Certification Examination* or the *National Association of Judiciary Interpreters and Translators*.)

GRAMÁTICA

Más narración en el pasado: ¿el pretérito o el imperfecto?

Para averiguar

1. Do you use the preterite or the imperfect to describe events that took place in a certain order? Which tense do you use to set the scene?
2. If you were describing a play, would you use the preterite or the imperfect to describe the scene when the curtain first went up? Which tense would you use to describe what the characters did, advancing the story?

Supplemental activities. **A.** Have students work in pairs to prepare five sentences describing what happened in a well-known movie without naming the characters. They then read the sentences one at a time to see how quickly their classmates can guess the name of the movie. *Modelo: Había una muchacha que vivía en Kansas. Tenía un pequeño perro. Un día se enojó y se fue de la casa. Después, regresó porque hacía muy mal tiempo. Se durmió y cuando se despertó estaba en otro país donde todos eran muy bajos. > El Mago de Oz.* **B.** Have students work in pairs to do *5-8 Una pareja feliz* on p. 137 using the preterite and imperfect, rather than the present.

When telling a story in the past, use the imperfect to set the scene and give background information that continued to be true through a sequence of events. Use the preterite for the sequence of events that advance the story line. For example, if you were describing a play, you would use the imperfect to describe the stage when the curtain went up.

> Una mujer y un hombre **estaban** en la cocina. El hombre **hablaba** por teléfono y la mujer **leía** el periódico. La cocina **era** pequeña y **había** sólo una mesa con dos sillas. El reloj **indicaba** que **eran** las nueve de la mañana…

In the preceding paragraph, nothing new happened advancing the story line. All the verbs are in the imperfect because they set the scene. The events that take place advancing the story are in the preterite.

> … El reloj indicaba que eran las nueve de la mañana. Después de algunos minutos un muchacho **abrió** la puerta y **entró. Abrazó** a su madre pero no le **dijo** nada a su padre.

The following diagram is useful to help visualize the use of the preterite and the imperfect when telling a story.

> Un muchacho **abrió** la puerta, **entró, se sentó** y **se comió** una manzana. **Tenía** el pelo rubio.
>
> | abrió | entró | se sentó | se comió |
> |---|---|---|---|
> | X | X | X | X |
>
> tenía el pelo rubio

The Xs represent events that can be sequenced in order (the preterite). The continuous arrow represents background information (the imperfect) that cannot be ordered in the sequence of events, but rather is true throughout the scene. In the example, the fact that the boy had blond hair continued to be true throughout the sequence of events.

℗ 7-27 911. Usted acaba de ser testigo/a de un accidente. Con otro/a estudiante, invente los detalles de un accidente que Ud. vio, para contestar las preguntas del/de la operador/a de emergencias del 911.

1. ¿Dónde ocurrió el accidente?
2. ¿A qué hora ocurrió?
3. ¿Hubo algún herido en el accidente? ¿Se necesita una ambulancia?
4. ¿Qué hacía Ud. cuando ocurrió?
5. ¿Había más gente (*people*) en la calle? ¿Qué estaban haciendo?

7-28 La Caperucita Roja. Complete el cuento de la Caperucita Roja, cambiando los verbos a la forma del pretérito o del imperfecto.

Hay (1) una niña muy bonita y simpática que *se llama* (2) Caperucita Roja porque siempre *lleva* (3) una caperuza roja. Un día *encuentra* (4) a un lobo *(wolf)* enorme mientras le *lleva* (5) unos pasteles a su abuelita que *vive* (6) al otro lado del bosque. El lobo *sale* (7) de entre los árboles y *saluda* (8) a Caperucita Roja preguntándole adónde *va* (9). Caperucita Roja *contesta* (10) que *trae* (11) comida para su abuelita y que *va* (12) a su casa.

El lobo *se despide* (13) y *se va* (14) corriendo a la casa de la abuelita para llegar primero. Cuando el lobo *llega* (15) a su casa, la abuelita *abre* (16) la puerta porque *piensa* (17) que *es* (18) Caperucita Roja. El lobo *devora* (19) a la abuelita toda entera *(whole)*, *se pone* (20) la ropa de ella y *se acuesta* (21) en su cama.

Luego Caperucita Roja *llega* (22) a la casa y *entra* (23), y cuando *ve* (24) a su abuelita *comenta* (25) que sus dientes *se ven* (26) muy grandes. En ese instante el lobo *se abalanza (pounces)* (27) sobre Caperucita Roja y *se la come* (28) toda entera. Mientras tanto, un cazador *(In the meantime, a hunter) pasa* (29) por la casa y *observa* (30) lo que *ocurre* (31). *Entra* (32) en la casa y *raja* (33) el vientre *(splits open the belly)* del lobo, y Caperucita Roja y su abuelita *salen* (34) vivas.

P Ahora imagine que Ud. es policía investigando la muerte del lobo y que no cree la historia de Caperucita Roja. En parejas, preparen cuatro preguntas para interrogarla sobre los detalles más increíbles.

> **Modelo**   **¿Por qué no te comió el lobo cuando te encontró mientras caminabas por el bosque?**

G **7-29 Testigos.** Imagine que ustedes fueron testigos de lo que pasó en esta fiesta y la policía quiere hacerles unas preguntas. En grupos de tres preparen una conversación en la cual uno/a de ustedes es el/la policía/mujer policía y les hace preguntas a los/las otros/as dos.

Vocabulario útil: una moto *(a motorcycle)*, **un/a motociclista** *(a biker)*, **caer a** *(to fall into)*.

¡Trato hecho!

En portada

REVISTA CULTURAL

The **¡Trato hecho!** section always opens with the **En portada** reading. The accompanying activities follow on the right page. Be sure to complete the **Antes de leer** activities (on the right page) before proceeding with the reading.

MI BARRIO, MI GENTE

La calle Caminito, Barrio de La Boca, Buenos Aires.

La Calle Ocho, Miami.

El barrio tiene ese sentimiento de comunidad tan **valorado** entre los hispanos, es el lugar donde **se echan** las primeras **raíces,** donde se empieza a formar nuestra identidad. Uno de los países donde el sentimiento de barrio está más **arraigado** es Argentina, y en especial en su capital Buenos Aires.

El hispano lleva esa idea de barrio **consigo** cuando emigra fuera de su país. Los Ángeles, Nueva York, Chicago, Miami, Houston y Riverside-San Bernardino, en California, son áreas de población con más de un millón de residentes latinos.

En estos lugares los barrios hispanos poseen características únicas que les dan una identidad propia. Cuando uno se pasea por Boyle Heights en Los Ángeles, por el Harlem español en Nueva York o por la pequeña Habana en Miami, se puede sentir en la misma Latinoamérica. En las calles se escucha el español, o el *espanglish*, se encuentran las bodegas del barrio, pequeños supermercados con productos típicos del país y lugares de reunión social, restaurantes con **sazón** latino, quioscos y librerías con publicaciones en español, oficinas de **envíos de dinero** y otros servicios para la comunidad hispana.

Laveta Terrace, Los Ángeles.

En estos barrios, los inmigrantes compran o alquilan casas o apartamentos y se desarrolla ese sentido de pertenencia.

Aunque el estado económico de la mayoría de los inmigrantes hispanos es a su llegada inferior al de la población norteamericana, también sueñan con tener su propia casa. De hecho, según un estudio reciente de la Fundación Fannie Mae, el 65% de los hispanos entrevistados indicaron que tener su propia casa es una prioridad importante.

Harlem, Nueva York.

Maxwell Street Market, Chicago.

---

valorado *valued* **se echan raíces** *people take root* **arraigado** *deep-rooted* **consigo** *with him/her* **sazón** *flavor* **envíos de dinero** *wired money orders*
aunque *although*

Desafortunadamente, la diferencia entre **los dueños** de viviendas todavía es significativa. Cerca del 67% de la población estadounidense es dueña de una vivienda, pero sólo un 46% de los hispanos son dueños de sus casas.

En propiedad.

Antes de leer

Observe con atención las fotos que acompañan a la lectura y describa los distintos ambientes (*environments*) que aparecen. ¿Qué ideas puede inferir de las fotos? ¿Cómo se relacionan con el título *Mi barrio, mi gente*?

Reading strategies: Activating existing background knowledge. When reading a foreign language, not only does your growing comprehension of the language help you understand a text, you also use your prior knowledge of the topic acquired through your own experiences, cultural background, and previous education. Activating background information and establishing connections between your own experiences and the topic will increase your comprehension and help you learn from a text, while stimulating your interest and curiosity.

7-30 Ahora Ud. ¿Con qué ideas asocia el concepto de barrio? ¿Cómo era el barrio donde creció? ¿Qué lugares recuerda especialmente de su barrio? Compare el barrio de su niñez con el barrio donde está su universidad.

Después de leer

P **7-31 El sentido de pertenencia.** En parejas, respondan a las siguientes preguntas relacionadas con la lectura *Mi barrio, mi gente*.

1. ¿Qué valor tiene el concepto de *barrio* en la cultura hispánica?
2. ¿Qué características forman la identidad de los barrios latinos en Estados Unidos?
3. ¿Cómo valora el hispano la propiedad de una vivienda? ¿Qué porcentaje de la población hispana es dueña de una vivienda en Estados Unidos?
4. ¿Hay algún vecindario latino cerca de su casa o cerca de su universidad? Describa el ambiente de este vecindario.

7-32 Comportamientos de grupo. Busque en la lectura las estructuras con *se impersonal*, indique el infinitivo del verbo y explique por qué aparece en tercera persona de singular o de plural.

G **7-33 El perfil del barrio.** El Harlem español, la pequeña Habana y Boyle Heights son algunos ejemplos de barrios latinos en Estados Unidos. Busque otros ejemplos en Internet y prepare una tabla comparativa de estos vecindarios y los mencionados, incluyendo el área geográfica donde están, el grupo predominante de inmigrantes y el porcentaje de población que representan en la región.

Note. Have students complete the *Antes de leer* section and *Ahora Ud.* before reading the article *Mi barrio, mi gente*.

Suggestion. The movie *Real Women Have Curves* by director Patricia Cardoso offers an excellent setting to discuss the *barrio* identity, the different attitudes of Hispanics toward the *barrio,* and family business and traditions. Students can watch the movie as a course assignment and conduct a guided discussion in class and/or write a reflection about the topics mentioned above.

Suggestion. A class discussion related to the concept of Spanglish and how it developed in the *barrios* could be an interesting activity to expand the reading. Have students conduct an Internet research on Spanglish, and encourage them to express their opinions regarding this topic.

desafortunadamente *unfortunately* **los dueños** *owners*

De puertas abiertas a la comunidad

📹 NIÑOS AYER, HÉROES HOY

7-34 Entrando en materia. Cuando usted era niño, ¿qué soñaba ser de mayor? ¿Qué profesiones admiraba más? ¿Por qué? ¿Quién era su héroe de la infancia? ¿Guiaron sus sueños de niño la dirección de su carrera actual? Al contestar estas preguntas, preste atención al uso del imperfecto.

> De niños todos soñamos con ser maestras, policías, bomberos, pilotos, médicas... Nuestros sueños de la niñez guían a veces la dirección que tomamos en nuestra vida. Otras veces vivimos una experiencia extraordinaria que nos abre la puerta a un nuevo destino. En este segmento de vídeo, van a escuchar los testimonios de varias personas que nos hablan de su **infancia** y de los recuerdos más bonitos. Van a ver también como esos niños ayer, son héroes hoy.

7-35 Recuerdos de la infancia. Analissa y Alejandro recuerdan sus días de la infancia. Complete los siguientes testimonios con el imperfecto o el pretérito de los verbos entre paréntesis, según corresponda.

Alejandro en la bodega

Yo ___me crié___ (1. criarse *to be brought up*) detrás del mostrador de mi negocio, bueno el negocio de mi padre en ese tiempo. Cuando yo ___era___ (2. ser) joven, mis padres me ___traían___ (3. traer) a la bodega todos los días e incluso (*even*) me ___compraron___ (4. comprar) una pequeña cuna (*cradle*) para el negocio. Me ___gustaba___ (5. gustar) pasar el rato aquí con mis padres, y normalmente ___ayudaba___ (6. ayudar) con las quehaceres: ___limpiaba___ (7. limpiar), ___movía___ (8. mover) bolsas.

Analissa y su chelo

Los recuerdos más bonitos de mi infancia son recuerdos de la música. Yo desde los diez años, con mi papá y mi mamá, y a veces con mis hermanos, ___viajaba___ (1. viajar) con mi chelo siempre. Nos ___íbamos___ (2. ir) a Zacatecas, ___estudiaba___ (3. estudiar, yo) en Bellas Artes en México en los veranos. Y siempre con mi chelo, siempre ___tenía___ (4. tener) mi chelo, tocando con mis amigos, con los maestros. La verdad es que no me acuerdo cómo ___era___ (5. ser) mi vida antes de la música.

7-36 Mi infancia fue... Escuche con atención el testimonio de Gloria Celaya sobre su infancia y su adolescencia. Luego, complete las siguientes frases con la forma adecuada del pretérito o del imperfecto de cada verbo.

1. Su infancia ___fue___ (ser) una infancia feliz.

2. Gloria ___tenía___ (tener) muchos tíos y tías que la ___cuidaban___ (cuidar *to take care of*).

---

infancia *childhood*

3. Gloria _____tenía_____ (tener) un tío compositor que _____influyó_____ (influir) mucho en su carrera artística.

4. Cuando _____tenía_____ (tener) 18 años / Gloria _____viajó_____ (viajar) a Francia con una beca (*scholarship*)..

5. Gloria _____vivió_____ (vivir) en Francia cinco años.

7-37 Háblenos de su infancia. ¿Qué recuerda usted de su infancia? ¿Cómo creció? ¿Qué cosas hacía con sus padres que le gustaban y todavía hoy recuerda? ¿Fue feliz creciendo en su barrio? Preste especial atención al uso del pretérito y del imperfecto en su testimonio.

7-38 Algo muy importante en mi vida. ¿Cuál fue el acontecimiento más importante en la vida de Alejandro? ¿Por qué fue tan importante para él? Y para usted, ¿cuál fue el acontecimiento más importante en su vida? ¿Por qué tiene este valor?

7-39 De niña quería ser... Bárbara Bonilla, hoy maestra de español, nos habla de qué quería ser de niña. Escuche su testimonio e indique si las siguientes afirmaciones son ciertas o falsas. Corrija las falsas.

	Cierto	Falso
1. De niña, Bárbara quería ser pintora.	☐	☒
2. Cuando tenía nueve años tenía una escuelita en el patio de su casa.	☒	☐
3. Nunca tenía estudiantes en su escuelita.	☐	☒
4. El papá de Bárbara le hacía las tarjetitas de notas para los comentarios de sus clases.	☒	☐
5. Nadie recuerda la escuelita de Bárbara.	☐	☒
6. Hace dos años, una vecina de su barrio viejo le regaló la tarjeta de notas que Bárbara escribió cuando era la "maestra" de su hija.	☒	☐

Answers for 7-38. *Algo muy importante en mi vida.* Un acontecimiento muy importante en la vida de Alejandro fue su graduación de la universidad. Fue muy importante para él porque él fue el primer miembro de su familia que se graduó de la universidad. Y este acontecimiento es un orgullo para su familia y para la comunidad latina de Estados Unidos en general.

Answers for 7-39. *De niña quería ser...* 1. Bárbara quería ser maestra. 3. Siempre tenía muchos niños en su escuelita. 5. Una vecina del barrio tomó la tarjetita de notas de su hija y se la dio a Bárbara con su firma y su comentario.

P **7-40 ¿Y Uds.?** ¿Qué quería ser usted de niño/a? Entreviste a un/a compañero/a sobre lo que le quería ser de niño/a y la dirección profesional que está tomando ahora. Informe después a la clase del testimonio de su compañero/a.

G **7-41 De profesión, bombero.** Cuando piensan en la profesión de bombero, ¿qué ideas les vienen a la mente (*come to mind*)? ¿Qué concepto tienen de la profesión de bombero? ¿Qué riesgos (*risks*) presenta este trabajo?

Completen el siguiente texto con las palabras de la caja que resulten apropiadas. Conjuguen los verbos cuando sea necesario.

orgulloso   resultar herido   humo   dedicarse   valiente   incendios

Rafael es un hombre muy (1) _____valiente_____. El trabajo de bombero tiene muchos riesgos. Rafael (2) _____se dedica_____ a ayudar a la gente cuando hay (3) _____incendios_____. Muchas veces las personas (4) _____resultan_____ _____heridas_____ y Rafael tiene que entrar en las casas y encontrar a las personas entre el fuego y el (5) _____humo_____ para rescatarlas. Rafael está muy (6) _____orgulloso_____ de servir a la comunidad con su trabajo.

Escapadas

BUENOS AIRES, "LA REINA DEL PLATA"

La Plaza de Mayo, Buenos Aires.

Buenos Aires, **"la reina del Plata"**, es una de las ciudades más cosmopolitas de Sudamérica, con una herencia cultural muy variada que se refleja en la personalidad de sus barrios. La presencia de la inmigración europea es evidente en muchos **rincones** de Buenos Aires.

El Barrio de San Telmo es el más viejo de la ciudad. Los primeros vecinos eran pescadores y trabajadores del **puerto** de origen italiano, irlandés, africano y **criollo.** Hoy San Telmo es un barrio de artistas y artesanos, que ocupan las casas coloniales renovadas. Todos los domingos se celebra **una feria de antigüedades** en la Plaza Dorrego, una auténtica atracción popular.

El Distrito de la Avenida de Mayo es conocido también como Distrito Español por su gran parecido con la arquitectura de Madrid. En los comienzos **del siglo XX** este barrio fue **el hogar** de muchos inmigrantes españoles, de origen gallego y asturiano en su mayoría. La Plaza de Mayo es el principal centro político de Buenos Aires. Allí están la Casa Rosada, residencia oficial del presidente, y el Cabildo, **sede** del gobierno local.

Tango en el Barrio de San Telmo.

La Casa Rosada, Buenos Aires.

la reina del Plata *The queen of the Río de la Plata* **rincones** *corners* **puerto** *port* **criollo** *Creole* **una feria de antigüedades** *an antique fair* **el siglo XX** *the 20th century* **el hogar** *the home* **sede** *headquarters, seat*

En el centro de la plaza se encuentra la Pirámide de Mayo, donde todavía hoy marchan cada jueves las Madres de la Plaza de Mayo en protesta por sus hijos **desaparecidos** durante **la dictadura** militar **impuesta** en el país entre 1976 y 1983.

La Recoleta es un barrio elegante donde se puede visitar uno de **los camposantos** más hermosos del mundo: el Cementerio de la Recoleta, donde están las tumbas de importantes personalidades argentinas como Eva Perón. Alrededor del cementerio están el Museo Nacional de Bellas Artes, la Biblioteca Nacional, la iglesia colonial de Nuestra Señora del Pilar y el Centro de Exposiciones del Gobierno de la ciudad de Buenos Aires.

Las Madres de la Plaza de Mayo.

El Barrio de la Boca es el más pintoresco de la ciudad. Allí se establecieron entre 1830 y 1852 inmigrantes italianos, dedicados a la industria pesquera. **El alma** del barrio es la calle Caminito, donde hay un museo al aire libre que es tributo al tango y a tantos artistas que allí **desarrollaron** su obra.

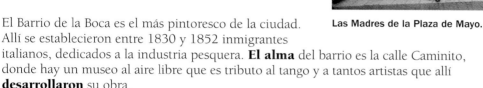

El Palacio Nacional de Congresos, Buenos Aires.

Buenos Aires es una ciudad misteriosa y bella y sus habitantes, los **porteños,** se sienten **orgullosos** de su pasado europeo y de su **mezcla** de tradición y modernidad.

La calle Caminito, Barrio de La Boca, Buenos Aires.

desaparecidos *missing* **la dictadura** *the dictatorship* **impuesta** *imposed* **los camposantos** *cemeteries* **el alma** *the soul* **desarrollaron** *developed* **porteños** *people from Buenos Aires* **orgullosos** *proud* **mezcla** *mix*

Suggestion. Encourage students to read about current events in Argentina, the economic crisis of the country, and its repercussions in people's lives. This could be an interesting topic for an in-class oral presentation.

Suggestion. Students can learn more about the totalitarian regime in Argentina between 1976 and 1983 and the story of *los desaparecidos,* by analyzing the film *La historia oficial.* A historical background of this period should precede the viewing of the movie.

Answers for 7-43. *¿Pretérito o imperfecto?* 1. viajamos 2. íbamos 3. nos divertíamos 4. pasamos 5. era 6. hacía 7. pudimos 8. Estuvimos 9. visitamos 10. fuimos 11. vimos 12. honraban 13. paseamos 14. conoció 15. sentíamos

℗ 7-42 Los barrios de Buenos Aires. ¿Qué saben sobre Buenos Aires? Contesten estas preguntas relacionadas con la lectura *Buenos Aires, "la reina del Plata".*

1. ¿Cuál es el barrio más antiguo de Buenos Aires? ¿Quiénes fueron los primeros vecinos? ¿Quién vive en este vecindario hoy?
2. ¿Cuál es la importancia de la Plaza de Mayo?
3. ¿Dónde está la calle Caminito? ¿Por qué es conocida (*well-known*) esta calle?
4. ¿Qué debe visitar el turista si va al barrio de La Recoleta?
5. ¿Con qué otro nombre se conoce el Distrito de la Avenida de Mayo? ¿Por qué?

7-43 ¿Pretérito o imperfecto? Complete la siguiente narración de un viaje a Buenos Aires con el verbo en la forma del pretérito o del imperfecto.

El verano de 2003 mi hermano y yo _____ (1. viajar) a Buenos Aires. Generalmente, él y yo _____ (2. ir) de vacaciones juntos en junio y siempre _____ (3. divertirse) mucho. Aquel verano _____ (4. pasar) diez días en la capital. Durante nuestro viaje _____ (5. ser) invierno en Argentina, y _____ (6. hacer) bastante frío, pero todavía nosotros _____ (7. poder) explorar la ciudad en profundidad. _____ (8. Estar) en los barrios más importantes de Buenos Aires: en La Recoleta, nosotros _____ (9. visitar) la tumba de Eva Perón; en San Telmo, _____ (10. ir) a la feria popular de antigüedades; en la Plaza de Mayo, _____ (11. ver) a las madres que _____ (12. honrar) (*to honor*) la memoria de sus hijos desaparecidos; en el Barrio de la Boca, _____ (13. pasear) por la calle Caminito admirando los murales y a los artistas callejeros, y mi hermano _____ (14. conocer) a una bailarina de tango bellísima (*extremely beautiful*). Después del viaje, nosotros _____ (15. sentir) nostalgia de la ciudad.

7-44 Nostalgia. ¿Siente usted nostalgia de algún lugar? Hable de los recuerdos que tiene de ese lugar especial utilizando los tiempos del pasado que estudió en el capítulo. ¿Cómo era? ¿Qué hizo en ese lugar?

Los muelles de Puerto Madero, Buenos Aires.

En palabras de...

UN INFORME POLICIAL

Imagine que fue testigo de un asalto cometido en las proximidades de su campus y ahora tiene que contar su testimonio a la policía. Piense en el incidente y trate de recordar el mayor número posible de detalles relacionados con el asalto: hora del día, apariencia física del asaltante y de la víctima, hechos concretos. Escriba después un informe (*report*) completo y objetivo del incidente.

Writing strategies: Preparing an incident report. An incident report is a factual-based description of an episode, and it should provide an accurate picture of the course of the events, the external circumstances, and the individuals involved. The first part of the report should set the scene describing when and where it was, who was there, and what they were doing. The second part should provide an orderly, linear, and objective narration of the facts recounting what happened step by step.

Antes de escribir

En preparación a su informe conteste las siguientes preguntas.

- ¿Quién sufrió el asalto? ¿Quién fue el asaltante?
- ¿Cómo, cuándo, y dónde ocurrió el asalto?

Prepare ahora su informe en dos párrafos. El primer párrafo debe situar la escena: quién, cuándo y dónde. El segundo párrafo debe narrar los hechos (*facts, actions*) de forma ordenada y objetiva.

Después de escribir

Revise y edite su informe prestando especial atención a las siguientes cuestiones:

 LISTA DE CONTROL:

___ ¿Incluyó todos los detalles del incidente?
___ ¿Utilizó el imperfecto para describir el marco (*frame*) contextual de los hechos y/o acciones en desarrollo (*in progress*)?
___ ¿Utilizó el pretérito para hablar de la secuencia de eventos?
___ ¿Contó los hechos de manera organizada y objetiva?

 **En la red**

¿Qué medidas de seguridad se pueden tomar en los campus universitarios? ¿Cómo se puede evitar (*to avoid*) ser víctima de un asalto? Prepare una lista de diez medidas de seguridad que la universidad y usted pueden aplicar para evitar incidentes en las proximidades del campus. Utilice las estructuras de *se impersonal*.

> **Modelo**   **Se necesitan alarmas en los dormitorios.**

Compare después su lista con las recomendaciones que las páginas web de distintas universidades del país ofrecen a sus estudiantes para prevenir este tipo de situaciones.

All the sources consulted for the readings are cited on the *¡Trato hecho!* Web site at **www.prenhall.com/trato**

VOCABULARIO

TEMA ①

Profesiones
un/a abogado/a *a lawyer*
un actor *an actor*
una actriz *an actress*
un/a agricultor/a *a farmer*
un/a artista *an artist, a performer*
un/a asistente social *a social worker*
un/a bombero/a *a firefighter*
un/a cantante *a singer*
un/a contador/a *an accountant*
un/a deportista *an athlete*
un/a diseñador/a de software *a software designer*
un/a enfermero/a *a nurse*
un hombre / una mujer de negocios *a businessman/woman*

un/a jugador/a de béisbol *a baseball player*
un/a maestro/a *a teacher*
un/a médico/a *a doctor, a physician*
un/a músico *a musician*
un/a obrero/a de fábrica *a factory worker*
un/a obrero/a de la construcción *a construction worker*
un/a pintor/a *a painter*
un policía / una mujer policía *a police officer*
un/a programador/a *a programmer*
un/a secretario/a *a secretary*

Verbos
dedicarse a *to do (for a living), to devote oneself to*
portarse *to behave*
soñar (ue) **con** *to dream of / about*

Otras palabras
un colegio *a high school*
de niño/a *as a child*
deportista (adj.) *athletic, fond of sports*
la niñez *childhood*
travieso/a *mischievous*
universitario/a (adj.)   *university*

TEMA ②

Acontecimientos
un acontecimiento *an event*
una boda *a wedding*
un campeonato *a championship*
un concurso *a contest*
una fiesta de cumpleaños *a birthday party*
un funeral *a funeral*
una graduación *a graduation*
una jubilación *a retirement*
una muerte *a death*
un nacimiento *a birth*
una quinceañera *a fifteenth birthday party*

Otros sustantivos
la belleza *beauty*
la edad *age*
un equipo *a team*
una licencia de manejar *a driver's license*
un/a novio/a *a groom/bride*
el patinaje *skating*
un recuerdo *a memory*

Verbos
celebrar *to celebrate*
cumplir *to turn (an age), to carry out*

ganar *to win*
graduarse *to graduate*
jubilarse *to retire*
manejar *to drive*
marcar un gol *to score a goal*
morir (ue, u) *to die*
nacer *to be born*
recordar (ue) *to remember*

Otras palabras y expresiones
al comienzo *at the beginning*
emocionado/a *excited*
orgulloso/a *proud*
preocupado/a *worried*

T E M A ❸

Sustantivos
un/a amante *a lover*
el amor *love*
un/a campesino/a *a country person, a peasant*
el cariño *affection*
la cortesía *courtesy*
un cuerpo *a body*
un deseo *a desire*
un fantasma *a ghost*
un grupo *a group*
un/a guerrero/a *a warrior*
una historia *a story*
el honor *honor*
una leyenda *a legend*
un lugar *a place*
el matrimonio *marriage, matrimony*
la paz *peace*

un soldado *a soldier*
una tumba *a tomb, grave*
el valor *bravery, courage*

Verbos
ahogar *to drown*
arrepentirse (ie, i) *to be sorry, to regret*
atacar *to attack*
echar(se) a *to start, to set off*
enterrar (ie) *to bury*
exagerar *to exaggerate*
huir *to flee*
informar *to inform, to report*
llorar *to cry*
luchar *to struggle, to fight*
matar *to kill*
obedecer *to obey*
replicar *to reply*

someterse (a) *to submit (to)*
tratarse de *to be about, to deal with*

Adjetivos
cruel *cruel*
enamorado/a *in love*
feliz *happy*
hermoso/a *beautiful*
secreto/a *secret*
valiente *brave, courageous*

Otras palabras y expresiones
alguna vez *ever*
bajo *under*
en aquella época *at that time*
en ruta a *en route to*
Érase una vez... *Once upon a time...*
me encanta(n) *I love it (them)*
pronto *soon*

T E M A ❹

En las calles
un accidente *an accident*
una acera *a sidewalk*
el aire *the air*
una autopista *a freeway*
un barrio *a neighborhood*
una carretera *a road*
un choque *a collision, a wreck*
un/a conductor/a *a driver*
la contaminación *pollution*
un espacio verde *a green area*
un estacionamiento *a parking lot*

una grúa *a tow truck*
un letrero *a sign*
un límite de velocidad *a speed limit*
una multa *a ticket*
una parada de autobús *a bus stop*
un peatón *a pedestrian*
los productos procesados *processed food*
un semáforo *a traffic light*
un taller *a mechanic's garage*
el tráfico *the traffic*

un vecindario *a neighborhood*
la vida *(the) life*

Verbos
andar a pie *to go on foot, to walk*
crecer *to grow (up)*
respirar *to breathe*

Otras palabras
demasiado/a *too much*
fresco/a *fresh*

T E M A ❺

Emergencias
una ambulancia *an ambulance*
un arresto *an arrest*
un carril *a lane*
un/a criminal *a criminal*
una denuncia *a police report, an accusation*
una dirección *a direction*
una emergencia *an emergency*
una escalera *a ladder, stairs*
un/a herido/a *an injured person*

el humo *smoke*
un incendio *a fire*
un/a paramédico/a *a paramedic*
los primeros auxilios *first aid*
un/a testigo *a witness*
una víctima *a victim*

Verbos
chocar *to have a wreck, to crash*
cruzar *to cross*
girar *to turn*

ocurrir *to occur*
resultar *to turn out*
resultar herido/a *to get injured*

Adjetivo
opuesto/a *opposite*

8

En el restaurante

In this chapter you will learn to...

- order in a restaurant
- describe meals and what you like to eat
- go to the market
- explain how to make a dish
- give advice on eating well
- discuss eating habits among Hispanics

You will use...

- indirect object pronouns
- verbs like **gustar**
- direct and indirect object pronouns together
- formal commands
- familiar commands

VOCABULARIO
¿Qué me recomienda?

TEMA ❶

Supplemental activities. **A.** ¿Qué palabra corresponde a cada definición? *Modelo:* una lista de los platos que se sirven en un restaurante > *el menú*
1. la persona que prepara la comida
2. la persona que sirve la comida en un restaurante
3. la lista de vinos
4. la suma que se debe pagar
5. el lugar donde se paga la cuenta
6. un objeto que se usa para cortar la carne
7. un plato que se usa para tomar sopa
8. el lugar donde se puede comer afuera
9. un recipiente que se usa para servir el vino
10. un recipiente que se usa para tomar vino
11. un recipiente que se usa para tomar café
B. ¿Quién habla, el cliente o el mesero?
1. ¿Están listos para pedir o necesitan más tiempo?
2. ¿Me trae un menú, por favor?
3. ¿Qué me recomienda Ud.?
4. ¿Qué desean beber?
5. ¿Cuál es el plato del día?
6. Otro vaso de agua, por favor.
7. ¿Puedo retirar este plato?
8. ¿Algo más?
9. La cuenta, por favor.

En un restaurante

la terraza

el/la dueño/a

el/la cocinero/a

el/la mesero/a

el menú

la carta de vinos

la propina

la caja

la cuenta

el carrito de postres

el comedor

una botella

un vaso

una copa

un mantel

una taza

una servilleta

un plato hondo

una cuchara

un tenedor

un plato llano

un cuchillo

¿Qué le dice el/la mesero/a al/a la cliente?

> ¿Está listo/a para pedir la comida?
> ¿Tiene preguntas **sobre** el menú?
> ¿Qué desea (**quisiera,** quiere) de **plato** principal? ¿de beber/tomar? ¿de **postre**?
> **¿Le traigo** (Necesita) algo más?
> ¿Puedo **retirar** este plato?

¿Qué le dice el/la cliente al/a la mesero/a?

> ¿Qué me recomienda…?
> ¿Con qué viene…?
> Me trae (Quisiera, Quiero, Necesito)…, por favor.
> La cuenta, por favor.

¡Ojo!

También se dice **ordenar** la comida en vez de **pedir** y **el/la camarero/a** en vez de **el/la mesero/a.**

---

sobre *over, about, on*   **quisiera** *I/you (formal)/he/she would like*   **plato** *dish, plate*   **postre** *dessert*   **¿Le traigo…** *Can I bring you…?*   **retirar** *to remove, to take away*

8-1 Una cena. Ponga los verbos en el pretérito o el imperfecto para describir la última vez que Alicia cenó en un restaurante.

> **Modelo**　*Son* las seis y media cuando Alicia *llega* al restaurante.
> **Eran las seis y media cuando Alicia llegó al restaurante.**

1. *Está* con su novio y *se quedan* dos horas en el restaurante.
2. *Hay* mucha gente en el restaurante y *tienen* que esperar mucho por una mesa.
3. El mesero *es* muy bueno y *sirve* la comida inmediatamente.
4. Cuando *trae* la comida *está* muy caliente.
5. *Tienen* mucha hambre y *comen* mucho.
6. No *pueden* comer toda la comida y *se llevan* un poco a casa.
7. El restaurante *es* muy caro y *pagan* con tarjeta de crédito.
8. *Llueve* cuando *salen* del restaurante.
9. Después de comer *tienen* ganas de descansar y *vuelven* a su casa.

Ahora cambie las oraciones anteriores para describir la última vez que usted comió en un restaurante con alguien.

> **Modelo**　**Era la una de la tarde cuando llegué al restaurante.**

G **8-2 Comparaciones.** En grupos de tres, hagan listas de las diferencias entre un restaurante de comida rápida y un restaurante elegante. ¿Qué grupo puede hacer la lista más larga?

> **Modelo**　**En un restaurante de comida rápida las servilletas son de papel, pero en un restaurante elegante son de algodón o de seda. No hay manteles en el restaurante de comida rápida…**

G **Conversaciones.** En grupos de tres, lean la siguiente conversación en la cual dos personas piden la comida en un restaurante de comida mexicana. Luego, cambien la conversación para pedir los platos de comida mexicana que ustedes prefieren. Una persona del grupo debe hacer el papel del/de la mesero/a.

— Buenas tardes. Voy a ser su mesero. ¿Qué **les** traigo de tomar?
— Me trae agua mineral, por favor.
— Y para mí, una limonada, por favor.
— ¿Ya saben lo que quieren comer o necesitan más tiempo?
— Creo que estamos listos. Yo quiero el plato de enchiladas verdes.
— ¿Con tortillas de **maíz** o de **harina**?
— De maíz, por favor.
— ¿Y para usted, señor?
— Me trae el **chile relleno,** por favor. Viene con **arroz** y **frijoles,** ¿verdad?
— Sí, correcto. ¿Les puedo ofrecer algo más?
— No, gracias, es todo.

---

les *to you* (plural)　**el maíz** *corn*　**la harina** *flour*　**chile relleno** *stuffed pepper*　**arroz** *rice*　**frijoles** *beans*

Follow-up for 8-1. *Una cena.* Have students ask a partner about the last time he/she ate out. *Modelos: ¿Qué hora era cuando llegaste al restaurante? ¿Con quién estabas? ¿Cuántas horas se quedaron en el restaurante?...*

Supplemental activity. Preguntas. ¿Siempre pone Ud. la mesa antes de comer? ¿Pone un mantel? ¿Cena Ud. en la cocina o en el comedor? Cuando Ud. come, ¿tiene el tenedor en la mano derecha o en la izquierda? ¿y el cuchillo? ¿Usa Ud. servilletas de papel, de algodón o de seda en casa? ¿Usa Ud. tenedores o cucharas de plástico a veces en casa? ¿Cuál es su restaurante preferido? ¿Sirven comida mexicana? Cuando come en un restaurante de comida mexicana, ¿qué pide generalmente de plato principal? ¿y de beber? ¿Come Ud. postre con frecuencia? ¿Le gusta la salsa picante? ¿Qué día come fuera con más frecuencia? ¿Come Ud. mucho en restaurantes de comida rápida? ¿Con quién sale a comer generalmente? ¿A qué hora le gusta cenar? Generalmente, ¿paga la cuenta con tarjeta de crédito? ¿Dónde desayunó hoy? ¿Dónde almorzó hoy/ayer?

AUDIO ¡A escuchar!

Escuchen otra conversación en la cual dos personas piden algo de comer en un restaurante. ¿Están en un restaurante de comida mexicana, italiana o china? ¿Qué piden de comer y de beber?

¡Ojo!

En España, la tortilla se hace con huevos, patatas y cebolla (*eggs, potatoes, and onion*).

¿Dónde cenó? ¿Cuándo fue la última vez que preparó la cena para otra persona? ¿Sabe cocinar bien? ¿Qué platos de países hispanos sabe hacer? ¿enchiladas? ¿guacamole? ¿mole? ¿paella? ¿un pastel de tres leches? ¿flan? ¿Le gustaría comer comida mexicana hoy o tiene ganas de comer otra cosa? ¿Tiene hambre ahora? ¿Tiene sed?

GRAMÁTICA

Hablar de intercambios: los pronombres de complemento indirecto, el verbo *dar*

When giving or telling something to someone, the thing being given or told is the direct object and the person to whom it is being given or told is the *indirect object*.

Do you recommend *this dish* **to us**?
     d.o.   i.o.
Can you tell **me** *the ingredients*?
     i.o.   d.o.

Indirect object pronouns in Spanish are the same as direct object pronouns, except **le** is used instead of **lo** or **la**, and **les** is used instead of **los** or **las.**

INDIRECT OBJECT PRONOUNS	
me (*to, for*) *me*	nos (*to, for*) *us*
te (*to, for*) *you* (fam. sing.)	os (*to, for*) *you* (fam. pl.)
le (*to, for*) *you* (form. sing.), *him, her*	les (*to, for*) *you* (pl.), *them*

Indirect object pronouns follow the same placement rules as direct object or reflexive pronouns.

Single conjugated verb	¿**Les** sirven la comida?
Conjugated verb + *infinitive*	¿**Les** van a servir la comida? ¿Van a servir**les** la comida?
With **estar + -ndo**	¿**Les** están sirviendo la comida? ¿Están sirviéndo**les** la comida?

Indirect objects are often used with the irregular verb **dar** (*to give*) and the other verbs listed in the margin that indicate exchange or communication.

	PRESENT	PRETERITE	IMPERFECT
yo	**doy**	**di**	**daba**
tú	**das**	**diste**	**dabas**
usted, él, ella	**da**	**dio**	**daba**
nosotros/as	**damos**	**dimos**	**dábamos**
vosotros/as	**dais**	**disteis**	**dabais**
ustedes, ellos, ellas	**dan**	**dieron**	**daban**

Indirect objects are also used to request favors or to say for whom they are done.

¿**Me** trae un café, por favor?   *Would you bring me a cup of coffee, please?*
Siempre **le** preparo la cena.   *I always prepare him dinner.*

Indirect object nouns are most often accompanied by the corresponding pronoun (clarifier) in the same sentence. This may seem repetitive, but it is normal in Spanish. The clarifier and the noun refer to the same person(s).

Le mandé flores **a mi novia.**   *I sent flowers to my girlfriend.*
Nunca **les** presto dinero **a mis amigos.**   *I never lend money to my friends.*

For clarification or emphasis, you may add the preposition **a** followed by a prepositional pronoun: **a (mí, ti, él, ella, usted, nosotros/as, vosotros/as, ustedes, ellos/as).**

Le digo todo **a ella** pero no **le** digo nada **a él.**

I tell her everything, but I don't tell him anything.

¿**Me** estás hablando **a mí**?

Are you talking to me?

8-3 En el restaurante. En un restaurante, ¿les hace el mesero las siguientes cosas a los clientes o viceversa?

> **Modelo** explicar el menú
> **El mesero les explica el menú a los clientes.**
> pedir la comida
> **Los clientes le piden la comida al mesero.**

1. traer el menú	**6.** servir la comida
2. hacer preguntas sobre el menú	**7.** pedir la cuenta
3. describir los platos	**8.** traer la cuenta
4. preguntar qué quieren beber	**9.** dar dinero
5. decir qué quieren	**10.** dar una propina

8-4 Interacciones. Complete las oraciones con el pronombre lógico: **me, nos, le** o **les.** Luego, cambie las oraciones para describir su propia situación.

> **Modelo** Cada año _____**le**_____ mando flores a mi madre por el Día de la Madre.
> **No le mando flores cada año, pero le mandé flores una vez.**

1. Generalmente, mis padres _____ dan dinero por mi cumpleaños.
2. Con frecuencia _____ pido mucho dinero a mis padres.
3. A veces _____ presto mi carro a mis amigos.
4. Cada semana mi novio/a (esposo/a) _____ escribe un poema.
5. Nunca _____ sirvo bebidas alcohólicas a mis amigos.
6. _____ podemos hacer preguntas en inglés al/a la profesor/a de español.
7. Nuestro/a profesor/a de español prefiere hablar_____ en español.

P 8-5 ¿A quién? Pregúntele a otro/a estudiante a quién le hace las siguientes cosas.

> **Modelo** deber dinero
> E1: **¿A quién le debes dinero?**
> E2: **Les debo dinero a mis padres. / No le debo dinero a nadie.**

1. mandar flores
2. pedir favores
3. prestar dinero
4. contar chistes
5. hablar en español
6. dar consejos (*advice*)

Ahora pregúntele a su compañero/a quién le hace las cosas anteriores a él/ella.

> **Modelo** deber dinero
> E1: **¿Quién te debe dinero?**
> E2: **Nadie me debe dinero.**

Suggestion for 8-3. *En el restaurante.* Point out to students again that it is normal to have both the indirect object pronoun and the noun in the same sentence.

Follow-up for 8-3. *En el restaurante.* En la recepción de un hotel, ¿le pide, le da, le pregunta o le dice Ud. las siguientes cosas al recepcionista? (Write the possible verbs on the board: *le pido, le doy, le pregunto, le digo*). *Modelo:* su tarjeta de crédito > *Le doy mi tarjeta de crédito.* (el número de su habitación, la llave, su pasaporte, a qué hora sirven el desayuno, cuánto tiempo va a estar en el hotel, el nombre y apellido de Ud., la dirección del hotel, si Ud. tiene un mensaje, un plano (map) de la ciudad, si hay un buen restaurante cerca del hotel, cómo llegar al restaurante) Ahora diga si el recepcionista le pide, le da, le pregunta o le dice las siguientes cosas a Ud.. *Modelo:* si tiene reserva > *Me pregunta si tengo reserva.* (su pasaporte, su nombre y apellido, el precio de la habitación, el número de la habitación, la llave)

Suggestion for 8-5. *¿A quién?* Point out the use of the personal *a* before *quién* and remind students to use it before *nadie* when it is an indirect object.

Follow-up for 8-5. *¿A quién?* Review the use of prepositional pronouns for emphasis with indirect objects and ask questions such as the following. *¿Cuál de las siguientes oraciones describe mejor su relación con su mejor amigo/a?* 1. Yo le presto más dinero a mi mejor amigo/a. — Él/Ella me presta más dinero a mí. 2. Yo le pido más favores a él/ella. — Él/Ella me pide más favores a mí. 3. Yo le hablo más de mis problemas a él/ella. — Él/Ella me habla más de sus problemas a mí. 4. Yo le doy más regalos a él/ella. — Él/Ella me da más regalos a mí.

VOCABULARIO
TEMA ② ¿Qué desea usted?

Supplemental activities. A. Remind students of the ending -*ería* in store names as on p. 148 and ask students: *¿Qué se vende en una pescadería (panadería, pastelería, carnicería, frutería, heladería, lechería, cafetería, tortillería, taquería)?* **B.** ¿Qué se usa para tomar café: un vaso, una copa o una taza? ¿para tomar una cola (agua, vino, té helado, té caliente, un refresco, leche)? ¿Qué bebidas se sirven en una botella? ¿Qué se usa para comer ensalada: una cuchara, un tenedor o un cuchillo? ¿y para comer cereales (pollo, helado, una chuleta de cerdo, flan, espárragos, una papa al horno, huevos, jamón, arroz)? ¿Qué se come con las manos? (las papas fritas, el flan, las enchiladas, los tacos, el pastel, el pan tostado, un bocadillo, la fruta, el pollo asado, el pollo frito, la sopa) ¿Se usa un plato hondo o un plato llano para tomar sopa? ¿Se usa una cuchara, un tenedor o un cuchillo? **C.** ¿Se usa sal o azúcar con las papas fritas (los huevos, el flan, la carne asada, los cereales, la sopa, el jamón, el helado, el té, el arroz, el pescado, el pastel, el café, el bistec, las verduras)? **D.** ¿Se sirve(n) frío/a(s), caliente(s) o a temperatura ambiente (*room temperature*)? *(la sopa, el vino blanco, el vino tinto, el bistec, el helado, el pastel, una papa al horno, las papas fritas, los huevos, las chuletas de cerdo, el jugo de naranja, la leche, el café, los refrescos, el té)*

El desayuno

el pan tostado   **los huevos**   **los cereales**   **el café, el jugo de naranja, la leche**   **la fruta**

El almuerzo

un bocadillo (de queso, de jamón)   **un refresco**   **el té helado/ caliente**   **la sal y la pimienta**

el azúcar   **las papas fritas**   **la ensalada de lechuga y tomate**

La cena

la sopa   **el pescado**   **los camarones**   **la papa al horno**   **el arroz**

la carne

el bistec   **el pollo**   **el jamón**   **la chuleta de cerdo**

las verduras   el postre

las zanahorias   **los espárragos**   **el flan**   **el pastel**   **el helado**

¿Prefiere Ud. la carne **asada, a la parrilla** o **al horno**? ¿Prefiere el bistec **poco cocido, término medio** o **bien cocido**?

8-6 Recomendaciones. Unos amigos quieren mejorar su salud (*improve their health*). ¿Cuál de las siguientes comidas les recomienda?

Modelo   la ensalada / las papas fritas
Les recomiendo la ensalada.

1. el café / el té verde
2. el pollo / la carne asada
3. el bistec / el pescado
4. el pollo asado / el pollo frito
5. el helado / la ensalada de fruta
6. el cóctel de camarones / la ensalada
7. el té con azúcar / el té sin azúcar
8. las verduras con sal / las verduras sin sal

8-7 Preferencias. Pregúntele a otro/a estudiante cuál de las comidas del ejercicio anterior prefiere. Luego, describe las preferencias de su pareja a la clase.

Modelo   E1: **¿Te gusta más la ensalada o te gustan más las papas fritas?**
E2: **Me gustan las papas fritas más que la ensalada. /**
Me gusta la ensalada tanto como las papas fritas.

Luego a la clase: **A Mónica le gustan las papas fritas más que la ensalada.**

8-8 Entrevista. Entreviste a otro/a estudiante con las siguientes preguntas.

1. ¿Qué preparas cuando tus amigos vienen a tu casa a cenar? ¿Qué les sirves de beber? Cuando tus amigos vienen a tu casa a comer, ¿te traen flores, chocolates o algo de tomar a veces? ¿Te ayudan a limpiar después de comer? Cuando unos amigos o familiares pasan la noche contigo, ¿les preparas un gran desayuno con huevos y pan tostado, les sirves cereales, les compras tacos en una taquería o van a un restaurante?
2. ¿Le das una propina al mesero si el servicio no es bueno? ¿Cuál fue el último restaurante que recuerdas donde el servicio era malo? ¿Por qué? ¿Tuviste que esperar mucho? ¿Te trajeron la comida fría? ¿No te gustó la comida?

Conversaciones. En parejas, lean la siguiente conversación en la cual dos compañeras de cuarto hablan de una cena que van a preparar. Luego, cambien la conversación para describir una cena que van a preparar para los padres, un/a novio/a o un/a amigo/a de uno/a de ustedes.

— ¿Tus padres vienen a cenar mañana? **Me encanta cocinar.** ¿Qué les vamos a servir? ¿Les puedo hacer carne asada?
— A mi padre le encanta la carne asada, pero a mi madre no le gusta tanto. Pienso hacerles pescado. Contiene menos **grasa** y además están a dieta.
— ¿Qué más les vas a servir?
— Voy a hacer arroz y les voy a preparar espárragos **al vapor.**
— **Me da hambre** hablar de eso. Me encantan los espárragos. ¿Tus padres están a dieta? ¿Qué les vas a servir de postre?
— Voy a hacer una ensalada de fruta.

¡Ojo!
También se dice **bien/poco hecho/a** en vez de **bien/poco cocido/a.**

Supplemental activities. A. ¿Qué comidas o bebidas asocia Ud. con estos nombres? *You may substitute brand names common in your region.* (Starbucks, Ben & Jerry's, Church's, Morton, Borden's, Subway, Sara Lee, Van Camp o Gorton, Souper Salad, McDonalds, Minute Maid) B. Normalmente, ¿se comen papas fritas o una papa preparada al horno con las hamburguesas? ¿Se comen espárragos o frijoles y arroz con las enchiladas? ¿Se comen los cereales con leche o con vino tinto? ¿Se toma vino tinto o vino blanco con el pescado? ¿y con el bistec? ¿Se comen muchos sándwiches de jamón con queso o de chuleta de cerdo con queso? ¿Se hace la ensalada o la sopa con lechuga y tomate? ¿Se hace pizza con queso y carne o con fruta y carne? ¿Se come el flan o el pastel con helado a veces? ¿Se prepara el pan o la carne a la parrilla? ¿Se prepara el pan o la ensalada al horno? ¿Se preparan las papas o los espárragos al horno? C. Generalmente, ¿asocia Ud. estas comidas o bebidas con el desayuno, el almuerzo o la cena? (el pan tostado, el bistec, el arroz, las chuletas de cerdo, las papas fritas,

AUDIO ¡A escuchar!
Escuchen otra conversación en la cual dos personas hablan de lo que van a preparar para la cena esta noche. ¿Qué deciden comer? ¿Cómo van a preparar la cena?

la ensalada, los huevos, el pastel, el helado, los cereales, el jugo de naranja, la leche, el vino, el té helado, el té caliente, el café) D. Point out that the verbs *desayunar, almorzar,* and *cenar* can be used to say what you have for those meals. *Modelo: Casi nunca desayuno huevos.* (I almost never have eggs for breakfast.) Then have students say how often they have the items pictured on the preceding page for each meal.

asado/a *roasted* a la parrilla *grilled, on the grill* al horno *baked, in the oven* poco cocido/a *rare* término medio *medium* bien cocido/a *well-done* me encanta *I love* cocinar *to cook* la grasa *fat* al vapor *steamed* darle hambre a alguien *to make someone hungry*

GRAMÁTICA
Expresar gustos e intereses: verbos como *gustar*

Para averiguar

1. What does **me gusta** literally mean?
2. When do you use the plural form **gustan**?
3. How do you say *we like, you (plural) like,* and *they like*?
4. What are seven other verbs that are used like **gustar**?

Supplemental activities. A. ¿Cuál de estas oraciones es más lógica para describir una relación feliz entre un hombre y su novia? *Modelo:* Le molesta con frecuencia a su novia. / Le gusta a su novia. > *Le gusta a su novia.* 1. A su novia le encanta darle un beso. / A su novia le da asco darle un beso. 2. Le compra flores con frecuencia a su novia. / Nunca le compra flores. 3. Nunca le dice a su novia que la quiere. / Le dice que la quiere todos los días. 4. Le pide dinero a su novia todo el tiempo. / Nunca le pide dinero. 5. Le prepara la cena a veces. / Nunca le prepara la cena. 6. Nunca le dice a su novia que es bonita. / Le dice con frecuencia que es bonita. 7. No le habla mucho a su novia. / Le cuenta todos su secretos a su novia. 8. Le importa mucho a su novia. / No le importa mucho a su novia. **B.** ¿Le gusta, le encanta, le gusta (bastante, un poco), no le interesa o le molesta hacer las siguientes cosas? (Write the options on the board.) *(salir a bailar los fines de semana, leer novelas de ciencia ficción, ver películas musicales, hablar de política, ir a partidos de fútbol americano, ver béisbol en la tele, ir de compras, escuchar música rap, cocinar, estudiar español)*

In your previous Spanish studies, you used the expression **me gusta(n)** to say what you *like* and later **me gustaría(n)** to say what you *would like*. The **me** of **me gusta(n)/me gustaría(n)** is an indirect object pronoun. Use the other indirect object pronouns with **gustar** like **me: me/te/le/nos/os/les gusta(n)**.

A phrase like **Nos gustan las verduras** literally means *Vegetables are pleasing to us.* **Gustar** agrees with the subject **las verduras** and not with **nos.** Note that the subject of **gustar** generally follows the verb and the definite article is used as well.

Les gusta la comida mexicana.	*They like Mexican food.* *(Mexican food is pleasing to them.)*
Les gustan las enchiladas.	*They like enchiladas.* *(Enchiladas are pleasing to them.)*

When followed by an infinitive or a series of infinitives, **gustar** is generally in the third-person singular form.

Les gusta comer fuera.	*They like to eat out.*
Les gusta comer, beber y bailar.	*They like to eat, drink, and dance.*

When you name a person who likes something (to whom something is pleasing), the name or noun is preceded by **a,** since it is an indirect object. Remember that an indirect object pronoun will be included in a statement along with the indirect object noun, even though it may seem redundant.

A mis padres no **les** gusta cocinar.	*My parents don't like to cook.*
A Juan le gusta mucho.	*Juan likes it a lot.* *(Cooking isn't pleasing to my parents.* *To Juan, it's very pleasing.)*

You may add the preposition **a** followed by a prepositional pronoun for emphasis or clarity.

A mí no **me** gusta el chocolate.	*I don't like chocolate.*
A él le gusta pero **a ella** no **le** gusta nada.	*He likes it, but she doesn't like it at all.*

The following verbs and expressions are used like **gustar.**

encantar	*to love*	Me encanta ese restaurante.
interesar	*to interest*	¿Te interesa la política?
faltar	*to be missing / to be needed*	Le falta sal a la sopa.
molestar	*to bother*	¿Te molesta si fumo?
importar	*to be important*	No nos importan tus problemas.
doler (ue)	*to hurt, to ache*	Me duele el estómago *(stomach).*
dar asco	*to be revolting, to not be able to stand*	Me dan asco los espárragos.

℗ 8-9 ¿Le gusta? Pregúntele a otro/a estudiante si le gustan las siguientes cosas.

Modelo   E1: **Marco, ¿te gusta el pollo?**
E2: **Sí, me gusta. / ¡Me encanta el pollo! / No, no me gusta mucho. / Me da asco el pollo.**

Follow-up for 8-9. *¿Le gusta?*
1. ¿Qué carne le gusta más? ¿Qué carnes no le gustan o le gustan menos? ¿Le gusta la pizza con carne o sin carne? 2. ¿Qué bebida le gusta más con las comidas? ¿Qué bebidas le gustan pero no con las comidas? ¿Qué bebidas no le gustan? ¿Le gusta más el té helado o el té caliente? ¿Le gusta el té con azúcar o sin azúcar? ¿Con limón o sin limón? ¿Cómo le gusta el café, con azúcar, con crema o solo? 3. ¿Le gusta más la comida italiana, mexicana, francesa, china, vietnamita o india? ¿Qué comida étnica no le gusta? 4. ¿Qué comidas o bebidas le encantan? ¿Qué comidas o bebidas le dan asco?

1.   **2.**   **3.**

4.   **5.**   **6.**

7.   **8.**   **9.**

Ahora descríbale los gustos de su compañero/a a la clase.

Modelo   **A Marco le gusta(n)… Le encanta(n)… No le gusta(n)… Le da(n) asco…**

8-10 ¿A quién? ¿A quién(es) de su familia le(s) gustan las siguientes cosas?

Modelo   el bistec poco cocido
A mi padre le gusta (A mi padre y a mí nos gusta / A mí me gusta / A todos nos gusta / A nadie le gusta) el bistec poco cocido.

Follow-up for 8-10. *¿A quién?* ¿A quién de su familia le interesan las siguientes cosas? 1. los deportes 2. la política 3. la física 4. las computadoras 5. los concursos de patinaje 6. viajar 7. probar platos nuevos 8. las telenovelas (*soap operas*) 9. la música 10. la ópera

1. cocinar
2. ir a McDonalds
3. los jalapeños
4. comer mucha ensalada
5. preparar la carne a la parrilla
6. la comida vegetariana
7. los postres
8. lavar los platos

℗ 8-11 Entrevista. Entreviste a otro/a estudiante con estas preguntas.

1. ¿Te interesa la cocina? ¿Te gusta cocinar? ¿Te molesta comer los mismos platos todos los días o no te importa?
2. ¿Dónde te gustaría cenar esta noche? ¿Te importan más los precios de un restaurante o el servicio? ¿Te gusta estar en la sección de fumadores de un restaurante o te molesta? ¿Te gusta el bistec bien cocido, término medio o poco cocido?
3. ¿Te gusta probar la comida de otros países? ¿Te duele el estómago (*stomach*) si comes jalapeños? ¿y si comes mucha salsa picante?
4. De niño/a, ¿a qué hora les gustaba cenar en tu familia? ¿Qué no te gustaba comer de niño/a que ahora sí te gusta? ¿Qué te encantaba comer de niño/a? ¿Te molestaba comer sobras (*leftovers*)?

TEMA 3

¡Ojo!

Hay muchas diferencias regionales en los nombres de las frutas y verduras.

las papas = las patatas
los plátanos = las bananas, los bananos, los guineos
las fresas = las frutillas
los chícharos = las arvejas, los guisantes
los ejotes = las judías verdes, las habichuelas
el maíz = el choclo, el elote

Note. You may wish to tell students that in Mexico, *un limón* is a lime and *un limón amarillo* is a lemon.

Supplemental activities. A. ¿Es una fruta, una verdura, una carne, una bebida, un postre o un recipiente? (You may wish to write the categories on the board.) *Modelo:* los espárragos > *Los espárragos son una verdura. (los plátanos, el jamón, la leche, el agua mineral, las uvas, las tazas, las espinacas, la lechuga, la limonada, los limones, el jamón, las fresas, el pastel, el brócoli, el jugo de naranja, las naranjas, el jugo de manzana, el helado, los platos, los vasos, el pollo, los melones, el vino tinto, las botellas, las copas, las cebollas, el flan)* As a follow-up, put students in pairs or groups of three and have them close their books and list as many items from *Tema 1* and this *Tema* as they can remember for each category. The group with the most complete lists wins. **B.** Play a chain game. *Vamos a preparar una gran cena para una fiesta. ¿Qué vamos a servir?* Each student adds a new food item after renaming from memory all of the items already named. **C.** ¿De qué color es/son...? *(las naranjas, las fresas, las piñas, los mangos, las manzanas, las uvas, la leche, el café, el vino tinto, las zanahorias, las cebollas, las papas, las espinacas, los plátanos, el brócoli, los limones)*

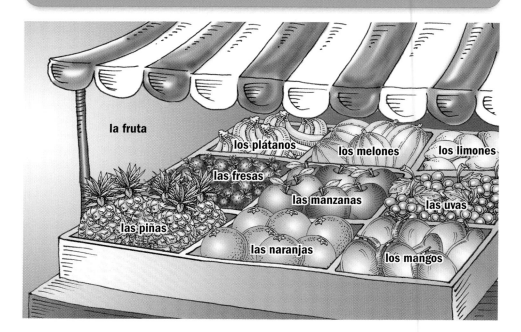

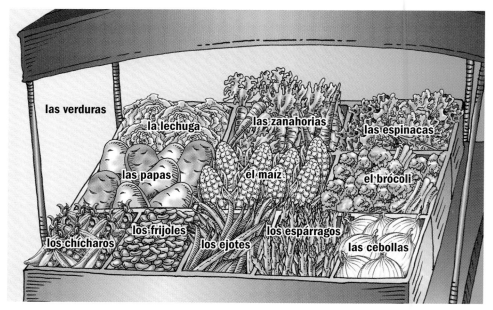

8-12 Grupos lógicos. ¿Cuál de las palabras no pertenece al grupo? Explique por qué.

Modelo las espinacas, las zanahorias, la lechuga, el brócoli
Las zanahorias porque las otras palabras son nombres de verduras verdes.

1. las fresas, las papas, las uvas, los plátanos
2. el pastel, el helado, las cebollas, el flan
3. la leche, los refrescos, el té, la sal
4. el pan, el bistec, el pollo, el jamón
5. los huevos, el melón, la piña, las naranjas
6. el maíz, las zanahorias, las espinacas, los mangos

G **8-13** **¿Qué falta?** Estos puestos de mercado son casi idénticos. ¿Cuántas diferencias pueden encontrar?

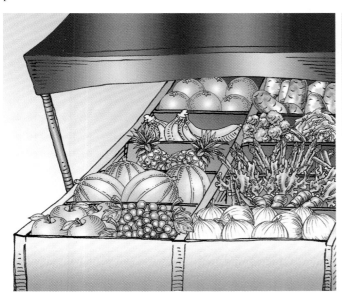 

P **8-14** **Entrevista.** Entreviste a otro/a estudiante con las siguientes preguntas.

1. ¿Qué verduras te gustan más? ¿Qué verduras no te gustan o te dan asco? ¿Te gusta más la sopa de verduras, de cebolla o de brócoli con queso?
2. ¿Qué frutas te gustan más? ¿Cuáles no te gustan o te dan asco? ¿Te gustan más las manzanas verdes o las rojas? ¿y las uvas? ¿Te gusta la pizza con piña?
3. ¿Te gusta más la ensalada de lechuga y tomate, de espinacas o de fruta? ¿Te gusta el brócoli en la ensalada? ¿y la cebolla? ¿Qué frutas no te gustan en la ensalada de fruta?
4. ¿Qué postre te gusta más: el pastel, el helado, el flan o la ensalada de fruta? ¿Te gusta más el pastel con helado o sin helado? ¿Te gusta más el helado de chocolate, de vainilla o de fresa?

P **Conversaciones.** En parejas, lean la siguiente conversación en la cual una mujer compra frutas y verduras en el mercado. Luego, cambien la conversación para comprar la verdura y la fruta que prefieren.

— Buenos días, señorita. ¿En qué le puedo servir?
— ¿Me da medio kilo de espárragos, por favor?
— Bueno, medio kilo de espárragos… ¿Le puedo ofrecer algo más?
— ¿Están buenos los melones hoy?
— Sí, están muy **dulces.**
— ¿Me da uno, por favor?
— ¿Es todo?
— Sí, ¿cuánto le debo, señor?
— Cuarenta y dos pesos con cincuenta centavos.

Supplemental activities. A. Have students secretly list the fruits from the preceding page in order of preference, with their favorite at the top. Then in pairs, have them determine the order of each other's list by asking either/or questions. *Modelo: — ¿Te gustan más las manzanas o las naranjas? — Me gustan más las naranjas.* Afterward, do the same with the vegetables. **B.** Para hacer una ensalada de fruta, ¿se usa(n) fresas (manzanas, maíz, espinacas, melón, uvas, frijoles, plátanos, zanahorias, lechuga, naranjas)?

AUDIO ¡A escuchar!

Escuchen otra conversación en la cual alguien compra comida en una tienda. ¿Está en una pescadería, una frutería o una carnicería? ¿Cuánto compra de cada cosa? ¿Cuánto paga?

¡Ojo!

Se usa el sistema métrico en los países hispanos.

1 kilo = 2.2 libras (*pounds*)
1 litro = 1.057 cuarto de galón

---

dulce *sweet*

GRAMÁTICA

Evitar la redundancia: la combinación de los pronombres de complemento directo e indirecto

The indirect object pronoun always precedes the direct object pronoun when they are used together. A written accent must be added to the stressed vowel of an infinitive or the **-ndo** form of the verb when two pronouns are attached to the end of the verb.

— ¿**Me** puedes dar **la receta para esa salsa**?
— Por supuesto que **te la** puedo dar. / Por supuesto que puedo dár**tela.**

— ¿Quién **nos** recomendó **este restaurante**?
— El recepcionista del hotel **nos lo** recomendó.

When both the direct and indirect object pronouns begin with the letter **l**, the indirect object pronoun changes to **se**.

— ¿**Les** vas a llevar **la cuenta a esos clientes**?
— Sí, **se la** voy a llevar ahorita.

— ¿**Le** diste **su dinero a ese señor**?
— Sí, **se lo** di.

Since **se** can have a variety of meanings when it replaces **le** (*to you, to him, to her*) or **les** (*to you, to them*), you may add the preposition **a** followed by a prepositional pronoun to clarify to whom you are referring.

Se lo di **a Ud. (a él, a ella, a Uds., a ellos/as).**   *I gave it to you (to him, to her, to you, to them).*

8-15 Favores. Hágale las siguientes preguntas a un/a compañero/a de clase. Luego, él/ella debe contestar con un pronombre de complemento directo.

Modelo E1: ¿Les prestas dinero a tus amigos?
E2: **Sí, a veces se lo presto. / No, nunca se lo presto.**

1. ¿Les prestas tu carro (ropa, tu apartamento/casa, dinero, libros, discos compactos, tu teléfono celular) a tus amigos?
2. ¿Le cuentas tus secretos (tus problemas, tus planes, chistes, mentiras [*lies*]) a tu mejor amigo/a con frecuencia?
3. ¿Tus padres te dan dinero para los estudios (consejos [*advice*], ropa, problemas, comida, libros, recetas [*recipes*]) con frecuencia?
4. ¿El/La profesor/a ya nos dio el teléfono de su oficina (sus horas de oficina, el programa de estudios [*syllabus*], la fecha del próximo examen, los resultados del último examen, la tarea para la próxima clase)?

G **8-16** **Recomendaciones.** Pídale recomendaciones a un/a compañero/a de clase. Luego, otro/a estudiante debe reaccionar a su recomendación.

> **Modelo** un restaurante de comida italiana
> E1: **Eric, ¿nos puedes recomendar un buen restaurante de comida italiana?**
> E2: **Les recomiendo Giovanni's.**
> E3: **Yo también se lo recomiendo. / Yo no se lo recomiendo. / No lo conozco.**

1. un café
2. una película
3. una heladería
4. una pastelería
5. un lugar para pasar las vacaciones
6. un restaurante de comida mexicana

P **8-17** **En el restaurante.** Dos amigos y un mesero hablan en un restaurante. En parejas, completen las oraciones con los pronombres lógicos.

1. — ¿Necesitan ver el menú?
   — Sí, _____ _____ trae, por favor.
2. — ¿Qué nos recomienda? ¿Qué tal está la paella hoy?
   — Está muy buena. _____ _____ recomiendo.
3. — Ud. desea el pastel, ¿verdad? ¿_____ _____ sirvo con o sin helado?
   — _____ _____ sirve sin helado, por favor, pero con una taza de café.
4. — ¿Están listos para la cuenta?
   — Sí, ¿ _____ _____ trae, por favor?
5. — Le diste tu tarjeta de crédito al mesero, ¿verdad?
   — Sí, _____ _____ di.
6. — ¿No le vas a dejar una propina al mesero?
   — Ya _____ _____ dejé.

P **8-18** **Relaciones.** Usando los verbos y las palabras de los cuadros, prepare cinco preguntas para su pareja sobre su relación con su mejor amigo/a, su novio/a o su esposo/a. Conteste las preguntas de su pareja con pronombres de complemento directo.

dar	prestar	contar	decir	preguntar	traer
pedir	explicar	comprar	preparar	servir	regalar

sentimientos	opinión	dinero	mentiras (lies)	galletas	la cena		flores
sueños		favores	problemas	ropa		vino	el desayuno	???

> **Modelo** E1: ¿Le regalas ropa a tu mejor amigo/a por su cumpleaños?
> E2: **Se la regalo a veces.**

Supplemental activities. A. ¿Les recomienda un médico las siguientes cosas a sus pacientes que quieren bajar de peso (*lose weight*)? *Modelo:* la ensalada > *Sí, se la recomienda.* (*las verduras, el helado, el pollo, la pizza, el flan, las espinacas, el té, el azúcar, la leche, los espárragos, el pastel, el chocolate, la cerveza, el vino, la fruta, el bistec, el brócoli*)
B. Ask students if they can serve the foods and drinks listed in section *A* to a diabetic. *Modelo:* la ensalada > *Sí, se la puedo servir. / Sí, puedo servírsela.*

Suggestion for 8-17. *En el restaurante.* Have students say who is talking, *el mesero y un cliente* or *los dos clientes.*

Follow-ups for 8-17. *En el restaurante.* **A.** Have students work in groups to prepare a conversation in a restaurant integrating some of the phrases from this activity and filling in the missing parts. Two students are customers, and one is a server.
B. Conteste las siguientes preguntas con pronombres de complemento directo. La última vez que Ud. comió en un restaurante con otra persona... 1. ¿El mesero les trajo el menú? 2. ¿Les dijo su nombre? 3. ¿Les sirvió vino? ¿café? ¿agua? ¿pan? 4. ¿Les pidió identificación? 5. ¿Les describió los platos del día? 6. ¿Les recomendó los platos preferidos de él? 7. ¿Les sirvió la comida inmediatamente? 8. ¿Les trajo la comida fría? 9. ¿Les ofreció postre? 10. ¿Les retiró los platos sucios inmediatamente? 11. ¿Les dio las sobras (*leftovers*)? 12. ¿Le dio la cuenta a Ud. o a la otra persona?

Suggestion for 8-18. *Relaciones.* Point out to students that the ??? in the box means that they can add other nouns of their choice.

VOCABULARIO

TEMA ④

Una receta

¿Qué ingredientes se necesitan?

tres cucharadas de mantequilla

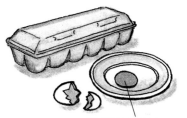

una yema de huevo

harina

media taza de leche

media taza de crema

media taza de queso
suizo rallado

la cuarta parte de una taza
de queso parmesano rallado

una cacerola

un recipiente
pequeño

Salsa Mornay

• Comience a prepararla 20 minutos antes de servirla.

• Contiene 164 calorías por 1/3 tz.

• Es una buena fuente de calcio y vitamina A.

Para preparar 2 1/3 tz:

3 cdas de mantequilla o margarina

2 cucharadas de harina

1 tz de caldo de pollo

1 tz de mitad leche y mitad crema

1 yema de huevo

1/2 tz de queso suizo rallado

1/4 tz de queso parmesano rallado

1 En una olla, a fuego mediano, derrita la mantequilla y agregue, revolviendo, la harina. Mezcle hasta que se unan bien.

2 Viértale, poco a poco, y revolviendo, la leche y el caldo de pollo. Mezcle hasta que se espese.

3 En un recipiente pequeño, y usando la escobilla de cocina o un batidor de alambre de mano, bata ligeramente la yema de huevo y agregue, revolviendo, un poquito de la mezcla anterior.

4 Únala lentamente a la mezcla caliente, revolviendo vigorosamente para evitar que se le formen grumos.

5 Agregue el queso y cocine a fuego de mediano a lento, revolviendo. Cocine hasta que se caliente bien, pero no lo deje hervir. Sirva caliente con vegetales cocinados, pescado, pollo asado o huevos poché.

8-19 Salsa Mornay. ¿Cuál de las definiciones de la lista va con los verbos de las instrucciones de la receta para hacer la salsa Mornay?

Suggestion for 8-19. *Salsa Mornay.* Encourage students to guess using context, even if they are not sure.

> beat   cook   add   blend   melt   mix   pour in   serve   start

1. *Comience* a prepararla 20 minutos antes de servirla.
2. *Derrita* la mantequilla y *agregue* la harina.
3. *Mezcle* hasta que se unan bien.
4. *Viértale* la leche y el caldo (*broth*) de pollo.
5. *Bata* la yema de huevo con la escobilla (*whisk*).
6. *Una* la yema de huevo a la mezcla (*mixture*) caliente.
7. *Cocine* hasta que se caliente bien.
8. *Sirva* caliente con vegetales cocidos, pescado o pollo asado.

¡Ojo!

También se usa **vegetales** en vez de **verduras** para decir *vegetables*.

8-20 ¿Cuánto? Conteste las preguntas con una cantidad lógica.

> una cucharada   una taza   media taza   dos tazas   un litro   medio kilo
> una botella   un kilo   dos kilos   un vaso   una copa   ???

1. ¿Cuánta leche necesita Ud. si come cereales por la mañana?
2. ¿Cuánto café necesita Ud. para despertarse por la mañana?
3. ¿Cuánto azúcar le pone a una taza de café?
4. ¿Cuántos refrescos toma Ud. a la semana? ¿cuánto vino? ¿cuánta leche?
5. ¿Cuánta carne necesita si prepara bistec a la parrilla para sus hermanos y sus padres?
6. ¿Cuánta mantequilla le pone al pan tostado? ¿Cuánto aderezo (*salad dressing*) le pone a una ensalada de lechuga y tomate?

(P)

Conversaciones. En parejas, lean la siguiente conversación en la cual una joven le explica a la madre de su compañera de cuarto cómo hacer la salsa Mornay. Luego, cambien la conversación para explicarle a la madre de un/a compañero/a cómo hacer un plato que usted sabe preparar.

— Esta salsa con el pescado está deliciosa. ¿Cómo se prepara?
— No es muy difícil. Primero, derrita tres cucharadas de mantequilla y luego agregue dos cucharadas de harina.
— Son dos cucharadas de harina con tres cucharadas de mantequilla **derretida,** ¿verdad?
— Sí, correcto. Luego, vierta una taza, mitad leche y mitad crema, y una taza de **caldo** de pollo y mézclelo todo por unos tres o cuatro minutos **hasta que se espese.** Luego, bata una yema de huevo y agréguela a la mezcla.
— A ver, se necesitan una taza, mitad leche y mitad crema, una taza de caldo de pollo y una yema de huevo **batida,** ¿verdad?
— Sí, **así es.** Finalmente, se agrega media taza de queso suizo rallado y la cuarta parte de una taza de queso parmesano rallado y se calienta un poco y **ya** está lista.

AUDIO ¡A escuchar!

Escuchen otra conversación en la cual alguien explica cómo preparar un plato al baño María (*in a double boiler*). ¿De qué plato hablan? ¿Qué ingredientes se usan y en qué orden?

---

derretido/a *melted*   **el caldo** *broth*   **hasta que se espese** *until it thickens*   **batido/a** *beaten*   **así es** *that's right*
ya *already*

GRAMÁTICA

Dar instrucciones y recomendaciones: los mandatos formales

To tell someone to do or not to do something, use the imperative (command form) of the verb. Form **Ud.** and **Uds.** commands by changing the present tense endings from **a** to **e** and **e** to **a**. Using the pronouns **Ud.** or **Uds.** after the verb is optional.

Present Indicative		Command	
Ud. habla	*you speak*	¡Hable (Ud.)!	*Speak!*
Uds. hablan	*you (plural) speak*	¡Hablen (Uds.)!	*Speak!*
Ud. duerme	*you sleep*	¡Duerma (Ud.)!	*Sleep!*
Uds. duermen	*you (plural) sleep*	¡Duerman (Uds.)!	*Sleep!*

Verbs ending with **-car, -gar,** and **-zar** have these spelling changes.

buscar (c > qu): bus**qu**e/bus**qu**en
pagar (g > gu): pa**gu**e/pa**gu**en
empezar (z > c): empie**c**e/empie**c**en

For any verb that has an irregular **yo** form in the present tense, use the **yo** form without the **o** ending to form the command. The command form endings are **-a/-an** for all of these verbs.

	Yo Form	Ud./Uds. Commands
tener (*to have*)	tengo	tenga/tengan
venir (*to come*)	vengo	venga/vengan
decir (*to say, to tell*)	digo	diga/digan
hacer (*to make, to do*)	hago	haga/hagan
poner (*to put, to place*)	pongo	ponga/pongan
traer (*to bring*)	traigo	traiga/traigan
salir (*to go out, to leave*)	salgo	salga/salgan
conocer (*to know*)	conozco	conozca/conozcan
ver (*to see*)	veo	vea/vean

The following verbs have irregular command forms.

ser (*to be*)	sea/sean	ir (*to go*)	vaya/vayan
estar (*to be*)	esté/estén	saber (*to know*)	sepa/sepan
dar (*to give*)	dé/den		

Reflexive, direct object, and indirect object pronouns are attached to the end of affirmative commands, but they are placed *before* negative commands. When attached to the end of verbs of more than one syllable, an accent mark is written on the stressed syllable.

Affirmative		Negative	
¡Levántense!	*Get up!*	¡No se levanten!	*Don't get up!*
¡Háganlo!	*Do it!*	¡No lo hagan!	*Don't do it!*
¡Dígamelo todo!	*Tell me everything!*	¡No me diga nada!	*Don't tell me anything!*

8-21 **¿Se lo doy?** Usted quiere que su hijo de cinco años coma bien. Dígale al mesero que le dé o que no le dé las siguientes comidas y bebidas.

Modelo   E1: ¿Le doy agua mineral?   E1: ¿Le doy vino?
E2: **Sí, desela.**   E2: **No, no se lo dé.**

¿Le doy…?

1. cola
2. jugo de fruta
3. ensalada
4. café
5. verduras
6. pastel
7. galletas
8. frijoles
9. zanahorias
10. helado
11. pollo
12. cerveza

8-22 **Consejos.** Usted le da consejos a un paciente que tiene mucho estrés y sufre de depresión. Dígale que haga o que no haga las siguientes cosas usando mandatos formales.

Modelo   tomar mucha cafeína
No tome Ud. mucha cafeína.

1. pensar en cosas negativas
2. ser optimista
3. fumar
4. practicar un deporte
5. hacer ejercicio
6. ir al trabajo
7. almorzar todos los días
8. tener una dieta equilibrada
9. comer comida rápida todos los días
10. salir con los amigos
11. quedarse en casa todo el tiempo
12. relajarse
13. enojarse
14. acostarse más temprano
15. dormir lo suficiente
16. ver la televisión toda la noche

G **8-23** **Meseros.** Ud. les explica a un grupo de meseros sin experiencia cómo hacer su trabajo. En grupos, preparen una lista de instrucciones usando mandatos.

Modelo   **Recomienden el vino blanco con el pescado.**
Pídanles identificación a los jóvenes si piden bebidas alcohólicas.

servir	dar	pedir	recomendar	retirar	ofrecer	preguntar
limpiar	ser	poner	llevar	contestar	venir	decir

G **8-24** **¿Diablo o ángel?** En grupos de cuatro, preparen mandatos para un grupo de jóvenes. Dos hacen el papel de ángel de la guardia y sugieren cosas buenas. Los otros dos hacen el papel de diablo y les dicen que hagan cosas malas.

Modelo   El ángel: **Hagan toda la tarea antes de salir con los amigos.**
El diablo: **Salgan con los amigos ahora y hagan la tarea después.**

Follow-ups for 8-21. *¿Se lo doy?*
A. Ud. se muda (*are moving*). Conteste con un mandato las preguntas de unos amigos que le ayudan. *Modelo:* ¿Dónde ponemos el sofá? > *Pónganlo en la sala.* ¿Dónde ponemos los platos (la cama, la ropa, el microondas, la nevera, el televisor, la computadora, la mesa, las cacerolas)? **B.** Name food items and have students tell you whether to eat them or not if you want to lose weight.

Follow-up for 8-22. *Consejos.* Put students in pairs and have them think of three or four more pieces of advice.

Supplemental activities. **A.** ¿Qué dice el/la profesor/a? Conteste las preguntas con mandatos y pronombres de complemento directo. *Modelos:* —¿Debemos hacer los ejercicios del cuaderno en casa? —*Sí, háganlos en casa.* / —¿Podemos abrir nuestros libros durante los exámenes? —*No, no los abran durante los exámenes.* 1. ¿Debemos escuchar los ejercicios del CD? 2. ¿Podemos hacer preguntas en inglés? 3. ¿Tenemos que contestar sus preguntas en español? 4. ¿Necesitamos leer las explicaciones del libro? 5. ¿Podemos comer sándwiches en clase? 6. ¿Debemos pronunciar la palabra "sándwich" como en inglés? 7. ¿Necesitamos traer nuestros libros a clase? 8. ¿Tenemos que aprender los mandatos para la próxima clase? 9. ¿Necesitamos aprender el vocabulario de este capítulo para el examen final? 10. ¿Necesitamos poner nuestra tarea en su mesa? **B.** Have students work in groups to list commands you frequently give them in class. **C.** Have students work in pairs to make a list of commands of things they want you to do. **D.** Give students the following verbs and have them give the class directions to their favorite restaurant in your area. The class listens to the directions and guesses the name of the restaurant. (*doblar/dar una vuelta, seguir recto, tomar, subir, bajar, cruzar*)

VOCABULARIO

TEMA 5

Una dieta

Follow-up for *16 formas de combatir el estrés y la fatiga.* Have students find the answers to the following questions in *16 formas de combatir el estrés y la fatiga.* 1. Según los estudios, ¿qué personas tienen menos síntomas de estrés? 2. ¿Cuándo es especialmente importante tomar agua? 3. ¿Qué le da el chocolate? 4. ¿Qué se pierde rápidamente cuando una persona está aburrida? 5. ¿Para qué es necesaria una alimentación equilibrada? 6. ¿Cuántas horas necesita dormir cada noche? ¿Cuántas horas duerme Ud.? 7. ¿Qué hace la cafeína? 8. ¿Qué hace la nicotina cuando una persona fuma? 9. ¿Qué le da el alcohol? 10. ¿Cuál es el resultado de dar y recibir afecto? 11. ¿Cuáles son algunas emociones negativas que afectan a su organismo? 12. ¿Cuál es el resultado de ser perfeccionista?

Si quieren **llevar una vida sana:**

Sigan una dieta sana y equilibrada.
Coman más verduras y fruta. Contienen muchas vitaminas.
Coman menos dulces, grasa y carbohidratos y más proteína.
Dejen de fumar.
Eviten el alcohol y la cafeína.

Aquí tienen algunas recomendaciones de la revista **Buena Salud** sobre cómo controlar el estrés.

16 formas de combatir el estrés y la fatiga

1. Sea optimista.
Los estudios han demostrado que los optimistas poseen menos síntomas mentales y físicos de estrés.

2. Beba agua.
Este líquido es esencial para la energía, especialmente durante el verano.

3. Coma un chocolate.
Puede comer uno a la hora del té y le permitirá recargar energías para terminar el día.

4. Elimine el aburrimiento.
Nada quita energías más rápido que el estar aburrido. Es importante encontrar formas de dar interés a las cosas de todos los días.

5. Practique yoga.
Esta disciplina le permitirá alcanzar la relajación y serenidad necesarias para combatir el estrés.

6. Piense como Peter Pan.
Usted se sentirá con energías siempre que esté en contacto con el impulsivo, curioso y libre personaje que era usted de niño.

7. Tenga una alimentación equilibrada.
La nutrición equilibrada es esencial para la buena salud y la resistencia al estrés.

8. Duerma ocho horas por noche.
La falta de sueño crónica crea un estado de agotamiento que disminuye la calidad de vida.

9. Limite su consumo de cafeína.
Un exceso de esta sustancia daña su salud e incrementa su susceptibilidad al estrés.

10. No fume.
Aunque la mayoría de los fumadores piensan que los cigarrillos los relajan, la nicotina, por lo contrario, es una sustancia que produce una respuesta artificial de estrés en el cuerpo.

11. Evite el alcohol.
Mucha gente bebe para dejar atrás un día difícil. Pero en realidad, el alcohol crea un desequilibrio químico en el cuerpo.

12. Sea afectivo.
Los investigadores han demostrado que las personas que regularmente dan y reciben afecto viven más tiempo.

13. Dedique tiempo a sus amigos.
Las invitaciones recíprocas, las llamadas telefónicas y los encuentros regulares con los amigos son eficaces en la lucha contra el estrés.

14. Elimine las emociones negativas.
La angustia, la ansiedad y la depresión son las emociones predominantes del estrés. Éstas afectan a su organismo y disminuyen su resistencia al estrés.

15. Organice su tiempo efectivamente.
Hacer demasiado en poco tiempo es un camino seguro hacia el estrés.

16. Sea menos perfeccionista.
Esto le permitirá tener más tiempo para hacer sus cosas.

---

llevar una vida sana *to lead a healthy life*   **seguir (i, i)** *to follow*   **dejar de** + infinitive *to stop …ing*   **evitar** *to avoid*   **Buena Salud** *Good Health*

8-25 **¿Y usted?** Diga si usted ya sigue las recomendaciones de *16 formas de combatir el estrés y la fatiga*, si necesita seguirlas o si no está de acuerdo (*do not agree*) con alguna recomendación.

> **Modelo**
> Sea optimista.
> **Necesito ser más optimista.**
> Beba agua.
> **Ya bebo ocho vasos de agua todos los días.**

Follow-up for 8-25. ¿Y usted? En grupos, preparen una lista de otros consejos sobre cómo mantenerse en buena salud. ¿Qué grupo puede hacer la lista más larga? *Modelo: No pase mucho tiempo en el sofá viendo la televisión.*

G **8-26** **¿Qué contienen?** En grupos de tres, hagan listas de las comidas o bebidas que contienen las sustancias de esta lista.

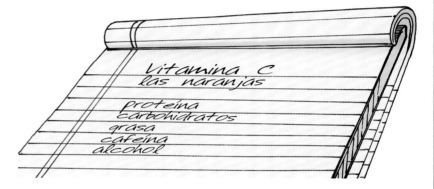

vitamina C
las naranjas

proteína
carbohidratos
grasa
cafeína
alcohol

Ahora pregúntele a uno/a de sus compañeros si come o bebe estas cosas con frecuencia.

> **Modelo**
> E1: **¿Comes naranjas con frecuencia?**
> E2: **Las como a veces, pero no muy a menudo (*often*).**

P **Conversaciones.** En parejas, lean la siguiente conversación en la cual un joven le pide **consejos** de salud a su amigo. Luego, cambien la conversación para pedirle consejos a su pareja sobre cómo mejorar (*improve*) sus hábitos de vida.

— Siempre me siento cansado. ¿Qué haces para **mantenerte en forma** y con tanta energía?

— Sigo la misma rutina todos los días. Me acuesto y me levanto a la misma hora y nunca **como** muy **fuerte**. Como comidas ligeras varias veces al día. ¿Duermes lo suficiente?

— Nunca duermo bien. Me despierto varias veces durante la noche y a veces no me vuelvo a dormir.

— ¿Cenas muy fuerte?

— Sí, no tengo tiempo para comer durante el día. Tomo un café o un refresco para tener un poco de energía en clase y en el trabajo.

— Si no tienes tiempo para comer mucho, come una fruta o una verdura cada tres o cuatro horas en vez de tomar cafeína. Vas a sentirte menos cansado y vas a dormir mejor.

AUDIO ¡A escuchar!

Escuchen otra conversación en la cual alguien le pide consejos a su médico durante su examen físico. ¿Cuál es su problema? ¿Qué alimentos (*foods*) le recomienda el médico y cuáles debe evitar?

Suggestion. Point out that the verbs *mantener(se)* and *contener*, like *obtener*, have *tener* as a root, which corresponds to the ending *-tain* in English. Have students guess the meaning of the following verbs: *detener, retener, sostener, abstenerse*.

---

consejos *advice*   **mantenerse en forma** *to stay in shape*   **comer fuerte** *to eat a lot*

GRAMÁTICA
Más instrucciones y recomendaciones: los mandatos familiares

Unlike the **Ud.** and **Uds.** commands, the form of commands for **tú** depends on whether you are telling someone to do something (an affirmative command) or not to do something (a negative command). Affirmative **tú** command forms of most verbs look like the **él/ella** form of the present indicative. In the negative, they are the same as **Ud.** commands with an **-s** added to the end.

	TÚ AFFIRMATIVE	TÚ NEGATIVE	USTED ALL COMMANDS	USTEDES ALL COMMANDS
hablar	habla	no hables	(no) hable	(no) hablen
jugar	juega	no juegues	(no) juegue	(no) jueguen
comer	come	no comas	(no) coma	(no) coman
volver	vuelve	no vuelvas	(no) vuelva	(no) vuelvan
abrir	abre	no abras	(no) abra	(no) abran
pedir	pide	no pidas	(no) pida	(no) pidan
traer	trae	no traigas	(no) traiga	(no) traigan
oír	oye	no oigas	(no) oiga	(no) oigan

The affirmative command forms for **tú** of the following verbs are irregular. Remember that the stems of the **usted, ustedes,** and negative **tú** commands of these verbs are obtained by dropping the final **-o** of the present indicative **yo** form. As with other verbs, the negative **tú** command is like the **usted** command with a final **-s.**

	TÚ AFFIRMATIVE	TÚ NEGATIVE	USTED ALL COMMANDS	USTEDES ALL COMMANDS
decir	di	no digas	(no) diga	(no) digan
hacer	haz	no hagas	(no) haga	(no) hagan
poner	pon	no pongas	(no) ponga	(no) pongan
salir	sal	no salgas	(no) salga	(no) salgan
tener	ten	no tengas	(no) tenga	(no) tengan
venir	ven	no vengas	(no) venga	(no) vengan

The following verbs are also irregular.

	TÚ AFFIRMATIVE	TÚ NEGATIVE	USTED ALL COMMANDS	USTEDES ALL COMMANDS
dar	da	no des	(no) dé	(no) den
estar	está	no estés	(no) esté	(no) estén
ir	ve	no vayas	(no) vaya	(no) vayan
ser	sé	no seas	(no) sea	(no) sean

Remember that object and reflexive pronouns are attached to the end of verbs in affirmative commands, but go before verbs in negative commands.

Hazlo. / No lo hagas.　　　　　*Do it. / Don't do it.*
Dime… / No me digas…　　　　*Tell me… / Don't tell me…*
Siéntate. / No te sientes.　　　*Sit down. / Don't sit down.*

8-27 Madre e hijo. Un hijo de seis años ayuda a su madre en la cocina. ¿Cuál de los siguientes mandatos le da la madre?

> **Modelo** (Juega / No juegues) con el cuchillo.
> **No juegues con el cuchillo.**

1. (Lávate / No te laves) las manos antes de empezar.
2. (Escúchame / No me escuches) bien.
3. (Sigue / No sigas) las instrucciones.
4. (Come / No comas) más azúcar.
5. (Cierra / No cierres) la puerta de la nevera.
6. (Lava / No laves) los platos después de usarlos.
7. (Pon / No pongas) la cuchara de plástico en la estufa.
8. (Juega / No juegues) cerca de la estufa.
9. (Toma / No tomes) el vino.
10. (Deja / No dejes) la basura (*trash*) en el piso.
11. (Saca / No saques) la basura.

Follow-ups for 8-27. *Madre e hijo.* **A.** ¿Les dicen los padres a los hijos que hagan o que no hagan estas cosas? Conteste con mandatos familiares. *Modelo:* comer con la boca (*mouth*) abierta. > *No comas con la boca abierta.* (comer con las manos, jugar con la comida, comer las verduras, sentarse recto, poner los pies en los muebles, hablar con gente desconocida (*unfamiliar*), irse con gente desconocida, llorar, portarse bien, acostarse tarde, lavarse los dientes, ponerse ropa limpia) Afterward, have students work with partners to think of more commands they used to hear as children. **B.** Have students work in groups to prepare a conversation where a mother explains to a child how to set the table. **C.** Redo 8-22 *Consejos* on p. 245 with students giving suggestions to a friend with *tú* commands.

8-28 Una madre sin paciencia. Lea la tira cómica y luego represente el papel (*role*) de la madre, diciéndoles a las siguientes personas que hagan o que no hagan las cosas indicadas entre paréntesis.

1. a su hija (escucharme, invitar a tus amigos, calmarte, ser educada, venir a saludar a Fefita)
2. a los amiguitos de su hija (venir a jugar aquí, traer sus juguetes, hacer ruido [*noise*], volver a su casa, regresar mañana)
3. a su amiga Fefita (pasar a la sala, sentarte, hacer como en tu casa, quedarte un rato, volver pronto)

8-29 Sugerencias. En grupos, hagan listas de dos o tres sugerencias para estas personas usando mandatos.

1. Los padres de su compañero/a de cuarto vienen a cenar y él/ella no sabe qué les va a servir.
2. Una amiga quiere sentirse mejor.
3. Su compañero/a de cuarto es muy perezoso/a y su apartamento está sucio.
4. Su hermana va a casarse mañana.
5. Un compañero de clase sufre de mucho estrés.
6. Un amigo quiere ir de vacaciones pero no sabe a donde ir.

¡Trato hecho!

En portada

Note: Have students complete the *Antes de leer, Reading strategies,* and *Ahora Ud.* activities before reading this article.

REVISTA CULTURAL

PRESERVAR EL SABOR LATINO

¡Salud!

¡Qué frescos!

La comida es una parte esencial y un modo de celebrar la cultura latina. Los hispanos **disfrutan** comiendo y compartiendo la hora de la comida y **la sobremesa** con sus familiares y amigos. La sobremesa es una costumbre muy latina; es el epílogo de una buena comida. Es el momento del café y la conversación y puede **durar** horas.

En Estados Unidos la población hispánica conserva en general sus hábitos **alimenticios,** aunque en algunos casos el proceso de asimilación cultural afecta a su dieta o a otros hábitos relacionados con las comidas. Los

¡A comer!

productos de su país nativo no están siempre disponibles en los supermercados norteamericanos y los platos pierden su sabor original. También el ritmo de vida en Estados Unidos es realmente **agitado** y el concepto de comida rápida, no muy extendido en los países hispanos, funciona mucho en la sociedad norteamericana.

La tradición juega **un papel** muy importante en la dieta de los latinos. Los hábitos del consumidor hispano en Estados Unidos **reflejan** esa inclinación por cocinar platos tradicionales en **el hogar.** Según un estudio reciente del *Food Market Institute,* un 85% de los hispanos entrevistados tratan de preservar el sabor latino en las comidas preparadas en casa. Su gusto por las comidas **caseras** se

ve reflejado en la tendencia a comprar productos frescos, especialmente carnes, verduras, frutas y productos **lácteos.**

El consumidor hispano gasta un promedio de 117 dólares a la semana en **comestibles,** superior a los 87 dólares que gasta el consumidor norteamericano no latino. Los supermercados son los lugares más frecuentados para la compra de sus comestibles, seguidos de tiendas especializadas como panaderías o carnicerías del barrio. El hispano valora mucho la presencia de productos **autóctonos** latinos en los supermercados, **de ahí** el gran **éxito** de compañías alimenticias como Goya.

Sin embargo, el proceso de asimilación del hispano en Estados Unidos presenta consecuencias negativas en sus hábitos de alimentación. Muchas madres trabajan fuera de la casa, y eso resulta en un mayor consumo de comida rápida y alimentos precocinados, y en un aumento de los índices de obesidad infantil: un 30.4% de los niños hispanos en Estados Unidos sufren de **sobrepeso,** frente al 25% de la población infantil de origen caucásico no latino. ¿Cómo encontrar un balance entre la tradición del buen comer y el estrés de la vida moderna?

Productos muy nuestros.

disfrutan *they enjoy*   **la sobremesa** *aftermeal conversation*   **durar** *to last*   **alimenticios** *eating*   **agitado** *busy*   **un papel** *a role*   **reflejan** *reflect*   **el hogar** *home*   **caseras** *homemade*   **lácteos** *dairy*   **comestibles** *groceries*   **autóctonos** *native, from the homeland*   **de ahí** *with the result*   **éxito** *success*   **sobrepeso** *excess weight*

Antes de leer

Reflexione un momento sobre los hábitos alimenticios de su familia. En casa de sus padres, ¿qué tipo de hábitos predominaban? ¿Son diferentes de sus hábitos alimenticios ahora que está en la universidad? ¿Qué productos consume con más frecuencia? ¿Le gusta la comida rápida? ¿Qué tipo de comida rápida prefiere?

Reading strategies: Reading the first sentence of the paragraph. A paragraph is a semantic unit on its own; it contains a thesis or main idea with supporting arguments or adjacent ideas. Each paragraph contributes to the general meaning of the text with its particular ideas. Paragraphs usually consist of a first sentence that defines the essence of the paragraph, and additional sentences that expand or support the main idea of the paragraph. Students can obtain a general overview of the text's main ideas by reading the first line of each paragraph. This opening sentence will help them to identify the main topics of the reading efficiently, and it will serve as an indication of how the ideas progress and develop throughout the text.

P **8-30 Ahora Ud.** Lean la primera oración de cada párrafo del artículo *Preservar el sabor latino* y preparen una lista de los temas (*topics*) principales que menciona la lectura. Después inventen un subtítulo para cada párrafo según la idea general que desarrolla (*develops*).

Después de leer

8-31 Les gusta… Indique si las siguientes afirmaciones son ciertas o falsas según el contenido de la lectura. Corrija las afirmaciones falsas.

	Cierto	Falso
1. En el mundo hispano la hora de la comida es una ocasión especial para disfrutar de la familia.	X	
2. A las familias hispanas en Estados Unidos no les importa preservar las tradiciones de su cocina autóctona.		X
3. Al consumidor hispano no le hace falta comprar alimentos frescos porque no prepara generalmente platos caseros.		X
4. Las familias hispanas compran sus comestibles generalmente en supermercados, panaderías y carnicerías.	X	
5. El consumidor hispano gasta menos en comestibles que la media nacional de consumidores no latinos.		X
6. Como resultado de la asimilación cultural, los hábitos alimenticios de la población hispana estadounidense están cambiando, especialmente en los niños.	X	

G **8-32 Asimilación cultural.** Discutan en grupos cómo se puede definir el concepto de asimilación cultural. La lectura menciona un resultado del proceso de asimilación cultural del hispano en Estados Unidos. ¿Qué otros resultados pueden mencionar?

8-33 Consejos. Dé seis consejos a los padres hispanos para evitar o combatir el sobrepeso en sus hijos. Utilice los mandatos formales que estudió en este capítulo.

Modelo   Haga ejercicio con sus hijos.

Suggestion. Bring student's attention to the concept of *sobremesa* and its cultural implications in the Hispanic world. Ask the class to think about or look for further information about Hispanic eating habits.

Answers for 8-31. *Les gusta…*
2. A las familias hispanas en Estados Unidos les importa preservar las tradiciones de la cocina de sus países de origen. 3. El consumidor hispano compra fundamentalmente productos frescos: carnes, verduras, frutas y productos lácteos, porque le gusta preparar comida casera.
5. El consumidor hispano gasta un promedio de 117 dólares a la semana en comestibles, superior a los 87 dólares que gasta el consumidor norteamericano no latino.

De puertas abiertas a la comunidad

📹 CON SAZÓN

⒢ 8-34 Entrando en materia. ¿Les gusta la cocina latina? ¿Qué platos conocen? ¿Creen que los platos varían dependiendo de los países hispánicos? ¿Qué ingredientes creen que son los más comunes? Preparen una lista con al menos (*at least*) seis platos típicos de la gastronomía hispana.

Answers for 8-35. *Una visita al restaurante El Quijote.* 1. la paella, la mariscada, la langosta, la paella valenciana o marinera, la sangría 2. La mariscada consiste en mariscos como las almejas, los mejillones, los camarones y las vieiras en diferentes salsas: salsa de ajo, salsa verde o salsa de tomate. 3. la paella 4. marisco, pollo y chorizo, almejas, mejillones, vieiras (*scallops*) y camarones 5. el vino español Rioja, blanco o tinto 6. el flan español, pastel de chocolate, de queso, queso con fresa, de piñón

La cocina latina ocupa un lugar importante en el panorama gastronómico estadounidense. La variedad de **sabores atrae** tanto al público hispano como al cliente de otras etnias que se deja seducir por **el tono sazonado** de los platos hispánicos. Pero los hábitos alimenticios de la población hispana en Estados Unidos están cambiando, especialmente entre los niños. Escuchen el testimonio de Jorge Yagual, un experto en nutrición hispano, que nos habla de este nuevo problema de la obesidad infantil y de otras tendencias en la alimentación de los hispanos que residen en Estados Unidos.

Vamos a visitar también el famoso restaurante El Quijote, en Chelsea, Nueva York, especializado en cocina española. Allí van a conocer a José Manuel Fernández, un **camarero** español, y a Adolfo Reinoso, de origen dominicano, que va a compartir con ustedes uno de los exquisitos platos del restaurante.

8-35 Una visita al restaurante El Quijote. Escuche con atención la información que José y Adolfo nos dan sobre las especialidades del restaurante El Quijote; luego conteste las siguientes preguntas.

1. ¿Cuáles son las especialidades del restaurante El Quijote?
2. ¿En qué consiste la mariscada?
3. ¿Cuál es el plato más popular del restaurante El Quijote?
4. ¿Qué ingredientes tiene?
5. ¿Qué vinos se sirven con más frecuencia en el restaurante?
6. ¿Cuáles son algunos de los postres más ricos?

sabores *flavors*   **atrae** *attracts*   **el tono sazonado** *the spicy nature*   **camarero = mesero**

8-36 ¿Cierto o falso? Seleccione el final o los finales adecuados para las siguientes afirmaciones que Jorge nos ofrece sobre los hábitos alimenticios de la población hispana.

1. Los hábitos de la población hispana son...
   a. malos.
   b. en general buenos.
   c. para los hispanos nacidos (*born*) en Estados Unidos, iguales a los de la población norteamericana.
2. Los hábitos de la población hispana están cambiando...
   a. por la influencia de la dieta norteamericana.
   b. en las personas que inmigraron en los últimos diez años.
   c. muy poco en general.
3. Entre la población más joven, Jorge atiende muchos casos de...
   a. malnutrición.
   b. obesidad.
   c. anorexia.
4. Entre la población adulta, el problema más común que Jorge trata es...
   a. la diabetes.
   b. la depresión.
   c. el estrés.

8-37   Guardar la línea... Escuche con atención lo que nos dice Jorge sobre su dieta, y compare la dieta de Jorge con su dieta utilizando verbos como **gustar.** ¿Hay muchas similitudes? ¿Hay diferencias?

LA DIETA DE JORGE	MI DIETA
muy balanceada	
muy colorida	
consume bastantes vegetales	
consume bastantes frutas	
consume arroz	

8-38   Recomendaciones para tener buena salud. ¿Qué recomendaciones les hace Jorge a los hispanos de Estados Unidos para tener buena salud? Preste atención a los mandatos formales en las respuestas.

Consejos para una buena salud

Jorge les dice a la población hispana de Estados Unidos....

que _____ ;

que _____ ;

que _____ ;

que _____ .

Answers for 8-38. *Recomendaciones para tener buena salud.* 1. mantengan una dieta balanceada, que consista principalmente de bastantes granos, vegetales y frutas 2. mantengan una actividad física 3. tres a cuatro veces a la semana caminen por lo menos treinta minutos 4. anden en bicicleta o salgan a caminar

Escapadas

PUERTO RICO, ISLA DEL ENCANTO

Puerto Rico, isla situada en el Mar Caribe a 1000 millas de Miami, es la más pequeña de las Antillas Mayores, que incluyen Cuba, Haití, la República Dominicana y Jamaica.

La isla estaba habitada originariamente por los indios taínos, gente de paz, que recibieron cordialmente a los españoles **al mando de** Cristóbal Colón en 1493, y que fueron colonizados en 1508 por Juan Ponce de León. **La riqueza** cultural de la isla deriva de su mezcla racial: junto con los indios taínos y los colonizadores españoles convivieron **esclavos** africanos, traídos por los españoles para trabajar en los campos, y también trabajadores franceses, irlandeses y escoceses, que favorecieron los matrimonios interraciales y la formación del rico grupo étnico de los criollos.

Estatua a Colón en el Viejo San Juan, Puerto Rico.

Productos de la tierra.

La influencia de estos distintos grupos se siente en la gastronomía puertorriqueña, conocida como la cocina criolla. La yuca, los pimientos y el maíz son productos autóctonos de la isla, protagonistas de muchos platos típicos: como los pasteles de plátano, **los surullitos de maíz** o **la gandinga**. De origen taíno también son las barbacoas. Los españoles introdujeron en la dieta **boricua** el aceite de oliva, **el ajo** y el cilantro. Los esclavos africanos dejaron su **huella** en la gastronomía del país con la introducción de su estilo de cocinar: **las frituras,** y productos como los plátanos, el coco y **el bacalao.** Otros platos típicos de la cocina criolla son el **asopao** de bacalao, el arroz con **gandules, el mofongo** y los **besitos de coco.**

La gastronomía boricua es sólo uno de los encantos de la isla. San Juan, la capital, es un tesoro arquitectónico y natural. El Viejo San Juan, con medio **siglo** de historia, ofrece al visitante casas coloniales del siglo XVI y XVII y plazas históricas, como la Plaza de Armas, centro social de la ciudad, con estatuas representativas de las cuatro estaciones; la Plaza de San José, con el famoso monumento a Ponce de León; y la Plaza del Quinto Centenario, en

La Plaza de Armas en el Viejo San Juan, Puerto Rico.

conmemoración de los quinientos años del **descubrimiento** de la isla por Colón.

---

al mando de *under the command of*   **la riqueza** *the richness*   **esclavos** *slaves*   **los surullitos de maíz** *corn fritters*   **la gandinga** *pork liver*   **boricua** *Puerto Rican*   **el ajo** *garlic*   **huella** *influence*   **las frituras** *fried food*   **el bacalao** *cod*   **asopao** *soup*   **gandules** *green pigeon peas*   **el mofongo** *fried plantains with pork and garlic*   **besitos de coco** *coconut kisses*   **siglo** *century*   **el descubrimiento** *the discovery*

Los monumentos militares son otro de los atractivos de la isla. La Fortaleza o Palacio de Santa Catalina, uno de los primeros **fuertes** de la isla, se terminó de construir en 1540, y **pasó a ser** después la residencia oficial del gobernador.

El Morro, fuerte de defensa de seis pisos **levantado** en 1589, es considerado hoy un símbolo nacional y ofrece magníficas vistas de **la bahía** de San Juan. **El Castillo** de San Cristóbal, terminado en 1771, de 150 pies de altura y 27 acres de **superficie,** constituye el mayor fuerte de defensa construido en las Américas.

La Plaza de San José en el Viejo San Juan, Puerto Rico.

Puerto Rico mantiene hoy relaciones **estrechas** con Estados Unidos. En 1952 **se convirtió** en **estado libre asociado** y los puertorriqueños son también **ciudadanos** norteamericanos: no necesitan visa para vivir o trabajar en Estados Unidos, pero no pagan **impuestos** federales ni pueden votar en las elecciones presidenciales. La mayoría de los boricuas son bilingües, **aunque** el español es la lengua oficial del país. Se estima que más de dos millones de puertorriqueños viven hoy en Estados Unidos, concentrados especialmente en el noreste del país.

La Fortaleza en el Viejo San Juan, Puerto Rico.

Fuerte de San Felipe del Morro, Puerto Rico.

fuertes *forts* **pasó a ser** *became* **levantado** *erected* **la bahía** *bay* **el castillo** *the castle* **superficie** *area* **estrechas** *close* **se convirtió** *it became* **estado libre asociado** *commonwealth* **ciudadanos** *citizens* **impuestos** *taxes* **aunque** *although*

P **8-39 ¿Qué saben de Puerto Rico?** Conteste las siguientes preguntas relacionadas con el contenido de la lectura.

1. ¿Quiénes eran los habitantes originarios de Puerto Rico? ¿Cómo se formó el grupo étnico criollo?
2. ¿Cuáles son algunos de los ingredientes de la cocina criolla? ¿De dónde proceden?
3. ¿Cuál es el barrio histórico por excelencia de San Juan? ¿Qué se puede visitar allí?
4. ¿Cómo se refleja en la arquitectura boricua la posición estratégica de la isla de Puerto Rico en el Caribe?
5. ¿En qué año adopta Puerto Rico el estatus de estado libre asociado? ¿Qué repercusiones tiene para los ciudadanos puertorriqueños este estatus?

8-40 Intercambios. Complete los siguientes datos sobre Puerto Rico con el verbo **dar** en el pretérito y el pronombre de complemento indirecto apropiado en cada caso. Después identifique también el complemento directo y escriba oraciones sustituyendo los dos pronombres.

Modelo   El gobierno de Estados Unidos ____les____ ____dio____ (dar) a los puertorriqueños el estatus de ciudadanos norteamericanos.
Complemento directo: el estatus de ciudadanos americanos (lo). El gobierno de Estados Unidos *se lo* dio (a los puertorriqueños).

1. Ponce de León ____le____ ____dio____ (dar) a la isla el nombre de Puerto Rico.
2. Los esclavos africanos ____le____ ____dieron____ (dar) a la gastronomía boricua un estilo personal: la fritura.
3. Las casas coloniales del Viejo San Juan ____le____ ____dieron____ (dar) a la ciudad un estilo muy español.
4. Los fuertes ____les____ ____dieron____ (dar) a los habitantes de Puerto Rico mayor seguridad en su territorio.
5. La condición de estado libre asociado no ____le____ ____dio____ (dar) al ciudadano boricua la oportunidad de votar en las elecciones presidenciales de Estados Unidos.

8-41 La cocina criolla. Busque la receta de uno de los platos criollos mencionados en la lectura y preséntela en la próxima clase. Utilice las estructuras adecuadas para describir los pasos de preparación de un plato que aprendió en este capítulo.

Callecita de San Juan, Puerto Rico.

En palabras de...

CRÍTICO GASTRONÓMICO

Imagine que tiene que escribir una reseña (*review*) de un restaurante latino de su ciudad para el periódico local. Piense en los restaurantes hispánicos que hay en el área y seleccione el más atractivo para usted. Debe mencionar en su reseña el origen de la cocina que allí se sirve, las especialidades del restaurante, su ambiente (*atmosphere*) y los precios.

Writing strategies: Writing a review. A review is a brief critical examination of a place, a product, or an event that offers the reader a relevant description of the topic from the personal perspective of the reviewer. Writing a review implies analyzing the topic selected, summarizing the significant details related to it, and persuading the reader of the excellence or the limitations of the place, product, or event reviewed.

Antes de escribir

En preparación a su reseña responda a las siguientes preguntas.

- ¿Cómo se llama el restaurante? ¿Cuál es el país de origen de su cocina?
- ¿Cuáles son los platos más típicos?
- ¿Cómo es el ambiente?
- ¿Tiene buenos precios?
- ¿Por qué recomienda este restaurante?

Prepare ahora su reseña en dos párrafos: el primer párrafo debe incluir una descripción objetiva del restaurante; el segundo párrafo debe presentar sus preferencias personales y por qué les recomienda el restaurante a los lectores.

Después de escribir

Revise y edite su informe asegurándose que incluyó las siguientes estructuras:

- ✓ vocabulario relacionado con la comida
- ✓ verbos que siguen el patrón de **gustar**
- ✓ estructuras para expresar recomendaciones

En la red

Busque información en Internet sobre un restaurante de comida latina famoso en una determinada región de Estados Unidos y compare la reseña de este restaurante con la que escribió usted. ¿Incluye información similar? ¿Qué elementos nuevos puede incorporar a su reseña?

All the sources consulted for the readings are cited on the *¡Trato hecho!* Web site at **www.prenhall.com/trato**

VOCABULARIO

TEMA ❶

En el restaurante
el arroz *rice*
una botella *a bottle*
un carrito de postres *a dessert cart*
una carta de vinos *a wine list*
un chile relleno *a stuffed pepper*
un/a cocinero/a *a cook*
una copa *a stemmed glass, a wine glass*
una cuchara *a spoon*
un cuchillo *a knife*
la cuenta *the bill, the check*
el/la dueño/a *the owner*
los frijoles *beans*
un mantel *a table cloth*
un menú *a menu*
un plato hondo *a bowl*
un plato llano *a plate*

un plato principal *a main dish, an entrée*
un postre *a dessert*
una propina *a tip*
una servilleta *a napkin*
una taza *a cup*
un tenedor *a fork*
una terraza *a terrace*
una tortilla de maíz/harina *a corn/flour tortilla*
un vaso *a glass*

Pronombres de complemento indirecto
me *(to, for) me*
te *(to, for) you (fam. sing.)*
le *(to, for) you (form. sing.), him, her*
nos *(to, for) us*

os *(to, for) you (fam. pl.)*
les *(to, for) you (pl.), them*

Verbos
dar *to give*
explicar *to explain*
ofrecer *to offer*
preguntar *to ask*
prestar *to lend*
quisiera *I/you/he/she would like*
regalar *to give (as a gift)*
retirar *to remove, to take away*
servir (i, i) *to serve*
vender *to sell*

Otra palabra
sobre *over, about, on*

TEMA ❷

Las comidas
el almuerzo *lunch*
la bebida *drink*
el bistec *steak*
los camarones *shrimp*
la carne *meat*
la cena *dinner, supper*
los cereales *cereal*
la chuleta de cerdo *pork chop*
la comida *food, meal*
el desayuno *breakfast*
la ensalada de lechuga y tomate *lettuce and tomato salad*
los espárragos *asparagus*
la fruta *fruit*
la grasa *fat*
los huevos *eggs*
el jugo de naranja *orange juice*
el pan tostado *toast*

la papa al horno *baked potato*
las papas fritas *French fries*
el pescado *fish*
la pimienta *pepper*
el pollo *chicken*
el postre *dessert*
la sal *salt*
el sándwich *sandwich*
la sopa *soup*
el té helado/caliente *iced/hot tea*
las verduras *vegetables*
las zanahorias *carrots*

La cocina
a la parrilla *on the grill, grilled*
al horno *in the oven, baked*
al vapor *steamed*
asado/a *roasted*
bien cocido/a *well-done*

poco cocido/a *rare*
preparado/a *prepared*
término medio *medium (meat)*

Verbos como gustar
dar asco *to be revolting, to not be able to stand*
doler (ue) *to hurt, to ache*
encantar *to love*
faltar *to be missing/needed*
importar *to be important*
interesar *to interest*
molestar *to bother*

Otras expresiones verbales
cocinar *to cook*
contener (ie) *to contain*
darle hambre a alguien *to make someone hungry*
estar a dieta *to be on a diet*

TEMA 3

En el mercado
el brócoli *broccoli*
la cebolla *onion*
un centavo *a cent*
los chícharos *peas*
los ejotes *green beans*
las espinacas *spinach*
las fresas *strawberries*
los frijoles *beans*

el limón *lemon*
un (medio) kilo *a (half) kilogram*
el maíz *corn*
el mango *mango*
la manzana *apple*
el melón *melon*
la naranja *orange*
la papa *potato*
un peso *a peso*

la piña *pineapple*
el plátano *banana*
las uvas *grapes*

Otras palabras y expresiones
dulce *sweet*
se *to you (formal, sing.), to him, to her, to you (pl.), to them*

TEMA 4

Las recetas
una cacerola *a pan*
el caldo de pollo *chicken broth*
la crema *cream*
la cuarta parte de *one fourth of*
una cucharada *a spoonful*
la harina *flour*
los ingredientes *ingredients*
la mantequilla *butter*
una media taza *half cup*
una mezcla *a mixture*
un minuto *a minute*
la mitad *half*
el queso suizo / parmesano *Swiss / Parmesan cheese*

una receta *a recipe*
un recipiente *a container, a receptacle*
la salsa *sauce*
una yema de huevo *an egg yolk*

Verbos
agregar *to add*
batir *to beat*
calentarse (ie) *to get warm*
comenzar (ie) *to begin*
derretir (i, i) *to melt*
espesarse *to thicken*
mezclar *to mix*
verter (ie) *to pour*

unir *to blend, to combine, to unite*

Adjetivos
batido/a *beaten*
delicioso/a *delicious*
derretido/a *melted*
rallado/a *grated*

Otras palabras y expresiones
¡Así es! *That's it! That's right!*
A ver… *Let's see…*
finalmente *finally*
ya *already*

TEMA 5

Sustantivos
el alcohol *alcohol*
la cafeína *caffeine*
los carbohidratos *carbohydrates*
los consejos *advice*
los dulces *sweets*
la energía *energy*
el estrés *stress*
la proteína *protein*

una recomendación *a recommendation*
una rutina *a routine*
la salud *health*
las vitaminas *vitamins*

Expresiones verbales
comer fuerte *to eat a lot*
controlar *to control*
dejar de + infinitive *to stop …ing*

evitar *to avoid*
llevar una vida *to lead a life*
mantenerse en forma *to stay in shape*
seguir (i, i) *to follow*

Otras palabras y expresiones
equilibrado/a *balanced*
ligero/a *light*
lo suficiente *sufficiently, enough*
sano/a *healthy*

9

Con el médico

In this chapter you will learn to...

- describe your body and talk about injuries
- suggest activities to friends
- describe symptoms of illnesses and ask for advice
- talk about how to stay healthy
- discuss how dieting affects your health
- talk about healthcare among Hispanics

You will use...

- more reflexive verbs
- **nosotros** form commands
- the subjunctive to influence others
- the subjunctive with impersonal expressions
- the subjunctive to express doubt

VOCABULARIO

TEMA **①**

¿Te lastimaste?

¡Ojo!

The verbs presented here are reflexive, except for **dolor (ue)** (*to hurt*), which is used like **gustar,** with indirect object pronouns.

A Juan le duelen los ojos.
Juan's eyes hurt.

Me caí y **me lastimé…**
Creo que **me rompí…**
Me torcí…
Me quemé…
Me duele…
Me di un golpe en…

El cuerpo

Supplemental activities.
A. Have students touch a part of the body as you name it. Follow up by having students name parts of the body as you touch them. **B.** ¿Para qué se usa(n) los ojos (la boca, las piernas, las manos, la cabeza, los dedos, los dientes)? Have students name as many verbs as they can think of. **C.** ¿Qué parte del cuerpo asocia Ud. con una jirafa (un elefante, un cocodrilo, un cíclope, la abuela de Caperucita Roja)? **D.** Play a chain game to see who is the biggest hypochondriac. One student says a part of his/her body hurts. The following students must say that the same parts of their bodies hurt and add one more. Point out that *me duele* becomes *me duelen* with plural nouns. **E.** Have different students describe the following features of a monster or an alien: *la cabeza, el pelo, los ojos, la nariz, la boca, las orejas, el pelo, el cuello, el pecho, el estómago, los brazos, las manos y los dedos, las piernas, los pies.* Students should draw the monster on a sheet of paper as it is being described, and afterward everyone shows his/her drawing. **F.** Have students name celebrities that have the following features: *piernas largas, ojos bonitos, pelo feo, una boca grande, brazos grandes, una nariz grande, orejas grandes.* **G.** ¿Qué parte del cuerpo asocia Ud. con estos artículos de ropa o de joyería? *(los zapatos, un sombrero, un cinturón, una corbata, los calcetines, la camisa, las gafas, los aretes, un anillo, un collar, las botas, los pantalones)*

el cabello
el ojo
el diente
el corazón
la piel
la nariz
la cara
la boca
el pecho
el estómago
el tobillo

la cabeza
la oreja
el cuello
la espalda
el brazo
la mano
los dedos
la pierna
el pie
la rodilla

---

caerse *to fall*   **lastimarse** *to hurt (yourself)*   **romperse (el brazo…)** *to break (your arm…)*   **torcerse (ue) (el tobillo)** *to twist, to sprain (your ankle)*   **quemarse** *to burn (yourself)*   **darse un golpe en…** *to bump/hit your...*

9-1 **¿Qué le duele?** ¿Qué parte del cuerpo le duele a una persona en las siguientes circunstancias?

Modelo   Acaba de caminar diez kilómetros sin zapatos.
Le duelen los pies.

1. Acaba de pasar toda la tarde en la playa sin crema protectora solar.
2. Acaba de leer por diez horas.
3. Acaba de tocar un plato muy caliente.
4. Durmió en el piso toda la noche.
5. Tiene alergia al polen.
6. Acaba de bailar toda la noche.
7. Bebió demasiado la noche anterior.
8. Acaba de cruzar un aeropuerto grande con tres maletas.
9. Acaba de comerse un jalapeño.
10. Acaba de escribir un ensayo de diez páginas en un examen.

9-2 **Expresiones idiomáticas.** Los nombres de las partes del cuerpo se usan en muchas expresiones idiomáticas. ¿Puede adivinar (*guess*) el equivalente en inglés de las siguientes expresiones?

1. costar un ojo de la cara
2. perder la cabeza
3. comer con los ojos
4. tomarle el pelo a alguien
5. romperse la cabeza
6. ser el brazo derecho de alguien
7. ir a pie
8. tener la cabeza bien puesta
9. ponerse de pie
10. hacer algo a espaldas de alguien
11. ver algo con buenos (malos) ojos
12. romperle el corazón a alguien
13. empezar el día con el pie izquierdo
14. tomar algo a pecho
15. no tener ni pies ni cabeza
16. hacérsele a alguien la boca agua
17. quedarse con la boca abierta
18. comerse a alguien con los ojos

P   **Conversaciones.** En parejas, lean la siguiente conversación en la cual una mujer explica cómo se lastimó. Luego, cambien la conversación para hablar de alguna vez que usted se rompió **un hueso** o se lastimó en un accidente o jugando a un deporte.

— Adela, ¿qué te **pasó**? ¿Por qué tienes el tobillo **vendado,** el brazo **enyesado** y andas con **muletas**?
— **Montaba a caballo** y me caí. Me rompí el brazo y me torcí el tobillo.
— ¿Te duele mucho?
— Al principio me dolía mucho pero **ya no** me duele **tanto**... pero no me gusta tener el brazo enyesado. No puedo escribir y es difícil manejar.
— ¿Cuándo te lo van a **quitar**?
— En tres semanas.
— Y las muletas, ¿hasta cuándo necesitas usarlas?
— Dos o tres días más.

---

un hueso *a bone* **pasar** *to happen* **vendado/a** *bandaged, wrapped* **enyesado/a** *in a cast* **las muletas** *crutches*
montar a caballo *to ride horseback* **ya no** *no longer* **tanto** *so much* **quitar** *to take off, to remove*

Supplemental activities. **A.** ¿Le duelen las siguientes partes del cuerpo a una persona por las alergias o por la artritis? (*la nariz, los pies, el brazo, los ojos, la cabeza, el tobillo, los dedos, las rodillas, las manos*) **B.** Have students work in groups to prepare an advertisement for a plastic surgeon. **C.** Explique qué estaba haciendo la última vez que Ud. se lastimó de las siguientes maneras. Complete las oraciones. *Modelo: Me torcí el tobillo bajando la escalera. / Nunca me torcí el tobillo.* 1. Me quemé la piel con el sol... 2. Me rompí el brazo... 3. Me corté un dedo... 4. Me lastimé un pie... 5. Me caí... 6. Me di un golpe en la cabeza...

Answers for 9-2. *Expresiones idiomáticas.* (Note that these expressions are used here to practice the names of body parts, and are not intended to be learned at this point as active vocabulary.) 1. *to cost an arm and a leg* 2. *to panic* 3. *to have eyes bigger than your stomach* 4. *to pull someone's leg* 5. *to rack your brains* 6. *to be someone's right hand* 7. *to go on foot* 8. *to have your head screwed on right* 9. *to stand up, to get on your feet* 10. *to do something behind someone's back* 11. *to (dis)approve* 12. *to break someone's heart* 13. *to start the day on the*

AUDIO ¡A escuchar!

Escuchen otra conversación en la cual alguien cuenta un pequeño incidente que tuvo. ¿Qué le duele? ¿Cómo se lastimó?

¡Ojo!

En España, también se dice **escayolado** en vez de **enyesado.**

wrong side of the bed 14. *to take something to heart* 15. *to be such that you cannot make heads or tails of it* 16. *to make your mouth water* 17. *to be dumbfounded (to stand there with your mouth open)* 18. *to devour someone with your eyes*

GRAMÁTICA

Más acciones reflexivas: repaso de los verbos reflexivos

Many verbs used to talk about health or accidents are reflexive. The reflexive verb **caerse** (*to fall*) has an irregular **yo** form in the present indicative and is like **leer** in the preterite.

	PRESENT	**PRETERITE**
yo	me caigo	me caí
tú	te caes	te caíste
Ud./él/ella	se cae	se cayó
nosotros/as	nos caemos	nos caímos
vosotros/as	os caéis	os caísteis
Uds./ellos/ellas	se caen	se cayeron

Use the command form to tell someone not to fall. Remember that for most verbs all commands except the affirmative **tú** form have the same stem as **yo** in the present indicative.

¡No te caigas! / ¡No se caiga! / ¡No se caigan!

The following reflexive verbs are also commonly used to talk about health. Note that reflexive verbs are often used to say that people do something to their own body or to indicate changes in physical or mental states.

cortarse	*to cut yourself*
darse un golpe (en la cabeza…) (contra…)	*to hit/bump (your head…) (against…)*
enfermarse	*to get sick*
lastimarse	*to hurt yourself*
ponerse (mal, nervioso/a…)	*to become (ill, nervous…)*
quemarse	*to burn yourself*
resfriarse	*to catch a cold*
romperse (el brazo…)	*to break (your arm…)*
sentirse (deprimido/a…)	*to feel (depressed…)*
torcerse (ue, yo form: **me tuerzo) (el tobillo…)**	*to twist/sprain (your ankle…)*

After reflexive verbs, the definite article is generally used with a part of the body where the possessive adjective is used in English.

Me lastimé **el** pie.	*I hurt **my** foot.*
Te vas a cortar **los** dedos.	*You're going to cut **your** fingers.*
Me lavé **el** cabello.	*I washed **my** hair.*

9-3 **¿Qué hicieron?** ¿Cómo se lastimaron estas personas?

> **Modelo** Se dio un golpe en la cabeza contra la mesa.

1.

2.

3.

4.

5.

6.

7.

G **9-4** **Consejos.** En grupos, preparen consejos lógicos para un amigo con las frases de las siguientes listas. Recuerden que los pronombres reflexivos se ponen al final del verbo en los mandatos afirmativos y antes del verbo en los mandatos negativos.

> **Modelo** **Ponte crema protectora solar si no quieres quemarte la piel.**

ponerse crema protectora solar
ponerse gafas del sol
relajarse
ponerse un suéter
divertirse con los amigos
no caerse
ponerse buenas botas
no darse un golpe contra la puerta
???

torcerse el tobillo
sentirse nervioso
quemarse la piel
lastimarse los ojos
sentirse deprimido
lastimarse la cabeza
resfriarse
romperse el brazo
???

P **9-5** **Entrevista.** Entreviste a otro/a estudiante con estas preguntas.

1. ¿En qué estación del año te enfermas más? ¿Tienes alergias? ¿Qué síntomas tienes? ¿Te resfrías mucho en invierno?
2. ¿Te tuerces el tobillo con frecuencia? ¿Te rompiste un hueso alguna vez? ¿Qué te rompiste? ¿Qué estabas haciendo cuando te lo (la, los, las) rompiste? ¿Lo (la, los, las) tuviste enyesado/a/os/as? ¿Por cuánto tiempo?
3. ¿Qué estabas haciendo la última vez que te lastimaste? ¿Qué parte del cuerpo te lastimaste? ¿Fuiste al médico?
4. ¿Tomas el sol con frecuencia? ¿Te quemas fácilmente con el sol? ¿Te pones crema protectora solar para protegerte (*protect yourself*) del sol?

VOCABULARIO
¡Cuídense!

TEMA 2

¿Qué necesita hacer Ud. para **cuidar** la salud y para mantenerse en forma? ¿Desea Ud. **bajar** o **subir de peso**?

Es importante seguir una dieta sana y equilibrada, comer menos grasa, más fruta, verduras y proteínas y tomar vitaminas. ¿Conoce Ud. la pirámide nutricional?

Las proteínas son necesarias para tener los músculos fuertes y para la reparación de tejidos. Se usan también para producir hormonas y enzimas. Comidas ricas en proteínas incluyen la carne, el pescado, la leche, el yogurt, los frijoles, el arroz, el maíz y otros cereales.

La vitamina D es necesaria para mantener los huesos, los dientes y el sistema nervioso fuertes y en buenas condiciones. Los alimentos como la leche, la mantequilla, el huevo, el queso, el salmón y el atún contienen esta vitamina.

La vitamina A es importante para la piel, el cabello, los ojos y los huesos. Se encuentra en el pescado, el melón, la zanahoria, el mango, las espinacas, la yema de huevo, la mantequilla y el queso.

La vitamina E ayuda a aliviar la fatiga, proteger los pulmones y el sistema inmunológico y previene el envejecimiento. Se encuentra en los cereales integrales, el maíz, las verduras verdes, la manzana, el plátano y la zanahoria.

La vitamina C es importante para prevenir enfermedades respiratorias y para el crecimiento de tejidos. Se encuentra en la fresa, el kiwi, el limón, el melón, la naranja, la piña y el mango.

Los carbohidratos dan la energía necesaria para las actividades físicas y mentales. Las papas, el arroz, los chícharos, la zanahoria, los frijoles, la piña, la miel, los cereales y el pan son alimentos ricos en carbohidratos.

---

cuidar *to take care of* **bajar/subir de peso** *to lose/gain weight* **prevenir** (conjugated like **venir**) *to prevent* **el crecimiento** *growth* **los tejidos** *tissues* **fuerte** *strong* **los alimentos** *foods* **el atún** *tuna* **ayudar** *to help* **aliviar** *to relieve* **proteger** *to protect* **los pulmones** *the lungs* **el envejecimiento** *aging* **integral** *whole-grain* **la miel** *honey* **rico** *rich*

9-6 La nutrición. De acuerdo con la información de la página anterior, ¿por qué son nutritivos los siguientes alimentos?

Modelo **La leche contiene mucha vitamina D. Es buena para los huesos, los dientes y el sistema nervioso.**

1.

2.

3.

4.

5.

6.

7.

G 9-7 La pirámide nutricional. Imaginen que tienen que darle una presentación sobre la nutrición a una clase bilingüe de una escuela primaria. En grupos de tres, preparen una descripción de la pirámide nutricional.

P Conversaciones. En parejas, lean la siguiente conversación en la cual un amigo le da consejos a otro sobre cómo mantenerse en forma haciendo ejercicio. Luego, cambien la conversación para dar consejos sobre cómo tener una dieta más saludable o cómo mantenerse en buena forma.

— ¡Siempre estás en buena forma y tienes mucha energía! ¿Cómo lo haces?
— Hago ejercicio en el gimnasio con regularidad. Me da **fuerza** y también me ayuda a controlar el estrés.
— No me gusta ir al gimnasio. Me siento **dolorido** cuando me despierto al día siguiente y me duele la espalda. No quiero levantarme de la cama.
— Necesitas **estirarte** antes de comenzar. Si no **tienes cuidado**, puedes lastimarte. Comienza con ejercicios ligeros y no **trates de** hacer ejercicios **pesados al principio.**

---

la fuerza *strength* **dolorido/a** *sore* **estirarse** *to stretch* **tener cuidado** *to be careful* **tratar de…** *to try to…* **pesado/a** *heavy* **al principio** *at first*

Follow-up for 9-7. *La pirámide nutricional.* Have one group give their presentation to the class. Students in the other groups should play the pupils and ask questions about good eating habits.

AUDIO ¡A escuchar!

Escuchen otra conversación en la cual dos amigos hablan de la dieta de uno de ellos. ¿Qué es lo que nunca come? ¿Qué come con muchas proteínas? ¿Qué es lo que más come para mantenerse en forma?

Follow-up for *Conversaciones.*
1. ¿Lleva Ud. una vida más o menos sana? ¿Mantiene una dieta equilibrada? ¿Fuma? ¿Qué hace para mantenerse en forma? ¿Qué necesita hacer para llevar una vida más sana?
2. ¿Hace ejercicio en un gimnasio con frecuencia? ¿Siempre se estira antes de hacer ejercicio? ¿Comienza con ejercicios ligeros? Para bajar de peso, ¿prefiere hacer ejercicio o ponerse a dieta? 3. ¿Tiene mucho estrés? ¿Por qué? ¿Qué hace para relajarse?

GRAMÁTICA

Hacer sugerencias: los mandatos con la forma *nosotros*

Para averiguar

1. What are two ways of saying *let's do something*?
2. What stem changes are there in **nosotros** commands of **-ir** verbs? Are there stem changes for **-ar** and **-er** verbs?
3. Where do you place object and reflexive pronouns with affirmative commands? with negative commands?
4. When do you drop the final **-s** from the end of the verb in **nosotros** commands?

¡Ojo!

¿Recuerda Ud. estos mandatos?

Infinitive	Ud. Command
caer	caiga
conocer	conozca
dar	dé
decir	diga
estar	esté
hacer	haga
ir	vaya
oír	oiga
poner	ponga
saber	sepa
salir	salga
ser	sea
tener	tenga
traer	traiga
venir	venga
ver	vea
-gar verbs	**(g > gu)**
pagar	pague
-car verbs	**(c > qu)**
sacar	saque
-zar verbs	**(z > c)**
rezar	rece

One way to suggest doing something with other people in Spanish is to use **vamos a** + infinitive to say *Let's* + verb.

| ¡Vamos a salir esta noche! | *Let's go out tonight!* |
| ¡Vamos a comer fuera! | *Let's eat out!* |

Nosotros commands can also be expressed by adding **-mos** to the **Ud.** command form. The written accents of the **Ud.** commands **dé** and **esté** are not needed in the **nosotros** commands.

¡**No salgamos** esta noche!	***Let's not go out** tonight!*
¡**Comamos** en el parque!	***Let's eat** at the park.*
¡**Seamos** pacientes!	***Let's be** patient.*
¡**Hagamos** ejercicio!	***Let's do** some exercise!*

The affimative **nosotros** command of **ir** is **vamos** instead of **vayamos.** In the negative, however, you do say **no vayamos.**

| ¡Vamos al gimnasio! | *Let's go to the gym!* |
| ¡No vayamos ahora! | *Let's not go now!* |

There is no stem change in **nosotros** commands of **-ar** and **-er** stem-changing verbs, but with **-ir** verbs **e** becomes **i** and **o** becomes **u.**

| ¡**Ce**rremos la puerta! | *Let's close the door!* |
| ¡**Vo**lvamos temprano! | *Let's return early!* |

but:

| ¡**Pi**damos algo de comer! | *Let's order something to eat!* |
| ¡**Du**rmamos un poco más! | *Let's sleep a little more!* |

Object pronouns and the reflexive pronoun **nos** are attached to the end of the verb in affirmative commands and an accent is written on the stressed vowel. They are placed before the verb in negative commands.

| ¡Hagámoslo mañana! | *Let's do it tomorrow!* |
| ¡No lo hagamos ahora! | *Let's not do it now!* |

The final **-s** of the command is dropped when the indirect object pronoun **se** or the reflexive pronoun **nos** is attached to the end of the verb.

¡Digámoselo!	*Let's tell it to them (him, her)!*
¡No se lo digamos!	*Let's not tell it to them (him, her)!*
¡Levantémonos tarde!	*Let's get up late!*
¡No nos levantemos temprano!	*Let's not get up early!*
¡Vámonos!	*Let's go!*

9-8 Sugerencias. Ud. y su amigo van a jugar tenis. Seleccionen la mejor opción para mantenerse sanos. Use mandatos en la forma **nosotros.**

> **Modelo** jugar al tenis / jugar a los videojuegos
> **No juguemos a los videojuegos. Juguemos al tenis.**

1. ir al parque en el carro / ir al parque en bicicleta
2. ponerse crema protectora solar / quemarse la piel
3. estirarse antes de jugar / lastimarse
4. tener cuidado / calentarse demasiado
5. comprar cerveza después de jugar / evitar el alcohol
6. tomar agua mineral / tomar refrescos
7. almorzar justo antes de jugar / comer después de jugar
8. comprar helado de postre / hacer ensalada de fruta

P 9-9 Invitaciones. Sugiérale a un/a compañero/a de clase que haga las siguientes cosas. Él/Ella debe aceptar y recomendar un lugar apropiado o sugerir otra actividad que prefiera.

> **Modelo** E1: **¡Durmamos una siesta!**
> E2: **Sí, vamos a casa. / No, no durmamos una siesta. Veamos una película.**

1.   **2.**

3.   **4.**   **5.**

P 9-10 Planes. Ud. va a salir con un/a amigo/a. Conteste sus preguntas con mandatos en la forma **nosotros** para expresar sus preferencias.

> **Modelo** ¿Qué quieres hacer esta noche?
> **Vamos a cenar.**

1. ¿Qué quieres hacer esta noche?
2. ¿A qué hora quieres salir?
3. ¿Adónde quieres ir?
4. ¿Quieres invitar a alguien más a salir con nosotros?
5. ¿Vamos juntos en mi carro?
6. ¿Le decimos a alguien adónde vamos?
7. ¿Quieres hacer algo más después?
8. ¿A qué hora quieres volver a casa?

Follow-ups for 9-8. *Sugerencias.*
A. Ud. habla con un/a amigo/a. Sugiérale que los/las dos hagan la actividad de su preferencia. *Modelo:* ¿Prefieres quedarte en casa esta noche o salir con los amigos? > *Quedémonos en casa esta noche. / Salgamos con los amigos.* ¿Prefieres (ver la tele o escuchar un CD, ir a bailar o ir al cine, cenar en un restaurante esta noche o cenar en casa, comer comida mexicana o italiana, estudiar en la biblioteca o ir a un café, ir al lago este fin de semana o ir de compras, pasar un fin de semana tranquilo en casa o hacer una fiesta, dormir hasta tarde el domingo o hacer algo temprano por la mañana, hacer la tarea el viernes por la noche o el domingo por la noche)? **B.** Have students work in groups to think of suggestions they might make to a professor so that they do not have to work too hard. *Modelo: Salgamos temprano de clase hoy.* **C.** Sugiérale un lugar específico u otra actividad a un/a amigo/a que tiene ganas de hacer las siguientes cosas con usted. *Modelo:* Tengo ganas de acampar. > *Yo también, vamos al río Brazos. / No, no acampemos este fin de semana. Vamos a la playa y alojémonos en un hotel.* Tengo ganas de comer comida china esta noche (ir de compras, nadar esta tarde, ver la nueva película de Walt Disney, alquilar un DVD, bailar, jugar al minigolf, jugar con los videojuegos, tomar una copa, tomar un café). **D.** Sugiérales a sus amigos que todos hagan algo juntos si va a hacer sol (va a hacer frío, va a llover, tienen mucho dinero, no tienen dinero).

VOCABULARIO

TEMA 3

¿Qué síntomas tiene?

Supplemental activities. A. Si alguien tiene alergia al polen, ¿tiene los siguientes síntomas a veces? 1. ¿Estornuda? 2. ¿Tiene fiebre? 3. ¿Le duelen los dedos? 4. ¿Le pican los ojos? 5. ¿Tiene tos? 6. ¿Vomita? 7. ¿Le duele la cabeza? 8. ¿Le duelen los oídos? 9. ¿Tiene los pies hinchados? 10. ¿Tiene los oídos hinchados? **B.** Complete las oraciones con el nombre de una parte del cuerpo lógica. 1. Tengo mucha tos. Me duele... 2. Estornudo mucho. Me duele... 3. No veo bien. Me pican... 4. Creo que voy a vomitar. Me duele mucho... 5. El médico me acaba de poner una inyección. Me duele... 6. No oigo nada. Me duelen... 7. Me caí de la bicicleta y no puedo levantarme. Me duelen... 8. Tengo un virus intestinal. Me duele... 9. Levanté algo pesado y ahora tengo que acostarme porque me lastimé un músculo de... 10. Antes de correr, necesita estirar los músculos de... **C.** ¿Es lógico? 1. Necesito una curita porque vomito. 2. Necesito muletas porque me torcí el tobillo. 3. Tengo tos porque tengo catarro. 4. Me duele la espalda porque tengo alergias. 5. Me tomo la temperatura porque creo que tengo fiebre. 6. Tengo el brazo enyesado porque estoy mareado. 7. Necesito una aspirina porque me duele la cabeza. 8. Tengo la mano hinchada porque está infectada. 9. Necesito una curita porque me corté el dedo. 10. El médico me examina la garganta porque me rompí la pierna.

Suggestion. You may wish to point out that some speakers say **una tirita** instead of **una curita.**

¿Qué dice el/la paciente? ¿Qué síntomas tiene?

**Estoy resfriado/a.
Tengo catarro. Estornudo.**

**Tengo tos.
Toso mucho.**

Me duele el oído.

Tengo fiebre.

Me pican los ojos.

**Me siento mareado/a.
Vomito.**

**Tengo el dedo hinchado
y adormecido.**

**Está infectado
Necesito una curita.**

¿Qué le hace el/la médico/a al/a la paciente?

**La examina la garganta
y le toma la temperatura.**

**Le receta medicamentos
(pastillas, aspirinas).**

Le pone una inyección.

---

el oído *the inner ear*   **hinchado/a** *swollen*   **adormecido/a** *numb*   **la garganta** *the throat*   **recetar** *to prescribe*
pastillas *tablets, pills*

9-11 ¿Quién lo hace? ¿Le hace el médico las siguientes cosas al paciente o viceversa?

Modelo tomar la temperatura
El médico le toma la temperatura al paciente.

1. describir los síntomas
2. examinar los oídos
3. explicar dónde le duele
4. tomar el pulso
5. pedir consejos
6. poner una inyección
7. recetar medicamentos
8. hacer preguntas sobre el uso de los medicamentos
9. pagar

Supplemental activities.
A. Generalmente, ¿puede tener una persona las siguientes cosas enyesadas? *(el brazo, el cabello, los ojos, las orejas, la pierna, el tobillo, la boca, los dedos)* **B.** ¿Se pone una persona una curita en las siguientes partes del cuerpo? *(la cara, el cabello, la oreja, el oído, los ojos, la rodilla, la nariz, los dientes, el cuello, el pie)*

(G) 9-12 ¿Cuáles son los síntomas? En grupos, preparen listas de los síntomas de una persona con estas enfermedades.

1. la gripe *(the flu)*
2. un catarro
3. un dedo infectado
4. un infarto *(heart attack)*
5. una sinusitis
6. una fractura del tobillo
7. una intoxicación por alimentos *(food poisoning)*

(G) 9-13 Uds. son médicos/as. Imagine que Uds. son médicos/as. En grupos, preparen una sugerencia para alguien que sufre de cada enfermedad de la actividad anterior. Utilicen mandatos en la forma **usted.**

(P) **Conversaciones.** En parejas, lean la siguiente conversación en la cual un paciente habla con el médico. Luego, cambien la conversación para representar una visita al doctor cuando usted estaba enfermo/a.

— Me siento muy mal. Tengo tos y no puedo respirar. Estoy congestionado y tengo la nariz **tapada.**
— ¿Le duelen los oídos?
— Sí, los tengo hinchados. No oigo bien y tengo **un dolor** de cabeza fuerte.
— Quítese la camisa y siéntese en la mesa… Abra la boca y diga aaah.
— Aaah.
— Ahora necesito que respire. No es nada **grave.** Tiene alergias y **sufre de** una sinusitis también. Le voy a recetar unos antibióticos. Tómese una pastilla cada doce horas y le **aconsejo** que **guarde cama** por unos días.

AUDIO ¡A escuchar!

Escuchen otra conversación en la cual un paciente habla con una médica. ¿Cómo le surgió el problema *(did the problem arise)*? ¿Qué tiene? ¿Qué tratamiento le da la médica?

---

tapado/a *stopped up* **un dolor** *an ache, a pain* **grave** *serious* **sufrir de** *to suffer from* **aconsejar** *to advise*
guardar cama *to stay in bed*

Para averiguar

1. When is the subjunctive used in a subordinate clause?
2. Which verb form that you have already learned is similar to the subjunctive?
3. Which five verbs are irregular in the subjunctive? Which two have accent changes?
4. What is the subjunctive of **hay**?
5. When do you use the infinitive after verbs like **querer** or **preferir** instead of the subjunctive?

Suggestion. Tell students to refer to the lists of *Ud.* commands on p. 268 as needed. Point out that the *Uds.* and *nosotros* forms of the subjunctive are like the commands, except for *vamos.*

Supplemental activity. Repita la oración que exprese su opinión.
1. Quiero que llueva mañana. / Quiero que haga sol mañana.
2. Quiero que mis padres vengan a mi casa este fin de semana. / Prefiero que no vengan a mi casa este fin de semana. 3. Espero que mi mejor amigo/a salga conmigo este sábado. / No quiero que mi mejor amigo/a salga conmigo este sábado. 4. Deseo que mi mejor amigo/a viva conmigo. / No quiero que viva conmigo. 5. Prohíbo que mis amigos fumen en mi casa. / Permito que mis amigos fumen en mi casa. 6. Prefiero que mis amigos me llamen por teléfono. / Prefiero que me escriban por correo electrónico. 7. Prefiero que alguien haga ejercicio conmigo. / Prefiero hacer ejercicio solo/a. 8. Deseo que mis amigos tomen una copa conmigo a veces. / Recomiendo que mis amigos eviten el alcohol. 9. Insisto en que mis amigos me lo digan si están enojados conmigo. / Prefiero que no me digan nada si están enojados conmigo. 10. Insisto en estar solo/a cuando estoy deprimido/a/. / Prefiero que alguien esté conmigo cuando estoy deprimido/a.

GRAMÁTICA

Expresar preferencias: el subjuntivo para influir sobre los demás

Up to this point you have been using verb forms in the indicative mood. The indicative mood is used to describe what the speaker considers to be reality. There is another mood called the *subjunctive*. The subjunctive form of the verb is used to express subjective opinions about what might or should happen.

The subjunctive is used in the subordinate (*usually the second*) clause of a sentence when the main (*usually the first*) clause expresses a wish, doubt, emotion, or attitude about what might or might not happen. Compare:

Indicative   Mi hijo **come** bien.

(The speaker assumes that it is a fact that his son eats well.)

Subjunctive   Quiero que mi hijo **coma** bien.

(The speaker does not necessarily assume it to be true that his son eats well. It is just what he wants to see happen.)

To form the subjunctive, use the same stem as for **Ud.** commands, which for most verbs is like the stem of the **yo** form in the present indicative. Subjunctive endings for **-ar** verbs have the vowel **e**, and **-er** and **-ir** verbs have the vowel **a**.

	HABLAR	COMER	VIVIR	HACER	IR
Ud. command	hable	coma	viva	haga	vaya
que yo	hable	coma	viva	haga	vaya
que tú	hables	comas	vivas	hagas	vayas
que Ud./él/ella	hable	coma	viva	haga	vaya
que nosotros/as	hablemos	comamos	vivamos	hagamos	vayamos
que vosotros/as	habléis	comáis	viváis	hagáis	vayáis
que Uds./ellos/ellas	hablen	coman	vivan	hagan	vayan

The subjunctive of **hay** is **haya,** and the verbs with irregular **Ud.** commands have the same stem in the subjunctive: **dar: dé, estar: esté, ir: vaya, ser: sea,** and **saber: sepa.** Note the accent changes on **dar** and **estar.**

    dar: dé, des, dé, demos, deis, den
    estar: esté, estés, esté, estemos, estéis, estén

When subjects of sentences have feelings or desires about what they do themselves, use the infinitive. When they have feelings or desires about what someone else does, use the subjunctive. The subjunctive is used following verbs such as: **aconsejar** (*to advise*), **desear, esperar** (*to hope*), **insistir (en), necesitar, pedir (i, i), permitir, preferir (ie, i), prohibir, querer (ie), recomendar (ie),** and **sugerir (ie, i)** (*to suggest*).

Feelings about themselves   **Feelings about others**
(Yo) Prefiero **ir.**   (Yo) Prefiero que (tú) **vayas.**
(Nosotros) Queremos **hacerlo.**   (Nosotros) Queremos que Uds. lo **hagan.**

Where Spanish has two clauses connected by **que,** English often has a different sentence structure.

Quiero que tengas esto.
I want you to have this.
(I want that you have this.)

Prefieren que vayamos.
They prefer for us to go.
(They prefer that we go.)

9-14 **¿Qué quieren?** Diga si las siguientes personas quieren las cosas indicadas entre paréntesis.

> **Modelo** Un médico (no) quiere que sus pacientes… (estar enfermos, dormir lo suficiente)
> **Un médico no quiere que sus pacientes estén enfermos.**
> **Un médico quiere que sus pacientes duerman lo suficiente.**

1. Un médico (no) quiere que (nosotros)… (fumar, dejar de fumar, evitar el alcohol, hacer ejercicio, pagarle, seguir sus recomendaciones, tener una dieta equilibrada, comer mucha grasa)

2. Generalmente, (no) quiero que el médico… (ponerme una inyección, darme medicamentos, decirme que estoy bien de salud, hacerme preguntas sobre mis síntomas, tomarme la temperatura, tener las manos frías)

3. Cuando me examina, el médico (no) quiere que (yo)… (abrir la boca, decir aaah, estornudar, tener frío, estar cómodo/a)

4. Los pacientes de un hospital (no) quieren que su habitación… (ser cómoda, estar sucia, tener un televisor, costar mucho, tener ventanas)

5. Los enfermeros (no) quieren que los pacientes… (ser antipáticos, estar cómodos, tener muchas visitas, comer bien, tomar sus medicamentos)

9-15 **¿Quién?** Ud. no puede levantarse de la cama porque está muy enfermo/a con fiebre alta y un amigo lo/la va a ayudar. ¿Necesita hacer las siguientes cosas Ud. mismo/a o necesita que su amigo se las haga?

> **Modelo** pasar el día en la cama
> **Yo necesito pasar el día en la cama.**
> ir al supermercado
> **Necesito que mi amigo vaya al supermercado.**

1. guardar cama
2. dormir mucho
3. llevar la receta a la farmacia
4. tomar los medicamentos
5. hacerme algo de comer
6. tomar muchos líquidos
7. traerme un vaso de agua
8. sentirme mejor

9-16 **La pareja ideal.** Escriba cinco oraciones describiendo rasgos (*traits*) que busca en una pareja. Utilice: **Quiero que…, Insisto en que…, Prefiero que…, Deseo que…** o **Espero que…**

> **Modelo** **Quiero que tenga un buen trabajo.**
> **Insisto en que no fume.**

Follow-ups for 9-14. **¿Qué quieren?**
A. ¿Quiere el médico que el paciente haga las siguientes cosas o viceversa? Comience cada oración con *El médico quiere que el paciente…* o *El paciente quiere que el médico… Modelo:* hablar con él después del examen físico > *El paciente quiere que el médico hable con él después del examen físico.*
1. describir bien los síntomas
2. saber mucho de medicina
3. bajar de peso 4. darle consejos de salud 5. pagar rápidamente
6. examinarle el cuerpo 7. sentirse mejor 8. recetarle pastillas 9. tomar los medicamentos como se indica
B. Practice the use of the infinitive instead of the subjunctive by having students say whether the patient needs to do each of the things in section *A,* or whether he needs the doctor to do them. **C.** En grupos, preparen dos listas: una de cosas que quieren que su profesor/a (no) haga y otra de cosas que su profesor/a quiere que Uds. (no) hagan. *Modelos: Lista 1: Queremos que el/la profesor/a nos dé buenas notas.* Lista 2: *El/La profesor/a quiere que vengamos a clase.* **D.** Haga una lista de cosas que otras personas quieren que Ud. haga pero que Ud. no quiere hacer. *Modelos: Mi profesor/a quiere que yo haga esta lista pero yo no quiero hacerla. / Con frecuencia mi mejor amigo quiere que yo juegue al tenis con él pero yo no quiero jugar.*

Follow-up for 9-16. *La pareja ideal.* Afterward, have students redo the activity describing the ideal house or apartment. *Modelo: Prefiero que mi apartamento esté cerca de la universidad.* You may also have them describe the ideal job. *Modelo: Quiero que mi trabajo sea interesante.*

VOCABULARIO
¿Quiere vivir 100 años?

Aquí hay una lista de consejos para vivir una vida larga. **¿Está de acuerdo?**

Una dieta rica en vitaminas le da más resistencia **ante** una enfermedad o una depresión.

Aprenda a controlar el estrés. Puede tener consecuencias negativas como la presión arterial alta o **un infarto**.

Evite el abuso de drogas o de alcohol y nunca maneja **ebrio/a**.

Note. The vocabulary in *25 Consejos para vivir 100 años* is not intended to be learned as active vocabulary at this point and is not included on the end-of-chapter vocabulary list.

Supplemental activities. *La lámpara de Aladino*. Ud. acaba de encontrar la lámpara de Aladino. Pídale tres deseos personales a la lámpara. *Modelo: Deseo vivir 100 años. Deseo perder unos kilos...* Luego, pídale tres deseos adicionales para otras personas. *Modelo: Deseo que mis padres vivan 100 años.* **B.** Have students pick out the five suggestions from *25 Consejos para vivir 100 años* that they find the most important. **C.** Ask students personal questions related to each of the *25 Consejos para vivir 100 años,* such as the following. 1. ¿Mantiene Ud. una dieta rica en frutas y verduras? ¿Cuántas frutas y verduras come Ud. todos los días? ¿Come Ud. más carne o más frutas y verduras? 2. ¿Cuántas horas necesita dormir todos los días? ¿Cuántas horas duerme? ¿Qué síntomas de fatiga tiene Ud. si no duerme lo suficiente? 3. ¿Sabe Ud. perdonar fácilmente? ¿Olvida Ud. rápidamente las peleas con los amigos o las recuerda por mucho tiempo? 4. ¿Lee Ud. mucho en la cama antes de dormir? ¿Prefiere Ud.

(Continued on the next page.)

Algunas normas que le ayudarán a llevar una vida mejor, más sana, más larga

25 Consejos para vivir 100 años

1. Mantenga una dieta rica en frutas y verduras.
2. Nunca duerma menos horas de las que necesita.
3. Si no puede perdonar, por lo menos olvide.
4. Tenga siempre un libro junto a su mesa de noche.
5. Camine un poquito diariamente.
6. Reúnase con frecuencia con sus viejos amigos.
7. No esconda sus sentimientos. Exprese lo que siente.
8. Para los que viven solos, una mascota es la mejor compañía.
9. Si se da baños de sol, escoja las horas en que es más benigno tomarlo.
10. Los chistes y la risa en general son una medicina maravillosa.
11. En la calle, maneje siempre su auto a la velocidad indicada.
12. No olvide ponerse el cinturón de seguridad siempre que maneje o permanezca en un auto.
13. Todos los días tome cinco o seis vasos de agua fresca.
14. Limite su consumo de carnes rojas.
15. Si no sabe mucho de electricidad, llame a un electricista.
16. Hágase un chequeo médico por lo menos una vez cada dos años, aunque no tenga ningún malestar.
17. Sométase a una prueba de mamografía una vez al año.
18. Duerma en un colchón duro para cuidar la espalda.
19. Al respirar, trate de hacer siempre inhalaciones profundas.
20. Medite todos los días por lo menos unos 15 minutos.
21. Manténgase en contacto directo con la naturaleza.
22. Báñese con jabones suaves y aceitosos para proteger su piel.
23. Pruebe las hierbas y los remedios naturales.
24. Dese un buen masaje de vez en cuando.
25. Si fuma, deje de hacerlo.

estar de acuerdo *to agree* **ante** *faced with* **un infarto** *a heart attack* **ebrio/a** *drunk*

9-17 ¿Y usted? ¿Cuáles de los *25 Consejos para vivir 100 años* ya sigue Ud.? ¿Cuáles necesita seguir?

Modelo   **Ya tengo una dieta rica en frutas y verduras.**
Necesito aprender a perdonar y olvidar.

G 9-18 ¿Qué más se puede hacer? En grupos de tres, preparen cuatro o cinco sugerencias más para agregar a la lista de *25 Consejos para vivir 100 años*.

Modelo   **Evite la autopista IH-35.**

9-19 Consejos. Lea los siguientes consejos de *Cómo actuar en caso de infarto* y diga qué es importante hacer.

Modelo   **Es importante telefonear rápidamente al médico.**

EL MÉDICO ACONSEJA

Cómo actuar en caso de infarto
Un infarto no tiene hora, lugar, ni edad. Actúe a tiempo.

+ Telefonee rápidamente al médico y si no puede localizarlo pida directamente una ambulancia.

+ El paciente debe estar en posición de descanso, sentado en una silla o acostado. No debe levantarse o caminar.

+ Permanezca al lado del paciente hasta que el médico llegue. Si el enfermo queda inconsciente, con pérdida de respiración y pulso, practique la respiración boca a boca y dele masaje cardíaco hasta que el médico llegue.

+ La gravedad de los síntomas varía desde un dolor muy agudo hasta una pequeña sensación de malestar. Incluso, es posible sufrir un infarto cardíaco asintomático (los diabéticos son los más propensos a este fenómeno).

+ En ocasiones el dolor puede ser más atípico y confundirse con una angina de pecho sin ninguna importancia.

P Conversaciones. En parejas, lean la siguiente conversación en la cual una amiga le habla a otra de su depresión. Luego, cambien la conversación para hablar de una situación estresante real o imaginaria de uno/a de ustedes.

— **Te veo** muy triste. ¡Vamos al lago para **levantarte el ánimo**!
— No, no tengo ganas de ir al lago.
— ¿Qué te pasa? ¡Te encanta ir al lago!
— **Desde que** perdí mi trabajo me siento muy mal y no tengo ganas de hacer nada. Estoy buscando otro empleo pero no puedo concentrarme. A veces quiero pasar todo el día en la cama y siento que no **valgo** nada.
— Escucha. Es normal estar deprimida después de perder el trabajo, pero si no tienes ganas de hacer nada, **más vale que** vayas al médico. Si no, puedes **desarrollar** una depresión profunda.
— Tal vez **tengas razón.** Voy a pedir **una cita.**

A. Follow-up for 9-17. **¿Y usted?** Have students change the commands from *25 Consejos para vivir 100 años* from formal to familiar command forms, telling a friend to do each one. Refer them to p. 248 to review command forms for *tú.*

Te veo… *You look… to me.* **levantarle el ánimo a alguien** *to cheer someone up, to lift someone's spirits*
Desde que *since* **valer (yo form: valgo)** *to be worth* **más vale que…** *one had better…* **desarrollar** *to develop*
tener razón *to be right* **una cita** *an appointment*

(*Continued from the previous page.*)
leer o ver la tele antes de acostarse? 5. ¿Camina Ud. todos los días? ¿Dónde prefiere caminar? ¿Prefiere caminar o correr? 6. ¿Con qué frecuencia ve Ud. a su mejor amigo/a? ¿Tiene contacto con sus viejos amigos de la escuela secundaria? 7. ¿Expresa Ud. sus sentimientos fácilmente? ¿Llora con frecuencia? ¿Con quién habla cuando necesita desahogarse (*to get something off your chest*)? 8. ¿Tiene Ud. un perro o un gato? ¿Es mejor compañía que sus amigos a veces? 9. ¿Toma Ud. el sol con frecuencia? ¿Se quema la piel con frecuencia? ¿Siempre se pone crema protectora solar? 10. ¿Les cuenta Ud. muchos chistes a sus amigos? 11. ¿Le gusta manejar rápido? ¿Siempre respeta el límite de velocidad? ¿Recibió una multa recientemente? 12. ¿Siempre se pone el cinturón de seguridad? 13. ¿Cuántos vasos de agua toma Ud.? ¿Compra Ud. agua mineral? 14. ¿Le gusta el bistec? ¿Come más carne roja o más pollo? 15. ¿Le gusta arreglar su casa Ud. mismo/a o prefiere que un profesional lo haga? 16. ¿Cuándo tuvo su último chequeo médico? ¿Se pone Ud. nervioso/a cuando va al médico? ¿Cuándo fue al dentista por última vez? 17. ¿Con qué frecuencia se debe hacer una mujer una mamografía? 18. ¿Duerme Ud. bien en un colchón duro? ¿Duerme Ud. bien en una cama de

AUDIO ¡A escuchar!

Escuchen otra conversación en la cual un hombre habla con su esposa de un problema médico. ¿Cuál es el problema? ¿Qué necesita hacer para aliviarlo? ¿Y si eso no funciona?

agua? 19. ¿Hace Ud. inhalaciones profundas? ¿Tiene asma o alergias? 20. ¿Medita Ud. a veces? ¿Practica yoga? 21. ¿Tiene muchas plantas? ¿Le gusta trabajar en el jardín? ¿Le gustan los animales? ¿Le gusta acampar? 22. ¿Cuáles son las mejores marcas de jabón para la piel? ¿Se lava Ud. las manos con frecuencia? 23. ¿Cree Ud. en los remedios naturales? ¿Qué hierbas usa? 24. ¿Cuándo fue la última vez que se dio un masaje? ¿En qué parte del cuerpo siente mucha tensión con frecuencia? 25. ¿Fuma Ud.? ¿Cuántos cigarrillos fuma al día? ¿Desea dejar de fumar? ¿Cuántos años tenía cuando empezó a fumar?

GRAMÁTICA
Hacer sugerencias: el subjuntivo con las expresiones impersonales

As you have already seen, you use the indicative to describe what actually happens and the subjunctive to express a desire for something to happen. The subjunctive is also used after the following expressions that make a subjective comment on whatever follows them. The **que** is often dropped from **Ojalá que.**

> **Es bueno/malo/mejor que…**
> **Es común que…**
> **Es increíble** (*incredible*) **que…**
> **Es importante que…**
> **Es lógico que…**
> **Es necesario que…**
> **Es normal que…**
> **Es preferible que…**
> **Es raro** (*strange*) **que…**
> **Es ridículo que…**
> **Es triste que…**
> **Es una lástima** (*a shame*) **que…**
> **Es urgente que…**
> **Más vale que…** (*One had better…*)
> **Ojalá (que)…** (*Let's hope that…*)

Es importante que vayas al médico.	*It's important that you go to the doctor.*
Es una lástima que no puedas ir ahora.	*It's a shame you can't go now.*
¡Ojalá que el médico te ayude!	*Let's hope that the doctor helps you!*

With all of these expressions except **Ojalá (que),** you may use an infinitive without the **que** to talk about people in general, rather than specific individuals.

Opinion about specific people

Es mejor que los niños descansen.	*It's better for the children to rest.*

General opinion

Es mejor descansar.	*It's better to rest.*

As in the present indicative, the **nosotros/as** and **vosotros/as** forms of stem-changing **-ar** and **-er** verbs have no stem change in the subjunctive. For stem-changing **-ir** verbs an **e** becomes **i** and an **o** becomes **u** in the **nosotros/as** and **vosotros/as** forms, just as with **nosotros** commands.

	CERRAR	VOLVER	SENTIR	DORMIR
Ud. command	cierre	vuelva	sienta	duerma
que yo	cierre	vuelva	sienta	duerma
que tú	cierres	vuelvas	sientas	duermas
que Ud./él/ella	cierre	vuelva	sienta	duerma
que nosotros/as	cerremos	volvamos	**sintamos**	**durmamos**
que vosotros/as	cerréis	volváis	**sintáis**	**durmáis**
que Uds./ellos/ellas	cierren	vuelvan	sientan	duerman

(Continued on the next page.)

9-20   ¿Es bueno? ¿Qué le diría (*would you say*) a un amigo que le hace los siguientes comentarios? Utilice una de las expresiones impersonales presentadas en la página anterior.

> **Modelo**   Me siento muy mal con frecuencia.
> **Es una lástima que te sientas mal con frecuencia.**

1. No tengo la presión arterial alta.
2. Fumo mucho.
3. Hago ejercicio todos los días.
4. Siempre me estiro un poco antes de hacer ejercicio.
5. Nunca voy al médico porque tengo miedo de las inyecciones.
6. Estoy un poco deprimido/a hoy.
7. Salgo con los amigos cuando estoy deprimido/a.
8. Nunca manejo después de tomar alcohol.

(G) 9-21   En el hospital. En grupos, hagan oraciones para describir un hospital. Utilicen un elemento de cada columna y terminen cada oración de manera original.

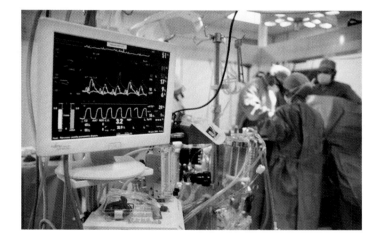

> **Modelo**   **Es importante que las habitaciones estén limpias.**
> **Es urgente que los pacientes con heridas graves reciban atención médica.**
> **Es mejor que los médicos siempre les digan la verdad a sus pacientes.**

(No)	Es importante que Es necesario que Es preferible Es mejor que Es malo que Es urgente que Es normal que	las habitaciones los médicos los pacientes los enfermeros el hospital	???

9-22   ¿Y Ud.? Prepare una lista explicando los cambios que Ud. y sus familiares necesitan hacer para llevar una vida más sana. Utilice las expresiones de la página anterior.

> **Modelo**   **Es importante que yo deje de fumar.**
> **Es preferible que todos comamos más verduras.**

(*Continued from the previous page.*)

preferible que bebas más (menos) agua. 10. Si tienes la presión arterial alta, es mejor que comas más (menos) grasa. 11. Si deseas bajar de peso, es mejor que hagas más (menos) ejercicio. **C.** Ud. es médico/a y su paciente tiene la gripe. Utilice una de las expresiones impersonales de la página 276 para contestar sus preguntas. *Modelo:* ¿Necesito comprar la receta inmediatamente? > *Sí, es preferible que la compre inmediatamente.* 1. ¿Necesito dormir mucho? 2. ¿Debo tomar muchos líquidos? 3. ¿Puedo salir al partido de fútbol con mis amigos esta noche? 4. ¿Necesito quedarme en casa? 5. ¿Puedo ir al trabajo mañana? 6. ¿Puedo manejar después de tomar los medicamentos? 7. ¿Debo tomar las pastillas con la comida? 8. ¿Necesito pagarle ahora?

TEMA 5

VOCABULARIO
La dieta y las enfermedades

Note. Only the names of the health problems and the labeled body parts on the realia are included with the active vocabulary at the end of the chapter.

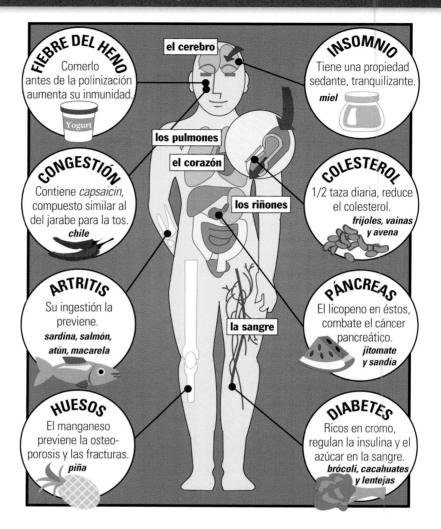

9-23 ¿Qué me recomienda? Dígale a un amigo que sufre de las siguientes afecciones (*conditions*) qué alimentos le recomienda.

Modelo   fiebre del heno (yogurt/piña)
Si sufres de fiebre del heno, te recomiendo que comas yogurt.

1. diabetes (brócoli/papas)
2. insomnio (salmón/miel)
3. artritis (pescado/carne)
4. congestión (zanahorias/chiles)
5. colesterol alto (frijoles/plátanos)
6. osteoporosis (piña/manzanas)

9-24 Remedios caseros. Exprese su opinión de los siguientes remedios caseros (*home remedies*) encontrados en Internet.

> Es cierto. Es posible. Es ridículo.

Modelo Tomar limón con miel es bueno para los resfriados y la bronquitis.
Es cierto.

1. El chocolate previene la aparición de las caries (*cavities*) porque contiene flúor y fosfatos.
2. Una mezcla de dos huevos crudos (*raw*) con un vaso de cognac es un remedio efectivo contra la ronquera (*hoarseness*).
3. Si uno/a se lava la cara con leche por la mañana y por la noche antes de acostarse la piel queda más suave (*soft*).
4. Una cebolla cortada por la mitad en la mesita de noche ayuda contra la tos y los resfriados.
5. Una mezcla de sábila (*aloe vera*) con miel es un buen remedio para las quemaduras y heridas.
6. La mitad de una papa aplicada a una quemadura alivia el dolor.
7. Comer zanahorias lo/la ayuda a broncearse (*to tan*).

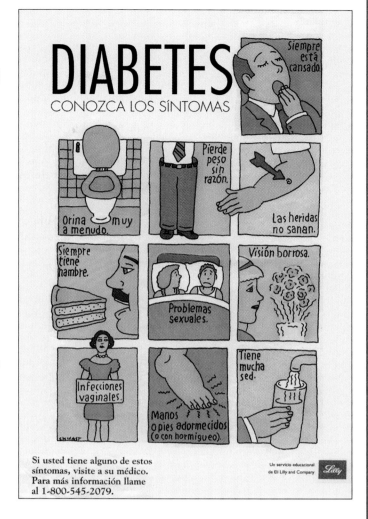

DIABETES
CONOZCA LOS SÍNTOMAS

Siempre está cansado.

Pierde peso sin razón.

Orina muy a menudo.

Las heridas no sanan.

Siempre tiene hambre.

Visión borrosa.

Problemas sexuales.

Infecciones vaginales.

Manos o pies adormecidos (o con hormigueo).

Tiene mucha sed.

Si usted tiene alguno de estos síntomas, visite a su médico. Para más información llame al 1-800-545-2079.

Un servicio educacional de Eli Lilly and Company *Lilly*

 Conversaciones. En parejas, lean la siguiente conversación en la cual un paciente habla de sus síntomas con su médico. Luego, preparen una conversación en la cual el/la paciente describe tres o cuatro de los síntomas de la diabetes u otra enfermedad y el/la médico/a da su diagnóstico.

— Dr. Láraga, me siento muy mal. Creo que tengo **pulmonía.**
— No, dudo que sea pulmonía. Quizás sea **gripe** porque hay una epidemia por toda la ciudad. ¿Qué síntomas tiene?
— Me duelen los oídos, la garganta y la cabeza, tengo tos y dolor muscular y no puedo respirar bien.
— Sí, tiene los pulmones muy congestionados y además tiene 39 grados de temperatura. Quiero que se cuide mucho y que no salga a la calle por unos días. Dudo que pueda volver al trabajo esta semana. Le voy a recetar un antibiótico. ¿Es usted alérgico a algo?
— Sí, soy alérgico a la penicilina.
— Aquí tiene una receta para unas pastillas. Le recomiendo que tome muchos líquidos y que guarde cama.

AUDIO ¡A escuchar!

Escuchen otra conversación en la cual dos personas se quejan de sus problemas médicos. ¿Cuál es el problema de cada una?

la pulmonía *pneumonia* **la gripe** *the flu*

GRAMÁTICA
Expresar duda: el subjuntivo con las expresiones de duda

Para averiguar

1. What are ten expressions of doubt or uncertainty that are followed by the subjunctive?
2. Can the conjunction **que** be dropped like *that* in English?
3. Why do you not use the subjunctive after **creer que, estar seguro/a de que, es cierto que,** and **es verdad que** in the affirmative? When do you use the subjunctive after these phrases in questions?
4. What are two ways of saying *perhaps* or *maybe*? When do you use the subjunctive with them?

The subjunctive is used after the following expressions of doubt and uncertainty, because they express situations that might not correspond to reality.

dudar que...	*to doubt that...*
es dudoso que...	*it's doubtful that...*
no creer que...	*to not believe that...*
no estar seguro/a de que...	*to not be sure that...*
no es cierto que...	*it's not true that...*
no es verdad que...	*it's not true that...*
es posible/imposible que...	*it's possible/impossible that...*
es probable/improbable que...	*it's probable/improbable that...*

Although the conjunction *that* is optional in English, **que** is required in Spanish.

Dudo que tengas pulmonía.	*I doubt (that) you have pneumonia.*
Es posible que sea gripe.	*It's possible (that) it might be the flu.*

Since **creer que, estar seguro/a de que, es cierto que,** and **es verdad que** indicate that the speaker considers his or her assumptions to be true, they take the indicative in affirmative statements. When these expressions are used in the negative, uncertainty is implied, and therefore they take the subjunctive.

Creo que **vienen** mañana.	*I believe they are coming tomorrow.*
No creo que **vengan** esta noche.	*I don't believe they are coming tonight.*

When these expressions are used in a question, they take the indicative when the speaker is merely seeking a confirmation, but use the subjunctive when verifying an opinion that was not expected or doubtful information.

Indicative: ¿Es verdad que te sientes mal?	*Is it true that you feel bad?*
Subjunctive: ¿Crees que sea gripe?	*Do you really think it is the flu?*

Use **quizás** or **tal vez** to say *maybe, perhaps*. The subjunctive is used after these expressions, unless the speaker feels quite sure that the assertion is true.

Quizás venga el médico.	*Perhaps the doctor might come.*
Tal vez sea mejor.	*Perhaps it might be better.*

9-25 En España. Ud. hace un viaje a España con un amigo y hablan de lo que deben hacer si se enferman. ¿Cree Ud. que las siguientes oraciones describan correctamente la situación en España?

> Modelo   Hay tantos hospitales como aquí.
> **Estoy seguro/a de que hay tantos hospitales como aquí. /**
> **Dudo que haya tantos hospitales como aquí.**

1. A veces los farmacéuticos (*pharmacists*) recetan medicinas.
2. Todos los médicos saben hablar inglés.
3. Se aceptan nuestros seguros (*insurance*) en los hospitales.
4. Muchos españoles no tienen seguro médico.
5. Hay asistencia médica universal para todos en España.
6. Tienen hospitales muy modernos.
7. Hay muchas enfermedades tropicales en Madrid.

Ⓖ 9-26 Cuídese Ud. y cuide a su bebé. Lea la siguiente información para las mujeres embarazadas (*pregnant*) que fuman. Luego, en grupos, preparen una lista de los posibles efectos del consumo de tabaco durante el embarazo y de recomendaciones para las personas que desean dejar de fumar.

> Modelo   **Si fuma durante el embarazo es posible que su bebé**
> **nazca prematuro.**
> **Si desea dejar de fumar, le recomiendo que tire a la**
> **basura todos los cigarrillos.**

Cuídese usted y a su bebé

La salud de su bebé comienza por usted. Aléjese de todo aquello que pueda perjudicarlos a los dos . . . como fumar.

Si usted fuma mientras está embarazada:

- Podría tener un aborto espontáneo o su bebé podría nacer muerto.

- Su bebé podría nacer prematuramente o demasiado pequeño. Los bebés que son demasiado pequeños al nacer pueden tener problemas respiratorios y otros problemas de salud general.

- Su bebé podría tener problemas de comportamiento y de aprendizaje más tarde en su niñez.

- Su bebé tiene un alto riesgo de morir del síndrome de la muerte súbita infantil. Esta enfermedad causa que un bebé que aparentemente está saludable muera sin ninguna indicación previa.

- Su bebé puede desarrollar asma u otros problemas respiratorios.

¿Por qué conviene dejar de fumar mientras está embarazada?

- Usted tendrá un embarazo más saludable.

- Su bebé, que está todavía por nacer, se desarrollará mejor porque le llegará más oxígeno y sustancias nutritivas.

- Su bebé tiene más probabilidades de nacer sano.

- Usted habrá tomado los pasos necesarios para dejar de fumar por el resto de su vida. Esto reducirá el riesgo de un ataque cardíaco, embolia cerebral y cáncer.

Cuando se sienta con deseos de fumar, haga lo siguiente:

- Cepíllese los dientes.

- Salga a caminar.

- Llame a un amigo o a una amiga.

- Tome agua o jugo de fruta.

- Mastique chicle sin azúcar o coma trocitos de zanahoria.

- Aspire profundamente y cuente hasta cinco. Exhale el aire lentamente. Repita esto cinco veces.

- Lea de nuevo su lista de razones para dejar de fumar.

- Mantenga las manos ocupadas. Busque cosas que pueda hacer con las manos para que no tenga cómo sostener el cigarrillo.

- Dígase a sí misma Yo puedo dejar de fumar.

Supplemental activities. A. Refer students to the poster showing symptoms of diabetes on p. 279 and have them make statements of possible signs of being a diabetic, using the expressions presented in this section or on p. 276. *Modelo: Es possible (común) que los diabéticos tengan mucha sed.* **B.** ¿Cree Ud. las siguientes ideas? Exprese su opinión. *Modelo: Las medicinas naturales son mejores que las recetas del médico. Sí, es cierto que las medicinas naturales son mejores. / No, dudo que las medicinas naturales sean mejores.* 1. Las medicinas nuevas son más eficientes que las viejas. 2. Siempre se debe aceptar la primera opinión del médico. 3. Necesitamos más hospitales en esta ciudad. 4. Los médicos ganan demasiado dinero. 5. Los médicos siempre saben cuál es el mejor tratamiento. 6. La aspirina ayuda a las personas con problemas del corazón. 7. Una copa de vino tinto todos los días evita los problemas del corazón. 8. Las espinacas transforman a las personas en Popeye. 9. El médico siempre tiene la razón. 10. Las mujeres son mejores enfermeras que los hombres. **C.** Have students redo *Activity 9-24 Remedios caseros* on p. 279, attaching *Dudo que* or *Creo que* to the beginning of each sentence.

Suggestion for 9-26. *Cuídese Ud. y cuide a su bebé.* Point out that *nacer* and other verbs that have infinitives ending with *-cer* are conjugated like *conocer.*

En portada

REVISTA CULTURAL

Note: Have students complete the *Antes de leer, Reading strategies,* and *Ahora Ud.* activities before reading this article.

LA SALUD PÚBLICA, ¿UN DERECHO?

En **la mayoría** de los países de Latinoamérica, España y el Caribe los servicios de salud pública son un derecho **garantizado** a los ciudadanos del país. A diferencia de lo que ocurre en Estados Unidos, todas las personas tienen acceso universal e **igualitario** al sistema de salud pública. Existen, como en Estados Unidos, planes privados de **sanidad,** pero la mayoría de los ciudadanos **se acogen** al sistema **gratuito.**

La atención médica pública en los países hispánicos está financiada por los trabajadores **mediante** contribuciones de su salario y, en su mayor parte, por el gobierno que **sostiene la red** de hospitales y ofrece **recursos** médicos y ayudas a **la investigación.**

Entre los países hispanos, Chile, Colombia, Costa Rica y España poseen sistemas de salud con más servicios y **cobertura** que Estados Unidos, según un estudio reciente realizado por la Organización Mundial de la Salud. Estados Unidos ocupa el puesto número treinta y siete en esta **encuesta** internacional de 191 países. A pesar de que Estados Unidos es la nación que gasta más dinero en asistencia médica,

3.700 dólares por persona, la Organización Mundial de la Salud dice que los resultados no son tan efectivos como los observados en muchos países con acceso universal a la sanidad.

En Estados Unidos no existe acceso universal al sistema de salud; esto significa que los individuos deben comprar planes privados de atención médica, pagando **de su propio bolsillo** o aceptando el beneficio que **la empresa** ofrece al **trabajador a tiempo completo.**

En Estados Unidos hay más de 43 millones de personas sin cobertura médica distribuidas entre los distintos grupos de población como sigue: un 10,7% de la población blanca, un 20,2% de la población afroamericana, un 18,4% de asiáticos y un 32,4% de latinos. **El riesgo** de no poseer seguro de asistencia médica es especialmente serio para los inmigrantes que no son ciudadanos: un 43,3% de inmigrantes no ciudadanos no tiene **seguro** médico.

Existen en el país servicios sociales médicos para las familias **con pocos recursos,** como Medicaid, pero para algunos el problema de la sanidad es serio en Estados Unidos, y con frecuencia se considera la posibilidad de establecer un sistema nacional de sanidad pública para **cubrir** las necesidades de todos los ciudadanos y evitar que las personas vivan sin cobertura médica.

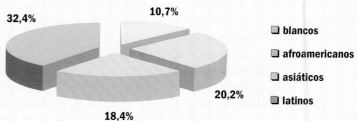

- 10,7% ▢ blancos
- 20,2% ▢ afroamericanos
- 18,4% ▢ asiáticos
- 32,4% ▢ latinos

---

un derecho *a right* **la mayoría** *the majority* **garantizado** *guaranteed* **igualitario** *equal* **sanidad** *health* **se acogen** *participate* **gratuito** *free* **mediante** *through* **sostiene** *supports* **la red** *the network* **recursos** *resources* **la investigación** *research* **cobertura** *coverage* **encuesta** *poll* **de su propio bolsillo** *out of their own pocket* **la empresa** *the company* **el trabajador a tiempo completo** *the full-time worker* **el riesgo** *the risk* **seguro** *insurance* **con pocos recursos** *low-income* **cubrir** *to cover*

Antes de leer

P Observen el título de la lectura, *La salud pública, ¿un derecho?* ¿Qué pueden anticipar del contenido del artículo? ¿Qué saben sobre el sistema de salud en Estados Unidos? ¿Con qué frecuencia usan usted y su familia los servicios médicos? ¿Son gratuitos (*free*) para ustedes?

Después de leer

Reading strategies: Outlining and summarizing. Outlining and summarizing are critical reading strategies that allow readers to grasp the main ideas of a text and separate them from the supporting information and specific examples. Outlining is the first step in the summarizing process. The outline should serve as a skeleton that restates the main ideas of a text condensed and rephrased in the reader's own words. The summary should reflect only the most essential and relevant information of the text. Outlining and summarizing lead to a deeper understanding of a reading by showing the reader how the components of a text fit together.

9-27 Ahora Ud. Identifique los puntos principales del artículo y prepare un esquema (*outline*) de la lectura con sus propias palabras. Después, utilizando su esquema como guía de escritura, prepare un resumen (*summary*) de la lectura en dos párrafos.

P **9-28 En cifras...** En parejas, observen la tabla que aparece con el texto y los datos que la acompañan y comenten las diferencias entre los distintos grupos de población.

1. ¿Qué sector de la población presenta el porcentaje más alto de individuos sin cobertura médica? latino
2. ¿Qué dos sectores de la población se encuentran cercanos (*close*) en sus índices de falta de cobertura médica? afroamericano y asiático
3. ¿Entre qué grupo parece estar más extendida la cobertura médica? blanco
4. En la actualidad se estima que viven en Estados Unidos más de 293 millones de personas. ¿Qué porcentaje de la población norteamericana no tiene cobertura médica? aproximadamente un 14,9% (43 millones) carece de cobertura médica

Ahora reflexione sobre las posibles causas que explican estas diferencias en relación a la cobertura médica en Estados Unidos.

9-29 Es urgente que... Reaccione a la información presentada en el artículo utilizando las estructuras impersonales con el subjuntivo introducidas en este capítulo.

> **Modelo** **Es importante que los servicios médicos estén disponibles para todos los ciudadanos.**

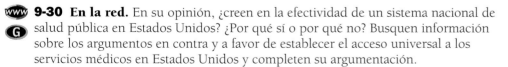 **9-30 En la red.** En su opinión, ¿creen en la efectividad de un sistema nacional de salud pública en Estados Unidos? ¿Por qué sí o por qué no? Busquen información sobre los argumentos en contra y a favor de establecer el acceso universal a los servicios médicos en Estados Unidos y completen su argumentación.

Suggestion. Have students prepare a debate on the issue, with half of the students preparing arguments for a universal healthcare system and half against.

De puertas abiertas a la comunidad

VIDEO MENTE SANA, CUERPO SANO

9-31 Entrando en materia. ¿Qué hace usted para mantenerse en forma? ¿Hace ejercicio con frecuencia? ¿Practica algún deporte? ¿Qué hace para no enfermarse?

Vamos a visitar el Centro Betances, un centro médico comunitario que ofrece servicios médicos **gratuitos** a **cualquier** paciente que necesita atención. Aquí vamos a hablar con Edith Quiñones, una trabajadora social que **asesora** a la comunidad hispana en temas de violencia doméstica y otros **trastornos** emocionales. Van a escuchar también a Teresa Cuadra, médica de familia en Betances, que atiende a familias y participa en los eventos que el centro organiza para la prevención de enfermedades y la sensibilización en materia de salud. La doctora Cuadra también nos habla del impacto que tuvo en su vida el Centro Comunitario Betances, un lugar que siempre tiene sus puertas abiertas a la comunidad que más lo necesita.

9-32 ¿Quién es quién? Lean la siguiente información y determinen a quién se refiere, a Teresa Cuadra, a Edith Quiñones o a ambas (*both*).

	Teresa Cuadra	Edith Quiñones	ambas
1. Soy de origen nicaragüense, nacida en San Francisco.	X	☐	☐
2. Soy colombiana, de Cali.	☐	X	☐
3. Trabajo en el Centro Comunitario Betances.	☐	☐	X
4. Quería trabajar con la comunidad latina y con gente con pocos recursos (*resources*) financieros.	X	☐	☐
5. Me dedico al trabajo social.	☐	X	☐
6. Soy doctora en la Universidad de Nueva York.	X	☐	☐
7. Trabajo con personas que necesitan apoyo (*support*) emocional.	☐	X	☐
8. Hablo con las familias sobre la importancia de tener buenos hábitos de salud.	X	☐	☐

G 9-33 En la consulta. Observen con atención las imágenes de la Doctora Cuadra con una paciente hispana. Completen la conversación imaginando por qué va Marta a la consulta de la Dra. Cuadra, y qué le dice la doctora. Utilicen el vocabulario del capítulo. Representen después la conversación en clase.

— Hola doctora, ¿cómo está? Buenos días.

— ¿Qué tal? ¡Qué gusto verla, Marta! ¿En qué la puedo servir?

Mente sana, cuerpo sano proverb "Healthy mind, healthy body" **gratuitos** *free* **cualquier** *any* **asesora** *advises* **trastornos** *disorders*

9-34 Un cambio en su carrera. Escuche con atención el testimonio de la Doctora Teresa Cuadra y conteste las siguientes preguntas con la información que oiga.

1. ¿Cuándo empezó a practicar la medicina la Dra. Cuadra?
2. ¿Cuál fue su primera especialidad? ¿Cuál es su especialidad ahora?
3. ¿Qué impacto tuvo el Centro Betances en la carrera de la Dra. Cuadra?
4. ¿Qué actividades realiza el Centro Betances para la sensibilización en materia de salud?

G **9-35 Es importante que...** ¿Qué desea la Dra. Cuadra para sus pacientes? Completen sus afirmaciones con el subjuntivo adecuado en cada caso.

La Dra. Cuadra desea que la familia ____forme____ (1. formar) unos buenos hábitos de salud. La doctora espera que los niños ____tengan____ (2. tener) una hora establecida para comer y para dormir. Ella les aconseja a los padres que ____les den____ (3. dar) comidas saludables a sus hijos y le pide a toda la familia que ____participe____ (4. participar) en los Festivales de Salud que organiza el Centro Betances. La doctora Cuadra insiste en que la familia ____lleve____ (5. llevar) un ritmo de vida constante.

¿Qué otros hábitos son importantes para mantener su salud? Utilicen las estructuras con subjuntivo que aprendieron en este capítulo.

1. Es importante que las personas _____.
2. Queremos que las personas _____.
3. Les aconsejamos a las personas que _____.
4. _____.
5. _____.

Answers for 9-34. *Un cambio en su carrera.* 1. La Dra. Cuadra empezó a practicar la medicina en 1985. 2. Su primera especialidad fue la obstetricia. Su especialidad ahora es la medicina de familia. 3. Es un lugar muy especial, porque allí conoció a médicos que querían trabajar con la comunidad hispana y con gente con pocos recursos financieros. 4. El Centro Betances organiza Festivales de Salud, donde invitan a toda la familia, donde tienen juegos para los niños y sirven comidas saludables. También dan clases de nutrición.

9-36 Mi trayectoria en el trabajo social. Conteste las siguientes preguntas con la información que Edith presentó en su testimonio.

1. ¿Cómo ha sido su trayectoria en el área del trabajo social? ¿Por qué?
2. ¿Cuáles son los casos más frecuentes con los que trabaja?
3. ¿Qué personas se ven afectadas por este problema?

9-37 A los jóvenes les diría... Escuche con atención los consejos que Edith le da a un joven universitario que desea involucrarse (*to get involved*) en el trabajo social. Preste atención al uso del subjuntivo en estos consejos.

Edith les recomienda a los jóvenes que desean involucrarse en el campo del trabajo social...

    Modelo   **que conozcan la cultura del paciente.**

1. que _____ hagan el trabajo de corazón _____.
2. que _____ se diviertan _____.
3. que _____ ayuden a otras personas y a ellos mismos _____.

Cambie ahora los consejos de Edith a la forma de mandatos con **nosotros.**

    Modelo   **Conozcamos la cultura del paciente.**

1. _____ Hagamos el trabajo de corazón _____.
2. _____ Divirtámonos _____.
3. _____ Ayudemos a otras personas y a nosotros mismos _____.

Answers for 9-36. *Mi trayectoria en el trabajo social.* 1. Su trayectoria en el trabajo social ha sido una experiencia muy bonita, porque ha podido comunicarse con las personas latinas, ayudarlas y entender sus necesidades. 2. Los casos más frecuentes con los que trabaja son

casos de violencia doméstica. 3. Los casos de violencia doméstica afectan principalmente a la mujer de clase obrera, a las mujeres que trabajan en restaurantes y salones de belleza, a las amas domésticas que les toca hacer los oficios en la casa y su marido tiene algún problema de uso de droga.

Escapadas

COSTA RICA, UN COMPROMISO CON LA TIERRA

Costa Rica, tierra de montañas, **llanuras** y mares, ocupa solamente el 0,001% de la superficie total del planeta y concentra en sus 50.900 **kilómetros cuadrados** de extensión el 6% de las especies animales y vegetales conocidas en el mundo. Costa Rica es un ejemplo del compromiso con la Tierra y la preservación del **medioambiente,** donde un 25% del territorio nacional representa **áreas naturales protegidas.**

Costa Rica es apreciada también por su estabilidad sociopolítica, con una democracia sólida, la ausencia de **ejército** profesional, uno de los mejores sistemas de salud pública y las tasas más altas de **alfabetización** de Latinoamérica. Sus habitantes, los ticos, están **orgullosos** de su tierra costarricense y son gente amable, relajada, que disfruta de la pura vida y que recibe a los visitantes con los brazos abiertos.

Costa Rica es el destino ideal para el ecoturismo. Las montañas y llanuras del norte son la región del país que se extiende hasta Nicaragua, especialmente atractiva por el volcán Arenal, en constante actividad. Cerca del volcán se puede visitar **la Catarata** de la Fortuna, de 70 metros **de altura,** y relajarse en las aguas termales del río Tabacón.

El volcán Arenal y las aguas termales del río Tabacón, Costa Rica.

---

compromiso *commitment*   **llanuras** *plains*   **kilómetros cuadrados** *square kilometers*   **el medioambiente** *the environment*   **áreas naturales protegidas** *environmental preserves*   **ejército** *army*   **alfabetización** *literacy*   **orgullosos** *proud*   **la catarata** *the waterfall*   **de altura** *high*

El Caribe costarricense es una región que se extiende desde la capital, San José, hasta la provincia de Limón. La ciudad de Limón es el puerto de exportación más activo de Costa Rica, y lugar de encuentro de las culturas tica, jamaicana, italiana y china. Desde esta pintoresca ciudad se puede viajar en barco hasta el Parque Nacional Tortuguero, una de las regiones más ricas en fauna y flora de Costa Rica, donde se puede observar **el desove** de **la tortuga** verde, una especie en peligro de extinción.

En el Valle Central el visitante puede pasearse por la capital, San José, con museos tan sorprendentes como el Museo Nacional del Jade, el único museo de jade precolombino existente con una colección incomparable, que exhibe también piezas **labradas en piedra** y cerámicas de ese mismo período. El Museo del Oro Precolombino contiene 1600 piezas de **orfebrería en oro** fechadas entre los años 300 y 1500 d.C. que reflejan la vida cotidiana de los pueblos precolombinos de Costa Rica, su organización social y su relación con la naturaleza. Desde la capital se pueden visitar hermosas plantaciones de café y los volcanes Irazú y Poás, donde la carretera llega casi hasta el mismo cráter.

¡Costa Rica, pura vida!

Celebración del Día de la Raza en Limón, Costa Rica.

El volcán Poás, Costa Rica.

La Basílica de Nuestra Señora de los Ángeles en San José, Costa Rica.

---

el desove *the spawning*   **la tortuga** *the turtle*   **labradas en piedra** *carved in stone*   **orfebrería en oro** *gold work*

(P) 9-38 Sobre la lectura... Conteste las siguientes preguntas relacionadas con la lectura *Costa Rica, un compromiso con la Tierra.*

1. Explique el significado del título del artículo *Costa Rica, un compromiso con la Tierra.*
2. Nombre cuatro de los hechos curiosos (*interesting facts*) mencionados en la lectura sobre Costa Rica.
3. ¿Qué tipo de turista cree que viajaría (*would travel*) a Costa Rica?
4. ¿Cuáles son las regiones más aptas para el ecoturismo y qué se puede visitar en ellas?
5. ¿Cuál es la capital de Costa Rica? ¿Cuáles son algunas de sus principales atracciones turísticas?
6. ¿Qué cree que significa la expresión costarricense *pura vida*?

9-39 ¡Vamos a Costa Rica! Después de leer la información sobre Costa Rica, usted quiere viajar allá con sus amigos. Escriba seis sugerencias utilizando la forma de mandatos con **nosotros** que aprendió en este capítulo.

> Modelo   **Viajemos en avión a San José y alquilemos un carro para ver el resto del país.**

(P) 9-40 Consejos para el turista. Cuando viajamos a un país extranjero debemos tomar ciertas precauciones para proteger nuestra salud. Preparen seis sugerencias dirigidas a un turista norteamericano que va a viajar a Costa Rica. Utilice las estructuras presentadas en el capítulo.

> Modelo   **Le recomiendo que lleve repelente de mosquitos. / Es importante que lleve repelente de mosquitos.**

Parque Nacional Guanacaste y la playa de Nancite, Costa Rica.

En palabras de...

POR UNA VIDA SIN ESTRÉS

Imagine que trabaja como voluntario para la agencia de salud pública de su ciudad y tiene que participar en el diseño de una campaña antiestrés para concienciar (*to make aware*) al público en general de la necesidad de vivir una vida más tranquila, sin tanto estrés.

Writing strategies: Designing a public awareness campaign. The major purpose of a public awareness campaign is to draw an audience's attention to a specific social problem, and ultimately to change the public's attitudes and perceptions about that particular issue. When developing a public awareness campaign, the following steps should be considered: describing the social issue, establishing the objective of the campaign, determining the target audience, planning the event and the activities to promote awareness on the specific social issue, and creating a slogan that reflects the essence of the campaign.

Antes de escribir

Comience con una reflexión sobre los factores más importantes que causan estrés en nuestra sociedad actual y ordene los factores según su orden de importancia.

Prepare ahora su campaña siguiendo los siguientes pasos:

Paso 1. Describa el objetivo principal de la campaña y su audiencia.

Paso 2. Escriba ocho consejos para una vida antiestrés.

Paso 3. Piense en actividades antiestrés que se pueden realizar en su ciudad.

Paso 4. Cree un eslogan atractivo para su campaña.

Después de escribir

Revise y edite su campaña asegurándose que incluyó las siguientes estructuras:

- ✓ vocabulario relacionado con el estrés
- ✓ verbos reflexivos
- ✓ el subjuntivo para influir sobre los demás
- ✓ el subjuntivo en estructuras impersonales

Incluya fotos y gráficos que ilustren el objetivo y/o las características de la campaña.

En la red

Busque información en Internet sobre una campaña de sensibilización pública similar a la suya (*yours*) y compare la información con la que escribió usted. ¿Incluye elementos similares? ¿Le parece suficientemente informativa? ¿Qué le llama la atención especialmente de esta campaña?

All the sources consulted for the readings are cited on the *¡Trato hecho!* Web site at **www.prenhall.com/trato**

VOCABULARIO

TEMA 1

El cuerpo
la boca *the mouth*
el brazo *the arm*
el cabello *the hair*
la cabeza *the head*
la cara *the face*
el corazón *the heart*
el cuello *the neck*
el cuerpo *the body*
los dedos *the fingers*
la espalda *the back*
el estómago *the stomach*
el hueso *the bone*
la mano *the hand*
la nariz *the nose*
la oreja *the ear*
el pecho *the chest*

el pie *the foot*
la piel *the skin*
la pierna *the leg*
la rodilla *the knee*
el tobillo *the ankle*

Verbos
caerse *to fall*
cortar(se) *to cut (yourself)*
darse un golpe (en la cabeza...) *to hit / bump (your head...)*
enfermarse *to get sick*
lastimar(se) *to hurt (yourself)*
montar a caballo *to ride horseback*
pasar *to happen*
ponerse (mal, nervioso/a...) *to become (ill, nervous...)*

quemar(se) *to burn (yourself)*
quitar(se) *to take off, to remove*
resfriarse *to catch a cold*
romper(se) (el brazo...) *to break (your arm...)*
torcer(se) (ue, yo form: **me tuerzo) (el tobillo...)** *to twist / sprain (your ankle...)*

Otras palabras y expresiones
contra *against*
deprimido/a *depressed*
enyesado/a *in a cast*
las muletas *the crutches*
tanto *so much*
vendado/a *wrapped, bandaged*
ya no *no longer, not any more*

TEMA 2

Sustantivos
los alimentos *food*
el atún *tuna*
el crecimiento *growth*
la enfermedad mental *mental illness*
el envejecimiento *aging*
la fatiga *fatigue*
la fuerza *strength*
la miel *honey*
los músculos *the muscles*
los pulmones *the lungs*
el salmón *salmon*
el sistema inmunológico *the immune system*
los tejidos *the tissues*
el yogurt *yoghurt*

Verbos
aliviar *to relieve*
ayudar *to help*
bajar / subir de peso *to lose / gain weight*
cuidar *to take care of*
encontrarse (ue) *to be found, to be located*
estirar(se) *to stretch*
incluir *to include*
mantener *to maintain*
prevenir (ie, **yo** form: **prevengo)** *to prevent*
producir (**yo** form: **produzco)** *to produce*
proteger (**yo** form: **protejo)** *to protect*

tener cuidado *to be careful*
tratar de... *to try to...*

Adjetivos
dolorido/a *sore*
físico/a *physical*
fuerte *strong*
integral *integral, whole-grain*
necesario/a *necessary*
pesado/a *heavy*
rico/a *rich*

Otras expresiones
al principio *at first*
con regularidad *regularly*
en buenas condiciones *in good condition*

TEMA 3

Sustantivos
una alergia *an allergy*
los antibióticos *antibiotics*
la aspirina *aspirin*
una curita *a band-aid*
un dolor de cabeza *a headache*
la fiebre *fever*
la garganta *the throat*
el oído *the inner ear*
un/a paciente *a patient*
una pastilla *a tablet*
un síntoma *a symptom*
una sinusitis *a sinus infection*
la temperatura *the temperature*

Verbos
aconsejar *to advise*
esperar *to hope*
estar resfriado/a *to have a cold*
estornudar *to sneeze*
examinar *to examine*
guardar cama *to stay in bed*
insistir (en) *to insist (on)*
permitir *to permit, to allow*
picar *to itch, to burn*
ponerle una inyección a alguien
    to give someone a shot
prohibir *to prohit, to forbid*
recetar *to prescribe*

sufrir (de) *to suffer (from)*
sugerir (ie, i) *to suggest*
tener catarro *to have a cold*
tener tos *to have a cough*
toser *to cough*
vomitar *to vomit, to throw up*

Adjetivos
adormecido/a *numb*
congestionado/a *congested*
grave *serious, grave*
hinchado/a *swollen*
infectado/a *infected*
mareado/a *dizzy, queasy*
tapado/a *stopped up, blocked*

TEMA 4

Sustantivos
el abuso de drogas *drug abuse*
una cita *an appointment*
las consecuencias (negativas)
    (negative) consequences
una depresión (profunda) *a*
    (deep) depression
un empleo *an employment, a job*
un infarto *a heart attack*
una lista *a list*
la presión arterial alta *high blood*
    pressure

la resistencia *resistance*

Verbos
desarrollar *to develop*
estar de acuerdo *to agree*
levantarle el ánimo a alguien *to*
    lift someone's spirits, to cheer
    someone up
tener razón *to be right*
valer (yo form: **valgo)** *to be worth*

Otras palabras y expresiones
ante *faced with, before*
desde que *since*
ebrio/a *drunk, inebriated*
más vale que… *one had better…*
¿Qué te pasa? *What's wrong with*
    you?
Te veo… *You look… to me.*

Para una lista de expresiones impersonales, vea la página 276.

TEMA 5

Sustantivos
la artritis *arthritis*
el cerebro *the brain*
el colesterol *cholesterol*
la congestión *congestion*
la diabetes *diabetes*
el dolor (muscular) *(muscular)*
    pain

la fiebre del heno *hay fever*
los grados *degrees*
la gripe *the flu*
el insomnio *insomnia*
el líquido *the liquid*
el páncreas *the pancreas*
la penicilina *penicillin*
la pulmonía *pneumonia*

los riñones *the kidneys*
la sangre *the blood*

Otras palabras y expresiones
quizás *maybe, perhaps*
ser alérgico/a a *to be allergic to*

Para las expresiones de duda, vea la página 280.

10

En la oficina

In this chapter you will learn to...

- describe the office where you work
- write your curriculum vitae
- tell about your work experience
- say what has been done
- describe bank transactions
- understand Hispanic influences on American business

You will use...

- present participles as adjectives
- **hace que** with the present and preterite tenses
- the present perfect
- object and reflexive pronouns with the present perfect
- expressions of emotion and the present perfect subjunctive

TEMA **1**

¡Ojo!

También se dice **prender la luz** en vez de **encender**. En España se dice **un ordenador** en vez de **una computadora** y en algunas regiones se dice **un computador**. Se usa **engrapadora** (**engrapar**) en algunas regiones y **grapadora** (**grapar**) en otras.

Suggestions. A. Point out that the word *teclado* is also used for a musical keyboard and *archivar* means *to save* a file on the computer, as well as *to file* in a cabinet. You may wish to write the names of these computer components on the board and have students guess what they are: *un puerto paralelo, un puerto en el panel trasero, un puerto serial, el bus del sistema, los chips, la placa madre, una ranura de extensión, la memoria RAM, el disco duro, un disquete = un disco flexible, la disquetera = la unidad para disquete, un módem, una tarjeta gráfica, una tarjeta de sonido, un escáner, un joystick, el hardware, el software.* Tell students that these words are just for those who are interested, and are not required vocabulary. **B.** Bring a calendar to class and review dates.

Supplemental activity. ¿Qué se usa para sacar copias (grapar papeles, leer algo en Internet, escribir algo en la computadora, buscar la fecha, imprimir documentos, archivar documentos, leer un libro por la noche)?

Supplemental activity. Preguntas auditivas. ¿Cuántos enchufes hay en el salón de clase? ¿Hay una computadora? ¿una impresora? ¿Hay suficiente luz? ¿Apago la luz a veces en clase? ¿Traigo una grapadora conmigo a clase? ¿Trae Ud. una grapadora en la mochila? ¿Saco muchas copias para Uds.?

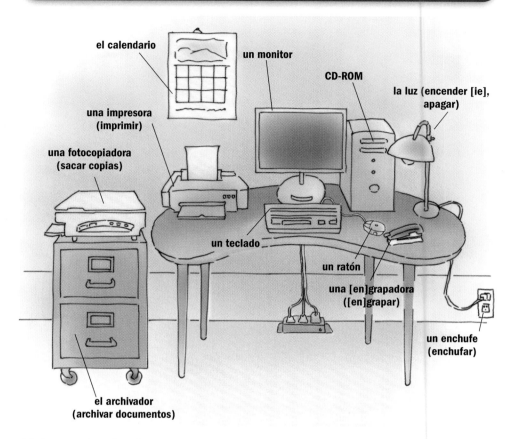

el calendario — un monitor — CD-ROM — la luz (encender [ie], apagar) — una impresora (imprimir) — una fotocopiadora (sacar copias) — un teclado — un ratón — una [en]grapadora ([en]grapar) — un enchufe (enchufar) — el archivador (archivar documentos)

10-1 **Cambio de oficina.** Una secretaria cambió de oficina. ¿Qué hizo ayer por la mañana?

archivar   organizar   colgar (*to hang*)   poner   instalar   conectar   limpiar

Modelo **Organizó su nueva oficina. Archivó...**

ayer por la mañana

esta mañana

P **10-2** **Entrevista.** Entreviste a otro/a estudiante con estas preguntas.

1. ¿Te gustaría trabajar en una oficina o prefieres trabajar en otro lugar como una escuela o una tienda? ¿Eres una persona organizada? ¿Mantienes tu escritorio ordenado o está desordenado con frecuencia?

2. ¿Apagas la computadora después de usarla o siempre la dejas encendida? ¿Sabes arreglar una computadora? ¿Sabes cambiar la placa madre (*motherboard*)? ¿Sabes conectar una impresora? ¿Sabes instalar software? ¿Qué programas de software sabes usar?

3. ¿Para qué clases preparas la tarea en la computadora? ¿Dónde se pueden imprimir documentos aquí en la universidad? ¿Para qué clases tienes que buscar información en Internet con frecuencia? ¿Se pueden tomar muchas clases por Internet aquí? ¿Te gustan esas clases o prefieres las clases tradicionales? ¿Por qué?

G **Conversaciones.** En grupos de tres, lean la siguiente conversación. Luego, preparen una conversación en la cual uno/a de Uds. llama a la oficina de su profesor/a y **marca** el número equivocado. Luego, vuelve a llamar y recibe su **buzón** de **voz**.

— Aló, **empresas** Betacom. ¿En qué puedo servirle?
— Quisiera hablar con el señor Roberto González en **recursos** humanos, por favor. Llamé al 223-5778 pero me dijeron que tenía el número **equivocado.**
— Sí, su número es el 223-4778. Un momento, por favor… Lo siento, su línea está ocupada en este momento. ¿Quisiera dejarle **un recado**? La puedo pasar a su buzón de voz.
— Sí, por favor. Gracias.
— *Ha llamado al buzón de Roberto González. No puedo contestar su llamada en este momento pero si deja su nombre, apellido y teléfono al oír el tono, le* **devolveré** *su llamada lo antes posible.*
— Me llamo Gloria García y llamo para obtener más información sobre la oferta de empleo publicada en su página web. ¿Puede llamarme al 454-6026, por favor? Gracias.

AUDIO ¡A escuchar!

Escuchen otra conversación en la cual alguien habla con un amigo sobre de su primer día en su nuevo trabajo. ¿Qué problemas tuvo?

---

marcar *to dial* **el buzón** *the mailbox* **la voz** *voice* **una empresa** *a company, an enterprise* **los recursos** *resources* **equivocado/a** *wrong, mistaken* **un recado** *a message* **devolveré** *I will return*

Para averiguar

1. What form of a verb can be used as an adjective?
2. What is the regular past participle ending in English? What ending is used to form past participles of **-ar** verbs in Spanish? What ending is used for regular **-er** and **-ir** verbs?
3. What are twelve verbs with irregular past participles in Spanish?
4. Do past participles agree with nouns when they are used as adjectives?

Suggestions. A. Tell students that the past participle of *dormir* is used to say *asleep*. **B.** Point out to students that English has many more irregular past participles than Spanish and have them give the past participle of the following verbs in English: *buy, see, do, win, fly, know, catch*. **C.** Point out that the following adjectives students have already learned are actually past participles and have students give the infinitive of each one and what it means: *organizado, cansado, enojado, interesado, sentado, ordenado, casado, divorciado, separado, despejado, nublado, helado, pasado, (aire) acondicionado, emocionado, preocupado, enamorado, procesado, mareado, resfriado, enyesado, vendado, hinchado, infectado, congestionado, tapado, equilibrado, (pan) tostado, asado, preparado, rallado, aburrido, (seres) queridos, incluido, herido, batido, derretido, deprimido, adormecido, confundido.*

GRAMÁTICA

Expresar estados resultantes: el participio pasado como adjetivo

The past participle is a verb form that can be used as an adjective. In English, regular past participles end in *-ed*. Note how the verbs *to reserve* and *to surprise* are used as adjectives in the following sentences.

The rooms are ***reserved.***	Las habitaciones están **reservadas.**
I'm very ***surprised.***	Estoy muy **sorprendido.**

Regular past participles are formed in Spanish by changing the ending of **-ar** verbs to **-ado** and the ending of **-er** or **-ir** verbs to **-ido.**

prepar**ar**	>	prepar**ado**	*prepared*
conoc**er**	>	conoc**ido**	*known*
prefer**ir**	>	prefer**ido**	*preferred, favorite*

The **-ido** ending of **-er** and **-ir** verbs has a written accent on the **-i-** when it directly follows the vowels **-a, -e,** or **-o.**

traer	>	tra**ído**
creer	>	cre**ído**
oír	>	o**ído**

The following verbs have irregular past participles.

abrir	**abierto**
decir	**dicho**
escribir	**escrito**
freír (*to fry*)	**frito**
hacer	**hecho**
imprimir	**impreso**
morir	**muerto**
poner	**puesto**
resolver	**resuelto**
romper	**roto**
ver	**visto**
volver	**vuelto**

When a past participle is used as an adjective, it agrees in number and gender with the noun it modifies.

cerrar:	La puerta está cerrad**a.**	*The door is closed.*
hacer:	Los informes están hech**os.**	*The reports are done.*

Follow-up for 10-3. ***¿Qué puede ser?*** Have students name the infinitive of the past participles.

10-3 ¿Qué puede ser? En el salón de clase, ¿a quién o qué objeto describen estos participios pasados?

Modelo roto/a
Esa silla está rota. / No hay nada roto en el salón de clase.

1. abierto/a
2. cerrado/a
3. interesado/a
4. confundido/a
5. enojado/a
6. sentado/a

10-4 ¿Está hecho? Su profesor/a quiere estar seguro/a de que todo está bien en la clase. Conteste con un participio pasado, como en el modelo.

> **Modelo** ¿Preparó Ud. los ejercicios del cuaderno para hoy?
> **Sí, están preparados.**

1. ¿Abrió Ud. el libro en la página 297?
2. ¿Cerró su libro?
3. ¿Encendió alguien las luces?
4. ¿Apagó Ud. su celular (*cell phone, m.*)?
5. ¿Escribió alguien las respuestas en la pizarra?
6. ¿Rompió Ud. su silla?
7. ¿Hizo Ud. su tarea para hoy?
8. ¿Perdió su tarea?

10-5 En la oficina. Describan las siguientes cosas y personas con el participio pasado de los verbos indicados.

> **Modelo** romper, cerrar, abrir
> **La ventana está rota.**
> **No está cerrada. Está abierta.**

1. encender, apagar, enchufar, desconectar

2. imprimir, grapar, archivar, perder

3. cansar, abrir, cerrar, ocupar, dormir, sentar, desordenar, enojar

ℙ **10-6 ¡Qué día tan horrible!** Imagine que Ud. vuelve a casa después de un día terrible en la oficina y le cuenta lo que pasó a su esposo/a o compañero/a de cuarto. En parejas, preparen una conversación usando al menos cinco participios pasados.

> **Modelo** **Estuve muy ocupado/a en la oficina hoy...**

> cansado/a roto/a enojado/a perdido/a muerto/a hinchado/a
> congestionado/a preparado/a equivocado/a ocupado/a deprimido/a
> confundido/a ???

Supplemental activities. **A.** Utilice el participio pasado de los siguientes verbos para describirse en este momento. *Modelo:* relajar > *Sí, estoy relajado/a. (No, no estoy relajado/a.)* (confundir, enojar, sentar, acostar, morir, preocupar, ocupar, vestir, dormir, resfriar, casar, interesar, perder, maquillar, jubilar, enterrar, preparar, descansar) **B.** Complete las siguientes oraciones de manera lógica con el participio pasado de uno de estos verbos: *aliviar, romper, tapar, infectar, enyesar, hinchar, herir, vendar, torcer, deprimir, quemar.* (Put the verbs on the board or a transparency.) *Modelo:* Me torcí el tobillo y ahora lo tengo *hinchado y vendado.* 1. Estoy resfriado/a y tengo los oídos y la nariz... 2. Me duele mucho mover la cabeza porque dormí con el cuello... 3. Pasé la tarde en la playa y ahora tengo la piel... 4. Ando con muletas porque tengo una pierna... 5. Me rompí el brazo y por eso lo tengo... 6. Tenía un dolor de cabeza, pero tomé una aspirina y ahora me siento... 7. Tuve un accidente y tengo la espalda... 8. No me limpié el dedo después de cortarme y ahora lo tengo... 9. Sufro de depresión. No sé por qué me siento tan... **C.** Conteste las siguientes preguntas usando un participio pasado. *Modelo:* ¿Le gusta más la comida que se sirve en la cafetería de aquí o la comida que se sirve en McDonalds? > *Me gusta más la comida servida en la cafetería de aquí/McDonalds.* ¿Le gusta(n) más...? 1. la ropa que se vende en (*name two local stores*) 2. los libros que se leen en la clase de historia / inglés 3. la música que se pone en (*name two local radio stations*) 4. las actividades que se hacen en parejas / con toda la clase 5. las cosas que se dicen en el show de Rush Limbaugh / Oprah Winfrey 6. las vacaciones que se pasan en la montaña / en la playa

TEMA ②

VOCABULARIO
Un currículum vitae

CURRÍCULUM VITAE

DATOS PERSONALES
Nombre y apellidos: Ana Guzmán Contreras
Fecha de nacimiento: 14 de agosto de 1982
Lugar de nacimiento: Monterrey, Nuevo León
Estado civil: soltera
Dirección: calle Morales, 214, Saltillo, Coahuila
Teléfono: (844) 4118009
E-mail: Ana814@hotmail.com

FORMACIÓN ACADÉMICA
Universitaria:
1999 – 2003   Licenciatura en Economía, Universidad Autónoma de Nuevo León, Monterrey, Nuevo León

Preparatoria:
1996 – 1999   Escuela Preparatoria 22, Guadalupe, Nuevo León

Secundaria:
1993 – 1996   Escuela Secundaria Técnica 27, Guadalupe, Nuevo León

Primaria:
1987 – 1993   Escuela Normal: Miguel F. Martínez, Monterrey, Nuevo León

EXPERIENCIA PROFESIONAL
2004 – 2005   Bancomex, Saltillo
2003   Contrato temporal en Empresa Texali, Monterrey

IDIOMAS
Inglés: Nivel alto
Francés: Nivel medio

INFORMÁTICA
Procesador de texto: Microsoft Word
Hojas de cálculo: Excel, Quatro Pro
Base de datos: Oracle
Programa de diseño gráfico: Photoshop
Internet y diseño de páginas Web

REFERENCIAS
Referencias disponibles a petición de la empresa.

un idioma = una lengua   escuela normal = escuela primaria   disponible a petición *available upon request*

10-7 **El currículum vitae.** Conteste las siguientes preguntas sobre el currículum vitae de la página anterior.

1. ¿Cómo se llama la candidata al puesto (*applicant*)?
2. ¿Cuántos años tiene?
3. ¿De dónde es originalmente? ¿Dónde vive ahora?
4. ¿En qué año se graduó de la universidad?
5. ¿Qué idiomas sabe hablar? ¿Cuál es su nivel?
6. ¿Qué software sabe usar?

(P) **10-8** **Factores de motivación.** En un papel, escriba los siguientes factores de motivación en la búsqueda de un empleo por orden de importancia para Ud. Luego, un/a compañero/a de clase determinará (*will determine*) el orden de su lista haciendo preguntas como las del modelo.

Modelo   E1: **Para ti, ¿el salario es más o menos importante que la ubicación?**
E2: **El salario es más importante para mí.**

- el salario
- la ubicación (*location*)
- las oportunidades de desarrollo profesional
- los beneficios: el seguro médico (*medical insurance*), las vacaciones pagadas, la pensión de jubilación (*retirement*)
- la compatibilidad con los colegas y los supervisores
- la necesidad o las oportunidades de viajar
- la satisfacción de sentirse útil
- las oportunidades de ser creativo/a

(P) **Conversaciones.** En parejas, lean la siguiente conversación en la cual dos amigos hablan del trabajo. Luego, preparen una conversación en la cual uno/a de Uds. habla de su trabajo (real o imaginario) y por qué le gusta o por qué quisiera cambiar de puesto.

— ¿Por qué quieres cambiar de trabajo?
— Por varios **motivos.** Primero, quiero un empleo a tiempo completo. No tengo seguro médico ahora porque trabajo a tiempo parcial. **Además,** hace tres años que trabajo en ese **puesto** sin aumento de **sueldo.**
— ¿Hay otros motivos para esta decisión?
— Sí, **el ambiente** de trabajo y la compatibilidad con mis colegas son muy importantes para mí. **El jefe** donde trabajo ahora es bien **gruñón.** Siempre **está de mal humor** y a veces **temo** verlo.
— Pero ahora trabajas a cinco minutos de tu casa.
— **La ubicación** de mi trabajo no es tan importante, **me** puedo **mudar** si encuentro un puesto interesante con oportunidades de desarrollo profesional.

Follow-up for *Conversaciones*. Ask those students from the class who work questions such as the following about their jobs: *¿Tiene trabajo a tiempo parcial o a tiempo completo? ¿Es un trabajo bien pagado o mal*

AUDIO ¡A escuchar!

Escuchen otra conversación en la cual alguien habla con un asesor de empleo (*employment adviser*). ¿Cuáles son los factores más importantes en su búsqueda de trabajo? ¿Qué factores no le parecen tan importantes? ¿Qué trabajos le recomienda el asesor?

pagado? ¿Dónde trabaja? ¿Está cerca o lejos de su casa? ¿Tiene oportunidades de ser creativo/a en el trabajo o es monótono? ¿Hay oportunidades de desarrollo profesional? ¿Se siente Ud. útil en ese puesto? ¿Utiliza una computadora en el trabajo? ¿Le dan seguro médico (vacaciones pagadas, aumentos de sueldo con frecuencia)? ¿Hay otros beneficios? ¿Cómo es su supervisor/a? Generalmente, ¿está de buen humor o de mal humor? ¿Cómo se lleva Ud. con él/ella? ¿y con los otros empleados? ¿Cuántos empleados hay? ¿Hay oportunidades de viajar? ¿Adónde? ¿Qué aspectos de su trabajo le gustan? ¿Qué aspectos no le gustan?

---

un motivo *a reason*   **además** *besides*   **un puesto** *a position*   **el sueldo** *the wages, the salary*
el ambiente *the environment*   **el/la jefe/a** *the boss*   **gruñón/gruñona** *grumpy*   **estar de buen/mal humor** *to be in a good/bad mood*   **temer** *to fear*   **la ubicación** *the location*   **mudarse** *to move*

GRAMÁTICA

Expresar la duración de una acción: *hace que*

Whereas the present perfect is used in English to describe an action that started in the past and continues in the present, the present indicative is used in Spanish, because the action still continues at present. In this context, use **desde hace** to say *for* how long someone has done something or just **desde** to say *since* a certain date or time.

PRESENT INDICATIVE IN SPANISH	PRESENT PERFECT IN ENGLISH
Trabajo aquí **desde hace** un mes.	*I have worked here for one month.*
Trabajo aquí **desde** enero.	*I have worked here since January.*
Los clientes **esperan desde hace** mucho tiempo.	*The customers have waited for a long time.*
Los clientes **esperan desde** las dos.	*The customers have been waiting since two o'clock.*

You may also use **hace… que** with the present tense to say how long someone has been doing something, as in the following examples.

Hace un mes **que trabajo** aquí.

I've worked here for one month. / It makes a month that I've worked here.

Hace mucho tiempo **que** los clientes **esperan.**

The customers have been waiting for a long time. / It has been a long time that the customers have been waiting.

Hace que is also used with the preterite to say how long *ago* someone did something. Compare the following sentences.

| Preterite: | **Hace** un mes **que** cambié de puesto. | (Completed in the past.) |
| | *I changed positions one month **ago.*** | |

| Present: | **Hace** un mes **que** tengo este puesto. | (Still going on at present.) |
| | *I've had this position **for** one month.* | |

10-9 ¿Presente o pretérito? Hágale las siguientes preguntas al/a la profesor/a. Si se trata de algo que el/la profesor/a todavía hace, utilice el presente, pero si es algo que terminó en el pasado, utilice el pretérito.

1. ¿Cuánto tiempo hace que Ud. (da, dio) clases de español?
2. ¿Cuánto tiempo hace que (se gradúa, se graduó) de la universidad?
3. ¿Cuánto tiempo hace que (enseña, enseñó) en esta universidad?
4. ¿Cuánto tiempo hace que (sabe, supo) hablar español? ¿e inglés?
5. ¿Cuánto tiempo hace que (viene, vino) a vivir a esta ciudad?
6. ¿Cuánto tiempo hace que (vive, vivió) en la casa o el apartamento donde vive ahora?

P 10-10 ¿Desde cuándo? Pregúntele a otro/a estudiante desde cuando hace las siguientes cosas. Su pareja debe contestar usando **desde hace.** Luego, debe repetir la información usando **hace que.**

Modelo   estudiar español
E1: **¿Cuánto tiempo hace que estudias español?**
E2: **Estudio español desde hace ocho meses. /
     Hace ocho meses que estudio español.**

1. ser estudiante universitario/a
2. estudiar aquí
3. querer aprender español
4. estar en clase hoy
5. vivir aquí
6. conocer a tu mejor amigo/a
7. saber manejar
8. tener tu carro

10-11 Un día laboral. Los relojes indican las horas en que Ramón, un hombre de negocios, empieza varias actividades. Complete las siguientes oraciones utilizando el pretérito de uno de los verbos entre paréntesis para hablar de una acción terminada y el presente del otro para hablar de algo en progreso.

> **Modelo** A las nueve y cuarenta, hace cuarenta minutos que **salió de la casa** y hace diez minutos que **está en la oficina** (estar en la oficina, salir de la casa).

1. A la una menos cuarto, hace más de tres horas que _____ y hace quince minutos que _____ (comer, llegar al trabajo).
2. A las dos y media, hace dos horas que _____ y hace treinta minutos que _____ (almorzar, dar la presentación).
3. A las tres, hace cinco horas y media que _____ y hace una hora que _____ (empezar su presentación, estar en la oficina).
4. A las cuatro, hace dos horas que _____ y hace unos minutos que _____ (hablar con los clients, salir de la presentación).
5. A las cinco, hace siete horas y media que _____ y hace una hora que _____ (despedirse de los clients, trabajar hoy).
6. A las seis y media, hace dos horas y media que _____ y hace quince minutos que _____ (cocinar, terminar su presentación).

VOCABULARIO
¿Qué experiencia tiene Ud.?

TEMA **3**

Suggestion. Remind students that although most nouns and adjectives ending with consonants have one form for both masculine and feminine, those ending with **-or** do have a feminine form with **-ora,** and those ending with **-ista** have just one form for both masculine and feminine.

¡Ojo!

En México, se usa **un camión** para decir *a bus* y **un tráiler** para decir *a (transport) truck.*

Supplemental activities. A. ¿Qué profesiones asocia Ud. con estas palabras? *(contar, vender, manejar, comunicar, enseñar, recetar medicamentos, arreglar un carro, escribir para un periódico, los estudiantes, una casa, la televisión, una inyección)* **B.** ¿Con qué profesiones se utiliza una computadora todos los días? ¿Dónde trabaja una maestra: en una universidad o en una escuela? ¿Trabaja un médico en una universidad o en un hospital? ¿Trabaja un agricultor en una oficina o en el campo? ¿Trabaja un chófer de camiones en las carreteras o en una oficina? ¿Trabaja un dependiente en una tienda o en una escuela? ¿Trabaja un obrero en una fábrica o en una oficina? ¿Trabaja un mecánico en una tienda o en un taller? ¿Trabaja un director de recursos humanos en una oficina o una tienda? ¿en una empresa grande o en una empresa muy pequeña? ¿Para qué profesiones se necesita estudiar en la universidad? ¿para cuáles no?

¿En qué **ha trabajado**? ¿en el sistema educativo? ¿en agricultura? ¿en medicina?

He trabajado en...

contabilidad (un/a contador/a)

atención al cliente
(un/a recepcionista)
o servicio técnico
(un/a programador/a)

recursos humanos
(un/a director/a)

ventas (un/a vendedor/a, un
dependiente/una dependienta)

publicidad (un/a diseñador/a
gráfico/a)

comunicaciones (**un/a
periodista,** un/a reportero/a)

transporte (un/a chófer de
autobús/taxi/**camión**)

mantenimiento (un/a
mecánico/a) o fabricación
(un/a obrero/a)

construcción (un/a
carpintero/a)

---

ha trabajado *have you worked*   **He trabajado en...** *I have worked in...*   **un/a periodista** *a journalist*
un camión *a (transport) truck*

10-12 **¿En qué sector?** ¿En qué trabajan las siguientes personas?

Modelo   un diseñador gráfico
   Un diseñador gráfico trabaja en publicidad.

1. una vendedora
2. un recepcionista
3. un chófer de autobús
4. una maestra de primaria
5. una contadora
6. un mecánico
7. un agricultor
8. un carpintero
9. una programadora de computadoras
10. una enfermera

G **10-13** **Aptitudes laborales.** Imaginen que son asesores (*advisers*) de empleo. En grupos, describan los rasgos necesarios para los diferentes empleos.

Modelo   **Para trabajar en atención al cliente, es importante ser paciente.**

contabilidad   atención al cliente   transporte mantenimiento
recursos humanos   ventas publicidad   servicio técnico
fabricación construcción   educación

paciente   fuerte   creativo   analítico   extrovertido   organizado
persuasivo   rápido   bueno en matemáticas   atento   dedicado
intuitivo   responsable   experto en nuevas tecnologías

P **Conversaciones.** En parejas, lean la siguiente entrevista en la cual un programador de computadoras quiere cambiar de trabajo. Luego, imaginen que uno/a de Uds. busca un empleo después de graduarse de la universidad. Cambien la conversación para hablar de su trabajo.

— ¿Ha trabajado Ud. en construcción e implementación de sitios web con una empresa como ésta?
— ¿Hace dos años que trabajo a tiempo parcial en la empresa Imaginex diseñando páginas web para varias tiendas y empresas. **Estoy encargado de** diseñar y mantener las páginas.
— ¿Trabaja en equipos de diseño o independientemente?
— Trabajo en un equipo de tres diseñadores.
— ¿Por qué quiere cambiar de empleo?
— Quiero trabajar a tiempo completo con mejor sueldo y mejores beneficios.

Supplemental activity. ¿Quién tiene la profesión mejor pagada? *(una médica o una enfermera, una recepcionista o una directora de recursos humanos, una vendedora de autos o una dependienta de una tienda de ropa, un mecánico o un chófer de autobús, una programadora de computadoras o una secretaria, un maestro de escuela primaria o un profesor universitario, un contador o un obrero de fábrica, un diseñador gráfico o un carpintero)*

Follow-up for 10-13. *Aptitudes laborales.* Have students pick the two traits from the box that describe them the best and the two that describe them the least. Also have them say in which areas they would prefer to work and in which they would not like to work. Have them explain why.

AUDIO ¡A escuchar!

Escuchen una entrevista de trabajo en una empresa de seguros médicos. ¿En qué ha trabajado la candidata al puesto? ¿Por qué quiere cambiar de trabajo?

_____

estar encargado/a de *to be in charge of*

GRAMÁTICA

Hablar de experiencias: el presente perfecto

Para averiguar

1. What auxiliary verb do you use with a past participle to say what you have done? What are its forms?
2. What is one case where the present perfect is used in English but not in Spanish?

Suggestion. Point out to students that the past participle of the verb *imprimir* is *impreso* when used as an adjective, but it is *imprimido* when used in the present perfect.

Supplemental activities. A. *¿Hemos hecho las siguientes cosas en clase hoy? Modelo: hablar mucho español > Sí, hemos hablado mucho español. / No, no hemos hablado mucho español. (abrir el libro, leer algo del libro, hacer ejercicios del libro, escribir algo en la pizarra, trabajar en grupos, decir algo en inglés, ver un vídeo, escuchar música, aprender algo nuevo, abrir el cuaderno de ejercicios, comenzar el Capítulo 11)* **B.** *¿Cuántas veces ha hecho Ud. las siguientes cosas este mes? (estar enfermo/a, comer en un restaurante, salir a bailar, ir al cine, jugar al tenis, dormir hasta las once de la mañana, ver a su mejor amigo/a, leer el periódico, escribir un ensayo para una clase, llegar tarde a la clase de español, venir a clase, ir a mi oficina)*

The present perfect (**el presente perfecto**) is used to say that you have done something. It is composed of the present tense of the auxiliary verb **haber** and the past participle. In the present perfect, the past participle always ends with **-o** and does not show agreement as with adjectives.

yo	**he** trabajado	*I have worked*
tú	**has** trabajado	*you have worked*
usted, él, ella	**ha** trabajado	*you have / he, she has worked*
nosotros/as	**hemos** trabajado	*we have worked*
vosotros/as	**habéis** trabajado	*you have worked*
ustedes, ellos, ellas	**han** trabajado	*you, they have worked*

¿Cuántos trabajos **ha tenido** Ud.? — *How many jobs have you had?*

He trabajado en muchos lugares, pero nunca **he hecho** esta clase de trabajo. — *I've worked in many places, but I've never done this sort of work.*

In Spanish, the present perfect is used as in English for the most part, but remember that there is one exception. Use the present tense with **hace que** or **desde hace** to say how long someone has done something still in progress.

Hace dos años que **vivo** aquí. — *I have lived here for two years.*

Tengo este puesto **desde hace** un mes. — *I have had this position for one month.*

10-14 ¿Lo has hecho? Pregúntele a otro/a estudiante si ha hecho las siguientes cosas. Él/Ella debe decir cuántas veces las ha hecho.

Modelo trabajar en una tienda
E1: **¿Has trabajado en una tienda?**
E2: **Sí, he trabajado en dos tiendas. /**
      No, nunca he trabajado en una tienda.

1. estudiar otros idiomas
2. arreglar una computadora
3. cambiar de empleo
4. ir a una entrevista importante
5. escribir un currículum vitae
6. diseñar una página web
7. comprar un auto
8. tener un accidente automovilístico
9. manejar un autobús
10. visitar otro país

10-15 ¿Quién? ¿Quién de su familia ha hecho las siguientes actividades?

Modelo viajar mucho
Todos hemos viajado mucho. / Mi padre ha viajado mucho. / Nadie ha viajado mucho.

1. estar en México
2. ir a Europa
3. visitar España
4. estudiar francés
5. trabajar en un restaurante
6. vivir en otro país
7. cambiar de trabajo
8. tener muchos empleos
9. vender un auto
10. celebrar su compleaños este mes
11. estar muy ocupado esta semana
12. dormir mucho esta semana

10-16 Una candidata. Complete la siguiente descripción de una candidata a un puesto con el presente o el presente perfecto de los verbos indicados.

1. A las dos de la tarde la candidata __ha llegado__ (llegar) para la entrevista pero la entrevista no __ha comenzado__ (comenzar).

2. Hace solamente diez minutos que la candidata __espera__ (esperar) cuando el director de recursos humanos viene a recibirla.

3. La candidata y el director de recursos humanos __hablan__ (hablar) desde hace quince minutos cuando la secretaria les trae café.

4. La candidata le habla al director del trabajo que __hace__ (hacer) actualmente y le da referencias de las empresas donde __ha trabajado__ (trabajar).

5. El director le pregunta cuánto tiempo hace que __busca__ (buscar) un nuevo puesto y por qué __ha decidido__ (decidir) cambiar de trabajo.

6. A las tres y veinte, la candidata ya __ha salido__ (salir) de la entrevista pero todavía no (*not yet*) __ha vuelto__ (volver) a su casa.

P 10-17 Entrevista. Entreviste a otro/a estudiante con estas preguntas.

1. ¿Cuánto tiempo hace que estudias aquí? ¿Has pensado mucho en qué quieres hacer después de graduarte? ¿Has decidido a qué quieres dedicarte? ¿Ya has hecho ese tipo de trabajo anteriormente?

2. ¿Has decidido dónde quieres vivir después de graduarte? ¿Cuánto tiempo hace que vives aquí? ¿Has comprado una casa? ¿En cuántas ciudades has vivido? ¿Qué ciudades has visitado que te gustan o que no te gustan?

3. ¿Dónde trabajas ahora? ¿Cuánto tiempo hace que estás empleado/a allí? ¿Cuántos empleos has tenido? ¿Dónde has trabajado? ¿Cuál de esos empleos te gustó más? ¿Has buscado un empleo recientemente? ¿Has ido a muchas entrevistas?

G 10-18 Consejos. Sus amigos hablan de sus problemas. En grupos, preparen preguntas sobre lo que han hecho para resolverlos.

Modelo   No puedo encontrar trabajo.
  ¿Has leído las ofertas de trabajo en el periódico? ¿Has mandado tu currículum vitae a muchas empresas? ¿Has tenido muchas entrevistas?

1. No comprendo nada en la clase de español.
2. Salimos de vacaciones en dos días y no estamos listos.
3. Siempre me siento cansada y estoy enferma con frecuencia.

Follow-up for 10-16. *Una candidata.* Refer students to the illustrations of the businessman's day on p. 301. Ask students if he has done the indicated things at the given times. *Modelo: A las nueve... (salir de la casa) > Sí, ha salido de la casa a las nueve.* 1. A las nueve y media... (empezar a trabajar, llegar al trabajo, dar su presentación) 2. A las doce y media... (pedir algo de comer, empezar a almorzar, comer toda la ensalada) 3. A las dos... (terminar el almuerzo, ir a la reunión con otros empleados, empezar su presentación, terminar su presentación) 4. A las cuatro... (terminar su presentación, volver a su oficina, volver a casa) 5. A las seis y cuarto de la tarde... (salir del trabajo, volver a la casa, empezar a preparar la cena, cenar)

Supplemental activities. A. Have students make a list of five things they haven't done lately that they need to do or things they have done that they shouldn't have. *Modelo: No he hablado con mis padres. He salido demasiado con los amigos y no he estudiado lo suficiente.* **B.** Have students make a list of three things they haven't done but would like to. *Modelos: No he visitado México pero me gustaría visitarlo. No he visto la nueva película de Halle Berry pero me gustaría verla.*

VOCABULARIO
¿Qué han hecho?

**el/la contador/a
(calcular el pago,
pagar las cuentas
y los impuestos)**

**el/la secretario/a
(distribuir el correo,
introducir datos, archivar
documentos, comprar
artículos de oficina)**

**el/la programador/a
(programar
las computadoras,
arreglar
las computadoras,
diseñar y mantener
las páginas web)**

**el/la director/a
de recursos humanos
(contratar/despedir (i,i)
a los empleados, recibir
solicitudes de empleo)**

**el/la supervisor/a
(entrenar a los empleados
y evaluar sus progresos,
aprobar (ue)
las decisiones)**

**el/la recepcionista
(contestar el teléfono,
recibir a los visitantes)**

**el/la diseñador/a
gráfico/a
(diseñar publicidad,
dibujar, pintar)**

---

los impuestos *the taxes* **introducir** *to input* **contratar** *to hire* **despedir (i, i)** *to fire*
una solicitud de empleo *a job application* **entrenar** *to train* **dibujar** *to draw* **pintar** *to paint*

10-19 ¿Lo han hecho? En una oficina, se ha hecho una de las siguientes cosas pero no se ha hecho la otra. ¿Cuál han hecho?

Modelo distribuir los cheques / calcular el pago
Han calculado el pago pero no han distribuido los cheques.

1. empezar a trabajar / llegar al trabajo
2. encender la fotocopiadora / sacar las copias
3. instalar la nueva computadora / conectar la impresora
4. contratar al nuevo empleado / recibir las solicitudes de empleo
5. entrenar a los empleados / evaluar sus progresos
6. despedir a la recepcionista / contratar a otra persona
7. publicar (*publish*) una oferta de empleo / recibir muchas solicitudes
8. volver a casa / apagar las luces

10-20 Problemas. Usted trabaja para una empresa grande y un colega le pregunta si ha hablado con las personas apropiadas para resolver estos problemas. ¿Qué le diría Ud. (*would you say*)?

Modelo Hay un problema con las computadoras.
¿Has hablado con los programadores en el servicio técnico?

1. Dijeron cosas falsas en mi evaluación.
2. Me retienen demasiado de mi sueldo en impuestos.
3. Envié (*I sent*) una solicitud para el nuevo puesto pero no me han llamado para una entrevista.
4. Un cliente viene a verme pero no sé si ha llegado.
5. Cada día recibo correo que no es para mí. Es para otra a persona.
6. Nadie me ha enseñado cómo hacer este trabajo.
7. La publicidad nueva de la empresa no me gusta.
8. La página web de la empresa no funciona bien. Cuando hago una búsqueda no localiza nada.

Conversaciones. Una supervisora habla con la secretaria de un problema en el trabajo. En parejas, lean la conversación; luego, preparen una conversación en la cual uno/a de Uds. habla con su supervisor/a o profesor/a de algún problema que ha encontrado en su trabajo o en una clase. Digan también qué ha hecho para resolverlo.

— ¿Ya ha introducido los datos que le di en la computadora?
— Todavía no. El sistema de computadoras no funciona otra vez. He llamado al departamento de servicio técnico, pero dudo que hayan resuelto el problema.
— ¿Han dicho cuánto tiempo vamos a estar sin acceso a las computadoras?
— No, no me han dicho nada. Dudo que funcionen por varias horas.
— ¿Cuántas veces **ha fallado** el sistema este mes?
— Ya van tres veces.

Supplemental activity. After presenting the placement of direct object pronouns in the present perfect on the next page, do the following continuation for 10-19. *¿Lo han hecho?* En una oficina, se ha hecho una de las siguientes cosas pero no se ha hecho la otra. ¿Cuál han hecho? Utilice un pronombre de complemento directo en la segunda parte de la oración. *Modelo:* sacar copias de los documentos / archivar los documentos > *Han sacado copias de los documentos pero no los han archivado.* 1. encender la computadora / enchufar la computadora 2. contratar a los nuevos empleados / entrenar a los nuevos empleados 3. distribuir los artículos de oficina / comprar los artículos de oficina 4. leer el correo / distribuir el correo 5. diseñar la publicidad / publicar la publicidad 6. tener muchos problemas con el nuevo empleado / despedir al nuevo empleado 7. pagar las cuentas / recibir las cuentas 8. traer la nueva fotocopiadora / pedir la nueva fotocopiadora

AUDIO ¡A escuchar!

Escuchen otra conversación en la cual dos colegas hablan de sus problemas con otro empleado. ¿Quién es y qué problemas tienen con él? ¿Por qué no lo despiden?

fallar *to fail, to be down*

GRAMÁTICA

Expresar acciones pasadas relevantes en el presente: los pronombres de complemento directo e indirecto con el presente perfecto

In the present perfect, reflexive and direct and indirect object pronouns are placed before the conjugated form of the auxiliary verb **haber.**

— ¿**Te** has familiarizado con esta cuenta?
— Sí, **me** he informado de todos los detalles.

— *Have you familiarized yourself with this account?*
— *Yes. I've found out all the details.*

— ¿Has preparado el informe?
— No, todavía no **lo** he hecho.

— *Have you prepared the report?*
— *No, I haven't done it yet.*

— ¿**Les** han escrito las cartas a los clientes?
— Sí, **se las** hemos escrito a todos.

— *Have you written the letters to the clients?*
— *Yes, I have written them to all of them.*

Review the forms of these pronouns. Remember that, as in the preceding example, the indirect object pronouns **le** and **les** change to **se** when followed by the direct object pronouns **lo, la, los,** or **las.**

REFLEXIVE	DIRECT OBJECT	INDIRECT OBJECT
me	me	me
te	te	te
se	lo	le
se	la	le
nos	nos	nos
os	os	os
se	los	les
se	las	les

10-21 Esta semana. Utilice el pronombre **me** con el presente perfecto de los verbos indicados para describir sus interacciones esta semana con las siguientes personas.

Modelo Mis padres… (ver)
Sí, mis padres me han visto esta semana. /
No, mis padres no me han visto esta semana.

1. Mis padres (ver, escribir un correo electrónico, llamar por teléfono, poner furioso/a, llevar a un restaurante)
2. Mi mejor amigo/a (invitar a salir, prestar dinero, pedir dinero, hablar mucho, visitar)
3. Mi profesor/a de español (hacer muchas preguntas, dar mucha tarea, decir la tarea para la próxima clase, ver todos los días)

ⓅP 10-22 ¿Qué has hecho? Es lunes y un amigo que llama a las horas indicadas le pregunta si ha hecho las siguientes cosas. En parejas, hagan los papeles.

> **Modelo**   a las ocho de la mañana
>
> E1: **¿Te has levantado?**
> E2: **Sí, me levanté hace una hora. /**
>   **No, no me he levantado. Todavía estoy en la cama.**

1. a las nueve de la mañana   **2.** a las diez de la mañana   **3.** a las once de la noche

Ahora, pregúntele si ha hecho estas cosas si es sábado.

10-23 ¿Quién? Un supervisor le pregunta a su secretaria si ha hecho las siguientes cosas. ¿Qué le pregunta? Utilice un pronombre de complemento directo con un verbo lógico.

organizar	hacer	conocer	distribuir	comprar
introducir	sacar	leer	pedir	archivar

> **Modelo**   el correo
> **¿Lo has distribuido? / ¿Lo has leído?**

1. los datos
2. mi oficina
3. el café
4. tu evaluación
5. los artículos de oficina que necesitamos
6. los documentos en mi escritorio que ya no necesito
7. las copias
8. la nueva empleada

ⓅP 10-24 ¿Y tú? Complete las oraciones y pregúntele a otro/a estudiante si está familiarizado/a con las cosas o los lugares mencionados. Utilice un verbo lógico como en el modelo.

> **Modelo**   Quiero ir a…
> E1: **Quiero ir a la Ciudad de México. ¿La has visitado?**
> E2: **No, no la he visitado. / Sí, la he visitado.**

1. Quiero ver la película…
2. Me gusta la nueva canción (*song*)…
3. Me gusta mucho el libro…
4. Quiero visitar la ciudad de…
5. Quiero estudiar…
6. Necesito aprender…
7. Nunca he comido…
8. Quiero probar el restaurante…

VOCABULARIO

TEMA 5

En el banco

un/a cajero/a

una ventanilla

depositar (un depósito, el depósito directo)

retirar (un retiro)

ahorrar (una cuenta de ahorros)

un/a banquero/a

obtener un préstamo, completar un formulario

un cajero automático

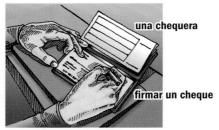

una chequera

firmar un cheque

una cuenta corriente

una tarjeta de débito

una tarjeta de crédito con una buena tasa de interés

un billete

dinero en efectivo

cambiar cheques de viaje

Supplemental activity. ¿Ha hecho Ud. las siguientes cosas este mes? *(depositar dinero en el banco, retirar dinero del banco, ir al banco, utilizar un cajero automático, obtener un préstamo, firmar muchos cheques, gastar mucho dinero, ahorrar mucho dinero, cargar mucho a una tarjeta de crédito)*

ahorrar *to save (money)* **un préstamo** *a loan* **una tasa de interés** *an interest rate*
una cuenta corriente *a checking account*

P **10-25** **Entrevista.** Entreviste a otro/a estudiante con estas preguntas.

1. ¿Te gusta tu banco? ¿Tienes acceso a tu cuenta por Internet? ¿Retiras dinero de los cajeros automáticos con frecuencia? ¿Cuánto te cobran (*charge*) si utilizas un cajero automático de otro banco?

2. ¿Cómo pagas generalmente cuando vas de compras? ¿con cheque? ¿con efectivo? ¿con tarjeta de crédito? ¿con tarjeta de débito? ¿Tienes tarjeta de crédito? ¿Cargas mucho a la tarjeta?

3. ¿Has obtenido un préstamo para pagar los estudios? ¿Cuál es la tasa de interés?

10-26 **Bancos.** Lea las descripciones de los servicios ofrecidos por un banco. ¿Son importantes para Ud. o no son necesarios?

Modelo **No es necesario que tengan muchas sucursales (*branches*) a través de todo el país.**

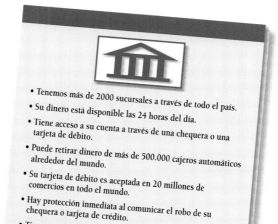

- Tenemos más de 2000 sucursales a través de todo el país.
- Su dinero está disponible las 24 horas del día.
- Tiene acceso a su cuenta a través de una chequera o una tarjeta de débito.
- Puede retirar dinero de más de 500.000 cajeros automáticos alrededor del mundo.
- Su tarjeta de débito es aceptada en 20 millones de comercios en todo el mundo.
- Hay protección inmediata al comunicar el robo de su chequera o tarjeta de crédito.
- Tiene permanente acceso sin costo a la información sobre su cuenta por Internet.

Suggestion for 10-26. *Bancos.* Use this activity to review the uses and forms of the subjunctive as a preview of the subjunctive with expressions of emotion and the present perfect subjunctive, which are presented on the next page.

P **Conversaciones.** En parejas, lean la siguiente conversación en la cual dos amigos hablan de sus bancos. Luego, preparen una conversación para hablar de sus propios bancos.

— Quiero cambiar de banco. ¿Conoces un buen banco con **una sucursal** cerca de aquí?

— Me gusta **el mío** pero no está cerca de aquí. Tengo depósito directo y hago casi todos mis **trámites** en línea o por teléfono. Siempre saco dinero de los cajeros automáticos. ¿Por qué quieres cambiar de banco?

— Si no tengo un depósito mínimo de 1.000 dólares me **cobran** 10 dólares al mes por mantener la cuenta corriente y tengo que pagar 2 dólares cada vez que utilizo un cajero automático.

— ¿De veras? Me **sorprende** que te cobren tanto.

— Sí, y además mi tarjeta de crédito con este banco tiene una tasa de interés del 18 por ciento.

— Debes probar mi banco en línea. No hay muchos cargos por los servicios y es muy práctico.

Follow-up for *Conversaciones.* Have students react to the following statements using *Es bueno que..., Es ridículo que..., Es una lástima que... Modelo:* Las tarjetas de crédito tienen una tasa de interés baja. > *Es bueno que las tarjetas de crédito tengan una tasa de interés baja.* 1. Le cobran diez dólares al mes por mantener una cuenta corriente. 2. Todos los trámites se hacen en línea. 3. Hay muchos cajeros automáticos cerca de su casa y su trabajo. 4. Los cajeros automáticos no funcionan con frecuencia. 5. No aceptan depósito directo. 6. Las sucursales están abiertas hasta las siete de la tarde. 7. No se puede sacar dinero si las computadoras del banco no funcionan. 8. Siempre hay muchos errores en su cuenta.

---

una sucursal *a branch office* **el/la mío/a** *mine* **un trámite** *a transaction* **cobrar** *to charge*
sorprender *to surprise*

GRAMÁTICA

Los sentimientos y la verificación: el subjuntivo para expresar las emociones y el presente perfecto del subjuntivo

Para averiguar

1. What are ten expressions of emotion that are followed by the subjunctive?
2. When do you use the present perfect subjunctive?
3. How do you form the present perfect subjunctive? What are the forms of **haber** in the subjunctive?

Suggestion. Point out to students that they have already seen *haya* as the subjunctive of *hay,* and that *haber* is the infinitive of *hay.* Ask them what the present perfect of *hay* (*there has been*) would be in Spanish.

Supplemental activity. In groups, have students complete the following statements with as many different endings as they can think of. 1. A los profesores les gusta (molesta) que los estudiantes... 2. A los estudiantes les gusta (molesta) que los profesores... 3. A los padres les gusta (molesta) que los hijos... 4. A los hijos les gusta (molesta) que los padres... 5. A los supervisores les gusta (molesta) que los empleados... 6. A los empleados les gusta (molesta) que los supervisores... 7. A los hombres les gusta (molesta) que las mujeres... 8. A las mujeres les gusta (molesta) que los hombres...

You have already used the subjunctive to express opinions or doubts about what should or might happen. It is also used to express feelings about what happens after the following expressions describing emotions.

alegrarse de que…	*to be happy that…*
estar contento/a de que…	*to be glad that…*
estar triste de que…	*to be sad that…*
sentir (ie) que…	*to be sorry that…*
temer que…	*to fear that…*
tener miedo de que…	*to be afraid that…*
me/te… gusta que…	*I/you… like that…*
me/te… encanta que…	*I/you… love that…*
me/te… molesta que…	*It bothers me/you… that…*
me/te… sorprende que…	*It surprises me/you… that…*

Me molesta que la fotocopiadora nunca **funcione.** Me sorprende que no **compren** una nueva.	*It bothers me that the copier never works. It surprises me that they don't buy a new one.*

Use the present perfect subjunctive to express feelings or doubts about what has happened or will have happened. The present perfect subjunctive is formed by using the subjunctive of the auxiliary verb **haber** and the past participle.

PRESENT PERFECT SUBJUNCTIVE	
que yo	**haya** trabajado
que tú	**hayas** trabajado
que usted, él, ella	**haya** trabajado
que nosotros/as	**hayamos** trabajado
que vosotros/as	**hayáis** trabajado
que ustedes, ellos, ellas	**hayan** trabajado

Me alegro de que **hayas tenido** varias entrevistas.	*I'm happy that you've had several interviews.*
Dudo que **hayan contratado** a otra persona.	*I doubt that they've hired another person.*

10-27 Los titulares. Exprese sus sentimientos sobre los siguientes titulares del periódico universitario.

Modelo   La matrícula (*tuition*) sube.
No me gusta que la matrícula suba.

10-28 Un puesto nuevo. Un amigo le habla del nuevo trabajo de su esposa. Reaccione a lo que dice, comenzando cada oración con **Me alegro de que…** o **Siento que….**

Modelo   Mi esposa tiene un nuevo trabajo.
Me alegro de que tenga un nuevo trabajo.

1. Le pagan mucho más.
2. Su trabajo es un poco aburrido.
3. Trabaja hasta tarde cada noche.
4. Su supervisor es gruñón.
5. Tiene beneficios excelentes.
6. Le dan cinco semanas de vacaciones pagadas.
7. No puede tomar vacaciones por un año.

Después de unos meses, el mismo amigo le dice las siguientes cosas. Reaccione, usando el presente perfecto del subjuntivo.

Modelo   Han despedido al supervisor gruñón de mi esposa.
Me alegro de que lo hayan despedido.

1. Le han dado un aumento a mi esposa.
2. La han hecho supervisora.
3. Ha tenido problemas con muchos de sus empleados.
4. No ha podido descansar desde que aceptó el puesto de supervisora.
5. Ha trabajado todos los sábados y domingos de este mes.
6. Ya ha resuelto casi todos los problemas en su oficina.

Un profesor de ciencias ecológicas recibe el Premio Nóbel.

Los profesores reciben más dinero.

Todos tienen que estudiar lenguas extranjeras.

CREAN MÁS LUGARES DE ESTACIONAMIENTO.

La policía da multas por comer o beber en la biblioteca.

LA BIBLIOTECA ESTÁ ABIERTA MÁS HORAS.

El nuevo estacionamiento cuesta dos dólares la hora.

Se permite fumar en las clases.

Hay menos ayuda financiera.

Más horas de matemáticas son necesarias para graduarse.

G 10-29 Una mentira. En un papel escriba dos cosas interesantes que haya hecho y una mentira (*a lie*) sobre algo que no haya hecho. Luego, lea las oraciones en voz alta y los otros miembros de su grupo dirán (*will say*) de cuál dudan.

Modelo   E1: **He vivido en México, he visto al presidente y he estado en España.**
E2: **Dudo que hayas vivido en México.**
E3: **Yo también dudo que hayas vivido en México.**
E4: **No, no es cierto que hayas visto al presidente.**
E1: **Tú tienes razón, Rick. No he visto al presidente.**

Follow-up for 10-28. *Un puesto nuevo.* Have students state good things or bad things that have happened to them recently. Then have another student express sympathy or joy using *Siento que…* or *Me alegro de que…*

Supplemental activities. A. ¿Ha hecho su mejor amigo/a las siguientes cosas hoy? Comience cada oración con *Estoy seguro/a de que, Es probable que* o *Dudo que…* Modelo: levantarse > *Estoy seguro/a de que se ha levantado. / Dudo que se haya levantado.* (salir de la casa, ir al trabajo, llegar a la universidad, almorzar / desayunar, ir a la iglesia, ir de compras, comprar un carro nuevo, quedarse en casa, dormir hasta ahora) B. Bring several gossip magazines to class and read statements of things that have supposedly happened. Students react with an expression of doubt or emotion. *Modelos:* Alguien ha visto a Elvis en un supermercado. > *Dudo que alguien haya visto a Elvis en un supermercado.* Han nominado a Jennifer López para el Oscar a la mejor actriz. > *(No) Me sorprende que la hayan nominado para el Oscar a la mejor actriz.* Depending on the level of your students and the amount of class time you have, you may wish to have groups of students prepare the statements, using the magazines. C. Have students think of two or three things that they hope have (not) happened when they return home today. *Modelos: Espero que mi compañero de casa haya limpiado el baño. Ojalá que no haya habido un incendio.*

Note: Have students complete the *Antes de leer, Reading strategies,* and *Ahora Ud.* activities before reading this article.

REVISTA CULTURAL

MÁS ALLÁ DE LAS FRONTERAS

La **creciente** población latina en Estados Unidos ha justificado la entrada en el mercado norteamericano de muchas compañías hispanas que han visto sus horizontes expandidos más allá de las fronteras de Latinoamérica. Hoy en día son muchas las empresas hispanas que tienen oficinas abiertas en Estados Unidos, o **acuerdos** establecidos con compañías norteamericanas para la distribución de sus productos en Estados Unidos.

Una de estas compañías es Novamex, subsidiaria de Axis Corporativo S.A, empresa con **sede central** en Ciudad Juárez, México. Novamex, **establecida** en El Paso, Texas, está especializada en la importación y distribución de alimentos y refrescos mexicanos en el mercado estadounidense. Novamex es una empresa bicultural, conocedora del consumidor mexicoamericano en Estados Unidos, que realiza sus comunicaciones de ventas en español.

La cadena de hoteles española Sol Meliá **se abre camino** en la industria hotelera estadounidense con la apertura en 2004 de su primer hotel en el país: el *Hard Rock Hotel Chicago*. Este proyecto es **fruto de** la alianza formada un año antes entre Sol Meliá y Rank Group, empresa **propietaria** de la cadena de hoteles y restaurantes Hard Rock. Los hoteles Hard Rock, de diseño moderno, están situados en los centros urbanos y ofrecen muchos atractivos al

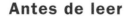

turista. Sol Meliá proyecta abrir próximamente nuevos hoteles Hard Rock en San Diego y Nueva York.

Otro ejemplo es ArtInSoft S.A., empresa pionera en el desarrollo del *software* en Costa Rica, que surgió como una alternativa a las **industrias bananeras** y del café. ArtInSoft estableció en el año 2001 acuerdos con Intel y Microsoft para **promover** la investigación y el desarrollo de nuevas tecnologías de *software*, y cuenta con oficinas en Colorado, Florida y Virginia.

El grupo financiero BBVA (Banco Bilbao Vizcaya Argentaria), fundado en 1857 en España, posee sucursales bancarias en 35 países de Asia, Europa, Latinoamérica y también Estados Unidos, en Miami y Nueva York. Recientemente el BBVA ha hecho su incursión en el mercado de la banca estadounidense con la adquisición del Valley Bank, un pequeño banco de California con sólo seis oficinas al sur de Los Ángeles. Esta experiencia piloto en California, el estado con más de diez millones de hispanos censados, va a permitir al BBVA explorar nuevas posibilidades de expansión en Estados Unidos.

Vivimos en la era de la globalización, donde se han abierto nuevos **caminos empresariales,** nuevas vías de desarrollo tecnológico y **canales** de exportación y distribución de productos nacionales, y **el empresario** latino es cada vez más consciente de estas oportunidades.

Antes de leer

Examine con atención los logotipos que acompañan a la lectura. ¿Con qué tipo de producto o servicio los asociaría (*would you associate them*)? ¿Qué tipo de compañía cree que representan? ¿Hay algún indicador en el nombre de las empresas del tipo de negocio que éstas realizan?

Reading strategies: Mapping. When reading a foreign language, it is often useful to organize the information that is given in a diagram. Such diagrams help you assimilate the content of a text by showing how its different elements are connected. You can use different types of maps—charts, trees, chains—to arrange the main elements and the secondary information of the reading. Look at the conceptual tree on the following page that provides a visual map of the accompanying text.

---

más allá de las fronteras *beyond the borders*   **creciente** *growing*   **acuerdos** *agreements*   **sede central** *headquarters*   **establecida** *established*
se abre camino *is making its way*   **fruto de** *the result of*   **propietaria** *owner*   **industria bananera** *banana industry*   **promover** *to promote*
caminos empresariales *business paths*   **canales** *channels*   **el empresario** *the entrepreneur*

Las empresarias hispanas son una floreciente comunidad que crea empleos y genera beneficios económicos para la nación.

Una de cada seis mujeres empresarias actualmente en California es hispana y en Nuevo México lo es una de cada cinco. La Asociación Nacional de Mujeres Hispanas de Negocios (NLBWA) indica que hay casi 500.000 empresas de mujeres hispanas en Estados Unidos, con capitales que ascienden a más de 29.400 millones de dólares anuales. La Asociación Nacional de Mujeres Hispanas de Negocios ofrece cursos interactivos de ocho semanas para las interesadas en iniciar su propia empresa. De acuerdo con las cifras del Censo, las empresarias hispanas ofrecen actualmente empleo a cerca de 200.000 personas en la nación y en diversas industrias.

María de Cárdenas es un modelo de empresaria hispana. Directora de comunicaciones de mercado de Cacique, una marca de quesos y otros derivados de leche en el área de Los Ángeles, es un vivo ejemplo de cómo combinar la profesión con el servicio social. Profesionalmente, ha contribuido a colocar la firma Cacique como líder entre las empresas de su categoría en la nación. En el área del servicio social, Cárdenas ha impulsado en los últimos años campañas en beneficio de organizaciones como el Hospital de los Niños de Los Ángeles, la Asociación Americana de Diabetes y el Hogar del Niño, entre otros.

Después de leer

10-30 Ahora Ud. ¿Cuál es el tema principal del artículo *Más allá de las fronteras*? ¿Cuáles son las ideas secundarias? Organice esta información en un árbol conceptual (*conceptual tree*) asegurándose que ofrece una visión completa.

10-31 A la caza de participios. Identifique los participios pasados que aparecen en la lectura *Más allá de las fronteras* y explique su significado.

PARTICIPIO	EQUIVALENTE EN INGLÉS
Modelo expandidos	*expanded*

10-32 Un paso más. Conteste las siguientes preguntas relacionadas con la lectura.

1. ¿Qué ha impulsado (*has driven*) la entrada de compañías latinas en el mercado norteamericano?
2. ¿Qué sectores empresariales se mencionan en el artículo?
3. ¿En qué estados han establecido oficinas las compañías mencionadas en el artículo? ¿Es relevante la localización geográfica de estas nuevas oficinas?
4. ¿Cuáles han sido algunas de las consecuencias positivas de la globalización?

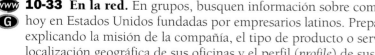

10-33 En la red. En grupos, busquen información sobre compañías que operan hoy en Estados Unidos fundadas por empresarios latinos. Preparen un informe explicando la misión de la compañía, el tipo de producto o servicio que ofrece, la localización geográfica de sus oficinas y el perfil (*profile*) de sus trabajadores. Presenten su informe en la próxima clase.

Ideas secundarias

- La presencia de empresarias hispanas es especialmente visible en California y Nuevo México.
- La Asociación Nacional de Mujeres Hispanas de Negocios informa del número de empresas dirigidas por hispanas y de los capitales anuales de estas empresas.
- La Asociación Nacional de Mujeres Hispanas de Negocios ofrece cursos interactivos para las mujeres interesadas en abrir un negocio.
- El modelo de empresaria hispana combina los negocios con el servicio social.

Ideas principales

- El número de mujeres hispanas que tienen su propia empresa en Estados Unidos aumenta.
- Las empresarias hispanas en Estados Unidos tienen mucho éxito en los negocios.
- Los negocios dirigidos por empresarias hispanas crean empleos y generan beneficios para la economía norteamericana.

Suggestions. Have students work in groups to discuss positive and negative effects of globalization.

De puertas abiertas a la comunidad

📹 EMPRESARIOS HISPANOS

Ⓟ 10-34   Entrando en materia. Piensen en pequeños negocios que haya en su vecindario. ¿Qué tipo de negocios son? ¿Qué productos venden? ¿Quiénes son sus dueños? ¿Creen que tienen dificultades compitiendo con grandes negocios?

> Las empresas latinas triunfan hoy en Estados Unidos y compiten ya con otros negocios nacionales. Cada vez son más los **empresarios** que, **respaldados** por **la Cámara de Comercio Hispana** de Estados Unidos, contribuyen a **fortalecer** la economía estadounidense con sus negocios. Muchas de las compañías fundadas por latinos en Estados Unidos son negocios familiares que generalmente están orientados a **mejorar** la calidad de vida de los hispanos, ofreciéndoles alternativas nuevas en los distintos sectores comerciales. En este capítulo van a escuchar el testimonio de dos de estos empresarios, dueños de pequeños negocios en la ciudad de Nueva York, Carlos Arias y Alejandro Cantagallo, que nos hablan de sus comienzos, del desarrollo de sus empresas, y de los servicios que ofrecen a la comunidad hispana de la ciudad. También vamos a escuchar una **voz representante** de la Cámara de Comercio Hispana de Manhattan, que nos ofrece información sobre las oportunidades empresariales para los latinos en la ciudad y los eventos que la institución realiza para fortalecer la presencia de negocios latinos en la economía norteamericana.

Ⓟ 10-35 Hace que... Lean con atención la información personal de María Álvarez y Carlos Arias y respondan a las preguntas que siguen utilizando la estructura **hace que** para expresar la duración de una acción.

> *María Álvarez Castro vive en la ciudad de Nueva York desde el año 1970. Es original de Guayaquil, Ecuador y trabaja como presidenta de la Cámara de Comercio Hispana desde el año 1989.*

> *Carlos Arias tiene veintiocho años de edad y es original de la República Dominicana. Vino a los Estados Unidos a los catorce años. Es dueño de un day spa que abrió en el año 2003.*

1. ¿Cuánto tiempo hace que María vive en la ciudad de Nueva York?

_____.

2. ¿Cuánto tiempo hace que María trabaja en la Cámara de Comercio Hispana?

_____.

3. ¿Cuánto tiempo hace que Carlos vino a los Estados Unidos?

_____.

4. ¿Cuánto tiempo hace que Carlos abrió su negocio?

_____.

---

empresarios *businessmen*   **respaldados** *supported*   **la Cámara de Comercio Hispana** *Hispanic Chamber of Commerce*   **fortalecer** *to strengthen*   **mejorar** *to improve*   **voz representante** *spokesperson*

10-36 La Cámara de Comercio Hispana. Complete la siguiente información sobre la Cámara de Comercio Hispana con la forma del presente perfecto de los verbos entre paréntesis.

La Cámara de Comercio Hispana de Nueva York ___ha tenido___ (1. tener) mucho éxito (*success*) en estos últimos años. Esta organización sin fines de lucro (*nonprofit*) ___ha ayudado___ (2. ayudar) a muchos empresarios a abrir nuevos negocios y ___ha hecho___ (3. hacer) crecer el número de negocios hispanos en la ciudad. María Álvarez ___ha visto___ (4. ver) las oportunidades que la Cámara les ___ha dado___ (5. dar) a los empresarios hispanos y ella, como presidenta, ___ha puesto___ (6. poner) a los empresarios hispanos en una posición mejor.

10-37 Un *day spa*. Conteste las siguientes preguntas relacionadas con el testimonio de Carlos Arias, dueño de un *day spa* en el Bronx, Nueva York.

1. ¿Cómo surgió (*came up*) la idea de su negocio?

_____.

2. ¿Con quién trabaja Carlos en el *day spa*?

_____.

3. ¿Qué servicios ofrecen en el *day spa*?

_____.

4. ¿Qué clientela cree usted que va a su negocio?

_____.

5. ¿Qué ha aprendido Carlos este año del negocio?

_____.

10-38 La bodega Don Francisco. Escuche con atención la información que Alejandro nos da sobre su bodega y cómo sirve a la comunidad hispana en su barrio. Luego, conteste las siguientes preguntas.

1. ¿Qué tipo de clientela viene a la bodega Don Francisco?

_____.

2. ¿Qué productos se venden más?

_____.

3. ¿Qué valor tiene la bodega para las personas del barrio?

_____.

(G) 10-39 Cualidades laborales. Imaginen qué aptitudes laborales necesitan las personas en el vídeo para hacer bien su trabajo.

> **Modelo**   **Para trabajar en el/la _____ es importante ser _____.**

APTITUDES LABORALES	
María en la Cámara de Comercio Hispana	
Alejandro en la bodega	
Carlos en el *day spa*	

10-40 Me alegra que... Después de escuchar los testimonios de estos pequeños empresarios, exprese sus sentimientos personales en relación al trabajo que realizan estas personas, a sus logros (*achievements*) y al futuro de sus negocios. Utilice las estructuras con subjuntivo que aprendió en el capítulo.

Answers for 10-37. Un *day spa*.
1. El negocio surgió de la idea y la cabeza de su mamá, que estaba trabajando en un salón de belleza y estaba haciendo tratamientos en la casa como un *part time*. 2. Carlos trabaja con su madre en el *day spa*. 3. Tratamientos faciales, masajes corporales, el parafango, que es un tratamiento para la piel, para la celulitis, la yesoterapia para rebajar de peso, depilaciones y maquillajes permanentes 4. *Answers will vary.* 5. *Answers will vary.*

Answers for 10-38. La bodega Don Francisco. 1. Una clientela muy internacional, de todas partes de Sur y Centroamérica: argentinos, uruguayos, colombianos, ecuatorianos, mexicanos y muchos centroamericanos. 2. El

producto más popular es la carne, los famosos chorizos de Don Francisco, y los productos importados de Argentina y de Uruguay. 3. Es un negocio donde se conoce al cliente. Es un lugar familiar adonde la gente viene a comer; es una cosa de todos los días para las personas del barrio venir a esta carnicería.

Escapadas

CHILE, ENIGMÁTICO

Chile se extiende **a orillas del** Océano Pacífico con su fina silueta alargada de aproximadamente 2.700 millas de **longitud** y sólo 150 millas de **anchura.** Sus países vecinos son al norte Perú, al noreste Bolivia y al este Argentina.

Aunque la población chilena es en su mayoría de ascendencia europea, todavía sobreviven las tradiciones de los indios araucanos en las celebraciones y el arte populares. Desde el silencioso desierto de Atacama al norte, con géisers impresionantes, hasta los glaciares de la Patagonia, Chile ofrece al visitante escenarios geográficos y culturales fascinantes.

Glaciares en el Parque Nacional Torres del Paine, Chile.

La Cordillera de la Sal, Desierto de Atacama, Chile.

La vendimia, viñedo de Cousino Macul, Santiago de Chile.

La capital, Santiago de Chile, es una ciudad moderna y es el centro financiero por excelencia del país, que posee hoy una de las economías más dinámicas de Sudamérica. Chile tiene, además de impresionantes recursos naturales, una importante **industria vinícola,** que lo convierte en el tercer mayor exportador de vinos del mundo. La ruta del vino en el Valle de Conchagua ofrece al visitante la oportunidad de **saborear** los vinos chilenos y aprender sobre su proceso de producción.

a orillas de *on the shore of* **longitud** *length* **anchura** *width* **aunque** *although* **industria vinícola** *wine industry* **saborear** *to taste*

Cerca de Santiago se encuentran **estaciones de esquí** sensacionales y las famosas playas de Valparaíso. Al norte de la capital se celebra uno de los festivales musicales de mayor fama internacional, el Festival Internacional de la Canción, en la preciosa ciudad marítima de Viña del Mar. Allí se reúnen todos los años en febrero talentos musicales de todo el mundo.

Cierto aire de misterio **envuelve** los territorios chilenos del sur, extendidos hasta la Antártida, y algunas de sus islas, como la Isla de Pascua. La Isla de Pascua, también conocida como "Los ojos que miran al cielo" en rapanui, su lengua **autóctona,** es un lugar enigmático que, **a pesar de** su **aislamiento,** ha conservado viva la cultura polinesia entre sus aproximadamente 3.300 habitantes. La Isla de Pascua está localizada a unos 3.800 kilómetros de la costa de Chile, y allí los habitantes viven de forma sencilla, alejados de la euforia de nuestra sociedad y dedicados a la pesca y a las artesanías.

Valparaíso, Chile.

Pescadores en el puerto de Hanga Roa, la Isla de Pascua, Chile.

Todavía hoy no se conoce el origen de las gigantescas estatuas de basalto volcánico, los moais, algunas de ellas de unos 13 pies de altura y 14 toneladas de peso, que **se elevan** en la Isla de Pascua a orillas del océano mirando al mar, contemplando desde la distancia el paso del tiempo.

La Isla de Pascua, Chile.

Los moais de la Isla de Pascua, Chile.

10-41 Sobre la lectura. Conteste las siguientes preguntas relacionadas con el contenido de la lectura.

1. ¿Cuáles son algunas de las características geográficas de Chile?
2. Mencione algunas de las actividades que el turista puede realizar durante su visita al país.
3. ¿Es Chile un país en vías (*in process*) de desarrollo económico?
4. ¿Dónde está situada la Isla de Pascua? ¿Quiénes son sus habitantes? ¿Cómo viven?
5. ¿Qué son los moais? ¿Por qué son tan misteriosos?

estaciones de esquí *ski resorts* **envuelve** *surrounds* **autóctona** *indigenous* **a pesar de** *despite* **aislamiento** *isolation* **se elevan** *rise*

10-42 Desde Chile con amor. Complete la postal (*postcard*) que Sofía le escribe a David desde Chile utilizando el presente de indicativo o el presente perfecto de los verbos en paréntesis.

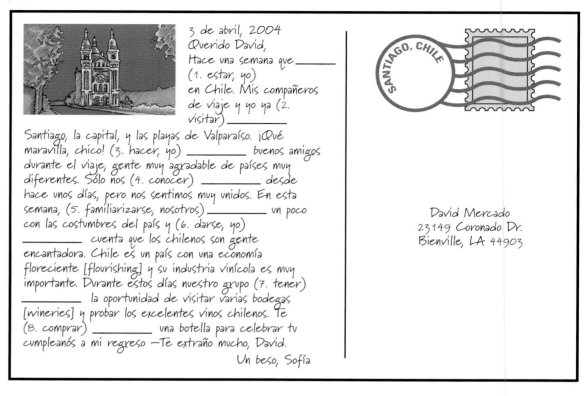

3 de abril, 2004
Querido David,
Hace una semana que _____ (1. estar, yo) en Chile. Mis compañeros de viaje y yo ya (2. visitar) _____ Santiago, la capital, y las playas de Valparaíso. ¡Qué maravilla, chico! (3. hacer, yo) _____ buenos amigos durante el viaje, gente muy agradable de países muy diferentes. Sólo nos (4. conocer) _____ desde hace unos días, pero nos sentimos muy unidos. En esta semana, (5. familiarizarse, nosotros) _____ un poco con las costumbres del país y (6. darse, yo) _____ cuenta que los chilenos son gente encantadora. Chile es un país con una economía floreciente [*flourishing*] y su industria vinícola es muy importante. Durante estos días nuestro grupo (7. tener) _____ la oportunidad de visitar varias bodegas [*wineries*] y probar los excelentes vinos chilenos. Te (8. comprar) _____ una botella para celebrar tu cumpleanós a mi regreso —Te extraño mucho, David.
Un beso, Sofía

SANTIAGO, CHILE

David Mercado
23149 Coronado Dr.
Bienville, LA 44903

10-43 ¿De veras? Reaccione a los siguientes comentarios utilizando una de las expresiones de la caja y el presente perfecto de subjuntivo.

> ¡Qué bueno que...!   Dudo que...   ¡Qué lástima que...!   Es importante que...
> ¡Qué curioso que...!   No creo que...   ¡Qué interesante que...!

1. En Calama, una ciudad en el desierto de Atacama en Chile, no ha llovido nunca.
2. Chile ha sido tradicionalmente el principal exportador de cobre (*copper*) del mundo.
3. Chile ha vendido en los años pasados más de cincuenta millones de litros de vino a Estados Unidos.
4. El mayor terremoto (*earthquake*) del mundo ocurrió en Valdivia, Chile, en 1960.
5. La Isla de Pascua ha recibido este nombre porque se descubrió durante la Pascua.
6. Los investigadores han identificado 887 moais en la Isla de Pascua.

10-44 Chile en imágenes. Imagine que ha hecho un viaje a la Isla de Pascua, Chile recientemente y quiere compartir sus experiencias con su profesor/a de español. Prepare un diario en imágenes, seleccionando fotos de la isla en Internet y explicando los detalles de su viaje.

- dónde está situada geográficamente la isla
- por qué es interesante para el turista
- cómo es la gente que vive allí
- qué lenguas se hablan en la isla
- por qué es un lugar tan misterioso

En palabras de...

LA CARTA DE PRESENTACIÓN

En esta sección van a escribir una carta de presentación en español para una oferta de trabajo donde se requieren conocimientos de español (*Spanish language skills*). Hablen de sus cualidades personales, de su experiencia laboral, de su interés en el trabajo y de sus metas (*objectives*) profesionales.

Writing strategies: Preparing a cover letter. As part of your job search you will have to write a cover letter introducing yourself to potential employers. Your cover letter should reflect your academic and professional strengths as well as any personal interests that make you a unique candidate for the position. Cover letters should be concise and well organized in order to be effective. Avoid syntactically complex sentences and include descriptive statements to present your qualifications, job experience, and career objectives.

Antes de escribir

Comience la elaboración de su carta preparando:

- una lista de las cualidades que usted tiene que son ideales para este puesto
- una descripción de su formación académica, los cursos que ha tomado, sus conocimientos de español
- una lista de los lugares donde ha trabajado y los trabajos que ha realizado

Escriba ahora su carta de forma simple, organizando la información que bosquejó (*drafted*) previamente. Seleccione un saludo y una despedida de los que le ofrecemos a continuación.

SALUDOS FORMALES		DESPEDIDAS FORMALES
Señor/Señora:	*Señores:*	*Atentamente,*
Estimado/a señor/a:	*Estimados señores:*	*Cordialmente,*
Distinguido/a señor/a:	*Distinguidos señores:*	*Atentos saludos,*
		Le saludo muy cordialmente,
		Me despido atentamente,

Después de escribir

Revise y edite su carta asegurándose que incluyó las siguientes estructuras:

✓ un saludo y una despedida formales
✓ estructuras para presentarse
✓ vocabulario para hablar de los cursos en la universidad
✓ el presente perfecto para hablar de experiencias pasadas recientes

En la red

Busque un modelo de carta de presentación en español y compárela con la que usted escribió. ¿Tienen una estructura similar? ¿Qué elementos nuevos puede incluir en su carta?

All the sources consulted for the readings are cited on the *¡Trato hecho!* Web site at **www.prenhall.com/trato**

VOCABULARIO

TEMA ①

Sustantivos
un apellido *a last name*
un archivador *a filing cabinet*
un buzón *a mailbox*
un calendario *a calendar*
un documento *a document*
una empresa *a company, an enterprise*
un enchufe *a socket*
una (en)grapadora *a stapler*
una fotocopiadora *a photocopier*
la información *the information*
la línea *the line*
la luz *the light*
un monitor *a monitor*

un nombre *a first name*
una oferta de empleo *a job offer*
un ratón *a mouse*
un recado *a message*
los recursos humanos *human resources*
un teclado *a keyboard*
un tono *a tone, a beep*
la voz *the voice*

Verbos
apagar *to turn off*
archivar *to file*
devolver (ue) *to return*
encender (ie) *to turn on*

enchufar *to plug in*
(en)grapar *to staple*
freír (i, i) *to fry*
imprimir *to print*
marcar *to dial*
obtener *to obtain*
resolver (ue) *to resolve*
sacar copias *to make copies*

Otras palabras y expresiones
equivocado/a *wrong, mistaken*
lo antes posible *as soon as possible*
publicado/a *published*

TEMA ②

Sustantivos
el ambiente *the environment*
un aumento *a raise*
una base de datos *a database*
un/a colega *a colleague*
la compatibilidad *compatibility*
un contrato temporal *a temporary contract*
un currículum vitae *a curriculum vitae, a résumé*
los datos personales *personal data*
una decisión *a decision*
el desarrollo *the development*
un empleo a tiempo completo/parcial *a full-time/part-time job*

el estado civil *marital status*
la experiencia profesional *professional experience*
la formación académica *education*
un idioma *a language*
un/a jefe/a *a boss*
un motivo *a reason*
un nivel básico/medio/alto *a basic/intermediate/high level*
una oportunidad *an opportunity*
la preparatoria *high school*
un procesador de texto *a word processor*
un programa de diseño gráfico *a graphic design program*
un puesto *a position*
una referencia *a reference*

el seguro médico *medical insurance*
el sueldo *the wage, the salary*
la ubicación *the location*

Otras palabras y expresiones
además *besides*
desde hace *for (how long)*
disponible a petición *available upon request*
estar de buen/mal humor *to be in a good/bad mood*
gruñona *grumpy*
mudarse *to move*
temer *to fear*

TEMA ③

Sustantivos
la agricultura *agriculture*
la atención al cliente *customer service*
un beneficio *a benefit*
un/a carpintero/a *a carpenter*
un/a chófer de autobús/taxi/camión *a bus/taxi/truck driver*
las comunicaciones *communications*
un/a contador/a *an accountant*

un/a director/a *a director*
un/a diseñador/a gráfico/a *a graphic artist*
la educación *education*
la fabricación *manufacturing*
la implementación *the implementation*
el mantenimiento *maintenance*
un/a mecánico/a *a mechanic*
la medicina *medicine*
un/a periodista *a journalist*

la publicidad *advertising*
un/a reportero/a *a reporter*
el transporte *transportation*
un/a vendedor/a *a salesperson*
las ventas *sales*

Otras palabras y expresiones
diseñar *to design*
estar encargado/a de *to be in charge of*
independientemente *independently*

TEMA ④

Sustantivos
el acceso *access*
los artículos de oficina *office supplies*
un departamento *a department*
un/a empleado/a *an employee*
los impuestos *taxes*
el pago *the pay*
el progreso *the progress*
una solicitud de empleo *a job application*

un/a supervisor/a *a supervisor*
un/a visitante *a visitor*

Verbos
aprobar (ue) *to approve*
calcular *to calculate*
contratar *to hire*
despedir (i, i) *to fire*
dibujar *to draw*
distribuir *to distribute*
entrenar *to train*

evaluar *to evaluate*
fallar *to fail, to be down*
introducir datos *to input data*
pintar *to paint*
programar *to program*

Otras expresiones
otra vez *again*
todavía no *not yet*

TEMA ⑤

Sustantivos
un/a banquero/a *a banker*
un billete *a bill*
un/a cajero/a *a teller, a cashier*
un cajero automático *an ATM machine*
un cargo *a charge*
una chequera *a checkbook*
una cuenta corriente / de ahorros *a checking / savings account*
un depósito *a deposit*
un dólar *a dollar*
un préstamo *a loan*
un retiro *a withdrawal*

una sucursal *a branch office*
una tasa de interés *an interest rate*
un trámite *a transaction*
una ventanilla *a counter window*

Verbos
ahorrar *to save*
alegrarse de que *to be happy that*
cobrar *to charge*
completar un formulario *to complete a form*
depositar *to deposit*
firmar un cheque *to sign a check*
retirar *to withdraw*

sentir (ie, i) que *to be sorry that*
sorprender *to surprise*
tener miedo de que *to be afraid that*
utilizar *to utilize, to use*

Otras palabras y expresiones
¿De veras? *Really?*
directo/a *direct*
el/la mío/a *mine*
mínimo/a *minimum*
práctico/a *practical*

11

En las noticias

In this chapter you will learn to...

- specify and describe people or things
- say what sort of people or things are needed
- talk about what will take place
- say when things will occur
- conjecture about what is happening or what might happen
- understand the growing importance of Spanish in the media in the United States

You will use...

- relative clauses
- the subjunctive in relative clauses
- the future tense
- the subjunctive in adverbial clauses
- the future to express probability or supposition

VOCABULARIO

¿Cómo se informa Ud.?

¡Ojo!

En España también se dice **telediario** en vez de **noticiero**.

¿Ve Ud. la televisión o escucha la radio? ¿Lee Ud. la prensa o se informa Ud. por Internet?

un noticiero (**un informe,** un/a reportero/a, un/a presentador/a de noticias, el pronóstico del tiempo)

un periódico o una revista (un artículo, un anuncio)

un buscador, un sitio web, una sala de chat

Suggestion. This chapter deals with the news and the media. Give students the stations and times of newscasts in Spanish in your area or addresses of web pages with current news. Have them watch the news or consult the web site each day and ask simple comprehension questions in the following class. You may wish to give extra credit to those who participate.

Supplemental activity. ¿Qué palabra de esta página asocia Ud. con las siguientes personas o cosas? *Newsweek, Yahoo, Peter Jennings, New York Times, Google,* (your school's web address), *The Tonight Show, Jay Leno,* (your local newspaper), (a well-known local journalist), *el canal Discovery, MSN.com.*

un documental sobre… (historia, medicina, economía…) un programa de entrevistas (**un anfitrión/una anfitriona,** un/a invitado/a, un/a comentarista)

---

un informe *a report*   **un anfitrión/una anfitriona** *a host*

11-1   Un sitio web. ¿Qué información puede obtener en este sitio web?

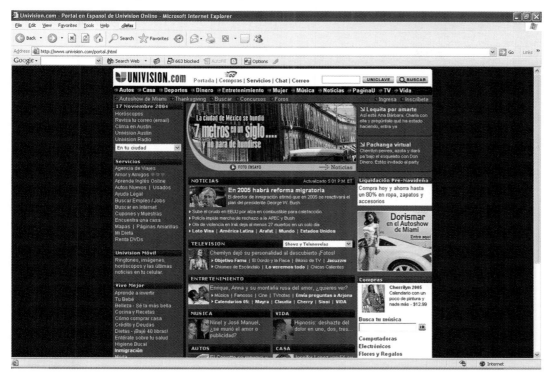

11-2   Entrevista. Entreviste a otro/a estudiante con estas preguntas.

1. ¿Cómo te informas de las noticias? ¿Qué periódico lees? ¿Qué canal de televisión tiene el mejor noticiero? ¿Lees una revista? ¿Consultas un sitio web para informarte?
2. ¿Viste un noticiero ayer? ¿Cuáles fueron las noticias más importantes? ¿Cuáles fueron las noticias de primera plana (*front page*) del periódico esta mañana?
3. ¿Qué buscador de Internet prefieres? ¿Te gusta participar en las salas de chat? ¿Cuáles te gustan más?

Conversaciones. En parejas, lean la siguiente conversación en la cual dos estudiantes hablan de una noticia reciente. Luego, cambien la conversación para hablar de un informe reciente de un noticiero de la televisión, de un artículo del periódico o de una revista.

— ¿Leíste el artículo del periódico sobre la universidad esta mañana?
— No, ¿por qué?
— Dicen que van a **aumentar la matrícula** el semestre que viene.
— Sí, hubo un informe sobre eso en el noticiero local de **la cadena** Univisión anoche pero no oí lo que dijeron.
— **Según** el periódico, la matrícula va a subir un diez por ciento.
— ¿Por qué lo van a aumentar tanto?
— Con la reducción de impuestos el año pasado, **el gobierno** tiene que **recortar** las contribuciones a las universidades.

AUDIO ¡A escuchar!

Escuchen otra conversación en la cual dos amigos hablan de una noticia. ¿Qué pasó y cómo se enteraron de eso?

---

aumentar *to raise*   **la matrícula** *tuition*   **la cadena** *network*   **según** *according to*   **el gobierno** *the government*
recortar *to cut back*

Para averiguar

1. What is a relative clause? What is a relative pronoun?
2. What can the relative pronoun **que** mean?
3. When do you use **quien** rather than **que** to say *who(m)*?
4. When do you use **lo que**?

Suggestion. Exemplify the use of relative pronouns by pretending that you are a visiting professor asking questions such as the following about students in the class: *¿Quién es el estudiante que... (lleva una camiseta amarilla, tiene barba, está detrás de Ud., no está en clase hoy...)?* Then continue by having students explain who different students are by completing sentences such as: *Caroline es la estudiante que...*

GRAMÁTICA

Expresar cualidades específicas: los pronombres relativos

A relative clause is a phrase that clarifies which noun you are talking about, or describes its characteristics. The word that begins the phrase, referring back to the noun described, is a relative pronoun. The most common relative pronoun in Spanish is **que** (*that, which, who*), which can be used to describe both people and things. Note how the following sets of phrases talking about the same nouns are connected by **que**. Relative clauses are placed immediately after the noun they describe.

> Me gusta **esa revista**. Estás leyendo **esa revista**.
> Me gusta **esa revista que** estás leyendo.
> *I like **that magazine that** you are reading.*

> **El periodista** es muy bueno. **Ese periodista** escribió este artículo.
> **El periodista que** escribió este artículo es muy bueno.
> ***The journalist who** wrote this article is very good.*

When a relative pronoun is the object of a preposition, use **quien(es)** instead of **que** to refer to people, but use **que** for things. Use the plural form **quienes** to refer to plural nouns. There is no accent on **quien(es)** or **que** when they are relative pronouns, rather than question words.

> ¿Cómo se llama **el reportero**? Hablaste **con ese reportero**.
> ¿Cómo se llama **el reportero con quien** hablaste?
> *What is the name of the reporter **with whom** you talked?*

To say *what* as a statement, rather than as a question, or to say *that which*, use **lo que**.

Question:	¿**Qué** dicen?	***What** do they say?*
Statement:	No creo **lo que** dicen.	*I don't believe **what** they say.*
Question:	¿**Qué** pasa?	***What's** happening?*
Statement:	**Lo que** pasa es esto…	***What's** happening is this...*

11-3 **¿Quiénes o qué son?** Combine las siguientes oraciones con el pronombre relativo **que**, diciendo quién o qué puede ser.

Modelo Es la cadena de televisión en español. Esa cadena de televisión en español tiene la mayor audiencia en Estados Unidos.
Univisión es la cadena de televisión en español que tiene la mayor audiencia en Estados Unidos.

1. Es una revista popular. Esa revista tiene muchos artículos sobre deportes.
2. Es el presentador de noticias de la cadena ABC. Ese presentador de noticias presenta las noticias nacionales.
3. Es un comentarista de la radio. Ese comentarista les gusta a muchas personas conservadoras (*conservative*).
4. Es un periódico con muchas fotos en color. Ese periódico se vende por todo el país.
5. Es el periodista del programa de televisión *Nightline*. *Nightline* se emite (*is broadcast*) cada noche en la cadena ABC después del noticiero local.
6. Es el anfitrión del programa de entrevistas de la cadena NBC. Ese programa de entrevistas se llama *The Tonight Show*.
7. Es la anfitriona de un programa de entrevistas de la tarde. Ella tiene una compañía de producción. Esa compañía de producción se llama *Harpo Enterprises*.
8. Es un buscador de Internet. Prefiero usar ese buscador de Internet.
9. Es el noticiero local. Veo ese noticiero local con más frecuencia.
10. Es un programa de televisión. Me gusta ver ese programa de televisión.
11. Es una emisora (*station*) de radio. La escucho con frecuencia en el carro.

Ⓟ 11-4 ¿Quién o qué? Complete las siguientes preguntas con **que, quien(es)** o **lo que.** Luego, entreviste a un/a compañero/a de clase.

1. ¿Cuáles son los temas de conversación ____que____ más te interesan? ¿Quién es el amigo o la amiga con ____quien____ más hablas de esos temas? Generalmente, ¿estás de acuerdo con ____lo que____ dice tu amigo/a?
2. ¿Quiénes son las personas de ____quienes____ más se habla en las noticias recientemente? ¿Estás interesado/a en ____lo que____ hacen esas personas? ¿Qué han hecho recientemente ____que____ salió en las noticias?
3. ¿Conoces a todas las personas con ____quienes____ te comunicas por Internet o te comunicas a veces con desconocidos (*strangers*)? Cuando hablas con los desconocidos por Internet, ¿te sientes más libre a veces de decirles cosas ____que____ nunca les dices a tus amigos?
4. ¿Quién es una persona famosa con ____quien____ te gustaría hablar? ¿Qué es ____lo que____ más te interesa de esa persona?

11-5 ¿Qué opina Ud.? Complete las siguientes oraciones expresando su opinión sobre los medios de comunicación locales, nacionales o internacionales.

> **Modelo** No creo todo lo que… **leo en Internet / dicen en el periódico local / veo en…**

1. No creo todo lo que…
2. Generalmente, estoy de acuerdo con lo que…
3. A veces, me sorprende lo que…
4. A veces, no me gusta lo que…
5. Lo que más me gusta ver en la televisión es / son…
6. Lo que más hago para informarme de las noticias es…

Answers for 11-3. *¿Quiénes o qué son?* 1. *Sports Illustrated* (*Answers may vary.*) 2. Peter Jennings 3. Rush Limbaugh (*Answers may vary.*) 4. *USA Today* 5. Ted Koppel 6. Jay Leno 7. Oprah Winfrey (*Answers will vary for items 8–11.*)

Follow-ups for 11-3. *¿Quiénes o qué son?* **A.** Using similar sentences with relative clauses, have groups of students write sentences explaining to someone who recently arrived from El Salvador who or what the following people or things are. (*Tom Brokaw, Peter Jennings, David Letterman, Newsweek, 60 Minutes, Howard Stern*) **B.** Have students write similar sentences with relative clauses giving information about a TV program, magazine, newspaper, journalist, or a show host that they like or dislike. Then have them read their sentences aloud and the rest of the class guesses whom or what they describe.

Follow-up for 11-5. *¿Qué opina Ud.?* Have students complete sentences such as the following. 1. En la clase de español, lo que hacemos más es… (Lo que me pone nervioso/a es/son…, Lo que más me gusta de la universidad es/son…., Lo que menos me gusta de la universidad es/son…) 2. Los fines de semana, lo que me gusta hacer es… (Lo que no me gusta hacer es…, Lo que más hago para divertirme es…) 3. Lo que más me gusta de mi apartamento/casa es/son… (Lo que menos me gusta es/son…) 4. Para ser feliz en la vida, lo que más necesito es/son… (En la vida, lo que no entiendo a veces es por qué…)

VOCABULARIO

TEMA ❷   ¿Qué noticias locales y nacionales hay?

Supplemental activity. Definiciones. Complete las siguientes oraciones con palabras lógicas de esta página. 1. Cuando los precios suben, hay... 2. Si muchas personas pierden su trabajo, hay mucho... 3. Si la productividad de un país baja, hay una... 4. Una persona que viene de otro país es... 5. Una persona que se presenta en las elecciones es... 6. Una persona que representa a uno de los cincuenta estados en el Congreso es... 7. Una persona que tiene la nacionalidad de un país es... 8. La administración política de un estado es el... 9. Un grupo de personas que respeta las mismas normas y leyes es una... 10. Los representantes y senadores que deliberan cambios de legislatura forman... 11. El desarrollo de las facultades intelectuales por la instrucción pública es la... 12. La actividad ilegal de una sociedad es la... 13. El abuso dentro de una familia es... 14. Un grupo de jóvenes delincuentes es una... 15. Una sustancia narcótica es una... 16. El trato imparcial para todos es... 17. Una persona encargada de resolver cuestiones de justicia es un... 18. La ayuda que un gobierno les da a los miembros de la sociedad es la...

Suggestion. Point out to students that *la criminalidad* refers to overall crime throughout society, and that one uses *un crimen* to talk about a particular incident of crime.

las elecciones   el/la candidato/a
el/la presidente/a   el/la senador/a
el/la representante

el gobierno   el Congreso   **las leyes**

la economía   la inflación   la depresión económica
el desempleo   la asistencia social

la sociedad   la educación   **el/la ciudadano/a**
la inmigración   los inmigrantes

la justicia   las cortes   **el/la juez**

la criminalidad   **las pandillas**   las drogas
el robo   la violencia doméstica

---

la ley *the law*   **el/la ciudadano/a** *the citizen*   **el/la juez** *the judge*   **la pandilla** *the gang*

11-6 Los titulares. Reaccione a los siguientes titulares (*headlines*) del periódico con **Estoy contento/a de que…** o **Es una lástima que…** .

Suggestion for 11-6. *Los titulares.* Use this activity to provide a quick review of familiar uses of the subjunctive as a transition to the following presentation of the use of the subjunctive in relative clauses.

Follow-up for 11-6. *Los titulares.* Have students work in groups to prepare two or three headlines describing real recent news and write them on the board. Then ask individuals to react to each one.

11-7 Un poco de historia. Complete las siguientes oraciones con **que** o **quien.** Luego, diga quién o qué es.

1. Es el presidente con _____ quien _____ Lyndon Johnson sirvió como vicepresidente.

2. Es el número de representantes _____ que _____ hay en la Cámara de Representantes de Estados Unidos.

3. Fue el candidato a presidente de Estados Unidos en el año 2000 por _____ quien _____ más personas votaron, pero _____ que _____ perdió la elección en el colegio electoral.

4. Fueron el primer padre e hijo _____ que _____ sirvieron como presidentes de Estados Unidos.

5. Es el presidente _____ que _____ renunció (*resigned*) a la presidencia por el escándalo de Watergate.

Answers for 11-7. *Un poco de historia.* 1. John Kennedy 2. 435 3. Al Gore 4. John Adams (1797–1801), John Quincy Adams (1825–1829) 5. Richard Nixon, 1974

Follow-up for 11-7. *Un poco de historia.* ¿Cuántos jueces hay en la Corte Suprema de Estados Unidos? (9) ¿Quién fue la primera mujer en la Corte Suprema? (Sandra Day O'Connor) ¿Cuántos senadores hay en el Congreso? (100) ¿Cómo se llaman los senadores de nuestro estado? ¿Quién es nuestro

G **Conversaciones.** En grupos, lean la siguiente conversación en la cual alguien está haciendo **una encuesta.** Luego, preparen una encuesta para la clase sobre algún problema social, los medios de comunicación o los hábitos de consumo.

— ¡Aló!
— Buenas tardes, llamo de parte de María Flores, su representante de la Cámara de Representantes en Washington, y estoy haciendo una breve encuesta sobre **los temas** más importantes para los votantes. ¿Me podría responder a tres preguntas sobre las prioridades del Congreso?
— Creo que sí.
— ¿Cuál debe ser la prioridad número uno del Congreso: la seguridad nacional, la economía, la educación o las reformas sobre la inmigración?
— La economía.
— Para salir de la depresión económica **actual,** ¿es más importante: **crear** nuevos empleos, controlar la inflación o recortar los impuestos?
— Para mí, es más importante crear nuevos empleos.
— Y la última pregunta es: ¿ha **mejorado** o **empeorado** su situación económica durante los últimos seis meses?
— Mi situación económica no ha cambiado.
— Eso es todo. Gracias por su participación.
— De nada.

AUDIO **¡A escuchar!**

Ahora escuchen otra encuesta. ¿De qué se trata? ¿Cuáles son las preguntas? ¿Tiene Ud. las mismas respuestas que la persona de esta entrevista?

representante en la Cámara de Representantes? ¿Quién fue presidente por doce años? (Franklin Roosevelt, 1933-1945) ¿Quién fue presidente por sólo 30 días? (William Harrison en 1841) ¿Quién fue el presidente durante la guerra entre Estados Unidos y México en 1846? (James Polk) ¿durante la guerra entre Estados Unidos y España en 1898? (William McKinley)

una encuesta *a survey* **los temas** *the topics* **actual** *current* **crear** *to create* **mejorar** *to improve* **empeorar** *to worsen*

GRAMÁTICA

Evocar personas o cosas desconocidas: el subjuntivo en las oraciones de relativo

Para averiguar

1. When do you use the indicative in a relative clause? When do you use the subjunctive?
2. Do you use the indicative or the subjunctive in a relative clause to describe a nonexistent noun after **nadie, nada,** and **ninguno/a**?

Suggestion. Refer students back to the forms of the subjunctive on pages 272 and 276 for a quick review.

You have seen that relative clauses are phrases that describe a noun in the main clause. Use the indicative in a relative clause to describe a person, place, or thing that is known to exist.

No creo lo que dijo el candidato que **acaba** de hablar.

I don't believe what the candidate who just spoke said.

Use the subjunctive in a relative clause to describe the characteristics of a person, place, or thing that is just imagined, but may not exist.

Quiero un candidato que **sea** menos dogmático y que **sepa** más.

I want a candidate who is less dogmatic and who knows more.

Compare the following sentences, which have the same translation in English. In the first sentence, the speaker has seen the Web site and knows it exists, but just cannot find it again. In the second sentence, the speaker doesn't know of such a Web site, but is looking for one.

Busco un sitio web que **tiene** información sobre ese tema.
Busco un sitio web que **tenga** información sobre ese tema.
I'm looking for a Web site that has information about that topic.

The subjunctive is also used after **nadie, nada,** or **ninguno/a** to describe a nonexistent noun.

No conozco a nadie que **sea** perfecto.
No tengo nada que **necesites.**

I don't know anyone who is perfect.
I don't have anything that you need.

Follow-up for 11-8. ¿Qué opina Ud.? Have students work in groups to think of other laws that they think are needed. Or have them think of silly, outrageous laws. *Modelo: Se necesitan leyes que prohíban más de una hora de tarea.*

11-8 ¿Qué opina Ud.? Complete las siguientes oraciónes con el final que mejor exprese su opinión. Utilice el subjuntivo.

Se necesitan leyes que…

Modelo   reducir los impuestos / reducir la asistencia social
**Se necesitan leyes que reduzcan los impuestos. /
Se necesitan leyes que reduzcan la asistencia social.**

1. controlar la contaminación industrial / darle más libertad a la industria
2. reconocer las contribuciones sociales y económicas de los inmigrantes / cerrar las fronteras (*borders*)
3. eliminar las reglas (*regulations*) que controlan la industria petrolera / desarrollar fuentes (*sources*) de energía alternativas como el sol, el viento y el agua
4. proteger los parques nacionales / abrir los parques nacionales a la explotación industrial
5. recortar los impuestos de las grandes empresas para estimular la economía / beneficiar a la clase media
6. prohibir la modificación genética en la agricultura / permitir la modificación genética de las plantas
7. imponer (*impose*) impuestos a los productos importados para proteger la industria norteamericana / abrir el mercado a los productos importados
8. limitar las demandas (*lawsuits*) frívolas e innecesarias contra los médicos / proteger sin límite a los pacientes contra la negligencia médica

11-9 ¿Es cierto? Un comentarista habla de política. Complete sus oraciones con la forma correcta de los verbos en el subjuntivo o en el indicativo. Luego, diga si Ud. está de acuerdo. Si no está de acuerdo, exprese su opinión.

1. Hay grupos de presión (*lobbies*) que _____tienen_____ (tener) mucha influencia sobre los miembros del Congreso.

2. Los candidatos que _____dicen_____ (decir) la verdad siempre ganan.

3. No hay nadie en Washington que siempre _____diga_____ (decir) la verdad.

4. Se necesitan más representantes que _____sean_____ (ser) ecologistas.

5. California es el estado que _____tiene_____ (tener) más representantes en el Congreso en Washington.

6. No hay ningún candidato que _____haga_____ (hacer) todo lo que promete hacer durante la campaña electoral.

7. Los representantes que _____sirven_____ (servir) en Washington necesitan un aumento de salario.

8. No hay nadie en el gobierno que _____esté_____ (estar) por encima de la ley.

Ⓟ 11-10 Una protesta. Un/a reportero/a contesta preguntas por teléfono sobre la manifestación (*demonstration*) de la foto. Con otro/a estudiante, preparen una conversación con el/la reportero/a utilizando preguntas como las siguientes.

¿Hay alguien que…?

¿Hay algún/alguna… que…?

¿No hay nadie que…?

¿Hay algo que…?

VOCABULARIO
¿Qué noticias internacionales hay?

TEMA **3**

Supplemental activity. Preguntas. *(Answers are provided in parentheses).* ¿En qué estado de Estados Unidos hay muchos terremotos? *(California)* ¿huracánes? *(Florida, Carolina del Norte, Texas, Luisiana...)* ¿En qué catástrofe natural perdieron más personas la vida en Estados Unidos? *(En el año 1900, más de 6.000 personas murieron en un huracán en Galveston, Texas.)* ¿En qué ciudad de Estados Unidos se encuentran las oficinas de las Naciones Unidas? *(Nueva York)* ¿Cuáles son los seis idiomas oficiales de las Naciones Unidas? *(árabe, chino, español, francés, inglés, ruso)* ¿En qué guerra perdieron más norteamericanos la vida: en la guerra civil, en la primera guerra mundial, en la segunda guerra mundial o en Vietnam? *(en la guerra civil, 620.000; en la segunda guerra mundial, 405.000; en la primera guerra mundial, 117.000; en Vietnam, 58.000)* ¿Durante cuál de esas guerras hubo muchas protestas y manifestaciones? *(Vietnam)* ¿En que año comenzó la guerra civil en Estados Unidos? *(1861)* ¿En qué año invadió Estados Unidos a México? *(1846)* ¿A qué países de Centroamérica ha invadido Estados Unidos y en qué año? *(a Panamá en 1989, a Guatemala en 1954, a Nicaragua en 1927, a Honduras en 1919)* ¿Después de qué guerra se hizo Puerto Rico territorio de Estados Unidos? *(la guerra entre Estados Unidos y España en 1898)* ¿En qué año impuso Estados Unidos sanciones económicas contra Cuba? *(1963)*

las Naciones Unidas
llegar a un acuerdo de paz
imponer sanciones contra...

una manifestación
las protestas
protestar contra...

la guerra
los conflictos
el terrorismo
el/la terrorista
atacar
invadir
amenazar

las catástrofes naturales
una inundación
un terremoto
un huracán

la contaminación
el calentamiento global
los recursos naturales

la salud
una epidemia
la malnutrición
la pobreza

---

amenazar *to threaten* **un terremoto** *an earthquake* **la pobreza** *poverty*

11-11 **¿Qué es?** Combine las siguientes oraciones usando un pronombre relativo y diga qué describe.

una manifestación	una epidemia	las Naciones Unidos
los recursos naturales	el calentamiento global	un huracán
un terremoto	la malnutrición	

Modelo   Es una organización. Esa organización resuelve problemas internacionales.
Las Naciones Unidas es una organización que resuelve problemas internacionales.

1. Es un cambio del clima. Ese cambio afecta a la temperatura del aire.
2. Muchos niños pobres sufren de esta enfermedad. Esos niños tienen hambre.
3. Son los elementos de la tierra. La industria los utiliza en la fabricación de productos.
4. Es una enfermedad contagiosa. Esa enfermedad ataca a muchas personas de una región.
5. Es un viento violento. Ese viento se forma sobre el océano en las zonas tropicales.
6. Es un movimiento del suelo. Ese movimiento puede destruir edificios.
7. Es la expresión pública de una opinión política de un grupo. Ese grupo está a favor o en contra de algo.

P **11-12** **Entrevista.** Entreviste a otro/a estudiante con estas preguntas.

1. ¿Ha habido manifestaciones recientemente en la universidad? ¿a favor o en contra de qué? ¿hace cuánto tiempo? ¿Has participado en una manifestación? ¿cuándo?
2. ¿Has trabajado como voluntario/a para alguna organización? ¿Te gustaría participar en una organización como el Cuerpo de Paz (*the Peace Corps*)? ¿Por qué (no)?
3. ¿Qué problema mundial (*world*) te preocupa (*worries*) más? ¿Qué debemos hacer para resolverlo?

P **Conversaciones.** En parejas, lean el comienzo de un noticiero en el cual dos presentadores comentan **los titulares** del día. Después, preparen un noticiero presentando noticias locales, nacionales o internacionales recientes.

— Muy buenas tardes. Éstas son las noticias más importantes del día.
— Ayuda humanitaria comienza a llegar a Nicaragua después de la devastación de la costa atlántica por el huracán Ignacio y las inundaciones.
— El presidente le pide al Congreso que revise las leyes de inmigración.
— Los nuevos indicadores económicos **muestran una mejora** en la tasa de desempleo.
— Reformas propuestas por el Departamento de Educación provocan protestas en la capital.
— **Tendremos** más información sobre estos temas y más a continuación en su noticiero del canal 54. ¡No se vayan!

Supplemental activity. Ud. oye los siguientes titulares en un noticiero de la radio. ¿Son noticias locales, nacionales o internacionales? 1. La universidad aumenta la matrícula para el año que viene. 2. Las Naciones Unidas proporciona más dinero para combatir la epidemia de SIDA en África. 3. Esta semana, representantes de las naciones industrializadas asisten a una conferencia en Tokio sobre el calentamiento global. 4. Un huracán en el Golfo de México amenaza la costa de Texas y Luisiana. 5. La tasa de desempleo baja en los estados del norte y del oeste. 6. Hay manifestaciones por la paz en cinco capitales de Europa. 7. Las inundaciones han dejado sin luz varios vecindarios al norte de la ciudad. 8. Hoy en la Casa Blanca, el Presidente dijo que la educación es su prioridad número uno para la próxima sesión del Congreso. 9. El Consejo Municipal anunció hoy la construcción de un nuevo parque en el centro. 10. El nuevo informe de la policía sobre la criminalidad indica un aumento en el número de robos de autos por toda la ciudad.

AUDIO **¡A escuchar!**

Ahora escuchen otra conversación en la cual dos presentadores de noticias abren un noticiero con los titulares del día. ¿Es un noticiero local o nacional? ¿De qué se tratan los titulares?

---

los titulares *top stories, headlines*   **mostrar (ue)** *to show*   **una mejora** *an improvement*   **tendremos** *we will have*

GRAMÁTICA

Hacer predicciones: el futuro

Para averiguar

1. What is the future stem of most verbs in Spanish? What are the endings?
2. What are ten verbs with irregular future tense stems?

Supplemental activities. **A.** ¿Hará o no hará Ud. las siguientes cosas si quiere mejorar su vida? *Modelo: hacer ejercicio > Sí, haré ejercicio. (tomar mucho alcohol, comer muchas frutas y verduras, trabajar, ser egoísta, ayudar a su familia, ser paciente, salir hasta tarde todas las noches, dormir lo suficiente, ver la televisión todo el tiempo, estudiar más español, viajar más)* **B.** After doing section A, have students write three resolutions for the future. **C.** ¿Quién de su familia hará las siguientes cosas mañana? *Modelo: ver las noticias en la tele > Mis padres verán las noticias en la tele. / Yo veré las noticias en la tele. / Todos veremos las noticias en la tele. / Nadie verá las noticias. (despertarse más temprano, dormir más, ir al trabajo, salir con amigos, estar en casa todo el día, ponerse vaqueros, ponerse un traje, venir a la universidad, poder descansar, volver más temprano/tarde a casa, preparar algo de comer, acostarse más tarde)*

You have learned to say what someone *is going to do* using **ir a +** an infinitive. Use the future tense to say what someone *will do*. The stem of the future tense of most verbs is the infinitive. There is a written accent on all of the endings except the **nosotros** form, and the endings are the same for all verbs.

	HABLAR	COMER	VIVIR
yo	hablar**é**	comer**é**	vivir**é**
tú	hablar**ás**	comer**ás**	vivir**ás**
usted, él, ella	hablar**á**	comer**á**	vivir**á**
nosotros/as	hablar**emos**	comer**emos**	vivir**emos**
vosotros/as	hablar**éis**	comer**éis**	vivir**éis**
ustedes, ellos, ellas	hablar**án**	comer**án**	vivir**án**

Las dos partes interesadas **llegarán** a un acuerdo. — *Both sides **will arrive** at an agreement.*
¿Qué candidato **ganará** las elecciones? — *What candidate **will win** the election?*
¿Quién **será** el nuevo presidente? — *Who **will be** the new president?*

The following verbs have irregular stems in the future, but use the same endings as regular verbs.

INFINITIVE	STEM	FUTURE
hacer	har-	haré, harás…
decir	dir-	diré, dirás…
querer	querr-	querré, querrás…
poder	podr-	podré, podrás…
salir	saldr-	saldré, saldrás…
tener	tendr-	tendré, tendrás…
venir	vendr-	vendré, vendrás…
poner	pondr-	pondré, pondrás…
saber	sabr-	sabré, sabrás…
haber (hay)	habr-	habré, habrás…(habrá)

Habrá más protestas contra la guerra. — ***There will be** more protests against the war.*
Tendremos que resolver estos problemas. — ***We will have** to solve these problems.*
El gobierno **impondrá** sanciones contra las empresas que contaminen. — *The government **will impose** sanctions against companies that pollute.*

As in English, use the future tense to say what will happen if circumstances are right, but use the present indicative in the clause with **si** (*if*).

Iré a la manifestación si vas conmigo. — ***I'll go** to the demonstration if you go with me.*

11-13 **Predicciones.** ¿Harán estas personas las cosas indicadas entre paréntesis? ¿Qué opina Ud.?

Modelo   yo (graduarse este año)
Sí, me graduaré este año. / No, no me graduaré este año.

1. yo (empezar un nuevo trabajo este año, casarse dentro de tres años, tomar una clase de español el próximo semestre, vivir en esta ciudad en cinco años)
2. mis padres (comprar un carro nuevo este año, mudarse dentro de tres años, tener más hijos, pagar mi matrícula el próximo semestre/trimestre, estar en casa esta noche)
3. en la clase de español, nosotros (tener un examen la semana que viene, venir a clase mañana, salir temprano de clase hoy, terminar este capítulo esta semana, hacer el capítulo 12 este semestre/trimestre)

11-14 **Un/a candidato/a perfecto/a.** Ud. es candidato/a al Congreso. Diga si hará o no hará las siguientes cosas.

Modelo   reducir la tasa de desempleo
Reduciré la tasa de desempleo.

1. aumentar los impuestos
2. decir la verdad sobre todo
3. luchar por la clase media
4. servir a los grupos de presión (*lobbies*)
5. escuchar a todos los ciudadanos
6. imponer sanciones duras contra las compañías que contaminen
7. hacer todo lo que los electores (*constituents*) le pidan
8. apoyar (*support*) un sistema de asistencia médica universal para todos
9. aceptar contribuciones políticas de las empresas grandes
10. proponer (*propose*) nuevas leyes regulando la posesión de armas

Ahora diga si cree que el presidente hará las cosas de la lista anterior.

Modelo   **Sí, reducirá la tasa de desempleo.**
No, no reducirá la tasa de desempleo.

P **11-15** **Entrevista.** Entreviste a otro/a estudiante con estas preguntas.

1. ¿Puedes imaginarte cómo será la vida en el año 2025? ¿Qué se hará con las computadoras? ¿Qué usaremos como dinero? ¿Cómo será una casa moderna? ¿y una universidad?
2. ¿Qué avances tecnológicos o científicos habrá en veinte años? ¿Habrá curas para algunas de las enfermedades de hoy? ¿para cuáles? ¿Qué pasará con nuestro planeta? ¿Crees que podremos viajar a otros planetas algún día? ¿Querrás viajar a otro planeta?
3. Dentro de diez años, ¿qué pasará con los problemas sociales? ¿Cuáles mejorarán? ¿Cuáles empeorarán? ¿Qué pasará con la economía?

VOCABULARIO
¿Qué cambiará y cuándo?

Supplemental activities. A. ¿Qué palabra(s) de esta página asocia Ud. con... (las escuelas y las universidades, el agua y el aire, las empresas multinacionales, la guerra, los médicos, las computadoras, una baja tasa de desempleo y de inflación, las Naciones Unidas, los medicamentos, un acuerdo de paz, la televisión o Internet, los recursos naturales, Watergate)? **B.** ¿Es Ud. optimista o pesimista? ¿Mejorarán o empeorarán las siguientes cosas en los próximos años o meses, o no cambiarán? *(la estabilidad económica, la tasa de desempleo, la tasa de criminalidad, la cooperación internacional, el terrorismo, los problemas ecológicos, la educación, los medios de comunicación, el calentamiento global, la comprensión internacional, su comprensión del español, su nota en la clase de español)*

¿En el futuro mejorarán o empeorarán las condiciones de vida? ¿Habrá más/menos…? ¿Habrá mejor(es) / peor(es)…?

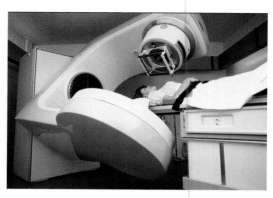

tratamientos para las enfermedades
curas
tecnología y medios de comunicación
educación
oportunidades

problemas ecológicos
contaminación
conflictos
comprensión
escándalos políticos

estabilidad económica
cooperación internacional
globalización
diversidad

11-16 Opiniones. Complete las siguientes oraciones para expresar su opinión.

1. En los últimos años, lo que ha mejorado más en mi vida es/son…
2. El sector de la economía que ha empeorado más recientemente es…
3. Lo que me preocupa más sobre el futuro es/son…
4. Lo que me da optimismo sobre el futuro es/son…

(G) 11-17 Comparaciones. En grupos, preparen cuatro oraciones comparando la vida de hoy día con la vida de hace 50 años. Luego, escriban cuatro predicciones sobre la vida en los próximos 50 años.

> **Modelo** **Hay mejores tratamientos médicos que hace 50 años.**
> **En cincuenta años muchas personas llegarán a la edad de 110 años**
> **o más.**

(G) 11-18 La globalización. En grupos, hagan una lista de los pros y los contras de la globalización. Consideren los aspectos mencionados a continuación. ¿Pueden pensar en otros efectos de la globalización?

¿Habrá más estabilidad económica y política? ¿Reducirá la globalización las estructuras económicas ineficaces (*inefficient*)? ¿Se usarán los recursos naturales con más eficiencia? ¿Quiénes controlarán la economía? ¿Habrá menos pobreza? ¿Habrá más cooperación internacional o más conflictos? ¿Perderemos la libertad o habrá nuevas fronteras para todos? ¿Habrá más control sobre los individuos? ¿Amenazará la globalización a la diversidad? ¿Habrá más cooperación en las investigaciones científicas? ¿Habrá más manipulación de la información o menos? ¿Será más fácil cometer actos de terrorismo o más difícil? ¿Habrá más sensibilidad hacia (*sensitivity towards*) los derechos humanos? ¿Habrá más estados autoritarios o menos?

(G) Conversaciones. En grupos de tres, lean la siguiente pausa comercial durante un noticiero. Luego, preparen una pausa comercial para un noticiero con anuncios para dos negocios de su ciudad.

— Ahora tenemos que hacer una pausa comercial, pero cuando regresemos iremos a Washington para escuchar un informe sobre las protestas contra la nominación del nuevo juez de la Corte Suprema. No se vayan, regresaremos **en seguida.**

— Hoy en su supermercado El Poblanito encontrará todo lo que su familia necesita a los mejores precios. Por ejemplo, esta semana puede comprar dos litros de su refresco preferido por 99 centavos o plátanos a 33 centavos la libra. Venga a vernos a El Poblanito en la calle Puebla porque no encontrará precios más bajos.

— ¿Busca un taller en el que pueda **confiar**? El taller Martínez lleva más de 25 años sirviendo a nuestra comunidad. Le explicaremos en español todos los arreglos necesarios y le daremos un precio garantizado. ¡Puede confiar en nosotros! ¡Le **aseguramos** que Ud. quedará satisfecho!

AUDIO ¡A escuchar!

Ahora escuchen el pronóstico del tiempo de un noticiero local. ¿Qué tiempo hizo hoy? ¿Qué tiempo hará mañana? ¿Cuándo habrá un gran cambio?

---

en seguida *right away*   **confiar** *to trust*   **asegurar** *to assure*

GRAMÁTICA
Definir momentos futuros: el subjuntivo en las oraciones temporales

Para averiguar

1. What are six conjunctions that are followed by the subjunctive when referring to future actions or events?
2. Which one of the six conjunctions is always followed by the subjunctive? Do you use the subjunctive or the indicative after the other five when talking about the past or what happens in general?
3. When do you use an infinitive after **después de, antes de,** and **hasta** without **que**?

Use the subjunctive in clauses after the following conjunctions when referring to future actions or potential events that may or may not happen. The verb in the main clause will be in the future.

cuando	*when*
antes (de) que	*before*
mientras	*while, as long as*
hasta que	*until*
después (de) que	*after*
tan pronto como	*as soon as*

Cuando **haya** elecciones, habrá muchos cambios.
When there are elections, there will be a lot of changes.
No llegarán a un acuerdo mientras las dos partes interesadas no **hablen.**
They won't reach an agreement as long as the two sides don't talk.

Use the present indicative or the preterite after all of the preceding conjunctions except **antes (de) que** when a sentence describes an activity completed in the past or one that recurs.

Cuando **hay** elecciones, siempre vemos mucha propaganda política en la tele.
When there are elections, we always see a lot of political advertising on TV.
Tan pronto como **propusieron** esa ley, hubo muchas protestas.
As soon as they proposed that law, there were a lot of protests.

The subjunctive is always used after **antes (de) que.**

A veces las cosas empeoran antes de que **mejoren.**
Sometimes things get worse before they improve.

Después de, antes de, and **hasta** are followed by an infinitive (without **que**) when there is no change of subject between the main clause and the subordinate clause.

Antes de cambiar la ley, los senadores debatieron los pros y los contras.
Before changing the law, the senators debated the pros and cons.

In some cases two options are accepted.

Hablarán **hasta llegar** a un acuerdo. / Hablarán **hasta que lleguen** a un acuerdo.
They will talk until they reach an agreement.

11-19 **Cuando yo sea presidente/a.** Imagínese que Ud. es candidato/a a la presidencia. Haga una lista de cosas que cambiarán cuando Ud. sea presidente/a.

> **Modelo** **Cuando yo sea presidente/a los estudiantes tendrán más ayuda para pagar la matrícula universitaria.**

11-20 **Sentimientos.** ¿Cuándo hará Ud. las siguientes cosas?

> **Modelo** casarse
> **Me casaré cuando encuentre al hombre/a la mujer perfecta. / Nunca me casaré.**

1. estar contento/a
2. divertirse
3. descansar
4. estar nervioso/a
5. saberlo todo
6. tener más tiempo
7. tener más dinero
8. buscar un nuevo empleo
9. comprar una casa

Ⓟ **11-21** **Entrevista.** Entreviste a otro/a estudiante con estas preguntas.

1. ¿Adónde irás cuando salgamos de clase hoy? ¿Volverás a casa? ¿Estará alguien en tu casa cuando vuelvas hoy?
2. ¿Qué harás cuando se termine este semestre/trimestre? ¿Harás un viaje? ¿Volverás a estudiar aquí el próximo semestre/trimestre?
3. ¿Cuántos años tendrás cuando te gradúes de la universidad? ¿Qué harás después de graduarte? ¿Dónde vivirás? ¿Cómo cambiará tu vida cuando ya no seas estudiante? ¿Mejorará?

Ⓟ **11-22** **Cambios.** En parejas, completen las siguientes oraciones de manera lógica.

1. Habrá menos delincuencia en este país cuando…
2. La vida mejorará cuando…
3. Siempre habrá conflictos en el mundo mientras…
4. Cuando las armas estén prohibidas en Estados Unidos…
5. Cuando haya las próximas elecciones para presidente...
6. Cuando tengamos 80 años…

Ⓖ **11-23** **Comentaristas.** En grupos, preparen una conversación basada en la siguiente situación. Uno de ustedes es periodista de un programa de televisión en el cual se debaten temas políticos. Los otros son invitados. El periodista hace cuatro o cinco preguntas sobre el futuro de la economía, problemas sociales u otros temas políticos. Cada invitado da su opinión.

Supplemental activities. A. Complete las siguientes oraciones. 1. Cuando salgamos de clase hoy... 2. Cuando yo vuelva a casa hoy... 3. Cuando terminemos este capítulo... 4. Cuando llegue el día del examen final... 5. Cuando yo tenga unos días de vacaciones... **B.** Have students write two goals for the future on a sheet of paper. Then ask them questions about when they plan to accomplish them, what they will have to do before reaching them, how they will feel or how their life will change when they accomplish them, and what they plan to do afterward.

VOCABULARIO

TEMA 5

¿Será posible?

¿Qué **chismes** hay en **el mundo de la farándula**? ¿Qué dicen los paparazzi?

¿Hay escándalos?

Una estrella de rock ha sido arrestada por actividades ilegales.

Un deportista profesional ha sido acusado de dopaje. Niega las acusaciones.

¿Hay rumores? ¿Son **mentiras**?

Una estrella famosa está embarazada. ¿Quién será el padre?

Un artista famoso se presentará como candidato a gobernador.

Una pareja famosa se casará/se divorciará. Hay una reconciliación de una pareja separada.

¡Ojo!

En español la palabra **artista** se usa para hablar no solamente de pintores, sino también de actores y cantantes. En este caso se usa la palabra *performers* en inglés.

---

los chismes *gossip*   **el mundo de la farándula** *the entertainment world*   **una estrella** *a star*
negar (ie) *to deny*   **una mentira** *a lie*   **embarazada** *pregnant*

11-24 Una telenovela. Dos amigos hablan de lo que va a pasar en una telenovela (*soap opera*). Complete las siguientes oraciones con la forma del futuro o del subjuntivo de los verbos. Siga el modelo de la primera oración.

— __Habrá__ (haber) una pelea cuando el novio __encuentre__ (encontrar) a su novia con otro muchacho.
— Él __volverá__ (1. volver) con su novia tan pronto como __sepa__ (2. saber) que está embarazada.
— Cuando (ella) se lo __diga__ (3. decir) a su padre, (ellos) __tendrán__ (4. tener) que casarse.
— Ella no __será__ (5. ser) feliz mientras __se quede__ (6. quedarse) con él. Algo __pasará__ (7. pasar) antes de que (ellos) __se casen__ (8. casarse) y (ellos) no __se casarán__ (9. casarse).
— (Nosotros) No __sabremos__ (10. saber) la verdad hasta que (nosotros) __veamos__ (11. ver) el último episodio.
— Tú __verás__ (12. ver) que todos los problemas __se resolverán__ (13. resolverse) antes de que __se termine__ (14. terminarse).
— (Yo) __Estaré__ (15. estar) muy triste cuando __llegue__ (16. llegar) al fin. ¿De qué __hablaremos__ (17. hablar) tú y yo?

(P) 11-25 Entrevista. Entreviste a otro/a estudiante con estas preguntas.

1. ¿Te interesa mucho lo que hacen las estrellas del cine o de la televisión? ¿Hablas mucho de los chismes con tus amigos? ¿Cuáles son los chismes más interesantes ahora? ¿Los crees?
2. ¿Crees que haya mucho dopaje entre los deportistas para mejorar el rendimiento (*performance*)? ¿Se deben hacer más exámenes de dopaje? ¿Se deben imponer sanciones contra los deportistas que dan positivo en los exámenes de dopaje? ¿En qué casos se deben imponer sanciones de por vida?

(P) Conversaciones. En parejas, lean la siguiente conversación en la cual dos paparazzi hablan de los escándalos más recientes en el mundo de la farándula. Luego, preparen una conversación hablando de chismes recientes verdaderos o imaginarios.

— Hace días, aparecieron fotos muy comprometedoras de los coprotagonistas de la telenovela *Destino de amor*, Ricardo Puente y Daniela Luna. Los dos artistas aseguran que estaban **grabando** un episodio de la telenovela pero según rumores están viviendo un romance en la vida real.
— El romance de la cantante Mónica Blanco con el guitarrista Marco Díaz **parece** haber terminado. La cantante niega **la ruptura,** pero la semana pasada él asistió a la presentación de los premios Grammy acompañado de otra mujer. Mónica Blanco no asistió.
— La presentadora del programa *24 horas*, Cristina Durán, anunció que está embarazada. Se casó con el representante de California, Daniel Cruz, en junio y los recién casados se sienten muy felices de estar esperando un bebé.

Suggestion for 11-24. *Una telenovela.* Tell students that unlike English-language soap operas in the U.S., soap operas from Latin America do not last more than several months.

Follow-up for 11-24. *Una telenovela.* Have students find classmates who watch the same television shows and prepare predictions about what will happen in upcoming episodes. If students are not familiar with the same television shows, have them make predictions about some situation in the news.

AUDIO ¡A escuchar!
Ahora escuchen otra conversación en la cual dos personas hablan de un escándalo. ¿Qué pasó y por qué? ¿Creen ellos que sea verdad?

grabar *to record*   **parecer** *to appear, to seem*   **la ruptura** *the breakup*

GRAMÁTICA

Hablar de situaciones hipotéticas: más usos del futuro

Para averiguar

1. What is another use of the future tense in Spanish, besides saying what *will happen*?
2. How might the future tense be translated in English when expressing probability or supposition?

In Spanish, the future tense can also be used to express probability, supposition, or rumors. When used in this way, the future is translated in a variety of ways in English: *probably, might, could, wonder, think,* and *bet* are some examples.

— ¿Dónde **estarán** los demás?   — *Where might the others be?*
— **Estarán** perdidos.   — *They are probably lost.*
— ¿**Habrán** tenido un accidente?   — *Could they have had an accident?*

— ¿Qué **estará** haciendo José?   — *What do you think José might be doing?*
— **Estará** estudiando.   — *I bet he's studying.*

— ¿Quién **será** ese hombre que está con ella?   — *I wonder who that man who is with her might be.*

11-26 Si son las... ¿Qué estarán haciendo las siguientes personas si son las horas indicadas?

> **Modelo**   usted (el sábado a las ocho de la mañana)
> **Estaré durmiendo. / Estaré desayunando.**

1. su mejor amigo (el sábado a las once de la noche, el domingo a las diez de la mañana, el lunes a las tres de la tarde)
2. su madre (el lunes a las diez de la mañana, el martes a las cinco y media de la tarde, el sábado a las nueve de la noche)
3. usted (el viernes a las seis de la tarde, el domingo a las siete de la mañana, el miércoles a las dos y media de la tarde)
4. usted y los estudiantes de la clase de español (en veinte minutos, el próximo día de clase, la noche antes del examen final)

P 11-27 ¿Qué estarán haciendo? ¿Qué estarán haciendo las siguientes personas en las siguientes situaciones? En parejas, preparen una descripción lógica.

> **Modelo**   Su madre está en el trabajo.
> **Estará hablando por teléfono con un cliente.**

1. Un compañero de clase está en la oficina del profesor.
2. Dos policías están en una casa/un apartamento en su calle.
3. Los miembros del equipo de fútbol americano universitario están en el estadio.
4. El presidente de Estados Unidos está en el Despacho Oval de la Casa Blanca.
5. Los senadores están en el Capitolio.
6. Peter Jennings está en los estudios de ABC.
7. Los miembros del Consejo General de las Naciones Unidas están reunidos (*meeting*).

11-28 **¿Quiénes serán?** En grupos, imaginen quiénes serán estas personas, dónde estarán y qué estarán haciendo.

1.

2.

3.

4.

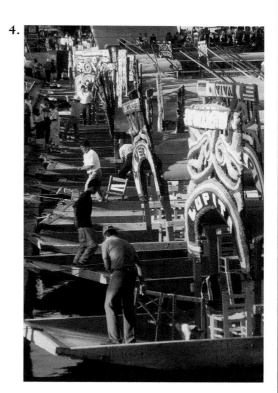

5.

Information for 11-28. *¿Quiénes serán?* 1. Desde el año 1977, las madres y abuelas de la Plaza de Mayo en Buenos Aires siguen protestando la desaparición de sus hijos y nietos durante la dictadura militar hace más de 25 años. 2. Unos voluntarios distribuyen agua potable después del huracán Mitch en Nicaragua. 3. Las calles se llenan de gente para celebrar la Semana Santa en Sevilla, España. 4. Unos trajineros trabajan en sus trajineras (canoas) en el parque Xochimilco en la Ciudad de México. 5. Los aymara celebran el Día de los Muertos en Perú.

¡Trato hecho!
En portada

Note: Have students complete the *Antes de leer, Reading strategies,* and *Ahora Ud.* activities before reading this article.

REVISTA CULTURAL

AL FILO DE LA NOTICIA

Financian programa de alfabetización del Instituto del Progreso Latino

07-10-2004
La institución bancaria Citibank concedió una beca de $50.000 al año durante dos años destinada a mejorar el programa vigente de alfabetización "Plaza Comunitaria E-México" del Instituto del Progreso Latino. La plaza comunitaria es una iniciativa del gobierno mexicano para proporcionar educación básica de alfabetización a adultos mexicanos y otras personas de habla hispana de Chicago, empleando tecnología de punta y las metodologías más actuales de enseñanza y aprendizaje.

La gran influencia de la lengua española en Estados Unidos y la fuerza de sus hablantes **se reflejan** también en la presencia de medios de comunicación en español en la **oferta mediática** norteamericana. Periódicos, revistas, noticieros de radio y televisión e Internet se encargan de informar al público hispano de Estados Unidos de las noticias nacionales e internacionales, de los chismes del mundo de la farándula, y de los eventos sociales, culturales y deportivos de actualidad.

El duelo del consuelo

07-24-2004
Para muchos el tercer lugar es poco consuelo, pero Uruguay buscará hoy derrotar a Colombia con el fin de quedarse con ese puesto en la Copa América y vengar la goleada que le propinó en las eliminatorias sudamericanas al Mundial del 2006.

La prensa escrita en español es especialmente fuerte en ciudades donde la población hispana es numerosa, pero hay periódicos en español por todo el país. Se estima que en el año 2003 se publicaron en Estados Unidos trescientos cuarenta y cuatro **diarios** y **semanarios** en español. Los **lectores** encuentran en estos periódicos noticias de **la actualidad** latinoamericana que los periódicos estadounidenses en inglés no siempre **cubren.**

A principios del año 2004 **se produjo la fusión** de los dos periódicos en español de mayor **tirada** en Estados Unidos, *La Opinión*

Una buena labor

07-28-2004
Gente Ayudando a Gente repara los hogares de los más necesitados

A través del programa Gente Ayudando a Gente, que trabaja junto con la institución World Changers, decenas de ancianos y personas discapacitadas reciben este tipo de ayuda para mejorar su calidad de vida. Luis Navas, 17, originario de Puerto Rico, tiene cuatro años como voluntario. Viene desde Oklahoma a Dallas una semana cada año para regalar su trabajo a personas que, como Florentina, no tienen más ayuda.

Día, publicado en Dallas, Texas, *El Nuevo Día*, diario puertorriqueño que ha iniciado su publicación en Orlando, Florida, e *Impacto USA*, semanario editado en Los Ángeles.

El impacto de la prensa en español es tan importante en Estados Unidos que diarios nacionales como *The Wall Street Journal* o *The Miami Herald* ya publican ediciones en español —*The Wall Street Journal Américas* y *El Nuevo Herald*— y otros periódicos como *The New York Times*, *USA Today* o *Los Angeles Times* podrán lanzar ediciones en español en el futuro.

de Los Ángeles —con lectores mayormente mexicanos, venezolanos y colombianos— y *El Diario/La Prensa* de Nueva York —con lectores en su mayoría centroamericanos y caribeños. En este último año también **se han lanzado** nuevos diarios en español, como *Al*

Telemundo va a por el público mexicano

07-24-2004
La cadena estadounidense quiere atraer al principal sector inmigrante con producciones como su miniserie 'Zapata'

La miniserie de seis capítulos *Zapata*, que relata la vida de uno de los héroes de la Revolución Mexicana Emiliano Zapata, será trasmitida en agosto por Telemundo y se lanzará al mercado hispano de EE.UU. en formato de DVD.

La constante llegada de nuevos lectores, el interés que la actualidad hispana genera en Estados Unidos y la **creciente** fuerza del español y de sus hablantes aseguran la continuidad y la difusión de periódicos y revistas en lengua española.

---

al filo de la noticia *on the edge of the news*   **se reflejan** *are reflected*   **oferta mediática** *media offerings*   **diarios** *daily newspapers*   **semanarios** *weekly newspapers*   **lectores** *readers*   **la actualidad** *current events*   **cubren** *cover*   **se produjo la fusión** *a merger occurred*   **tirada** *distribution*   **se han lanzado** *have been launched*   **creciente** *growing*

Antes de leer

¿Cómo se informa usted? ¿Qué medio de comunicación utiliza con mayor frecuencia para obtener información de la actualidad nacional e internacional? ¿Por qué?

Reading strategies: Self-monitoring. As you become more experienced reading Spanish, you should be capable of self-monitoring your understanding of texts to determine whether to carry on reading or to stop and self-correct. You can self-monitor your understanding by asking yourself a content-based question after each paragraph. By responding to the question posed, you will verify that your understanding of the piece is appropriate, and you can move forward in the reading.

11-29 Ahora Ud. Lea el primer párrafo de la lectura *Al filo de la noticia* y conteste la primera pregunta a continuación. Si su respuesta es correcta, repita el mismo procedimiento con los cuatro párrafos restantes (*remaining*).

1. ¿Cómo afecta la gran influencia de la lengua española a los medios de comunicación en Estados Unidos?
2. ¿Es fuerte la presencia de la prensa escrita en español en Estados Unidos?
3. ¿Cuáles son algunos de los periódicos en español de mayor tirada en Estados Unidos? ¿Dónde se publican?
4. ¿Existen ediciones españolas de periódicos nacionales norteamericanos?
5. ¿Qué circunstancias aseguran la continuidad y la difusión de periódicos y revistas en lengua española en Estados Unidos?

Después de leer

11-30 Titulares. Asocie los titulares de las noticias que aparecen en el artículo con estas secciones del periódico. Después, visite la página web de un periódico en español y seleccione una noticia de interés para usted. Preséntela con sus propias palabras en la próxima sesión de clase.

Internacional	**A**
Nacional – Sociedad	**B**
Deportes	**C**
Nacional – Educación	**D**
Entretenimiento	**E**

11-31 ¿Indicativo o subjuntivo? Complete las siguientes oraciones con el verbo entre paréntesis en indicativo o en subjuntivo según convenga.

1. En Estados Unidos se publican muchos diarios y semanarios que ____están____ (estar) dirigidos fundamentalmente al lector hispano.
2. Los periódicos en español informan al lector hispano de los eventos que ____ocurren____ (ocurrir) en sus países de origen.
3. Los medios de comunicación quieren crear programas de radio y televisión que ____lleguen____ (llegar) a la audiencia hispana.
4. Los periódicos y revistas en español son más abundantes en los estados que ____poseen____ (poseer) una alta concentración de hispanos.
5. Las editoriales (*publishing companies*) buscan medios que ____aumenten____ (aumentar) el número de lectores y de ventas de publicaciones en español en el futuro.
6. No hay nadie que ____crea____ (creer) que los medios de comunicación en español van a desaparecer en Estados Unidos.

De puertas abiertas a la comunidad

VIDEO ¡QUÉ AUDIENCIA!

11-32   Entrando en materia. ¿Qué canales de información en español conoce? ¿Qué periódicos o revistas en inglés tienen versión en español? ¿Sabe cuál es el canal de televisión en español de mayor audiencia en Estados Unidos? ¿Cuáles son algunos de los programas que se presentan en este canal?

¿Cómo se informa la audiencia hispana? ¿Qué programas de radio y televisión prefieren? ¿Cuáles son los usos que hacen de Internet? Michelle Vélez, experta en mercadotecnia de medios de comunicación en español, nos explica las estrategias más efectivas para llegar al **oyente** y al espectador hispano, según sus hábitos **mediáticos.** Vamos a escuchar también a Pablo Escarpellini, jefe de la sección internacional del periódico *Hoy,* quien nos habla del tipo de información que interesa al público hispano.

Distintos grupos de la audiencia hispana nos hablarán también de cómo se informan, de los periódicos y revistas que leen y del uso que hacen de Internet.

11-33   ¿Quién es quién? Asocie la siguiente información con la persona que corresponda, Michelle, Pablo o ambos (*both*).

	Michelle	Pablo	ambos
1. Es de origen español.	☐	X	☐
2. Es de origen mexicano.	X	☐	☐
3. Es especialista en mercadotecnia y trabaja para TV Azteca en Nueva York.	X	☐	☐
4. Es periodista y trabaja para el periódico *Hoy* en Nueva York.	☐	X	☐
5. Dirige la sección de noticias internacionales de Latinoamérica.	☐	X	☐
6. Diseña campañas publicitarias dirigidas al público hispano.	X	☐	☐
7. Cree que al público hispano le interesan mucho las noticias sobre el fútbol.	☐	☐	X
8. Cree que al público hispano le interesa saber qué pasa en sus países de origen.	☐	☐	X

oyente *listener*   **mediáticos** *media related*

11-34 Programas que venden. Escuche con atención la información que Michelle Vélez nos ofrece sobre los programas preferidos por el público hispano; luego conteste las siguientes preguntas.

1. ¿Qué programas prefiere la audiencia masculina?

_____

2. ¿Qué programas prefieren las amas de casa (*housewives*)?

_____

3. ¿Qué otro programa está entre los "top tres"? ¿Por qué es tan popular este programa?

_____

Answers for 11-34. *Programas que venden.* 1. La audiencia masculina prefiere el fútbol. 2. Las amas de casa prefieren los programas de chismes, de cotilleos y los *talk shows.* 3. Otro programa que está entre los *top tres* son los noticieros, porque la gente necesita estar informada de lo que pasa en su país de origen.

G 11-35 Estrategias de mercado. Según Michelle, ¿cuáles son las características ideales que debe tener una buena campaña mediática dirigida a atraer (*to attract*) a la audiencia hispana? ¿Pueden añadir (*to add*) otras que crean interesantes? Preste atención al uso del subjuntivo en las cláusulas relativas que describen esta campaña.

Answers for 11-35. *Estrategias de mercado.* Debe ser una campaña que tenga un mensaje claro, que se pueda entender. Debe ser una campaña que genere un valor a la audiencia, que sea atractiva, que deje a la audiencia con un mensaje de recordación.

Modelo **Debe ser una campaña que esté diseñada en español.**

11-36 La audiencia hispana. Complete la siguiente tabla con la información que la audiencia hispana entrevistada nos ofrece en el vídeo.

Los informantes	Las preguntas
Luis	¿Usa Internet?
Dennis	¿Para qué usa Internet?
Analissa	¿Lee periódicos o revistas?
Rosal	¿Qué periódicos lee?

G 11-37 La nueva onda. Ahora que saben un poco más de las preferencias televisivas del público hispano de los Estados Unidos, diseñen un programa de televisión nuevo dirigido (*directed*) a esta audiencia. Incluyan la siguiente información.

✔ LISTA DE CONTROL:

___ ¿Qué tipo de programa es? ¿un noticiero, un concurso (*contest*), una telenovela, un programa de entrevistas (*talk show*), un documental?
___ ¿Cuál es el nombre del programa?
___ ¿Qué día/s a la semana se transmite y a qué hora?
___ ¿A qué público va dirigido? ¿a jóvenes, adultos, niños, todos los públicos?
___ ¿Por qué creen que tendrá éxito el programa?

Answers for 11-36. *La audiencia hispana.* *Luis:* usa Internet muchísimo; usa Internet para comprar libros, para comunicarse; lee periódicos, lee todos los días el *New York Times*, está suscrito al *New York Times*; *Dennis:* usa Internet muchísimo; usa mucho Google, como consulta para escribir sus artículos; lee periódicos y revistas, mitad en inglés y mitad en español; *Analissa:* usa Internet; usa Internet para su trabajo, para mantener y formar contactos en otros países; no menciona si lee periódicos o revistas; *Rosal:* usa Internet, usa Internet para la escuela, para investigar, como un recurso para las clases; lee periódicos a veces; lee el *New York Times*, y de vez en cuando *El Diario*; no le gusta leer revistas.

Escapadas

GUANAJUATO, CIUDAD DE YACIMIENTOS

Mina de La Valenciana, con el Templo de San Cayetano al fondo, Guanajuato.

Guanajuato, situada en una zona montañosa y aislada del centro de México, estaba habitada originalmente por los indios chichimecas y fue descubierta por los españoles en **el siglo** XVI. En el siglo XVIII, Guanajuato fue especialmente próspera por la explotación de sus **yacimientos** de oro y de plata. Algunas de estas minas **permanecen** activas todavía hoy, y tienen una **profundidad** de hasta 600 metros, como la Boca del Infierno.

De esta época colonial son las extraordinarias construcciones barrocas, como la Basílica de Nuestra Señora de Guanajuato, el templo de San Diego y las bellísimas iglesias de La Compañía y La Valenciana, que han influido considerablemente en el barroco mexicano de la zona.

Templo de San Diego, Guanajuato.

Calle Hidalgo, Guanajuato.

Vestigios de este pasado se observan también hoy en las bellas calles **subterráneas,** como la Calle Hidalgo, los majestuosos palacios y mansiones, las populares plazas, como el Jardín de la Unión, y en los estrechos **callejones,** como el romántico Callejón del Beso.

---

el siglo *the century*   **yacimientos** *deposits*   **permanecen** *remain*   **profundidad** *depth*   **vestigios** *vestiges*
subterráneas *underground*   **callejones** *alleys*

La ciudad tiene un colorido muy peculiar de tonos rosados, rojizos y verdes, **reflejo** de los distintos materiales utilizados en la construcción de sus edificios. Los edificios más importantes se fabricaron de **cantera** rosa mientras que los más **humildes** se hicieron de adobe.

Colorido en la colina, Guanajuato.

Guanajuato es un foco histórico y cultural prominente. Jugó un papel importante en la independencia de México y es la **ciudad natal** de Diego Rivera. Rivera es un famoso muralista mexicano del siglo XX conocido por su arte popular —sus murales—comprometidos con la causa social y los **derechos** de su pueblo mexicano. En Guanajuato el turista puede visitar la casa natal del pintor y admirar algunas de sus obras.

Don Quijote y Sancho Panza, Guanajuato.

En la ciudad se celebra también desde hace más de veinte años el Festival de Teatro Cervantino. Allí se concentran cada mes de octubre actores, **bailarines,** músicos y espectadores de muy variada procedencia.

La activa Universidad de Guanajuato organiza también festivales culturales **al aire libre** en la Plazuela de San Roque, como el festival de **entremeses,** piezas teatrales breves de gran interés.

La Universidad de Guanajuato, en el centro de la ciudad histórica.

reflejo *reflection* **cantera** *(a type of stone)* **humildes** *humble* **ciudad natal** *birthplace* **derechos** *rights*
bailarines *dancers* **al aire libre** *outdoor* **entremeses** *short theater pieces*

11-38 **Vamos a contar mentiras.** Lea con atención las siguientes afirmaciones falsas sobre la ciudad de Guanajuato y corrija la información incorrecta.

1. Guanajuato es una ciudad mexicana situada en la costa del Caribe.
2. Guanajuato fue durante el siglo XVIII una ciudad pobre que vivía de la agricultura.
3. Todas las minas de Guanajuato están cerradas hoy en día.
4. Los edificios antiguos de Guanajuato no presentan una arquitectura relevante (*notable*).
5. Guanajuato es una ciudad oscura (*dark*) con casas hechas de piedra (*stone*) gris.
6. La actividad cultural de Guanajuato es mínima. No se celebran festivales al aire libre y la atmósfera no atrae a personas de distinta procedencia.
7. Guanajuato es la ciudad natal de la famosa pintora mexicana Frida Kahlo.
8. Guanajuato no es una ciudad atractiva para los estudiantes universitarios.

11-39 **Mis planes de viaje.** Imagine que va a hacer un viaje a la ciudad de Guanajuato, y le cuenta a un/a amigo/a sus planes de viaje, los días que estará en el país, los lugares que visitará y las actividades que realizará. Utilice la información de la lectura y otra información adicional que pueda encontrar en las guías de viaje o en la red. Preste atención al uso del futuro en la expresión de sus planes de viaje.

Modelo   **La primavera próxima viajaré a Guanajuato, México.**

www **11-40** **Diego Rivera, originario de Guanajuato.** Busque en Internet una de las obras de Diego Rivera y tráigala a su próxima clase. Explique qué elementos aparecen en la pintura y por qué escogió esa obra en particular.

"Study of a Sleeping Woman," 1921, Diego Rivera.

En palabras de...

CARTAS AL EDITOR

Ud. va a escribir una carta al editor de un periódico hispano expresando su preocupación y descontento ante un problema social o político que afecta a la comunidad hispana hoy. Describa esta realidad problemática y sugiera soluciones para mejorar la situación. Explique también las repercusiones posibles de llevar a cabo acciones correctas o incorrectas para resolver dicho problema.

Writing strategies: Writing a letter to the editor. Letters to the editor are a powerful instrument to bring up social, cultural, or political issues that are not always addressed in a news article. Letters to the editor voice people's concerns about or support for a certain issue. When writing a letter to the editor, make one point, two at the most, preferably in the first sentence; be sure that you keep the text of the letter brief and state your arguments clearly. The tone of the letter should not be aggressive. Challenge or support specific statements, address relevant information that might have been ignored in the media, but avoid destructive argumentation.

Antes de escribir

Comience la elaboración de su carta preparando:

- una lista con los principales problemas sociales y económicos que afectan a la comunidad hispana en nuestra sociedad actual.
- una lista con posibles soluciones a los problemas mencionados.
- una lista con las posibles repercusiones positivas y negativas en caso de atender (*to pay attention*) o no atender a este problema.

Seleccione el problema que crea más grave y escriba su carta destacando la necesidad de atender a esta situación y presentando las soluciones que considera más adecuadas. Explique también cómo mejorará o empeorará la situación en caso de llevar a cabo las acciones correctas o incorrectas.

Después de escribir

Revise y edite su carta comprobando que incluyó las siguientes estructuras:

- ✓ vocabulario relacionado con los problemas sociales y la política
- ✓ estructuras para hablar del futuro
- ✓ oraciones de relativo con indicativo
- ✓ oraciones de relativo con subjuntivo

En la red

Consulte las ediciones electrónicas de periódicos en español y busque ejemplos de cartas al editor que hablen de problemas sociales o políticos que afectan a la comunidad hispana. ¿Cómo es el tono de estas cartas? ¿Presentan soluciones al problema denunciado? ¿Son similares a la suya? ¿En qué son diferentes?

All the sources consulted for the readings are cited on the *¡Trato hecho!* Web site at **www.prenhall.com/trato**

VOCABULARIO

TEMA 1

Sustantivos

un anfitrión/una anfitriona *a (show) host/hostess*

un anuncio *an advertisement, an announcement*

un artículo *an article*

un buscador *a search engine*

una cadena *a (television) network*

un/a comentarista *a commentator*

una contribución *a contribution*

un documental *a documentary*

la economía *the economy*

el gobierno *the government*

un informe *a report*

un/a invitado/a *a guest*

la matrícula *tuition, registration fee*

un noticiero *a newscast*

la prensa *the press*

un/a presentador/a de noticias *a newscaster*

un programa de entrevistas *a talk show*

un pronóstico del tiempo *a weather forecast*

una reducción *a reduction*

Otras palabras

aumentar *to raise, to increase*

local *local*

lo que *what, that which*

recortar *to cut (back)*

según *according to*

TEMA 2

Sustantivos

la asistencia social *social assistance, welfare*

la Cámara de Representantes *the House of Representatives*

un/a candidato/a (a) *a candidate (for)*

un/a ciudadano/a *a citizen*

el Congreso *the Congress*

la corte *the court*

un crimen *a crime*

la criminalidad *crime (as a whole)*

el desempleo *unemployment*

las elecciones *the elections*

una encuesta *a survey, a poll*

la inflación *inflation*

la inmigración *immigration*

un/a inmigrante *an immigrant*

un/a juez *a judge*

la justicia *justice*

una ley *a law*

los medios de comunicación *the media*

una pandilla *a gang*

la participación *the participation*

el/la presidente/a *the president*

la prioridad *the priority*

un problema *a problem*

una reforma *a reform*

un/a representante *a representative*

el robo *theft*

la seguridad nacional *national security*

un/a senador/a *a senator*

la situación *the situation*

la sociedad *society*

la violencia doméstica *domestic violence*

un/a votante *a voter*

Verbos

crear *to create*

empeorar *to worsen*

mejorar *to improve*

reducir *to reduce*

responder *to respond, to answer*

Otras palabras y expresiones

actual *current, present*

breve *brief*

de parte de *on behalf of*

TEMA ❸

Sustantivos

un acuerdo de paz *a peace agreement*
la ayuda humanitaria *humanitarian aid*
el calentamiento global *global warming*
un canal *a channel*
la capital *the capital*
una catástrofe natural *a natural disaster*
un conflicto *a conflict*
la costa *the coast*
la devastación *the devastation*
una epidemia *an epidemic*
una guerra *a war*
un huracán *a hurricane*

los indicadores económicos *the economic indicators*
una inundación *a flood*
la malnutrición *malnutrition*
una manifestación *a demonstration*
una mejora *an improvement*
las Naciones Unidas *the United Nations*
la pobreza *poverty*
la protesta *the protest*
los recursos naturales *natural resources*
las sanciones *sanctions*
un terremoto *an earthquake*
el terrorismo *terrorism*
un/a terrorista *a terrorist*

los titulares *the headlines, the top stories*

Verbos

amenazar *to threaten*
imponer *to impose*
invadir *to invade*
mostrar (ue) *to show*
protestar (contra) *to protest (against)*
provocar *to provoke, to cause*
revisar *to review*

Otras palabras y expresiones

a continuación *following, next*
propuesto/a *proposed*

TEMA ❹

Sustantivos

un arreglo *a repair*
la comprensión *understanding*
una comunidad *a community*
un conflicto *a conflict*
la cooperación *cooperation*
una cura *a cure*
la diversidad *diversity*
un escándalo *a scandal*
la estabilidad *stability*
el futuro *the future*
la globalización *globalization*
una libra *a pound*

un litro *a liter*
la nominación *the nomination*
una pausa comercial *a commercial break*
la tecnología *technology*
el tratamiento *the treatment*

Verbos

asegurar *to assure*
confiar en *to trust, to confide in*
llevar... años... *to have... years experience*
quedar *to end up, to be*

Otras palabras y expresiones

bajo/a *low*
ecológico/a *ecological*
en seguida *right away*
garantizado/a *guaranteed*
mientras *while, as long as*
por ejemplo *for example*
satisfecho/a *satisfied*

TEMA ❺

Sustantivos

una acusación *an accusation*
un bebé *a baby*
los chismes *gossip*
un/a coprotagonista *a costar*
un/a deportista profesional *a professional athlete*
el dopaje *doping, drug use*
un episodio *an episode*
una estrella de rock *a rock star*
un/a gobernador/a *a governor*
un/a guitarrista *a guitarist*
una mentira *a lie*
el mundo de la farándula *the world of entertainment*
una pareja *a couple, a pair*

un premio *an award*
la presentación *the presentation*
los recién casados *newlyweds*
una reconciliación *a reconciliation*
un romance *a romance*
un rumor *a rumor*
una ruptura *a breakup*
una telenovela *a soap opera*

Verbos

anunciar *to announce*
aparecer *to appear*
divorciarse *to divorce*
esperar *to expect*
grabar *to record*
negar (ie) *to deny*

parecer *to seem*
presentarse como candidato/a (a) *to run as a candidate (for)*
terminar *to finish*

Adjetivos

acompañado/a *accompanied*
acusado/a *accused*
arrestado/a *arrested*
comprometedor/a *compromising*
embarazada *pregnant*
famoso/a *famous*
ilegal *illegal*
real *real*
separado/a *separated*

12

En el extranjero

● In this chapter you will learn or review how to...

- indicate who did what to whom
- express opinions or doubts about what might happen or used to happen
- say what would happen under different conditions
- tell what people used to want to happen
- talk about hypothetical situations
- make plans to live or study abroad

● You will use...

- all the pronouns you have learned
- the present subjunctive
- the conditional
- the imperfect subjunctive
- *if/then* clauses

TEMA **1**

VOCABULARIO
¿Qué les dijeron?

Suggestion. Much of this chapter deals with studying and living abroad. You may wish to discuss with students your own experiences living abroad, encouraging them to consider studying abroad and providing relevant information.

Supplemental activities. A. Una estudiante estudió un semestre en una universidad en España. ¿Hizo las siguientes cosas antes de salir para España o después de llegar? *Modelo: matricularse en la universidad > Se matriculó en la universidad después de llegar. (informarse sobre las universidades con programas para extranjeros, escoger una universidad, presentarse en la oficina de estudiantes extranjeros, solicitar la admisión al programa de estudios, ir a sus clases, obtener una visa, obtener una tarjeta de identificación, pagar la matrícula, escribir cartas o correos electrónicos para obtener información sobre los programas de estudios, renovar su visa para quedarse más tiempo)* **B.** ¿Qué hace un estudiante primero? *Modelo: ¿Solicita la admisión al programa de estudios o escoge una universidad? > Escoge una universidad.* 1. ¿Solicita la admisión a un programa de estudios o se matricula? 2. ¿Habla con un asesor o se matricula? 3. ¿Paga la matrícula o se matricula? 4. ¿Se matricula o escoge las clases? 5. ¿Solicita la admisión a un programa de estudios o paga la matrícula? 6. ¿Se gradúa o escoge una universidad? 7. ¿Escoge una universidad u obtiene una tarjeta de identificación?

¿Qué trámites se hacen para estudiar **en el extranjero**? Los estudiantes necesitan…

escoger una universidad y un plan de estudios
solicitar la admisión al programa de estudios antes de **la fecha límite**
encontrar **alojamiento**

Después de llegar, deben…

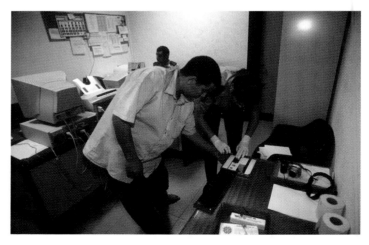

presentarse en la oficina de estudiantes extranjeros para obtener una tarjeta de identificación
hablar con **un/a asesor/a** antes de escoger las clases
matricularse en la universidad y pagar la matrícula
renovar su visa si deciden prolongar su **estancia**

---

en el extranjero *abroad*   **escoger** *to pick*   **solicitar** *to apply for*   **la fecha límite** *the deadline*
el alojamiento *housing, lodging*   **un/a asesor/a** *an advisor*   **matricularse** *to register*   **una estancia** *a stay*

12-1   Preguntas. Usted trabaja en la oficina de estudiantes extranjeros de su universidad y alguien le hace las siguientes preguntas. ¿Sabe las respuestas?

1. Para tomar clases en el otoño, ¿cuál es la fecha límite para solicitar la admisión en la universidad?
2. ¿Puedo completar la solicitud de admisión por Internet, necesito enviarla (*to send it*) por correo tradicional o tengo que presentarme en la oficina de admisiones y registro?
3. ¿Necesito hablar con un asesor antes de escoger mis clases?
4. ¿Puedo matricularme por Internet?
5. ¿Cuándo puedo matricularme para el próximo semestre?
6. ¿Puedo pagar la matrícula con tarjeta de crédito?
7. ¿Cuánto cuesta la matrícula semestral/trimestral?
8. ¿Cómo obtengo una tarjeta de identificación?

Ⓟ **12-2   Entrevista.** Entreviste a otro/a estudiante con estas preguntas.

1. ¿Por qué escogiste esta universidad? ¿A cuántas universidades solicitaste la admisión? ¿Visitaste el campus de otras universidades? ¿Cuáles te gustaron y cuáles no? ¿Por qué? ¿Vas a terminar los estudios aquí o quieres ir a otra universidad para terminarlos?
2. ¿Hablaste con un asesor antes de matricularte este semestre? ¿Te matriculaste con tiempo o en el último momento? ¿Todavía había muchas clases disponibles cuando te matriculaste este semestre/trimestre? ¿Pudiste matricularte en todas las clases que querías? Si no, ¿en qué clase no pudiste matricularte? ¿Cuánto te costó la matrícula?
3. ¿En qué otro país te gustaría estudiar? ¿Por qué? ¿Por cuánto tiempo?

Ⓟ **Conversaciones.** En parejas, lean la siguiente conversación en la cual un estudiante extranjero habla con una asesora sobre su solicitud de admisión a un programa de estudios. Luego, cambien la conversación para explicarle a un estudiante de Sudamérica la misma información sobre su universidad.

— Buenos días, ¿en qué lo puedo **atender**?
— Quisiera estudiar aquí el año que viene. ¿Me podría explicar **los pasos** a seguir para ser admitido?
— Aquí tiene los formularios para solicitar la admisión a los distintos programas de estudios y una guía universitaria para estudiantes extranjeros. Esta guía le explica todos los trámites que necesita hacer y las fechas límites.
— ¿Cuál es la fecha límite para ser admitido como **alumno de nuevo ingreso** el próximo otoño?
— Necesita **entregar** su solicitud de admisión antes del primero de marzo, y el primer **plazo de matrícula** para alumnos de nuevo ingreso empezará en julio.

Follow-ups for *Conversaciones*.
A. Preguntas. 1. ¿Se puede utilizar la biblioteca sin tarjeta de identificación? 2. ¿En cuántas horas de clases se puede matricular uno? Para ser estudiante a tiempo completo, ¿se puede matricular uno en menos de 12 horas? Para mantener una visa, ¿los estudiantes extranjeros necesitan ser estudiantes a tiempo completo? 3. ¿Cuesta la matrícula lo mismo para todos los estudiantes? Si no, ¿cuáles son las diferencias? 4. Para ser admitido como alumno de nuevo ingreso a esta universidad en el otoño, ¿cuál es la fecha límite para entregar la solicitud de admisión? 5. ¿Cuándo empieza el plazo de matrícula para el otoño? ¿para la primavera? ¿Pueden matricularse todos los estudiantes al mismo tiempo o tienen algunos prioridad? ¿Cómo se determina quiénes pueden matricularse primero? **B.** Have students work in groups to prepare suggestions of how to simplify the required transactions to be admitted to the university and to register, or to make the process fairer for all.

AUDIO ¡A escuchar!

Escuchen una conversación en la cual una estudiante habla con su compañera de cuarto de sus planes para estudiar en el extranjero. ¿Cuáles son las diferencias entre los dos programas que está considerando?

---

atender (ie) *to wait on, to serve*   **los pasos** *the steps*   **un/a alumno/a de nuevo ingreso** *an entering student*
entregar *to turn in*   **el plazo de matrícula** *the registration period*

Para averiguar

1. What are five sets of personal pronouns?
2. Which three groups of pronouns follow the same placement rules? When must they go before the verb? When must they be attached to the end of the verb? When is there an option?
3. When do you use the prepositional pronouns? Which two do not look like the subject pronouns?

Supplemental activities. A. ¿Hacen los estudiantes extranjeros las siguientes cosas antes de ser admitidos a una universidad o después? Utilice un pronombre de complemento directo en las respuestas. *Modelo:* escoger su plan de estudios > *Lo escogen antes de ser admitidos. (pedir información sobre la universidad, escoger la universidad, solicitar la admisión a la universidad, pagar la matrícula, pedir ayuda financiera, escoger las clases, obtener una visa de estudiante, renovar su visa de estudiante, visitar el campus por primera vez)*
B. ¿Hacen los buenos estudiantes o los malos estudiantes las siguientes cosas? *Modelo:* obtener becas > *Los buenos estudiantes las obtienen. (sacar malas notas, tomar las clases más difíciles, leer todos los libros, utilizar Cliff Notes en vez de leer los libros, leer todas las explicaciones del libro, hacer su tarea en el último momento, copiar las respuestas de un amigo, completar toda la tarea, saber todas las respuestas, obtener su diploma)*

¡Ojo!

Use **conmigo** and **contigo** instead of **mí** and **ti** with **con.**

¿Vienes **conmigo**?
Are you coming with me?

GRAMÁTICA

Indicar quién: resumen de los pronombres personales

The personal pronouns that you have learned are summarized below.

Subject	Reflexive/ Reciprocal	Direct object	Indirect object	Prepositional
yo	me	me	me	mí
tú	te	te	te	ti
él	se	lo	le	él
ella	se	la	le	ella
usted	se	lo/la	le	usted
nosotros/as	nos	nos	nos	nosotros/as
vosotros/as	os	os	os	vosotros/as
ellos	se	los	les	ellos
ellas	se	las	les	ellas
ustedes	se	los/las	les	ustedes

Subject pronouns are generally used only when needed for clarity, to stress the subject, or to contrast the subject with someone else.

Yo llegué primero y **ellos** llegaron después. — ***I*** *arrived first and* ***they*** *arrived afterwards.*

Reflexive/reciprocal, direct object, and indirect object pronouns all follow the same placement rules, which are summarized in the following chart.

	Before a conjugated verb	Attached to the end of a verb
Single conjugated verb	**Me** atienden.	—
Conjugated verb + infinitive	**Me** van a atender.	Van a atender**me.**
estar + -ndo form of the verb	**Me** están atendiendo.	Están atendiéndo**me.**
Present perfect	**Me** han atendido.	—

The direct object pronoun **lo** may be used to refer to a whole idea.

— ¿Entiendes **cómo matricularte**? — *Do you understand* ***how to register****?*
— No, no **lo** entiendo. — *No, I don't understand (****it****).*

The indirect object pronouns **le** and **les** become **se** when followed by **lo, la, los,** or **las.**

— ¿**Me** dio Ud. su pasaporte? — *Did you give* ***me*** *your passport?*
— Sí, **se lo** di hace un rato. — *Yes, I gave* ***it to you*** *a little while ago.*

Prepositional pronouns follow a preposition.

No hay nadie detrás de **mí.** — *There isn't anybody behind* ***me.***

12-3 Mejores amigos. Sustituya con pronombres las palabras en cursiva de las siguientes oraciones describiendo su relación con su mejor amigo/a. Luego, diga si cada oración es cierta o falsa y corrija las oraciones falsas.

> **Modelo** Conocí *a mi mejor amigo/a* en la escuela secundaria.
> **Lo/La conocí en la escuela secundaria.**
> **Falso: Lo/La conocí antes de ir a la escuela primaria.**

1. Veo *a mi mejor amigo/a* todos los días.
2. Vivo con *mi mejor amigo/a*.
3. Me gusta salir a bailar con *mi mejor amigo/a*.
4. *Le* escribo *correos electrónicos* con frecuencia.
5. Yo *le* presto *dinero* a *mi mejor amigo/a* a veces, pero *mi mejor amigo/a* nunca me presta *dinero* a mí.
6. Mi relación con *mi mejor amigo/a* es muy importante. Para mí, no hay nadie más importante que *mi mejor amigo/a*.

12-4 Su primer día. Un amigo habla de la llegada de una estudiante extranjera a una universidad donde estudia español por un año. Sustituya con pronombres las palabras en cursiva para evitar la repetición.

Catherine fue a la universidad para matricular *a Catherine* en la oficina de estudiantes extranjeros, pero no podía encontrar *la oficina de estudiantes extranjeros*. Entonces, le preguntó a un señor que vio en la calle dónde se encontraba y *ese señor* le explicó *dónde se encontraba*, pero Catherine todavía no entendía muy bien *dónde se encontraba*. El señor era muy simpático y cuando vio que Catherine no entendía *dónde se encontraba*, ofreció acompañar *a Catherine* a la oficina. Entonces Catherine fue con *ese señor*, y por el camino *(on the way)* hablaron un poco. *Catherine* le preguntó si era profesor y *ese señor* le dijo que les enseñaba español a los extranjeros como *Catherine*. En la oficina de estudiantes extranjeros habló con varios asesores. Pasó mucho tiempo con *los asesores* y estos ayudaron *a Catherine* a matricular *a Catherine*. Unos días más tarde fue a su primera clase y ¿sabes quién era el profesor? Era el mismo señor que llevó *a Catherine* a la oficina de estudiantes extranjeros cuando no podía encontrar *la oficina de estudiantes extranjeros*.

ℙ 12-5 Entrevista. Entreviste a otro/a estudiante con las siguientes preguntas. Conteste sustituyendo con pronombres las palabras en cursiva.

1. ¿Quién te explicó *cómo matricularte la primera vez*? ¿Quién te ayudó a escoger tus clases el primer semestre/trimestre? ¿Conocías bien *el campus* tu primer día de clase? ¿Te lo enseñó alguien?
2. ¿Sabías *quién iba a enseñar esta clase* cuando te matriculaste? ¿Cuántas veces has visitado *al profesor (a la profesora)* durante sus horas de oficina? ¿Cuántas veces le has escrito *correos electrónicos*?
3. ¿Ves *a muchos estudiantes extranjeros que hablen español* en el campus? ¿Les hablas a veces? ¿Practicas *español* con ellos a veces?

Answers for 12-4. *Su primer dia.*
Catherine fue a la universidad para matricularse en la oficina de estudiantes extranjeros, pero no podia encontrarla. Entonces, le preguntó a un señor que vio en la calle dónde se encontraba y él se lo explicó, pero Catherine todavía no lo entendía muy bien. El señor era muy simpático y cuando vio que Catherine no lo entendía, ofreció acompañarla a la oficina. Entonces Catherine fue con él, y por el camino (*on the way*) hablaron un poco. Ella le preguntó si era profesor y él le dijo que les enseñaba español a los extranjeros como ella. En la oficina de estudiantes extranjeros habló con varios asesores. Pasó mucho tiempo con ellos y estos la ayudaron a matricularse. Unos días más tarde fue a su primera clase y ¿sabes quién era el profesor? Era el mismo señor que la llevó a la oficina de estudiantes extranjeros cuando no podía encontrarla.

Expansion for 12-5. *Entrevista.*
1. ¿Traes *tu tarjeta de identificación* todos los días? ¿La utilizas con frecuencia? ¿Para qué? 2. ¿Tienes clases con *tu mejor amigo/a*? ¿Estudias con él/ella a veces? ¿Te ayuda con tu tarea a veces? 3. ¿Te pagas *la matrícula* tú mismo/a o te la pagan tus padres? ¿Te dan *dinero* para comprar *los libros*? 4. ¿Ya has tomado todas *tus clases optativas*? ¿Has escogido *las clases* para el semestre/trimestre que viene? 5. ¿Has hablado con *tu asesor/a académico/a* recientemente? ¿Te ayuda mucho con la selección de clases? ¿Siempre te da *la información que necesitas*?

VOCABULARIO

¿Podría Ud....? ¿Debería...? ¿Le importaría a Ud.?

TEMA 2

Para pedir o dar información, se puede decir...

¿Me podría…?

enviar más información, **asesorar,**

confirmar sus datos personales, explicar los pasos a seguir

¿Qué **debería** obtener? ¿Qué documentos debería llevar?

un acta de nacimiento original
  legalizada por el Cónsul
un certificado de secundaria legalizado
  por un notario público
una carta de solvencia
un pasaporte **vigente**
una visa

¿Me podría…? *Could you… (to, for) me?* **enviar** *to send* **asesorar** *to advise* **debería** *should I*
legalizar *to authenticate* **una carta de solvencia** *a letter of financial standing* **vigente** *valid*

12-6 **¿Me podría...?** Ud. quiere ser admitido/a a un nuevo programa de estudios y pide muchos favores. ¿Cuántas peticiones (*requests*) lógicas puede componer utilizando un elemento de cada grupo u otras palabras?

Modelo **¿Me podría confirmar las fechas límites?**

Me podría	enviar explicar confirmar asesorar dar enseñar ???	las fechas límites los formularios más información sobre las clases la oficina los pasos a seguir ???

12-7 **¿Qué debería llevar?** ¿Qué deberían hacer las siguientes personas en estas situaciones? Trabajen en parejas.

Modelo Un viajero va de vacaciones a Europa y va a visitar varios países.
Debería (*He/She should*) obtener cheques de viaje.
Debería llevar su pasaporte...

1. Un inmigrante quiere trabajar aquí.
2. Un estudiante solicita la admisión a un programa de estudios en el extranjero.

Conversaciones. En parejas, lean la siguiente conversación en la cual una estudiante extranjera se presenta para matricularse después de ser admitida a la universidad. Luego, cambien la conversación para dar la misma información sobre su universidad.

— Buenas tardes. Quisiera matricularme en el programa de español para estudiantes extranjeros.
— Primero necesita pasar por la oficina de admisiones y registro por **el sobre** de matrícula con **el impreso** de datos personales y **una ficha** para la tarjeta de identificación. También necesitará una foto de **tamaño** pasaporte.
— Ya tengo todos esos documentos y los **he rellenado.**
— ¿Me los permite, por favor?
— Sí, por supuesto.
— Gracias. Aquí tiene una lista de todas **las asignaturas** obligatorias y optativas para su programa de estudios y un horario de clases. Después de escoger sus clases, alguien la atenderá.
— ¿Cuándo necesito pagar?
— Tiene hasta el 28 de agosto para pagar.

Follow-up for 12-6. ¿Me podría...? Have students work in pairs to prepare three requests with *nos podría* that they might give you.

Follow-up for *Conversaciones*. Preguntas. ¿Cuáles de las clases que Ud. toma este semestre/trimestre son asignaturas obligatorias y cuáles son optativas? En su plan de estudios, ¿cuántos cursos optativos hay? ¿Ya tomó Ud. todos los cursos optativos? Si no, ¿qué piensa tomar? ¿Le gusta su horario de clases este semestre/trimestre? ¿Por qué sí o por qué no? ¿En qué asignaturas no hay suficientes clases ofrecidas cada semestre/trimestre? ¿Es difícil matricularse en algunas de sus asignaturas obligatorias? En las tarjetas de identificación de esta universidad, ¿hay una foto de los estudiantes? ¿Qué otros datos hay? ¿Es necesario renovar su tarjeta de identificación cada semestre/trimestre? ¿cada año? ¿Tenía Ud. tarjeta de identificación en la escuela secundaria?

AUDIO **¡A escuchar!**

Escuchen una conversación en la cual una estudiante habla con un asesor de su programa de estudios. ¿Cuáles son las asignaturas obligatorias que debe tomar y qué cursos optativos se recomiendan? ¿Qué necesita hacer la estudiante antes de escoger sus clases?

el sobre *the envelope*   **el impreso** *the printout, the form*   **una ficha** *a card*   **el tamaño** *the size*
rellenar *to fill out*   **las asignaturas** *the subjects*

GRAMÁTICA

Expresar condiciones y cortesía: el condicional

Para averiguar

1. How is the conditional generally translated in English?
2. The stem of the conditional is the same as what other tense? What other tense has the same endings?

Use the conditional to say that someone *would do* something or that something *would happen* under certain circumstances. You have already used the conditional in **me gustaría** to say that you would like to do something. Form the conditional using the same verb stem as for the future tense and the same endings as for the imperfect of **-er/-ir** verbs.

	HABLAR	COMER	VIVIR	HACER
yo	hablar**ía**	comer**ía**	vivir**ía**	har**ía**
tú	hablar**ías**	comer**ías**	vivir**ías**	har**ías**
usted, él, ella	hablar**ía**	comer**ía**	vivir**ía**	har**ía**
nosotros/as	hablar**íamos**	comer**íamos**	vivir**íamos**	har**íamos**
vosotros/as	hablar**íais**	comer**íais**	vivir**íais**	har**íais**
ustedes, ellos, ellas	hablar**ían**	comer**ían**	vivir**ían**	har**ían**

¡Ojo!

Do you remember the following irregular future/conditional stems?

hacer:	har-
decir:	dir-
querer:	querr-
poder:	podr-
salir:	saldr-
tener:	tendr-
venir:	vendr-
poner:	pondr-
saber:	sabr-
haber:	habr-

— ¿Qué **harías** en mi lugar?   — *What would you do in my place?*
— Yo **diría** la verdad.   — *I would tell the truth.*

— ¿Te **gustaría** estudiar en España?   — *Would you like to study in Spain?*
— Me **encantaría. Sería** estupendo.   — *I would love to. It would be great.*

The conditional may be used to make polite requests or suggestions.

¿**Podría** Ud. ayudarme?	*Could you help me?*
¿Me **diría** Ud. la hora?	*Would you tell me the time?*
Deberíamos volver más tarde.	*We should return later.*

Just as in English, the conditional is used to report what someone said or knew would happen.

Me dijeron que **estaría** listo.   *They told me that it would be ready.*

Supplemental activities. A. ¿Haría Ud. las siguientes cosas con más dinero o con más tiempo? *Modelo: salir más a bailar > Sí, saldría más a bailar. / No, no saldría más a bailar.* (estudiar más, trabajar menos, dormir más, salir más a cenar, aprender a tocar un instrumento, pasar más tiempo con la familia, hacer más ejercicio, tener menos estrés, ser más feliz, viajar más, ver más la televisión, ir más al cine, ir de compras con más frecuencia, trabajar más en el jardín) **B.** Si Ud. fuera (were) el/la profesor/a, ¿haríamos las siguientes cosas en esta clase? *Modelo: trabajar mucho en grupos > Sí, trabajaríamos mucho en grupos. / No, no trabajaríamos mucho en grupos.* (tener más exámenes, hablar más inglés en clase, salir temprano de la clase hoy, hacer mucha tarea para la próxima clase, poder utilizar el libro durante los exámenes, divertirse en clase)

12-8 **¿Qué dijo?** Otro estudiante de la clase le dice las siguientes cosas. Confirme si es algo dicho por su profesor/a. Comience cada oración con **Sí, el/la profesor/a dijo que…** o **No, el/la profesor/a no dijo que…**

> **Modelo**   Tendremos un examen la próxima vez, ¿verdad?
> **Sí, el/la profesor/a dijo que tendríamos un examen. /**
> **No, el/la profesor/a no dijo que tendríamos un examen.**

1. El/La profesor/a nos ayudará durante sus horas de oficina, ¿verdad?
2. El/La profesor/a estará en su oficina hoy después de clase, ¿verdad?
3. No habrá clase la próxima semana, ¿verdad?
4. Terminaremos este capítulo antes del próximo examen, ¿verdad?
5. No tendremos otro examen antes del examen final, ¿verdad?
6. El examen final no será difícil, ¿verdad?
7. Podremos utilizar el libro durante el examen final, ¿verdad?
8. No haremos más tarea este semestre, ¿verdad?

P 12-9 **¿Lobo o cordero?** Complete el siguiente prueba de personalidad con otro/a estudiante para determinar si el/ella es lobo (*wolf*) o cordero (*lamb*) cuando interactúa con otras personas.

¿LOBO O CORDERO?

1. ¿Dirías una mentira sobre ti para impresionar a una persona que no te conoce bien?
2. En una tienda, ¿le indicarías un error a favor tuyo al dependiente que te devuelve el cambio?
3. ¿Preferirías pasar las vacaciones sin tu pareja?
4. ¿Te gustaría más tener un gato que otros animales?
5. ¿Volverías con gusto a ver viejas películas que te habían gustado en otro momento?
6. ¿Te **lanzarías en paracaídas**?
7. ¿Tendrías la misma profesión que tus padres?
8. ¿Llevarías ropa muy original y algo **vistosa**?
9. ¿Aceptarías una invitación de una persona a quien no conoces bien?

10. ¿Te gustaría volver a revivir el pasado?
11. ¿Te describirías como una persona optimista?
12. ¿Te molestaría encontrar a un ex amor con otra pareja?
13. ¿Saldrías con alguien de la edad de tus padres?
14. ¿Te gustaría ser abogado/a?

RESULTADOS:
Suma un punto por cada respuesta que coincida con las siguientes:
1. sí 2. no 3. sí 4. sí 5. no 6. sí 7. no 8. sí 9. sí 10. no 11. sí 12. no 13. sí 14. sí

De 1-5 puntos:	Eres un corderito tierno e indefenso. Tímido/a, romántico/a y dulce.
De 6-10 puntos:	Eres una persona equilibrada y razonable.
De 11-14 puntos:	Eres un verdadero lobo.

lanzarse en paracaídas *to jump with a parachute*   **vistoso/a** *loud* (clothing)

12-10 **Una educación perfecta.** Primero diga si las siguientes oraciones acerca de (*about*) los estudios universitarios son ciertas o falsas. Luego, diga si la situación cambiaría en un sistema de educación perfecto.

Modelo   Muchos jóvenes inteligentes no pueden estudiar en la universidad.
Sí, es cierto. En un sistema perfecto, todos los jóvenes inteligentes podrían estudiar en la universidad.

1. Todos los estudiantes saben hablar una lengua extranjera al graduarse de la universidad.
2. Los estudios universitarios son gratuitos (*free of charge*).
3. Hay muchas becas y ayuda financiera para los estudiantes sin muchos recursos económicos.
4. Muchos estudiantes no tienen suficiente tiempo para estudiar porque necesitan trabajar para pagarse la matrícula.
5. En muchas universidades, los resultados del equipo de fútbol americano son más importantes que los resultados académicos.
6. En algunas universidades, es posible vivir lejos de la universidad y tomar todas las clases en línea.
7. Los estudiantes pasan más tiempo divirtiéndose que estudiando.

P 12-11 **Estudiantes extranjeros.** Pregúntele a otro/a estudiante qué haría con una beca (*scholarship*) para estudiar en el extranjero por un año.

¿A qué país irías? ¿Estarías nervioso/a? ¿Vivirías en una residencia universitaria, en un apartamento o con una familia? ¿Volverías a Estados Unidos entre semestres? Si no, ¿qué harías? ¿Te comunicarías todos los días con tus padres por teléfono? ¿por correo electrónico? ¿Te gustaría vivir en otro país por un año? ¿En qué país? ¿Por qué?

Follow-up for 12-11. Estudiantes extranjeros. ¿Haría Ud. las siguientes cosas si estudiara en España por un año? Modelo: hablar mucho español. > Sí, hablaría mucho español. (hablar inglés todo el tiempo, pasar todo su tiempo con otros estudiantes norteamericanos, visitar los sitios históricos, visitar otros países de Europa, comprar un coche, tomar el autobús, aprender mucho, estudiar todo el tiempo, sacar muchas fotos)

Supplemental activities. **A.** Si pudiera cambiar (*If you could change*) a las siguientes personas o cosas, ¿cómo serían o qué harían? *Modelo:* su profesor/a de español > *Mi profesor de español me daría menos tarea. Haría exámenes más fáciles. Hablaría más despacio...* 1. su mejor amigo/a 2. sus vecinos 3. sus padres 4. su compañero/a de cuarto/casa 5. el presidente de Estados Unidos 6. Ud. mismo/a **B.** Si pudiera volver a vivir los años de la escuela secundaria, ¿cuáles son tres cosas que haría de otra manera?

Follow-ups for 12-10. *Una educación perfecta.* **A.** Have students work in groups to think of two more changes they would make to improve education in this country. **B.** Give students statements such as the following and have them say whether they agree and what the situation would be in a perfect world. *Modelo:* Hay mucha gente sin hogar. > *Sí es verdad. En un mundo perfecto, no habría gente sin hogar.* 1. Tenemos mucho estrés en la vida diaria. 2. Las mujeres tienen las mismas oportunidades que los hombres. 3. El aire está contaminado. 4. Hay muchas enfermedades. 5. Todos los enfermos pueden ver a un médico. 6. Los tratamientos médicos cuestan mucho dinero. 7. Es difícil encontrar trabajo.

TEMA 3

¿Es necesario?

¿Qué hacen los funcionarios en el Servicio de Ciudadanía e Inmigración?

Atienden a la gente.
Proporcionan información.
Revisan las solicitudes para obtener la ciudadanía o la residencia permanente.
Tramitan las solicitudes de renovación de visa.

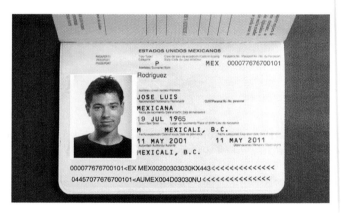

¿Cuál es su nacionalidad? ¿Es Ud…?

argentino/a	dominicano/a	nicaragüense
boliviano/a	ecuatoriano/a	panameño/a
canadiense	español/a	paraguayo/a
chileno/a	estadounidense	peruano/a
colombiano/a	guatemalteco/a	salvadoreño/a
costarricense	hondureño/a	uruguayo/a
cubano/a	mexicano/a	venezolano/a

12-12 Inmigrantes. Adivine (*Guess*) qué nacionalidad corresponde a los siguientes números de inmigrantes viviendo en Estados Unidos.

los colombianos	los cubanos	los dominicanos
los ecuatorianos	los guatemaltecos	los hondureños
los mexicanos	los peruanos	los salvadoreños

proporcionar *to provide* **tramitar** *to process, to handle*

Supplemental activities. A. ¿Cuál es la nacionalidad de cada persona? *Modelo:* Felicia es de Caracas. > *Es venezolana.* 1. Ramón es de Quito. 2. Cecilia es de Buenos Aires. 3. Jorge es de La Habana. 4. Fidencio es de Tegucigalpa. 5. Beatriz es de Santo Domingo. 6. Ximena es de Lima. 7. Isabel es de Santiago. 8. Natalia es de Managua. 9. Carlos es de Bogotá. 10. Víctor es de San José. 11. Victoria es de Madrid. 12. David es de Washington. **B.** *(The correct answer is italicized.)* 1. ¿Shakira es *colombiana* o peruana? 2. Sammy Sosa es puertorriqueño o *dominicano*? 3. Antonio Banderas es argentino o *español*? 4. ¿La familia de Jennifer López es de origen *puertorriqueño* o cubano? 5. ¿Salma Hayek es *mexicana* o guatemalteca? 6. ¿La familia de Christina Aguilera es de origen peruano o *ecuatoriano*?

Suggestion. Point out to students that nationalities are not capitalized in Spanish.

¡Ojo!

Los puertorriqueños tienen nacionalidad estadounidense.

Suggestion. Explain to students that in order to promote diversity, the U.S. gives out 50,000 green cards by lottery each year. Since the purpose of the lottery is to promote diversity, countries whose citizens received more than 50,000 green cards over the previous five years are not eligible. Have students guess which Hispanic nationalities are not eligible (as of 2004). (los mexicanos, dominicanos, salvadoreños y colombianos)

1. 9.162.419	**4.** 710.985	**7.** 281.137
2. 878.085	**5.** 500.413	**8.** 268.896
3. 824.692	**6.** 468.583	**9.** 253.615

12-13 **¿Quiénes eran?** ¿Qué persona corresponde a cada descripción?

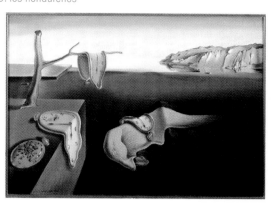

La persistencia de la memoria.

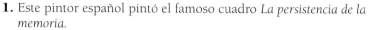

Salvador Dalí	Frida Kahlo	César Chávez	Che Guevara
Simón Bolívar	José Martí	Eva Perón (Evita)	

1. Este pintor español pintó el famoso cuadro *La persistencia de la memoria*.

2. Esta pintora mexicana pintó muchos autorretratos (*self-portraits*).

3. Este activista estadounidense luchó por los derechos de los inmigrantes.

4. Esta esposa de un presidente argentino murió en 1952 a la edad de 33 años.

5. Este revolucionario y poeta cubano luchó por la independencia de Cuba y escribió los *Versos sencillos*.

6. Este revolucionario venezolano luchó contra España por la independencia de varios países de Sudamérica.

7. La imagen de este revolucionario argentino marxista se ve con frecuencia en las camisetas.

Ⓟ **Conversaciones.** En parejas, lean la siguiente conversación en la cual una estudiante extranjera se presenta para obtener una visa de estudiante. Luego, cambien la conversación para representar la siguiente situación: uno/a de ustedes es estudiante extranjero/a de Guatemala y desea obtener una visa para terminar sus estudios en su universidad.

— Buenos días. Tengo una visa de turista y necesito obtener una visa de estudiante F-1 para estudiar en Providence College. ¿Qué necesito hacer?
— ¿Cuál es su nacionalidad?
— Panameña.
— Se necesitan los siguientes documentos: el formulario I-20 de la institución donde desea estudiar, un pasaporte con validez superior a seis meses, un comprobante de solvencia y una foto de tamaño pasaporte.
— Creo que tengo todo eso menos el comprobante de solvencia. ¿Me podría explicar en qué consiste exactamente?
— Necesita probar que tiene los recursos para pagar todos **los gastos** durante su estancia. Puede ser **un estado de cuenta** de su banco o del banco de sus padres o **una beca.**
— Me voy a graduar en cuatro años. ¿Puedo obtener una visa para una estancia de más de un año?
— Sí, la visa **permanece** vigente hasta el término de los estudios **con tal que** esté matriculada en la institución.

AUDIO ¡A escuchar!

Escuchen una conversación en la cual un estudiante llama al Consulado de Ecuador para averiguar si necesita una visa para estudiar un semestre en Quito. ¿Qué documentos necesita presentar? ¿Cuánto debe pagar?

---

los gastos *expenses* **un estado de cuenta** *a (bank) statement* **una beca** *a scholarship* **permanecer** *to remain* **con tal que** (+ subjunctive) *provided that*

GRAMÁTICA

Expresar acciones virtuales: repaso del presente del subjuntivo

Para averiguar

1. When do you use the subjunctive in relative clauses?
2. When do you use the subjunctive after conjunctions like **cuando** or **hasta que**?
3. What are three other conjunctions that are followed by the subjunctive?
4. What are five other uses of the subjunctive?

Review the forms of the present subjunctive presented on pages 272 and 276. Use the subjunctive…

- to express desire or preference about what someone might do.

  Quiero que **vayas** conmigo.   *I want you to go with me.*

- to express the need for something to happen.

  Necesito que me lo **explique.**   *I need you to explain it to me.*

- to express doubt about what might or might not happen.

  Dudo que me **den** una visa.   *I doubt that they will give me a visa.*

- to express emotions and feelings about what happens.

  Estoy contento de que no **haya** cola.   *I'm happy there's no line.*

- to say what someone is told or asked to do.

  Díganles que **vuelvan** más tarde.   *Tell them to come back later.*

- in a relative clause, to describe nouns that do not or possibly may not exist.

  ¿Hay alguien que me **pueda** atender?   *Is there anyone who can wait on me?*

- after the conjunctions **cuando, después (de) que, tan pronto como,** and **hasta que** to talk about the future, and always after **antes (de) que.**

  Necesita firmar su pasaporte tan   *You need to sign your passport as soon*
  pronto como lo **reciba.**   *as you receive it.*

Also use the subjunctive after the following conjunctions:

para que   Necesito ver al asesor **para que** me **ayude.**
so that, for   *I need to see the advisor so that he might help me.*

a menos que   Los inmigrantes no pueden trabajar **a menos que**
unless   **tengan** una visa H1-B o una tarjeta de residencia.
                         Immigrants cannot work unless they have an H1-B visa
                         or a green card.

con tal (de) que   No tienen que hacer cola **con tal que hagan** una cita.
provided that   *They don't have to stand in line provided that they make*
                         an appointment.

12-14 ¿Qué prefieren? Diga si los clientes quieren que los funcionarios hagan las siguientes cosas en las oficinas administrativas y viceversa.

1. Los clientes (no) quieren que los funcionarios… (atenderlos rápidamente, estar de mal humor, saber su idioma, decirles que esperen, tener paciencia)
2. Los funcionarios (no) quieren que los clientes… (llegar tarde, traer todos los documentos, completar los formularios antes de llegar, enojarse, perder la paciencia, esperar su turno)

12-15 Reglamentos. Imagine que Ud. trabaja en la oficina de estudiantes extranjeros. Complete las siguientes oraciones de manera lógica con la conjunción **para que, a menos que** o **con tal que** y la forma correcta del verbo entre paréntesis.

> **Modelo** Los estudiantes extranjeros no pueden estudiar aquí **a menos que** ___**tengan**___ (tener) una visa.

1. Necesitan ser admitidos a una universidad __para que__ el Servicio de Inmigración les ___dé___ (dar) una visa.
2. Sus visas permanecen vigentes __con tal que__ ___sean___ (ser) estudiantes de tiempo completo.
3. Generalmente no se consideran estudiantes de tiempo completo __a menos que__ __se matriculen__ (matricularse) en doce horas de clases.
4. Necesitan presentar una carta de solvencia __a menos que__ ___tengan___ (tener) una beca.
5. Pueden matricularse en clases con estudiantes del país __con tal que__ ___sepan___ (saber) hablar inglés.

Ⓖ 12-16 Recomendaciones. Un amigo va a estudiar un año en otro país. En grupos, preparen una lista de recomendaciones.

> Es necesario que… Es importante que… Es mejor que…
> Te recomiendo que…

> **Modelo** **Te recomiendo que hables con un asesor.**

1. llevar…
2. pedir…
3. encontrar…
4. hablar con…
5. confirmar…
6. obtener…
7. solicitar…
8. saber…
9. informarse…
10. ???

12-17 En el extranjero. ¿Qué prefiere Ud. si estudia en un país hispano?

> **Modelo** Prefiero una universidad que… (tener residencias / ofrecer alojamiento con familias)
> **Prefiero una universidad que tenga residencias.**

1. Prefiero una universidad que… (estar en una ciudad grande / estar en las provincias, estar en México / estar en España, tener un campus moderno / tener muchos edificios históricos)
2. Prefiero un/a compañero/a de cuarto que… (fumar / no fumar, ser de allí / ser estudiante extranjero/a, sólo hablar español / hablar inglés, estudiar ciencias / estudiar literatura o arte)

Supplemental activity. Diga si cree las siguientes afirmaciones sobre las universidades en España. Comience cada oración con **Dudo que…, Es posible que…** o **Estoy seguro/a de que…** 1. Las universidades en España son en su mayoría públicas. 2. Los estudiantes universitarios con mejores notas son generalmente las muchachas. 3. Las carreras universitarias en España son de tres o de cinco años. 4. En España, las universidades privadas tienen más recursos que las universidades públicas. 5. En las universidades públicas hay muchos más estudiantes por clase que en las universidades privadas.

VOCABULARIO
¿Qué le dijeron que hiciera?

En las oficinas del gobierno **hay que...**

hacer una cita

acudir a la hora prevista

hacer cola, esperar su turno

hablar con los funcionarios

completar los formularios

entregar los documentos y pagar las tarifas

---

hay que... *one must...* **acudir** *to come, to show up* **previsto/a** *planned, arranged, scheduled* **una tarifa** *a fee*

12-18 **El Servicio de Ciudadanía e Inmigración.** Complete la siguiente descripción del Servicio de Ciudadanía e Inmigración de Estados Unidos con las palabras lógicas de la lista.

Supplemental activities. A. Imagine que Ud. es un/a inmigrante ilegal. En grupos, preparen al menos tres oraciones describiendo cómo sería su vida. *Modelo: Sería difícil encontrar un buen trabajo.* **B.** En grupos, preparen argumentos a favor y en contra de abrir las fronteras abiertas a los inmigrantes.

> proporcionan   acuden   atienden   tarifa   cola
> ciudadanía   cita   funcionarios   solicitudes

En el año 2003, el Servicio de Inmigración y Naturalización de Estados Unidos se convirtió en el Servicio de Ciudadanía e Inmigración, donde unos 15.000 (1) _funcionarios_ (2) _atienden_ a más de 5.000.000 de clientes que (3) _acuden_ a sus oficinas cada año. Además, tramitan unos 6.000.000 de (4) _solicitudes_ de ciudadanía o de visa cada año y les (5) _proporcionan_ información a unos 14.000.000 de clientes por teléfono. Para evitar que los clientes hagan (6) _cola_, en muchas oficinas se puede hacer una (7) _cita_ por Internet. Los inmigrantes pagan una (8) _tarifa_ de 240 dólares con su solicitud de ciudadanía. En promedio, unos 600.000 inmigrantes obtienen la (9) _ciudadanía_ cada año.

12-19 **Consejos.** Alguien le da consejos a un amigo que quiere solicitar la ciudadanía. Complete las siguientes oraciones con verbos lógicos.

Suggestion for 12-19. *Consejos.* Remind students to use the subjunctive after these conjunctions.

1. No tendrás que hacer cola con tal que _hagas_ una cita.
2. No te atenderán a menos que _acudas_ a la hora prevista.
3. Necesitas hablar con un funcionario del Servicio de Ciudadanía e Inmigración para que te _dé_ más información.
4. No tramitarán tu solicitud a menos que _completes_ todos los documentos necesarios.
5. Te doy estos consejos para que no _tengas_ problemas.

P

Conversaciones. En parejas, lean la siguiente conversación en la cual un inmigrante habla de todos los trámites burocráticos y **papeleo** en el Servicio de Ciudadanía e Inmigración. Luego, cambien la conversación para describir una situación en la cual uno/a de Uds. tuvo que **realizar** muchos trámites burocráticos.

AUDIO ¡A escuchar!

Escuchen una conversación en la cual una estudiante habla de los problemas que tuvo cuando fue por su tarjeta de identificación. ¿Qué problemas tuvo?

— ¿Cómo te fue con la renovación de tu visa?
— Pasé todo el día ayer en el Servicio de Cuidadanía e Inmigración y tuve que regresar esta mañana. Salí con un dolor de cabeza tremendo. Hay tanto papeleo.
— ¿Qué pasó?
— Ayer tenía una cita para las nueve de la mañana pero fui a la oficina equivocada. Cuando llegué eran casi las diez y no me atendieron por dos horas.
— ¿Por qué tuviste que regresar esta mañana?
— Cuando les entregué mis documentos me dijeron que faltaba el comprobante de domicilio. Tuve que volver esta mañana regrese con una copia del recibo de la luz para probar dónde vivo.

---

el papeleo *paperwork, red tape*   **realizar** *to carry out, to perform*

Para averiguar

1. What form of the subjunctive do you use when the main verb is in a past tense?
2. What verb form is used to determine the stem of the imperfect subjunctive? What do you drop from it to obtain the imperfect subjunctive stem?
3. What are the endings for the imperfect subjunctive?
4. What is the only form of the imperfect subjunctive with a written accent?
5. When do you use the imperfect subjunctive with **ojalá (que)**?

GRAMÁTICA
Expresar sugerencias en relación al pasado: el imperfecto del subjuntivo

Just as the indicative mood has present and past tense forms, so does the subjunctive. Use the imperfect subjunctive to talk about the past. To form the imperfect subjunctive, remove the final **-on** ending from the **ellos/ellas** form of the preterite and add the following endings. The imperfect subjunctive of **hay** is **hubiera**.

	HABLAR	COMER	VIVIR	HACER
preterite of **ellos:**	hablarøn	comierøn	vivierøn	hicierøn
yo	hablar**a**	comier**a**	vivier**a**	hicier**a**
tú	hablar**as**	comier**as**	vivier**as**	hicier**as**
usted, él, ella	hablar**a**	comier**a**	vivier**a**	hicier**a**
nosotros/as	hablár**amos**	comiér**amos**	viviér**amos**	hiciér**amos**
vosotros/as	hablar**ais**	comier**ais**	vivier**ais**	hicier**ais**
ustedes, ellos, ellas	hablar**an**	comier**an**	vivier**an**	hicier**an**

Use the imperfect subjunctive to talk about past desires, needs, doubts, or emotions, just as one uses the present subjunctive to talk about the present or the future. Whether you use the present or imperfect subjunctive depends on whether the main verb is in the present tense or a past tense.

Quiero que vengas. / *I want you to come.*
Quería que vinieras. / *I wanted you to come.*

No creo que él sepa la verdad. / *I don't believe that he knows the truth.*
No creía que él supiera la verdad. / *I didn't believe that he knew the truth.*

Use the present subjunctive after **ojalá (que)** to say what you hope will happen, but use the imperfect subjunctive to say what you wish were true. The use of **que** is optional after **ojalá.**

Present subjunctive: Ojalá (que) **haga** buen tiempo. / *I hope the weather's nice.*
Imperfect subjunctive: Ojalá (que) **hiciera** buen tiempo. / *I wish the weather were nice.*

¡Ojo!

Do you remember the preterite form for **ellos** of these irregular verbs?

decir:	dijeron
dar:	dieron
estar:	estuvieron
hacer:	hicieron
ir/ser:	fueron
poder:	pudieron
poner:	pusieron
querer:	quisieron
saber:	supieron
traer:	trajeron
tener:	tuvieron
venir:	vinieron

And of stem-changing **-ir** verbs?

dormir:	durmieron
servir:	sirvieron

Supplemental activity. Trabajando en grupos, preparen listas de cosas que yo le dije a algún estudiante o a la clase que hicieran desde el comienzo de la clase hoy o de esta semana. ¿Qué grupo puede hacer la lista más detallada? *Modelos: Le dije a Ángela que fuera a la pizarra. Nos dijo que entregáramos la tarea.*

12-20 En el colegio. ¿Qué deseaban sus padres cuando Ud. era estudiante de la secundaria? Utilice un elemento de cada grupo para formar oraciones.

(No) Querían que (No) Insistían en que (No) Me permitían que (No) Les importaba que	(yo)	hablara mucho con ellos. trabajara. saliera con los amigos todos los días. pasara mucho tiempo con ellos. sacara buenas notas. volviera a casa muy tarde los sábados. fuera feliz. ayudara en casa. fuera a la iglesia/sinagoga/mezquita. comiera bien.

12-21 ¿Quién? ¿Quién le dijo o le pidió al otro que hiciera las siguientes cosas en la oficina de inmigración?

El funcionario le dijo al inmigrante que…

El inmigrante le pidió al funcionario que…

Modelo traer todos los documentos
El funcionario le dijo al inmigrante que trajera todos los documentos.

1. hacer cola
2. explicarle los formularios
3. no llegar tarde a su cita
4. atenderlo con paciencia

5. volver a una segunda cita
6. venir a su oficina
7. darle una visa
8. enseñarle su pasaporte

Ⓖ 12-22 Preferencias. En grupos, comparen lo que les parecía más importante en la selección de una universidad.

Modelo tener un campus bonito
E1: **Yo quería una universidad que tuviera un campus bonito.**
E2: **A mí no me importaba que tuviera un campus bonito.**

1. tener un buen equipo de…
2. estar cerca/lejos de la casa de mis padres
3. tener un campus bonito
4. estar en una ciudad grande/pequeña
5. tener clases pequeñas
6. no costar mucho
7. ser conocida por su departamento de…
8. dar muchos cursos por Internet
9. darme una beca

12-23 Ojalá. Complete las siguientes oraciones describiendo sus deseos.

Modelo Ojalá que pudiera…
Ojalá que pudiera tomar unas vacaciones.

1. Ojalá que tuviera…
2. Ojalá que no tuviera que…
3. Ojalá que supiera…
4. Ojalá que mi mejor amigo/a y yo pudiéramos…
5. Ojalá que mi mejor amigo/a fuera…

Ⓟ 12-24 Entrevista. Entreviste a otro/a estudiante con estas preguntas.

En la escuela secundaria, ¿te gustaba que tus padres te hicieran muchas preguntas acerca de (*about*) tus amigos o te molestaba? ¿Te permitían que salieras hasta tarde los fines de semana? ¿A qué hora querían que volvieras a casa si salías los sábados? ¿Insistían en que les dijeras adónde ibas cuando salías? ¿Qué cosas no te permitían que hicieras con los amigos? ¿Te enojaba que te dijeran que no hicieras esas cosas? ¿Insistían en que sacaras buenas notas en la escuela? ¿Querían que trabajaras durante el verano?

VOCABULARIO
Les agradecería...

Para comenzar una carta o un correo electrónico en situaciones formales, se puede decir…

Señores…
Estimado/a señor/a…
A quien corresponda…

Para explicar por qué escribe, se puede decir…

Me dirijo a usted(es) con la intención de…
Con referencia a…
Quisiera saber más sobre…
Les agradecería me enviaran más información **acerca de…**
Deseo confirmar que…
Adjunto le(s) envío…

Para cerrar la carta o el correo electrónico se puede decir…

Atentamente,
A la espera de su respuesta…

12-25 Les agradecería me… Escriban oraciones lógicas utilizando el imperfecto del subjuntivo como en el modelo.

> Modelo **Le agradecería me explicara los formularios.**

Le agradecería me	dar enviar proporcionar explicar enseñar ayudar con confirmar	un ejemplo los formularios los datos las fechas límites los pasos a seguir más información los trámites los documentos necesarios

Suggestion for 12-25. *Les agradecería me…* Point out to students the use of the imperfect subjunctive with this expression and check that they understand its meaning by having a volunteer translate the model sentence.

A quien corresponda *To whom it may concern* **Me dirijo a usted(es)…** *I'm writing/contacting you…*
les agradecería + imperfect subjunctive *I would be grateful if you would…* **acerca de** *about* **adjunto** *attached*
atentamente *sincerely*

12-26　Una carta. Complete la siguiente carta con palabras lógicas.

Joel Martínez
305 East 50ᵗʰ Street
Austin, Texas 78751
Estados Unidos

21 de noviembre de 2005

Instituto Cervantes
San Juan, 84
28020 Madrid
España

(1) __Estimados__ señores:

Me (2) ____dirijo____ a Uds. con la intención de obtener información
(3) __acerca de__ su programa de español para estudiantes extranjeros para el
verano que viene. Les (4) __agradecería__ me enviaran información acerca de los
cursos que se ofrecerán y el costo. Además (5) __quisiera/deseo__ saber si habrá
alojamiento disponible y confirmar los documentos necesarios y la fecha
límite para ser admitido al programa.

(6) __Atentamente__,

Joel Martínez

Note: Answers may vary.

G　Conversaciones. En grupos, lean la siguiente conversación en la cual dos
estudiantes extranjeros escriben una carta a la oficina de admisiones de su
universidad. Luego, imaginen que se habla español en su universidad y que
ustedes le escriben una carta al presidente (a la presidenta) o a otro
departamento de su universidad con alguna recomendación.

— Le estoy escribiendo una carta a la oficina de admisiones con nuestras
recomendaciones de cómo atender mejor a los estudiantes extranjeros.
¿A quién le dirijo la carta? ¿Comienzo con *A quien corresponda*?
— Sí, creo que está bien. ¿Qué les vas a decir?
— Les voy a recomendar que hagan una lista de estudiantes de lenguas
extranjeras de esta universidad que quisieran conocer a estudiantes
extranjeros. Al llegar a la universidad, les sería útil a los estudiantes
extranjeros conocer a alguien de aquí que los ayude a adaptarse al nuevo
sistema. También les sería útil a los estudiantes norteamericanos conocer a
estudiantes extranjeros para practicar las lenguas que estudian. Aprenderían
mucho de los estudiantes extranjeros y podrían hacer amistades.
— Es buena idea. Deberías enviarles esta carta a los departamentos de
lenguas extranjeras también.
— Voy a terminar la carta con *Atentamente*… ¿Quieres firmarla también?
— Sí. ¡Claro! Me habría sido de gran ayuda conocer a estudiantes de aquí
durante los primeros días en la universidad.

AUDIO ¡A escuchar!

Escuchen una conversación en la
cual dos amigos hablan de un
correo electrónico que uno de
ellos recibió de una amiga que
estudia en el extranjero. ¿Cuáles
son dos cosas que haría de
manera diferente si volviera a
comenzar?

Follow-up for *Conversaciones*. As a
writing assignment, have students
write the letter they discuss in their
adaptation of the dialogue.

GRAMÁTICA

Evocar situaciones ficticias: las oraciones de *si* + imperfecto del subjuntivo

Para averiguar

When talking about hypothetical circumstances, which tense do you use for verbs in the clause with **si** (*if*)? Which tense do you use in the result clause saying what would happen?

Use the conditional to say what would happen under different circumstances and use the imperfect subjunctive in the clause with **si** to state the circumstances.

Si **tuviera** más dinero, **compraría** una casa.	*If I had more money, I would buy a house.*
Si yo **fuera** usted, **llegaría** muy temprano.	*If I were you, I would arrive very early.*

The order of the clauses may be reversed without changing the meaning of sentences.

Si me dijeran eso, estaría furioso. / Estaría furioso si me dijeran eso.	*If they told me that, I would be furious. / I would be furious if they told me that.*

12-27 Reacciones. ¿Cómo reaccionaría Ud. en las siguientes situaciones si tuviera que hacer unos trámites en el Servicio de Cuidadanía e Inmigración?

> me enojaría   me quejaría   se lo agradecería   no haría nada   ???

1. Si tuviera que esperar más de cinco horas para que me atendieran…
2. Si pudiera hacer todos los trámites en línea…
3. Si el funcionario perdiera todos mis documentos…
4. Si el funcionario tramitara rápidamente mi solicitud…
5. Si me explicaran todos los trámites y formularios en mi propio idioma…
6. Si un asesor me diera la información equivocada…
7. Si alguien no hiciera cola como los otros clientes para esperar su turno…
8. Si me dijeran que volviera otro día después de hacer cola por dos horas…

Follow-up for 12-28. *Situaciones hipotéticas.* Have students think of one more ending for each of the sentences.

12-28 Situaciones hipotéticas. Complete las oraciones diciendo si Ud. haría las cosas indicadas entre paréntesis.

1. Si no tuviera clase hoy… (estar en casa, ir a la biblioteca, ir al lago, dormir todo el día)
2. Si fuera el/la profesor/a de español… (dar mucha tarea hoy, hacer exámenes muy difíciles, hablar mucho español)
3. Si ganara diez millones de dólares… (seguir trabajando, comprar un carro muy caro, viajar, darles mucho dinero a organizaciones humanitarias)
4. Si estuviera de vacaciones esta semana… (ir a la playa, quedarse en casa, visitar a sus padres, poder descansar, hacer un viaje a México)
5. Si hubiera un examen sobre este capítulo hoy… (estar listo/a, saber todas las respuestas, ponerse nervioso/a)

12-29 Si… Complete las siguientes oraciones.

Suggestion for 12-29. *Si…* Give students time to prepare.

> **Modelo**   Tendría más energía si **durmiera más y comiera mejor.**

1. Me gustarían más mis clases si…
2. Estudiaría más si…
3. Comprendería mejor los contenidos de esta clase si…
4. Pasaría más tiempo con mi familia si…
5. Me llevaría mejor con mi compañero/a de cuarto (mis padres) si…
6. Perdería menos la paciencia si…
7. Sería más feliz si…

12-30 Pretextos. Un amigo le hace las siguientes sugerencias. Conteste sus sugerencias con un pretexto lógico.

> **Modelo**   ¿Por qué no haces más ejercicio?
> **Haría más ejercicio si tuviera tiempo.**

1. ¿Por que no visitas más a tus padres?
2. ¿Por qué no te quedas más en casa?
3. ¿Por qué no trabajas menos?
4. ¿Por qué no estudias en el extranjero por un semestre?
5. ¿Me puedes prestar tu carro?
6. ¿Me puedes dar 20 dólares?
7. ¿Me puedes explicar el uso del subjuntivo en español?

Ⓟ 12-31 Psicólogo. Complete las siguientes preguntas con la forma correcta de cada verbo entre paréntesis y entreviste a otro/a estudiante.

1. Si ___fueras___ (ser: tú) una persona famosa, ¿quién te ___gustaría___ (gustar) ser? ¿Por qué? ¿Cómo ___sería___ (ser) la vida si ___fueras___ (ser: tú) esa persona?

2. Si ___pudieras___ (poder: tú) hablar con cualquier (*any*) persona del pasado, ¿con quién ___hablarías___ (hablar: tú)? Si ___vivieras___ (vivir: tú) en cualquier época (*time period*) del pasado, ¿cuándo ___preferirías___ (preferir: tú) vivir?

3. Si ___pudieras___ (poder: tú) vivir en cualquier ciudad del mundo, ¿qué ciudad ___escogerías___ (escoger: tú)? ¿Qué ___harías___ (hacer: tú) si ___vivieras___ (vivir: tú) en esa ciudad?

4. Si ___pudieras___ (poder: tú) cambiar algo en el mundo, ¿qué ___sería___ (ser)?

5. Si ___volvieras___ (volver: tú) a vivir los últimos diez años de tu vida, ¿qué ___cambiarías___ (cambiar: tú)?

6. Si ___hicieran___ (hacer: ellos) una película sobre tu vida, ¿___Sería___ (ser) una comedia, una película de acción, una película de amor o una película de terror? ¿Quién ___sería___ (ser) el actor/la actriz principal? ¿___Escogerías___ (escoger: tú) música latina, clásica, country, rock, rap o jazz para la película?

7. Si ___escribieras___ (escribir: tú) una autobiografía hasta el presente, ¿cómo ___se llamaría___ (llamarse) el libro? ¿Qué parte del libro ___sería___ (ser) la más interesante, el comienzo, los capítulos centrales o el final? ¿Qué parte ___sería___ (ser) la menos interesante?

¡Trato hecho!

En portada

REVISTA CULTURAL

Note: Have students complete the *Antes de leer, Reading strategies,* and *Ahora Ud.* activities before reading this article.

CONECTAR CON LA LENGUA EN SU ELEMENTO

¿Qué significa conocer una lengua? ¿Entender su gramática? ¿Tener un amplio vocabulario? ¿Poder interactuar con sus **hablantes**? Las lenguas son la expresión viva de la cultura y las tradiciones de sus hablantes, del pensamiento y de la idiosincrasia de su pueblo. Por eso, debemos complementar la práctica activa de la lengua en el salón de clase con su experiencia directa en las sociedades que la hablan. El contacto directo con hablantes nativos nos ayudará a obtener un buen conocimiento de la lengua en situaciones

¡En el extranjero!

reales de comunicación.

Estudiar en el extranjero, conectar con la lengua en su elemento y aprender la cultura de sus hablantes nos dan la oportunidad de vivir la lengua en todas sus dimensiones. La oferta de programas para estudiar español en Latinoamérica y España es muy variada. ¿Cómo escoger el programa adecuado? Muchas universidades norteamericanas poseen **convenios** con instituciones en países hispanos que nos facilitan

¿Cómo escoger?

la transición académica para solicitar la admisión al programa de estudios y pasar un año, un semestre o un verano estudiando en el extranjero.

Pero no estamos limitados a estos convenios. Internet nos permite acceder directamente a las páginas web de las instituciones

Voluntarios sin fronteras.

extranjeras y obtener información sobre la ubicación de la institución, sus ofertas académicas y **el perfil** de sus estudiantes. A la hora de escoger un programa debemos pensar en las razones para estudiar en el extranjero: ¿conocer un nuevo país y su gente? ¿practicar la lengua? ¿dar un servicio a la comunidad?

Los programas tradicionales ofrecen clases de lengua, cultura, arte, política y negocios que generalmente son transferibles al plan de estudios de la universidad norteamericana. Una alternativa muy **altruista** a estos programas son los programas de **voluntariado** que combinan el estudio de la lengua y la cultura con la participación en tareas sociales de ayuda a la comunidad.

Celebración del Cinco de Mayo en Los Ángeles, California.

También es importante recordar la increíble riqueza cultural hispana que Estados Unidos ofrece. En nuestra sociedad podemos entrar en contacto con la diversidad de culturas hispanas que viven en este país. **Acérquense a** esta comunidad y conecten con la lengua en su elemento; la lengua y su gente están esperándolos.

---

hablantes *speakers*   **convenios** *agreements*   **el perfil** *profile*   **altruista** *altruist*   **voluntariado** *volunteering*   **acérquense a** *reach out to*

Antes de leer

¿Cree que es importante estudiar en el extranjero? ¿Cuáles son algunas de las razones por las que cree que sería beneficioso para usted pasar un semestre o un verano estudiando en una universidad hispanoamericana?

Después de leer

Reading strategies: Reacting to a text. As a reader you bring to the reading process an array of relevant opinions and experiences related to the topic or topics presented in the text. Identifying main ideas, understanding the author's point of view, and reacting to the text are essential parts of the critical reading process. The reader can react to a reading, expressing opinions about the issues addressed in the text, and contrasting his/her ideas with the author's point of view.

12-32 Ahora Ud. ¿Está de acuerdo o no con las siguientes opiniones que presenta el autor en el artículo *Conectar con la lengua en su elemento*? Explique por qué.

1. Las lenguas son la expresión viva de la cultura y de las tradiciones de sus hablantes.
2. Debemos complementar la práctica activa de la lengua en el salón de clase con su experiencia directa en las sociedades que la manejan (*use it*).
3. El contacto directo con hablantes nativos nos facilita alcanzar (*to reach*) un buen conocimiento de la lengua.
4. No debemos sentirnos limitados por los convenios de nuestra universidad para estudiar en el extranjero.
5. Podemos conectar con la lengua española a través de las comunidades hispanas de Estados Unidos.

12-33 Espero que tengas suerte. Un/a amigo/a le cuenta que piensa estudiar un semestre en el extranjero. Hágale algunas sugerencias utilizando las expresiones impersonales con subjuntivo.

> Modelo   **Es importante que escojas una buena universidad.**

12-34 Quiero un programa que... ¿Cuáles son las características que busca en un programa de estudios en el extranjero? Describa este programa ideal utilizando el subjuntivo en las cláusulas relativas.

> Modelo   **Busco un programa que ofrezca cursos de arte.**

12-35 Si pudiera... Si pudiera estudiar en un país de habla hispana, ¿qué país escogería? ¿Por qué? ¿En qué universidad estudiaría? ¿Cuánto tiempo pasaría allí? ¿Viviría con una familia? ¿Qué cursos tomaría? ¿Combinaría sus estudios con actividades de voluntariado?

Escriba un párrafo respondiendo a estas preguntas y añadiendo (*adding*) otros detalles que crea importantes.

> Modelo   **Si pudiera estudiar en un país de habla hispana, escogería Chile.**

12-36 En mi universidad... ¿Qué programas ofrece su universidad para estudiar en el extranjero? ¿Le interesa algún programa en particular? ¿Qué opinión tienen los estudiantes de estos programas? Hable con varios estudiantes en el campus que hayan participado en programas en el extranjero y presente sus testimonios al resto de la clase. Si no encuentra estudiantes que hayan estudiado en el extranjero, hable con estudiantes de programas de ESL (*English as a Second Language*) y pregúnteles sobre las diferencias entre el sistema de estudios en su país y el sistema de estudios norteamericano.

Suggestion. Have students summarize the main ideas of the article before completing the activity *Ahora Ud.* The summary will allow them to present their own understanding of the reading.

Suggestion. Have any students who have studied abroad narrate their experience to the class using the past tenses and give advice to the rest of the class about studying abroad.

De puertas abiertas a la comunidad

🎥 SUEÑOS

12-37 Entrando en materia. ¿Es usted idealista? ¿Cree que la situación social actual puede mejorarse? ¿Cuáles son sus sueños (*dreams*)? ¿Piensa que el futuro le sonreirá (*will smile on you*)? ¿Cómo sería su vida ideal?

> La realidad social que vive la población hispana en Estados Unidos no siempre es óptima. Desde las oficinas del gobernador del estado de Nueva York nos habla Javier Gómez, subsecretario de prensa puertorriqueño, muy informado de los aspectos que preocupan a la comunidad hispana y con ideas brillantes sobre cómo llegar al público hispano e **involucrarlo** en asuntos políticos y sociales.
>
> El sentimiento de solidaridad existente entre los hispanos de los Estados Unidos es muy profundo. No importa el origen mexicano, guatemalteco, nicaragüense, chileno, colombiano, dominicano o puertorriqueño, todos se sienten hermanos, y están bien **orgullosos** de ser hispanos y de compartir una misma lengua: el español. Sus sueños son grandes, algunos ya los están viviendo, escúchenlos, están llenos de **esperanza.**

Answers for 12-38. ¿Cierto o falso?
2. Están llegando millones de inmigrantes de zonas donde antes no había una ola migratoria tan marcada.
3. El inmigrante está preocupado por encontrar un trabajo.

12-38 ¿Cierto o falso? Escuche con atención el testimonio de Javier González e indique si las siguientes afirmaciones son ciertas o falsas. Corrija las falsas.

	Cierto	Falso
1. El inmigrante hispano viene a los Estados Unidos buscando el sueño americano.	X	
2. La inmigración hispana no es muy abundante en los últimos años.		X
3. El desempleo no preocupa a los inmigrantes hispanos.		X
4. El reto (*challenge*) del gobierno está en proveer oportunidades para los nuevos inmigrantes.	X	
5. Los hispanos están preocupados por dar a su familia una casa segura.	X	

12-39 El sueño americano. Javier menciona que el inmigrante hispano viene a los Estados Unidos buscando el sueño americano. ¿Qué es para usted el sueño americano? ¿Qué representa para un inmigrante obtener este sueño?

Answers for 12-40. Preocupaciones.
A los hispanos les preocupa la inmigración y la educación, porque la educación abre la puerta a la oportunidad y permite conseguir un empleo con solvencia económica y posibilidades de ascenso, posibilidades de aumento. También les preocupa el desarrollo económico (¿empleo o desempleo? ¿dónde trabajar? ¿cómo ahorrar?) y la vivienda (¿cómo adquirir? ¿cómo ser propietario? y ¿cómo poder tener un techo seguro?).

12-40 Preocupaciones. Javier nos habla de los principales aspectos que preocupan a la población hispana. ¿Podría mencionar estos aspectos? ¿Por qué le preocupan a la comunidad hispana estas cuestiones?

---

involucrarlo *to engage them*   **orgullosos** *proud*   **esperanza** *hope*

12-41 La educación. ¿Qué opinión tiene Javier sobre recibir una buena educación? ¿Cuál es la opinión personal de usted sobre este tema? ¿Qué puertas cree usted que abre el haber recibido una buena educación? Utilice en su respuesta verbos como **(no) pensar/(no) creer/(no) estar seguro** y estructuras impersonales como **es importante/increíble/lógico/necesario/preferible.** Preste atención al uso del subjuntivo.

G 12-42 Madera de líder. ¿Creen ustedes que Javier tiene un futuro brillante en la política? ¿Creen que tiene "madera de líder" (*the makings of a leader*)? ¿Por qué sí o por qué no? ¿Qué características creen que debe tener un buen político? Usen el subjuntivo en cláusulas relativas para hacer su descripción de un buen político.

12-43 ¿Quién sueña? Escuche con atención los grandes sueños de los hispanos que han participado en este vídeo y asocie cada sueño con la persona que corresponda.

1.

2.

3.

4.

5.

6.

a. comenzar otros negocios
b. continuar haciendo una diferencia positiva
c. producir documentales y escribir
d. siempre tener la música en mi vida
e. crear una sociedad de respeto mutuo entre las personas
f. formar una familia

G 12-44 Sueños hechos realidad. Escuchen los sueños que las personas en el vídeo han compartido con nosotros. Identifiquen a las personas que están viviendo su sueño y expliquen cómo están viviendo ese sueño en sus vidas.

G 12-45 Hay esperanza... Seleccionen el sueño de una de las personas entrevistadas en el vídeo, el que más le haya gustado, y expliquen a la clase por qué les ha causado impacto el sueño de esa persona en particular.

Escapadas

ECUADOR MÁGICO, INSPIRACIÓN NATURAL

Ecuador es un país lleno de contrastes, por su variedad geográfica, étnica y cultural. Su nombre viene de la línea imaginaria del ecuador, que **atraviesa** el país y divide la Tierra en el hemisferio norte y el hemisferio sur. Los países vecinos de Ecuador son al norte Colombia y al sureste Perú; al oeste tiene el Océano Pacífico, donde están las famosas Islas Galápagos, territorio ecuatoriano.

Las Islas Galápagos.

La variedad geográfica de Ecuador se refleja en la belleza de sus montañas, los Andes, de su **selva amazónica,** de sus volcanes, de sus playas y de sus islas en el Pacífico. La riqueza cultural ecuatoriana **deriva de** su gran herencia indígena: un 52% de la población es india **quechua,** un 40% mestiza, y el 8% restante es de origen español o africano. La lengua oficial es el español, pero también se habla el quechua, una lengua indígena de la región.

Herencia indígena.

La capital, Quito, es una de las ciudades más antiguas de América del Sur. El Quito colonial es un **entresijo** de callejuelas y edificios de origen español, mezclados con mercados indígenas. La Catedral, la Iglesia de la Compañía y el Convento de San Francisco, conocido como *El Escorial de Los Andes*, son algunos de los ejemplos más importantes de la arquitectura colonial de Quito.

El Quito colonial.

La Iglesia de la Compañía, Quito.

Monte Chimborazo, los Andes.

---

atraviesa *crosses* **selva amazónica** *Amazonian jungle* **deriva de** *comes from* **quechua** *indigenous people from Ecuador* **entresijo** *maze*

Viajando unas horas hacia el norte a través de las montañas de los Andes, se encuentra el magnífico Mercado de Otavalo, el más rico de Sudamérica en su clase, donde los indígenas ofrecen sus artesanías, sus coloridos ponchos de lana y su **bisutería andina.** El mejor día para ir al mercado es el sábado, cuando una multitud de artesanos **se reúnen** en Otavalo.

Venta de ponchos en el Mercado de Otavalo.

Bisutería andina en el Mercado de Otavalo.

Sin duda, el destino estelar de Ecuador son las Islas Galápagos, cuyo nombre oficial es el Archipiélago Colón. Las islas, situadas a 590 millas de la costa de Ecuador, son el laboratorio natural con mayor biodiversidad del planeta. Las islas son de origen volcánico y las más antiguas emergieron hace unos cinco millones de años. Familias de reptiles como tortugas gigantes, iguanas y **lagartijas de lava, conviven** con pingüinos, cormoranes, albatros, leones marinos y delfines en este santuario natural, que inspiró a Charles Darwin a desarrollar su teoría de la evolución.

Ecuador mágico, inspiración natural.

Tortuga gigante a los pies del Volcán Alcedo, Islas Galápagos.

León de mar tomando el sol en las Islas Galápagos.

Pareja de albatros en las Islas Galápagos.

bisutería andina *Andean costume jewelry* **se reúnen** *gather* **lagartijas de lava** *lava lizards* **conviven** *live together*

12-46 Errores. Alguien le ha dado información errónea sobre Ecuador. Ahora que sabe un poco más sobre el país, explique por qué las siguientes afirmaciones son falsas.

1. Ecuador está situado en el Mar Caribe.
2. No se sabe de dónde viene el nombre del país.
3. La herencia indígena no es especialmente visible en Ecuador.
4. La capital de Ecuador, Guayaquil, es una ciudad moderna.
5. Los mercados indígenas no son típicos de Ecuador.
6. Las Islas Galápagos son territorio chileno.
7. No han sobrevivido muchas especies animales en las Islas Galápagos.
8. Las especies animales de las Islas Galápagos viven aisladas (*isolated*) unas de otras.

12-47 ¿Te acuerdas de nuestro viaje a Ecuador? Escriban una conversación entre dos amigos/as que hablan de su viaje a Ecuador. ¿Qué visitaron? ¿Qué impresión tuvieron de la gente de Ecuador? ¿Qué compras hicieron? Después escenifiquen la conversación para el resto de la clase.

12-48 Ecuador mágico. Imaginen que tienen que desarrollar una campaña para promocionar el turismo en Ecuador. En grupos preparen un anuncio con fotos, texto y música, destacando los atractivos del país y las razones por las cuales es un lugar mágico para el turista.

12-49 Me encantaría... Después de leer *Ecuador mágico, inspiración natural,* ¿cree que le gustaría visitar Ecuador? ¿Estudiaría un semestre o un verano allí? Explique sus razones. Si es necesario, puede buscar información adicional en Internet sobre el país y sobre las ofertas académicas.

El Convento de San Francisco, Quito.

En palabras de...

CORRESPONDENCIA FORMAL

Ud. está pensando en pasar un semestre o un verano estudiando en un país de Latinoamérica, pero le gustaría obtener información más detallada sobre el programa. Ud. decide escribir una carta al programa de estudios en el extranjero de la universidad que ha escogido expresando su interés en el programa y solicitando más detalles sobre el mismo.

Writing strategies: Writing a letter requesting information.
When we write a letter requesting information, it is essential to organize it logically, greeting the addressee appropriately: **Señores...; Muy señor/a mío/a...; Estimado/a señor/a...**, stating the purpose of the letter early on: **Me dirijo a ustedes con el objeto de...**; making any further request that you might have, and thanking the addressee in advance for the time and the information that will be provided to you: **Le agradezco su colaboración en este asunto / Gracias por su atención en este particular.**

It is also very important to consider the tone of the letter. Make your request formal, polite, and clear.

Antes de escribir

Comience la elaboración de su carta preparando:

- una lista de los centros universitarios de Latinoamérica donde le gustaría estudiar;
- una lista de las razones por las que le gustaría estudiar en esos centros;
- una lista de los aspectos a considerar a la hora de estudiar en el extranjero.

Seleccione la universidad que le parezca más atractiva y escriba una carta al/a la director/a del programa solicitando información sobre los aspectos que mencionó en su lista relacionados con los estudios en el extranjero.

Después de escribir

Revise y edite su carta asegurándose que incluyó las siguientes estructuras:

- ✓ expresiones formales de saludo
- ✓ estructuras para expresar interés y deseo
- ✓ expresiones formales para solicitar información
- ✓ el condicional de cortesía
- ✓ expresiones formales para cerrar la carta

 **En la red**

Visite la página web de organizaciones para estudiar en el extranjero, como *International Studies Abroad* para asegurarse que incluyó en su carta todos los detalles interesantes y necesarios sobre cursar estudios en el extranjero y para leer algunos de los testimonios de los estudiantes que han participado de esta experiencia.

All the sources consulted for the readings are cited on the *¡Trato hecho!* Web site at **www.prenhall.com/trato**

VOCABULARIO

TEMA ❶

Sustantivos
la admisión *admission*
el alojamiento *housing, lodging*
un/a alumno/a (de nuevo ingreso) *a(n) (entering) student*
un/a asesor/a *an advisor*
una estancia *a stay*
la fecha límite *the deadline*
los pasos *the steps*
un plan de estudios *a plan of studies, a degree plan, curriculum*

el plazo de matrícula *the registration period*
una tarjeta de identificación *an identification card*

Expresiones verbales
atender (ie) *to wait on*
entregar *to turn/hand in*
escoger *to pick*
explicar *to explain*
matricularse *to register*

presentarse *to show up, to be present*
prolongar *to prolong, to extend*
renovar (ue) *to renew*
ser admitido/a *to be admitted*
solicitar *to apply for*

Otras palabras y expresiones
en el extranjero *abroad*
varios *various*

TEMA ❷

Sustantivos
un acta de nacimiento *a birth certificate*
una asignatura *a (school) subject*
una carta de solvencia *a letter of financial standing*
un certificado de secundaria *a high-school diploma*
un cónsul *a consul*
una ficha *a card*
un impreso *a printout, a form*

un/a notario/a público/a *a notary public*
la oficina de admisiones y registro *the Registrar's Office*
un sobre *an envelope*
el tamaño *the size*

Verbos
asesorar *to advise*
confirmar *to confirm*
debería *I/he/she should*
enviar *to send*

legalizar *to authenticate*
rellenar *to fill out*

Adjetivos
obligatorio/a *required, obligatory*
optativo/a *optional, elective*
original *original*
vigente *valid*

Otra expresión
por supuesto *of course*

TEMA ❸

Sustantivos
una beca *a scholarship*
un/a funcionario/a *a government employee*
la gente *people*
la ciudadanía *citizenship*
un estado de cuenta *a (bank) statement*
los gastos *the expenses*
la nacionalidad *the nationality*
la renovación *the renovation, the renewal*

la residencia permanente *permanent residency*
el término *the end, the conclusion*
un/a turista *a tourist*

Verbos
permanecer *to remain*
probar (ue) *to prove*
proporcionar *to provide*
tramitar *to handle, to deal with*

Otras palabras y expresiones
a menos que *unless*
con tal (de) que *provided that, as long as*
con validez superior a... *valid for more than...*
en qué consiste *of what it consists, what it is*
exactamente *exactly*
para que *so (that)*

Para los adjetivos de nacionalidad, vea la página 366.

TEMA 4

Sustantivos
el domicilio *the domicile, the place of residence*
el papeleo *the paperwork, the red tape*
las tarifas *the fees*
el turno *the turn*

Expresiones verbales
acudir *to come, to show up*
hacer cola *to stand in line*
realizar *to carry out, to perform*

Otras palabras y expresiones
hay que... *one must...*
previsto/a *planned, arranged*
tremendo/a *tremendous*

TEMA 5

La correspondencia
adjunto *attached*
A la espera de *Awaiting...*
A quien corresponda *To Whom it May Concern*
Atentamente... *Sincerely...*
Estimado/a... *Dear... (in a formal letter)*

Me dirijo a usted(es) con la intención de... *I'm writing to you for the purpose of...*
Te/Le/Les agradecería *I would be grateful if you would...*

Otras palabras y expresiones
acerca de *about*

adaptarse *to adapt*
formal *formal*
hacer amistades *to make friends, to develop friendships*
una idea *an idea*
Me habría sido de gran ayuda... *It would have helped me a lot...*

Regular Verbs: Simple Tenses

TABLAS DE VERBOS

Infinitive Present Participle Past Participle	Indicative						Subjunctive		Imperative
	Present	Imperfect	Preterite	Future	Conditional		Present	Imperfect	
hablar hablando hablado	hablo hablas habla hablamos habláis hablan	hablaba hablabas hablaba hablábamos hablabais hablaban	hablé hablaste habló hablamos hablasteis hablaron	hablaré hablarás hablará hablaremos hablaréis hablarán	hablaría hablarías hablaría hablaríamos hablaríais hablarían		hable hables hable hablemos habléis hablen	hablara hablaras hablara habláramos hablarais hablaran	habla tú, no hables hable Ud. hablemos hablen Uds.
comer comiendo comido	como comes come comemos coméis comen	comía comías comía comíamos comíais comían	comí comiste comió comimos comisteis comieron	comeré comerás comerá comeremos comeréis comerán	comería comerías comería comeríamos comeríais comerían		coma comas coma comamos comáis coman	comiera comieras comiera comiéramos comierais comieran	come tú, no comas coma Ud. comamos coman Uds.
vivir viviendo vivido	vivo vives vive vivimos vivís viven	vivía vivías vivía vivíamos vivíais vivían	viví viviste vivió vivimos vivisteis vivieron	viviré vivirás vivirá viviremos viviréis vivirán	viviría vivirías viviría viviríamos viviríais vivirían		viva vivas viva vivamos viváis vivan	viviera vivieras viviera viviéramos vivierais vivieran	vive tú, no vivas viva Ud. vivamos vivan Uds.

Vosotros Commands

hablar	hablad, no habléis	comer	comed, no comáis	vivir	vivid, no viváis

Regular Verbs: Perfect Tenses

	Indicative					Subjunctive	
	Present Perfect	**Past Perfect**	**Preterite Perfect**	**Future Perfect**	**Conditional Perfect**	**Present Perfect**	**Past Perfect**
	he	había	hube	habré	habría	haya	hubiera
	has	habías	hubiste	habrás	habrías	hayas	hubieras
	ha hablado	había hablado	hubo hablado	habrá hablado	habría hablado	haya hablado	hubiera hablado
	hemos comido	habíamos comido	hubimos comido	habremos comido	habríamos comido	hayamos comido	hubiéramos comido
	habéis vivido	habíais vivido	hubisteis vivido	habréis vivido	habríais vivido	hayáis vivido	hubierais vivido
	han	habían	hubieron	habrán	habrían	hayan	hubieran

Irregular Verbs

Infinitive Present Participle Past Participle	Indicative					Subjunctive		Imperative
	Present	**Imperfect**	**Preterite**	**Future**	**Conditional**	**Present**	**Imperfect**	
andar andando andado	ando	andaba	anduve	andaré	andaría	ande	anduviera	anda tú,
	andas	andabas	anduviste	andarás	andarías	andes	anduvieras	no andes
	anda	andaba	anduvo	andará	andaría	ande	anduviera	ande Ud.
	andamos	andábamos	anduvimos	andaremos	andaríamos	andemos	anduviéramos	andemos
	andáis	andabais	anduvisteis	andaréis	andaríais	andéis	anduvierais	anden Uds.
	andan	andaban	anduvieron	andarán	andarían	anden	anduvieran	
caer cayendo caído	caigo	caía	caí	caeré	caería	caiga	cayera	cae tú,
	caes	caías	caíste	caerás	caerías	caigas	cayeras	no caigas
	cae	caía	cayó	caerá	caería	caiga	cayera	caiga Ud.
	caemos	caíamos	caímos	caeremos	caeríamos	caigamos	cayéramos	caigamos
	caéis	caíais	caísteis	caeréis	caeríais	caigáis	cayerais	caigan Uds.
	caen	caían	cayeron	caerán	caerían	caigan	cayeran	
dar dando dado	doy	daba	di	daré	daría	dé	diera	da tú,
	das	dabas	diste	darás	darías	des	dieras	no des
	da	daba	dio	dará	daría	dé	diera	dé Ud.
	damos	dábamos	dimos	daremos	daríamos	demos	diéramos	demos
	dais	dabais	disteis	daréis	daríais	deis	dierais	den Uds.
	dan	daban	dieron	darán	darían	den	dieran	

Irregular Verbs

Infinitive Present Participle Past Participle	Indicative					Subjunctive		Imperative
	Present	Imperfect	Preterite	Future	Conditional	Present	Imperfect	
decir diciendo dicho	digo dices dice decimos decís dicen	decía decías decía decíamos decíais decían	dije dijiste dijo dijimos dijisteis dijeron	diré dirás dirá diremos diréis dirán	diría dirías diría diríamos diríais dirían	diga digas diga digamos digáis digan	dijera dijeras dijera dijéramos dijerais dijeran	di tú, no digas diga Ud. digamos decid vosotros, no digáis digan Uds.
estar estando estado	estoy estás está estamos estáis están	estaba estabas estaba estábamos estabais estaban	estuve estuviste estuvo estuvimos estuvisteis estuvieron	estaré estarás estará estaremos estaréis estarán	estaría estarías estaría estaríamos estaríais estarían	esté estés esté estemos estéis estén	estuviera estuvieras estuviera estuviéramos estuvierais estuvieran	está tú, no estés esté Ud. estemos estad vosotros, no estéis estén Uds.
haber habiendo habido	he has ha hemos habéis han	había habías había habíamos habíais habían	hube hubiste hubo hubimos hubisteis hubieron	habré habrás habrá habremos habréis habrán	habría habrías habría habríamos habríais habrían	haya hayas haya hayamos hayáis hayan	hubiera hubieras hubiera hubiéramos hubierais hubieran	
hacer haciendo hecho	hago haces hace hacemos hacéis hacen	hacía hacías hacía hacíamos hacíais hacían	hice hiciste hizo hicimos hicisteis hicieron	haré harás hará haremos haréis harán	haría harías haría haríamos haríais harían	haga hagas haga hagamos hagáis hagan	hiciera hicieras hiciera hiciéramos hicierais hicieran	haz tú, no hagas haga Ud. hagamos haced vosotros, no hagáis hagan Uds.
ir yendo ido	voy vas va vamos vais van	iba ibas iba íbamos ibais iban	fui fuiste fue fuimos fuisteis fueron	iré irás irá iremos iréis irán	iría irías iría iríamos iríais irían	vaya vayas vaya vayamos vayáis vayan	fuera fueras fuera fuéramos fuerais fueran	ve tú, no vayas vaya Ud. vamos, no vayamos id vosotros, no vayáis vayan Uds.

Irregular Verbs (continued)

Infinitive / Present Participle / Past Participle	Indicative					Subjunctive		Imperative
	Present	Imperfect	Preterite	Future	Conditional	Present	Imperfect	
oír / oyendo / oído	oigo / oyes / oye / oímos / oís / oyen	oía / oías / oía / oíamos / oíais / oían	oí / oíste / oyó / oímos / oísteis / oyeron	oiré / oirás / oirá / oiremos / oiréis / oirán	oiría / oirías / oiría / oiríamos / oiríais / oirían	oiga / oigas / oiga / oigamos / oigáis / oigan	oyera / oyeras / oyera / oyéramos / oyerais / oyeran	oye tú, no oigas / oiga Ud. / oigamos / oigan Uds.
poder / pudiendo / podido	puedo / puedes / puede / podemos / podéis / pueden	podía / podías / podía / podíamos / podíais / podían	pude / pudiste / pudo / pudimos / pudisteis / pudieron	podré / podrás / podrá / podremos / podréis / podrán	podría / podrías / podría / podríamos / podríais / podrían	pueda / puedas / pueda / podamos / podáis / puedan	pudiera / pudieras / pudiera / pudiéramos / pudierais / pudieran	
poner / poniendo / puesto	pongo / pones / pone / ponemos / ponéis / ponen	ponía / ponías / ponía / poníamos / poníais / ponían	puse / pusiste / puso / pusimos / pusisteis / pusieron	pondré / pondrás / pondrá / pondremos / pondréis / pondrán	pondría / pondrías / pondría / pondríamos / pondríais / pondrían	ponga / pongas / ponga / pongamos / pongáis / pongan	pusiera / pusieras / pusiera / pusiéramos / pusierais / pusieran	pon tú, no pongas / ponga Ud. / pongamos / pongan Uds.
querer / queriendo / querido	quiero / quieres / quiere / queremos / queréis / quieren	quería / querías / quería / queríamos / queríais / querían	quise / quisiste / quiso / quisimos / quisisteis / quisieron	querré / querrás / querrá / querremos / querréis / querrán	querría / querrías / querría / querríamos / querríais / querrían	quiera / quieras / quiera / queramos / queráis / quieran	quisiera / quisieras / quisiera / quisiéramos / quisierais / quisieran	quiere tú, no quieras / quiera Ud. / queramos / quieran Uds.
saber / sabiendo / sabido	sé / sabes / sabe / sabemos / sabéis / saben	sabía / sabías / sabía / sabíamos / sabíais / sabían	supe / supiste / supo / supimos / supisteis / supieron	sabré / sabrás / sabrá / sabremos / sabréis / sabrán	sabría / sabrías / sabría / sabríamos / sabríais / sabrían	sepa / sepas / sepa / sepamos / sepáis / sepan	supiera / supieras / supiera / supiéramos / supierais / supieran	sabe tú, no sepas / sepa Ud. / sepamos / sepan Uds.
salir / saliendo / salido	salgo / sales / sale / salimos / salís / salen	salía / salías / salía / salíamos / salíais / salían	salí / saliste / salió / salimos / salisteis / salieron	saldré / saldrás / saldrá / saldremos / saldréis / saldrán	saldría / saldrías / saldría / saldríamos / saldríais / saldrían	salga / salgas / salga / salgamos / salgáis / salgan	saliera / salieras / saliera / saliéramos / salierais / salieran	sal tú, no salgas / salga Ud. / salgamos / salgan Uds.

Irregular Verbs (continued)

Infinitive Present Participle Past Participle	Indicative Present	Imperfect	Preterite	Future	Conditional	Subjunctive Present	Imperfect	Imperative

ser
siendo
sido
	soy
	eres
	es
	somos
	sois
	son
		era
		eras
		era
		éramos
		erais
		eran
			fui
			fuiste
			fue
			fuimos
			fuisteis
			fueron
				seré
				serás
				será
				seremos
				seréis
				serán
					sería
					serías
					sería
					seríamos
					seríais
					serían
						sea
						seas
						sea
						seamos
						seáis
						sean
							fuera
							fueras
							fuera
							fuéramos
							fuerais
							fueran
								sé tú,
								  no seas
								sea Ud.
								seamos
								sed vosotros,
								  no seáis
								sean Uds.

tener
teniendo
tenido
	tengo
	tienes
	tiene
	tenemos
	tenéis
	tienen
		tenía
		tenías
		tenía
		teníamos
		teníais
		tenían
			tuve
			tuviste
			tuvo
			tuvimos
			tuvisteis
			tuvieron
				tendré
				tendrás
				tendrá
				tendremos
				tendréis
				tendrán
					tendría
					tendrías
					tendría
					tendríamos
					tendríais
					tendrían
						tenga
						tengas
						tenga
						tengamos
						tengáis
						tengan
							tuviera
							tuvieras
							tuviera
							tuviéramos
							tuvierais
							tuvieran
								ten tú,
								  no tengas
								tenga Ud.
								tengamos
								tened vosotros,
								  no tengáis
								tengan Uds.

traer
trayendo
traído
	traigo
	traes
	trae
	traemos
	traéis
	traen
		traía
		traías
		traía
		traíamos
		traíais
		traían
			traje
			trajiste
			trajo
			trajimos
			trajisteis
			trajeron
				traeré
				traerás
				traerá
				traeremos
				traeréis
				traerán
					traería
					traerías
					traería
					traeríamos
					traeríais
					traerían
						traiga
						traigas
						traiga
						traigamos
						traigáis
						traigan
							trajera
							trajeras
							trajera
							trajéramos
							trajerais
							trajeran
								trae tú,
								  no traigas
								traiga Ud.
								traigamos
								traed vosotros,
								  no traigáis
								traigan Uds.

venir
viniendo
venido
	vengo
	vienes
	viene
	venimos
	venís
	vienen
		venía
		venías
		venía
		veníamos
		veníais
		venían
			vine
			viniste
			vino
			vinimos
			vinisteis
			vinieron
				vendré
				vendrás
				vendrá
				vendremos
				vendréis
				vendrán
					vendría
					vendrías
					vendría
					vendríamos
					vendríais
					vendrían
						venga
						vengas
						venga
						vengamos
						vengáis
						vengan
							viniera
							vinieras
							viniera
							viniéramos
							vinierais
							vinieran
								ven tú,
								  no vengas
								venga Ud.
								vengamos
								venid vosotros,
								  no vengáis
								vengan Uds.

ver
viendo
visto
	veo
	ves
	ve
	vemos
	veis
	ven
		veía
		veías
		veía
		veíamos
		veíais
		veían
			vi
			viste
			vio
			vimos
			visteis
			vieron
				veré
				verás
				verá
				veremos
				veréis
				verán
					vería
					verías
					vería
					veríamos
					veríais
					verían
						vea
						veas
						vea
						veamos
						veáis
						vean
							viera
							vieras
							viera
							viéramos
							vierais
							vieran
								ve tú,
								  no veas
								vea Ud.
								veamos
								ved vosotros,
								  no veáis
								vean Uds.

Stem-Changing and Orthographic-Changing Verbs

Infinitive Present Participle Past Participle	Indicative						Subjunctive		Imperative
	Present	Imperfect	Preterite	Future	Conditional		Present	Imperfect	
dormir (ue, u) durmiendo dormido	duermo duermes duerme dormimos dormís duermen	dormía dormías dormía dormíamos dormíais dormían	dormí dormiste durmió dormimos dormisteis durmieron	dormiré dormirás dormirá dormiremos dormiréis dormirán	dormiría dormirías dormiría dormiríamos dormiríais dormirían		duerma duermas duerma durmamos durmáis duerman	durmiera durmieras durmiera durmiéramos durmierais durmieran	duerme tú, no duermas duerma Ud. durmamos dormid vosotros, no durmáis duerman Uds.
incluir (y) incluyendo incluido	incluyo incluyes incluye incluimos incluís incluyen	incluía incluías incluía incluíamos incluíais incluían	incluí incluiste incluyó incluimos incluisteis incluyeron	incluiré incluirás incluirá incluiremos incluiréis incluirán	incluiría incluirías incluiría incluiríamos incluiríais incluirían		incluya incluyas incluya incluyamos incluyáis incluyan	incluyera incluyeras incluyera incluyéramos incluyerais incluyeran	incluye tú, no incluyas incluya Ud. incluyamos incluid vosotros, no incluyáis incluyan Uds.
pedir (i, i) pidiendo pedido	pido pides pide pedimos pedís piden	pedía pedías pedía pedíamos pedíais pedían	pedí pediste pidió pedimos pedisteis pidieron	pediré pedirás pedirá pediremos pediréis pedirán	pediría pedirías pediría pediríamos pediríais pedirían		pida pidas pida pidamos pidáis pidan	pidiera pidieras pidiera pidiéramos pidierais pidieran	pide tú, no pidas pida Ud. pidamos pedid vosotros, no pidáis pidan Uds.
pensar (ie) pensando pensado	pienso piensas piensa pensamos pensáis piensan	pensaba pensabas pensaba pensábamos pensabais pensaban	pensé pensaste pensó pensamos pensasteis pensaron	pensaré pensarás pensará pensaremos pensaréis pensarán	pensaría pensarías pensaría pensaríamos pensaríais pensarían		piense pienses piense pensemos penséis piensen	pensara pensaras pensara pensáramos pensarais pensaran	piensa tú, no pienses piense Ud. pensemos pensad vosotros, no penséis piensen Uds.

Stem-Changing and Orthographic-Changing Verbs (continued)

Infinitive Present Participle Past Participle	Indicative						Subjunctive		Imperative
	Present	Imperfect	Preterite	Future	Conditional		Present	Imperfect	
producir (zc) produciendo producido	produzco produces produce producimos producís producen	producía producías producía producíamos producíais producían	produje produjiste produjo produjimos produjisteis produjeron	produciré producirás producirá produciremos produciréis producirán	produciría producirías produciría produciríamos produciríais producirían		produzca produzcas produzca produzcamos produzcáis produzcan	produjera produjeras produjera produjéramos produjerais produjeran	produce tú, no produzcas produzca Ud. produzcamos producid vosotros, no produzcáis produzcan Uds.
reír (i, i) riendo reído	río ríes ríe reímos reís ríen	reía reías reía reíamos reíais reían	reí reíste rió reímos reísteis rieron	reiré reirás reirá reiremos reiréis reirán	reiría reirías reiría reiríamos reiríais reirían		ría rías ría riamos riáis rían	riera rieras riera riéramos rierais rieran	ríe tú, no rías ría Ud. riamos reíd vosotros, no riáis rían Uds.
seguir (i, i) (ga) siguiendo seguido	sigo sigues sigue seguimos seguís siguen	seguía seguías seguía seguíamos seguíais seguían	seguí seguiste siguió seguimos seguisteis siguieron	seguiré seguirás seguirá seguiremos seguiréis seguirán	seguiría seguirías seguiría seguiríamos seguiríais seguirían		siga sigas siga sigamos sigáis sigan	siguiera siguieras siguiera siguiéramos siguierais siguieran	sigue tú, no sigas siga Ud. sigamos seguid vosotros, no sigáis sigan Uds.
sentir (ie, i) sintiendo sentido	siento sientes siente sentimos sentís sienten	sentía sentías sentía sentíamos sentíais sentían	sentí sentiste sintió sentimos sentisteis sintieron	sentiré sentirás sentirá sentiremos sentiréis sentirán	sentiría sentirías sentiría sentiríamos sentiríais sentirían		sienta sientas sienta sintamos sintáis sientan	sintiera sintieras sintiera sintiéramos sintierais sintieran	siente tú, no sientas sienta Ud. sintamos sentid vosotros, no sintáis sientan Uds.
volver (ue) volviendo vuelto	vuelvo vuelves vuelve volvemos volvéis vuelven	volvía volvías volvía volvíamos volvíais volvían	volví volviste volvió volvimos volvisteis volvieron	volveré volverás volverá volveremos volveréis volverán	volvería volverías volvería volveríamos volveríais volverían		vuelva vuelvas vuelva volvamos volváis vuelvan	volviera volvieras volviera volviéramos volvierais volvieran	vuelve tú, no vuelvas vuelva Ud. volvamos volved vosotros, no volváis vuelvan Uds.

VOCABULARIO ESPAÑOL-INGLÉS

The **Vocabulario español-inglés** presents all active vocabulary presented in *¡Trato hecho!*, as well as all words used in the readings, except for exact cognates. Numbers following entries indicate the chapter where words are introduced as active vocabulary. All translations separated by commas before a number are considered active in that chapter. Gender of nouns in Spanish is indicated by (*m*) for masculine and (*f*) for feminine. Nouns referring to people that have both masculine and feminine forms are indicated by (*m/f*), and those that are generally used in the plural are followed by (*pl*).

A

a to 1, at 1; **a la parrilla** on the grill, grilled 8; **a las dos (tres..)** at two (three…) o'clock 1; **al + *infinitive*** as soon as you + *verb*, upon …ing 6; **al comienzo** at the beginning 7; **al día siguiente** on the next day 6; **al horno** in the oven, baked 8; **a lo largo de** along; **a lo personal** from a personal point of view; **al principio** at first 9; **al vapor** steamed 8; **a menos que** unless 12; **a partir de** starting; **¿A qué hora?** At what time? 1; **A quien corresponda** To Whom It May Concern 12; **a su paso** as one goes through; **a través de** through, by means of; **a veces** sometimes, at times 2; **A ver…** Let's see… 8; **de… a…** from… to… 1; **subir a** get on/in, go up 6
a.C. B.C.
abierto/a open 2
abogado/a (*m/f*) lawyer 7
abordar board 6
abrazarse hug each other 5
abrazo (*m*) hug 5
abrigo (*m*) overcoat 5
abril (*m*) April 4
abrir open 3; **¡Abran…!** Open…! 2; **abrir camino** make one's way
abrocharse el cinturón de seguridad buckle your seatbelt 6
abuela (*f*) grandmother 3
abuelo (*m*) grandfather 3; **abuelos** (*mpl*) grandparents 3
abundante abundant
aburrido/a boring 1, bored 2
abuso (*m*) **de drogas** drug abuse 9
acá here 5; **por acá** over here 5
acabar de + *infinitive* to have just + *past participle* 5
académico/a academic; **formación académica** (*f*) education 10
acampar camp 6
acantilado (*m*) cliff
acceder a have access to 12
acceso (*m*) access 10
accidente (*m*) accident 7
acción (*f*) action
aceite (*m*) **de oliva** olive oil
acento (*m*) accent 1; **con o sin acento** with or without an accent 1; **acento gráfico** written accent; **acento tónico** (*m*) stress

aceptar accept 5; **aceptado/a** accepted
acera (*f*) sidewalk 7
acerca de about 12
acercarse a come/go/get closer to
acertado/a accurate
acogerse a participate in
acompañar accompany; **acompañado/a** accompanied 11
acondicionado/a conditioned; **aire acondicionado** (*m*) air conditioning 6
aconsejar advise 9
acontecimiento (*m*) event 7
acordarse (ue) remember
acostarse (ue) lie down, go to bed 5
acre (*m*) acre
acta (*f*) **de nacimiento** birth certificate 12
actividad (*f*) activity 1
activo/a active
actor (*m*) actor 7
actriz (*f*) actress 7
actual current, present 11
actualidad (*f*) current events, current situation; **en la actualidad** currently
acuario (*m*) aquarium
acuático/a water, aquatic
acudir come, show up 12
acuerdo (*m*) agreement 11; **acuerdo** (*m*) **de paz** peace agreement 11; **de acuerdo con** according to; **estar de acuerdo** agree 9
acusación (*f*) accusation 11
acusado/a accused 11
adaptarse adapt 12
adecuado/a suitable, adequate
además (de) besides 10
adicional additional
adiós good-bye 1
adjetivo (*m*) adjective
adjunto attached 12
administración (*f*) administration; **administración** (*f*) **de empresas** business (studies) 1
administrado/a administered, managed
admirar admire
admisión (*f*) admission 12; **oficina** (*f*) **de admisiones y registro** Admissions and Registrar's Office 12
admitido/a admitted 12
adolescencia (*f*) adolescence
adolescente (*m/f*) teenager, adolescent

¿adónde? (to) where? 4
adoptar adopt
adormecido/a numb 9
adquirir (ie) acquire, obtain
adquisición (*f*) acquisition
adquisitivo: poder (*m*) **adquisitivo** buying power
aduana (*f*) customs 6
adulto/a (*m/f*) adult
aeróbico: hacer ejercicio aeróbico do aerobics 4
aerolínea (*f*) airline 6
aeropuerto (*m*) airport 6
afectar affect; **afectado/a por** affected by
aficionado/a (*m/f*) fan
afirmación (*f*) affirmation
africano/a African
afroamericano/a African-American
afuera outside 3
afueras (*fpl*) outskirts 3
agencia (*f*) agency; **agencia de viajes** travel agency 6
agitado/a agitated
agosto (*m*) August 4
agradable pleasant, nice 3
agradecer thank; **Te/Le/Les agradecería…** I would be grateful if you would… 12
agregar add 8
agricultor/a (*m/f*) farmer 7
agricultura (*f*) agriculture 10
agua (*f*) water 4
ahí there; **de ahí** with the result
ahogar drown 7
ahora now 1
ahorita right now
ahorrar save 10
ahorro (*m*) saving; **cuenta** (*f*) **de ahorros** savings account 10
aire (*m*) air 7; **aire acondicionado** (*m*) air conditioning 6; **al aire libre** outdoor
aislado/a isolated
aislamiento (*m*) isolation
ajedrez (*m*) chess 4
ajo (*m*) garlic
alargado/a lengthened
albatros (*m*) albatross
albergar accommodate
albergue (*m*) hostel, inn, shelter
alcanzar reach
alcohol (*m*) alcohol 8
alegrarse de que be happy that 10

alejado/a remote, at a distance
alemán/alemana German
Alemania (f) Germany
alergia (f) allergy 9
alérgico/a: ser alérgico/a a be allergic to 9
alfabetización (f) literacy
alfombra (f) rug 3
algo something 2; **¿Algo más?** Anything else? 4; **echar algo al correo** mail something 6
algodón (m) cotton 5
alguien someone, somebody 3
alguno/a(s) (algún) some, any 4; **alguna vez** ever 7
alianza (f) alliance
alimentación (f) diet, feeding
alimenticio/a eating, nutricional; **hábitos alimenticios** (mpl) eating habits
alimento (m) food 9
aliviar relieve 9
allá there; **más allá de** beyond
allí there
alma (f) soul
almacén (m) department store 5
almohada (f) pillow 6
almorzar (ue) eat lunch, have lunch 4
almuerzo (m) lunch 8
aló hello (on the phone) 4
alojamiento (m) housing, lodging 12
alojarse en stay at 6
alquilar rent 3
alquiler (m) rent 3
alrededor de around
alternativa (f) alternative
alto/a tall 3, high; **presión arterial alta** (f) high blood pressure 9
altruista altruist
altura (f) height; **de... pies de altura** ...feet high
alumno/a (m/f) **(de nuevo ingreso)** a(n) (entering) student 12
ama (f) **de casa** housewife
amable kind
amante (m/f) lover 7
amarillo/a yellow 3
amazónico/a Amazonian
ambicioso/a ambitious 1
ambiente (m) environment 10; atmosphere
ámbito (m) field, area, sphere
ambos/as both
ambulancia (f) ambulance 7
amenaza (f) threat
amenazar threaten 11
América (f) America; **América del Norte/Sur** North/South America
americano/a American
amigo/a friend 1; **mi mejor amigo/a** my best friend 1
amistad (f) friendship; **hacer amistades** make friends, develop friendships 12
amor (m) love 7
ampliar broaden
amplio/a wide
anaranjado/a orange 3
anchura (f) width
anciano/a elderly

andar a pie go on foot, walk 7
andino/a Andean
anfitrión/anfitriona (m/f) (show) host/hostess 11
anillo (m) ring 5
animal (m) animal 3
anoche last night 6
Antártida: la Antártida (f) the Antarctic
ante faced with, before 9
antelación: con... de antelación ...in advance 6
anterioridad: con anterioridad previously
antes de before 2; **lo antes posible** as soon as possible 10
antibióticos (mpl) antibiotics 9
anticipar anticipate
antiestrés antistress
antigüedad (f) antiquity, antique
antiguo/a ancient, old
Antillas Mayores Greater Antilles
antipático/a unpleasant 1
anual annual
anualmente annually
anunciar announce 11
anuncio (m) advertisement, announcement 11
añadir add
año year 2; **una vez al año** once per year 2; **tener... años** be... years old 3
apagar turn off 10
aparecer appear 11
apariencia (f) appearance
apartamento (m) apartment 2
apellido (m) last name 10
apertura (f) opening
aplicar apply
apóstol (m) apostle
apoyar support
apoyo (m) support
apreciar appreciate; **apreciado/a** appreciated
aprender (a...) learn (to...) 3; **¡Aprendan...!** Learn...! 2
aprobar (ue) approve 10
apropiado/a appropriate
aprovechar take advantage of
aproximadamente approximately
aptitud (f) aptitude
apto/a suitable, right
aquel/aquella (aquellos/as) that (those) 5; **en aquella época** at that time 7
aquí here 1; **Aquí lo/la tiene.** Here it is. 5
árbol (m) tree 3
archipiélago (m) archipelago
archivador (m) filing cabinet 10
archivar file 10
archivo (m) file
área (f) area
arete (m) earring 5
argentino/a Argentinian 12
argumentación (f) line of argument
argumento (m) argument
arma (f) arm, weapon
armario (m) closet, wardrobe 3
arqueológico/a archaeological
arquitectónico/a architectural
arquitectura (f) architecture

arraigado/a deep-rooted
arrecife (m) **de coral** coral reef
arreglar fix, repair 6
arreglo (m) repair 11
arrepentirse (ie, i) be sorry, regret 7
arrestado/a arrested 11
arresto (m) arrest 7
arriba up, above
arroz (m) rice 8
arte (m) (feminine in the plural) art 1; **artes escénicas** theater arts; **artes plásticas** plastic arts; **bellas artes** fine arts
arterial: presión arterial alta (f) high blood pressure 9
artesanía (f) craft, handicraft
artesano/a (m/f) artisan, craftsman
artículo (m) article 11; **artículos** (mpl) **de oficina** office supplies 10
artista (m/f) artist, performer 7
artístico/a artistic
artritis (f) arthritis 9
asado/a roasted 8
asaltante (m/f) robber, attacker, assailant
asalto (m) robbery, holdup, assault
ascendencia (f) heritage
ascensor (m) elevator 6
asco (m) disgust; **dar asco** be revolting, not be able to stand 8
asegurar assure 11; **asegurarse** make sure
asesor/a (m/f) advisor 12
asesorar advise 12
así thus, so; **así como** just like; **¡Así es!** That's it! That's right! 8
asiático/a Asian
asiento (m) seat 6
asignatura (f) (school) subject 12
asimilación (f) assimilation
asistencia (f) assistance; **asistencia social** social assistance, welfare 11
asistente (m/f) assistant; **asistente de vuelo** flight attendant 6; **asistente social** social worker 7
asistir (a) attend 3
asociación (f) association
asociar associate
asopao (m) soup
aspecto (m) aspect; **en el aspecto físico** in appearance 3
aspirina (f) aspirin 9
asturiano/a Asturian
asunto (m) matter
atacar attack 7
atención (f) attention; **atención al cliente** customer service 10
atender (ie) wait on 12; tend to
Atentamente... Sincerely... 12
atento/a attentive
aterrizar land 6
Atlántico: océano Atlántico (m) Atlantic ocean
atlético/a athletic 1
atmósfera (f) atmosphere
atracción (f) attraction; **parque** (m) **de atracciones** amusement park 6
atractivo (m) attractive
atractivo/a attractive

atraer attract
atrás back, backwards
atravesar (ie) cross
atún (*m*) tuna 9
audiencia (*f*) audience
aumentar raise, increase 11
aumento (*m*) raise 10
aún yet, even; **aún hoy** even today
aunque although
ausencia (*f*) absence
auténtico/a authentic
auto (*m*) auto, car
autobiografía (*f*) autobiography
autobús (*m*) bus 2; **chófer** (*m/f*) **de autobús** bus driver 10; **en autobús** by bus 2; **parada** (*f*) **de autobús** bus stop 7
autóctono/a indigenous
automático/a automatic; **cajero automático** (*m*) ATM machine 10
automóvil (*m*) automobile
autónomo/a autonomous
autopista (*f*) freeway 7
autor/a (*m/f*) author
auxilio (*m*) help; **primeros auxilios** (*mpl*) first aid 7
avalancha (*f*) avalanche
ave (*f*) bird
avenida (*f*) avenue
aventura (*f*) adventure; **película** (*f*) **de aventuras** adventure movie 2
averiguar verify, check
avión (*m*) airplane 6; **pasaje** (*m*) **de avión** plane ticket 6
ayer yesterday 6
ayuda (*f*) help; **ayuda humanitaria** humanitarian aid 11; **Me habría sido de gran ayuda...** It would have helped me a lot... 12
ayudar help 9
azúcar (*m*) sugar 4
azul blue 3

B

bacalao (*m*) cod
bahía (*f*) bay
bailar dance 2
bailarín/bailarina (*m/f*) dancer
baile (*m*) dance
bajar de get off/out of, go down 6; **bajar de peso** lose weight 9
bajo under, below 7
bajo/a short (*in height*) 3; low 11; **planta baja** (*f*) ground floor 6
balcón (*m*) balcony 6
baloncesto (*m*) basketball 4
bananero/a: industria bananera banana industry
banca (*f*) banking
bancario/a banking
banco (*m*) bank 6
banquero/a (*m/f*) banker 10
bañarse bathe, take a bath 5
baño (*m*) bathroom 3; **traje** (*m*) **de baño** swimsuit 5
bar (*m*) bar 3

barato/a cheap 5
barba (*f*) beard 3
barbacoa (*f*) barbecue
barco (*m*) boat, ship
barrera (*f*) barrier
barrio (*m*) neighborhood 3
barroco/a baroque
basalto (*m*) basalt
base (*f*) **de datos** database 10
basílica (*f*) basilica
bastante enough, plenty of, quite a few of
batir beat 8; **batido/a** beaten 8
bebé (*m*) baby 11
beber drink 3
bebida (*f*) drink 8
beca (*f*) scholarship 12
beige beige 3
béisbol (*m*) baseball 7; **jugador/a de béisbol** (*m/f*) baseball player 7
bellas artes (*fpl*) fine arts 1
belleza (*f*) beauty 7
bello/a beautiful; **bellísimo/a** very beautiful
beneficio (*m*) benefit 10
beneficioso/a beneficial
besar(se) kiss (each other) 5
beso (*m*) kiss 5; **besito de coco** coconut kiss
biblioteca (*f*) library 1
bicicleta (*f*) bicycle
bien well 1; **bien cocido/a** well-done 8; **¿Está bien?** Okay? 2; **llevarse bien** get along well 5; **¡Qué bien!** How nice!
bienvenido/a welcome 6
bigote (*m*) mustache 3
bilingüe bilingual
billete (*m*) ticket 6, bill 10
biodiversidad (*f*) biodiversity
biografía (*f*) biography
biología (*f*) biology 1
bistec (*m*) steak 8
bisutería (*f*) jewelry
blanco/a white 3; **vino blanco** (*m*) white wine 4
blusa (*f*) blouse 5
boca (*f*) mouth 9
bocadillo (*m*) **(de queso/de jamón)** (cheese/ham) sandwich 4
bocado (*m*) bite
boda (*f*) wedding 5
bodega (*f*) winery, grocery store
boleto (*m*) ticket 6
bolígrafo (*m*) pen 2
boliviano/a Bolivian 12
bolsa (*f*) purse 5
bolsillo (*m*) pocket; **de su propio bolsillo** out of one's own pocket
bombero/a (*m/f*) firefighter 7
bonito/a pretty 1, nice
boricua Puerto Rican
borrador (*m*) draft
bosque (*m*) woods, forest 6; **bosque de lluvia** rain forest
bosquejar draft
bota (*f*) boot 5
botella (*f*) bottle 8
botones (*m*) bellhop 6
boutique (*f*) boutique 5

brasileño/a Brazilian
brazo (*m*) arm 9; **romper(se) el brazo...** break your arm... 9
breve brief 11
brillante brilliant
brócoli (*m*) broccoli 8
buceo (*m*) diving
budista (*m/f*) Buddhist
Buenas noches. Good evening. Good night. 1
Buenas tardes. Good afternoon. 1
buen(o)/a good 1; **Buenos días.** Good morning. 1
buscador (*m*) search engine 11
buscar look for 5
búsqueda (*f*) search
buzón (*m*) mailbox 10

C

caballo (*m*) horse; **a caballo** horseback; **montar a caballo** ride horseback 9
cabello (*m*) hair 9
cabeza (*f*) head 9; **darse un golpe en la cabeza** hit/bump (your head...) 9; **dolor** (*m*) **de cabeza** headache 9
cabo: llevar a cabo carry out
cacerola (*f*) pan 8
cada every, each 2; **cada vez más** more and more
cadena (*f*) chain 5; **cadena de televisión** television network 11
caerse fall 9
café (*m*) café 2, coffee 3; **color café** brown 3
cafeína (*f*) caffeine 8
cafetería (*f*) cafeteria 1
caja (*f*) cash register 5, box
cajero/a (*m/f*) teller, cashier 10; **cajero automático** (*m*) ATM machine 10
calcetín (*m*) sock 5
calculadora (*f*) calculator 2
calcular calculate 10
cálculo (*m*) calculation, calculus; **hoja** (*f*) **de cálculo** spreadsheet 10
caldo (*m*) **de pollo** chicken broth 8
calefacción (*f*) heating 6
calendario (*m*) calendar 10
calentamiento global (*m*) global warming 11
calentarse (ie) get hot 8
calidad (*f*) quality; **calidad de vida** quality of life
caliente (*m*) hot 4; **té** (*m*) **caliente** hot tea 8
calle (*f*) street 2
callejero/a from the street, stray
callejón (*m*) alley
callejuela (*f*) alley
calor: Hace (mucho) calor. It's (very) hot. 4
cama (*f*) bed 3; **cama matrimonial** double bed 6; **guardar cama** stay in bed 9
cámara (*f*) camera 6, chamber; **Cámara de Representantes** House of Representatives 11; **Cámara de Comercio** Chamber of Commerce
camaradería (*f*) camaraderie

camarera/o (f) maid 6, waiter

camarón (m) shrimp 8

cambiar change, exchange 6

cambio (m) change

caminar walk

camino (m) road, path, way; **abrir camino** make one's way; **camino empresarial** business path

camión (transport) truck; **chófer** (m/f) **de camión** truck driver 10

camisa (f) shirt 5

camiseta (f) T-shirt 5

campaña (f) campaign; **campaña publicitaria** advertising campaign

campeonato (m) championship 7

campesino/a (m/f) country person, peasant 7

camping (m) camping area

campo (m) country 3; field

camposanto (m) cemetery

canadiense Canadian 12

canal (m) channel 11, canal

canción (f) song

candidato/a (m/f) **(a)** candidate (for) 11; **presentarse como candidato/a** run as a candidate 11

canoa (f) canoe 6

canoso/a gray/white hair 3

cansado/a tired 2

cantante (m/f) singer 7

cantar sing 2

cantera (f) a type of stone

capital (f) capital 11

capítulo (m) chapter

capuchino (m) cappuccino 4

cara (f) face 9

carácter (m) character, personality; **en el carácter** as for personality 3

característica (f) characteristic

caracterizarse be characterized

caramelito (m) piece of candy

carbohidratos (mpl) carbohydrates 8

cargo (m) charge 10; **a cargo** in charge

Caribe: Mar (m) **Caribe** Caribbean Sea

caribeño/a Caribbean

cariño (m) affection 7

carne (f) meat 8

carnicería (f) butcher's shop 5

caro/a expensive 3

carpintero/a (m/f) carpenter 10

carrera (f) career, degree, race

carretera (f) road 7

carril (m) lane 7

carrito (m) **de postres** dessert cart 8

carro (m) car 3

carta (f) letter 3; **carta de solvencia** letter of financial standing 12; **carta de vinos** wine list 8; **cartas** (fpl) cards 4

cartera (f) wallet, billfold 5

casa (f) house 3; **casa rural** country home; **compañero/a** (m/f) **de casa** housemate 3

casado/a married 3; **pareja casada** (f) married couple; **recién casados** (mpl) newlyweds 11

casarse (con) get married (to) 5

casero/a homemade

casi almost 2

caso (m) case; **en ese caso** in that case 6

castaño/a brown (hair) 3

castillo (m) castle

catarata (f) waterfall

catarro: tener catarro have a cold 9

catástrofe natural (f) natural catastrophe, natural disaster 11

catedral (f) cathedral

categoría (f) category

católico/a Catholic

catorce fourteen 1

caucásico/a Caucasian

causa (f) cause; **causa social** social cause

causar cause

cautivar capture

CD (m) CD 3

cebolla (f) onion 8

celebración (f) celebration

celebrar celebrate 7; **celebrarse** be celebrated

cementerio (m) cemetery

cena (f) dinner, supper 2

cenar eat dinner, have (for) dinner 4

cenicero (m) ashtray 6

censado/a assessed

centavo (m) cent 8

centro (m) center, downtown 3; **centro comercial** (m) mall, shopping center 4

Centroamérica (f) Central America

centroamericano/a Central American

cerámica (f) ceramics

cerca de near 2

cercano/a close, near

cerdo (m) pig; **chuleta** (f) **de cerdo** pork chop 8

cereales (mpl) cereal 8

cerebro (m) brain 9

cero zero 1

cerrar (ie) close 4

certificado (m) certificate; **certificado de secundaria** high-school diploma 12

cerveza (f) beer 4

champú (m) shampoo 6

chaqueta (f) jacket 5

chau ciao, bye 4

cheque (m) check 10; **cheque de viaje** traveler's check 6

chequera (f) checkbook 10

chícharos (mpl) peas 8

chico/a (m/f) boy/girl

chico/a small

chile relleno (m) stuffed pepper 8

chileno/a Chilean 12

chino/a Chinese 4

chisme (m) piece of gossip 11

chiste (m) joke 4; **contar chistes** tell jokes 4

chocar to have a wreck, to crash 7

chocolate (m) chocolate 4; **chocolate caliente** hot chocolate 4

chófer (m/f) **de autobús/taxi/camión** bus/taxi/truck driver 10

choque (m) wreck, collision 7

chuleta (f) **de cerdo** pork chop 8

cielo sky 4; **El cielo está despejado.** The sky's clear. 4; **El cielo está nublado.** The sky's cloudy. 4

cien one hundred 1; **ciento…** one hundred and… 3; **descuento** (m) **del… por ciento** a… percent discount 5

ciencias (fpl) sciences 1; **ciencias políticas** political science, government 1; **ciencias sociales** social sciences 1

ciertamente certainly

cierto/a true 9

cifra (f) figure, number

cigarro (m) cigar

cilantro (m) coriander

cinco five 1

cincuenta fifty 1

cine (m) movie theater, cinema 2; **ir al cine** to go to the movies 2

cinturón (m) belt 5; **abrocharse el cinturón de seguridad** buckle your seatbelt 6

circunstancia (f) circumstance

cita (f) appointment 9, date

ciudad (f) city 3; **plano** (m) **de la ciudad** city map 6

ciudadanía (f) citizenship 12

ciudadano/a (m/f) citizen 11

civil: estado civil (m) marital status 10

¡Claro! Sure! 1

clase (f) class 1; **¿Cuál es la tarea para la próxima clase?** What is the homework for the next class? 2; **compañero/a** (m/f) **de clase** classmate 1; **en clase** in class 1; **salón** (m) **de clase** classroom 2

cláusula (f) clause

cliente/clienta (m/f) customer 5; **atención** (f) **al cliente** customer service 10

clientela (f) clientele

club nocturno (m) night club 2

cobertura (f) coverage

cobrar charge 10

cobre (m) copper

coche (m) car 2; **en mi coche** in my car 2

cocido/a: bien cocido/a well-done 8; **poco cocido/a** rare 8

cocina (f) kitchen 3; cuisine, cooking

cocinar cook 8

cocinero/a (m/f) cook 8

coco (m) coconut

cola: hacer cola stand in line 12

colega (m/f) colleague 10

colegio high school 7

colesterol (m) cholesterol 9

collar (m) **de plata** silver necklace 5

colombiano/a Colombian 12

colonia (f) colony, neighborhood

colonización (f) colonization

colonizado/a colonized

colonizador/a (m/f) colonizer

color (m) color 3; **color café** brown 3; **¿De qué color es…?** What color is…? 3; **de un solo color** solid-colored 5

colorido (m) coloring

combatir combat

combinar combine

comedia (f) comedy

comedor (*m*) dining room 3
comentar comment on, talk about
comentario (*m*) commentary
comentarista (*m/f*) commentator 11
comenzar (ie) begin 8
comer eat 2; **comer fuerte** eat a lot 8
comercial commercial; **centro comercial** (*m*) mall, shopping center 4; **pausa comercial** (*f*) commercial break 11
comercio (*m*) commerce, business, trade
comestibles (*mpl*) groceries
cómico/a comical, funny 1
comida (*f*) food 2, meal 8; **restaurante** (*m*) **de comida mexicana** Mexican food restaurant 2
comienzo (*m*) beginning; **al comienzo** at the beginning 7
comité (*m*) committee
cómo: ¿cómo? how? 2; **¿Cómo es…?** What's… like? 1; **¿Cómo está usted?** How are you? (*formal*) 1; **¿Cómo estás?** How are you? (*familiar*) 1; **¿Cómo se dice… en español?** How do you say… in Spanish? 2; **¿Cómo se escribe…?** How is… written? 1; **¿Cómo se llama usted?** What is your name? (*formal*) 1; **¿Cómo te llamas?** What is your name? (*familiar*) 1; **Sí, cómo no.** Yes, of course. 5
como like, as 1; **tan… como** as…as 1
cómoda (*f*) chest (of drawers) 3
comodidad (*f*) comfort
cómodo/a comfortable 5
compañero/a (*m/f*) partner; **compañero/a de casa** housemate 3; **compañero/a de clase** classmate 1; **compañero/a de trabajo** fellow worker
compañía (*f*) company
comparación (*f*) comparison
comparativo/a (*m*) comparative
compartir share 3
compatibilidad (*f*) compatibility 10
competencia (*f*) competition
competir (i, i) compete
complejo/a complex
complementar complement
complemento (*m*) accessory; **complemento directo** (*m*) direct object
completar complete 10
completo/a complete 2; **a tiempo completo** full-time 10
comportamiento (*m*) behavior
compositor/a (*m/f*) composer
compra (*f*) purchase; **ir de compras** go shopping 4
comprador/a (*m/f*) purchaser, buyer
comprar buy 2
comprender understand 3; **No comprendo.** I don't understand. 2
comprensión (*f*) understanding 11
comprobante (*m*) receipt, proof 6
comprobar (ue) prove, check
comprometedor/a compromising 11
comprometido/a committed, engaged
compromiso (*m*) **con** commitment to
computadora (*f*) computer 2

común common 9; **en común** in common
comunicación (*f*) communication; **comunicaciones** (*fpl*) communications 10; **comunicación** (*f*) **de ventas** sales report
comunicar connect, communicate; **comunicarse** get in touch with each other, contact each other 5; **¿Podría(s) comunicarme con… ?** Could you connect me with…? 6
comunidad (*f*) community 11
comunitario/a community
con with 1; **casarse con** get married (to) 5; **con… de antelación** …in advance 6; **con frecuencia** frequently 2; **Con mucho gusto.** Gladly., I'd be happy to. 6; **con o sin acento** with or without an accent 1; **con regularidad** with regularity 9; **con tal que** provided that, as long as 12; **con validez superior a…** valid for more than… 12; **soñar (ue) con** dream of/about 7
concentrado/a concentrated
concentrar concentrate
concepto (*m*) concept
concienciar make aware
concierto (*m*) concert 3
concreto/a concrete
concurso (*m*) contest 7
condado (*m*) county
condición (*f*) condition 9; **en buenas condiciones** in good condition 9
condicional (*m*) conditional
conducir drive
conductor/a (*m/f*) driver 7
conectado/a connected
conectar connect
confiar (en) confide (in), trust (in) 11
confirmar confirm 12
conflicto (*m*) conflict 11
confrontar confront
confundido/a confused 2
congestión (*f*) congestion 9
congestionado/a congested 9
Congreso (*m*) Congress 11
conjugar conjugate
conmemoración (*f*) commemoration
conmigo with me 1
conocedor/a (*m/f*) connoisseur, expert
conocer know, be familiar with, be acquainted with, meet 6; **conocido/a** known
conocimiento (*m*) knowledge
conquistado/a conquered
consciente conscious
consecuencia (*f*) consequence 9
consejo (*m*) piece of advice 8
conservar conserve, keep
considerablemente considerably
considerar consider; **considerado/a** considered, considerate
consigo with oneself
consistir consist; **en qué consiste** of what it consists 12
constante constant

constitución (*f*) constitution
construcción (*f*) construction 7
construir build, construct; **construido/a por** constructed by
Cónsul (*m*) Consul 12
consulado (*m*) consulate
consultar consult 6
consumidor/a (*m/f*) consumer
consumir consume
consumo (*m*) consumption
contabilidad (*f*) accounting 1
contacto (*m*) contact
contador/a (*m/f*) accountant 7
contaminación (*f*) pollution 7
contar (ue) count, tell 4; **contar con** have
contemplar contemplate
contemporáneo/a contemporary
contener (ie) contain 8
contenido (*m*) content
contento/a happy 2
contestar answer 2; **¡Contesten…!** Answer…! 2
contexto (*m*) context
contigo with you 2
continente (*m*) continent
continuación: a continuación following, next 11
continuamente continually
continuar continue
continuidad (*f*) continuity
contra against 11
contraste (*m*) contrast
contratar hire 10
contrato temporal (*m*) temporary contract 10
contribución (*f*) contribution 11
contribuir contribute
control: lista (*f*) **de control** checklist
controlar control 8
convenio (*m*) agreement
convenir fit, be appropriate
convento (*m*) convent
conversación (*f*) conversation
convertir (ie, i) convert; **convertirse (ie)** become
convivir live together
cooperación (*f*) cooperation 11
coordinador/a (*m/f*) coordinator
copa (*f*) stemmed glass, wine glass 8; **tomar una copa** have a drink 4
copia (*f*) copy; **sacar copias** make copies 10
coprotagonista (*m/f*) costar 11
corazón (*m*) heart 9; **de corazón** from the heart
corbata (*f*) necktie 5
cordialmente cordially
cormorán (*m*) cormorant
corona (*f*) crown
correcto/a right, correct 6
corregir (i, i) correct
correo (*m*) mail; **correo electrónico** (*m*) e-mail 3; **echar algo al correo** mail something 6; **oficina** (*f*) **de correos** post office 6
correr run 3

corresponder correspond; **A quien corresponda** To Whom It May Concern 12

correspondiente corresponding

corriente: cuenta (*f*) **corriente** checking account 10

cortar(se) cut (yourself) 9; **cortarse el pelo** get one's hair cut, cut one's hair 5

corte (*f*) court 11

cortesía (*f*) courtesy 7

corto/a short (*in length*) 3; **pantalones cortos** (*mpl*) shorts 5

cosa (*f*) thing 5

cosmopolita cosmopolitan

costa (*f*) coast 11

costar (ue) cost; **¿Cuánto cuesta(n)?** How much does it (do they) cost? 5

costarricense Costa Rican 12

costo (*m*) cost

costumbre (*f*) custom

cotidiano/a daily

creación (*f*) creation

crear create 11

creatividad (*f*) creativity

crecer grow (up) 7

creciente growing

crecimiento (*m*) growth 9

crédito: tarjeta (*f*) **de crédito** credit card 5

creencia (*f*) belief

creer believe 3

crema (*f*) cream 4; **crema protectora solar** (*f*) sunscreen 6

crimen (*m*) crime 11

criminal (*m*) criminal 7

criminalidad (*f*) crime (*as a whole*) 11

criollo/a Creole

cristianismo (*m*) Christianity

cristiano/a Christian

crítico/a (*m/f*) critic

cruel cruel 7

crucero (*m*) cruise; **hacer un crucero** take a cruise 6

cruzar cross 7

cuaderno (*m*) notebook 2; **cuaderno** (*m*) **de ejercicios** workbook 2

cuadra (*f*) (city) block 6

cuadrado/a square

cuadros: de cuadros checkered, plaid 5

cuál: ¿cuál(es)? which?, what? 2; **¿Cuál es la tarea para la próxima clase?** What is the homework for the next class? 2

cualidad (*f*) quality

cualquier(a) (just) any

¿cuándo? when? 2

¿cuánto/a? how much? 2; **¿cuántos/as?** how many? 1; **¿Cuánto cuesta(n)?** How much does it (do they) cost? 5; **¿Cuántos son en…?** How many are there in…? 3

cuarenta forty 1

cuarta parte (*f*) **de** one fourth of 8

cuarto (*m*) room 2; quarter 1; **Es la/Son las… y cuarto.** It's a quarter past… 1

cuarto/a fourth 6

cuatro four 1

cuatrocientos/as four hundred 3

cubano/a Cuban 12

cubrir cover

cuchara (*f*) spoon 8

cucharada (*f*) spoonful 8

cuchillo (*m*) knife 8

cuello (*m*) neck 9

cuenta (*f*) bill, check 8; account 10; **cuenta corriente/de ahorros** checking/savings account 10; **estado** (*m*) **de cuenta** statement (of an account) 12; **vivir por su cuenta** live on one's own

cuero (*m*) leather 5

cuerpo (*m*) body 7

cuestión (*f*) question, matter

cuestionario (*m*) questionnaire

cuidado: tener cuidado be careful 9

cuidar take care of 9

cultura (*f*) culture

cumpleaños (*m*) birthday 7; **fiesta** (*f*) **de cumpleaños** birthday party 7

cumplir turn (an age), carry out 7

cuna (*f*) cradle

cura (*f*) cure 11

curioso/a interesting

curita (*f*) band-aid 9

currículum vitae (*m*) curriculum vitae, resumé 10

cursar estudios study, attend school

cursiva: en cursiva in italics

curso (*m*) course 1; **curso técnico** technical course 1

cuyo/a whose

D

danza (*f*) dance

dar give 8; **dar asco** be revolting, not be able to stand 8; **darle hambre a alguien** make someone hungry 8; **darse la mano** shake hands 5; **darse un abrazo/un beso** give each other a hug/a kiss 5; **darse un golpe (en la cabeza…)** hit/bump (your head…) 9

datos (*mpl*) information, data 10; **datos personales** personal data 10; **introducir datos** input data 10

de from 1, of 2; **antes de** before 2; **bajar de** get off / out of, go down 6; **cerca de** near 2; **de… a…** from… to… 1; **de acuerdo con** according to; **debajo de** below 2; **de cuadros** checkered, plaid 5; **¿De dónde eres?** Where are you from? (*familiar*) 1; **¿De dónde es usted?** Where are you from? (*formal*) 1; **de estatura mediana** of medium height 3; **de (no) fumadores** (non-)smoking 6; **de la mañana** in the morning 1; **de mediana edad** middle-aged 3; **de niño/a** as a child 7; **de oferta** on sale 5; **de parte de** on behalf of 11; **de rayas** striped 5; **de… pies de altura** …feet high; **¿De qué color es…?** What color is…? 3; **después de** after 2; **detrás de** behind 2; **de un solo color** solid-colored 5; **de una manera…** in a… way; **¿De veras?** Really? 10; **Eso depende de…** That depends on… 2; **hablar de** talk about; **más de** + *number* more than + *number* 6

deber should, ought to, owe 3; **debería** I/he/she should 12

débito: tarjeta (*f*) **de débito** debit card 5

década (*f*) decade

decidir decide 6

décimo/a tenth 6

decir say, tell 4; **¿Cómo se dice… en español?** How do you say… in Spanish? 2

decisión (*f*) decision 10

declarar declare

dedicación (*f*) dedication

dedicar dedicate; **dedicarse** do (for a living), devote oneself to 7; **dedicado/a** dedicated

dedo (*m*) finger 9

defensa (*f*) defense

definición (*f*) definition

definir define; **definido/a** defined

dejar leave (*something somewhere*) 3; let; **dejarse** let oneself; **dejar de** + *infinitive* stop …ing 8

delante de ahead of, in front of 2

delfín (*m*) dolphin

delgado/a thin 3

delicioso/a delicious 8

demás: los/las demás the rest, the others

demasiado/a too, too much 7

democracia (*f*) democracy

democrático/a democratic

demostrativo/a demonstrative

dentro de within

denuncia (*f*) police report, accusation 7

denunciado/a reported, denounced

departamento (*m*) department 10

depender depend; **dependiendo de** depending on; **Eso depende de…** That depends on… 2

dependiente/dependienta (*m/f*) salesclerk 5

deporte (*m*) sport 2

deportista athletic, fond of sports 7

deportista (*m/f*) athlete 7

deportivo/a sports

depositar deposit 10

depósito (*m*) deposit 10

depresión (*f*) depression 9

deprimido/a depressed 9

derecha: a la derecha de to the right of 2

derecho (*m*) right

derivar de come from; **derivado/a** derived

derretir (i, i) melt 8; **derretido/a** melted 8

desafío (*m*) challenge

desafortunadamente unfortunately 3

desaparecer disappear; **desaparecido/a** missing

desarrollar develop 9

desarrollo (*m*) development 10

desayunar eat breakfast, have (for) breakfast 4

desayuno (*m*) breakfast 6

descansar rest 2

descanso (*m*) break

descargar download; unload

descender (ie) go down, descend 6

descontento (*m*) dissatisfaction
describir describe
descripción (*f*) description
descubierto/a (por) discovered (by)
descubrimiento (*m*) discovery
descubrir discover
descuento (*m*) **del... por ciento...** percent discount 5
desde from; **desde hace** for 10; **desde que** since 9
desear wish, desire 4
desempleo (*m*) unemployment 11
deseo (*m*) desire 7
deserción escolar (*f*) dropping out of school
desértico/a desert
desfile (*m*) parade
desierto (*m*) desert
desordenado/a messy 3
desove (*m*) spawning
despedida (*f*) good-bye, farewell
despedir (i, i) fire 10; **despedirse (i)** say good-bye 5
despegar take off 6
despejado/a: El cielo está despejado. The sky's clear. 4
despertador (*m*) alarm clock 6
despertarse (ie) wake up 5
después de after 2
destacar emphasize, stress, bring out
destino (*m*) destination; destiny
detallado/a detailed
detalle (*m*) detail
detenerse stop
determinar determine
detrás de behind 2
devastación (*f*) devastation 11
devolver (ue) return 10
día (*m*) day; **al día siguiente** on the next day 6; **Buenos días.** Good morning. 1; **hoy en día** nowadays; **¿Qué día es hoy?** What day is today? 1; **todo el día** all day 1; **todos los días** every day 2
diabetes (*f*) diabetes 9
diariamente daily
diario (*m*) diary, daily newspaper
diario/a daily
dibujar draw 10
diciembre (*m*) December 4
dictadura (*f*) dictatorship
dicho/a mentioned
diecinueve nineteen 1
dieciocho eighteen 1
dieciséis sixteen 1
diecisiete seventeen 1
diente (*m*) tooth 5; **lavarse los dientes** brush your teeth 5
dieta (*f*) diet; **estar a dieta** be on a diet 8
diez ten 1
diferencia (*f*) difference; **a diferencia de** different from
diferente different
difícil difficult 1
dificultad (*f*) difficulty
difundir spread, diffuse
difusión (*f*) spreading, diffusion
dinámica (*f*) dynamics

dinámico/a dynamic
dinero (*m*) money 3; **cambiar dinero** change / exchange money 6
dirección (*f*) address 3; direction 7
directamente directly
directo/a direct 10; **complemento directo** (*m*) direct object
director/a (*m/f*) director 10
dirigir direct; **dirigido/a** directed; **Me dirijo a usted(es) con la intención de...** I'm writing to you for the purpose of... 12
disciplina (*f*) discipline
disculpar pardon, excuse; **¡Disculpe!** Excuse me!, Pardon me! 6
discurso (*m*) speech, discourse
discutir discuss, argue
diseñador/a (*m/f*) designer; **diseñador/a de moda** fashion designer; **diseñador/a de software** software designer 7; **diseñador/a gráfico/a** graphic artist 10
diseñar design 10
diseño (*m*) design; **programa** (*m*) **de diseño gráfico** graphic design program 10
disfrutar de enjoy
disponible available 6; **disponible a petición** available upon request 10
distancia (*f*) distance; **llamada** (*f*) **de larga distancia** long distance call 6
distinguido/a distinguished
distinto/a different
distribución (*f*) distribution
distribuir distribute 10; **distribuido/a** distributed
distrito (*m*) district
diversidad (*f*) diversity 11
divertido/a fun 1
divertirse (ie) have fun, amuse oneself 5
dividir divide
divorciarse divorce 11; **divorciado/a** divorced 3
doble double; **habitación doble** (*f*) double room 6
doce twelve 1
doctor/a (*m/f*) doctor 2
documentación (*f*) documentation
documental (*m*) documentary 11
documentar document
documento (*m*) document 10
dólar (*m*) dollar 10
doler (ue) hurt, ache 8
dolor (*m*) pain, ache; **dolor de cabeza** headache 9; **dolor muscular** muscular pain 9
dolorido/a sore 9
doméstico/a (*f*) domestic 11
domicilio (*m*) domicile, place of residence 12
dominar dominate
domingo (*m*) Sunday 1
dominicano/a Dominican 12
dominico (*m*) Dominican
¿dónde? where? 1; **¿de dónde?** from where? 2
dopaje (*m*) doping, drug use 11
dormir (ue) sleep 4; **dormir hasta tarde** sleep late 4; **dormir una siesta** take a nap; **saco de dormir** (*m*) sleeping bag 6

dormitorio (*m*) bedroom 3
dos two 1
doscientos/as two hundred 3
drama (*m*) drama
droga (*f*) drug; **abuso** (*m*) **de drogas** drug abuse 9
ducha (*f*) shower 6
ducharse shower, take a shower 5
duda (*f*) doubt
dudar doubt 9
dudoso/a doubtful 9
dueño/a (*m/f*) owner 8
dulce sweet 8
dulces (*mpl*) sweets 8
durante during 6
durar last 6
DVD: reproductor (*m*) **de DVD** DVD player 3

E

e and (*used instead of* **y** *before the letters* **i** *and* **hi**) 1
ebrio/a drunk, inebriated 9
ecológico/a ecological 11
economía (*f*) economics 1; economy 11
económico/a economic 11; **indicadores económicos** (*mpl*) economic indicators 11
economista (*m/f*) economist
ecosistema (*m*) ecosystem
ecoturismo (*m*) ecotourism
ecuador (*m*) equator
ecuatoriano/a Ecuatorian 12
echar(se) a start, set off 7; **echar algo al correo** mail something 6; **echarse raíces** put down roots
edad (*f*) age 7; **de mediana edad** middle-aged 3; **Edad Media** (*f*) Middle Ages
edición (*f*) edition
edificio (*m*) building 1
editar edit; **editado/a** edited
editor/a (*m/f*) editor
editorial (*f*) publishing company
educación (*f*) education 10
educador/a (*m/f*) educator
educativo/a educational
efectividad (*f*) effectiveness
efectivo (*m*) cash 5
efectivo/a effective
Egipto (*m*) Egypt
egoísta selfish, egotistical 1
ejemplo (*m*) example; **por ejemplo** for example 11
ejercicio (*m*) exercise 2; **cuaderno** (*m*) **de ejercicios** workbook 2; **hacer ejercicio** exercise 7; **hacer ejercicio aeróbico** do aerobics 4
ejército (*m*) army
ejotes (*mpl*) green beans 8
el the 1; **el (lunes...)** on (Monday...) (*a particular week*) 1; **el/la mío/a** mine 10
él he 1; him 2
elaboración (*f*) elaboration
elecciones (*fpl*) election 11; **elección múltiple** multiple choice

electrónico/a electronic; **correo electrónico** (m) e-mail 3
elegir (i, i) select
elemental elementary
elemento (m) element
elevarse rise
ella she 1, her 2
ellos/as they 1, them 2
emancipación (f) emancipation
embajada (f) embassy
embarazada pregnant 11
embargo: sin embargo nevertheless, however
embarque: tarjeta (f) **de embarque** boarding pass 6
emergencia (f) emergency 7
emerger emerge
emigrante (m/f) emigrant
emigrar emigrate
emitirse be broadcast
emocionado/a excited 7
emocional emotional 1
emocionante exciting
empeorar worsen 11
empezar (ie) begin 4
empleado/a (m/f) employee 10
empleo (m) employment 9; **empleo** (m) **a tiempo completo/parcial** full-time/part-time employment 10; **oferta** (f) **de empleo** job offer 10; **solicitud** (f) **de empleo** job application 10
empresa (f) company, enterprise 10; **administración** (f) **de empresas** business (studies) 1
empresarial business; **camino empresarial** (m) business path
empresario/a (m/f) entrepreneur
en at, in, 1, on 2; **en aquella época** at that time 7; **en autobús** by bus 2; **en bicicleta** by bicycle; **en casa** at home 1; **en clase** in class 1; **en el extranjero** abroad 12; **en el trabajo** at work 1; **en mi coche** in my car 2; **en portada** on the front page; **en qué consiste** of what it consists 12; **en seguida** right away 11; **en torno** around; **¿En qué puedo servirle?** How may I help you? 5
enamorado/a in love 7
encantar love 8; **me encanta(n)** I love it (them) 7
encanto (m) enchantment
encargado/a: estar encargado/a de be in charge of 10
encargarse take care of
encarnación (f) incarnation
encender (ie) turn on 10
enchufar plug in 10
enchufe (m) socket 10
encima de on top of 2
enclave (m) crossroad
encontrar (ue) find 4; **encontrarse (ue)** get together, meet one another 5; be found, be located 9
encuentro (m) meeting; **lugar** (m) **de encuentro** meeting place

encuesta (f) survey, poll 11
energía (f) energy 8
enero (m) January 4
enfermarse get sick 9
enfermedad (mental) (f) (mental) illness 9
enfermero/a (m/f) nurse 7
enfermo/a sick, ill 2
enfrentar face; **enfrentarse (con)** confront
enfrente de across from, facing 2
engrapadora (f) stapler 10
engrapar staple 10
enigmático/a enigmatic
enojado/a angry, mad 2
enojarse get angry 5
enorgullecerse pride oneself, be proud
enorme enormous
ensalada (f) salad 4; **ensalada de lechuga y tomate** lettuce and tomato salad 8
ensayo (m) essay, paper 3
enseñanza (f) teaching
enseñar teach 2
entender (ie) understand 4; **entenderse** get along
enterrar (ie) bury 7
entonces so, then 4
entrada (f) entrance 6
entrar enter
entre between 2; among
entregar turn/hand in 12
entremés (m) short theater piece
entrenar train 10
entresijo (m) maze
entrevista (f) interview; **programa** (m) **de entrevistas** talk show 11
entrevistado/a (m/f) interviewee
envejecimiento (m) aging 9
enviar send 12
envío (m) sending; **envío de dinero** money order
envolver (ue) surround
enyesado/a in a cast 9
epidemia (f) epidemic 11
epílogo (f) epilogue
episodio (m) episode 11
época (f) time period 7; **en aquella época** at that time 7
equilibrado/a balanced 8
equipaje (m) luggage 6; **facturar el equipaje** check your luggage 6
equipo (m) team 7
equivocado/a wrong, mistaken 10
era (f) era, age
Érase una vez… Once upon a time… 7
erróneo/a wrong, erroneous
escala stopover 6; **hacer escala** make a stopover 6
escalera (f) stairs 6; ladder 7
escándalo (m) scandal 11
escapada (f) escape
escena (f) scene
escenario (m) stage, scene
esclavo/a (m/f) slave
esclusa (f) gate
escocés/escocesa Scottish
escoger pick, choose 12

escolar school; **deserción escolar** dropping out of school
escribir write 3; **¡Escriban…!** Write…! 2; **¿Cómo se escribe…?** How is… written? 1; **Se escribe…** It's written… 1
escritorio (m) desk 2
escritura (f) writing
escuchar listen (to) 2
escuela (f) **(primaria, secundaria)** (primary, secondary) school 2
escuelita (f) little school
escultura (f) sculpture
ese/a that 4; **esos/as** those 5
esencial essential
eslogan (m) slogan
esnórquel (m) snorkeling
eso that 2; **Eso depende de..** That depends on… 2; **por eso** therefore, that's why
espacio (m) space; **espacio de encuentro** meeting space; **espacio verde** green area 7
espalda (f) back 9
España (f) Spain
español (m) Spanish 1; **¿Cómo se dice… en español?** How do you say… in Spanish? 2
español/a Spanish 12
espárragos (mpl) asparagus 8
especial special; **nada en especial** nothing in particular 3
especialidad (f) specialty
especialista (m/f) specialist
especializado/a specialized
especialmente especially
especie (f) species
específico/a specific
espectador/a (m/f) spectator
espejo (m) mirror 3
espera (f) wait; **A la espera de…** Awaiting… 12; **sala** (f) **de espera** waiting room 6
esperanza (f) hope
esperar wait (for) 6; hope 9; expect 11
espesarse thicken 8
espinacas (fpl) spinach 8
esposa (f) wife, spouse 1
esposo (m) husband, spouse 1
esquema (m) outline
esquiar ski 4
esquina (f) corner 6
estabilidad (f) stability 11
establecer establish; **establecerse** be established; **establecido/a** established
estación (f) station 6, season; **estación de esquí** ski resort; **estación de servicio** service station, 6; **estación de trenes** train station
estacionamiento (m) parking lot 7
estadio (m) stadium 2
estado (m) state, status; **estado civil** marital status 10; **estado de cuenta** statement (of an account) 12; **estado libre asociado** (m) commonwealth; **Estados Unidos** United States
estadounidense American 12
estancia (f) stay 12
estante (m) shelf 2

estar be 2; **estoy** I am, I'm 1; **¿Cómo está usted?** How are you? (formal) 1; **¿Cómo estás?** How are you? (familiar) 1; **¿Está bien?** Okay? 2; **estar a dieta** be on a diet 8; **estar de acuerdo** agree 9; **estar de buen/mal humor** be in a good/bad mood 10; **estar de moda** be in fashion 5; **estar encargado/a de** be in charge of 10; **estar resfriado/a** have a cold 9

estatua (f) statue

estatura (f) stature; height; **de estatura mediana** of medium height 3

estatus (m) status

este (m) east

este/esta (estos/as) this (these) 5; **este fin de semana** this weekend 1; **esta mañana/tarde** this morning/afternoon 4; **esta noche** tonight, this evening 4; **esta semana** (f) this week 1

estelar star, stellar

estilo (m) style; **estilo de vida** lifestyle

Estimado/a... Dear... 12

estimar estimate; **estimarse** be estimated

estirar(se) stretch 9

estómago (m) stomach 9

estornudar sneeze 9

estrategia (f) strategy

estrecho/a close, narrow, tight

estrella (f) **de rock** rock star 11

estrés (m) stress 8

estresante stressful

estructura (f) structure

estudiante (m/f) student 1

estudiar study 1

estudio (m) study; **plan** (m) **de estudios** plan of studies, degree plan 12

estufa (f) stove 3

estupendo/a great 2

etapa (f) step

etnia (f) ethnicity

étnico/a ethnic

euforia (f) euphoria

Europa (f) Europe

europeo/a European

evaluar evaluate 10

evento (m) event

evidente evident

evitar avoid 8

evolución (f) evolution

exactamente exactly 12

exagerar exaggerate 7

examen (m) exam 1

examinar examine 9

excelencia (f) excellency; **por excelencia** quintessential

excursión (f) outing, hike 6; **hacer una excursión** go for a hike

exhibición (f) exhibit, exhibition

exhibir exhibit

existente existing

existir exist

éxito (m) success

expandido/a expanded

experiencia (f) experience 10

experto/a (m/f) expert

explicación (f) explanation

explicar explain 8

exploración (f) exploration

explorar explore

explotación (f) exploitation

exportación (f) exportation

exportador/a (m/f) exporter

exposición (f) exhibition 4

expresar express

expresión (f) expression

expulsar drive out, expel

exquisito/a exquisite

extenderse (ie) be extended; **extendido/a** widespread, extended

extenso/a extense

extinción (f) extinction

extranjero/a foreign 2

extranjero: en el extranjero abroad 12

extraordinario/a extraordinary

extravagante extravagant

extrovertido/a outgoing, extroverted 1

F

fábrica (f) factory 7

fabricación (f) manufacturing 10

fabricarse be made/fabricated

fácil easy 1

facilitar facilitate

facturar el equipaje check your luggage 6

falda (f) skirt 5

fallar fail, be down 10

falso/a false

falta (f) lack; **hacer falta** need

faltar be missing / needed 8

fama (f) fame

familia (f) family 1

familiar family

famoso/a famous 11

fantasma (m) ghost 7

farándula: mundo (m) **de la farándula** world of entertainment 11

farmacia (f) pharmacy 6

fascinante fascinating

fatiga (f) fatigue 9

favor (m) favor; **a favor** in favor; **por favor** please 2

favorecer favor

favorito/a favorite 2

febrero (m) February 4

fecha (f) date 4; **¿Cuál es la fecha (de...)?** What is the date (of...)? 4; **fecha límite** deadline 12

fechado/a dated

feliz happy 7

femenino/a feminine

feo/a ugly 1

feria (f) fair, festival

festivo/a festive

ficha (f) card 12

fiebre (f) fever 9; **fiebre del heno** hay fever 9; **fiebre viajera** traveling frenzy

fiesta (f) party; **hacer una fiesta** have a party 3; **fiesta de cumpleaños** birthday party 7

fijarse en focus on

filo (m) cutting edge; **al filo de la noticia** on the edge of the news

filosofía (f) philosophy 1

fin (m) end; **este fin de semana** this weekend 1; **los fines de semana** weekends 2; **sin fines de lucro** nonprofit

finalmente finally 8

financiado/a por financed by

financiero/a financial

firmar sign 5

física (f) physics 1

físico/a physical 9; **en el aspecto físico** in appearance 3

flan (m) flan 4

flor (f) flower 3

floreciente flourishing

fluidez (f) fluency, fluidity

foco (m) focus

folleto (m) brochure

fondo: al fondo (de) at the back (of) 2

forma (f) shape, way; **mantenerse en forma** stay in shape 8; **de forma sencilla** in a simple way

formación (f) formation; **formación académica** (f) education 10

formal formal 12

formar form; **formado/a** formed; **formar parte de** be part of

formular formulate

formulario (m) form 10

fortalecer strengthen

fortaleza (f) fortress

fortuna (f) fortune

foto (f) photo 4; **sacar una foto** take a picture 4

fotocopiadora (f) photocopier 10

fotografía (f) photocopy

fragmento (m) fragment

francés (m) French 1

francés/francesa French

Francia (f) France

franco/a frank; **zona franca** free-trade zone

frase (f) phrase

frecuencia (f) frequency; **con frecuencia** frequently 2

frecuentado/a frequented

frecuente frequent

freír (i, i) fry 10

frente al facing

fresas (fpl) strawberries 8

fresco/a fresh 7; **Hace fresco.** It's cool. 4

frijoles (mpl) beans 8

frío (m) cold; **Hace (mucho) frío.** It's (very) cold. 4

frito/a fried; **papas fritas** (fpl) French fries 8; **papitas fritas** (fpl) potato chips 4

frituras (fpl) fried food

frontera (f) border

fruta (f) fruit 8

fruto (m) fruit; **el fruto de** the result of

fuego (m) fire

fuera de out(side) of

fuerte (m) fort

fuerte strong 9, loud; **comer fuerte** eat a lot 8

fuerza (f) strength 9, force
fumador/a (m/f) smoker **de (no) fumadores** (non-) smoking 6
fumar smoke 3
funcionar work, function 6
funcionario/a (m/f) government employee 12
fundación (f) foundation
fundamentalmente mainly, principally
fundarse be founded; **fundado/a** founded
funeral (m) funeral 7
fusión (f) merger, fusion
fusionar merge
fútbol (m) soccer 2; **fútbol americano** (m) football 2
futuro (m) future 11

G

gafas (fpl) glasses 3; **gafas de sol** sunglasses 6
gallego/a Galician
galleta (f) cookie 4
ganar win 7, earn
ganas: tener ganas de + infinitive feel like …ing 4
gandinga (f) pork liver
garaje (m) garage 3
garantizado/a guaranteed 11
garganta (f) throat 9
gasolina (f) gasoline 6
gasolinera (f) gas station 6
gastar spend 5
gasto (m) expense 12
gastronomía (f) gastronomy
gastronómico/a gastronomical
gato (m) cat 3
géiser (m) geyser
generación (f) generation
generacional generation
general general; **en general** in general; **por lo general** in general 5
generalmente generally 1
generar generate
género (m) genre, type
gente (f) people 12
geografía (f) geography
geográfico/a geographical
gigante giant
gigantesco/a gigantic
gimnasio (m) gymnasium 1
girar turn 7
glaciar (m) glacier
global global 11; **calentamiento global** (m) global warming 11
globalización (f) globalization 11
globo (m) balloon
gobernador/a (m/f) governor 11
gobierno (m) government 11
gol (m) goal 7; **marcar un gol** score a goal 7
golpe (m) blow; **darse un golpe (en la cabeza…)** hit/bump (your head…) 9
gordo/a fat 3
gorra (f) cap 5
gótico/a Gothic
grabar record 11
gracias thank you 1

grado (m) grade; **grados** (mpl) degrees 9
graduación (f) graduation 7
graduarse graduate 7
gráfico (m) graph
gráfico/a graphic; **acento gráfico** (m) written accent; **diseñador/a gráfico/a** (m/f) graphic artist 10; **programa** (m) **de diseño gráfico** graphic design program 10
gramática (f) grammar
gran great 3
grande big 1
grapadora (f) stapler 10
grapar staple 10
grasa (f) fat 8
gratis free
gratuitamente for free
gratuito/a free
grave serious, grave 9
gripe (f) flu 9
gris gray 3
grúa (f) wrecker 7
gruñón/gruñona grumpy 10
grupo (m) group 7; **grupo minoritario** (m) minority group
guapo/a handsome, beautiful 3
guardar keep, save, put away; **guardar cama** stay in bed 9
guatemalteco/a Guatemalan 12
guerra (f) war 11
guerrero/a (m/f) warrior 7
guía (m/f) guide 6; **guía turística** (f) tourist guide (book) 6
guiar guide
guitarra (f) guitar 2
guitarrista (m/f) guitarist 11
gustar: me gusta(n) I like 1; **Me/Te/Le gustaría…** I/You/He, She, You would like… 3; **te gusta(n)** you like 1; **le gusta(n)** you like (formal), he likes, she likes 1
gusto (m) taste; **Con mucho gusto.** Gladly., I'd be happy to. 6; **Mucho gusto.** Pleased to meet you. 1

H

haber have
habitación (f) room 6; **habitación sencilla/doble** single/double room 6; **servicio** (m) **de habitaciones** room service 6
habitado/a inhabited
habitante (m/f) inhabitant
hábito (m) habit; **hábitos alimenticios** (mpl) eating habits
habitualmente usually
hablante (m/f) speaker
hablar speak, talk 2; **hablar de** talk about; **hablar por teléfono** talk on the phone 2; **hablarse** talk to each other 5
hacer do 2, make 3; **¡Hagan…!** Do…! 2; **Hace buen/mal tiempo.** The weather's good/bad. 4; **hace tres días** three days ago 6; **hacer amistades** make friends, develop friendships 12; **hacer cola** stand in line 12; **hacer ejercicio** exercise 3;

hacer falta need; **hacer la maleta** pack your suitcase 6; **hacer mandados** run errands 5; **hacerse** become; **hacer un crucero** take a cruise 6; **hacer una excursión** go for a hike 6; **hacer una fiesta** have a party 3; **hacer una pregunta** ask a question 3; **hacer yoga** do yoga 4; **¿Qué tiempo hace?** What's the weather like? 4
hacia toward(s)
hambre (f) hunger; **darle hambre a alguien** make someone hungry 8; **tener hambre** be hungry 4
harina (f) flour; **tortilla** (f) **de harina** flour tortilla 8
hasta until 2, up to, even; **Hasta luego.** See you later. 1; **Hasta mañana.** See you tomorrow. 1; **¡Hasta pronto!** See you soon!; **dormir hasta tarde** sleep late 4
hay there is, there are, is there, are there 1; **hay que…** one must… 12
hecho (m) fact; **de hecho** in fact; **¡Trato hecho!** It's a deal!
helado (m) **(de vainilla/de chocolate)** (vanilla/chocolate) ice cream 4
helado/a iced; **té** (m) **helado** iced tea 8
hemisferio (m) hemisphere
heno (m) hay; **fiebre** (f) **del heno** hay fever 9
herencia (f) heritage
herido/a (m/f) injured person 7
herido/a injured; **resultar herido/a** get injured 7
hermana (f) sister 1
hermano (m) brother 1; **hermanos** (mpl) brothers and sisters 3
hermoso/a beautiful 7
héroe (m) hero
herramienta (f) tool
hielo (m) ice 4
higiénico/a: papel higiénico (m) toilet paper 6
hija (f) daughter 3
hijo (m) son 3; **hijos** (mpl) children 3
hinchado/a swollen 9
hispánico/a Hispanic
hispano/a Hispanic
hispanoamericano/a Hispanic American
historia (f) history 1; story 7
histórico/a historic 6
hogar (m) home
hoja (f) **de cálculo** spreadsheet 10
Hola. Hi. 1
hombre (m) man; **hombre de negocios** businessman 7
hondo/a: plato hondo (m) bowl 8
hondureño/a Honduran 12
honesto/a honest
honor (m) honor 7
hora (f) hour 1; **¿A qué hora?** At what time? 1; **¿Qué hora es?** What time is it? 1; **a la hora de** at the time of; when it comes time to
horario (m) schedule 1
horizonte (m) horizon
horno (m) oven; **papa** (f) **al horno** baked potato 8

hospedería (*f*) lodge
hospital (*m*) hospital 7
hotel (*m*) hotel 6
hotelero/a hotel
hoy today 1; **hoy en día** nowadays; **¿Qué día es hoy?** What day is today? 1
huella (*f*) influence, print
hueso (*m*) bone 9
huésped (*m/f*) guest 6
huevo (*m*) egg 8; **yema** (*f*) **de huevo** egg yolk 8
huir flee 7
humanidades (*fpl*) humanities 1
humanitario/a: ayuda humanitaria (*f*) humanitarian aid 11
humanos: recursos humanos (*mpl*) human resources 10
humilde humble
humo (*m*) smoke 7
humor: estar de buen/mal humor be in a good/bad mood 10
huracán (*m*) hurricane 11

I

idea (*f*) idea 12
idealista idealistic
identidad (*f*) identity
identificación (*f*) identification 6
identificar identify
idioma (*m*) language 10
idiosincrasia (*f*) idiosyncrasy
iglesia (f) church 4
igual equal, the same
igualitario/a equal
igualmente likewise 1
ilegal illegal 11
ilustrativo/a illustrative
imagen (*f*) image
imaginar imagine
imaginario/a imaginary
impacto (*m*) impact
imperfecto (*m*) imperfect
impermeable (*m*) raincoat 5
implementación (*f*) implementation 10
imponer impose 11
importación (*f*) importation
importancia (*f*) importance
importante important 9
importar be important 8; import
imposible impossible 9
impresión (*f*) impression
impresionante impressive
impreso (*m*) printout, form 12
impresora (*f*) printer 3
imprimir print 10
improbable improbable 9
impuesto (*m*) tax 10; **libres de impuestos** duty free
impuesto/a imposed
impulsar drive
impulsivo/a impulsive 1
incendio (*m*) fire 7
incidente (*m*) incident
inclinación (*f*) inclination
incluido/a included 6

incluir include 9
incluso even, including
incorporar incorporate
incorrecto/a incorrect
increíble incredible 9
incursión (*f*) incursion, raid
independencia (*f*) independence
independiente independent
independientemente independently 10
independizarse become independent
indicador (*m*) indicator 11; **indicadores económicos** (*mpl*) economic indicators 11
indicar indicate 11
indicativo (*m*) indicative
índice (*m*) index
indígena native
indio/a (*m/f*) Indian; **indio/a araucano/a** Araucanian Indian
individuo (*m*) individual
industria (*f*) industry
inestabilidad (*f*) instability
infancia (*f*) childhood
infantil childhood; childish
infarto (*m*) heart attack 9
infectado/a infected 9
inferir (ie, i) infer
infierno (*m*) hell, inferno
infinitivo (*m*) infinitive
inflación (*f*) inflation 11
influencia (*f*) influence
influir influence
información (*f*) information 10
informar inform, report 7; **informado/a** informed; **informarse** get informed
informática (*f*) computer science 1
informativo/a informative
informe (*m*) report 11
infraestructura (*f*) infrastructure
inglés (*m*) English 1; **¿Qué significa… en inglés?** What does… mean in English? 2
ingrediente (*m*) ingredient 8
ingreso (*m*) entry; **alumno/a** (*m/f*) **de nuevo ingreso** an entering student 12
inicialmente initially
iniciar start; **iniciarse** begin
iniciativa (*f*) initiative
inigualable incomparable
inmigración (*f*) immigration 11
inmigrante (*m/f*) immigrant 11
inmigrar immigrate
inmunológico/a: sistema (*m*) **inmunológico** immune system 9
innovador/a innovative
insistir (en) insist (on) 9
insomnio (*m*) insomnia 9
inspiración (*f*) inspiration
inspirar inspire; **inspirado/a** inspired
instantáneo/a instantaneous
institución (*f*) institution
instituto (*m*) institute
instrucción (*f*) instruction
integral integral, whole-grain 9
intelectual intellectual 1
inteligente intelligent 1

intención (*f*) intention 12; **Me dirijo a usted(es) con la intención de…** I'm writing to you for the purpose of… 12
interactuar interact
intercambio (*m*) exchange
interés (*m*) interest; **tasa** (*f*) **de interés** interest rate 10
interesante interesting 1
interesar interest 8; **interesado/a** interested 2
internacional international 6
intriga (*f*) intrigue
introducción (*f*) introduction
introducir introduce, bring in; **introducido/a** introduced; **introducir datos** input data 10
inundación (*f*) flood 11
invadir invade 11
inventar invent
investigación (*f*) research
invierno (*m*) winter 4
invitado/a (*m/f*) guest 11
involucrar involve; **involucrarse** get involved; **involucrado/a** involved
inyección (*f*) shot; **ponerle una inyección a alguien** give someone a shot 9
ir go 2; **ir a** + *infinitive* be going to + *verb* 4; **ir de compras** go shopping 4; **ir de excursión** go on an outing, go on a hike 6; **ir de vacaciones** go on vacation 6; **¡Vayan…!** Go…! 2
irlandés/irlandesa Irish
irse leave, go away 5
isla (*f*) island
islamismo (*m*) Islamism
italiano/a Italian 2
itinerario (*m*) itinerary 6
izquierda: a la izquierda de to the left of 2

J

jabón (*m*) soap 6
jade (*m*) jade
jamón (*m*) ham 4
jardín (*m*) garden, yard 3
jefe/a (*m/f*) boss 10
jóven (*m/f*) young person
joven young 3
joyería (*f*) jewelry store 5
jubilación (*f*) retirement 7
jubilado/a (*m/f*) retiree
jubilarse retire 7
judaísmo (*m*) Judaism
judío/a (*m/f*) Jew
jueves (*m*) Thursday 1
juez (*m/f*) judge 11
jugador/a de béisbol (*m/f*) baseball player 7
jugar (ue) (al tenis) play (tennis) 4
jugo (*m*) **(de naranja)** (orange) juice 8
juguete (*m*) toy 5
julio (*m*) July 4
junio (*m*) June 4
junto a next to 6; **junto con** together with
juntos/as together 2
justicia (*f*) justice 11

justificar justify
juventud (f) youth

K

kilo (m) kilogram 8
kilómetro (m) kilometer

L

la the; **Es la una.** It's one o'clock. 1
la you, her, it 5; **Aquí la tiene.** Here it is. 5
labor (f) labor, work
laboral work; **experiencia laboral** (f) work experience
laboratorio (m) **de lenguas** language lab 1
labrado/a en piedra carved in stone
lácteo/a milk
lado (m) side; **al lado de** next to 2; **por todos lados** everywhere 3
lagartija (f) lizard
lago (m) lake 4
laguna (f) lagoon
laico/a secular, lay
lámpara (f) lamp 3
lana (f) wool 5
lanzarse launch
lápiz (m) pencil 2
largo (m) length; **a lo largo** along
largo/a long 3; **llamada** (f) **de larga distancia** long distance call 6
las the 1; **Son las dos (tres…).** It's two (three…) o'clock. 1
las you, them 5
lástima (f) shame 9
lastimar(se) hurt (yourself) 9
latino/a Latino
Latinoamérica (f) Latin America
lavabo (m) sink 6
lavandería (f) laundry; **servicio** (m) **de lavandería** laundry service 6
lavarse el pelo wash your hair 5; **lavarse los dientes** brush your teeth 5
le (to, for) you (form. sing.), him, her 8; **le gusta(n)** you like (formal), he likes, she likes 1; **Le gustaría…** He/She/You would like… 3
lechuga lettuce 8; **ensalada** (f) **de lechuga y tomate** lettuce and tomato salad 8
lector/a (m/f) reader
lectura (f) reading
leche (f) milk 4
leer read 3; **¡Lean…!** Read…! 2
legado (m) legacy
legalizar authenticate 12
lejos de far from 2
lengua (f) language 1; **laboratorio** (m) **de lenguas** language lab 1
león (m) lion; **león marino** (m) sea lion
les (to, for) you (form. pl.), them 8
letrero (m) sign 7
levantado/a erected, raised
levantar raise; **levantar pesas** lift weights 4; **levantarle el ánimo a alguien** lift someone's spirits, cheer someone up 9; **levantarse** get up 5

ley (f) law 11
leyenda (f) legend 7
liberal liberal 1
libertad (f) freedom, liberty
libra (f) pound 11
libre free; **al aire libre** outdoor; **ratos libres** (m) free time 4
libremente freely
librería (f) bookstore 2
libro (m) book 2; **libro de texto** textbook 3
licencia (f) **de manejar** driver's license 7
licenciatura (f) degree
líder (m/f) leader
ligero/a light 8
limitado/a limited
límite (m) limit 7; **fecha** (f) **límite** deadline 12; **límite de velocidad** speed limit 7
limón (m) lemon 8
limonada (f) lemonade 4
limpiar clean 2
limpio/a clean 3
línea (f) line 10, figure; **en línea** on line
lingüístico/a linguistic
líquido (m) liquid 9
lista (f) list 9
listo/a ready, smart 2
literatura (f) literature 1
litro (m) liter 11
llamada (f) **(de larga distancia)** (long distance) call 6
llamar call 6; **llamarse** be called/named 5; **¿Cómo se llama usted?** What is your name? (formal) 1; **¿Cómo te llamas?** What is your name? (familiar) 1; **Me llamo…** My name is… 1; **Se llama (Se llaman)…** His/Her name is (Their names are)… 3
llanura (f) plain
llave (f) key 6
llegada (f) arrival 6
llegar arrive 2; **llegar al público** reach the public
lleno/a full
llevar take, carry, wear 5; **llevar a cabo** carry out; **llevar una vida** lead a life 8; **llevar… años…** have… years experience 11; **llevarse** take 5; **llevarse bien/mal** get along well/badly 5
llorar cry 7
llover (ue) rain 4; **Llueve.** It rains., It's raining. 4
lluvia (f) rain; **bosque** (m) **de lluvia** rain forest
lo the; **lo antes posible** as soon as possible 10; **lo que** what, that which 11; **lo suficiente** sufficiently, enough 8
lo you, him, it 5; **Aquí lo tiene.** Here it is. 5; **Lo siento.** I'm sorry. 6
local local 11
localización (f) location
localizado/a located, localized
lógico/a logical 9
logotipo (m) logo
logro (m) achievement
longitud (f) length
los the 1; **los (lunes…)** on (Mondays…) (every week) 1; **los fines de semana**

weekends 2; **los/las que** the ones that
los you, them 5
lucha (f) struggle, fight
luchar (por) struggle, fight (for) 7
lucro: sin fines de lucro nonprofit
luego then, next 2; **Hasta luego.** See you later. 1
lugar (m) place 7; **lugar de trabajo** workplace
lunes (m) Monday 1
luz (f) light 10

M

madera (f) wood; makings
madre (f) mother 1
maestro/a (m/f) teacher 7
mágico/a magical
magnífico/a magnificent
maíz (m) corn 8; **tortilla** (f) **de maíz** corn tortilla 8
majestuoso/a majestic
mal badly 1; **llevarse mal** get along badly 5; **ponerse mal** become ill 9
maleta (f) suitcase 6; **hacer la maleta** pack your suitcase 6
malnutrición (f) malnutrition 11
mal(o)/a bad 1
mandado (m) errand; **hacer mandados** run errands 5
mandar send 6
mandato (m) command
mando: al mando de under the command of
manejar drive 7; use, manage; **licencia** (f) **de manejar** driver's license 7
manera (f) manner, way; **de una manera…** in a… way
mango (m) mango 8
manifestación (f) demonstration 11
mano (m) hand 9; **darse la mano** shake hands 5
mansión (f) mansion
mantel (m) tablecloth 8
mantener maintain 9; **mantenerse en forma** stay in shape 8; **mantenido/a** maintained
mantenimiento (m) maintenance 10
mantequilla (f) butter 8
manzana (f) apple 8
mañana morning 4; **de/por la mañana** in the morning 1; **esta mañana** this morning 4; **mañana por la mañana** tomorrow morning 4
mañana tomorrow 1; **Hasta mañana.** See you tomorrow. 1; **mañana por la tarde** tomorrow afternoon 4
maquillarse put on make-up 5
mar (m) sea 6
maravilloso/a marvelous
marcar dial 10; **marcar un gol** score a goal 7; **marcado/a** marked
marchar march, work; **marcharse** leave
marco (m) frame
mareado/a dizzy, queasy 9
mariposa (f) butterfly
mariposario (m) butterfly pavilion
mariscos (mpl) seafood

marítimo/a maritime, coastal
marrón brown 3
martes (m) Tuesday 1
marzo (m) March 4
más more 2; **¿Algo más?** Anything else? 4; **cada vez más** more and more; **más allá de** beyond; **más de** + *number* more than + *number* 6; **más tarde** later; **más vale que** one had better 9; **más... que** more... than, -er... than 1
masculino/a masculine
matar kill 7
matemáticas (fpl) mathematics 1
materia (f) material, matter; **en materia de** on the subject of
matrícula (f) tuition, registration fee 11; **plazo** (m) **de matrícula** registration period 12
matricularse register 12
matrimonial: cama matrimonial (f) double bed 6
matrimonio (m) matrimony 7; married couple
máximo/a maximum
maya Mayan 6
mayo (m) May 4
mayor (m/f) adult
mayor older, oldest 3; greater, greatest; **el/la tercer/a mayor** the third largest; **la mayor parte** the majority, the most part
mayoría (f) majority; **en su mayoría** for the most part
mayormente mainly
me me, myself 5; (to, for) me 8; **me encanta(n)** I love it (them) 7; **Me llamo...** My name is... 1; **me gusta(n)** I like 1; **Me gustaría(n)...** I would like... 3; **Me habría sido de gran ayuda...** It would have helped me a lot... 12; **Me parece(n)...** It seems (They seem)... to me. 5; **Me permite...** May I see... 6
mecánico/a (m/f) mechanic 10
media (f) average
mediano/a: de estatura mediana of medium height 3; **de mediana edad** middle-aged 3
medianoche (f) midnight 1
mediante through
mediático/a media
medicamento (m) medicine 6
medicina (f) medicine 10
médico/a (m/f) doctor, physician 7
médico/a medical; **seguro médico** (m) medical insurance 10
medida (f) measure
medio/a half; **Es la / Son las... y media.** It's half past... 1; **la Edad Media** (f) the Middle Ages; **medio kilo** half kilogram 8; **término medio** medium (*meat*) 8
medioambiente (m) environment
mediodía (m) noon 1
medios (mpl) **de comunicación** mass media 11
mejor better, best 3; **mejor amigo/a** (m/f) best friend 1
mejora (f) improvement 11
mejorar(se) improve 11

melón (m) melon 8
mencionar mention; **mencionarse** be mentioned; **mencionado/a** mentioned
menor younger, youngest 3
menos less, minus 1; fewer 3; **menos... que** less... than 1; fewer... than 3; **a menos que** unless 12; **al menos** at least
mensaje (m) message 6
mensajería instantánea (f) instant messaging
mental mental 9; **enfermedad mental** (f) mental illness 9
mente (f) mind
mentira (f) lie 11
menú (m) menu 8
mercado (m) market(place) 6; **mercado de trabajo** job market
mercancía (f) merchandise
mes month 2; **una vez al mes** once per month 2
mesa (f) table 2
mesero/a (m/f) server 4
mestizo/a of mixed blood
meta (f) objective, goal
metro (m) subway
mexicano/a Mexican 2
mexicoamericano/a Mexican American
mezcla (f) mixture 8
mezclar mix 8; **mezclado/a** mixed
mezclilla (f) denim 5
mezquita (f) mosque 4
mi(s) my 1
mí me 2
microondas (m) microwave oven 3
miedo (m) fear; **tener miedo (de que)** be afraid (that) 10
miel (f) honey 9
miembro (m) member
mientras while, as long as 11
miércoles (m) Wednesday 1
mil one thousand 3
milenario/a thousand-year-old
militar military
milla (f) mile
millón (m) million 3
mina (f) mine
mineral mineral 4; **agua** (f) **mineral** mineral water 4
mínimo/a minimum 10
minoría (f) minority
minuto (m) minute 8
mirar look at, watch 2
misa (m) mass
misión (f) mission
misionero/a (m/f) missionary
mismo/a same 2; **por sí mismo/a** for oneself, by oneself
misterio (m) mystery
misterioso/a mysterious
mitad (f) half 8
mochila (f) bookbag, backpack 2
moda (f) fashion; **estar de moda** be in fashion 5
modernidad (f) modernness, modernity
moderno/a modern 1
modo (m) way

mofongo (m) fried plantains with pork and garlic
molestar bother 8
momento (m) moment 4
monitor (m) monitor 10
montaña (f) mountain 3
montañoso/a mountainous
montar a caballo ride horseback 9
monumento (m) monument
morado/a purple 3
moreno/a dark-haired, dark-skinned 3
morir(se) (ue, u) die 7
mostrador (m) counter
mostrar (ue) show 11
motivo (m) reason 10
mucho/a much, a lot (of) 1; **muchos/as** many, a lot (of) 1; **Mucho gusto.** Pleased to meet you. 1; **Con mucho gusto.** Gladly., I'd be happy to. 6; **Hace mucho calor.** It's very hot. 4; **hace mucho tiempo** a long time ago 6
mudarse move 10
muebles (mpl) furniture 3
muerte (f) death 7
muerto/a dead 3
muestra (f) sample, example
mujer (f) woman; **mujer de negocios** businesswoman 7; **mujer policía** female police officer 7
muletas (fpl) crutches 9
multa (f) ticket 7
multiculturalismo (m) multiculturalism
multilingüismo multilingualism
multitud (f) crowd
mundial world(wide)
mundo (m) world 11; **mundo de la farándula** world of entertainment 11; **Tercer Mundo** Third World
muralista (m/f) muralist
muscular muscular 9
músculo (m) muscle 9
museo (m) museum 4
música (f) music 1
músico (m/f) musician 7
musulmán/musulmana (m/f) Moslem
mutuo/a mutual
muy very 1

N

nacer be born 7; **nacido/a (en)** born (in)
nacimiento (m) birth 7; **acta** (f) **de nacimiento** birth certificate 12
nación (f) nation
nacional national 11
nacionalidad (f) nationality 12
Naciones Unidas (fpl) United Nations 11
nada nothing, (not) anything 3; **nada en especial** nothing in particular 3
nadar swim 4
nadie nobody, (not) anyone 4
naranja (f) orange 8; **jugo** (m) **de naranja** orange juice 8
nariz (f) nose 9
narración (f) narration
narrar narrate

natal native; **ciudad natal** (f) birthplace
nativo/a native
natural natural 11; **catástrofe natural** (f) natural catastrophe, natural disaster 11; **recursos naturales** (mpl) natural resources 11
naturaleza (f) nature
navarro/a from Navarre
Navidad (f) Christmas
necesario/a necessary 9
necesidad (f) necessity
necesitar need 2
negar (ie) deny 11
negativo/a negative 9
negocio (m) business; **hombre** (m) **de negocios** businessman 7; **mujer** (f) **de negocios** businesswoman 7
negrita: en negrita in boldface
negro/a black 3
nervioso/a nervous 2; **ponerse nervioso/a** become/get nervous 9
nevar (ie) snow; **Nieva.** It snows., It's snowing. 4
nevera (f) refrigerator 3
ni nor 2; **ni…ni…** neither… nor 4
nicaragüense Nicaraguan 12
nieta (f) granddaughter 3
nieto (m) grandson 3; **nietos** (mpl) grandchildren 3
ninguno/a (ningún) none, not any 4
niñez (f) childhood 7
niño/a boy/girl; **de niño/a** as a child 7
nivel level 10; **nivel básico/medio/alto** (m) basic/intermediate/high level 10
no no, not 1; **no… nada** not… anything 3
noche (f) night 1; **Buenas noches.** Good evening. Good night. 1; **de/por la noche** in the evening, at night 1; **esta noche** tonight, this evening 4
nombre (m) first name 10
nominación (f) nomination 11
noreste (m) Northeast
normal normal 9
normalmente normally
norte (m) north
norteamericano/a (North) American
nos us 5; (to, for) us 8; ourselves, each other, one another 5
nosotros/as we 1; us 2
nostalgia (f) nostalgia, homesickness
notario/a público/a (m/f) notary public 12
noticia (f) piece of news; **presentador/a** (m/f) **de noticias** newscaster 11
noticiero (m) newscast 11
novecientos/as nine hundred 3
novela (f) soap opera
noveno/a ninth 6
noventa ninety 1
novia (f) girlfriend 1; bride 7
noviembre (m) November 4
novio (m) boyfriend 1; groom 7
nublado/a: El cielo está nublado. The sky's cloudy. 4
núcleo (m) nucleus
nuestro/a/os/as our 3
nueve nine 1

nuevo/a new 1
número (m) number 1; **número de teléfono** telephone number 1
numeroso/a large, numerous
nunca never 2
nutrición (f) nutrition
nutrirse (de) be nourished (by), feed (on)

O

o or 1
obedecer obey 7
obesidad (f) obesity
objetivo (m) objective, goal
objetivo/a objective
obligatorio/a required, obligatory 12
obra (f) work; **obra de teatro** play 4
obrero/a (m/f) worker 7; **obrero/a de la construcción** construction worker 7; **obrero/a de fábrica** factory worker 7
observar observe; **observado/a** observed
obtener obtain 10; **obtenido/a** obtained
ocasión (f) occasion
occidente (m) west
océano (m) ocean; **Océano Pacífico** Pacific Ocean
ochenta eighty 1
ocho eight 1
ochocientos/as eight hundred 3
ocio (f) leisure
octavo/a eighth 6
octubre (m) October 4
ocupar occupy; **ocupado/a** busy 2, occupied
ocurrir occur 7
oeste (m) west
oferta (f) offer, offering; **oferta mediática** media offerings; **oferta de empleo** job offer 10; **de oferta** on sale 5
oficina (f) office 2; **artículos** (mpl) **de oficina** office supplies 10; **oficina de admisiones y registro** Admissions and Registrar's Office 12; **oficina de correos** post office 6
ofrecer offer 8
oído (m) inner ear 9
oír hear, listen to 3
Ojalá (que)… Let's hope (that)… 9
ojos eyes 3
oliva (f) olive
once eleven 1
onda (f) wave; **nueva onda** new wave
opción (f) option
operación (f) operation
operar operate
operario/a (m/f) operative
opinar think; have the opinion that
oportunidad (f) opportunity 10, chance
optativo/a optional, elective 12
optimista optimistic 1
óptimo/a ideal
opuesto/a opposite 7
oración (f) sentence 2
orden order (f) (command), (m) (sequence)
ordenado/a neat, straightened up 3
ordenar put in order

oreja (f) ear 9
orfebrería (f) **en oro** gold work
organizar organize; **organizado/a** organized 1
orgullo (m) pride
orgulloso/a proud 7
orientado/a oriented
oriente (m) east
origen (m) origin
original original 12
originalmente originally
originariamente originally
orilla (f) (river) bank; **a orillas de** on the shore of
oro (m) gold; **cadena** (f) **de oro** golden chain 5
os you 5; (to, for) you (fam. pl.) 8; yourselves, each other, one another 5
oscuro/a dark
otoño (m) autumn, fall 4
otro/a other, another 1; **otra vez** again 10; **unos a los otros** one to another
oyente (m/f) listener, auditor

P

paciencia (f) patience
paciente (m/f) patient 9
paciente patient 1
Pacífico: Océano Pacífico (m) Pacific Ocean
padre (m) father 1; **padres** (mpl) parents 3
padrino (m) godfather
pagar pay 3
página (f) page 2
pago (m) pay 10
país (m) country 6
paisaje (m) countryside
palabra (f) word 2
palacio (m) palace
pan bread; **pan tostado** (m) toast 8
panadería (f) bakery
panameño/a Panamanian 12
páncreas (m) pancreas 9
pandilla (f) gang 11
pantalla (f) screen 10
pantalones (mpl) pants 5; **pantalones cortos** (mpl) shorts 5
papa (f) potato 8; **papa al horno** baked potato 8; **papas fritas** (fpl) French fries 8
papel (m) paper 2, role; **papel higiénico** toilet paper 6
papeleo (m) paperwork, red tape 12
papitas fritas (fpl) potato chips 4
paquete vacacional (m) vacation package
par (m) pair, couple
para for 1; **para** + *infinitive* (in order) to + *verb* 4; **para mí** for me 4; **para que** so (that) 12
parada (f) **de autobús** bus stop 7
paraguas (m) umbrella 5
paraguayo/a Paraguayan 12
paraíso (m) paradise, heaven
paramédico/a (m/f) paramedic 7
parcial: empleo (m) **a tiempo parcial** part-time employment 10

parecer seem 11; **Me parece(n)…** It seems (They seem)… to me. 5; **parecido/a** alike, similar; **Se parece a…** He/She looks like… 3

parecido (m) similarity

pared (f) wall 3

pareja (f) pair 2, couple 11; **en parejas** in pairs 2

parentesco (m) relationship, kindred

paréntesis: entre paréntesis in parentheses

pariente (m/f) relative

parmesano: queso parmesano (m) Parmesan cheese 8

parque (m) park 2; **parque de atracciones** amusement park 6

párrafo (m) paragraph

parrilla (f) grill; **a la parrilla** on the grill, grilled 8

parte (f) part; **cuarta parte de** one fourth of 8; **de parte de** on behalf of 11; **la mayor parte** the majority

participación (f) participation 11

participar participate 2

particular (m) matter; **en este particular** in this matter

partido (m) **de fútbol (fútbol americano)** soccer (football) game 2

partir: a partir de starting in

pasado (m) past

pasado/a last, past 6

pasaje (m) **de avión** plane ticket 6

pasajero/a (m/f) passenger 6

pasaporte (m) passport 6

pasar pass, spend (time) 2; happen 9; **pasar a ser** become; **¿Qué te pasa?** What's wrong with you? 9

pasatiempo (m) pastime

pasear walk, go for a walk 4

pasillo (m) aisle, hall 6

paso (m) step 12; **paso del tiempo** passing of time

pastel (m) cake 4

pastelería (f) pastry shop, bakery 5

pastilla (f) tablet 9

patinaje (m) skating 7

patio (m) patio, backyard

patrón (m) pattern

pausa comercial (f) commercial break 11

paz (f) peace 7; **acuerdo** (m) **de paz** peace agreement 11

peatón (m) pedestrian 7

pecho (m) chest 9

peculiar particular

pedir (i, i) ask for, order 4

pelearse fight 5

pelícano (m) pelican

película (f) **(extranjera, de aventuras, de terror)** (foreign, adventure, horror) movie 2; **rollo** (m) **de película** roll of film 6

peligro (m) danger

pelirrojo/a redheaded 3

pelo (m) hair 3; **lavarse el pelo** wash one's hair 5; **cortarse el pelo** get one's hair cut, cut one's hair 5

peluquería (f) hair salon 5

pena: redimir sus penas redeem their sins

penicilina (f) penicillin 9

pensamiento (m) thought

pensar (ie) think 4; **pensar +** *infinitive* intend to + *verb* 4

peor worse 3, worst

pequeño/a little, small 1

perder (ie) lose, miss 4

peregrino/a (m/f) pilgrims

perezoso/a lazy 1

perfecto/a perfect 2

perfil (m) profile

periódico (m) newspaper 3; periodical 6; **quiosco** (m) **de periódicos** newsstand 6

periodista (m/f) journalist 10

periodo (m) period

permanecer remain 12

permanencia stay, continuance

permanente: residencia permanente (f) permanent residency 12

permitir permit, allow 9; **Me permite…** May I see… 6

pero but 1

perro (m) dog 3

persecución (f) persecution

persona (f) person 3

personal personal 10; **a lo personal** from a personal point of view

personalidad (f) personality

perspectiva (f) perspective

pertenencia (f) belonging

peruano/a Peruvian 12

pesado/a heavy 9

pesar: a pesar de despite

pesas: levantar pesas lift weights 4

pesca (f) fishing; **ir de pesca** go fishing

pescadería (f) seafood shop 5

pescado (m) fish 8

pescador/a (m/f) fisherman/fisherwoman

pescar fish 6

pesimista pessimistic 1

peso (m) peso 8, weight 9; **bajar/subir de peso** lose/gain weight 9

pesquero/a fishing

petición (f) request 12; **disponible a petición** available upon request 10

pez (m) fish

picar itch, burn 9

pie (m) foot 9; **andar a pie** go on foot, walk 7; **a pie** on foot; **de… pies de altura** …feet high

piedra (f) stone

piel (f) skin 9

pierna (f) leg 9

pieza (f) piece; **pieza teatral** play

piloto (m/f) pilot

pimienta (f) pepper 8

pimiento verde (m) green pepper

pingüino (m) penguin

pintar paint 10

pintor/a (m/f) painter 7

pintoresco/a picturesque

pintura (f) painting 3

piña (f) pineapple 8

pionero/a (m/f) pioneer

pirámide (f) pyramid

piscina (f) swimming pool 3

pizarra (f) blackboard 2

pizza (f) pizza 4

plan (m) plan 12; **plan de estudios** plan of studies, degree plan 12

planear plan

planeta (m) planet

planificar plan

plano (m) **de la ciudad** city map 6; **plano personal** personal level

planta (f) plant 2; **planta baja** ground floor 6

plata (f) silver 5; **collar** (m) **de plata** silver necklace 5

plátano (m) banana 8

plato (m) dish, plate 6; **plato hondo** bowl 8; **plato llano** flat plate 8; **plato principal** main dish, entrée 8

playa (f) beach 3

plazo (m) **de matrícula** registration period 12

población (f) population

pobre poor

pobreza (f) poverty 11

poco/a little; **pocos/as** few 2; **un poco** a little 1; **poco cocido/a** rare 8

poder (m) power; **poder adquisitivo** buying power

poder (ue) be able, can 4; **¿En qué puedo servirle?** How may I help you? 5; **¿Podría(s) comunicarme con… ?** Could you connect me with…? 6; **se puede…** one can… 6

policía / mujer policía (m/f) police officer 7

policial police

polinesio/a Polynesian

política (f) politics

político/a political

pollo (m) chicken 8; **caldo** (m) **de pollo** chicken broth 8

poner put, place, set, turn on 3; **ponerle una inyección a alguien** give someone a shot 9; **ponerse (la ropa)** put on (clothes) 5; **ponerse (mal, nervioso/a…)** become (ill, nervous…) 9

pontificio/a papal

popular popular 6

popularización (f) popularization

por for, through, because of 5; **descuento** (m) **del… por ciento…** percent discount 5; **hablar (por teléfono)** speak, talk (on the phone) 2; **por acá** over here 5; **por ciento** percent; **por ejemplo** for example 11; **por eso** therefore, that's why; **por favor** please 2; **por la mañana** in the morning 1; **por lo general** in general 5; **por supuesto** of course 12; **por todo el país** throughout the country; **por todos lados** everywhere 3

porcentaje (m) percentage

¿por qué? why? 1

porque because 1

portada (f) front page

portarse behave 7

porteño/a from Buenos Aires

poseer possess

posesión (f) possession
posibilidad (f) possibility
posible possible 9; **lo antes posible** as soon as possible 10
posición (f) position
positivo/a positive
postal postal; **tarjeta postal** postcard
postre (m) dessert 8
práctica (f) practice
practicar practice; **practicar un deporte** play a sport
práctico/a practical 10
precaución (f) precaution
precio (m) price 5
precioso/a precious
precocinado/a precooked
precolombino/a pre-Columbian
predominante predominant
predominar predominate
preferencia (f) preference
preferible preferable 9
preferir (ie, i) prefer 4; **preferido/a** favorite, preferred; **Prefiero…** I prefer… 2
pregunta (f) question 2; **hacer una pregunta** ask a question 3
preguntar ask 8
prehispánico/a pre-Hispanic
premio (m) award 11
prenda (f) garment
prensa (f) press 11
preocupación (f) worry, preoccupation
preocupado/a worried 7
preocupar worry, preoccupy
preparación preparation
preparar prepare 2; **prepararse** get ready, prepare oneself; **preparado/a** prepared 8
preparatoria (f) high school 10
preposición (f) preposition
prerrománico/a pre-Roman
presencia (f) presence
presentación (f) presentation 11
presentador/a (m/f) **de noticias** newscaster 11
presentar present; **Quiero presentarte/le a…** I want you to meet… 1; **presentado/a** presented; **presentarse como candidato/a** run as a candidate 11; **presentarse** show up, be present 12
presente (m) present
preservar preserve
presidencial presidential
presidente/a (m/f) president 11
presión (f) pressure 9; **presión arterial alta** high blood pressure 9
préstamo (m) loan 10
prestar lend 8; **prestar atención** pay attention
pretérito (m) preterite
prevención (f) prevention
prevenir prevent 9
previamente previously
previo/a previous
previsto/a planned, arranged 12
primario/a primary; **escuela** (f) **primaria** primary school 2
primavera (f) spring 4

primer(o)/a first 2; **Es el primero de…** It's the first of…4; **primeros auxilios** (mpl) first aid 7
primo/a (m/f) cousin 3
principal (m) main 8
principio (m) beginning; **a principios de** at the beginning of; **al principio** at first 9
prioridad (f) priority 11
privado/a private
probable probable 9
probador (m) fitting room 5
probar (ue) try 6; prove 12; **probarse (ue)** try on 5
problema (m) problem 11
problemático/a problematic
procedencia (f) origin
proceder proceed, come from
procedimiento (m) procedure
procesado/a (m) processed 7
procesador (m) **de texto** word processor 10
proceso (m) process, trial
proclamar proclaim
producción (f) production
producir produce 9; **producirse** be produced
producto (m) product; **productos procesados** (mpl) processed food 7
profesión (f) profession
profesional professional 10
profesor/a (m/f) professor 1
profundidad (f) depth
profundo/a (f) deep 9
programa (m) program 12; **programa de diseño gráfico** graphic design program 10; **programa de entrevistas** talk show 11
programador/a (m/f) programmer 7
programar program 10
progreso (m) progress 10
prohibir prohibit, forbid 9
prolongar prolong 12
promedio (m) average
prominente prominent
promocionar promote
promover (ue) promote
pronombre (m) pronoun
pronóstico (m) **del tiempo** weather forecast 11
pronto soon 7; **¡Hasta pronto!** See you soon!
pronunciar pronounce; **¿Cómo se pronuncia…?** How is… pronounced?
propiedad (f) property
propietario/a (m/f) owner
propina (f) tip 8
propio/a own 3
proporcionar provide 12
propósito (m) purpose
propuesto/a proposed 11
próspero/a prosperous
protagonista (m/f) protagonist
protectora: crema protectora solar (f) sunscreen 6
proteger protect 9; **protegido/a** protected
proteína (f) protein 8
protesta (f) protest 11

protestar (contra) protest (against) 11
proveer provide
provincia (f) province
provocar provoke, cause 11
próximamente soon, shortly
proximidad (f) proximity
próximo/a next 2; **¿Cuál es la tarea para la próxima clase?** What is the homework for the next class? 2
proyectar plan, project
proyecto (m) plan, project
prueba (f) test, proof
pruebita (f) quiz 2
psicología (f) psychology 1
publicación (f) publication
publicado/a published 10
publicar publish; **publicarse** be published
publicidad (f) advertising 10
publicitario/a advertising; **campaña publicitaria** (f) advertising campaign
público (m) public
público/a public 6
pueblo (m) people; town
puerta (f) door 2; gate 6; **puerto** (m) port
puertorriqueño/a Puerto Rican
pues well
puesto (m) position 10
pulmones (mpl) lungs 9
pulmonía (f) pneumonia 9
punto (m) point
pupitre (m) student desk 2
puro/a pure

Q

¿qué? what? 2; **¿A qué hora?** At what time? 1; **¿En qué puedo servirle?** How may I help you? 5; **lo que** what, that which 11; **más… que** more… than, , -er… than 1; **menos… que** less… than 1; **¿Qué día es hoy?** What day is today? 1; **¿Qué hora es?** What time is it? 1; **¿Qué significa… en inglés?** What does… mean in English? 2; **¿Qué tal…?** How was/were…? 6; **¿Qué te pasa?** What's wrong with you? 9; **¿Qué tiempo hace?** What's the weather like? 4
quechua (m) Quechua
quedarse stay 5; end up, be 11; **quedar atrás** stay behind
quemar(se) burn (yourself) 9
querer (ie) want 4, love; **¿Quieres…?** Do you want…? 1; **Quiero…** I want… 1; **quererse (ie)** love each other 5; **querido/a** dear; **ser** (m) **querido** loved one
queso (m) cheese 4; **queso suizo/ parmesano** Swiss/Parmesan cheese 8
¿quién(es)? who? 2; **A quien corresponda** To Whom it May Concern 12; **¿con quién(es)?** with whom? 2
química (f) chemistry 1
quince fifteen 1
quinceañera (f) fifteenth birthday party 7
quinientos/as five hundred 3
quinto/a fifth 6

quiosco (*m*) **de periódicos** newsstand 6
quisiera I/you (formal)/he/she would like 8
quitar(se) take off, remove 9
quizás maybe, perhaps 9

R

radio (*f*) radio 3
raíz (*f*) root; **echarse raíces** establish roots
rallado/a grated 8
rápido/a fast
raro/a strange 9
rato (*m*) while; **pasar el rato** spend a while;
    ratos libres free time 4
rayas (*f*) stripes; **de rayas** striped 5
razón (*f*) reason; **tener razón** be right 9
razonable reasonable 5
real real 11, royal
realidad (*f*) reality
realizar carry out, do, perform 12;
    realizado/a realized, made real, done
realmente really
rebelde rebellious 1
recado (*m*) message 10
recepción (*f*) front desk 6
recepcionista (*m/f*) receptionist 6
receta (*f*) recipe 8; prescription
recetar prescribe 9
recibir receive 3
recibo (*m*) receipt 5
recién casados (*mpl*) newlyweds 11
reciente recent
recientemente recently
recipiente (*m*) container, receptacle 8
recoger pick up, gather 6
recogido/a collected
recomendación (*f*) recommendation 8
recomendar (ie) recommend 6
reconciliación (*f*) reconciliation 11
reconciliarse make up 5
reconocer recognize, admit
reconquista (*f*) reconquest
recordar (ue) remember 7
recorrer travel across
recortar cut (back) 11
recto/a straight; **seguir (i, i) recto** continue
    straight (ahead) 6
recuerdo (*m*) souvenir 6; memory 7
recurso (*m*) resource 10; **con pocos**
    recursos low-income; **recursos**
    humanos (*mpl*) human resources 10;
    recursos naturales (*mpl*) natural
    resources 11
red (*f*) net, web
redimir sus penas redeem one's sins
reducción (*f*) reduction 11
reducir reduce 11
referencia (*f*) reference 10
referirse (ie) refer
reflejar reflect; **reflejarse** be reflected
reflejo (*m*) reflection
reflexión (*f*) reflection
reflexionar reflect
reflexivo/a reflexive
reforma (*f*) reform 11
refresco (*m*) soft drink 4

regalar give (*as a gift*) 7
regalo (*m*) gift, present 5
región (*f*) region
regional regional 6
registrar register
registro: oficina (*f*) **de admisiones y**
    registro Admissions and Registrar's
    Office 12
regla (*f*) rule, ruler
regresar return 2
regular as usual, regular 1
regularidad: con regularidad with
    regularity 9
reina (*f*) queen
relación (*f*) relationship
relacionarse be related; **relacionado/a con**
    related to
relajarse relax 5; **relajado/a** relaxed
relativo/a relative
relevante notable
religión (*f*) religion
religioso/a religious 1
rellenar fill out 12
relleno/a: chile relleno (*m*) stuffed pepper 8
reloj (*m*) clock, watch 2
renacimiento (*m*) Renaissance
renovación (*f*) renovation, renewal 12
renovado/a renovated
renovar (ue) renew 12
repercusión (*f*) repercussion
repetir (i, i) repeat 4; **¡Repitan…!**
    Repeat…! 2
replicar reply 7
reportero/a (*m/f*) reporter 10
representación (*f*) performance
representante (*m/f*) representative 11;
    Cámara (*f*) **de Representantes** House of
    Representatives 11
representar represent
representativo/a representative
reproductor (*m*) **de DVD** DVD player 3
reptil (*m*) reptile
república (*f*) republic
requerir (ie) require; **requerido/a** required
rescatar rescue
reseña (*f*) review
reserva (*f*) reservation, reserving
reservación (*f*) reservation
reservar reserve 6
resfriado/a: estar resfriado/a have a cold 9
resfriarse catch a cold 9
residencia (*f*) residence hall, dormitory 1;
    residencia permanente permanent
    residency 12
residente (*m/f*) resident
residir reside
resistencia (*f*) resistance 9
resolver (ue) resolve 10
respaldado/a supported
respetar respect; **respetarse** be respected
respeto (*m*) respect
respirar breathe 7
responder respond, answer 11
responsabilidad (*f*) responsibility
responsable responsible 1
respuesta (*f*) answer 2

restante remaining
restaurante (*m*) restaurant 2; **restaurante**
    de comida mexicana/italiana Mexican
    food/Italian restaurant 2
resto (*m*) rest
resultado (*m*) result
resultar turn out 7; **resultar herido/a** get
    injured 7
resumen (*m*) summary
retirar remove, take away 8; withdraw 10
retiro (*m*) withdrawal 10
reto (*m*) challenge
reuma (*m*) rheumatism
reunión (*f*) meeting; **reunión familiar**
    family reunion
reunir bring together; **reunirse** gather
revisar review 11, revise
revista (*f*) magazine 3
revolución (*f*) revolution
rey (*m*) king
rezar pray 4
rico/a rich 9, tasty
ridículo/a ridiculous 9
riesgo (*m*) risk
rincón (*m*) corner
riñones (*mpl*) kidneys 9
río (*m*) river 6
riqueza (*f*) richness
ritmo (*m*) rhythm
robo (*m*) theft 11
rock (*m*) rock (music); **estrella** (*f*) **de rock**
    rock star 11
rodilla (*f*) knee 9
rojizo/a reddish
rojo/a red 3
rollo (*m*) **de película** roll of film 6
romance (*m*) romance 11
románico/a Roman
romano/a (*m/f*) Roman
romántico/a romantic 1
romper(se) (el brazo…) break (your
    arm…) 9
ropa (*f*) clothes 5; **ponerse (la ropa)** put on
    (clothes) 5; **tienda** (*f*) **(de ropa)**
    (clothing) store 2
rosa pink 3
rosado/a pink 3
roto/a torn 5, broken 10
rubio/a blond(e) 3
ruinas (*f*) ruin 6
rumor (*m*) rumor 11
ruptura (*f*) breakup 11
ruta: en ruta a en route to 7
rutina (*f*) routine 8

S

sábado (*m*) Saturday 1
sábana (*f*) (bed)sheet 6
saber know, find out 6; **No sé.** I don't know. 2
sabor (*m*) flavor, taste
saborear taste
sacar take, take out, get 6; **¡Saquen…!** Take
    out…! 2; **sacar copias** make copies 10;
    sacar una foto take a picture 4
saco de dormir (*m*) sleeping bag 6

sagrado/a sacred
sal (f) salt 8
sala (f) living room 3; **sala de espera** waiting room 6
salario (m) salary
salida (f) departure, exit 6
salir leave 3, go out 2
salmón (m) salmon 9
salón (m) **de clase** classroom 2
salsa (f) sauce 8
salud (f) health 8
saludo (m) greeting
salvadoreño/a Salvadoran 12
sanciones (f) sanctions 11
sandalia (f) sandal 5
sándwich (m) sandwich 8
sangre (f) blood 9
sanidad (f) health
sano/a healthy 8
santuario (m) sanctuary
satisfacer satisfy; **satisfecho/a** satisfied 11
sazón (f) seasoning, flavor
sazonado/a seasoned
se himself, herself, yourself, yourselves, themselves, each other, one another 5; to you, to him, to her, to you, to them 8; **¿Cómo se dice… en español?** How do you say… in Spanish? 2; **¿Cómo se escribe…?** How is… written? 1; **¿Cómo se escribe?** How is it written? 2; **¿Cómo se llama usted?** What is your name? *(formal)* 1; **Se escribe…** It's written… 1; **Se llama (Se llaman)…** His/Her name is (Their names are)… ; **Se parece a…** He/She looks like… 3; **se puede…** one can… 6
sección (f) section
secretario/a (m/f) secretary 7
secreto/a secret 7
secuencia (f) sequence
secundaria secondary; **certificado** (m) **de secundaria** high-school diploma 12; **escuela secundaria** (f) secondary school 2
sed (f) thirst; **tener sed** be thirsty 4
seda (f) silk 5
sede (f) seat; **sede central** (f) headquarters
seducir seduce
segmento (m) segment
seguida: en seguida right away 11
seguir (i, i) continue 6; follow 8; **seguir recto** continue straight (ahead) 6; **seguido/a por** followed by
según according to 11
segundo/a second 6
seguridad (f) safety; **abrocharse el cinturón de seguridad** buckle your seatbelt 6; **seguridad nacional** (f) national security 11
seguro médico (m) medical insurance 10
seguro/a sure, safe 2
seis six 1
seiscientos/as six hundred 3
seleccionar select
sello (m) stamp 6
selva (f) jungle
semáforo (m) traffic light 7

semana (f) week; **esta semana** (f) this week 1; **este fin de semana** this weekend 1; **los fines de semana** weekends 2; **una vez a la semana** once per week 2
semanario (m) weekly newpaper
semestre (m) semester
senador/a (m/f) senator 11
sencillo/a simple; **habitación sencilla** (f) single room 6
sensacional sensational
sensibilización (f) raising awareness
sentarse (ie) sit (down) 5
sentido (m) sense
sentimiento (m) feeling, sentiment
sentir(se) (ie, i) feel 5; **Lo siento.** I'm sorry. 6; **sentir que** be sorry that 10
seña (f) sign
señor Mr., sir 1
señora Mrs., Mme. 1
señorita Miss 1
separado/a separated 11
septiembre (m) September 4
séptimo/a seventh 6
ser querido (m) loved one
ser be 1; **¡Así es!** That's it! That's right! 8; **¿Cómo es…?** What's… like? 1; **¿Cuántos son en…?** How many are there in…? 3; **¿De dónde eres?** Where are you from? 1; **Me habría sido de gran ayuda…** It would have helped me a lot… 12; **son** equals 1; **Son las dos (tres…)** It's two (three…) o'clock. 1
sereno/a serene
serio/a serious 1; **¡En serio!** Seriously!
servicio (m) service; **estación** (f) **de servicio** service station, 6; **servicio de habitaciones** room service 6; **servicio de lavandería** laundry service 6
servilleta (f) napkin 8
servir (i, i) serve 4; **¿En qué puedo servirle?** How may I help you? 5
sesenta sixty 1
sesión (f) session
setecientos/as seven hundred 3
setenta seventy 1
sexto/a sixth 6
sí: por sí mismo/a for oneself, by oneself
sicología (f) psychology
siempre always 2
siesta (f) nap; **dormir (ue, u) una siesta** take a nap
siete seven 1
siglo (m) century
significado (m) meaning
significar mean, signify; **¿Qué significa… en inglés?** What does… mean in English? 2
significativo/a significant
siguiente following 2; **al día siguiente** on the next day 6
silencioso/a silent
silueta (f) silhouette
silla (f) chair 2
símbolo (m) symbol
similitud (f) similarity
simpático/a nice 1

sin without 1; **sin embargo** nevertheless, however; **sin fines de lucro** non profit
sinagoga (f) synagogue 4
sino rather, but; **sino también** but also
síntoma (m) symptom 9
sinuoso/a winding
sinusitis (f) sinus infection 9
sistema (m) system 9; **sistema inmunológico** (m) immune system 9
sitio (m) site 6, place
situación (f) situation 11
situar situate, locate; **situado/a** located
sobre (m) envelope 12
sobre about, on, over 8
sobremesa (f) after-dinner conversation
sobrepeso (m) excess weight
sobrevivir survive
sobrina (f) niece 3
sobrino (m) nephew 3; **sobrinos** (mpl) nephews and nieces 3
social social 1
sociedad (f) society 11
sociopolítico/a sociopolitical
sofá (m) sofa 3
software: diseñador/a (m/f) **de software** software designer 7
sol (m) sun; **gafas** (fpl) **de sol** sunglasses 6; **Hace sol.** It's sunny. 4; **tomar el sol** sunbathe 4
solamente only
solar solar; **crema protectora solar** (f) sunscreen 6
soldado (m) soldier 7
solicitar apply for 12
solicitud (f) **de empleo** job application 10
solidaridad (f) solidarity
sólido/a solid
sólo only 3
solo/a alone 1; **de un solo color** solid-colored 5
soltero/a single 3
solución (f) solution
solvencia (f) solvency; **carta** (f) **de solvencia** letter of financial standing 12
sombrero (m) hat 5
someterse (a) submit (to) 7
sonreír (i, i) smile
soñar (ue) con dream of/about 7
sopa (f) soup 8
sorprendente surprising
sorprender surprise 10
sorpresa (f) surprise
sostener support
su(s) your, his, her 1; its, their 3
subdirector/a (m/f) assistant director
subir a get on/in, go up 6; **subir de peso** gain weight 9
subjuntivo (m) subjunctive
subsecretario/a de prensa deputy press secretary
subsidiaria (f) subsidiary
subterráneo/a underground
subtítulo (m) subtitle
suceso (m) event
sucio/a dirty 3
sucursal (f) branch office 10

sudadera (f) sweatshirt 5
Sudamérica (f) South America
sueldo (m) wage, salary 10
suelo (m) ground, floor 3
sueño (m) dream
suerte (f) luck; **tener suerte** be lucky
suéter (m) sweater 5
suficiente sufficient; **lo suficiente** sufficiently, enough 8
suficientemente sufficiently
sufrir (de) suffer from 9
sugerencia (f) suggestion
sugerir (ie, i) suggest 9; **sugerido/a** suggested
suizo/a Swiss 8
superficie (f) surface, area
superior superior; **con validez superior a…** valid for more than… 12
supermercado (m) supermarket 2
supervisor/a (m/f) supervisor 10
supuesto: por supuesto of course 12
sur (m) south
sureste (m) southeast
surgir arise
suroeste (m) southwest
surullito (m) corn fritter
sustituir substitute
suyo/a his, her, its, your, their

T

tabacalero/a tobacco
tabla (f) table, chart
tal such; **tal vez** maybe, perhaps 5; **¿Qué tal…?** How was/were…? 6; **con tal que** provided that, as long as 12
talento (m) talent
talla (f) size 5
taller (m) mechanic's garage 7
tamaño (m) size 12
también too, also 1
tampoco neither, not either 3
tan so 2; **tan… como** as… as 1
tanto so much 9; **tanto/a/os/as… como** as much… as, as many… as 3
tapado/a stopped up, blocked 9
tardar (en) delay (in), take a long time
tarde afternoon 1; **Buenas tardes.** Good afternoon. 1; **de/por la tarde** in the afternoon 1; **esta tarde** this afternoon 4
tarde late 2
tardío/a late
tarea (f) homework 1, task; **¿Cuál es la tarea para la próxima clase?** What is the homework for the next class? 2
tarifa (f) fee 12
tarjeta (f) card 5; **tarjeta de crédito** credit card 5; **tarjeta de débito** debit card 5; **tarjeta de embarque** boarding pass 6; **tarjeta de identificación** identification card 12; **tarjeta postal** postcard; **tarjeta telefónica** phone card 6
tasa (f) rate; **tasa de interés** interest rate 10
taxi (m) taxi 6; **chófer** (m/f) **de taxi** taxi driver 10
taza (f) cup 8

te (familiar) you, yourself 5; (to, for) you 8; **¿Cómo te llamas?** What is your name? (familiar) 1; **te gusta(n)** you like 1; **Te gustaría(n)…** You would like… 3; **Te veo…** You look… to me. 9
té (m) tea 4; **té helado/caliente** iced/hot tea 8
teatro (m) theater (for live performances) 4; **obra** (f) **de teatro** play 4
teclado (m) keyboard 10
técnico/a technical 1
tecnología (f) technology 11
tecnológico/a technological
tejido (m) tissue 9; fabric
tele (f) TV 2
telefónico/a telephone; **tarjeta telefónica** (f) phone card 6
teléfono (m) telephone 6; **hablar (por teléfono)** speak, talk (on the phone) 2; **número** (m) **de teléfono** telephone number 1
telenovela (f) soap opera 11
televisión (f) television 2
televisivo/a television
televisor (m) television set 3
tema (m) topic 11
temer fear 10
temperatura (f) temperature 9
templo (m) temple 4
temporada (f) season
temporal temporary 10
temprano early 4
tendencia (f) tendency
tenedor (m) fork 8
tener have 3; **Aquí lo/la tiene.** Here it is. 5; **tener catarro** have a cold 9; **tener cuidado** be careful 9; **tener ganas de +** infinitive feel like …ing 4; **tener hambre** be hungry 4; **tener miedo de que** be afraid that 10; **tener que +** infinitive have to + verb 3; **tener razón** be right 9; **tener sed** be thirsty 4; **tener… años** be… years old 3; **(No) tengo** I (don't) have 1
tenis (m) tennis 4; **tenis** (mpl) tennis shoes 5
teoría (f) theory
tercer(o)/a third 6; **Tercer Mundo** (m) Third World
termal thermal
terminar finish 11
término (m) end, conclusion 12; **término medio** medium (meat) 8
terraza (f) terrace 8
terremoto (m) earthquake 11
territorio (m) territory
terrorismo (m) terrorism 11
terrorista (m/f) terrorist 11
tesoro (m) treasure
testigo (m/f) witness 7
testimonio (m) testimony
texano/a Texan
texto (m) text; **libro** (m) **de texto** textbook 3; **procesador** (m) **de texto** word processor 10
ti you 2
tía (f) aunt 3
tico/a Costa Rican

tiempo (m) time 2; **hace mucho tiempo** a long time ago 6; **Necesito más tiempo.** I need more time. 2; **tiempo pretérito** (m) preterite tense; **¿Qué tiempo hace?** What's the weather like? 4; **a tiempo completo** full-time; **Hace buen/mal tiempo.** The weather's good/bad. 4; **pronóstico** (m) **del tiempo** weather forecast 11
tienda (f) store 2
tierra (f) land; **Tierra** (f) Earth
tímido/a shy, timid 1
tinto: vino tinto (m) red wine 4
tío (m) uncle 3; **tíos** (mpl) aunts and uncles 3
típicamente typically
típico/a typical 6
tipo (m) type
tirada (f) circulation, distribution
titular (m) headline, top story 11
título (m) title; **título** (m) **universitario** university degree
toalla (f) towel 6
tobillo (m) ankle 9; **torcerse (ue) el tobillo…** twist/sprain your ankle… 9
tocar play (an instrument) 2; **tocar la guitarra** play the guitar 4
todavía still; **todavía no** not yet 10
todo/a/os/as all, every 2; **por todos lados** everywhere 3; **todo el día** all day 1; **todos los días** every day 2
todos everyone 4
tolerancia (f) tolerance
tomar drink, take 2; **tomar el sol** sunbathe 4; **tomar una copa** have a drink 4
tomate (m) tomato; **ensalada** (f) **de lechuga y tomate** lettuce and tomato salad 8
tonelada (f) ton
tónico stressed; **acento tónico** (m) stress
tono (m) tone, beep 10
torcer(se) (ue) (el tobillo…) twist/sprain (your ankle…) 9
torre (f) tower
tortilla (f) **de maíz/harina** corn/flour tortilla 8
tortuga (f) turtle
tos (f) cough 9
toser cough 9
tostado/a: pan tostado (m) toast 8
trabajador/a (m/f) worker
trabajador/a hard-working 1
trabajar work 2; **¿Qué días trabajas?** What days do you work? 1; **Trabajo el (lunes…)** I work on (Monday…) (a particular week) 1
trabajo (m) work 1; **compañero/a** (m/f) **de trabajo** fellow worker; **en el trabajo** at work 1; **lugar** (m) **de trabajo** workplace; **mercado** (m) **de trabajo** job market
tradición (f) tradition
tradicional traditional
tradicionalmente traditionally
traer bring 3; **traído/a** brought
tráfico (m) traffic 7
traición (f) betrayal, treason

traje (m) suit 5; **traje** (m) **de baño** swimsuit 5
tramitación (f) handling
tramitar handle, deal with 12
trámite (m) transaction 10
tranquilo/a calm, tranquil
transferible transferable
transición (f) transition
transmitir transmit, broadcast
transporte (m) transportation 10
trastorno (m) disorder
tratamiento (m) treatment 11
tratar treat; **tratar (de)** try (to) 9; **tratarse de** be about, deal with 7
trato (m) treatment, deal; **¡Trato hecho!** It's a deal!
través: a través de across, though, by means of
travieso/a mischievous 7
trayectoria (f) trajectory, path
trece thirteen 1
treinta thirty 1
tremendo/a tremendous 12
tren (m) train; **estación** (f) **de trenes** train station
tres three 1
trescientos/as three hundred 3
tributo (m) tribute
trimestre (m) trimester
triste sad 2
triunfar triumph
trozo (m) slice 4
tú you (familiar) 1; **¿Y tú?** And you? 1
tu/s your (familiar) 1
tumba (f) tomb, grave 7
turismo (m) tourism
turista (m/f) tourist 12
turístico/a: guía turística (f) tourist guide 6
turno (m) turn 12

U

u or (used instead of **o** before **o** or **ho**)
ubicación (f) location 10
ultimar finalize, complete
último/a last 2
un/a/os/as a, an, some 2; **un poco** a little 1; **unos a los otros** one to another
único/a unique
unidad (f) unity
unido/a united; **Estados Unidos** United States; **Naciones Unidas** (fpl) United Nations 11
unión (f) union
unir blend, combine, unite 8; connect
universidad (f) university 1
universitario/a university 7
uno (un, una) one 1; **Es la una.** It's one o'clock. 1
urbano/a urban
urbe (f) large city
urgente urgent 9
uruguayo/a Uruguayan 12
usar wear, use 3

uso (m) use
usted you 1; **¿Y usted?** And you? 1; **ustedes** you 1
usuario/a (m/f) user
útil useful 1
utilizar utilize, use 10
uvas (fpl) grapes 8

V

vacacional vacation; **paquete vacacional** (m) vacation package
vacaciones (fpl) vacation; **ir de vacaciones** go on vacation 6
vainilla (f) vanilla 4
valer (yo valgo) be worth 9; **Más vale que…** One had better… 9
validez (f) validity; **con validez superior a…** valid for more than… 12
valiente brave, courageous 7
valioso/a valuable
valle (m) valley
valor (m) bravery, courage 7; value
valorar value, assess; **valorado/a** valued, assessed
vapor (m) steam; **al vapor** steamed 8
vaqueros (mpl) jeans 5
variar vary; **variado/a** varied
variedad (f) variety
varios various; **varios/as** several 2
vasco/a Basque
vaso (m) glass 8
vecindario (m) neighborhood 7
vecino/a (m/f) neighbor 3
vegetal plant, vegetable
veinte twenty 1
veinticinco twenty-five 1
veinticuatro twenty-four 1
veintidós twenty-two 1
veintinueve twenty-nine 1
veintiocho twenty-eight 1
veintiséis twenty-six 1
veintisiete twenty-seven 1
veintitrés twenty-three 1
veintiuno twenty-one 1
velero (m) sailboat 6
velocidad (f) speed; **límite** (m) **de velocidad** speed limit 7
vencer defeat
vendado/a wrapped, bandaged 9
vendedor/a (m/f) salesperson 10
vender sell 3; **vendido/a** sold
venezolano/a Venezuelan 12
venir (ie, yo vengo) come 4; **la semana (el mes, el año) que viene** next week (month, year) 4
venta (f) sale (10); **comunicación** (f) **de ventas** sales report
ventana (f) window 2
ventanilla (f) window (of a vehicle) 6; counter window 10
ver see 3; **A ver…** Let's see… 8; **Te veo…** You look… to me. 9; **verse** see one another 5
verano (m) summer 4

veras: ¿De veras? Really? 10
verbo (m) verb
verdad (f) truth 9; **¿verdad?** right? 6
verde green 3; **espacio verde** (m) green area 7
verdura (f) vegetable 8
versión (f) version
verter (ie) pour 8
vestido (m) dress 5
vestigio (m) vestige
vestir (m) wardrobe
vestirse (i, i) get dressed 5
vez time (2); **a veces** sometimes, at times 2; **cada vez más** more and more; **Érase una vez…** Once upon a time… 7; **tal vez** maybe, perhaps 5; **una vez (dos veces) a la semana/al mes/al año** once (twice) per week/per month/per year 2
vía (f) way, road; **en vías de** in the process of
viajar travel 6
viaje (m) trip 3; **agencia** (f) **de viajes** travel agency 6; **cheque** (m) **de viaje** traveler's check 6; **hacer un viaje** take a trip 3
viajero/a (m/f) traveler
viajero/a traveling
víctima (f) victim 7
vida (f) life 7; **calidad** (f) **de vida** quality of life; **estilo** (m) **de vida** lifestyle; **llevar una vida** lead a life 8; **vida diaria** (f) daily life
vídeo (m) video 3
videojuego (m) video game 4
viejo/a old 1
viento (m) wind; **Hace (mucho) viento.** It's (very) windy. 4
viernes (m) Friday 1
vigente valid 12
vinícola: industria vinícola (f) wine industry
vino (m) wine 8; **carta** (f) **de vinos** wine list 8; **vino (tinto/blanco)** (red/white) wine 4
violencia (doméstica) (f) (domestic) violence 11
visa (f) visa 6
visigodo/a Visigoth
visitante (m/f) visitor 10
visitar visit 6
vistas (a) (fpl) view (of) 6
vitae: currículum vitae (m) curriculum vitae, resumé 10
vitamina (f) vitamin 8
vivienda (f) housing
viviente living
vivir live 3; **vivir por su cuenta** live on one's own
vivo/a alive, living
vocabulario (m) vocabulary 2
volar (ue) fly
volcán (m) volcano
volcánico/a volcanic
voléibol (m) volleyball 4
voluntariado (m) volunteering
voluntario/a (m/f) volunteer

volver (ue) return 4; **volver a** + *infinitive* to + *verb* again 4

vomitar vomit, throw up 9

vosotros/as you 1

votante *(m/f)* voter 11

votar vote

voz *(f)* voice 10; **voz representante** spokesperson

vuelo *(m)* flight 6; **asistente** *(m/f)* **de vuelo** flight attendant 6

vuestro/a/os/as your 3

y and 1; **¿Y tú/usted?** And you? *(familiar/formal)* 1

ya already 8; **ya no...** no longer..., not... any more 9

yacimiento *(m)* deposit

yema *(f)* **de huevo** egg yolk 8

yo I 1

yoga *(m)* yoga; **hacer yoga** do yoga 4

yogurt *(m)* yoghurt 9

yuca *(f)* yucca, cassava

zanahoria *(f)* carrot 8

zapatería *(f)* shoe store 5

zapato *(m)* shoe 5

zona *(f)* zone; **zona franca** free-trade zone

VOCABULARIO INGLÉS-ESPAÑOL

The **Vocabulario inglés-español** includes all active vocabulary presented in *¡Trato hecho!*, as well as other high frequency words. Numbers following entries indicate the chapter where words are introduced. All translations separated by commas before a number are considered active in that chapter. Gender of nouns in Spanish is indicated by (*m*) for masculine and (*f*) for feminine. Nouns refering to people that have both masculine and feminine forms are indicated by (*m/f*), and those that are generally used in the plural are followed by (*pl*).

A

a, an un/a 2; **a little** un poco 1; **a lot (of)** mucho/a 1

able: be able poder (ue) 4

about acerca de 12; **about five** unos/as cinco; **be about** tratarse de 7; **talk about** hablar de

abroad en el extranjero 12

abuse: drug abuse abuso (*m*) de drogas 9

accent: with or without an accent con o sin acento 1

accept aceptar 5

accident accidente (*m*) 7

accompany acompañar; **accompanied** acompañado/a 11

according to según 11

account: checking/savings account cuenta (*f*) corriente/de ahorros 10

accountant contador/a (*m/f*) 7

accounting contabilidad (*f*) 1

accusation acusación (*f*) 11

accused acusado/a 11

ache doler (ue) 8

acquainted: be acquainted with conocer 6

across from enfrente de 2

activity actividad (*f*) 1

actor actor (*m*) 7

actress actriz (*f*) 7

adapt adaptarse 12

add agregar 8

address dirección (*f*) 3

admission admisión (*f*) 12; **Admissions and Registrar's Office** oficina (*f*) de admisiones y registro 12

admitted: be admitted ser admitido/a 12

advance: ...in advance con... de antelación 6

adventure aventura (*f*); **adventure movie** película (*f*) de aventuras 2

advertisement anuncio (*m*) 11

advertising publicidad (*f*) 10

advice: piece of advice consejo (*m*) 8

advise aconsejar 9; asesorar 12

advisor asesor/a (*m/f*) 12

affection cariño (*m*) 7

afraid: be afraid that tener miedo de que 10

after después de 2

afternoon tarde (*f*) 1; **Good afternoon.** Buenas tardes. 1; **in the afternoon** de la tarde (*with a specific hour*), por la tarde (*with no hour given*) 1; **this afternoon** esta tarde 4; **tomorrow afternoon** mañana por la tarde 4; **yesterday afternoon** ayer (por la tarde) 6

again otra vez 10; **to +** *verb* **again,** volver (ue) a + *infinitive* 4

age edad (*f*) 7; **middle-aged** de mediana edad 3

agency: travel agency agencia (*f*) de viajes 6

aging envejecimiento (*m*) 9

ago: three days ago hace tres días 6

agree estar de acuerdo 9

agreement acuerdo (*m*) 11

agriculture agricultura (*f*) 10

ahead of delante de 2

aid ayuda (*f*) 11

air aire (*m*) 7; **air conditioning** aire acondicionado (*m*) 6

airline aerolínea (*f*) 6

airplane avión (*m*) 6

airport aeropuerto (*m*) 6

aisle pasillo (*m*) 6

alarm clock despertador (*m*) 6

alcohol alcohol (*m*) 8

allergy alergia (*f*) 9

almost casi 2

alone solo/a 1

along a lo largo de, por; **get along well/badly** llevarse bien/mal 5

already ya 8

also también 1

always siempre 2

all todo/a/os/as 2; **all day** todo el día 1

allergic: be allergic to ser alérgico/a a 9

allow permitir 9

ambitious ambicioso/a 1

ambulance ambulancia (*f*) 7

American estadounidense 12

amuse oneself divertirse (ie, i) 5

amusement park parque (*m*) de atracciones 6

and y, e (*used instead of* **y** *before the letters* **i** *and* **hi**) 1; **And you?** ¿Y tú/usted? (*familiar/formal*) 1

angry enojado/a 2; **get angry** enojarse 5

animal animal (*m*) 3

ankle tobillo (*m*) 9

announce anunciar 11

announcement anuncio (*m*) 11

another otro/a 1; **meet one another** encontrarse (ue) 5; **one another** se, nos, os 5

answer contestar 2; responder 11; **Answer...!** ¡Contesten...! 2

answer respuesta (*f*) 2

antibiotics antibióticos (*mpl*) 9

any alguno/a(s) (algún) 4; **not any** ninguno/a (ningún) 4

anyone: not anyone nadie 4

anything: Anything else? ¿Algo más? 4; **not... anything** no... nada 3

apartment apartamento (*m*) 2

appear aparecer 11

appearance: in appearance en el aspecto físico 3

apple manzana (*f*) 8

application: job application solicitud (*f*) de empleo 10

apply for solicitar 12

appointment cita (*f*) 9

approve aprobar (ue) 10

April abril (*m*) 4

area: green area espacio verde (*m*) 7

Argentinian argentino/a 12

arm brazo (*m*) 9

arranged previsto/a 12

arrest arresto (*m*) 7; arrestado/a 11

arrival llegada (*f*) 6

arrive llegar 2

art arte (*m*) 1

arthritis artritis (*f*) 9

article artículo (*m*) 11

artist artista (*m/f*) 7; **graphic artist** diseñador/a gráfico/a (*m/f*) 10

as como 3; **as... as** tan... como 1; **as a child** (de niño/a 7); **as long as** mientras 11, con tal que 12; **as much... as** tanto/a ... como 3; **as many... as** tantos/as... como 3; **as soon as possible** lo antes posible 10; **as soon as you +** *verb* al + *infinitive* 6; **as usual** regular 1

ashtray cenicero (*m*) 6

ask preguntar 8; **ask a question** hacer una pregunta 3; **ask for** pedir (i, i) 4

asparagus espárragos (*mpl*) 8

aspirin aspirina (*f*) 9

assistance asistencia (*f*) 11

assure asegurar 11

at en 1; **at first** al principio 9; **at home** en casa 1; **at one o'clock** a la una 1; **at the back (of)** al fondo (de) 2; **at times** a veces 2; **at two o'clock** a las dos 1; **At what time?** ¿A qué hora? 1; **at work** en el trabajo 1

athlete deportista (*m/f*) 7
athletic atlético/a 1; deportista 7
ATM machine cajero automático (*m*) 10
attached adjunto 12
attack atacar 7; **heart attack** infarto (*m*) 9
attend asistir (a) 3
attendant: flight attendant asistente (*m/f*) de vuelo 6
August agosto (*m*) 4
aunt tía (*f*) 3; **aunts and uncles** tíos (*mpl*) 3
authenticate legalizar 12
autumn otoño (*m*) 4
available disponible 6; **available upon request** disponible a petición 10
avoid evitar 8
await esperar; **Awaiting…** A la espera de… 12
award premio (*m*) 11
away: go away irse 5; **right away** en seguida 11; **take away** retirar 8

B

baby bebé (*m*) 11
back espalda (*f*) 9; **at the back (of)** al fondo (de) 2
backpack mochila (*f*) 2
bad mal(o)/a 1
badly mal 1
bag bolsa; **sleeping bag** saco de dormir (*m*) 6
baked potato papa (*f*) al horno 8
bakery pastelería (*f*) 5
balanced equilibrado/a 8
balcony balcón (*m*) 6
banana plátano (*m*) 8
bandaged vendado/a 9
band-aid curita (*f*) 9
bank banco (*m*) 6
banker banquero/a (*m/f*) 10
bar bar (*m*) 3
baseball player jugador/a de béisbol (*m/f*) 7
basic level nivel básico (*m*) 10
basketball básquetbol (2); baloncesto (*m*) 4
bath: take a bath bañarse 5
bathe bañarse 5
bathroom baño (*m*) 3
be ser 1, estar 2; **be able** poder (ue) 4; **be about** tratarse de 7; **be acquainted with** conocer 6; **be born** nacer 7; **be called/named** llamarse 5; **be careful** tener cuidado 9; **be down** fallar 10; **be familiar with** conocer 6; **be going to +** *verb* ir a + *infinitive* 4; **be hungry** tener hambre 4; **be important** importar 8; **be in fashion** estar de moda 5; **be located, be found** encontrarse (ue) 9; **be missing/needed** faltar 8; **be right** tener razón 9; **be sorry** arrepentirse (ie, i) 7; **be thirsty** tener sed 4; **be worth** valer (yo form: valgo) 9; **be… years old** tener… años 3; **How are you?** ¿Cómo está usted? ¿Cómo estás? 1; **How is… written?** ¿Cómo se escribe…? 1; **I am, I'm** estoy, soy 1; **It's (very) hot.** Hace (mucho) calor. 4; **It's written…** Se escribe… 1; **My name is…** Me llamo…

1; **there is, there are, is there, are there** hay 1; **What is your name?** ¿Cómo se llama usted?, ¿Cómo te llamas? 1; **Where are you from?** ¿De dónde eres? ¿De dónde es usted? 1
beach playa (*f*) 3
beans frijoles (*mpl*) 8; **green beans** ejotes (*mpl*) 8
beard barba (*f*) 3
beat batir 8; **beaten** batido/a 8
beautiful guapo/a 3; hermoso/a 7
beauty belleza (*f*) 7
because porque 1; **because of** por 5
become (ill, nervous…) ponerse (mal, nervioso/a…) 9
bed cama (*f*) 3; **double bed** cama matrimonial (*f*) 6; **go to bed** acostarse (ue) 5; **stay in bed** guardar cama 9
bedroom dormitorio (*m*) 3
bedsheets sábanas (*fpl*) 6
beep tono (*m*) 10
beer cerveza (*f*) 4
before antes de 2; ante 9
begin empezar (ie) 4; comenzar (ie) 8
beginning comienzo (*m*); **at the beginning** al comienzo 7
behalf: on behalf of de parte de 11
behave portarse 7
behind detrás de 2
beige beige 3
believe creer 3
bellhop botones (*m*) 6
belt cinturón (*m*) 5
benefit beneficio (*m*) 10
besides además 10
best mejor 3; **best friend** mejor amigo/a (*m/f*) 1
better mejor 1; **one had better** más vale que 9
between entre 2
big grande 1
bill cuenta (*f*) 8; billete (*m*) 10
billfold cartera (*f*) 5
biology biología (*f*) 1
birth nacimiento (*m*) 7; **birth certificate** acta (*f*) de nacimiento 12
birthday cumpleaños (*m*) 7; **birthday party** fiesta (*f*) de cumpleaños 7; **fifteenth birthday party** quinceañera (*f*) 7
black negro/a 3
blackboard pizarra (*f*) 2
blend unir 8
block cuadra (*f*) 6
blocked tapado/a 9
blond(e) rubio/a 3
blood sangre (*f*) 9; **high blood pressure** presión arterial alta (*f*) 9
blouse blusa (*f*) 5
blue azul 3
board abordar 6
boarding pass tarjeta (*f*) de embarque 6
body cuerpo (*m*) 7
Bolivian boliviano/a 12
bone hueso (*m*) 9
book libro (*m*) 2
bookbag mochila (*f*) 2

bookstore librería (*f*) 2
boot bota (*f*) 5
bored aburrido/a 2
boring aburrido/a 1
born: be born nacer 7
boss jefe/a (*m/f*) 10
bother molestar 8
bottle botella (*f*) 8
boutique boutique (*f*) 5
bowl plato hondo (*m*) 8
boyfriend novio (*m*) 1
brain cerebro (*m*) 9
branch office sucursal (*f*) 10
brave valiente 7
bravery valor (*m*) 7
break: commercial break pausa comercial (*f*) 11
break (your arm…) romper(se) (el brazo…) 9
breakfast desayuno (*m*) 6; **eat breakfast, have breakfast** desayunar 4
breakup ruptura (*f*) 11
breath respirar 7
bride novia (*f*) 7
brief breve 11
bring traer 3
broccoli brócoli (*m*) 8
broth: chicken broth caldo (*m*) de pollo 8
brother hermano (*m*) 1; **brothers and sisters** hermanos (*mpl*) 3
brown marrón, color café, castaño/a (*hair*) 3
brush your teeth lavarse los dientes 5
buckle your seatbelt abrocharse el cinturón de seguridad 6
building edificio (*m*) 1
bump (your head…) darse un golpe (en la cabeza…) 9
burn (yourself) quemar(se), picar 9
bury enterrar (ie) 7
bus autobús (*m*) 2; **by bus** en autobús 2; **bus stop** parada (*f*) de autobús 7
business (studies) administración (*f*) de empresas 1
businessman hombre (*m*) de negocios 7
businesswoman mujer (*f*) de negocios 7
busy ocupado/a 2
but pero 1
butcher's shop carnicería (*f*) 5
butter mantequilla (*f*) 8
buy comprar 2
by cerca de, en 2; por 5; **by bus** en autobús 2
Bye. Chau. 4

C

cabinet: filing cabinet archivador (*m*) 10
café café (*m*) 2
cafeteria cafetería (*f*) 1
caffeine cafeína (*f*) 8
cake pastel (*m*) 4
calculate calcular 10
calculator calculadora (*f*) 2
calendar calendario (*m*) 10
call llamada (*f*) 6
call llamar (a) 6; **be called** llamarse 5

camera cámara (f) 6
camp acampar 6
can poder (ue) 4; **one can...** se puede... 6
Canadian canadiense 12
candidate (for) candidato/a (m/f) (a) 11; **run as a candidate** presentarse como candidato/a 11
canoe canoa (f) 6
cap gorra (f) 5
capital capital (f) 11
cappuccino capuchino (m) 4
car carro (m) 3, coche (m) 2; **in my car** en mi coche 2
carbohydrates carbohidratos (mpl) 8
card tarjeta (f) (5), ficha (f) 12; **cards** cartas (fpl) 4; **credit card** tarjeta (f) de crédito 5
care: take care of cuidar 9
careful: be careful tener cuidado 9
carpenter carpintero/a (m/f) 10
carrot zanahoria (f) 8
carry llevar 5; **carry out** cumplir 7; realizar 12
cart carrito (m) 8
case: in that case en ese caso 6
cash efectivo (m) 5; **cash register** caja (f) 5
cashier cajero/a (m/f) 10
cast: in a cast enyesado/a 9
cat gato (m) 3
catastrophe catástrofe (f) 11
catch a cold resfriarse 9
cause provocar 11
CD CD (m) 3
celebrate celebrar 7
cent centavo (m) 8
center centro (m) 3; **shopping center** centro comercial (m) 4
cereal cereales (mpl) 8
certificate: birth certificate acta (f) de nacimiento 12
chain cadena (f) 5
chair silla (f) 2
championship campeonato (m) 7
change cambiar 6
channel canal (m) 11
charge cargo (m) 10
charge: be in charge of estar encargado/a de 10
charge cobrar 10
cheap barato/a 5
check cuenta (f) 8, cheque (m) 10; **traveler's check** cheque (m) de viaje 6
check your luggage facturar el equipaje 6
checkbook chequera (f) 10
checkered de cuadros 5
checking account cuenta (f) corriente 10
cheer someone up levantarle el ánimo a alguien 9
cheese queso (m) 4; **sandwich** bocadillo (m) de queso 4; **Swiss/Parmesan cheese** queso suizo/parmesano (m) 8
chemistry química (f) 1
chess ajedrez (m) 4
chest pecho (m) 9; **chest (of drawers)** cómoda (f) 3

chicken pollo (m) 8; **chicken broth** caldo (m) de pollo 8
child niño/a (m/f) 7; **as a child** de niño/a 7; **children** hijos (mpl) 3
childhood niñez (f) 7
Chilean chileno/a 12
Chinese food comida china (f) 4
chips: potato chips papitas fritas (fpl) 4
chocolate chocolate (m) 4; **chocolate ice cream** helado (m) de chocolate 4; **hot chocolate** chocolate caliente (m) 4
cholesterol colesterol (m) 9
chop: pork chop chuleta (f) de cerdo 8
church iglesia (f) 4
Ciao. Chau. 4
cinema cine (m) 2
citizen ciudadano/a (m/f) 11
citizenship ciudadanía (f) 12
city ciudad (f) 3; **city block** cuadra (f) 6; **city map** plano (m) de la ciudad 6
class clase (f) 1; **What classes do you have this semester/trimester?** ¿Qué clases tienes este semestre/trimestre? 1; **What is the homework for the next class?** ¿Cuál es la tarea para la próxima clase? 2
classmate compañero/a (m/f) de clase 1
classroom salón (m) de clase 2
clean limpiar 2
clean limpio/a 3
clear: The sky's clear. El cielo está despejado. 4
clock reloj (m) 2; **alarm clock** despertador (m) 6
close cerrar (ie) 4
closet armario (m) 3
clothes ropa (f) 5
clothing store tienda (f) de ropa 2
cloudy: The sky's cloudy. El cielo está nublado. 4
club club (m) 2; **night club** club nocturno (m) 2
coast costa (f) 11
coffee café (m) 3
cold frío/a; **be cold** tener frío; **catch a cold** resfriarse 9; **have a cold** estar resfriado/a, tener catarro 9; **It's (very) cold.** Hace (mucho) frío. 4
colleague colega (m/f) 10
collision choque (m) 7
Colombian colombiano/a 12
color color (m) 3; **What color is...?** ¿De qué color es...? 3
combine unir 8
come acudir 12
come venir (ie) (yo vengo) 4
comfortable cómodo/a 5
comical cómico/a 1
commentator comentarista (m/f) 11
commercial break pausa comercial (f) 11
common común 9
communications comunicaciones (fpl) 10
community comunidad (f) 11
company empresa (f) 10
compatibility compatibilidad (f) 10
complete completar 10
complete completo/a 2

compromising comprometedor/a 11
computer computadora (f) 2; **computer science** informática (f) 1
concern: To Whom It May Concern A quien corresponda 12
concert concierto (m) 3
conclusion término (m) 12
condition: in good condition en buenas condiciones 9
confide in confiar en 11
confirm confirmar 12
conflict conflicto (m) 11
confused confundido/a 2
congested congestionado/a 9
congestion congestión (f) 9
Congress Congreso (m) 11
connect: Could you connect me with...? ¿Podría(s) comunicarme con... ? 6
consequences consecuencias (fpl) 9
consist: of what it consists en qué consiste 12
construction worker obrero/a (m/f) de la construcción 7
Consul Cónsul (m) 12
consult consultar 6
contact each other comunicarse 5
contain contener (ie) 8
container recipiente (m) 8
contest concurso (m) 7
continue straight (ahead) seguir (i, i) recto 6
contract contrato (m) 10
contribution contribución (f) 11
control controlar 8
cook cocinero/a (m/f) 8
cook cocinar 8
cookie galleta (f) 4
cool: It's cool. Hace fresco. 4
cooperation cooperación (f) 11
copy copia (f) 10
corn maíz (m) 8; **corn tortilla** tortilla (f) de maíz 8
corner esquina (f) 6
correct correcto/a 6
cost costar (ue); **How much does it (do they) cost?** ¿Cuánto cuesta(n)? 5
Costa Rican costarricense 12
costar coprotagonista (m/f) 11
cotton algodón (m) 5
cough tos (f) 9
cough toser 9
Could you...? ¿Podría(s)...? 6
count contar (ue) 4
counter window ventanilla (f) 10
country (nation) país (m) 6, (countryside) campo (m) 3; **country person** campesino/a (m/f) 7
couple pareja (f) 11
courage valor (m) 7
courageous valiente 7
course curso (m) 1; **of course** por supuesto 12; **Yes, of course.** Sí, cómo no. 5
court corte (f) 11
courtesy cortesía (f) 7
cousin primo/a (m/f) 3
crash chocar 7
cream crema (f) 4; **ice cream** helado (m) 4

create crear 11
credit card tarjeta (f) de crédito 5
crime (as a whole) criminalidad (f), crimen (m) 11
criminal criminal (m) 7
cross cruzar 7
cruel cruel 7
cruise crucero (m) 6
crutches muletas (fpl) 9
cry llorar 7
Cuban cubano/a 12
cup taza (f) 8
cure cura (f) 11
current actual 11
curriculum vitae currículum vitae (m) 10
customer cliente (m), clienta (f) 5; **customer service** atención (f) al cliente 10
customs aduana (f) 6
cut (yourself) cortar(se) 9; **cut (back)** recortar 11; **get one's hair cut, cut one's hair** cortarse el pelo 5

D

dance bailar 2
dark-haired moreno/a 3
dark-skinned moreno/a 3
data datos (mpl) 10
database base (f) de datos 10
date fecha (f) 4; **What is the date (of…)?** ¿Cuál es la fecha (de…)? 4
daughter hija (f) 3
day día (m) 1; **all day** todo el día 1; **every day** todos los días 2; **What day is today?** ¿Qué día es hoy? 1
dead muerto/a 3
deadline fecha (f) límite 12
deal with tratarse de 7, tramitar 12
Dear… Querido/a (familiar), Estimado/a… (formal) 12
death muerte (f) 7
debajo de below 2
debit card tarjeta (f) de débito 5
December diciembre (m) 4
decide decidir 6
decision decisión (f) 10
deep profundo/a (f) 9
degree plan plan (m) de estudios 12
degrees grados (mpl) 9
delicious delicioso/a 8
demonstration manifestación (f) 11
denim mezclilla (f) 5
deny negar (ie) 11
department departamento (m) 10; **department store** almacén (m) 5
departure salida (f) 6
depends: That depends on… Eso depende de… 2
deposit depósito (m) 10
deposit depositar 10
depressed deprimido/a 9
depression depresión (f) 9
descend descender (ie) 6
design diseño (m) (10); **graphic design program** programa (m) de diseño gráfico 10

design diseñar 10
designer diseñador/a (m/f) 7
desire deseo (m) 7
desire desear 4
desk escritorio (m) 2; **front desk** recepción (f) 6; **student desk** pupitre (m) 1
dessert postre (m) 8; **dessert cart** carrito (m) de postres 8
devastation devastación (f) 11
develop desarrollar 9; **develop friendships** hacer amistades 12
development desarrollo (m) 10
devote oneself to dedicarse a 7
diabetes diabetes (f) 9
dial marcar 10
die morir(se) (ue, u) 7
diet: be on a diet estar a dieta 8
difficult difícil 1
dining room comedor (m) 3
dinner cena (f) 2; **eat dinner, have (for) dinner** cenar 4
diploma: high-school diploma certificado (m) de secundaria 12
direct directo/a 10
direction dirección (f) 7
director director/a (m/f) 10
dirty sucio/a 3
disaster: natural disaster catástrofe natural (f) 11
discount: percent discount descuento (m) del… por ciento… 5
dish plato (m) 6; **main dish** plato principal (m) 8
distance: long distance call llamada (f) de larga distancia 6
distribute distribuir 10
diversity diversidad (f) 11
divorce divorciarse 11; **divorced** divorciado/a 3
dizzy mareado/a 9
do hacer 2; **Do…!** ¡Hagan…! 2; **do (for a living)** dedicarse a 7; **do aerobics** hacer ejercicio aeróbico 4; **Do we need…?** ¿Necesitamos…? 2; **don't** no 1; **do yoga** hacer yoga 4; **Do you want…?** ¿Quieres…? 1
doctor doctor/a (m/f) 2; médico/a (m/f) 7
document documento (m) 10
documentary documental (m) 11
dog perro (m) 3
dollar dólar (m) 10
domestic violence violencia doméstica (f) 11
domicile domicilio (m) 12
Dominican dominicano/a 12
done: well-done (meat) bien cocido/a 8
door puerta (f) 2
doping dopaje (m) 11
dormitory residencia (f) 1
double: double bed cama matrimonial (f) 6; **double room** habitación doble (f) 6
doubt dudar 9
doubtful dudoso/a 9
down abajo; **be down** (machine) fallar 10; **go down** bajar 6, descender (ie) 6; **lie down** acostarse (ue) 5

downtown centro (m) 3
draw dibujar 10
drawer: chest (of drawers) cómoda (f) 3
dream (of/about) soñar (ue) (con) 7
dress vestido (m) 5
dress vestir(se) (i, i) 5; **get dressed** vestirse (i, i) 5
drink bebida (f) 8; **have a drink** tomar una copa 4; **soft drink** refresco (m) 4
drink tomar 2, beber 3
drive manejar 7
driver conductor/a (m/f) 7; **bus/taxi/truck driver** chófer (m/f) de autobús/taxi/camión 10; **driver's license** licencia (f) de manejar 7
drown ahogar 7
drug droga (f) 9; (medication) medicamento (m) 6; **drug abuse** abuso (m) de drogas 9; **drug use** dopaje (m) 11
drunk ebrio/a 9
during durante 6
DVD player reproductor (m) de DVD 3

E

each cada 2; **each other** se, nos, os 5
ear oreja (f) 9; **inner ear** oído (m) 9
early temprano 4
earring arete (m) 5
earthquake terremoto (m) 11
easy fácil 1
eat comer 2; **eat a lot** comer fuerte 8; **eat breakfast** desayunar 4; **eat dinner** cenar 4, **eat lunch** almorzar (ue) 4
ecological ecológico/a 11
economics economía (f) 1, **economic indicators** indicadores económicos (mpl) 10
economy economía (f) 11
Ecuatorian ecuatoriano/a 12
education educación (f) 10, formación académica (f) 10
egg huevo (m) 8; **egg yolk** yema (f) de huevo 8
egotistical egoísta 1
eight ocho 1; **eight hundred** ochocientos/as 3
eighteen dieciocho 1
eighth octavo/a 6
eighty ochenta 1
either cualquiera; **either… or** o… o; **not either** tampoco 3
elections elecciones (fpl) 11
elevator ascensor (m) 6
eleven once 1
else: Anything else? ¿Algo más? 4
e-mail correo electrónico (m) 3
emergency emergencia (f) 7
emotional emocional 1
employee empleado/a (m/f) 10; **government employee** funcionario/a (m/f) 12
employment empleo (m) 9
end término (m) 12
end terminar 11; **end up** quedar 11
energy energía (f) 8
engine: search engine buscador (m) 11

English inglés (m) 1; **What does... mean in English?** ¿Qué significa... en inglés? 2
enough lo suficiente 8
enter entrar; **entering student** alumno/a (m/f) de nuevo ingreso 12
enterprise empresa (f) 10
entertainment entretenimiento (m); **world of entertainment** mundo (m) de la farándula 11
entrance entrada (f) 6
entrée plato principal (m) 8
envelope sobre (m) 12
environment ambiente (m) 10
epidemic epidemia (f) 11
episode episodio (m) 11
errands: run errands hacer mandados 5
essay ensayo (m) 3
evaluate evaluar 10
evening noche (f) 1, **Good evening.** Buenas noches. 1; **in the evening** de la noche (with a specific hour), por la noche (with no hour given) 1; **this evening** esta noche 4
event acontecimiento (m) 7
ever alguna vez 7
every todo/a/os/as 2; **every day** todos los días 2
everyone todos 4
everywhere por todos lados 3
exactly exactamente 12
exaggerate exagerar 7
exam examen (m) 1
examine examinar 9
example: for example por ejemplo 11
exchange money cambiar dinero 6
excited emocionado/a 7
Excuse me! ¡Disculpe! 6
exercise ejercicio (m) 2
exercise hacer ejercicio 3
exhibition exposición (f) 4
expect esperar 11
expense gasto (m) 12
expensive caro/a 3
experience experiencia (f) 10; **have... years experience** llevar... años... 11
explain explicar 8
eye ojo (m) 3

face cara (f) 9
faced with ante 9
facing enfrente de 2
factory fábrica (f) 7; **factory worker** obrero/a (m/f) de fábrica 7
fail fallar 10
fall otoño (m) 4
fall caerse 9
familiar: be familiar with conocer 6
family familia (f) 1
famous famoso/a 11
far from lejos de 2
farmer agricultor/a (m/f) 7
fat grasa (f) 8
fat gordo/a 3
father padre (m) 1

fatigue fatiga (f) 9
favorite favorito/a 2; preferido/a
fear temer 10
February febrero (m) 4
fee tarifa (f) 12; **registration fee** matrícula (f) 11
feel like ...ing tener ganas de + infinitive 4
feel sentirse (ie, i) 5
fever fiebre (f) 9; **hay fever** fiebre (f) del heno 9
few pocos/as 2
fifteen quince 1
fifteenth birthday party quinceañera (f) 7
fifth quinto/a 6
fifty cincuenta 1
fight pelearse 5, luchar 7
file archivar 10
filing cabinet archivador (m) 10
fill out rellenar 12
film película (2); **roll of film** rollo (m) de película 6
finally finalmente 8
financial: letter of financial standing carta (f) de solvencia 12
find encontrar (ue) 4; **find out** saber 6
fine arts bellas artes (fpl) 1
finger dedo (m) 9
finish terminar 11
fire (disaster) incendio (m) 7, fuego (m)
fire despedir (i, i) 10
firefighter bombero/a (m/f) 7
first primer(o)/a 2; **at first** al principio 9; **first aid** los primeros auxilios (mpl) 7; **first name** nombre (m) 10
fish pescado (food) (m) 8; pez (m) (animal)
fish pescar 6
fitting room probador (m) 5
five cinco 1; **five hundred** quinientos/as 3
fix arreglar 6
flan flan (m) 4
flee huir 7
flight vuelo (m) 6; **flight attendant** asistente (m/f) de vuelo 6
flood inundación (f) 11
floor suelo (m) 3; **ground floor** planta baja (f) 6
flour harina (f) (8); **flour tortilla** tortilla (f) de harina 8
flower flor (f) 3
flu gripe (f) 9
follow seguir (i, i) 8
following siguiente 2; a continuación 11
fond of sports deportista 7
food comida (f) 8, alimento (m) 9; **Chinese food** comida china (f) 4; **Mexican food restaurant** restaurante (m) de comida mexicana 2
foot pie (m) 9; **go on foot** andar a pie 7
football fútbol americano (m) 2; **football game** partido (m) de fútbol americano 2
for para 1, por 5, desde hace 10; **for me** para mí 4
forbid prohibir 9
forecast: weather forecast pronóstico (m) del tiempo 11

foreign extranjero/a (m) 2; **foreign movie** película (f) extranjera 2
forest bosque (m) 6
fork tenedor (m) 8
form formulario (m) 10, impreso (m) 12
formal formal 12
forty cuarenta 1
found: be found encontrarse (ue) 9
four cuatro 1; **four hundred** cuatrocientos/as 3
fourteen catorce 1
fourth cuarto/a 6; **one fourth of** la cuarta parte (f) de 8
free libre, (of charge) gratis; **free time** los ratos libres (m) 4
freeway autopista (f) 7
French francés (m) 1, francesa (f); **French fries** papas fritas (fpl) 8
frequently con frecuencia 2
fresh fresco/a 7
Friday viernes (m) 1
friend amigo/a (m/f) 1; **make friends** hacer amistades 12
friendships: develop friendships hacer amistades 12
fries: French fries papas fritas (fpl) 8
from de 1; **from where?** ¿de dónde? 2; **from... to...** de... a... 1; **Where are you from?** ¿De dónde eres? ¿De dónde es usted? 1
front frente (m); **front desk** recepción (f) 6; **in front of** delante de 2
fruit fruta (f) 8
fry freír (i, i) 10
full lleno/a; **full-time** a tiempo completo 10
fun: have fun divertirse (ie, i) 5
fun divertido/a 1
function funcionar 6
funeral funeral (m) 7
funny cómico/a 1, chistoso
furniture muebles (mpl) 3
future futuro (m) 11

gain weight subir de peso 9
game partido (m) 2; **soccer game** partido (m) de fútbol 2; **video games** videojuegos 4
gang pandilla (f) 11
garage garaje (m) 3; **mechanic's garage** taller (m) 7
garden jardín (m) 3
gas station gasolinera (f), estación (f) de servicio 6
gasoline gasolina (f) 6
gate puerta (f) 6
gather recoger 6
general: in general por lo general 5
generally generalmente 1
get sacar 6, obtener; **get along well/badly** llevarse bien/mal 5; **get angry** enojarse 5; **get dressed** vestirse (i, i) 5; **get hot** calentarse (ie) 8; **get in touch with each other** comunicarse 5; **get injured** resultar herido/a 7; **get married (to)** casarse (con) 5; **get off / out of** bajar de

6; **get on / in** subir a 6; **get one's hair cut** cortarse el pelo 5; **get sick** enfermarse 9; **get together** encontrarse (ue) 5; **get up** levantarse 5

ghost fantasma (m) 7

gift regalo (m) 5

girlfriend novia (f) 1

give dar 8, (as a gift) regalar 8; **give each other a hug** darse un abrazo 5; **give someone a shot** ponerle una inyección a alguien 9

Gladly. Con mucho gusto. 6

glass vaso (m) 8; **glasses** gafas (fpl) 3; **wine glass, stemmed glass** copa (f) 8

global warming calentamiento global (m) 11

globalization globalización (f) 11

go ir 2; **Go…!** ¡Vayan…! 2; **be going to +** *verb* ir a + *infinitive* 4; **go away** irse 5; **go down** bajar de 6; **go down** descender (ie) 6; **go for a walk** pasear 4; **go on foot** andar a pie 7; **go out** salir 2; **go shopping** ir de compras 4; **go to bed** acostarse (ue) 5; **go up** subir a 6

goal: score a goal marcar un gol 7

gold(en) chain cadena (f) de oro 5

good buen(o)/a 1; **Good afternoon.** Buenas tardes. 1; **Good evening. Good night.** Buenas noches. 1; **Good morning.** Buenos días. 1

Good-bye. Adiós. 1; **say good-bye** despedirse (i, i) 5

gossip: piece of gossip chisme (m) 11

government gobierno (m) 11; (course) ciencias políticas (fpl) 1; **government employee** funcionario/a (m/f) 12

governor gobernador/a (m/f) 11

graduate graduarse 7

graduation graduación (f) 7

grandchildren nietos (mpl) 3

granddaughter nieta (f) 3

grandfather abuelo (m) 3

grandmother abuela (f) 3

grandparents abuelos (mpl) 3

grandson nieto (m) 3

grapes uvas (fpl) 8

graphic gráfico/a; **graphic artist** diseñador/a gráfico/a (m/f) 10; **graphic design program** programa (m) de diseño gráfico 10

grated rallado/a 8

grateful: I would be grateful if you would… Te/Le/Les agradecería… 12

grave grave 9

gray gris 3, (hair) canoso/a 3

great estupendo/a 2

green verde 3; **green area** espacio verde (m) 7; **green beans** ejotes (mpl) 8

grill: on the grill a la parrilla 8

grilled a la parrilla 8

groom novio (m) 7

ground suelo (m) 3; **ground floor** planta baja (f) 6

group grupo (m) 7

grow (up) crecer 7

growth crecimiento (m) 9

grumpy gruñón (gruñona) 10

guaranteed garantizado/a 11

Guatemalan guatemalteco/a 12

guest huésped (m/f) 6, invitado/a (m/f) 11

guide: tourist guide guía turística (f) 6

guitar guitarra (f) 2; **play the guitar** tocar la guitarra 4

guitarist guitarrista (m/f) 11

gymnasium gimnasio (m) 1

H

hair pelo (m) 3, cabello (m) 9; **hair salon** peluquería (f) 5; **get one's hair cut, cut one's hair** cortarse el pelo 5

half mitad (f) 8; **It's half past six.** Son las seis y media. 1; **half kilogram** medio kilo (m) 8

hall pasillo (m) 6; **residence hall** residencia (f) 1

ham jamón (m) 4; **ham sandwich** bocadillo (m) de jamón 4

hand mano (m) 9; **shake hands** darse la mano 5

hand in entregar 12

handle tramitar 12

handsome guapo/a 3

happen pasar 9

happy contento/a 2, feliz 7; **be happy that** alegrarse de que 10; **I'd be happy to.** Con mucho gusto. 6

hard-working trabajador/a 1

hat sombrero (m) 5

have tener 3; **have access to** acceder a 12; **have a cold** estar resfriado/a, tener catarro 9; **have a cough** tener tos 9; **have a drink** tomar una copa 4; **have a party** hacer una fiesta 3; **have a wreck** chocar 7; **have breakfast** desayunar 4; **have dinner** cenar 4; **have fun** divertirse (ie, i) 5; **have just +** *past participle* acabar de + *infinitive* 5; **have lunch** almorzar (ue) 4; **have… years experience** llevar… años… 11; **I have** tengo 1; **one had better** más vale que 9; **What classes do you have this semester/trimester?** ¿Qué clases tienes este semestre/trimestre? 1

hay fever fiebre (f) del heno 9

he él 1; **he likes** le gusta(n) 1; **He would like…** Le gustaría(n)… 3

head cabeza (f) 9

headache dolor (m) de cabeza 9

headlines titulares (mpl) 11

health salud (f) 8

healthy sano/a 8

hear oír 3

heart corazón (m) 9; **heart attack** infarto (m) 9

heating calefacción (f) 6

heavy pesado/a 9

height: of medium height de estatura mediana 3

hello (on the phone) aló 4

help ayudar 9; **How may I help you?** ¿En qué puedo servirle? 5; **It would have helped me a lot…** Me habría sido de gran ayuda… 12

her ella 2, la 5; **(to, for) her** le, se 8

her su(s) 1

here aquí 1; **Here it is.** Aquí lo/la tiene. 5

herself se 5

Hi. Hola. 1

high alto/a; **high level** nivel alto (m) 10; **high school** colegio 7, preparatoria (f) 10; **high-school diploma** certificado (m) de secundaria 12

hike: go on a hike ir de excursión 6

him él 2, lo 5; **(to, for) him** le, se 8

himself se 5

hire contratar 10

his su(s) 1

historic histórico/a 6

history historia (f) 1

hit pegar; **hit (your head…)** darse un golpe (en la cabeza…) 9

home hogar (m); **at home** en casa 1

homework tarea (f) 1; **What is the homework for the next class?** ¿Cuál es la tarea para la próxima clase? 2

Honduran hondureño/a 12

honey miel (f) 9

honor honor (m) 7

hope esperanza (f)

hope esperar 9; **Let's hope (that)…** Ojalá (que)… 9

horror movie película (f) de terror 2

horseback: ride horseback montar a caballo 9

host/hostess (of a show) anfitrión/anfitriona (m/f) 11

hot caliente 4; **be/feel hot** tener calor 4; **hot chocolate** chocolate caliente (m) 4; **hot tea** té caliente (m) 8; **get hot** calentarse (ie) 8; **It's (very) hot.** Hace (mucho) calor. 4

hotel hotel (m) 6

hour hora (f) 1

house casa (f) 3; **House of Representatives** Cámara (f) de Representantes 11

housemate compañero/a (m/f) de casa 3

housing alojamiento (m) 12

how? ¿cómo? 1; **How are you?** ¿Cómo está usted? ¿Cómo estás? 1; **How do you say… in Spanish?** ¿Cómo se dice… en español? 2; **How is… written?** ¿Cómo se escribe…? 1; **how many** ¿cuántos/as? 1; **How many are there in…?** ¿Cuántos son en…? 3; **How may I help you?** ¿En qué puedo servirle? 5; **How much does it (do they) cost?** ¿Cuánto cuesta(n)? 5; **how much?** ¿cuánto/a? 2; **How was/were…?** ¿Qué tal…? 6; **How's the weather?** ¿Qué tiempo hace? 4

hug abrazo (m) 5

hug each other abrazarse 5

human resources recursos humanos (mpl) 10

humanitarian aid ayuda humanitaria (f) 11

humanities humanidades (fpl) 1

hundred: one hundred cien 1; **one hundred and…** ciento… 3; **five hundred** quinientos/as 3; **two hundred** doscientos/as 3

hungry: be hungry tener hambre 4; **make someone hungry** darle hambre a alguien 8
hurricane huracán (m) 11
hurt doler (ue) 8; **hurt (yourself)** lastimar(se) 9
husband esposo (m) 1

I

I yo 1; **I am, I'm** estoy, soy 1; **I don't understand.** No comprendo. 2; **I have** tengo 1; **I like** me gusta(n) 1; **I need more time.** Necesito más tiempo. 2; **I would like…** Me gustaría(n)… 3
ice hielo (m) 4; **ice cream** helado (m) 4
iced tea té (m) helado 8
idea idea 12
identification identificación (f) 6; **identification card** tarjeta (f) de identificación 12
ill enfermo/a 2
illegal ilegal 11
illness enfermedad (f) 9
immigrant inmigrante (m/f) 11
immigration inmigración (f) 11
immune system sistema inmunológico (m) 9
implementation implementación (f) 10
important importante 9; **be important** importar 8
impose imponer 11
impossible imposible 9
improbable improbable 9
improve mejorar 11
improvement mejora (f) 11
impulsive impulsivo/a 1
in en 1; **in class** en clase 1; **in front of** delante de 2; **in general** por lo general 5; **in love** enamorado/a 7; **in my car** en mi coche 2; **in order to** + verb para + infinitive 4; **in pairs** en parejas 2; **in the morning** de la mañana (with a specific hour), por la mañana (with no hour given) 1; **get in** subir a 6
include incluir 9; **included** incluido/a 6
increase aumentar 11
incredible increíble 9
independently independientemente 10
indicate indicar 11
indicators: economic indicators indicadores económicos (mpl) 11
inebriated ebrio/a 9
infected infectado/a 9
infection infección (f); **sinus infection** sinusitis (f) 9
inflation inflación (f) 11
inform informar 7
information información (f) 10
ingredient ingrediente (m) 8
injured person herido/a (m/f) 7; **get injured** resultar herido/a 7
inner ear oído (m) 9
input data introducir datos 10
insist (on) insistir (en) 9
insomnia insomnio (m) 9
insurance: medical insurance seguro médico (m) 10

integral integral 9
intellectual intelectual 1
intelligent inteligente 1
intend to + verb pensar (ie) + infinitive 4
interest interesar 8
interest rate tasa (f) de interés 10
interested interesado/a 2
interesting interesante 1
intermediate level nivel medio (m) 10
international internacional 6
invade invadir 11
it lo, la 5; **Here it is.** Aquí lo/la tiene. 5; **That's it!** ¡Así es! 8; **What time is it?** ¿Qué hora es? 1; **It's a quarter past three.** Son las tres y cuarto. 1; **It's half past six.** Son las seis y media. 1; **It's one o'clock.** Es la una. 1; **It's two o'clock.** Son las dos. 1; **It's written…** Se escribe… 1
Italian italiano/a; **Italian restaurant** restaurante (m) de comida italiana 2
itch picar 9; **My eyes itch.** Me pican los ojos. 9
itinerary itinerario (m) 6

J

jacket chaqueta (f) 5
January enero (m) 4
jeans vaqueros (mpl) 5
jewelry store joyería (f) 5
job empleo (m) 10, trabajo (m) 1; **job application** solicitud (f) de empleo 10; **job offer** oferta (f) de empleo 10
joke chiste (m); **tell jokes** contar chistes 4
journalist periodista (m/f) 10
judge juez (m/f) 11
juice jugo (m) (8); **orange juice** jugo (m) de naranja 8
July julio (m) 4
June junio (m) 4
just sólo; **to have just** + past participle acabar de + infinitive 5
justice justicia (f) 11

K

key llave (f) 6
keyboard teclado (m) 10
kidneys riñones (mpl) 9
kilogram kilo (m) 8
kill matar 7
kiss beso (m) 5
kiss each other besarse 5
kitchen cocina (f) 3
knee rodilla (f) 9
knife cuchillo (m) 8
know conocer 6; saber 6; **I don't know.** No sé. 2

L

ladder escalera (f) 7
lake lago (m) 4
lamp lámpara (f) 3
land aterrizar 6

lane carril (m) 7
language lengua (f) 1; idioma (m) 10; **language lab** laboratorio (m) de lenguas 1
last durar 6
last último/a 2, pasado/a 6; **last month** el mes pasado 6; **last name** apellido (m) 10; **last night** anoche 6; **last week** la semana pasada 6
late tarde 2; **sleep late** dormir (ue, u) hasta tarde 4; **See you later.** Hasta luego. 1
laundry service servicio (m) de lavandería 6
law ley (f) 11
lawyer abogado/a (m/f) 7
lazy perezoso/a 1
lead a life llevar una vida 8
learn (to…) aprender (a…) 3; **Learn…!** ¡Aprendan…! 2
leather cuero (m) 5
leave salir 3, irse 5, (something somewhere) dejar 3
left: to the left of a la izquierda de 2
leg pierna (f) 9
legend leyenda (f) 7
lemon limón (m) 8
lemonade limonada (f) 4
lend prestar 8
less… than menos… que 1
let dejar; **Let's hope (that)…** Ojalá (que)… 9; **Let's see…** A ver… 8
letter carta (f) 3; **letter of financial standing** carta (f) de solvencia 12
lettuce lechuga (f) 8
level: basic/intermediate/high level nivel básico/medio/alto (m) 10
liberal liberal 1
library biblioteca (f) 1
license: driver's license licencia (f) de manejar 7
lie mentira (f) 11
lie mentir (ie, i) 9; **lie down** acostarse (ue) 5
life vida (f) 7; **lead a life** llevar una vida 8
lift levantar; **lift someone's spirits** levantarle el ánimo a alguien 9; **lift weights** levantar pesas 4
light (weight) ligero/a 9, (color) claro
light luz (f) 10; **traffic light** semáforo (m) 7
like como 3; **feel like …ing** tener ganas de + infinitive 4; **He/She looks like…** Se parece a… 3; **What's… like?** ¿Cómo es…? 1
like: I like me gusta(n) 1; **you like** te gusta(n)/le gusta(n) 1; **he likes/she likes** le gusta(n) 1; **I/You/He/She/You would like…** Me/Te/Le gustaría(n)… 3; **I/you/he/she would like** quisiera 8
Likewise. Igualmente. 1
line línea (f) 10; **on line** en línea; **stand in line** hacer cola 12
liquid líquido (m) 9
list lista (f) 9; **wine list** carta (f) de vinos 8
listen (to) escuchar 2; oír 3
liter litro (m) 11
literature literatura (f) 1
little pequeño/a 1
little poco/a/os/as 2; **a little** un poco 1

live vivir 3
living room sala (f) 3
loan préstamo (m) 10
local local 11
located: be located encontrarse (ue) 9
location ubicación (f) 10
lodging alojamiento (m) 12
logical lógico 9
long largo/a 3; **a long time ago** hace mucho tiempo 6; **as long as** con tal que 12; mientras 11; **long distance call** llamada (f) de larga distancia 6; **no longer** ya no 9
look (at) mirar 2; **look for** buscar 5; **He/She looks like…** Se parece a… 3; **You look… to me.** Te veo… 9
lose perder (ie) 4; **lose weight** bajar de peso 9
lot: a lot (of) mucho/a 1; **eat a lot** comer fuerte 8; **parking lot** estacionamiento (m) 7
love amor (m) 7; **in love** enamorado/a 7
love encantar 8, querer (ie); **love each other** quererse (ie) 5; **I love it (them)** me encanta(n) 7
lover amante (m/f) 7
low bajo 11
luggage equipaje (m) 6
lunch almuerzo (m) 8; **eat lunch, have lunch** almorzar (ue) 4
lungs pulmones (mpl) 9

M

mad enojado/a 2
magazine revista (f) 3
maid camarera (f) 6
mail something echar algo al correo 6
mailbox buzón (m) 10
main principal; **main dish** plato principal (m) 8
maintain mantener 9
maintenance mantenimiento (m) 10
make hacer 3; **make a stopover** hacer escala 6; **make copies** sacar copias 10; **make friends** hacer amistades 12; **make someone hungry** darle hambre a alguien 8; **make up** reconciliarse 5
make-up: put on make-up maquillarse 5
mall centro comercial (m) 4
malnutrition malnutrición (f) 11
mango mango (m) 8
manufacturing fabricación (f) 10
many muchos/as 1; **as many… as** tantos/as… como 3; **how many?** ¿cuántos/as? 1; **How many are there in…?** ¿Cuántos son en…? 3
map mapa (m); **city map** plano (m) de la ciudad 6
March marzo (m) 4
marital status estado civil (m) 10
market(place) mercado (m) 6
marry: get married (to) casarse (con) 5
mass media medios (mpl) de comunicación 11
mathematics matemáticas (fpl) 1
matrimony matrimonio (m) 7

May mayo (m) 4
may poder (ue) (4); **How may I help you?** ¿En qué puedo servirle? 5; **May I see…** Me permite… 6
Mayan maya 6
maybe quizás 9; tal vez 5
me me 5, mí 2; **(to, for) me** me 8; **for me** para mí 4; **with me** conmigo 1
meal comida (f) 8
mean: What does… mean in English? ¿Qué significa… en inglés? 2
meat carne (f) 8
mechanic mecánico/a (m/f) 10; **mechanic's garage** taller (m) 7
media medios (mpl) de comunicación 11
medical insurance seguro médico (m) 10
medicine medicamento (m) 6; medicina (f) 10
medium mediano/a; (meat) término medio 8; **of medium height** de estatura mediana 3
meet (for the first time) conocer 6; **meet one another** encontrarse (ue) 5; **I want you to meet…** Quiero presentar/le a… (familiar/formal) 1; **Pleased to meet you.** Mucho gusto. 1
melon melón (m) 8
melt derretir (i, i) 8; **melted** derretido/a 8
memory recuerdo (m) 7
mental illness enfermedad mental (f) 9
menu menú (m) 8
message mensaje (m) 6; recado (m) 10
messy desordenado/a 3
Mexican mexicano/a 2; **Mexican food restaurant** restaurante (m) de comida mexicana 2
microwave oven microondas (m) 3
middle medio (m); **in the middle of** en medio de; **middle-aged** de mediana edad 3
midnight medianoche (f) 1
milk leche (f) 4
million: one million un millón (de) 3
mine el/la mío/a 10
mineral water agua (f) mineral 4
minimum mínimo/a 10
minute minuto (m) 8
mirror espejo (m) 3
mischievous travieso/a 7
Miss señorita 1
miss perder (ie) 4
missing: be missing faltar 8
mistaken equivocado/a 10
mix mezclar 8
mixture mezcla (f) 8
Mme. señora 1
modern moderno/a 1
moment momento (m) 4
Monday lunes (m) 1
money dinero (m) 3
monitor monitor (m) 10
month: per month al mes 2
mood: be in a good/bad mood estar de buen/mal humor 10
more más 1; **more… than** más… que 1; **I need more time.** Necesito más tiempo.

2; **more than** + number más de + number 6, superior a… 12; **not any more** ya no 9
morning mañana (f) 1; **Good morning.** Buenos días. 1; **in the morning** de la mañana (with a specific hour), por la mañana (with no hour given) 1; **this morning** esta mañana 4; **tomorrow morning** mañana por la mañana 4; **yesterday morning** ayer por la mañana 6
mosque mezquita (f) 4
mother madre (f) 1
mountain montaña (f) 3
mouth boca (f) 9
move mudarse 10
movie película (f) 2; **(foreign, adventure, horror) movie** película (f) (extranjera, de aventuras, de terror) 2; **movie theater** cine (m) 2; **go to the movies** ir al cine 2
Mr. señor 1
Mrs. señora 1
much mucho/a 1; **as much… as** tanto/a… como 3; **How much does it (do they) cost?** ¿Cuánto cuesta(n)? 5; **how much?** ¿cuánto/a? 2; **so much** tanto 9
muscle músculo (m) 9
muscular pain dolor muscular (m) 9
museum museo (m) 4
music música (f) 1
musician músico (m/f) 7
must tener que, deber 3; **one must…** hay que… 12
mustache bigote (m) 3
my mi(s) 1; **My name is…** Me llamo… 1
myself me 5

N

name nombrar; **be named** llamarse 5
name nombre (m) 10; **His/Her name is (Their names are)…** Se llama (Se llaman)… 3; **last name** apellido (m) 10; **My name is…** Me llamo… 1; **What is your name?** ¿Cómo se llama usted? ¿Cómo te llamas? 1
napkin servilleta (f) 8
nation nación (f) 11; **the United Nations** las Naciones Unidas (fpl) 11
national security seguridad nacional (f) 11
nationality nacionalidad (f) 12
natural natural (m) 11; **natural disaster, natural catastrophe** catástrofe natural (f) 11
near cerca de 2
neat ordenado/a 3
necessary necesario/a 9
neck cuello (m) 9
necklace collar (m) 5
necktie corbata (f) 5
need necesitar 2; **I need more time.** Necesito más tiempo. 2; **be needed** faltar 8
negative negativo/a 9
neighbor vecino/a (m/f) 3
neighborhood vecindario (m) 7, barrio (m) 3
neither tampoco 3; **neither… nor** ni… ni… 4

nephew sobrino (m) 3; **nephews and nieces** sobrinos (mpl) 3
nervous nervioso/a 2; **get nervous** ponerse nervioso/a 9
network cadena (f) (television) 11
never nunca 2
new nuevo/a 1
newlyweds recién casados (mpl) 11
newscast noticiero (m) 11
newscaster presentador/a (m/f) de noticias 11
newspaper periódico (m) 3
newsstand quiosco (m) de periódicos 6
next próximo/a 2, luego 2, a continuación 11; **next month** el mes que viene 4; **next to** al lado de 2; junto a 6; **next week** la semana que viene 4; **next year** el año que viene 4; **on the next day** al día siguiente 6; **What is the homework for the next class?** ¿Cuál es la tarea para la próxima clase? 2
Nicaraguan nicaragüense 12
nice simpático/a 1, agradable 3
niece sobrina (f) 3; **nephews and nieces** sobrinos (mpl) 3
night noche (f) 1; **at night** de la noche (with a specific hour), por la noche (with no hour given) 1; **Good night.** Buenas noches. 1; **night club** club nocturno (m) 2
nine nueve 1; **nine hundred** novecientos/as 3
nineteen diecinueve 1
ninety noventa 1
ninth noveno/a 6
no no 1; **no longer** ya no 9
nobody nadie 4
nomination nominación (f) 11
none ninguno/a (ningún) 4
non-smoking de no fumadores 6
noon mediodía (m) 1
nor ni 2; **neither... nor** ni... ni... 4
normal normal 9
nose nariz (f) 9
not no 1; **not any more** ya no 9; **not either** tampoco 3; **not yet** todavía no 10; **not... anything** no... nada 3
notary: notary public notario/a público/a (m/f) 12
notebook cuaderno (m) 2
nothing nada 4; **nothing in particular** nada en especial 3
November noviembre (m) 4
now ahora 1
numb adormecido/a 9
nurse enfermero/a (m/f) 7

O

obey obedecer 7
obligatory obligatorio/a 12
obtain obtener 10
occur ocurrir 7
o'clock: It's one o'clock. Es la una. 1; **It's two o'clock.** Son las dos. 1
October octubre (m) 4
of de 2; **a lot of** mucho/a 1; **of course** por supuesto 12; **Yes, of course.** Sí, cómo no. 5

off apagado/a 10; **get off** bajar de 6; **turn off** apagar 10
offer: job offer oferta (f) de empleo 10
offer ofrecer 8
office oficina (f) 2; **branch office** sucursal (f) 10
officer: police officer policía/mujer policía (m/f) 7
Okay? ¿Está bien? 2
old viejo/a 1; **be... years old** tener... años 3; **older** mayor 3; **oldest** mayor 3
on en 2, sobre 8, encendido/a 10; **on sale** de oferta 5; **on the next day** al día siguiente 6; **on top of** encima de 2; **get on** subir a 6; **on Monday** (a particular week) el lunes 1; **on Mondays** (every week) los lunes... 1; **on the phone** por teléfono 2; **That depends on...** Eso depende de.. 2; **turn on** encender (ie) 10
once una vez 2; **Once upon a time...** Érase una vez... 7
one uno (un, una) 1; **one another** se, nos, os 5; **one can...** se puede... 6; **one hundred** cien 1; **one hundred and...** ciento... 3; **one million** un millón (de) 3; **one thousand** mil 3; **It's one o'clock.** Es la una. 1
onion cebolla (f) 8
only sólo 3
open abrir 3; abierto/a 2; **Open...!** ¡Abran...! 2
opportunity oportunidad (f) 10
opposite opuesto/a 7
optimistic optimista 1
optional optativo/a 12
orange naranja (f) 8; **orange juice** jugo (m) de naranja 8
orange anaranjado/a 3
order (sequence) orden (m); (command) orden (f); **in order to** + verb para + infinitive 4
order pedir (i, i) 4
organize organizar; **organized** organizado/a 1
original original 12
other otro/a 1; **each other** se, nos, os 5
ought to deber 3
our nuestro/a/os/as 3
ourselves nos 5
out fuera; **get out of** bajar de 6; **go out** salir 3; **take out** sacar 6; **turn out** resultar 7
outgoing extrovertido/a 1
outing: go on an outing ir de excursión 6
outside afuera 3
outskirts las afueras (fpl) 3
oven horno (m) 8; **microwave oven** microondas (m) 3
over sobre 8; **over here** por acá 5
overcoat abrigo (m) 5
owe deber 3
own propio/a 3
owner dueño/a (m/f) 8

P

pack your suitcase hacer la maleta 6
page página (f) 2
pain dolor (m) 9

paint pintar 10
painter pintor/a (m/f) 7
painting pintura (f) 3
pair pareja (f) 11
pan cacerola (f) 8
Panamanian panameño/a 12
pancreas páncreas (m) 9
pants pantalones (mpl) 5
paper papel (m) 2; (essay) ensayo (m) 3
paperwork papeleo (m) 12
Paraguayan paraguayo/a 12
paramedic paramédico/a (m/f) 7
Pardon me! ¡Disculpe! 6
parents padres (mpl) 3
park parque (m) 2; **amusement park** parque (m) de atracciones 6
parking lot estacionamiento (m) 7
Parmesan cheese queso parmesano (m) 8
participate participar 2
participation participación (f) 11
particular: nothing in particular nada en especial 3
part-time a tiempo parcial 10
party fiesta 3; **birthday party** fiesta (f) de cumpleaños 7; **fifteenth birthday party** quinceañera (f) 7; **have a party** hacer una fiesta 3
pass pasar 2; **boarding pass** tarjeta (f) de embarque 6
passenger pasajero/a (m/f) 6
passport pasaporte (m) 6
past pasado/a; **It's a quarter past three.** Son las tres y cuarto. 1; **It's half past six.** Son las seis y media. 1
pastry shop pastelería (f) 5
patient paciente (m/f) 9
patient paciente 1
pay pagar 3
pay pago (m) 10
peace paz (f) 7; **peace agreement** acuerdo (m) de paz 11
peas chícharos (mpl) 8
peasant campesino/a (m/f) 7
pedestrian peatón (m) 7
pen bolígrafo (m) 2
pencil lápiz (m) 2
penicillin penicilina (f) 9
people gente (f) 12
pepper pimienta (f) 8; **stuffed pepper** chile relleno (m) 8
per week/per month/per year a la semana / al mes/al año 2
percent discount descuento (m) del... por ciento a... 5
perfect perfecto/a 2
perform realizar 12
performer artista (m/f) 7
perhaps quizás 9; tal vez 5
period época (f); **registration period** plazo (m) de matrícula 12
periodical periódico (m) 6
permanent permanente 12
permit permitir 9
person persona (f) 3; **country person** campesino/a (m/f) 7; **injured person** herido/a (m/f) 7

personal personal 10
personality carácter (*m*) 3, personalidad (*f*); **as for personality** en el carácter 3
Peruvian peruano/a 12
pessimistic pesimista 1
peso peso (*m*) 8
pharmacy farmacia (*f*) 6
philosophy filosofía (*f*) 1
phone teléfono (*m*) 2; **phone card** tarjeta telefónica (*f*) 6; **talk on the phone** hablar por teléfono 2
photo foto (*f*) 6; **take a photo** sacar una foto 4
photocopier fotocopiadora (*f*) 10
physical físico/a 9
physician médico/a (*m/f*) 7
physics física (*f*) 1
pick escoger 12; **pick up** recoger 6
picture pintura (*f*) 3; foto (*f*) 4; **take a picture** sacar una foto 4
piece trozo (*m*) 4; **piece of advice** consejo (*m*) 8; **piece of gossip** chisme (*m*) 11
pillow almohada (*f*) 6
pineapple piña (*f*) 8
pink rosado/a, rosa 3
pizza pizza (*f*) 4
place lugar (*m*) 7; **place of residence** domicilio (*m*) 12
place poner 3
plaid de cuadros 5
plan plan (*m*) 12; **plan of studies, degree plan** plan de estudios 12
plane avión (*m*) 6; **plane ticket** pasaje (*m*) de avión 6
planned previsto/a 12
plant planta (*f*) 2
plate plato (*m*) 6
play (*an instrument*) tocar 2; (*games*) jugar 4
play obra (*f*) de teatro 4
player: DVD player reproductor (*m*) de DVD 3
pleasant agradable 3
please por favor 2; **Pleased to meet you.** Mucho gusto. 1
plug in enchufar 10
pneumonia pulmonía (*f*) 9
police policía (*f*); **police officer** policía/mujer policía (*m/f*) 7; **police report** denuncia (*f*) 7
political science ciencias políticas (*fpl*) 1
poll encuesta (*f*) 11
pollution contaminación (*f*) 7
pool: swimming pool piscina (*f*) 3
popular popular 6
pork chop chuleta (*f*) de cerdo 8
position puesto (*m*) 10
possible posible 9
possible: as soon as possible lo antes posible 10
post office oficina (*f*) de correos 6
potato papa (*f*) 8; **potato chips** papitas fritas (*fpl*) 4; **baked potato** papa (*f*) al horno 8
pound libra (*f*) 11
pour verter (ie) 8
poverty pobreza (*f*) 11

practical práctico/a 10
pray rezar 4
prefer preferir (ie) 4; **I prefer…** Prefiero… 2
preferable preferible 9
pregnant embarazada 11
prepare preparar 2; **prepared** preparado/a 8
prescribe recetar 9
present regalo (*m*) 5
present actual 11, presente; **be present** presentarse 12
presentation presentación (*f*) 11
president presidente/a (*m/f*) 11
press prensa (*m/f*) 11
pressure: high blood pressure presión arterial alta (*f*) 9
pretty bonito/a 1
prevent prevenir 9
price precio (*m*) 5
primary school escuela primaria (*f*) 2
print imprimir 10
printer impresora (*f*) 3
printout impreso (*m*) 12
priority prioridad (*f*) 11
probable probable 9
problem problema (*m*) 11
processed procesado/a (*m*) 7; **processed food** los productos procesados (*m*) 7
processor: word processor procesador (*m*) de texto 10
produce producir 9
professional profesional 10
professor profesor/a (*m/f*) 1
program programa (*m*) 10
program programar 10
programmer programador/a (*m/f*) 7
progress progreso (*m*) 10
prohibit prohibir 9
prolong prolongar 12
proof comprobante (*m*) 6
proposed propuesto/a 11
protect proteger 9
protein proteína (*f*) 8
protest protesta (*f*) 11
protest (against) protestar (contra) 11
proud orgulloso/a 7
prove probar (ue) 12
provide proporcionar 12; **provided that** con tal que 12
provoke provocar 11
psychology (p)sicología (*f*) 1
public público/a 6; **notary public** notario/a público/a (*m/f*) 12
published publicado/a 10
purple morado/a 3
purpose: I'm writing to you for the purpose of… Me dirijo a usted(es) con la intención de… 12
purse bolsa (*f*) 5
put poner 3; **put on (clothes)** ponerse (la ropa) 5; **put on make-up** maquillarse 5

Q

quarter: It's a quarter past three. Son las tres y cuarto. 1
queasy mareado/a 9

question pregunta (*f*) 2; **ask a question** hacer una pregunta 3
quiz pruebita (*f*) 2

R

radio radio (*f*) 3
rain llover (ue) 4
raincoat impermeable (*m*) 5
raise aumento (*m*) 10
raise aumentar 11
rare poco cocido/a 8
rate: interest rate tasa (*f*) de interés 10
read leer 3; **Read…!** ¡Lean…! 2
ready listo/a 2
real real 11
Really? ¿De veras? 10
reason motivo (*m*) 10
reasonable razonable 5
rebellious rebelde 1
receipt comprobante (*m*) 6; recibo (*m*) 5
receive recibir 3
receptacle recipiente (*m*) 8
receptionist recepcionista (*m/f*) 6
recipe receta (*f*) 8
recommend recomendar (ie) 6
recommendation recomendación (*f*) 8
reconciliation reconciliación (*f*) 11
record grabar 11
red rojo/a 3; **red tape** papeleo (*m*) 12
redheaded pelirrojo/a 3
reduce reducir 11
reduction reducción (*f*) 11
reference referencia (*f*) 10
reform reforma (*f*) 11
refrigerator nevera (*f*) 3
regional regional 6
register matricularse 12; **cash register** caja (*f*) 5
registrar: Admissions and Registrar's Office oficina (*f*) de admisiones y registro 12
registration matrícula (*f*) 11; **registration period** plazo (*m*) de matrícula 12
regret arrepentirse (ie, i) 7
regularity: with regularity con regularidad 9
relax relajarse 5
relieve aliviar 9
religious religioso/a 1
remain permanecer 12
remember recordar (ue) 7
remove quitar 9; retirar 8
renew renovar (ue) 12
renovation renovación (*f*) 12
rent alquiler (*m*) 3
rent alquilar 3
repair arreglo (*m*) 11
repair arreglar 6
repeat repetir (i, i) 4; **Repeat…!** ¡Repitan…! 2
reply replicar 7
report informe (*m*) 11; **police report** denuncia (*f*) 7
report informar 7
reporter reportero/a (*m/f*) 10

representative representante *(m/f)* 11;
   House of Representatives Cámara *(f)* de
   Representantes 11
request petición *(f)* 10; **available upon
   request** disponible a petición 10
required obligatorio/a 12
reserve reservar 6
residence: place of residence domicilio *(m)*
   12; **residence hall** residencia *(f)* 1
residency residencia *(f)* 12
resistance resistencia *(f)* 9
resolve resolver (ue) 10
resources recursos *(m)* 11; **human
   resources** recursos humanos *(mpl)* 10
respond responder 11
responsible responsable 1
rest descansar 2
restaurant restaurante *(m)* 2;
   Mexican/Italian restaurant restaurante
   (m) de comida mexicana/italiana 2
resumé currículum vitae *(m)* 10
resources recursos *(mpl)* 10
retire jubilarse 7
retirement jubilación *(f)* 7
return regresar 2; volver (ue) 4; *(something)*
   devolver (ue) 10
review revisar 11
revolting: be revolting dar asco 8
rice arroz *(m)* 8
rich rico/a 9
ride horseback montar a caballo 9
ridiculous ridículo 9
right correcto/a 6; **right?** ¿verdad? 6; **be
   right** tener razón 9; **right away** en
   seguida 11; **That's right!** ¡Así es! 8; **to
   the right of** a la derecha de 2
ring anillo *(m)* 5
river río *(m)* 6
road carretera *(f)* 7
roasted asado/a 8
rock star estrella *(f)* de rock 11
roll of film rollo *(m)* de película 6
romance romance *(m)* 11
romantic romántico/a 1
room cuarto *(m)* 2, habitación *(f)* 6; **room
   service** servicio *(m)* de habitaciones 6;
   dining room comedor *(m)* 3; **living room**
   sala *(f)* 3; **waiting room** sala *(f)* de espera 6
route: en route to en ruta a 7
routine rutina *(f)* 8
rug alfombra *(f)* 3
ruins ruinas *(fpl)* 6
rumor rumor *(m)* 11
run correr 3; **run as a candidate**
   presentarse como candidato/a 11; **run
   errands** hacer mandados 5

S

sad triste 2
safe seguro/a 2
sailboat velero *(m)* 6
salad ensalada *(f)* 4
salary sueldo *(m)* 10
sale: on sale de oferta 5; **sales** las ventas
   (fpl) 10

salesclerk dependiente *(m)*, dependienta *(f)* 5
salesperson vendedor/a *(m/f)* 10
salmon salmón *(m)* 9
salon: hair salon peluquería *(f)* 5
salt sal *(f)* 8
Salvadoran salvadoreño/a 12
same mismo/a 2
sanctions sanciones *(fpl)* 11
sandal sandalia *(f)* 5
sandwich bocadillo *(m)* 4, sándwich *(m)* 8
satisfied satisfecho/a 11
Saturday sábado *(m)* 1
sauce salsa *(f)* 8
save ahorrar 10
savings account cuenta *(f)* de ahorros 10
say decir 4; **How do you say… in
   Spanish?** ¿Cómo se dice… en español?
   2; **say good-bye** despedirse (i) 5
scandal escándalo *(m)* 11
sciences ciencias *(fpl)* 1; **political science**
   ciencias políticas *(fpl)* 1
schedule horario *(m)* 1
scholarship beca *(f)* 12
school escuela *(f)* 2; **high school** colegio 7,
   preparatoria *(f)* 10
score a goal marcar un gol 7
screen pantalla *(f)* 10
sea mar *(m)* 6
seafood shop pescadería *(f)* 5
search engine buscador *(m)* 11
season estación *(f)* 4
seat asiento *(m)* 6
seatbelt cinturón *(m)* de seguridad 6
second segundo/a 6
secondary school escuela secundaria *(f)* 2
secret secreto/a 7
secretary secretario/a *(m/f)* 7
security seguridad *(f)* 11
see ver 3; **see one another** verse 5; **See you
   later.** Hasta luego. 1; **See you
   tomorrow.** Hasta mañana. 1; **Let's see…**
   A ver… 8; **May I see…** Me permite… 6
seem parecer 11; **It seems (They seem)…
   to me.** Me parece(n)… 5
selfish egoísta 1
sell vender 3
**semester: What classes do you have this
   semester?** ¿Qué clases tienes este
   semestre? 1
senator senador/a *(m/f)* 11
send enviar 12, mandar 6
sentence oración *(f)* 2
separated separado/a 11
September septiembre *(m)* 4
serious serio/a 1, grave 9
serve servir (i, i) 4
server mesero/a *(m/f)* 4
service servicio *(m)* 6; **service station**
   estación *(f)* de servicio 6; **customer
   service** atención *(f)* al cliente 10; **room
   service** servicio *(m)* de habitación 6
set: television set televisor *(m)* 3
set poner 3; **set off** echar(se) a 7
seven siete 1; **seven hundred** setecientos/as 3
seventeen diecisiete 1
seventh séptimo/a 6

seventy setenta 1
several varios/as 2
shake hands darse la mano 5
shame: It's a shame that… Es una lástima
   que… 9
shampoo champú *(m)* 6
shape: stay in shape mantenerse en forma 8
share compartir 3
she ella 1; **she likes** le gusta(n) 1; **She
   would like…** Le gustaría(n)… 3
sheets sábanas *(fpl)* 6
shelf estante *(m)* 2
shirt camisa *(f)* 5; **T-shirt** camiseta *(f)* 5
shoe zapato *(m)* 5; **shoe store** zapatería *(f)* 5
shopping: go shopping ir de compras 4;
   shopping center centro comercial *(m)* 4
short *(in height)* bajo/a 3, *(in length)* corto/a 3
shorts pantalones cortos *(mpl)* 5
shot: give someone a shot ponerle una
   inyección a alguien 9
should deber 3; **I/he/she should** debería 12
show programa *(m)* 11; **talk show** programa
   (m) de entrevistas 11
show mostrar (ue) 11; **show up** acudir 12;
   show up presentarse 12
shower ducha *(f)* 6; **take a shower**
   ducharse 5
shrimp camarón *(m)* 8
shy tímido/a 1
sick enfermo/a 2; **get sick** enfermarse 9
sidewalk acera *(f)* 7
sign letrero *(m)* 7
sign firmar 5
silk seda *(f)* 5
silver necklace collar *(m)* de plata 5
since desde que 9
Sincerely… Atentamente… 12
sing cantar 2
singer cantante *(m/f)* 7
single soltero/a 3; **single room** habitación
   sencilla *(f)* 6
sink lavabo *(m)* 6
sinus infection sinusitis *(f)* 9
sir señor 1
sister hermana *(f)* 1; **brothers and sisters**
   hermanos *(mpl)* 3
sit (down) sentarse (ie) 5
site sitio *(m)* 6
situation situación *(f)* 11
six seis 1; **six hundred** seiscientos/as 3
sixteen dieciséis 1
sixth sexto/a 6
sixty sesenta 1
size talla *(f)* 5; tamaño *(m)* 12
skating patinaje *(m)* 7
ski esquiar 4
skin piel *(f)* 9
skirt falda *(f)* 5
sky cielo *(m)* 4; **The sky's clear.** El cielo está
   despejado. 4; **The sky's cloudy.** El cielo
   está nublado. 4
sleep dormir (ue, u) 4; **sleep late** dormir
   hasta tarde 4
sleeping bag saco de dormir *(m)* 6
slice trozo *(m)* 4
small pequeño/a 1

smart listo/a 2
smoke humo (m) 7
smoke fumar 3
smoking de fumadores 6
sneeze estornudar 9
snow nevar (ie) 4
so tan 2; entonces 4; **so (that)** para que 12; **so much** tanto 7
soap jabón (m) 6; **soap opera** telenovela (f) 11
soccer fútbol (m) 2; **soccer game** partido (m) de fútbol 2
social social 1; **social assistance** asistencia social (f) 11; **social sciences** ciencias sociales (fpl) 1; **social worker** asistente social (m/f) 7
society sociedad (f) 11
sock calcetín (m) 5
socket enchufe (m) 10
sofa sofá (m) 3
soft drink refresco (m) 4
software designer diseñador/a (m/f) de software 7
soldier soldado (m/f) 7
solid-colored de un solo color 5
some unos/as 2, alguno/a(s) (algún) 4
somebody alguien 3
someone alguien 3
something algo 4
sometimes a veces 4
son hijo (m) 3
soon pronto 7; **as soon as possible** lo antes posible 10; **as soon as you** + verb al + infinitive 6
sore dolorido/a 9
sorry: be sorry arrepentirse (ie, i) 7; **be sorry that** sentir (ie, i) que 10; **I'm sorry.** Lo siento. 6
soup sopa (f) 8
souvenir recuerdo (m) 6
Spanish español (m) 1; **How do you say… in Spanish?** ¿Cómo se dice… en español? 2
Spanish español/a 12
speak hablar 2; **speak on the phone** hablar por teléfono 2
speed limit límite (m) de velocidad 7
spend (time) pasar 2, (money) gastar 5
spinach espinacas (fpl) 8
spirits: lift someone's spirits levantarle el ánimo a alguien 9
spoon cuchara (f) 8
spoonful cucharada (f) 8
sport deporte (m) 2; **fond of sports** deportista 7
spouse esposo/a (m/f) 1
sprain (your ankle…) torcer(se) (ue) (el tobillo…) 9
spreadsheet hoja (f) de cálculo 10
spring primavera (f) 4
stability estabilidad (f) 11
stadium estadio (m) 2
stairs escalera (f) 6
stamp sello (m) 6
stand up levantarse 5; **stand in line** hacer cola 12; **not be able to stand** dar asco 8

staple (en)grapar 10
stapler (en)grapadora (f) 10
star: rock star estrella (f) de rock 11
start empezar (ie) 4; comenzar (ie) 8; echar(se) a 7
statement (of an account) estado (m) de cuenta 12
station: service station estación (f) de servicio, 6; **gas station** gasolinera (f) 6
status: marital status estado civil (m) 10
stay estancia (f) 12
stay quedarse 5; **stay at** (on trips) alojarse en 6; **stay in bed** guardar cama 9; **stay in shape** mantenerse en forma 8
steak bistec (m) 8
steamed al vapor 8
stemmed glass copa (f) 8
step paso (m) 12
stomach estómago (m) 9
stop: bus stop parada (f) de autobús 7
stop …ing dejar de + infinitive 8
stopover: make a stopover hacer escala 6
stopped up tapado/a 9
store tienda (f) 2; **clothing store** tienda (f) de ropa 2; **department store** almacén (m) 5; **jewelry store** joyería (f) 5
story historia (f) 7; **top stories** titulares (mpl) 11
stove estufa (f) 3
straight: continue straight (ahead) seguir (i, i) recto 6
straightened up ordenado/a 3
strange raro/a 9
strawberry fresa (f) 8
street calle (f) 2
strength fuerza (f) 9
stress estrés (m) 8
stretch estirar(se) 9
striped de rayas 5
strong fuerte 9
struggle luchar 7
student estudiante (m/f) 1; **student desk** pupitre (m) 2; **entering student** alumno/a (m/f) de nuevo ingreso 12
studies: plan of studies plan (m) de estudios 12
study estudiar 1
stuffed pepper chile relleno (m) 8
subject (school) asignatura (f) 12
submit (to) someterse (a) 7
suffer from sufrir (de) 9
sufficiently lo suficiente 8
sugar azúcar (m) 4
suggest sugerir (ie, i) 9
suit traje (m) 5
suitcase maleta (f) 6
summer verano (m) 4
sunbathe tomar el sol 4
Sunday domingo (m) 1
sunglasses gafas (fpl) de sol 6
sunny: It's sunny. Hace sol. 4
sunscreen crema protectora solar (f) 6
supermarket supermercado (m) 2
supervisor supervisor/a (m/f) 10
supper cena (f) 8

supplies: office supplies los artículos (mpl) de oficina 10
sure seguro/a 2, **Sure!** ¡Claro! 1
surprise sorprender 10
survey encuesta (f) 11
sweater suéter (m) 5
sweatshirt sudadera (f) 5
sweet dulce 8
sweets los dulces (mpl) 8
swim nadar 4
swimming pool piscina (f) 3
swimsuit traje (m) de baño 5
Swiss cheese queso suizo (m) 8
swollen hinchado/a 9
symptom síntoma (m) 9
synagogue sinagoga (f) 4
system sistema (m) 9

T

table mesa (f) 2; **table cloth** mantel (m) 8
tablet pastilla (f) 9
take tomar 2, llevar 5, llevarse 5; **take a bath** bañarse 5; **take a cruise** hacer un crucero 6; **take a nap** dormir (ue, u) una siesta; **take a picture** sacar una foto 4; **take a shower** ducharse 5; **take a trip** hacer un viaje 3; **take away** retirar 8; **take care of** cuidar 9; **take off** (on a plane) despegar 6; (remove) quitar(se) 9; **Take out…!** ¡Saquen…! 2; **take out** sacar 6
talk hablar 2; **talk on the phone** hablar por teléfono 2; **talk show** programa (m) de entrevistas 11; **talk to each other** hablarse 5
tall alto/a 3
tape cinta adhesiva (f); **red tape** papeleo (m) 12
tax impuesto (m) 10
taxi taxi (m) 6
tea té (m) 4; **iced/hot tea** té (m) helado/caliente 8
teach enseñar 2
teacher maestro/a (m/f) 7
team equipo (m) 7
technical técnico/a 1
technology tecnología (f) 11
teeth dientes (mpl) 5
telephone teléfono (m) 6; **telephone number** número (m) de teléfono 1
television televisión (f) 2; **television set** televisor (m) 3
tell decir 4; contar (ue) 4; **tell jokes** contar chistes 4
teller cajero/a (m/f) 10
temperature temperatura (f) 9
temple templo (m) 4
temporary temporal (m) 10
ten diez 1
tennis tenis (m) 4; **tennis shoes** tenis (mpl) 5
tenth décimo/a 6
terrace terraza (f) 8
terrorism terrorismo (m) 11
terrorist terrorista (m/f) 11
textbook libro (m) de texto 3

than: less… than menos… que 1; **more… than** más… que 1

thank you gracias 1

that (those) ese/esa (esos/as) 5; aquel/aquella (aquellos/as) 5; **That depends on…** Eso depende de… 2; **that which** lo que 11; **That's it! That's right!** ¡Así es! 8

theater *(for live performances)* teatro *(m)* 4; **movie theater** cine *(m)* 2

theft robo *(m)* 11

their su/s 3

them ellos/as 2; los, las 5; les, se 8

themselves se 5

then luego 2, entonces 4

there allí; **there is, there are, is there, are there** hay 1; **How many are there in…?** ¿Cuántos son en…? 3

they ellos/as 1

thicken espesarse 8

thin delgado/a 3

thing cosa *(f)* 5

think pensar (ie) 4

third tercer(o)/a 6; **Third World** Tercer Mundo *(m)*

thirsty: be thirsty tener sed 4

thirteen trece 1

thirty treinta 1

this (these) este/esta (estos/as) 5; **this afternoon** esta tarde 4; **this evening** esta noche 4; **this morning** esta mañana 4; **this week** esta semana *(f)* 1; **this weekend** este fin de semana 1; **What classes do you have this semester?** ¿Qué clases tienes este semestre? 1

thousand: one thousand mil 3

threaten amenazar 11

three tres 1; **three hundred** trescientos/as 3

throat garganta *(f)* 9

through por (5)

throw up vomitar 9

Thursday jueves *(m)* 1

ticket billete *(m)* 6; boleto *(m)* 6; *(fine)* multa *(f)* 7; **plane ticket** pasaje *(m)* de avión 6

time tiempo *(m)* 2; **a long time ago** hace mucho tiempo 6; **at that time** en aquella época 7; **at times** a veces 2; **At what time?** ¿A qué hora? 1; **I need more time.** Necesito más tiempo. 2; **Once upon a time…** Érase una vez… 7; **What time is it?** ¿Qué hora es? 1

timid tímido/a 1

tip propina *(f)* 8

tired cansado/a 2

tissue tejido *(m)* 9

to a 4; **from… to…** de… a… 1; **(in order) to** + *verb* para + *infinitive* 4; **to have to** + *verb* tener que + *infinitive* 3; **to the left of** a la izquierda de 2; **to the right of** a la derecha de 2; **to where** adónde 4

toast pan tostado *(m)* 8

today hoy 1; **What day is today?** ¿Qué día es hoy? 1

together juntos/as 2; **get together** encontrarse (ue) 5

toilet paper papel higiénico *(m)* 6

tomato tomate *(m)* 8

tomb tumba *(f)* 7

tomorrow (afternoon) mañana (por la tarde) 4; **See you tomorrow.** Hasta mañana. 1

tone tono *(m)* 10

tonight esta noche 4

too también 1

top parte *(f)* de arriba; **top stories** titulares *(mpl)* 11; **on top of** encima de 2

topic tema *(m)* 11

torn roto/a 9

tortilla: corn/flour tortilla tortilla *(f)* de maíz/harina 8

touch tocar; **get in touch with each other** comunicarse 5

tourist turista *(m/f)* 12; **tourist guide** guía turística *(f)* 6

towel toalla *(f)* 6

toy juguete *(m)* 5

traffic tráfico *(m)* 7; **traffic light** semáforo *(m)* 7

train tren *(m)*

train entrenar 10

transaction trámite *(m)* 10

transportation transporte *(m)* 10

travel viajar 6; **travel agency** agencia *(f)* de viajes 6

traveler's check cheque *(m)* de viaje 6

treatment tratamiento *(m)* 11

tree árbol *(m)* 3

tremendous tremendo/a 12

trimester: What classes do you have this trimester? ¿Qué clases tienes este trimestre? 1

trip viaje *(m)* 3; **take a trip** hacer un viaje 3

true cierto/a 9, verdad 9

trust confiar en 11

try probar (ue) 6; **try (to..)** tratar de 9; **try on** probarse (ue) 5

T-shirt camiseta *(f)* 5

Tuesday martes *(m)* 1

tuition matrícula *(f)* 11

tuna atún *(m)* 9

turn turno *(m)* 12

turn girar 7; **turn (an age)** cumplir 7; **turn in** entregar 12; **turn off** apagar 10; **turn on** encender (ie) 10, poner 3; **turn out** resultar 7

TV tele *(f)* 2

twelve doce 1

twenty veinte 1; **twenty-eight** veintiocho 1; **twenty-five** veinticinco 1; **twenty-four** veinticuatro 1; **twenty-nine** veintinueve 1; **twenty-one** veintiuno 1; **twenty-seven** veintisiete 1; **twenty-six** veintiséis 1; **twenty-three** veintitrés 1; **twenty-two** veintidós 1

twice dos veces 2

twist (your ankle…) torcer(se) (ue) (el tobillo…) 9

two dos 1; **two hundred** doscientos/as 3

typical típico/a 6

U

ugly feo/a 1

umbrella paraguas *(m)* 5

uncle tío *(m)* 3; **aunts and uncles** tíos *(mpl)* 3

under bajo 7

understand comprender 3; entender (ie) 4; **I don't understand.** No comprendo. 2

understanding comprensión *(f)* 11

unemployment desempleo *(m)* 11

unfortunately desafortunadamente 3

unite unir 8; **United Nations** Naciones Unidas *(fpl)* 11

university universidad *(f)* 1

university universitario/a *(adj.)* 7

unless a menos que 12

unpleasant antipático/a 1

until hasta 2

up arriba; **get up** levantarse 5; **go up** subir 6

upon encima de 2, sobre 8; **Once upon a time…** Érase una vez… 7; **upon …ing** al + *infinitive* 6

urgent urgente 9

Uruguayan uruguayo/a 12

us nosotros/as 2, nos 5

use uso *(m)*; **drug use** dopaje *(m)* 11

use usar 3, utilizar 10

useful útil 1

usual: as usual regular 1

utilize utilizar 10

V

vacation vacaciones *(fpl)* 6; **go on vacation** ir de vacaciones 6

valid vigente 12; **valid for more than…** con validez superior a… 12

vanilla vainilla *(f)* 4; **vanilla ice cream** helado *(m)* de vainilla 4

various varios 12

vegetable verdura *(f)* 8

Venezuelan venezolano/a 12

very muy 1

victim víctima *(f)* 7

video vídeo *(m)* 3; **video game** videojuego *(m)* 4

view (of) vistas (a) *(fpl)* 6

visa visa *(f)* 6

visit visitar 6

visitor visitante *(m/f)* 10

vitae: curriculum vitae currículum vitae *(m)* 10

vitamin vitamina *(f)* 8

vocabulary vocabulario *(m)* 2

voice voz *(f)* 10

volleyball vóleibol *(m)* 4

vomit vomitar 9

voter votante *(m/f)* 11

W

wage sueldo *(m)* 10

wait (for) esperar 6; **wait on** atender (ie) 12

waiting room sala *(f)* de espera 6

wake up despertarse (ie) 5

walk pasear 4, andar a pie 7, caminar; **go for a walk** pasear 4

wall pared (f) 3

wallet cartera (f) 5

want querer (ie) 4; **Do you want…?** ¿Quieres…? 1; **I want you to meet…** Quiero presentarte/le a… (familiar/formal) 1

war guerra (f) 11

wardrobe armario (m) 3

warming: global warming calentamiento global (m) 11

warrior guerrero/a (m/f) 7

wash (your hair) lavarse (el pelo) 5

watch reloj (m) 2

watch mirar 2

water agua (f) 4; **mineral water** agua (f) mineral 4

waterski hacer esquí acuático 4

we nosotros/as 1

wear llevar 5; usar 3

weather tiempo (m) 4; **weather forecast** pronóstico (m) del tiempo 11; **What's the weather like?** ¿Qué tiempo hace? 4; **The weather's good/bad.** Hace buen/mal tiempo. 4

wedding boda (f) 5

Wednesday miércoles (m) 1

week semana (f) 1; **this week** esta semana (f) 1; **per week** a la semana 2

weekend fin (m) de semana 1; **this weekend** este fin de semana 1; **weekends** los fines de semana 2

weight peso (m); **lift weights** levantar pesas 4; **lose/gain weight** bajar/subir de peso 9

welcome bienvenido/a 6

welfare asistencia social (f) 11

well bien 1

well-done (meat) bien cocido/a 8

what? ¿qué? 1, ¿cuál(es)? 1, lo que 11; **At what time?** ¿A qué hora? 1; **What color is…?** ¿De qué color es…? 3; **What day is today?** ¿Qué día es hoy? 1; **What days do you work?** ¿Qué días trabajas? 1; **What does… mean in English?** ¿Qué significa… en inglés? 2; **What is the date (of…)?** ¿Cuál es la fecha (de…)? 4; **What is the homework for the next class?** ¿Cuál es la tarea para la próxima clase? 2; **What is your name?** ¿Cómo se llama usted? (formal) 1; **What is your name?** ¿Cómo te llamas? (familiar) 1;

What time is it? ¿Qué hora es? 1; **What's the weather like?** ¿Qué tiempo hace? 4; **What's… like?** ¿Cómo es…? 1

when? ¿cuándo? 2

where ¿dónde? 1; **from where?** ¿de dónde? 2; **Where are you from?** ¿De dónde eres? ¿De dónde es usted? 1; **(to) where?** ¿adónde? 4

which? ¿cuál(es)? 2; **that which** lo que 11

while mientras 11

white blanco/a 3; (hair) canoso/a 3

who? ¿quién(es)? 2

whole-grain integral 9

whom: To Whom It May Concern A quien corresponda 12

why? ¿por qué? 1

wife esposa (f) 1

win ganar 7

window ventana (f) 2; (of a vehicle) ventanilla (f) 6; **counter window** ventanilla (f) 10

windy: It's (very) windy. Hace (mucho) viento. 4

wine vino (m); **red wine** vino tinto 4; **white wine** vino blanco 4; **wine glass** copa (f) 8; **wine list** carta (f) de vinos 8

winter invierno (m) 4

wish desear 4

with con 1; **with me** conmigo 1; **with or without an accent** con o sin acento 1; **with whom?** ¿con quién(es)? 2; **with you** contigo 2

withdraw retirar 10

withdrawal retiro (m) 10

without sin 1

witness testigo (m/f) 7

woods bosque (m) 6

wool lana (f) 5

word palabra (f) 2; **word processor** procesador (m) de texto 10

work trabajo (m) 1; **at work** en el trabajo 1

work trabajar 2, funcionar 6; **What days do you work?** ¿Qué días trabajas? 1; **I work** trabajo 1

workbook cuaderno (m) de ejercicios 2

worker obrero/a (m/f) 7; **social worker** asistente social (m/f) 7

world mundo (m) 11; **Third World** Tercer Mundo (m); **world of entertainment** mundo (m) de la farándula 11

worried preocupado/a 7

worse peor 3

worsen empeorar 11

worth: be worth valer 9

would: I would be grateful if you would… Te/Le/Les agradecería… 12; **It would have helped me a lot…** Me habría sido de gran ayuda… 12; **I/You/He/She/You would like…** Me/Te/Le gustaría(n)… 3; **I/you (formal)/he/she would like** quisiera 8

wrapped vendado/a 9

wreck choque (m) 7; **have a wreck** chocar 7

wrecker grúa (f) 7

write escribir 3; **Write…!** ¡Escriban…! 2; **How is… written?** ¿Cómo se escribe…? 1; **I'm writing to you for the purpose of…** Me dirijo a usted(es) con la intención de… 12; **It's written…** Se escribe… 1

wrong equivocado/a 10; **What's wrong with you?** ¿Qué te pasa? 9

Y

yard jardín (m) 3

year año (m) 2; **be… years old** tener… años 3; **per year** al año 2

yellow amarillo/a 3

yesterday (morning) ayer (por la mañana) 6

yet: not yet todavía no 10

yoghurt yogur (m) 9

yolk: egg yolk yema (f) de huevo 8

you tú (familiar), usted (formal), ustedes (plural), vosotros/as (plural, familiar) 1; te, lo, la, los, las, os 5; ti 2; **(to, for) you** te, le, os, les, se 8; **And you?** ¿Y tú/usted? (familiar/formal) 1; **I want you to meet…** Quiero presentarte/le a… (familiar/formal) 1; **Pleased to meet you.** Mucho gusto. 1; **See you later.** Hasta luego. 1; **See you tomorrow.** Hasta mañana. 1; **thank you** gracias 1; **you like:** te gusta(n) (familiar), le gusta(n) (formal) 1; **You (familiar)/You (formal) would like…** Te/Le gustaría(n)… 3; **with you** contigo (familiar) 2

young joven 3; **younger, youngest** menor 3

your tu(s) (familiar) 1, su(s) (formal or plural), vuestro/a/os/as (familiar plural) 3

yourself te 5; **yourselves** se 5, os 5;

Z

zero cero 1

CREDITS

Cover: © Digital Vision Ltd; **page 3:** © Bob Daemmrich/The Image Works; **page 4 (top):** © Peter Menzel Photography; **page 4 (bottom):** Triangle Images/Digital Vision Ltd.; **page 6 (left):** Terry Vine/Getty Images Inc./Stone Allstock; **page 6 (right):** Juan Silva/Getty Images Inc./Image Bank; **page 8 (top):** Arthur Tilley/Getty Images, Inc./Taxi; **page 8 (middle):** Ryan McVay/Getty Images, Inc./Photodisc; **page 8 (bottom):** Photolibrary.Com; **page 16:** PhotoDisc/Getty Images; **page 24 (top right):** © Nik Wheeler/CORBIS; **page 24 (bottom right):** © Bob Daemmrich Photography, Inc.; **page 24 (top left):** © Robert Brenner/PhotoEdit; **page 24 (bottom left):** © Comstock Images; **page 25 (top):** courtesy of Hispanic Heritage Festival; **page 28 (top left):** © John M. Roberts/The Stock Market; **page 28 (middle left):** © Buddy Mays/CORBIS; **page 28 (top right):** Heidi Grassley © Dorling Kindersley; **page 28 (bottom left):** © Steve Jay Crise/CORBIS; **page 28 (bottom right):** © Mark Richards/PhotoEdit; **page 29:** Francesca Yorke © Dorling Kindersley; **page 60 (bottom):** © Robert Frerck/Odyssey/Chicago; **page 35:** David Mendelsohn/Masterfile USA Corporation; **page 56 (top left):** Spencer Grant/PhotoEdit; **page 56 (bottom left and right):** © Will Hart; **page 59 (middle):** © Hispana Magazine; **page 60 (top):** © Robert Frerck/Odyssey/Chicago; **page 60 (bottom):** © Gonzalo Azumendi/AGE Fotostock America, Inc.; **page 61 (top):** © Comstock Images; **page 61 (bottom):** SuperStock, Inc.; **page 62:** Stephen Simpson/Getty Images, Inc./Taxi; **page 63:** Peter Wilson/David Alfaro Siqueiros's mural "The People for the University, the University for the People" (1952–6) is a relief mosaic at Mexico City's main university. © Estate of David Alfaro Siqueiros/SOMAAP, Mexico/VAGA, New York; **page 67:** Andrew Wakeford/Getty Images, Inc./Photodisc.; **page 88 (clockwise from top left):** © Bill Lai/Image Works; © Jose Carrillo/PhotoEdit; David Hanover/Getty Images Inc./Stone Allstock; Hoby Finn/Getty Images, Inc./Photodisc; EyeWire Collection/Getty Images/Photodisc; Laurence Monneret/Getty Images Inc./Stone Allstock; Christopher Bissell/Getty Images Inc./Stone Allstock; **page 89:** Rob Lewine/The Stock Market; **page 92 (top):** Luis Viega/Getty Images Inc./Image Bank; **page 92 (bottom):** José Enrique Molina/AGE Fotostock; **page 93 (top):** Simon D. Pollard/Photo Researchers, Inc.; **page 93 (bottom):** Linda Whitwam © Dorling Kindersley; **page 94:** Luis Viega/Getty Images Inc./Image Bank; **page 95:** © Karen Strattner; **page 99:** © Comstock Images; **page 104 (from top):** © David R. Frazier Photolibrary, Inc.; Kim Sayer © Dorling Kindersley; © Antipodes/Getty Images, Inc/Liaison; © Ken Welsh/AGE Fotostock America, Inc.; **page 113:** © D. Donne Bryant Stock Photography; **page 120 (VIVE.com, clockwise from upper left):** Lynn Johnson/Aurora & Quanta Productions Inc; Stockbyte; Richard Price /Taxi/Getty Images; © AP/Wide World Photos; **page 120 (bottom, left to right):** © Michael Keller/Corbis/Stock Market; © David Young-Wolff/PhotoEdit; © David Young-Wolff/PhotoEdit; **page 121 (left to right):** © David Young-Wolff/PhotoEdit; © Tony Freeman/PhotoEdit; **page 124 (from top):** © Danny Lehman/CORBIS; © Ken Gillham/Robert Harding World Imagery; Brown W. Cannon III/Getty Images Inc.; Cary Wolinsky/Aurora & Quanta Productions Inc; **page 125:** © Wolfgang Kaehler; **page 126 (bottom):** © José Fuste Raga/AGE Fotostock America, Inc.; **page 127:** Jay Belmore/Getty Images Inc./Image Bank; **page 131:** Stockbyte; **page 152 (clockwise, from top left):** Stephen Simpson/Getty Images, Inc./Taxi; © Tom Stillo/Omni-Photo Communications, Inc.; Stockbyte; © David Young-Wolff/PhotoEdit; Photolibrary.Com; © Pablo Woll; **page 156 (from top):** © Max Alexander/Robert Harding World Imagery; © Paolo Koch/Photo Researchers, Inc.; © Max Alexander/Dorling Kindersley Media Library; **page 157 (from top):** © Beryl Goldberg; © David Barnes/AGE Fotostock America, Inc.; © Scala/Art Resource, N.Y.; **page 159:** Lockyer, Romilly/Getty Images Inc./Image Bank; **page 163:** © J.D. Dallet/AGE Fotostock America, Inc.; **page 164 (clockwise from top left):** Steve Smith/Getty Images/Taxi; Matthias Clamer/Getty Images Inc./Stone Allstock; Picture Finders Ltd./eStock Photography, LLC; © Robert Frerck/Woodfin Camp and Associates; **page 165:** © Adalberto Rios/Getty Images, Inc./Photodisc.; **page 171:** Jack Hollingsworth/Getty Images, Inc./Photodisc.; **page 173 (left):** © Suzanne Murphy-Larronde; **page 173 (right):** Patricia Rush; **page 183:** © José Fuste Raga/AGE Fotostock America, Inc.; **page 184 (clockwise, from top):** Sami Sarkis/Getty Images, Inc./Photodisc.; © Reuters NewMedia Inc./CORBIS; © Bob Thomas/Getty Images Inc./Stone Allstock; Andrew Wakeford/Getty Images, Inc./Photodisc.; Alan Schein Photography/CORBIS; **page 187 (bottom):** courtesy Consulado General de Costa Rica; **page 188 (from top):** © Duncan Maxwell/Robert Harding World Imagery; © Miguel Angel Muñoz/AGE Fotostock America, Inc.; © Robert Frerck/Getty Images Inc./Stone Allstock; **page 189 (top):** © Ken Gillham/Robert Harding World Imagery; **page 189 (bottom):** Robin MacDougall/Getty Images/Taxi; **page 190 (clockwise, from upper left):** Frank Herholdt/Getty Images Inc./Stone Allstock; © George Haling/AGE Fotostock America, Inc.; © Fritz Poelking/AGE Fotostock America, Inc.; © José Fusta Raga/AGE Fotostock America, Inc.; © J Lightfoot/Firecrest Pictures/Robert Harding World Imagery; Hans Weisenhoffer/Getty Images, Inc./Photodisc.; **page 191:** Jude Maceren/Spots on the Spot; **page 195:** © Corbis Digital Stock; **page 196 (top row, from left):** © Bob Daemmrich/The Image Works; © Reuters NewMedia Inc./Corbis; Lynton Gardiner © Dorling Kindersley; **page 196 (middle row, from left):** A. Ramey/PhotoEdit; © David Young-Wolff/PhotoEdit; © Juan Carlos Ulate/REUTERS/Archive Photos; **page 196 (bottom row, from left):** Marks, Inc., Stephen/Getty Images Inc./Image Bank; © Walter Hodges/Getty Images Inc./Stone Allstock; **page 200 (top to bottom, left to right):** © CC Studio/Science Photo Library/Photo Researchers, Inc.; © Tony Freeman/PhotoEdit; © Richard Hutchings/PhotoEdit; © Jose Carillo/PhotoEdit; © Tony Freeman/PhotoEdit; © Spencer Grant/PhotoEdit; © Alan Oddie/PhotoEdit; © Michael Newman/PhotoEdit; Dick Luria/Getty Images, Inc./Taxi; **page 203 (top):** Robert Van Der Hilst/Getty Images Inc./Stone Allstock; **page 203 (bottom):** Bil Bachman/PhotoEdit; **page 213:** Robert Frerck/Getty Images Inc./Stone Allstock; **page 214 (top to bottom):** Nigel Shuttleworth/Life File/Photodisc/Getty Images; Fountain Group/Digital Vision Ltd.; Michael Newman/PhotoEdit; © **page 218 (clockwise from top left):** © Sergio Pitamitz/AGE Fotostock America, Inc.; John

Nordell/The Image Group; © Andrew Leyerle © Dorling Kindersley; Dave King © Dorling Kindersley; © Rudi Von Briel/PhotoEdit; **page 219:** © Tony Freeman/PhotoEdit; **page 222 (from top):** Index Stock Imagery, Inc.; © Alvaro de Leiva/AGE Fotostock America, Inc.; © José Fuste Raga/AGE Fotostock America, Inc.; **page 223 (from top):** © Robert Frerck/Odyssey Productions, Inc.; © Stefano Cellai/AGE Fotostock America, Inc.; © Sergio Pitamitz/AGE Fotostock America, Inc.; © **page 224:** © Sergio Pitamitz/AGE Fotostock America, Inc.; **page 225:** Chad J. Shaffer/Spots on the Spot; **page 229:** © John Neubauer/PhotoEdit; **page 246 (top):** Neil Beer/Getty Images, Inc./Photodisc; **page 246 (bottom)** © AP Wide World Photos; **page 249:** Lillo/*Buenhogar*, May 31, 1994; **page 250 (clockwise from top left):** Uwe Krejci/Getty Images Inc./Stone Allstock; © Michael Newman/Photo Edit; © Robert Brenner/PhotoEdit; Jose Carrillo/PhotoEdit; **page 254 (top):** John Neubauer/PhotoEdit; **page 254 (middle):** John Davis/Dorling Kindersley Media Library; **page 254 (bottom):** © Atlantide S.N.C./AGE Fotostock America, Inc.; **page 255 (from top):** © Puerto Rico Tourism Development Company; John Neubauer/PhotoEdit; © John Neubauer/PhotoEdit; **page 256:** © Phyllis Picardi/Stock Boston; **page 257:** Betsie Van der Meer/Getty Images, Inc./Stone Allstock; **page 261:** Ken Chernus/Getty Images, Inc./Taxi; **page 266:** Jenny Mills/ Photolibrary.Com; **page 274 (left to right):** Ryan McVay/Getty Images, Inc./Photodisc; Adam Smith/Getty Images, Inc./ Taxi; Doug Menuez/Getty Images, Inc./Photodisc; **page 274 (bottom):** Will & Deni McIntyre/Getty Images Inc./ Stone Allstock; **page 277:** Danilo Balducci/Das Fotoarchiv/Peter Arnold, Inc.; **page 278:** reprinted by permission of *Revista Mía de México*; **page 279:** reprinted by permission of Eli Lilly and Company; **page 281:** reprinted by permission of March of Dimes Birth Defects Foundation; **page 282 (top left):** Stockbyte; **page 282 (bottom left):** Mark Harmel/Getty Images, Inc./Taxi; **page 282 (right):** Kevin A. Short/Spots on the Spot; **page 286 (top):** © Michael Fogden/DRK Photo; **page 286 (middle):** Jerry Dreindl/Getty Images, Inc./Taxi; **page 286 (bottom):** © Kevin Schafer/Corbis; **page 287 (top right):** © Kevin Schafer/Corbis/Bettmann; **page 287 (from top):** © Joe Viesti/The Viesti Collection, Inc; © AP Wide World Photos; Harvey Lloyd/Getty Images, Inc./Taxi; **page 288:** Kevin Schafer/Corbis/Bettman; **page 289:** Noma/Spots on the Spot; **page 293:** Photolibrary.Com; **page 298:** Stephen Simpson/Getty Images, Inc./Taxi; **page 302 (left to right, top to bottom):** © Elena Rooraid/PhotoEdit; G & M David de Lossy/Getty Images Inc./Image Bank; PBJ Pictures/Getty Images Inc./Stone Allstock; Juan Silva/Getty Images Inc./Image Bank; Michael Newman/PhotoEdit; © Dana White/Photo Edit; David Buffington/Getty Images, Inc./Photodisc.; Chris Salvo/Getty Images, Inc./Taxi; Rob Melnychuk/Getty Images, Inc./ Photodisc.; **page 314 (top):** courtesy Novamex; **page 314 (middle):** courtesy Artinsoft; **page 314 (bottom):** courtesy BBVA; **page 318 (top):** © Jordi Cam/AGE Fotostock America, Inc.; **page 318 (middle):** Walter Bibikow/Getty Images, Inc./Taxi; **page 318 (bottom):** © B. Gleasner/The Viesti Collection, Inc.; **page 319 (clockwise):** Adalberto Rios/Getty Images, Inc./Photodisc; © Don and Elaine Dvorak; © Wolfgang Kaehler/Corbis/Bettmann; © Geoff Renner/Robert Harding World Imagery; **page 325:** © Pearson Education U.S. ELT/Scott Foresman; **page 326 (top to bottom):** © Spencer Grant/PhotoEdit; © Luis Diez Solano/The Image Works; © Shelley Rotner/Omni-Photo Communications, Inc.; © David Young-Wolff/PhotoEdit; **page 327:** courtesy Univision; **page 328:** © Patricio Crooker/fotosbolivia/The Image Works; **page 330 (left to right, top to bottom):** © Dario Lopez-Mills/AP Wide World Photos; © Richard During/Getty Images Inc./Stone Allstock; © Ron Giling/Peter Arnold, Inc.; © Danny Johnston/AP Wide World Photos; © Tom Fox/AP Wide World Photos; © Jean Marc Giboux/Liaison/Getty Images, Inc./Liaison; **page 333:** © Jay W. Sharp/D. Donne Bryant Stock Photography; **page 334 (left to right, top to bottom):** © Carl Dekeyzer/Magnum Photos, Inc.; © C. Carrion/Corbis/ Sygma; © Sestini Agency/Getty Images, Inc./Liaison; © Richard Figueroa/AP Wide World Photos; © Jose Luis Magana/AP Wide World Photos; © Vera Lentz/Black Star; **page 338 (top to bottom):** © Keith Dannemiller/Corbis/SABA Press Photos, Inc.; © Reujh, Juan M./Animals Animals/Earth Scenes; © Stephen McBrady/PhotoEdit; **page 341:** Ryan McVay/Getty Images, Inc./Photodisc**; page 345 (top to bottom):** © Rafael Wollmann/Getty Images, Inc./Liaison; Esbin/Anderson/ Omni-Photo Communications, Inc.; © AFP/CORBIS; © Victor Englebert/Englebert Photography, Inc; Peter Wilson © Dorling Kindersley; **page 346 (top left):** Michael Newman/PhotoEdit; **(bottom left):** © Patricio Crooker/fotosbolivia/ The Image Works; **(top right):** Bob Daemmrich/The Image Works; **(bottom right):** © David Young-Wolff/PhotoEdit; **page 350 (top to bottom):** Francesca Yorke © Dorling Kindersley; © José Fuste Raga/AGE Fotostock America, Inc.; **page 351 (top to bottom):** Spike/Getty Images, Inc./Photodisc.; Diego Rivera (Guanajuato, Mexico, 1886–1957, Mexico City). "Study of a Sleeping Woman," 1921, black crayon on off-white laid paper, 62.7 cm x 46.9 cm. 1965.436. Courtesy of the Fogg Art Museum, Harvard University Art Museums. Bequest of Meta and Paul; Jan Murray/Alamy Images; © José Fuste Raga/AGE Fotostock America, Inc.; **page 353:** Dave Cutler/Spots on the Spot; **page 357:** © A. Ramey/PhotoEdit; **page 358 (top):** Jay Penni/Prentice Hall School Division; **page 358 (bottom):** Markus Matzel/Das Fotoarchiv./Peter Arnold, Inc.; **page 361:** Pearson Education/PH College; **page 362 (top to bottom):** Bill Aron/PhotoEdit; © Bob Daemmrich/Bob Daemmrich Photography, Inc.; John Morrison/Prentice Hall School Division; **page 365:** "¿Lobo o cordero?" reprinted by permission of *Clara mensual con mil ideas*, Barcelona, España; **page 366 (top):** © A. Ramey/PhotoEdit; **page 366 (bottom):** Latin Focus.com; **page 367:** Photograph © Topham/The Image Works © 2004 Kingdom of Spain, Gala-Salvador Dali Foundation/Artists Rights Society (ARS), New York.; **page 373:** Joan Farre © Dorling Kindersley; **page 374:** Gary Buss/Getty Images, Inc./Taxi; **page 378 (clockwise from upper left):** Christopher Vorlet/Spots on the Spot; © Steve Maines/Stock Boston; © Gary Conner/PhotoEdit; Photolibrary.Com; **page 382 (clockwise from upper left):** © Barbara C. Rowell/DRK Photo; W. Lynn Seldon Jr./Omni-Photo Communications, Inc.; Angel Hurtado/Art Museum of the Americas; Jeff Greenberg/PhotoEdit; © Rob Cousins/Robert Harding World Imagery; **page 383 (clockwise from top right):** Fabian/Corbis/Sygma; © Tui De Roy/Bruce Coleman Inc.; © Tui De Roy/Minden Pictures; Jeff Greenberg/Omni-Photo Communications, Inc.; © Robert Frerck/Odyssey/Chicago; **page 384:** Paul Harris/Getty Images Inc./Stone Allstock; **page 385:** Bruno Budrovic/Spots on the Spot.

ÍNDICE

Mar Caribe

OCÉANO
ATLÁNTICO

Barranquilla
Cartagena
Maracaibo
Caracas
Barquisimeto
VENEZUELA
Río Orinoco
Georgetown
Paramaribo
GUYANA
SURINAM
Cayenne
GUAYANA
FRANCESA
(Francia)
Medellín
Salto
Ángel
Manizales
Bogotá
Cali
COLOMBIA
Quito
ECUADOR
Ecuador
Guayaquil
Cuenca
Iquitos
Manaus
Río Amazonas
Belém
Islas
Galápagos
(Ec.)
Fortaleza
Cajamarca
CORDILLERA DE LOS ANDES
Río Madeira
Trujillo
PERÚ
Río Branco
B R A S I L
Recife
Machu
Picchu
Lima
Ayacucho
Cuzco
BOLIVIA
Salvador
Arequipa
Lago
Titicaca
La Paz
Cochabamba
Santa Cruz
Brasília
Belo
Horizonte
Arica
Sucre
Potosí
Iquique
PARAGUAY
São Paulo
Río de Janeiro
Antofagasta
Santos
Trópico de Capricornio
Salta
Asunción
Salto
Iguazú
CHILE
San Miguel
de Tucumán
Coquimbo
ARGENTINA
Pôrto Alegre
Córdoba
Rivera
Valparaíso
Rosario
Río Paraná
Río Uruguay
URUGUAY
Santiago
Mendoza
Buenos Aires
La Plata
Montevideo
OCÉANO
ATLÁNTICO
CORDILLERA DE LOS ANDES
Desierto de Atacama
Concepción
Bahía Blanca
Río de la Plata
Puerto Montt

OCÉANO
PACÍFICO

Estrecho de
Magallanes
Islas
Malvinas
(Br.)
Punta Arenas
TIERRA DEL FUEGO
Cabo de Hornos

OCÉANO
PACÍFICO
I. Pinta
I. Fernandina
I. Marchena
I. San Salvador
Santa Cruz
I. Isabela
I. Santa Cruz
Puerto
Ayora
Puerto
Villamil
I. San
Cristóbal
Puerto
Baquerizo
Moreno
ISLAS GALÁPAGOS
(ECUADOR)

OCÉANO
PACÍFICO
Cabo Norte
Volcán
Katiki
Hanga Roa
Cabo
Cumming
Mataveri
ISLA de PASCUA
(CHILE)

América del Sur